THE

WILLARD J. GRAHAM SERIES

IN ACCOUNTING

BOOKS IN
THE WILLARD J. GRAHAM SERIES IN ACCOUNTING

CONSULTING EDITOR   ROBERT N. ANTHONY   *Harvard University*

Principles of auditing

Principles of auditing

WALTER B. MEIGS, Ph.D., C.P.A.
Professor of Accounting
University of Southern California

E. JOHN LARSEN, D.B.A., C.P.A.
Associate Professor of Accounting
University of Southern California

ROBERT F. MEIGS, D.B.A.
Assistant Professor of Accounting
California State University at San Diego

Fifth Edition · 1973
RICHARD D. IRWIN, INC. *Homewood, Illinois 60430*
IRWIN-DORSEY LIMITED *Georgetown, Ontario*

Fifth Edition

First Printing, February 1973

ISBN 0-256-01423-X
Library of Congress Catalog Card No. 72–90775
Printed in the United States of America

Preface

Current developments in the public accounting profession

THIS FIFTH EDITION of *Principles of Auditing* reflects the dramatic changes currently taking place in the profession of public accounting. In the four years since publication of the preceding edition, the wave of litigation naming CPA firms as defendants has continued to grow. Many of these new court cases have shed additional light on the CPA's responsibility to clients and to third parties. Chapter 3 is a new chapter, devoted entirely to the legal liability of auditors, and contains summaries of major court cases involving CPAs.

The recently adopted Code of Professional Ethics of the American Institute of Certified Public Accountants represents a complete restatement of ethical standards. Chapter 2 includes the major portions of the new Code, including the entire text of the Rules of Conduct. This completely rewritten chapter analyzes and explains the ethical concepts set forth by the AICPA and relates these concepts to the actions of the Securities and Exchange Commission.

The ever-increasing importance of electronic data processing systems to the auditor is recognized in an expanded chapter on this topic. New emphasis is placed on the use of the computer as an auditing tool of great value on many engagements. On-line, real-time systems, time sharing, service bureaus, and generalized computer audit programs are discussed in simple, understandable terms, yet in sufficient depth to give the student a real appreciation of the increased importance of the computer to virtually every CPA. In addition, illustrations of accounting and auditing applications of the computer are included in several other chapters.

Statistical sampling is an increasingly popular tool for audit tests relating to receivables, inventories, and many other portions of an audit engagement. The coverage of discovery sampling and of estimation sampling for variables has been significantly expanded in Chapter 8.

Other new features of the fifth edition include:

1. Expanded coverage of flowcharting in Chapter 5, Internal Control.
2. Discussion of receivables and sales as a unit in Chapter 13.
3. Discussion of inventories and cost of sales as a unit in Chapter 14.
4. Comprehensive illustration of a current form of report on internal control in Chapter 5.
5. Segregation of most illustrative working papers into a separate supplement, while retaining illustrations of the most critical working papers in the text itself.

Objective tests and examinations

A complete set of achievement tests and a comprehensive examination (all in objective form) will be available in quantity to adopters. Each achievement test covers about four chapters and the comprehensive examination covers the entire book. The achievement tests are of a length that may conveniently be fitted into the normal class meeting time, and the comprehensive examination may be used as a final examination. The CPA Examination in Auditing has used objective questions extensively in recent years. Many of the questions in the achievement tests and comprehensive examination have been drawn from this source. Thus, they may serve the dual purpose of providing a rapid efficient means of testing student understanding of course content and also giving the student some first-hand experience with the kinds of questions now playing such an important role in the CPA Examination in Auditing.

Reduction in number of chapters

In recognition of the tightness of many curricula with a limited number of units made available for the study of auditing, every effort has been made in this edition to condense the coverage of less vital topics. The total number of chapters has been reduced from 23 to 21. The discussion of all interest-bearing debt (both long-term and current) has been combined in a single chapter (Chapter 18).

Continued emphasis on internal control

The strong emphasis on internal control which characterized the preceding editions is continued in this fifth edition. When appropriate, those auditing procedures associated with internal control tests of transactions have been segregated from "year-end" auditing procedures. The advent of the computer has caused some changes in the concepts of internal control but has not lessened its importance. An internal control questionnaire designed by the national public accounting firm of Laventhol, Krekstein, Horwath & Horwath for the audit of clients with computerized systems is presented as an appendix to Chapter 6.

Questions, problems, and case studies

The questions, problems, and case materials at the end of each chapter are divided as follows: Group I—Review Questions; Group II—Questions Requiring Analysis; Group III—Problems; and Group IV—Case Studies in Auditing.

The review questions are closely related to the material in the chapter and provide a convenient means of determining whether the student has grasped the major ideas and implications contained in that chapter.

The questions requiring analysis call for thoughtful appraisal of realistic auditing situations and the application of generally accepted auditing standards. Many of these Group II questions are taken from CPA examinations, others from actual audit engagements. These thought-provoking questions requiring analysis differ from the Group III Problems in that they are generally shorter and tend to stress value judgments and conflicting opinions.

Most of the Group III Problems have been drawn from CPA examinations; in the selection of these problems consideration was given to all auditing problems which have appeared in CPA examinations for the past 15 years. Other problems reflect actual audit situations from the experience of practicing accountants. Many of the problems are new, but problems appearing in the previous editions have been retained (usually with some modification) if they were superior to other available problems. In response to the recent shift in content of the auditing section of the CPA examination, problems requiring extensive working papers and quantitative applications have been minimized, and short case-type questions have been emphasized.

Case studies in auditing

The 12 case studies in auditing appear at the ends of the chapters on Legal Liability of Auditors; Audit Working Papers; Cash; Accounts and Notes Receivable and Sales Transactions; Inventories and Cost of Sales; Prepaid Expenses, Deferred Charges, and Intangible Assets; Accounts Payable and Other Liabilities; Interest-Bearing Debt and Interest Expense; Owners' Equity; Further Verification of Revenue and Expenses (2 case studies); and Financial Statements and Audit Reports. These cases present specific issues covered in these chapters, but they also place these issues in proper perspective in relation to the entire examination and to the issuance of an audit report.

The authors' experience in teaching the auditing course has been that the use of case studies at strategic intervals is one of the highlights of the course. Case studies in auditing are a means of viewing audit engagements through the eyes of a partner in a CPA firm and also from the viewpoint of the client. Students enjoy the cases thoroughly because of the lively class discussions they produce and the arguments of opposing views. In preparing and discussing these cases the student must identify the important issues, weigh the opposing arguments, and then reach a conclusion. Class discussions in which each student evaluates the arguments of others and participates in reaching common grounds of agreement can bring the auditing course close to the realities of the professional practice of the certified public accountant.

References to American Institute of Certified Public Accountants

Extensive references are made to the pronouncements of the American Institute of Certified Public Accountants, especially to such recent publications as the Code of Professional Ethics, Statements on Auditing Procedure, Accounting Principles Board Opinions, Statements on Responsibilities in Tax Practice, Industry Audit Guides, and An Auditor's Approach to Statistical Sampling. The cooperation of this professional organization in permitting the use of its published materials and of questions from the Uniform CPA Examination brings to an auditing text an element of authority not otherwise available.

Contributions by others

We gratefully acknowledge the able and thorough reviews of the Fourth Edition provided by Professor John W. Cook of Georgia State University and by Professor John H. Ziegler of California State University —Chico. Their many suggestions for this Fifth Edition were most valuable.

Our special thanks go to Mr. Edwin M. Lamb, Partner, Arthur Young & Company, who has contributed importantly to the content of Chapter 8, Statistical Sampling.

Mr. Charles Chazen, Partner, Laventhol Krekstein Horwath & Horwath, made possible the inclusion of an internal control questionnaire developed by that firm for the audit of electronic data processing installations.

Mr. Robert Dodson, Partner, Touche Ross & Co., was also most helpful with respect to Chapter 6 on the audit of electronic data processing systems.

Finally, to the many faculty members at various schools who used the preceding editions and offered constructive suggestions, and to the students in the auditing courses taught by the authors—our sincere thanks.

January 1973

WALTER B. MEIGS
E. JOHN LARSEN
ROBERT F. MEIGS

Contents

internal control for an EDP system. Internal control questionnaire for EDP systems. Flowchart analysis. Test decks. Controlled programs. Generalized (computer) audit programs. Implications of on-line, real-time systems. Computer service centers. Time-sharing systems. Auditing EDP Systems—a look to the future. GLOSSARY OF SELECTED EDP TERMS.

Auditor's opinion based on evidence. Auditing procedures—a means of gathering evidence. Evidence needed for material items. Quantity and quality of evidence. Types of evidence. Internal control as evidence. Physical evidence. Documentary evidence. Ledgers and journals as evidence. Comparisons and ratios as evidence. Computations as evidence. Oral evidence. The cost of obtaining evidence. Calculated risk. Relative risk. Evidence provided by subsequent events. Footnote disclosure of subsequent events. The auditor's responsibility for subsequent events. TESTS AND SAMPLES: Reliance by the auditor upon tests and samples. Selecting audit samples. Judgment block samples. Judgment random samples. Judgment stratified sampling. Evaluation of errors found by sampling. Size of judgment audit samples. Sampling and the detection of fraud. Working rules for audit tests. Criticism of judgment approach to audit test checking. Statistical sampling.

Statistical sampling versus random sampling. Statistical selection and statistical measurement. STATISTICAL SELECTION: Random number table selection. Using the random number table. Random number generator. Systematic selection. Stratified selection. Cluster selection. STATISTICAL MEASUREMENT: Precision. Confidence level. Sample size. Why sample size need not increase proportionately with population. Acceptance sampling. Estimation sampling for attributes. Illustration of estimation sampling for attributes. Definition of audit exceptions. Discovery sampling. Estimation sampling for variables. Theory of sampling for variables. Determination of sample size. Illustration of estimation sampling for variables. Combined use of sampling for attributes, sampling for variables, and discovery sampling. Advantages of statistical sampling.

Definition of working papers. Confidential nature of working papers. Ownership and control of working papers. Purposes of audit working papers. Working papers and auditing standards. Working papers and accountants' liability. Essentials of good working papers. Planning working papers. The content of working papers. Adjusting journal entries and reclassification entries. Distinction between adjusting entries and reclassification entries. Adjusting entries for material items only. Auditor's adjusting entries recorded by client. Supporting schedules. Working paper for analysis of a ledger account. Computational working papers. Copies of minutes and other records or documents. Letters of representations provided by clients. The permanent file. Indexing and preserving working papers. Standards for preparation of working papers.

Relationship with clients. Beginning the audit. Inspection tour of plant and offices. Review of general records. REVIEW OF NONFINANCIAL RECORDS: Corporate charter and bylaws. Partnership agreement. Corporate minutes book. Contracts held or issued by client. Government regulations. Correspondence files. REVIEW OF FINANCIAL RECORDS: Income tax returns of prior years. Financial statements and annual reports of prior years. Reports to the SEC. REVIEW OF ACCOUNTING RECORDS: The general ledger. The general journal. Auditor's description of his examination of accounting records. Interim examination of general records. Organization of succeeding chapters.

What is the auditor looking for? The auditor's objectives in examination of cash. How much audit time for cash? Internal control over cash transactions. Internal control over cash sales. Internal control over collections from customers. Internal control over cash disbursements. Internal control aspects of petty cash funds. Internal control and the computer. Audit working papers for cash. Audit program for cash. Interim audit work on cash.

The auditor's objectives in examination of securities. Internal control for securities. Internal control questionnaire. Audit working papers for securities. Audit program for securities. OTHER INVESTMENTS: Balance sheet presentation of other investments.

Meaning of accounts receivable. Meaning of notes receivable. The auditor's objectives in examination of receivables and sales. Internal control of sales transactions and accounts receivable. Internal control of notes receivable. Internal control and the computer. Audit working papers for receivables and sales. Audit program for receivables and sales transactions. Interim audit work on receivables *and* sales.

Critical importance of inventories to the auditor. The auditor's objectives in examination of inventories and cost of sales. Internal control of inventories and cost of sales. Physical control. Record control. Internal control and the computer. Audit working papers for inventories and cost of sales. Audit program for inventories and cost of sales.

The auditor's objectives in examination of property, plant and equipment. Contrast with audit of current assets. Cost as the basis of valuation. Use of a general price index to adjust depreciation. Internal controls over plant and equipment. The plant and equipment budget. Other major control devices. Audit working papers. Initial audits and repeat engagements. Audit program for property, plant and equipment. Depreciation. The auditor's objectives in review of depreciation. Audit program—depreciation and depreciation allowances. Testing the client's provision for depreciation. Analysis of accumulated depreciation accounts. Audit procedures for depletion of natural resources. Examination of plant and equipment in advance of the balance sheet date.

PREPAID EXPENSES AND DEFERRED CHARGES: Internal control of prepaid expenses and deferred charges. The auditor's objectives in examination of prepaid expenses and deferred charges. Concurrent verification of related expense and liability accounts. Audit working papers for prepaid expenses and deferred charges. Unexpired insurance. Taxes paid in advance. Rent paid in advance. Other prepaid expenses. Deferred charges. INTANGIBLE ASSETS: Generally accepted accounting principles for intangible assets. The auditor's objectives in examination of intangible assets. Internal control. Acquisition of intangibles from insiders. Audit working papers for intangible assets. Goodwill. Organization costs. Patents. Research and development costs. Leases and leasehold improvements. Other intangible assets. Time of examination.

Meaning of accounts payable. The auditor's objectives in examination of accounts payable. Internal control. Internal control and the computer. Audit working papers for accounts payable. Audit program. OTHER LIABILITIES: Amounts withheld from employees' pay. Sales taxes payable. Unclaimed wages. Customers' deposits. Liabilities for fines or other penalties. Accrued liabilities. Deferred credits to revenue. Balance sheet presentation. Time of examination.

The auditor's objectives in examination of interest-bearing debt. Internal control over interest-bearing debt. Audit working papers. Internal control questionnaire. Audit program for interest-bearing debt. Time of examination. CONTINGENT LIABILITIES: General audit procedures. Liability representation. Balance sheet presentation. COMMITMENTS.

1

The role of the auditor in the American economy

Communication of economic data

IN OUR complex, highly industrialized society the communication of financial and other economic data is vitally important. Our economy is characterized by large corporate organizations which have gathered capital from millions of investors and which control economic resources spread throughout the country or even throughout the world. Top management in the corporate headquarters is remote from the operations of company plants and branches and must rely on financial reports and other communications of economic data to control its far-flung resources. The millions of individuals who have entrusted their savings to corporations by the purchase of securities are also remote from the resources in which they have acquired an interest. This remoteness forces them to rely upon annual financial statements for assurance that their invested funds are being used honestly and efficiently.

The federal government expends an increasing share of the gross national product and in so doing relies upon the communication of financial data to assure that the costs it incurs are reasonable, regardless of whether the project be a trip to the moon, a mass transit system, or a foreign aid program. The revenues of the federal government are derived in large part from corporate income taxes. Thus the financial support of the government rests on the measurement and communication of these data concerning taxable income.

Finally, most of our national policies such as increasing employment,

1

controlling inflation, combatting pollution, and maintaining a satisfactory international balance of payments rely directly on quantitative measurement of economic activity and the communication of these data. Appropriate accounting standards and effective financial reporting are thus key factors in the pursuit of our economic and social goals.

Contribution of the independent auditor to financial reporting

Both the day-to-day operation of our economy and its long-run success are highly dependent on communication of financial data. How then do we gain assurance that the data being reported are properly measured and fairly presented? A major share of the answer lies in the audits performed by independent public accountants. Audited financial statements are now the accepted means by which American business concerns report to their stockholders, bankers, creditors, and to government. The word "audited" when applied to financial statements means that the balance sheet, statement of income and retained earnings, and statement of changes in financial position are accompanied by an audit report prepared by an independent public accountant, expressing his professional opinion as to the fairness of the company's statements.

Unaudited financial statements—the credibility gap

Financial statements prepared by management and transmitted to outsiders without first being audited by independent accountants leave a credibility gap. In reporting on its own administration of the business, management can hardly be expected to be entirely impartial and unbiased, any more than a football coach could be expected to serve as both coach and official referee in the same game.

Unaudited financial statements are not acceptable to absentee owners or other outsiders for several reasons. The statements may have been honestly but carelessly prepared. Liabilities may have been overlooked and omitted from the balance sheet. Assets may have been overstated as a result of arithmetical errors or through violation of generally accepted accounting principles. Net income may have been exaggerated because revenue expenditures were capitalized or because sales transactions were recorded in advance of delivery dates.

Finally, there is the possibility that unaudited financial statements have been deliberately falsified in order to conceal theft and fraud, or as a means of inducing the reader to invest in the business or to extend credit. Although deliberate falsification in financial statements is not common, it has occurred and has caused disastrous losses to persons who relied upon such misleading statements.

For all these reasons (accidental errors, deviation from accounting principles, unintentional bias, and deliberate falsification) unaudited annual financial statements are not acceptable in the business community.

ILLUSTRATIVE CASE. A few years ago, the bankruptcy of Allied Crude Vegetable Oil Corporation, a major exporter of vegetable oils, stunned the world of finance. Fifty-one companies and banks which were creditors of Allied held warehouse receipts for nearly two billion pounds of salad oil purportedly owned by Allied. Investigation disclosed that the bulk of the warehouse receipts, ostensibly issued by a warehousing subsidiary of American Express Company, had been forged, and that an inventory of salad oil with a reported value of $175 million did not exist.

Bankruptcy hearings disclosed that none of the creditors received current audited financial statements of Allied before making loans to the company. Had the creditors insisted upon receiving audited statements before granting or renewing loans to Allied, the shortages would have been discovered by the auditors before reaching large amounts.

Auditing—then and now

Although the objectives and concepts which guide present-day audits were almost unknown 75 years ago, audits of one type or another have been made throughout the recorded history of commerce and of government finance. From medieval times on through the Industrial Revolution, audits were made to determine whether persons in positions of fiscal responsibility in government and commerce were acting and reporting in an honest manner. During the Industrial Revolution, as manufacturing concerns grew in size, their owners began to use the services of hired managers. With this separation of the ownership and management groups, the absentee owners turned increasingly to auditors to protect themselves against the danger of fraud by both managers and employees. Prior to 1900 auditing was concerned principally with the detection of fraud. In the 20th century the direction of audit work has turned away from fraud detection toward the new goal of determining whether financial statements give a fair picture of financial position, operating results, and changes in financial position.

In Great Britain, which is often regarded as the birthplace of auditing, the growth of business enterprise during and following the Industrial Revolution was accompanied by improved accounting systems. As corporations became the dominant form of organization and professional managers replaced individual owners, accounting systems were improved and standardized. A fairly complete and systematic accounting program was recognized as a necessary step in preventing fraud and in providing dependable financial reporting. As stockholders in these expanding corporations struggled to verify the reports and records of the companies they owned, the need for professionally trained auditors became apparent. To conduct an efficient audit of a large corporation was clearly beyond the ability of an amateur.

The attest function

The separation of ownership and management in English companies made stockholders aware that they needed the protection of an independent audit. Although the business enterprise which prepares financial statements is primarily responsible for the data reported, an independent public accountant who examines the data and supporting evidence may "attest" to their reliability by attaching his written opinion to the financial statements. To **attest** to financial statements means to affirm their truthfulness—to bear witness as to their validity. One reason for inviting an independent public accountant to attest to financial statements is the **conflict of interest** which may exist between the company preparing the financial statements and those persons who use the statements. The users of financial statements whose interests may differ from that of the reporting entity include bankers, creditors, stockholders, and governmental agencies.

Recognition of the responsibility of independent accountants to third parties led to the organization in Scotland and England of Institutes of Chartered Accountants. The technical competence of persons desiring to become chartered accountants was tested by examinations. Independence, integrity, and professional responsibility were recognized as qualities quite as important in chartered accountants as technical skill. Through the Institutes of Chartered Accountants, ethical principles were evolved to encourage auditors to follow professional standards in performing the attest function of auditing.

A new objective—determining fairness of financial statements

Shortly before 1900 many Scottish and English chartered accountants came to the United States to represent British investors in this era of rapid industrialization in America. These men were influential in the formation of an American accounting profession. In 1896 legislation was enacted by New York providing for the first licensing of certified public accountants in the United States.

In 1900 auditing work was concentrated on the balance sheet; in fact most companies at that time regarded the income statement as confidential information not to be made available to outsiders. The principal distribution of audited financial data outside the company was to bankers from whom loans were being requested. These bankers were interested in the balance sheet rather than the income statement and they were strongly in favor of a conservative valuation of assets. In brief, they wanted assurance of debt-paying ability. The independent public accountants of this era were much influenced by the attitudes of bankers because they represented the major users of audited financial statements. Today, regular releases of corporate income data, audited by independent public accountants, are eagerly awaited by the public and by government as the most significant measure of business trends.

The public accounting profession in the United States emerging about 1900 was concerned with an important new objective—determining the fairness of financial statements. After 1900 the auditor's role as a detective was gradually pushed into the background. The principal objective of auditing changed from fraud detection to determining the fairness with which the financial statements presented financial position and operating results. The advent of federal income taxes added another dimension to the auditor's work; it involved not only the preparation of tax returns but also a new emphasis upon the government's interest in the fairness of reported income. This interest was given further impetus by the enactment of the Securities Act of 1933 and the Securities Exchange Act of 1934—the "truth in securities" laws.

This new concept of auditing was a natural outgrowth of an era in which corporations grew to gigantic size with widespread public ownership of corporate securities. Now that the financing of business enterprise is accomplished in large part by selling securities to millions of small investors, an annual independent audit is essential to assure the public of the fairness of the results being reported.

Development of sampling techniques

In the early days of the auditing profession, a proper audit was one which included a ***complete review of all transactions.*** However, about 1900, as large-scale business enterprise developed rapidly in both Great Britain and the United States, auditors were forced to adopt a ***sampling technique.*** This new auditing technique transformed the audit process into the making of tests of selected transactions rather than the verification of all transactions. Auditors and businessmen gradually came to accept the proposition that careful examination of a few transactions selected at random would give a reliable indication of the accuracy of other similar transactions.

Internal control as a basis for testing and sampling

As auditors gained experience with the technique of sampling, they became aware of the importance of the system of internal control. The meaning of internal control and the methods by which the auditor evaluates the system of internal control are thoroughly explored in Chapter

5 and illustrated throughout this book. At this point a concise definition will serve to explain why good internal control makes it possible for auditors to rely greatly upon sampling techniques. A system of internal control consists of all measures used by a business for the purposes of (1) safeguarding its resources against waste, fraud, and inefficiency; (2) promoting accuracy and reliability in accounting and operating data; (3) encouraging and measuring compliance with company policy; and (4) judging the efficiency of operations in all divisions of the business.

One very simple example of internal control is an organization plan which separates the custody of assets from the function of record keeping. Thus, a person handling cash should not also maintain accounting records. Another example is the subdivision of duties so that no one person handles a transaction in its entirety, and the work of one employee serves to prove the accuracy of the work of another.

Evaluation of internal control became recognized as a prerequisite to successful use of sampling techniques. Auditors found that by studying the client's accounting system and by considering the flow of accounting work and the methods provided for automatic proof of recorded data, they could determine the extent and direction of the tests needed for a satisfactory audit of the financial statements. *The stronger the system of internal control, the less testing required by the auditor.* For any section of the accounts or any phase of financial operations in which controls were weak, the auditor learned he must expand the scope and intensity of his tests.

The advent of electronic data processing

As more and more business concerns have developed electronic data processing systems, dramatic changes have taken place in the form and nature of accounting records and in the "information system" as a whole. One of the challenging tasks confronting the auditor in recent years has been to modify his traditional procedures to fit the computer age. The accounting data which he wishes to verify may, for example, be stored on magnetic tape rather than in loose-leaf ledgers. The auditor must, therefore, be familiar with electronic data processing systems and their impact upon internal controls and the information system; he must also be competent to use the computer as a tool for performing audit functions.

Major auditing developments of the 20th century

Many of the ideas mentioned in this brief historical sketch of the development of auditing will be analyzed in detail in later sections of this book. Our purpose at this point is merely to orient ourselves with a quick overall look at some of the major auditing developments of the 20th century:

1. The change of objectives from the detection of fraud to the determination of fairness of financial statements.
2. Increased responsibility of the auditor to "third parties," such as governmental agencies, stock exchanges, and an investing public numbered in the millions.
3. The change of auditing method from detailed examination of individual transactions to use of sampling techniques, including statistical sampling.
4. Recognition of the need to evaluate the system of internal control as a guide to the direction and amount of testing and sampling to be performed.
5. Development of new auditing procedures applicable to electronic data processing systems, and use of the computer as an auditing tool.

The examination—a basis for the auditor's opinion

Before the independent public accountant can express an opinion on a company's financial statements, he must make an examination or audit of those statements. The audit consists of a searching analytical review of the balance sheet, statement of income and retained earnings, and statement of changes in financial position, and of the accounting records and other evidence supporting those statements. This examination provides objective evidence that the amounts on the financial statements are valid, genuine, and trustworthy—and not mere optimistic estimates or fanciful conjectures.

For example, the evidence gathered by the auditor during his examination will prove that the assets listed in the balance sheet really exist, that the company has title to these assets, and that the valuations assigned to these assets have been established in accordance with generally accepted accounting principles. Evidence will be gathered to show that the balance sheet contains *all* the liabilities of the company; otherwise it might be grossly misleading because certain important liabilities had been deliberately or accidentally omitted. Similarly, the auditor will gather information about the statement of income and retained earnings. He will demand proof that the reported sales really occurred; proof that the goods were actually shipped to customers; and proof that the recorded costs and expenses are applicable to the current period and that all expenses have been recognized.

After completing an examination the auditor has a sound basis for expressing an opinion about the company's financial statements. He has satisfied himself by a variety of tests, inquiries, inspection of assets, and other audit procedures that the financial statements have been properly prepared from the accounting records and give a fair and dependable picture of the company. The auditor's examination is thus the basis for an audit report.

Never does the auditor express an opinion on financial statements without first making an audit. Personal acquaintance with the business, audits in past years, belief in the integrity of the owners and managers—none of these factors is sufficient to warrant an expression of opinion on the financial statements by the independent public accountant. Either he makes an audit of the current year's financial statements or he does not. If he does not perform an audit, he does not express an opinion on the fairness of the financial statements.

The audit procedures comprising an examination will vary considerably from one engagement to the next. Many of the procedures appropriate to the audit of a small retail store would not be appropriate for the audit of a giant manufacturing corporation such as General Motors. Auditors make examinations of all types of business enterprise, and of nonprofit organizations as well. Banks and breweries, factories and stores, colleges and churches, airlines and labor unions—all of these are regularly visited by auditors. The selection of the audit procedures best suited to each engagement requires the exercise of professional skill and judgment.

The certified public accountant

In recognition of the public trust imposed upon independent public accountants, each state recognizes public accountancy as a profession and issues the certificate of Certified Public Accountant. The CPA certificate is not only a license to practice but also a symbol of technical competence. This official recognition by the state is comparable to that accorded to the legal, medical, and other professions. A CPA certificate is issued by state and territorial governments to those individuals who have demonstrated through written examinations and the satisfaction of educational and experience requirements their qualifications for entry to the public accounting profession.

Why should the states license independent accountants by granting CPA certificates? Such action by the various state governments is based on the assumption that the public interest will be protected by an official identification of competent professional accountants who offer their services to the public. The opinion of an independent public accountant concerning the fairness of a set of financial statements is the factor that causes these statements to be generally accepted by bankers, investors, and government agencies. To sustain such confidence, the independent public accountant must be a professional person of the highest integrity.

In addition to passing an examination and meeting certain educational requirements, the candidate for a CPA certificate in many states must also complete from one to five years of public accounting experience. The requirements as to amount of education and public accounting experience differ considerably among the various states. Since there are 54 sets of rules involved (50 states, three territories, and the District of Columbia), the standards for licensing of certified public accountants are less uniform than might be desirable. As a practical matter, a college education with major work in accounting is the only adequate preparation for the examination, and probably 80 percent or more of persons currently passing the examination are college graduates. The rigor of the examinations seems to have been more influential than state laws in raising the educational standards for admission to the profession. Some states require candidates to be college graduates, but other states have more lenient educational requirements. More rigorous educational requirements are needed to keep pace with the development of the profession. With the expansion of collegiate programs in accounting there appears to be a trend toward emphasizing education rather than practical experience as the primary qualification for issuance of a CPA certificate. The American Institute of Certified Public Accountants (AICPA), the national professional organization of CPAs, has taken a position that five years of college study, and passing the CPA examination, should be the only requirements for entry into the public accounting profession.

In recognition of the increasing complexity of public accounting practice, the AICPA has recently urged that each state require its licensed CPAs, as a condition precedent to relicensing, to demonstrate that they are continuing their professional education. A few states have already enacted continuing education laws for CPAs.

Although the profession of public accounting is only about 80 years old in this country, it is the fastest growing profession. There are presently about 125,000 certified public accountants in the United States. More than half of these are relatively young persons who have received their certificates within the past 10 years. Despite this tremendous growth of the profession, the demand for the services of CPAs appears to be growing even faster.

A sharp distinction must be drawn between the terms "Certified Public Accountant" and "Public Accountant." The requirements for a license as a "Public Accountant" are in general less rigorous than for a CPA certificate and usually do not include the taking of an examination. The requirements as to accounting experience and other qualifications vary considerably from state to state. Some states restrict only the use of the CPA title and permit anyone to practice as a public accountant.

In other states, laws have been adopted with the intent of ultimately limiting the professional practice of accounting to certified public accountants, after an initial licensing of all persons engaged in public accounting at the time the laws were enacted.

In addition to the making of audits, nearly all CPA firms do a substantial amount of professional work in the fields of taxation and management advisory services. Tax work includes advising clients on business policies which will hold the burden of taxation to a minimum as well as the actual preparation of income and other tax returns. Management advisory services include a wide range of activities such as the design and installation of accounting systems, budgeting, and financial forecasting.

The CPA examination

Although certified public accountants are licensed by State Boards of Accountancy, a uniform examination is given twice a year on a national basis. The examination function is performed for the state boards by the AICPA.

The CPA examination is essentially an academic one; in most states candidates are not required to have any work experience to sit for the examination. In the opinion of the authors, the ideal time to take the examination is immediately after the completion of a comprehensive program of accounting courses in a college or university. The examination extends over two and a half days and covers four fields: auditing, accounting theory, accounting practice, and business law. Although the subject of federal income taxes is not presented as a separate field, this topic is usually emphasized in several parts of the examination. In most states the examination is given twice a year, in May and November.

The compilation of the questions and problems included in this textbook involved a review of all CPA examinations of the past 20 years and the selection of representative questions and problems. Use of this material is with the consent of the American Institute of Certified Public Accountants. Many other problems and questions (not from CPA examinations) are included with each chapter.

American Institute of Certified Public Accountants

The AICPA is the national organization of certified public accountants engaged in promoting and maintaining high professional standards of practice. During the 80 years of its existence the Institute has contributed enormously to the evolution of generally accepted accounting principles as well as to development of auditing standards. The many technical divisions and committees of the Institute (such as the Committee on Auditing Procedure) provide a means of focusing the collective experience and ability of the profession on current problems.

The development of a *Code of Professional Ethics* and the enforcement of this code represent another achievement of the AICPA. Governmental agencies such as the Securities and Exchange Commission (SEC) and the Internal Revenue Service continually seek the advice and cooperation of the Institute in improving laws and regulations relating to accounting matters.

Research and publications of the AICPA—auditing literature

Among the most important AICPA publications bearing directly on the work of the CPA are the following:

Accounting Trends & Techniques (published annually since 1947)
Code of Professional Ethics
Internal Control
Statements on Auditing Procedure
Statements on Management Advisory Services
Statements on Responsibilities in Tax Practice
The Journal of Accountancy (published monthly since 1906)
Management Adviser (published bimonthly since 1964)
The Tax Adviser (published monthly since 1970)

In addition to the above, the Institute has published several industry audit guides, such as *Audits of Fire and Casualty Insurance Companies*. The AICPA also offers a continuing program of professional development courses, conferences, and training programs designed to strengthen the position of public accounting as a learned profession.

Opinions of the Accounting Principles Board

Since its inception the AICPA has been concerned with divergences in accounting practice which tend to reduce the comparability of financial statements. A research program designed to cope with controversial accounting issues was launched in 1938 and led to the publication of a series of 51 *Accounting Research Bulletins* and 4 *Accounting Terminology Bulletins* between 1939 and 1959. A restatement and revision of this series entitled *Accounting Research and Terminology Bulletins, Final Edition,* was published in 1961.

The Accounting Principles Board of the AICPA was formed in 1959 to carry on a new and more ambitious program of research publication.

The board superseded the former committees on accounting procedure and terminology.

The serially numbered *Opinions* issued by the Accounting Principles Board provide substantial authoritative support in clarifying the phrase "generally accepted accounting principles" used in the audit report. The APB *Opinions* must be followed in the preparation of financial statements, or any departures from these recommended principles must be disclosed in notes attached to the statements or in the report of the independent auditors. In the continuing drive to establish a clear and authoritative meaning for the term "accounting principles," the *Opinions* of the Accounting Principles Board must be regarded as one of the most significant developments of recent years. However, opposition to *APB Opinions* and criticism of the Board for not playing a more vigorous role in developing new concepts of financial accounting increased in the latter portion of its 13 year life. The Accounting Principles Board was superseded in 1973 by the Financial Accounting Standards Board, a smaller, full-time and highly paid group.

Financial Accounting Standards Board

Reacting to dissatisfaction both within and without the public accounting profession as to the Accounting Principles Board's format and output, the AICPA's president in 1971 appointed a seven-member study group to make recommendations for improving the process of establishing accounting principles. The report issued by the study group in 1972 was quickly accepted by the AICPA's governing hierarchy, and the recommended structure was fully operational in 1973. The new structure for establishing accounting rules is comprised of the following three bodies:

1. A Financial Accounting Foundation of nine trustees, separate from all existing professional bodies. One trustee is the AICPA's president; the other eight trustees are appointed for three-year terms by the AICPA's board of directors. Four appointed trustees are CPAs in public practice, two are financial executives, one is a financial analyst, and one is an accounting educator. Duties of the Financial Accounting Foundation include appointing members of the Financial Accounting Standards Board, raising and allocating required funds, and reviewing the operations and effectiveness of the new structure.
2. A Financial Accounting Standards Board of seven full-time salaried members serving five-year terms with the possibility of reappointment for a second term. Four Standards Board members are CPAs from public practice; the other three need not be CPAs but must

have extensive experience in financial reporting. Financial accounting standards promulgated by the Standards Board require an affirmative vote of at least five members.

3. A Financial Accounting Standards Advisory Council with approximately 20 members serving one-year terms which may be renewed indefinitely. The Advisory Council members, drawn from a variety of occupations, advise the Financial Accounting Standards Board on its priorities and in the investigation of matters considered by the Standards Board.

The new structure for establishing accounting principles should satisfy many of the critics of the Accounting Principles Board for two principal reasons. The AICPA is no longer the sole authority; groups such as the Financial Executives Institute and the American Accounting Association now have a voice in establishing accounting principles. In addition, the seven Financial Accounting Standards Board members must sever all connections with other employers to devote their full-time efforts to the work of the Standards Board.

Securities and Exchange Commission

It is the responsibility of the SEC to require good financial reporting by companies offering their securities to the public. In meeting this responsibility, the SEC has necessarily been deeply concerned with the strengthening of auditing standards. Publications by the SEC of particular importance to the auditor are *Regulation S–X (Form and Content of Financial Statements)* and *Accounting Series Releases* (includes reports on investigations and opinions by the Chief Accountant of the SEC). Late in 1972, the chairman of the SEC stated publicly that the Commission is moving to a more active role in proposing and adopting accounting standards.

The audit report

A principal purpose of most audits is to enable an independent public accountant to form an opinion as to the fairness of the client's financial statements. This opinion is given in the form of a written report, which often consists of only two short paragraphs. The first paragraph is a concise statement of the scope of the examination; the second paragraph is an equally concise statement of the auditor's opinion based on this examination. The wording of this short-form audit report usually follows quite closely the pattern recommended by the Committee on Auditing Procedure of the AICPA.

SHORT-FORM AUDIT REPORT

To the Board of Directors,
XYZ Company:

We have examined the balance sheet of XYZ Company as of December 31, 19—, and the related statements of income and retained earnings and changes in financial position for the year then ended. Our examination was made in accordance with generally accepted auditing standards, and accordingly included such tests of the accounting records and such other auditing procedures as we considered necessary in the circumstances.

In our opinion, the aforementioned financial statements present fairly the financial position of XYZ Company at December 31, 19—, and the results of its operations and the changes in its financial position for the year then ended, in conformity with generally accepted accounting principles applied on a basis consistent with that of the preceding year.

CERTIFIED PUBLIC ACCOUNTANTS
February 26, 19—

The audit report is addressed to the person or persons who retained the auditor; in the case of corporations, the selection of an auditing firm is usually made by the board of directors or by the stockholders. Although the auditor is paid by the client company and addresses his report to the board of directors, the report is intended for use primarily by such outsiders as bankers, investors, and creditors. Unless the auditor is truly independent and free from any restraint or influence by the client, his report would be of little value to these outside users of the company's financial statements. It is the *independent status* of the auditor which gives value and significance to audit reports.

The long-form report

In most audit engagements, the auditor is requested to submit only the short-form report previously discussed. In other engagements, however, the auditor will prepare two separate types of reports:

1. A short-form report intended for distribution with published financial statements to stockholders, creditors, and other interested outside parties.
2. A long-form report intended for use by management and including discussion of the company's financial position and operating results, analytical schedules and ratios, and comments on various phases of the examination.

The long-form report has the merit of giving management a fresh viewpoint on the financial phases of the business, a view based on a thorough investigation by an independent expert. This report is usually regarded as a confidential document available only to the management of the company, although in many cases the client will agree to provide a copy to his banker. Most bankers feel that study of a long-form report prepared by a certified public accountant is a necessary prerequisite to the granting of a large loan.

The long-form report usually includes the same two paragraphs comprising the short-form report: a statement of scope of the examination and the auditor's opinion based on such examination. The remainder of the long-form report is less standardized and may contain any analyses or recommendations which are useful to management or creditors. Since the long-form report includes the same statements used in the short-form report, we may say that the standards of reporting are the same regardless of whether a short-form or long-form report is being prepared.

Importance of the auditor's report

The writing of the auditor's report is the *final* step in completing an examination. Why, then, should we study the auditor's report at the *beginning* of a course in auditing? The answer is that if one appreciates the significance of an auditor's report, understands why it is prepared and how it is used as a basis for financial decisions, he is then in an excellent position to understand the purpose of the various audit procedures which comprise an examination. Every step in the auditing process is taken to enable the auditor to express an informed opinion on the fairness of the client's financial statements. Later chapters of this book present the auditor's work in verification of cash, inventories, and other financial statement topics. In these chapters the student may appropriately ask himself at each step: How does this verification work relate to the preparation of the auditor's report?

Since the auditor's report is so very briefly and concisely worded, a full understanding of its meaning requires that we consider the significance of each of the phrases included. Phrases such as "generally accepted auditing standards" and "generally accepted accounting principles" mean very different things, and a clear understanding of each is essential to an appreciation of the purpose and nature of auditing. In the following sections of this chapter we shall, therefore, give careful consideration to each of the main ideas in the auditor's short-form report.

Auditors' reports and clients' financial statements

In the scope paragraph of the auditor's report, the first sentence reads: "We have examined the balance sheet of XYZ Company as of December

31, 19—, and the related statements of income and retained earnings and changes in financial position for the year then ended." To gain a full understanding of this sentence we need to emphasize the following four points:

1. *The client, not the auditor, is primarily responsible for the financial statements.*

The management of a company has the responsibility of maintaining adequate accounting records and of preparing proper financial statements for the use of stockholders and creditors. These reporting obligations cannot be discharged merely by arranging for an audit by certified public accountants. However, the retaining of auditors indicates good faith on the part of management and is an important step toward meeting obligations of financial reporting. The management, not the auditor, is *primarily* responsible for the accuracy and adequacy of the financial statements. Even though the statements are sometimes constructed and typed in the auditor's office, primary responsibility for the statements remains with management. For this reason the first sentence of the auditor's report indicates that he has examined the financial statements of the client, that is, statements prepared and issued by the client.

The auditor's product is his report. It is a separate document from the client's financial statements, although the two are closely related and often transmitted together to stockholders and to creditors.

Once we recognize that the financial statements are the statements of the company and not of the auditor, we realize that the auditor has no right to make changes in the financial statements. What action then should the auditor take if he does not agree with the presentation of a material item in the balance sheet or income statement? Assume, for example, that the allowance for uncollectible accounts is not sufficient (in the auditor's opinion) to cover the probable collection losses in the accounts receivable.

The auditor will first discuss the problem with management and point out why he believes the valuation allowance to be inadequate. If management agrees to the desirability of increasing the allowance for uncollectible accounts, an adjusting entry will be made for that purpose, and the problem is solved. If management is not convinced by the auditor's arguments and declines to increase the uncollectible accounts allowance, the auditor will probably qualify his opinion by stating in his report that the financial statements reflect fairly the company's financial position and operating results, except that the provision for uncollectible account losses appears to be insufficient.

Usually such issues are satisfactorily disposed of in discussions between the auditor and the client, and a qualification of the auditor's opinion is avoided. The point to be stressed, however, is that only the management has the power to change the financial statements. The auditor often recommends changes, and generally these changes are agreed to by management. A full consideration of the use of qualifications in the auditor's report is presented in Chapter 21.

2. The auditor does not express an opinion on financial statements without first performing an audit.

The assertion in the report that the auditor has made an examination precludes the possibility that an auditor might issue an opinion merely on the basis of having done some accounting work for a client such as adjusting and closing the books and preparing monthly statements.

When retained to perform an audit, especially of small business concerns, the CPA sometimes finds that the accounting records have not been kept up to date and that the ledgers are not in balance. Considerable work in recording transactions may be necessary before the records will be ready for audit. In such cases the CPA should make clear to the client that a normal audit does not include part-time accounting services; if such work is to be performed by the CPA he must charge professional rates for it in addition to his audit fee. The use of professional auditors to perform routine accounting work is not economical for the businessman, nor is it an attractive form of engagement for the CPA.

3. The auditor's examination and opinion cover not only the balance sheet but the statement of income and retained earnings and the statement of changes in financial position as well.

In the early days of public accounting when audit reports were used principally by short-term creditors, the auditor often limited his investigation to the balance sheet and his examination was referred to as a "balance sheet audit." Many companies considered the income statement confidential and did not release it to outsiders. This situation no longer exists. The measurement of periodic income is perhaps the most important step in the accounting process, and figures for annual earnings are of great interest to investors; consequently, the auditor's examination covers revenue and expense accounts as well as assets and liabilities. The auditor's opinion on the fairness of the net income reported for the period is just as important as his opinion on the fairness of the balance sheet.

In *Opinion No. 19*, the AICPA's Accounting Principles Board held that information concerning the financing and investing of a business enterprise and the changes in its financial position for a period is essential for financial statement users in making economic decisions. Accordingly, the auditor now covers the *statement of changes in financial position* in his examination and opinion.

**4.   The auditor's examination is centered on the financial
statements, not on the accounting records.**

The auditor investigates every item on the financial statements; this
investigation includes reference to the accounting records but is not
limited to the company's books. The auditor's examination includes
physical inspection of assets and the gathering of evidence from outsiders
(such as banks, customers, and suppliers) as well as analysis of the
client's accounting records.

It is true that a principal means of establishing the validity of a
balance sheet and income statement is to trace the statement figures
to the accounting records and back through the records to original evidence of transactions. However, the auditor's use of the accounting
records is merely a part of his examination. It is, therefore, appropriate
for the auditor to state in his report that he has made an examination
of the *financial statements* rather than to say that he has made an examination of the accounting records.

Auditing standards

The second sentence in the scope paragraph of the auditor's report
indicates whether the examination was made in accordance with generally accepted auditing standards and included all auditing procedures
which the auditor considered to be necessary. The sentence reads as
follows: "Our examination was made in accordance with generally accepted auditing standards, and accordingly included such tests of the
accounting records and such other auditing procedures as we considered
necessary in the circumstances."

Standards are authoritative rules for measuring the *quality* of performance. The existence of generally accepted auditing standards is evidence that auditors are much concerned with the maintenance of a
uniformly high quality of audit work by all independent public accountants. If every certified public accountant has adequate technical training
and performs audits with skill, care, and professional judgment, the
prestige of the profession will rise, and the public will attribute more
and more significance to the auditor's opinion attached to financial
statements.

The stature of any profession is largely dependent upon the quality
of the daily work being performed by its members. A uniformly high
quality of work by a professional group is possible only when there
is general recognition and acceptance of specific standards. The development of generally accepted auditing standards has been one of the major
accomplishments of the public accounting profession during the last
quarter of a century. Without these standards, public accounting could
hardly be considered a profession.

What are the standards developed by the public accounting profession? The AICPA Committee on Auditing Procedure has set forth the following description of auditing standards:

GENERAL STANDARDS

1. The examination is to be performed by a person or persons having adequate technical training and proficiency as an auditor.

2. In all matters relating to the assignment an independence in mental attitude is to be maintained by the auditor or auditors.

3. Due professional care is to be exercised in the performance of the examination and the preparation of the report.

STANDARDS OF FIELD WORK

1. The work is to be adequately planned and assistants, if any, are to be properly supervised.

2. There is to be a proper study and evaluation of the existing internal control as a basis for reliance thereon and for the determination of the resultant extent of the tests to which auditing procedures are to be restricted.

3. Sufficient competent evidential matter is to be obtained through inspection, observation, inquiries and confirmations to afford a reasonable basis for an opinion regarding the financial statements under examination.

STANDARDS OF REPORTING

1. The report shall state whether the financial statements are presented in accordance with generally accepted principles of accounting.

2. The report shall state whether such principles have been consistently observed in the current period in relation to the preceding period.

3. Informative disclosures in the financial statements are to be regarded as reasonably adequate unless otherwise stated in the report.

4. The report shall either contain an expression of opinion regarding the financial statements, taken as a whole, or an assertion to the effect that an opinion cannot be expressed. When an over-all opinion cannot be expressed, the reasons therefor should be stated. In all cases where an auditor's name is associated with financial statements the report should contain a clear-cut indication of the character of the auditor's examination, if any, and the degree of responsibility he is taking.

This statement of auditing standards has been officially adopted by the membership of the AICPA. The expression "generally accepted auditing standards" as used in the short-form audit report refers to the 10 standards listed above.

Application of auditing standards

The 10 standards set forth by the AICPA Committee on Auditing Procedure include such intangible and subjective terms of measurement as *"adequate* planning," *"proper* evaluation of internal control," *"suffi-*

cient competent evidential matter," and "*adequate* disclosure." To decide under the circumstances of each audit engagement what is adequate, proper, and sufficient requires the exercise of professional judgment. Auditing cannot be reduced to rote; the exercise of judgment by the auditor is vital at numerous points in every examination. However, the formulation and publication of carefully worded auditing standards are of immense aid in raising the quality of audit work, even though these standards require professional judgment in their application.

If auditing standards are generally accepted, then it can be assumed that each independent public accountant is aware of the quality level expected and maintained by other members of the profession. The conclusions reached by one auditor should be substantially the same as those reached by another if both are confronted with identical sets of accounting data. The publications of the AICPA, the releases of the SEC, and the meetings and committee activities of the several state societies of certified public accountants have all been instrumental in creating a uniform concept of what constitutes acceptable quality in audit work.

Training and proficiency

How does the independent auditor achieve the "adequate technical training and proficiency" required by the first general standard? The AICPA's position on pre-entry education and continuing education was described earlier in this chapter; the key point is that *continuing* education is considered to be essential. The practicing CPA must be given on-the-job training during every audit assignment, must participate in formal training programs of the CPA firm or the AICPA, and must continually read and study current literature in accounting and related fields. This dedication to continuing education and training is essential to meet the requirements of the first general standard.

Independence—the most important auditing standard

An opinion by an independent public accountant as to the fairness of a company's financial statements is of no value unless the accountant is truly independent. Consequently, the auditing standard that "in all matters relating to the assignment an independence in mental attitude is to be maintained by the auditor" is perhaps the most essential factor in the existence of a public accounting profession.

If an auditor owned stock in a company which he audited or if he served as a member of the board of directors, he might subconsciously be biased in the performance of auditing duties. The CPA should therefore avoid any relationship with a client which would cause an outsider who had knowledge of all the facts to doubt the CPA's independence. It is not enough that the CPA be independent; he must conduct himself in such a manner that informed members of the public will have no reason to doubt his independence.

A possible difficulty in the maintenance by the auditor of an attitude of independence lies in the fact that he is selected and paid by the management of the company he audits. Moreover, he often serves as a financial adviser and consultant to management. These circumstances naturally create in the auditor a tendency to react sympathetically toward the attitudes and objectives of management and to identify himself with the management group. One indication of this "management viewpoint" by the auditor is found in the number of cases in which auditors leave the field of public accounting to accept executive positions with client companies.

The principal danger inherent in this close association and feeling of mutual interest between the auditor and the management of the company under audit is that the objectives and interest of management may at times be opposed to the objectives and interests of other groups such as creditors, stockholders, employees, or regulatory authorities. For example, a company may be in desperate need of a bank loan. Bankers and all other outside groups are entitled to a fair and impartial report on the financial position and operations of the company, even though they do not directly employ the auditor or work closely with him.

The long-run welfare of the public accounting profession—in fact, its very existence and recognition as a profession—is dependent upon the independence and integrity of the auditor. If he assumes the role of a partisan spokesman for management, he thereby sacrifices his professional status as an independent public accountant.

Auditing standards contrasted with auditing procedures

Auditing standards must not be confused with auditing procedures. Auditing standards are basic principles governing the nature and extent of the investigation necessary on each examination; auditing procedures, on the other hand, are the detailed acts or steps comprising the auditor's investigation. A familiar example of an audit procedure is the inspection and counting of a client's assets such as cash, marketable securities, and notes receivable.

To illustrate the distinction between auditing standards and procedures, let us consider the auditor's work on inventories. One of the standards of field work stated by the AICPA Committee on Auditing Procedure is the obtaining of "sufficient competent evidential matter" to provide a basis for an opinion. As related to inventory this standard requires evidence as to quantities and prices of merchandise on hand.

One phase of the standard requires that the auditor satisfy himself that the merchandise on hand is fairly priced. To meet this standard the auditor might utilize such auditing *procedures* as (*a*) compare prices applied to the inventory with prices on purchase invoices, (*b*) investigate current market prices, and (*c*) verify the accuracy of footings and extensions on the inventory sheets. These three investigative steps are auditing procedures.

A decision as to how many purchase invoices should be examined and how extensive the comparison with current market prices should be requires the exercise of judgment by the auditor and invokes an auditing standard—the judging of how much evidence is sufficient under the circumstances. This decision should ideally be the same if made by different auditors facing the same set of circumstances.

No single set of procedures will fit all examinations. In each engagement the nature of the accounting records, the quality of the internal control, and other circumstances peculiar to the company will dictate the audit procedures to be used. Auditing standards, however, do not and should not vary from one examination to the next. Standards should be uniform; procedures should vary to fit the circumstances of each engagement.

Audit procedures not determined by the client

The independent status of the auditor is indicated by the fact that the auditor, and not the client, determines the procedures to be employed. The owner or manager of a business instructs his employees as to the procedures they are to follow: he cannot, however, specify the procedures to be followed by the CPA auditing the business. The report states that the auditor used all procedures which *he* considered necessary in the circumstances. This statement indicates that the audit work was in no way restricted or guided by the client and that the auditor assumes full responsibility for the adequacy and scope of his work. The procedures followed are not listed in the report; the users of audited financial statements must rely upon the professional competence of the auditor for assurance that the procedures selected were appropriate under the circumstances.

The opinion paragraph of the auditor's report

In preceding sections of this chapter, the scope paragraph of the auditor's report has been analyzed, with particular emphasis being placed on the reference to generally accepted auditing standards. Now that we have examined the basis for the auditor's opinion, as set forth in the scope paragraph, we are ready to consider the nature of the opinion itself.

The opinion paragraph consists of only one sentence, which is restated here with certain significant phrases shown in italics:

In our opinion, the aforementioned financial statements *present fairly* the financial position of XYZ Company at December 31, 19___, and the results of its operations and the changes in its financial position for the year then ended, in conformity with *generally accepted accounting principles* applied on a basis *consistent with that of the preceding year.*

Each of the italicized phrases has a special significance. The first phrase, "in our opinion," makes clear that the auditor is expressing nothing more than an informed opinion; he is not guaranteeing or certifying that the statements are accurate, correct, or true. In an earlier period of public accounting, the wording of the audit report contained the phrase "I certify that . . . ," but this expression was discontinued on the grounds that it was misleading. To "certify" implies a positive assurance of accuracy which an audit simply does not provide.

The auditor cannot guarantee the correctness of the financial statements because the statements themselves are largely matters of opinion rather than of absolute fact. Furthermore, the auditor does not make a complete and detailed examination of all transactions. His examination is limited to a program of tests which leaves the possibility of some errors going undetected. Because of limitations inherent in the accounting process and because of practical limitations of time and cost in the making of an audit, the auditor's work culminates in the expression of an opinion and not in the issuance of a guarantee of accuracy. The growth of public accounting and the increased confidence placed in audited statements by all sectors of the economy indicate that the auditor's opinion is usually sufficient assurance that the statements may be relied upon.

The statements "present fairly . . ."

The next phrase of the opinion paragraph which requires special consideration is the expression "present fairly." Use of these words by the auditor means that he has concluded that the statements are dependable and free from material errors. Since many of the items in financial statements cannot be measured exactly, the auditor cannot say that the statements "present exactly" the financial position or operating results. Fairness in financial statements means two things: first, freedom from bias and dishonesty; and, second, completeness of information. This concept is applicable not only to the dollar amounts and descriptive titles but also to the propriety of classifications, as in the distinction drawn between current and noncurrent assets.

Adequate informative disclosure

If financial statements are to *present fairly* the financial position and operating results of a company, there must be adequate disclosure of all essential information. A financial statement may be misleading if its does not give a complete picture. For example, if an extraordinary gain arising from the sale of plant and equipment were combined with operating revenue and not clearly identified, the reader might be misled as to the earning power of the company. Of course it might be argued that the management already knows the details of the extraordinary gain realized during the year, and it is, therefore, unimportant whether the item is separately identified in the statements. The answering argument is that the auditor cannot count on all readers of the statement having supplementary knowledge of the company's affairs which will enable them to "read between the lines."

"Adequate informative" disclosure is not "full" disclosure. Premature disclosure of a prospective merger, for example, might injure a company's position. Disclosure of an out-of-court settlement of a single pending lawsuit among a number of interrelated suits might also prove injurious to the company.

Materiality

The preceding paragraphs have indicated that disclosure of essential information is necessary if the statements are to *present fairly* the financial position and operating results of a company. In achieving adequate disclosure, however, it is important not to clutter up the statements with unimportant details. Disclosure is needed only for material facts. The concept of materiality as used in accounting has been defined as a state of relative importance. Unfortunately there is no handy rule of thumb to tell us whether a given item is material. Some accountants have tended to dismiss the concept of materiality as meaning nothing more than "if it isn't important, don't bother with it." In actual auditing practice, however, one of the most significant elements of professional judgment is the ability to draw the line between material and immaterial errors or departures from good accounting practice. The auditor who raises objections and creates crises over immaterial items will soon lose the respect of his clients and associates.

For example, the acquisition of a new delivery truck for $5,000 by a small drugstore would be a relatively important transaction. This $5,000 truck, appearing in the plant and equipment classification, might represent 5 percent or more of the total assets of a small store and would be regarded as material in amount. On the other hand, equipment costing $5,000 would definitely not be a material item on the balance sheet of Sears, Roebuck and Company which has total assets in excess of a billion dollars.

The relative dollar amounts involved are an important consideration in gauging materiality, but they are not necessarily the controlling factor. If a corporation sells assets to a member of its top-management group and he in turn sells the same assets back to the corporation at a profit, the transaction warrants disclosure even though the dollar amounts are not large in relation to the financial statements as a whole. Such a transaction suggests a conflict of interests and warrants disclosure. Both quantitative and qualitative elements warrant consideration in the determination of materiality. Overemphasis on disclosure can detract from the usefulness of a financial statement by obscuring important elements with a mass of trivial details.

Perhaps the most useful working rule in applying the test of materiality is to ask the question: "Is the item of sufficient importance to influence the conclusions which will be reached by users of the financial statements?" This view of materiality has been well expressed by the American Accounting Association in *Accounting and Reporting Standards for Corporate Financial Statements:*

The materiality of an item may depend on its size, its nature, or a combination of both. An item should be regarded as material if there is reason to believe that knowledge of it would influence the decisions of an informed investor.

Generally accepted accounting principles

In our study of the main ideas contained in the auditor's report, the next key phrase to be considered is "generally accepted accounting principles." Of all the phrases we have considered, this one is by far the most difficult to define. Yet a clear definition and widespread understanding of "generally accepted accounting principles" are essential to the preparation of financial statements which will permit comparisons between companies. Bankers, creditors, and investors are constantly weighing the merits of one company against another. By close study of the financial statements of many companies, the professional analyst is able to judge the degree of credit risk or the earning capacity of each company as compared with others in the industry. Decisions to extend credit or to buy or sell an interest in an enterprise are generally based on comparisons of financial statements; if these comparisons are to be valid, the statements of the several companies must be prepared according to the same set of accounting principles.

Comparability in financial statements is not possible unless business enterprise as a whole follows generally accepted accounting principles. The importance of comparability in financial statements can hardly be overemphasized. Financial statements indicate which companies and which industries are employing capital most successfully; and under our free enterprise system, capital flows toward the areas in which earnings are highest. This method of allocating our economic resources works efficiently only if the measurement and reporting of business income are comparable for all sectors of the economy. The CPA thus serves a vital function in the economy when he improves the quality and comparability of financial statements. Further progress in this direction, however, is dependent in large part upon the ability of the accounting profession to reach a clearer, better defined agreement upon the meaning of generally accepted accounting principles.

What are generally accepted accounting principles? No official list exists, but the AICPA's Accounting Principles Board has made a substantial contribution to the compilation of generally accepted accounting principles in *Statement No. 4—Basic Concepts and Accounting Principles Underlying Financial Statements of Business Enterprises.* In this *Statement* (which does not have the force and effect of a formal *Opinion*), the board defines generally accepted accounting principles as "the conventions, rules, and procedures necessary to define accepted accounting practice at a particular time." The *Statement* subdivides present generally accepted accounting principles into three sections—*pervasive principles, broad operating principles,* and *detailed principles.* The pervasive principles, which relate to financial accounting as a whole and provide a basis for the other principles, and the broad operating principles, which guide the recording, measuring, and communicating processes of financial accounting, are listed in *Statement No. 4.* The detailed principles—those which involve the practical application of the pervasive and broad operating principles—are not enumerated in the *Statement.* The board points out that many detailed principles are already found in the board's *Opinions* and in the *Accounting Research Bulletins.*

Another source of detailed accounting principles is the series of accounting releases by the SEC which is stated to be a "program for the publication, from time to time, of opinions on accounting principles for the purpose of contributing to the development of uniform standards and practices on major accounting questions." The American Accounting Association has contributed significantly to the development of a unified body of accounting standards by such publications as its *Accounting and Reporting Standards for Corporate Financial Statements.*

Consistency

Another key phrase in the opinion paragraph of the auditor's report is the statement that accounting principles have been applied on a basis *consistent with that of the preceding year.* The privilege of choosing from among a number of alternative accounting methods carries with it an obligation to use the selected methods in a consistent manner. Inventory, for example, may be valued by such diverse methods as Lifo, Fifo, and average cost, even by companies in the same industry. Whichever method is selected by a given company, however, must be followed consistently to obtain comparable statements from year to year. In this regard, the AICPA's Accounting Principles Board, in *Opinion No. 20*, has held that in the preparation of financial statements there is a presumption that an accounting principle once adopted should not be changed in accounting for events and transactions of a similar type.

A change in the application of accounting principles may cause a distortion of net income for the period in which the change is made. In consequence, the nature of and justification for a change in accounting principle and its effect on income should be disclosed in the financial statements of the period in which the change is made. The justification for the change should explain clearly why the newly adopted principle is preferable. In this situation the auditor cannot issue the standard short-form report as previously illustrated; he must revise the wording of the opinion paragraph to point out the break in consistency of application of accounting principles. In summary we may say that the doctrine of consistency does not make a choice of accounting method an irrevocable decision; it does however prevent a continual switching from one method to another, and also requires disclosure of the effect on net income of any change in method, and the justification for the change.

Other types of auditor's reports

The form of auditor's report discussed in this chapter is called an *unqualified opinion.* Such a report may be regarded as a "clean bill of health" issued by the auditor. An unqualified opinion denotes that the examination was adequate in scope and that the financial statements present fairly financial position and results of operations in conformity with generally accepted accounting principles applied on a basis consistent with that of the preceding year. Under these circumstances the auditor is taking no exceptions and inserting no qualifications in his report.

In many audit engagements, however, the auditor finds that one or more items in the financial statements are not stated in accordance with generally accepted accounting principles. Also, he may find that accounting methods have been changed during the year; hence there is an inconsistency with prior years. Perhaps the client imposes some restriction on the scope of the auditor's examination (as, for example, not authorizing the auditor to visit a distant branch).

Under any of these circumstances the auditor cannot issue the unqualified report previously described. If he finds extremely material
departures from generally accepted accounting principles, he will issue
an *adverse* opinion, which states that the financial statements are *not*
fairly presented. If restrictions imposed by clients are of such import
that they materially limit the auditor's compliance with generally accepted auditing standards, he will *disclaim* an opinion on the financial
statements. If in the auditor's judgment his exceptions as to fairness
of the financial statements or as to his compliance with auditing
standards are cause for concern but are not sufficiently material to warrant an adverse opinion or a disclaimer, respectively, he may issue a
qualified opinion on the financial statements, stating clearly his exceptions. In more extreme cases he may deem it necessary to withdraw
from the engagement. The subject of qualifications and exceptions in
the auditor's report will be considered in detail in Chapter 21.

The audit trail

The financial statements which the auditor is retained to examine
may be thought of as an end product of the accounting system. By
way of background let us consider for a moment the nature of a conventional manual accounting system. The flow of accounting data begins
with the recording of thousands of individual transactions on documents
such as invoices and checks. The information recorded on these original
documents is summarized in journals; and at the end of each month,
the totals of the journals are computed and posted to ledger accounts.
At the end of the year the balances in the ledger accounts are arranged
in the form of a balance sheet and income statement.

In thinking of the accounting records as a whole, we may say that
a continuous trail of evidence exists—a trail of evidence which links
the thousands of individual transactions comprising a year's business
with the summary figures in the financial statements. The great mass
of detailed information originally recorded is condensed and summarized
as it is carried forward through the records so that it finally appears
in the financial statements as a concise overall picture of the company's
affairs.

When punched card accounting systems replace manual systems, the
audit trail still exists. If an electronic data processing system is installed,
audits will still be necessary and care should be taken to maintain the
audit trail of evidence. However, the complexity of electronic data
processing systems has radically altered the nature of the audit trail;
this problem will be discussed in Chapter 6.

It is the job of the auditor to determine whether the concise overall
picture presented in the financial statements is dependable and complete.

One approach used by the auditor is to follow the stream of evidence back to its sources. This type of verification consists of tracing the various items in the statements (such as cash, receivables, sales, and expenses) back to the ledger accounts, and from the ledgers on back through the journals to original documents evidencing transactions. This process of working backward from the statement figures to the detailed evidence of individual transactions is the exact opposite of the accounting process. In accounting work we record a great mass of information, classify and summarize this information, and mold it into a summary report. In auditing work, on the other hand, the starting point is the summary report or financial statement: the auditor's work consists of following the amounts in the financial statements back through the accounts to basic documentary evidence of business transactions. This procedure will not disclose **omitted** transactions; we shall consider in later chapters specific audit techniques for disclosing unrecorded transactions.

Of course the auditor is concerned with more than the agreement of the dollar amounts in the statements with those in the records; he must also determine whether transactions were interpreted and recorded in accordance with generally accepted accounting principles, applied on a basis consistent with that of the preceding year. Although the audit technique of working backward from the figures in the financial statements to the accounting records is a fundamental one, it is important to bear in mind that the auditor also utilizes other types of evidence obtained from sources other than the accounting records.

Extensions of the auditor's attest function

In recent years, the auditor has gradually extended his attest function from reporting only on financial statements. The auditor currently issues reports on a client's internal control (discussed in Chapter 5), reports to various governmental regulatory agencies, and letters to underwriters of a securities issue and other "special reports" (elaborated upon in Chapter 21). The growth of multinational corporations has caused the auditor to report on the financial statements of foreign subsidiaries and divisions which involve accounting principles of the countries involved. In addition, there have been pressures on the independent auditor to further extend his attest function.

Securities analysts are giving increasing attention to companies' financial forecasts and budgets and are requesting the auditor to attest to these "forward-looking" data. A forecast of earnings, or at least a cash budget, may soon be included in a prospectus describing a new issue of securities. The growing interest in the capabilities of a company's managers has generated proposals that the auditor conduct "management audits" and attest to management's performance. Finally, the rising importance of publicly owned companies' quarterly earnings reports has created pressures for the auditor to attest to the fairness of these reports in addition to the annual financial statements. The SEC has recently urged CPAs to review the quarterly statements of their clients before these interim statements are issued to the public, and to consult with clients on reporting problems as they arise.

All of these previously uncharted areas of attestation involve new and difficult challenges. To maintain his professional stature, the auditor must meet these challenges with the same rigorous standards he presently follows in the examination of annual financial statements.

GROUP I
REVIEW QUESTIONS

1–1.   Select the best answer for each of the following items:

a)   The general group of the generally accepted auditing standards includes a requirement that—

(1)   The auditor maintain an independent mental attitude.

(2)   The audit be conducted in conformity with generally accepted accounting principles.

(3)   Assistants, if any, be properly supervised.

(4)   There be a proper study and evaluation of internal control.

b)   The essence of a CPA's independence is—

(1)   Avoiding significant financial interest in the client.

(2)   Maintaining a mental attitude of impartiality.

(3)   Performing the examination from the viewpoint of the stockholders.

(4)   Being sure no relatives or personal friends are employed by the client.

c)   The general group of the generally accepted auditing standards is primarily concerned with—

(1)   The personal qualifications of CPAs.

(2)   Negotiation with the client about the audit engagement and arrangements for the audit.

(3)   Conformity to generally accepted accounting principles.

(4)   The overall audit program including provision for a review of internal control.

d)   An unqualified standard short-form report by a CPA normally does not explicitly state—

(1)   The CPA's opinion that the financial statements comply with generally accepted accounting principles.

(2)   That generally accepted auditing standards were followed in the conduct of the audit.

(3)   That the internal control system of the client was found to be satisfactory.

(4)   The subjects of the audit examination.

e) In his auditor's report, the CPA states that he has examined the—

    (1) Books and other records of the client.

    (2) Financial statements of the client.

    (3) Financial condition and operating results of the client.

    (4) Client's transactions, adjustments, and summaries thereof for the audit period. (AICPA, adapted)

1–2. Bowling Corporation has had an annual audit performed by the same firm of certified public accountants for many years. The financial statements and copies of the audit report are distributed to stockholders each year shortly after completion of the audit. Who is primarily responsible for the fairness of these financial statements? Explain.

1–3. An attitude of independence is a most essential element of an audit by a certified public accountant. Describe several situations in which the CPA might find it somewhat difficult to maintain this independent point of view.

1–4. List some of the more important contributions to auditing literature by the American Institute of Certified Public Accountants.

1–5. Draft the standard form of audit report commonly issued after a satisfactory examination of a client's financial statements.

1–6. One of the directors of the Ralston Corporation suggested that the corporation appoint as controller a certified public accountant on the staff of the auditing firm that had made annual audits of Ralston Corporation for many years. The director expressed the opinion that this move would effect a considerable saving in professional fees as annual audits would no longer be needed. He proposed to give the controller, if appointed, sufficient staff to carry on such continuing investigations of accounting data as appeared necessary. Evaluate this proposal.

1–7. The role of the auditor in the American economy has changed over the years in response to changes in our economic and political institutions. Consequently, the nature of an audit today is quite different from that of an audit performed in the year 1900. Classify the following phrases into two groups: (1) phrases more applicable to an audit performed in 1900, and (2) phrases more applicable to an audit performed today.

    a) Complete review of all transactions.

    b) Evaluation of the system of internal control.

    c) Balance sheet audit.

    d) Emphasis upon use of sampling techniques.

    e) Determination of fairness of financial statements.

    f) Audit procedures to prevent or detect fraud on the part of all employees and managers.

    g) Primary emphasis upon verification of balance sheet amounts.

    h) Responsibility of the auditor for the fairness of reported income.

    i) Influence of stock exchanges and the investing public upon use of independent auditors.

    j) Generally accepted auditing standards.

\ *k)*   Bankers and short-term creditors as principal users of audit reports.

\ *l)*   Certification by the auditor.

1–8.   What professional services other than auditing are commonly offered by CPAs?

1–9.   Under what circumstances may the auditor be unable to issue an unqualified opinion after completing his examination?

1–10.   "I have never issued a qualified report," said Accountant X. "Such reports satisfy no one. I find it much simpler to change the financial statements if the client is using unacceptable accounting methods." Criticize this quotation.

1–11.   The accountant does not guarantee the financial soundness of a client when he renders an opinion on financial statements, nor does the accountant guarantee the absolute accuracy of the statements. Yet the accountant's opinion is respected and accepted. What is expected of the accountant in order to merit such confidence? (AICPA)

1–12.   What is the principal use and significance of an audit report to a large corporation with securities listed on a stock exchange? To a small, family-owned enterprise?

1–13.   State the three principal representations made by the auditor in the opinion paragraph of the standard short-form report.

1–14.   Alan Weston, CPA, completed an examination of the Kirsten Manufacturing Company and issued an unqualified short-form audit report. What does this tell us about the extent of the auditing procedures included in the examination?

1–15.   List some of the social and economic factors which have encouraged the development of the attest function to its present importance in the United States.

1–16.   Contrast the objectives of auditing in the late 19th century with the objectives of auditing today.

1–17.   What were some of the factors that caused auditors to adopt a sampling technique rather than make a complete review of all transactions?

1–18.   Describe several business situations which would create a need for a report by an independent public accountant concerning the fairness of a company's financial statements.

1–19.   Why should the state license certified public accountants?

1–20.   A student of auditing, when asked to distinguish between auditing standards and auditing procedures, stated that auditing standards relate to the preparation of the audit report whereas auditing procedures are concerned with the examination of the accounts prior to writing the report. Do you agree? Explain.

1–21.   If an auditor has made a thorough professional examination of a client's financial statements, should he not be able to issue a report dealing with facts rather than the mere expression of an opinion? Explain.

1–22.   Why did the auditors of a generation ago usually limit their examinations principally to balance sheet accounts?

1–23.   The short-form audit report usually contains a sentence such as the following: "Our examination was made in accordance with generally accepted auditing standards, and included all auditing procedures which we considered necessary in the circumstances."

     a)   Distinguish between auditing standards and auditing procedures.

     b)   Quote or state in your own words four generally accepted auditing standards. (AICPA)

GROUP II
QUESTIONS REQUIRING ANALYSIS

1–24.   While working as a member of the audit staff of Larkin & Walsh, CPAs, Robert Davis was assigned to the audit of Winslow Corporation. During the next several years, Davis regularly participated in the audit of this client and eventually was placed in charge of the Winslow engagement. During this period he received his CPA certificate. Finally, Davis, who had made a very favorable impression upon the officers of Winslow Corporation, was offered a position as controller of the company. He accepted the position. Immediately after this appointment, a member of the board of directors introduced a motion for discontinuance of the annual audit on the grounds that the corporation now had the services of Mr. Davis on a full-time basis.

     While considering this motion, the board invited Mr. Davis to express his views. Put yourself in the role of the new controller and explain fully your views on the proposed discontinuance of the annual audit.

1–25.   The valuation methods applied to certain assets by the Parsons Manufacturing Corporation did not meet with the approval of Roberts and Hawes, CPAs, engaged to audit the company for the first time. Should the auditors change the financial statements to reflect proper valuation of the items in question, or should they qualify the audit report by indicating that generally accepted accounting principles had not been followed in certain respects? Explain.

1–26.   For several years you have made annual audits of the Winchester Corporation and have issued unqualified audit reports. You have also suggested to management several steps for improving internal control and accounting procedures. One of your recommendations has been for a change in the method of inventory valuation from first-in, first-out to last-in, first-out. Assuming that the change is made, what effect if any, would this action have upon the audit report at the time of the next annual examination?

1–27.   Assume that you were retained by the Powell Corporation to perform an examination of its financial statements. You have completed the examination in accordance with generally accepted auditing standards and are satisfied with the results of your work.

Required:

a) What effect, if any, would there be on your issuing an audit opinion if the client company had a loan payable to a finance company in which your brother was the principal stockholder? Assume that the loan was material in relation to the other elements in Powell Corporation's statements. Discuss.

b) Assume that your son, age 16, owns 100 shares of the 50,000 shares of the Powell Corporation common stock outstanding at the balance sheet date. Would this fact have any effect on your issuance of an opinion as an independent auditor? Discuss. (AICPA, adapted)

1–28.   Assume that you are a senior member of an audit staff and are in charge of the audit of a medium-sized manufacturing company whose unaudited financial statements show total assets, $250,000; stockholders' equity, $100,000; net sales, $500,000; and net income, $40,000. One of your less-experienced assistants informs you that he has discovered several irregularities while performing the audit tasks assigned to him, but that he is uncertain whether these errors are sufficiently material to warrant any action. The errors noted were as follows:

(1) Petty cash fund of $100 shown by count at the balance sheet date to be $1 short.

(2) An expenditure of $200 for stationery had been charged to the Miscellaneous Office Expense account, although other expenditures of similar nature were charged to Office Supplies Expense, which had a balance of $1,800.

(3) A few entries for amounts less than $100 had been entered directly in general ledger accounts without the use of journal entries.

Do you think that any of these items should be disclosed in the financial statements or in the audit report, or that any other action by you as auditor is called for? Explain fully.

GROUP III
PROBLEMS

1–29.   Lawrence Wilson, a partner in the CPA firm of Wilson and Milligan, received the following memorandum from Wayne Johnson, president of Johnson Products Corporation, an audit client of many years.

DEAR LARRY:

I have a new type of engagement for you. You are familiar with how much time and money we have been spending in installing equipment to eliminate the air and water pollution caused by our manufacturing plant. We have changed our production processes to reduce discharge of gases; we have changed to more expensive fuel sources with less pollution potential; and we have even discontinued some products because we couldn't produce them without causing considerable pollution.

I don't think the stockholders and the public are aware of the efforts we have made, and I want to inform them of our accomplishments in avoiding damage to the environment. We will devote a major part of our annual report to this topic, stressing that our company is the leader of the entire industry in combatting pollution. To make this publicity more convincing, I would like to retain your firm to study what we have done and to attest as independent accountants that our operations are the best in the industry as far as preventing pollution is concerned.

To justify your statement, you are welcome to investigate every aspect of our operations as fully as you wish. We will pay for your services at your regular audit rates and will publish your "pollution opinion" in our annual report to stockholders immediately following some pictures and discussion of our special equipment and processes for preventing industrial pollution. We may put this section of the annual report in a separate cover and distribute it free to the public. Please let me know at once if this engagement is acceptable to you.

Required:

Put yourself in Lawrence Wilson's position and write a reply to this client's request. Indicate clearly whether you are willing to accept the engagement and explain your attitude toward this proposed extension of the auditor's attest function.

1–30. Thomas Vance, president of Whitehall Corporation, has become convinced that the quality of work being performed in the company's accounting operations has not shown the progress achieved in some other sections of the company. To remedy this situation, Mr. Vance decides to retain the services of a firm of certified public accountants. The company has never been audited. Mr. Vance, on October 1, invites you as a CPA, to conduct an audit covering the current calendar year. The request by Mr. Vance includes mention of the fact that subsidiary ledgers are not in balance with control accounts, the posting of transactions is approximately two months in arrears, and bank statements have not been reconciled for several months.

Required:

You are to evaluate each of the following courses of action and state which, if any, you would follow. Give reasons for your choice. If none of the suggested courses of action is satisfactory in your opinion, describe what you consider to be the appropriate action by the auditor. In drafting your answer to this problem, prepare a separate section for each of the six alternative courses of action.

a) Urge the management to take whatever steps are necessary to have the books in balance and all transactions recorded on a current basis before the end of the year, so that the audit work can begin as scheduled and be completed in a reasonable time.

b) Advise the management of the serious deficiencies in operation of the accounting department, and explain that one of the benefits of your audit will be the balancing of subsidiary ledgers with control accounts and the bringing of the posting work up to date.

c) Offer to make an immediate analysis of the condition of the records, and then to undertake the necessary corrective work as a separate engagement, prior to the year-end audit already agreed upon.

    d)   Offer to make an immediate analysis of the records and a review of accounting personnel with the objective of making recommendations which will aid the client's own staff in getting the records into acceptable condition.

    e)   Advise the client that no corrective action is feasible until after the year-end audit. Explain that the performance of that audit will provide information on the nature and source of bookkeeping shortcomings which should permit more efficient operation in the future.

    f)   Advise the client that you cannot accept the engagement, as you would not be able to express an opinion on the financial statements of a business having such poorly kept records.

1–31.   Nelson Marsh, a college student majoring in accounting, helped finance his education with a part-time job maintaining all accounting records for a small company, Horton Company, located near the campus. Upon graduation, Marsh passed the CPA examination and joined the audit staff of a national CPA firm. However, he continued to perform all accounting work for Horton Company during his "leisure time." Two years later Marsh received his CPA certificate and decided to give up his part-time work with Horton Company. He notified Mr. Horton that he would no longer be available after preparing the year-end financial statements.

    On January 7, Marsh delivered the annual financial statements as his final act for the Horton Company. Mr. Horton then made the following request: "Nelson, I am applying for a substantial bank loan, and the bank loan officer insists upon getting audited financial statements to support my loan application. You are now a CPA and you know everything that's happened in this company and everything that's included in these financial statements, and you know they give a fair picture. I would appreciate it if you would write out the standard short-form audit report and attach it to the financial statements. Then I'll be able to get some fast action on my loan application."

Required:

    a)   Would Marsh be justified in complying with Mr. Horton's request for an auditor's opinion? Explain.

    b)   If you think Marsh should issue the audit report, do you think he should first perform an audit of the company despite his detailed knowledge of the company's affairs? Explain.

    c)   If Mr. Horton had requested an audit by the national CPA firm for which Marsh worked, would it have been reasonable for that firm to accept and to assign Marsh to perform the audit? Explain.

1–32.   William Ball was engaged in the December 31, 1974 year-end audit of Cypress Corporation during the month of January 1975. One of the first matters that came to his attention was the heavy damage to one of the client's two plants caused by a fire on January 1, 1975. The loss from the fire was not covered by insurance. The spectacular fire at this plant was fully described by newspapers, but the December 31, 1974 financial statements and appended notes as prepared by the client did not disclose the loss caused by the fire. The CPA is now in the process of preparing his short-form report. Which of the following courses of action do you think he should follow? Base your answer on the *Generally Accepted Auditing Standards* published by the AICPA and indicate which standard or standards you utilize. Discuss.

a) He need make no mention of the fire loss because the event has been widely publicized and interested parties may be considered as having been notified.

b) A fire loss need not be disclosed because disclosure of such an event frequently creates doubt as to the reason therefor.

c) If the client is not willing to disclose the fire loss in the statements or notes, the CPA should include its mention in his report, probably in a middle paragraph, to assure proper interpretation of the financial statements.

d) If the client is unwilling to disclose the fire loss in the financial statements, the auditor should withdraw from the engagement. (AICPA, adapted)

1–33. The following audit report is deficient in a number of respects. You are to criticize the report systematically from beginning to end, considering each sentence in turn. Use a separate paragraph with identifying heading for each point, as for example, Paragraph 1, Sentence 1. You may also wish to make comments on the overall contents of each paragraph and upon any omissions. Give reasons to support your views. After completing this critical review of the report, draft a revised report, on the assumption that your examination was adequate in all respects and disclosed no significant deficiencies.

To Whom It May Concern:

We have examined the accounting records of the Garland Corporation for the year ended June 30, 1974. We counted the cash and marketable securities, studied the accounting methods in use (which were consistently followed throughout the year), and made tests of the ledger accounts for assets and liabilities. The system of internal control contained no weaknesses.

In our opinion the accompanying balance sheet and related income statement present correctly the financial condition of the corporation at June 30, 1974.

The accounting records of Garland Corporation are maintained in accordance with accounting principles generally observed throughout the industry. Our examination was made in accordance with generally accepted auditing standards, and we certify the records and financial statements without qualifications.

2

Professional ethics

ETHICS—meaning moral principles and standards of conduct—is an essential element of any occupation claiming to be a profession. The term "professional ethics," however, involves more than moral principles; each of the leading professions has developed a code of proper conduct for its members which guides their actions in many ways, including some which are not moral issues. To advertise, for example, is not immoral but is unethical for lawyers, physicians, certified public accountants, and other professional groups. Thus, professional ethics means not only the observing of moral concepts but also specific practical rules designed to guide individual members in a pattern of conduct which will enhance the status of the professional group. Existence of a system of professional ethics inspires public confidence in a profession, and may even be regarded as consideration received by the public in exchange for licensing the professional person.

Professional ethics in public accounting

A physician, lawyer, certified public accountant, or any other professional person, to be successful must have the confidence of his clients. To the certified public accountant, however, public confidence is of special significance; he must have the confidence not only of his clients but also of investors, creditors, bankers, and other "outsiders" who rely upon the auditor's report. These interested third parties will not usually be personally acquainted with the CPA issuing the audit report; their acceptance of the report is based on respect for and confidence in certified public accountants as a professional group.

Professional ethics in public accounting as in other professions has developed gradually and is still in a process of change as the practice of accounting itself changes. Often new concepts are added as a result of unfortunate incidents which reflect unfavorably upon the profession, although not specifically in violation of existing standards.

Evidence that public accounting has achieved the status of a profession is found in the willingness of its members to accept voluntarily standards of conduct more rigorous than those imposed by law. These standards of conduct cover the relationships of the CPA with his clients, with fellow practitioners, and with the public. To be effective, a body of professional ethics must be attainable and enforceable; it must consist not merely of abstract ideals but of attainable goals and practical working rules which can be enforced.

In the short run the restraints imposed on the individual CPA by a body of professional ethics may sometimes appear to constitute a hardship. From a long-run point of view, however, it is clear that the individual practitioner, the profession as a whole, and the public all benefit from the existence of a well-defined body of professional ethics. Certainly, no one would care to engage an independent public accountant if he were known to put the earning of his fee ahead of service to the client, or if he could not be trusted to hold in confidence information given him about his client's financial affairs. Since clients and outside users of audited data are seldom in a position to judge firsthand the quality of the public accountant's work, they must trust him and believe in his competence. Thus the reputation of the CPA is his most valuable asset, and the reputation of CPAs as a group gives professional status to each person licensed as a certified public accountant.

The AICPA Code of Professional Ethics

A principal factor in maintaining high professional standards of practice has been the development of a code of professional ethics under the leadership of the American Institute of Certified Public Accountants. Lack of integrity or careless work on the part of any CPA is a reflection upon the entire profession. Consequently, the members of the profession have acted in unison through their national organization to devise a code of ethics. This code provides practical guidance to the individual member in maintaining a professional attitude. In addition this code gives assurance to clients and to the public that the profession intends to maintain high standards and to enforce compliance by individual members.

The AICPA *Code of Professional Ethics* consists of three parts. The first part, "Concepts of Professional Ethics," is a philosophical discussion which is not intended to establish enforceable standards of ethics. The second part, "Rules of Conduct," is a group of enforceable ethical standards approved by the membership of the AICPA. "Interpretations of Rules of Conduct" issued by the AICPA's Division of Professional Ethics comprise the third part of the code.

A portion of the Concepts of Professional Ethics section is quoted below, followed by that portion of the code which sets forth specific Rules of Conduct.

A distinguishing mark of a professional is his acceptance of responsibility to the public. All true professions have therefore deemed it essential to promulgate codes of ethics and to establish means for ensuring their observance.

The reliance of the public, the government and the business community on sound financial reporting and advice on business affairs, and the importance of these matters to the economic and social aspects of life impose particular obligations on certified public accountants.

Ordinarily those who depend upon a certified public accountant find it difficult to assess the quality of his services; they have a right to expect, however, that he is a person of competence and integrity. A man or woman who enters the profession of accountancy is assumed to accept an obligation to uphold its principles, to work for the increase of knowledge in the art and for the improvement of methods, and to abide by the profession's ethical and technical standards.

The ethical Code of the American Institute emphasizes the profession's responsibility to the public, a responsibility that has grown as the number of investors has grown, as the relationship between corporate managers and stockholders has become more impersonal and as government increasingly relies on accounting information.

The Code also stresses the CPA's responsibility to clients and colleagues, since his behavior in these relationships cannot fail to affect the responsibilities of the profession as a whole to the public.

The Institute's Rules of Conduct set forth minimum levels of acceptable conduct and are mandatory and enforceable. However, it is in the best interests of the profession that CPAs strive for conduct beyond that indicated merely by prohibitions. Ethical conduct, in the true sense, is more than merely abiding by the letter of explicit prohibitions. Rather it requires unswerving commitment to honorable behavior, even at the sacrifice of personal advantage.

The conduct toward which CPAs should strive is embodied in five broad concepts stated as affirmative Ethical Principles:

Independence, integrity and objectivity. A certified public accountant should maintain his integrity and objectivity and, when engaged in the practice of public accounting, be independent of those he serves.

Competence and technical standards. A certified public accountant should observe the profession's technical standards and strive continually to improve his competence and the quality of his services.

Responsibilities to clients. A certified public accountant should be fair and candid with his clients and serve them to the best of his ability, with professional concern for their best interests, consistent with his responsibilities to the public.

Responsibilities to colleagues. A certified public accountant should conduct himself in a manner which will promote cooperation and good relations among members of the profession.

Other responsibilities and practices. A certified public accountant should conduct himself in a manner which will enhance the stature of the profession and its ability to serve the public.

The foregoing Ethical Principles are intended as broad guidelines as distinguished from enforceable Rules of Conduct. Even though they do not provide a basis for disciplinary action, they constitute the philosophical foundation upon which the Rules of Conduct are based.

RULES OF CONDUCT

Applicability of rules

The Institute's Code of Professional Ethics derives its authority from the bylaws of the Institute which provide that the Trial Board may, after a hearing, admonish, suspend or expel a member who is found guilty of infringing any of the bylaws or any provisions of the Rules of Conduct.

The Rules of Conduct which follow apply to all services performed in the practice of public accounting including tax and management advisory services except (*a*) where the wording of the rule indicates otherwise and (*b*) that a member who is practicing outside the United States will not be subject to discipline for departing from any of the rules stated herein so long as his conduct is in accord with the rules of the organized accounting profession in the country in which he is practicing. However, where a member's name is associated with financial statements in such a manner as to imply that he is acting as an independent public accountant and under circumstances that would entitle the reader to assume that United States practices were followed, he must comply with the requirements of Rules 202 and 203.

A member may be held responsible for compliance with the Rules of Conduct by all persons associated with him in the practice of public accounting who are either under his supervision or are his partners or shareholders in the practice.

A member engaged in the practice of public accounting must observe all the Rules of Conduct. A member not engaged in the practice of public accounting must observe only Rules 102 and 501 since all other Rules of Conduct relate solely to the practice of public accounting.

A member shall not permit others to carry out on his behalf, either with or without compensation, acts which, if carried out by the member, would place him in violation of the Rules of Conduct.

Independence, integrity and objectivity

Rule 101—Independence. A member or a firm of which he is a partner or shareholder shall not express an opinion on financial statements of an enterprise unless he and his firm are independent with respect to such enterprise. Independence will be considered to be impaired if, for example:

A. During the period of his professional engagement, or at the time of expressing his opinion, he or his firm

1. Had or was committed to acquire any direct or material indirect financial interest in the enterprise; or

2. Had any joint closely held business investment with the enterprise or any officer, director or principal stockholder thereof which was material in relation to his or his firm's net worth; or

3. Had any loan to or from the enterprise or any officer, director or principal stockholder thereof. This latter proscription does not apply to the following loans from a financial institution when made under normal lending procedures, terms and requirements:

   (a) Loans obtained by a member or his firm which are not material in relation to the net worth of such borrower.

   (b) Home mortgages.

   (c) Other secured loans, except loans guaranteed by a member's firm which are otherwise unsecured.

B. During the period covered by the financial statements, during the period of the professional engagement or at the time of expressing an opinion, he or his firm

1. Was connected with the enterprise as a promoter, underwriter or voting trustee, a director or officer or in any capacity equivalent to that of a member of management or of an employee; or

2. Was a trustee of any trust or executor or administrator of any estate if such trust or estate had a direct or material indirect financial interest in the enterprise; or was a trustee for any pension or profit-sharing trust of the enterprise.

The above examples are not intended to be all-inclusive.

Rule 102—Integrity and objectivity. A member shall not knowingly misrepresent facts, and when engaged in the practice of public accounting, including the rendering of tax and management advisory services, shall not subordinate his judgment to others. In tax practice, a member may resolve doubt in favor of his client as long as there is reasonable support for his position.

Competence and technical standards

Rule 201—Competence. A member shall not undertake any engagement which he or his firm cannot reasonably expect to complete with professional competence.

Rule 202—Auditing standards. A member shall not permit his name to be associated with financial statements in such a manner as to imply that he is acting as an independent public accountant unless he has complied with the applicable generally accepted auditing standards promulgated by the Institute. Statements on Auditing Procedure issued by the Institute's committee on auditing procedure are, for purposes of this rule, considered to be interpretations of the generally accepted auditing standards, and departures from such statements must be justified by those who do not follow them.

Rule 203—*Accounting principles.* A member shall not express an opinion that financial statements are presented in conformity with generally accepted accounting principles if such statements contain any departure from an accounting principle promulgated by the body designated by Council to establish such principles which has a material effect on the statements taken as a whole, unless the member can demonstrate that due to unusual circumstances the financial statements would otherwise have been misleading. In such cases his report must describe the departure, the approximate effects thereof, if practicable, and the reasons why compliance with the principle would result in a misleading statement.

Rule 204—*Forecasts.* A member shall not permit his name to be used in conjunction with any forecast of future transactions in a manner which may lead to the belief that the member vouches for the achievability of the forecast.

Responsibilities to clients

Rule 301—*Confidential client information.* A member shall not disclose any confidential information obtained in the course of a professional engagement except with the consent of the client.

This rule shall not be construed (a) to relieve a member of his obligation under Rules 202 and 203, (b) to affect in any way his compliance with a validly issued subpoena or summons enforceable by order of a court, (c) to prohibit review of a member's professional practices as a part of voluntary quality review under Institute authorization or (d) to preclude a member from responding to any inquiry made by the ethics division or Trial Board of the Institute, by a duly constituted investigative or disciplinary body of a state CPA society, or under state statutes.

Members of the ethics division and Trial Board of the Institute and professional practice reviewers under Institute authorization shall not disclose any confidential client information which comes to their attention from members in disciplinary proceedings or otherwise in carrying out their official responsibilities. However, this prohibition shall not restrict the exchange of information with an aforementioned duly constituted investigative or disciplinary body.

Rule 302—*Contingent fees.* Professional services shall not be offered or rendered under an arrangement whereby no fee will be charged unless a specified finding or result is attained, or where the fee is otherwise contingent upon the findings or results of such services. However, a member's fees may vary depending, for example, on the complexity of the service rendered.

Fees are not regarded as being contingent if fixed by courts or other public authorities or, in tax matters, if determined based on the results of judicial proceedings or the findings of governmental agencies.

Responsibilities to colleagues

Rule 401—Encroachment. A member shall not endeavor to provide a person or entity with a professional service which is currently provided by another public accountant except:

1.   He may respond to a request for a proposal to render services and may furnish service to those who request it. However, if an audit client of another independent public accountant requests a member to provide professional advice on accounting or auditing matters in connection with an expression of opinion on financial statements, the member must first consult with the other accountant to ascertain that the member is aware of all the available relevant facts.

2.   Where a member is required to express an opinion on combined or consolidated financial statements which include a subsidiary, branch or other component audited by another independent public accountant, he may insist on auditing any such component which in his judgment is necessary to warrant the expression of his opinion.

A member who receives an engagement for services by referral from another public accountant shall not accept the client's request to extend his service beyond the specific engagement without first notifying the referring accountant, nor shall he seek to obtain any additional engagement from the client.

Rule 402—Offers of employment. A member in public practice shall not make a direct or indirect offer of employment to an employee of another public accountant on his own behalf or that of his client without first informing such accountant. This rule shall not apply if the employee of his own initiative or in response to a public advertisement applies for employment.

Other responsibilities and practices

Rule 501—Acts discreditable. A member shall not commit an act discreditable to the profession.

Rule 502—Solicitation and advertising. A member shall not seek to obtain clients by solicitation. Advertising is a form of solicitation and is prohibited.

Rule 503—Commissions. A member shall not pay a commission to obtain a client, nor shall he accept a commission for a referral to a client of products or services of others. This rule shall not prohibit payments for the purchase of an accounting practice or retirement payments to individuals formerly engaged in the practice of public accounting or payments to their heirs or estates.

Rule 504—Incompatible occupations. A member who is engaged in the practice of public accounting shall not concurrently engage in any business or occupation which impairs his objectivity in rendering professional services or serves as a feeder to his practice.

Rule 505—Form of practice and name. A member may practice public accounting, whether as an owner or employee, only in the form of a proprietorship, a partnership or a professional corporation whose characteristics conform to resolutions of Council.

A member shall not practice under a firm name which includes any fictitious name, indicates specialization or is misleading as to the type of organization (proprietorship, partnership or corporation). However, names of one or more past partners or shareholders may be included in the firm name of a successor partnership or corporation. Also, a partner surviving the death or withdrawal of all other partners may continue to practice under the partnership name for up to two years after becoming a sole practitioner.

A firm may not designate itself as "Members of the American Institute of Certified Public Accountants" unless all of its partners or shareholders are members of the Institute.

Analysis of AICPA Code of Professional Ethics

Some of the rules stated in the *Code of Professional Ethics* are self-explanatory, but discussion and illustration may be necessary to a full understanding of several other sections of the code.

Independence.   The first AICPA Rule of Conduct is concerned with the problem of independence. Two distinct ideas are involved: first, the accountant must *in fact* be independent of any enterprise which he audits; and, second, the relationships of the CPA with his client must be such that he will *appear* independent to third parties.

The point concerning *appearance of independence* to an informed third party was only recently added to the code. Previously accountants had been prone to say that independence was a state of mind, a mental attitude, which was not subject to objective measurement and therefore could only be judged by the CPA himself. For example, a CPA who owned stock in a corporation or served as a director might argue that his financial interest in the company did not modify by one hair his objective approach to the annual audit. Despite such arguments it seems reasonable that an investor or banker using audited financial statements would prefer that the audit be performed by a CPA who had no financial interest in the company and therefore had no problem of conflicting interests. The standard stated in Rule 101 which holds that any direct financial interest or connection such as director or promoter of a client company will render the CPA *not independent* is comparable to the policy of requiring that the Secretary of Defense and other high government officials have no financial interest in companies holding government contracts. Although such relationships would not necessarily cause an official to act in a biased manner, the public will have greater confidence in government officials who do not have such investments.

Although experience has shown that most audited financial statements are dependable, occasionally material fraud will occur and not immediately be discovered by the auditors for the company. When the fraud does come to light, the reaction of creditors, investors, and the public would be far more critical if it were then discovered that the "independent" accountants who audited the company's financial statements were also part owners of the company even if that ownership interest was quite small. Under these circumstances the publicity which always stems from fraud cases is sure to lessen public confidence in the public accounting profession. It is beside the point as to whether the auditors would in fact be influenced by their financial interest in the client company. The CPA must not only *be* independent of the company on whose statements he reports; he must also *appear* independent to outsiders who are given all pertinent information about the relationships between the auditor and the company being audited.

Auditing standards and accounting principles.   Rule 202 obligates a CPA to comply with the 10 generally accepted auditing standards discussed in Chapter 1 and clarifies the enforceability of Statements on Auditing Procedure. Rule 203 requires the CPA to recognize the pronouncements of the Financial Accounting Standards Board and its predecessor, the Accounting Principles Board, as primary sources of generally accepted accounting principles.

The consequence of these two rules is a strengthening of the authority of the AICPA and the Financial Accounting Standards Board and a lessening of the opportunities for wide variations in the quality of auditing services or the options available for accounting procedures.

Forecasts of future transactions.   Owners of a business who wish to sell all or part of the enterprise sometimes prepare optimistic forecasts of expected future earnings. Similar projections may be prepared to support an application for a bank loan. To make these forecasts more convincing the businessman may seek to have them endorsed by a certified public accountant. Such endorsements are not permitted under the *Code of Professional Ethics.* The accountant can make an objective verification of *past* earnings and vouch for their fairness; he cannot read the future and therefore he must not vouch for the achievability of an estimate of *future* earnings. To do so would tend to cheapen the professional status of the CPA.

Rule 204, in prohibiting AICPA members from vouching for the achievability of forecasts, does not prevent the auditor from aiding management in preparing budgets, pro forma financial statements, cash forecasts, etc. These studies are essential tools of management and aid in the formulation of sound decisions. The CPA may prepare or assist the client in preparing such statements and analyses; however, if his name is associated with this work he must indicate clearly in writing the assumptions made, the source of the data, the responsibility he has assumed, and the fact that he does *not* vouch for the achievability of the forecast.

Confidential client information.   Rule 301 stresses the confidential nature of the information obtained by a CPA from his client. The nature of the accountant's work makes it necessary for him to have access to the client's most confidential financial affairs. The independent accountant may thus gain knowledge of impending mergers, purchases of businesses, proposed financing, prospective stock splits or dividend changes, contracts being negotiated, and other confidential information which if disclosed or otherwise improperly used could bring the accountant quick monetary profits. Of course the client would be financially injured, as well as embarrassed, if the CPA were to "leak" such information. The accountant must not only keep quiet as to his client's business plans but he rarely even mentions in public the names of his clients. Any loose talk by an independent public accountant concerning his clients' affairs would immediately brand him as lacking in professional ethics.

The communications of a client to a certified public accountant are not privileged under common law as are communications to a lawyer, clergyman, or physician. However, some states have adopted statutes indicating that a public accountant should not be required in court to give evidence gained by him in confidence from a client. In the course of an audit, independent accountants sometimes become aware of illegal transactions. In such cases, do the responsibilities of the auditor as a law-abiding private citizen compel him to report the illegal transactions to the authorities, or is he bound by the confidential relationship with his client to keep silent? There is an old adage which says that "an auditor is neither a reformer nor an informer"; however, most members of the public accounting profession would certainly not accept as a client any company engaging in illegal practices. As to whether the auditor would take the initiative in reporting an illegal action by a client, no general answer can be given; the auditor's decision would have to be governed by the seriousness of the illegal act and by all of the attendant circumstances.

Contingent fees. An accountant is prohibited (Rule 302) from making an audit on a contingent fee basis. For example, a company in need of an auditor's report to support its application for a bank loan might offer to make the auditor's fee contingent upon approval of the loan by the bank. Such an arrangement would create an undesirable temptation for the auditor to abandon his independent viewpoint and to lend his support to the statements prepared by management. In the handling of tax work, on the other hand, the accountant does not assume an independent status, and contingent fees are permissible if they are determined as a result of judicial proceedings or government agency findings.

A major purpose of the Rules of Conduct is to cause the auditor to avoid situations in which he will face a strong temptation to sacrifice his independence. As a parallel illustration, a bank does not permit even its most trusted officers and employees to take the bank's cash home at night. Regardless of the fact that an auditor may have demonstrated repeatedly his independence and integrity, it is desirable that he avoid situations which present unusual temptations.

Encroachment.   Rule 401 bans encroachment by one CPA upon the practice of another. The need for such a prohibition is apparent; without it, distrust and hostility would pervade relationships between public accountants.

Rule 401 also contains a safeguard against the undesirable practice known as "shopping for principles." In the past, a CPA who took a stand against what he considered to be an improper accounting presentation or disclosure by a client might find himself discharged by the client and replaced by another CPA whose professional judgment sanctioned the disputed presentation or disclosure. Such an occurrence obviously had a detrimental effect upon the relationship between the two CPA firms involved and upon the public accounting profession as a whole. The requirement that a public accountant who is approached by the audit client of another CPA must consult with the other accountant before rendering professional services should contribute a great deal toward curbing any "shopping for principles." Recent action by the SEC, requiring companies subject to its jurisdiction to report reasons for auditor replacement directly to the Commission, and providing for corroboration from the replaced CPA firm, should also help curb such "shopping."

Solicitation and advertising.   Rule 502 prohibits solicitation of clients and bans advertising, which is a form of solicitation. The related interpretations by the Division of Professional Ethics of the AICPA prohibit the CPA from advertising his services in any form, even from publishing in newspapers a small "card" or announcement of change in address or change in personnel of a firm. The use of radio or television advertising, outdoor signs, bold-type listing in telephone directories, stationery with headings describing services offered, and similar practices are all unacceptable for a member of a profession. Also prohibited is the practice of distributing tax booklets or newsletters with the name of the accountant imprinted thereon, unless he is the author of the publication. A businessman may appropriately advertise the merits of the products he sells, but the professional man cannot appropriately advertise his own intelligence, education, and knowledge.

To illustrate the breadth of application of this rule, let us assume that a certified public accountant appears on television during the income tax season in an educational-type program discussing some of the problems commonly encountered by taxpayers in the preparation of tax returns. Such appearances are in the public interest and are entirely within the bounds of professional ethics, *provided* the accountant does not at any time during the program mention his business address or otherwise intimate that he is available for tax work, and *provided* that he is not introduced or described by the announcer as available for tax services.

Previous versions of the AICPA *Code of Professional Ethics* contained prohibitions against competitive bidding by CPAs for professional engagements. Competitive bidding for audit work was stated to be a form of solicitation, unprofessional, and not in the public interest. However, the Institute's legal counsel recommended this rule not be enforced because of possible violation of federal antitrust laws. In 1972 a suit by the U.S. Department of Justice against the AICPA for violation of the price-fixing prohibitions of the Sherman Antitrust Act was settled by a consent decree. Meanwhile, the new Rules of Conduct now in effect had been prepared without any prohibition against competitive bidding.

Incompatible occupations. Rule 504 prohibits the AICPA member from engaging "in any business or occupation which impairs his objectivity in rendering professional services or serves as a feeder for his (public accounting) practice." For example, an accountant should not act as an insurance agent because one of the normal procedures in an audit is a review of the adequacy of the client's insurance coverage. An objective appraisal of insurance coverage would be difficult if the accountant were in a position to benefit personally by the sale of insurance. Another objection to carrying on an insurance business conjointly with a public accounting practice is that any advertising incident to the insurance business might be regarded as an indirect means of advertising accounting services.

Enforcement of professional ethics

The AICPA *Code of Professional Ethics* is binding only upon accountants who are members of the AICPA. Violation of the code may result in reprimand, suspension, or expulsion of the offending member. Although expulsion from the AICPA would not in itself cause the loss of a CPA license and would not prevent the expelled member from continuing the practice of public accounting, the damage to his professional reputation would probably be so great as to make this penalty disastrous to the individual or firm.

Many provisions of the AICPA Rules of Conduct have been adopted by numerous states as part of state accountancy acts; in these states the revocation of license to practice is a possible consequence of the violation of the standards previously discussed. The several state societies of certified public accountants also follow the leadership of the AICPA to a great extent in urging compliance by their members with the policies set forth in the code. In summary, a problem of enforcing professional ethics exists and will no doubt continue to exist, but with a few exceptions most public accounting firms recognize the value of professional ethics and attempt to conform fully with the standards enunciated by the AICPA.

Securities and Exchange Commission—impact on professional ethics

A discussion of professional ethics would be incomplete without considering the important role played by the Securities and Exchange Commission. A principal aim of the Commission throughout its existence has been the improvement of auditing standards and the establishment of high levels of professional conduct by the independent public accountants practicing before the Commission.

The SEC is an independent, quasi-judicial agency of the U.S. government. It administers the Securities Act of 1933, the Securities Exchange Act of 1934, and other legislation concerning securities and financial matters. The function of the SEC is to protect the interests of investors and the public by requiring full disclosure of financial information by companies offering securities for public sale. A second objective is to prevent misrepresentation, deceit, or other fraud in the sale of securities. The "disclosure doctrine" of protecting investors was extended by the Securities Exchange Act of 1934 to all securities listed on national stock exchanges. At present all over-the-counter companies with total assets exceeding $1 million and 500 or more stockholders are subject to the same disclosure requirements previously applicable only to companies listed on major stock exchanges.[1]

The term *registration statement* is an important one in any discussion of the impact of the SEC on accounting practice. To *register* securities means to qualify them for sale to the public by filing with the SEC financial statements and other data in a form acceptable to the Commission. A registration statement varies by type of company but generally calls for (*a*) description of the business, (*b*) description of the securities offered and other outstanding securities, (*c*) information on management, and (*d*) *audited financial statements,* including a balance sheet and income statements for a three-year period. The legislation creating the SEC made the Commission responsible for determining whether the financial statements presented to it reflected proper application of accounting principles. To aid the Commission in discharging this responsibility, the Securities Acts provided for an examination and report by an *independent* public accountant. Thus, from its beginning, the Securities and Exchange Commission has been a major user of audited financial statements and has exercised great influence upon the development of

[1] Certain over-the-counter companies having as few as 300 shareholders may be required to file periodic reports with the SEC subsequent to registering a new securities issue with the Commission under provisions of the Securities Act of 1933.

accounting principles, the strengthening of auditing standards, and especially upon the concept of independence.

Protection of investors, of course, requires that the public have available the information contained in a registration statement concerning a proposed issue of securities. The issuing company is therefore required to deliver to prospective buyers of securities a *prospectus* or selling circular based on the registration statement. The registration of securities does not insure investors against loss; the SEC definitely does not pass on the merit of securities. There is in fact only one purpose of registration: that purpose is to provide disclosure of the important facts so that the investor has available all pertinent information on which to base an intelligent decision on whether to buy a given security.

If the SEC believes that a given registration statement does not meet its standards of disclosure, it may require amendment of the statement or may issue a stop order preventing sale of the securities. However, the fairness of the pricing of the securities or the prospects for successful operation of the business are not factors bearing on registration—the only standard to be met is that of adequate disclosure. Certain security offerings are presently exempt from the requirements of registration; these include certain offerings not in excess of $500,000, offerings restricted to residents of a single state, private offerings to a limited number of persons, and governmental securities. In appraising the impact of the SEC upon the practice of public accountants, it should be borne in mind that annual financial statements as well as registration statements must be filed with the Commission by all companies with securities listed on national stock exchanges.

To improve the quality of the financial statements filed with it and the professional standards of the independent accountants who report on these statements, the SEC has adopted a basic accounting regulation known as *Regulation S–X* and entitled *Form and Content of Financial Statements*. The Commission has also published, in *Accounting Series Releases*, its decisions on accounting issues presented in important cases, and opinions of the Commission's Chief Accountant on many complex accounting problems. These publications, along with the studies and recommendations of professional accounting societies mentioned in Chapter 1, have been most influential in the improvement of accounting practices and auditing standards.

Extent of SEC coverage of financial reporting

The laws administered by the SEC require that the financial statements filed with the Commission be audited by an independent public or certified public accountant. In 1936, shortly after the SEC had begun its operations, the number of issuing companies filing registration statements was over 2,000, and the securities involved amounted to nearly $5 billion. In a recent year, more than 18,000 companies were required to file annual reports and over 3,400 filed registration statements. The fallacious notion that only the large national CPA firms are concerned with SEC requirements is quickly dispelled by a review of the records. Many CPA firms each year audit annual reports filed by their clients with the SEC. Some of these CPA firms are relatively small and have among their clients only one or two companies coming under SEC jurisdiction. Nevertheless, these firms as well as the national public accounting organizations must be familiar with SEC accounting practices and requirements.

Independence as defined by the SEC

The laws administered by the SEC require that financial statements be examined by "independent public or certified public accountants." The Commission therefore faces the task of deciding upon the meaning of "independence" on the part of accountants. The following was adopted as part of Rule 2–01 of *Regulation S–X:*

The Commission will not recognize any certified public accountant . . . as independent who is not in fact independent. For example, an accountant will be considered not independent with respect to any person . . . (1) in which, during the period of his professional engagement to examine the financial statements being reported on or at the date of his report, he or his firm or a member thereof had, or was committed to acquire, any direct financial interest or any material indirect financial interest; or (2) with which, during the period of his professional engagement to examine the financial statements being reported on, at the date of his report or during the period covered by the financial statements, he or his firm or a member thereof was connected as a promoter, underwriter, voting trustee, director, officer, or employee, . . . For the purposes of Rule 2–01 the term "member" means all partners in the firm and all professional employees participating in the audit or located in an office of the firm participating in a significant portion of the audit.

In applying this rule to specific cases the SEC has held that the public accountant was not independent in the following situations, among others:

1. The public accountant or one of his employees was an officer or director of the client company.
2. The public accountant or one of his employees performed the month-end accounting work of the client, including the making of general ledger entries and closing entries.
3. The public accountant and the client made personal loans of material amount to each other.

SEC rules compared with AICPA Code of Professional Ethics

Some differences have existed between the concept of independence required by the SEC and that set forth in the AICPA *Code of Professional Ethics*. One point of difference has been the much-discussed question of whether the CPA who performs bookkeeping services for a client, such as posting the general ledger, making monthly closing entries, and preparing monthly financial statements, can also serve as independent auditor for the company. The SEC answer is no; the CPA is not independent under these circumstances. The auditor should be an outsider who reviews the work performed by the client's accounting employees; if the auditor performs the original bookkeeping work, he cannot maintain the posture of an outside critic. In *Accounting Series Release No. 126,* the SEC stated: "The Commission is of the opinion that an accountant cannot objectively audit books and records which he has maintained for a client."

ILLUSTRATIVE CASE. The SEC found in one famous case (In the Mattter of Interstate Hosiery Mills, Inc., 4 SEC 706, 717 [1939]) that a staff member of the CPA firm had been keeping the books of a client; the financial statements had been falsified, and the audit staff member was responsible for the falsification. Clearly the dual role of bookkeeper and independent auditor played by this individual had resulted in defeating the purpose of the audit.

The AICPA, on the other hand, has often considered the propriety of combining the performance of manual or automated bookkeeping services with the conduct of an independent audit for a client, but has not opposed the practice as damaging to the auditor's independence. Such a ruling would no doubt be a blow to many small public accounting firms with practices including considerable "write-up work" and occasional audits for "write-up" clients. Despite this attitude of the AICPA, the SEC position denying the independence of an auditor-bookkeeper appears much sounder in terms of basic auditing philosophy.

The CPA as tax adviser—ethical problems

What is the responsibility of the CPA in serving as tax adviser? He has a primary responsibility to his client: that is, to see that his client pays the proper amount of tax and no more. Rule of Conduct No. 102 provides that in his role as tax adviser, the CPA may properly resolve questionable issues in favor of the client; the CPA is not obliged to maintain the posture of independence required in his audit work. When he expresses an opinion on financial statements he must be unbiased; freedom from bias is not required in serving as a tax adviser. On the other hand, the CPA must adhere to the same standards of truth and personal integrity in tax work as in all other professional activities. Any departure from these standards on a tax engagement would surely destroy the reputation of the CPA in performing his work as independent auditor.

A second responsibility of the CPA on a tax engagement is to the public whose interests are represented by the government, more specifically by the Internal Revenue Service. To meet this responsibility, the CPA must observe the preparer's declaration on the tax returns he prepares. This declaration requires him to state that the return is "true, correct, and complete . . . based on all information of which he has any knowledge." To comply with this declaration, what steps must the CPA take to acquire knowledge relating to the tax return? He is not required to make an audit; his knowledge of the return may be limited to information supplied him by the taxpayer. However, if this information appears unreasonable or contradictory, he is obligated to make sufficient inquiries to resolve these issues. Information which appears plausible to a layman might appear unreasonable to the CPA, since he is an expert in evaluating financial data. The CPA is not obligated to investigate any and all information provided by the taxpayer, but he cannot ignore clues which cast doubt on the accuracy of these data.

In addition to being guided by the declaration on the tax return, the CPA is also bound by the AICPA *Code of Professional Ethics.* This code is in general applicable to every type of work which the CPA undertakes, although those portions of the Rules of Conduct relating to the examination of financial statements *are clearly not applicable to tax engagements.* However, in tax work as in auditing or any other area of his practice, the CPA is pledged to high standards of morality and integrity. Only by unswerving conformance with these standards can he uphold the dignity and honor of the accounting profession.

To further identify appropriate standards of tax practice for CPAs, the AICPA in 1964 initiated a series of *Statements on Responsibilities in Tax Practice.* The eight statements issued to date have focused on the CPA's responsibilities, in varying circumstances, for signing the preparer's declaration on tax returns which he has prepared or reviewed; for use of estimates in preparing returns; for errors in previously filed returns or client failure to file returns; and for advice to clients on tax matters. A proposed ninth statement deals with procedural aspects of preparing tax returns.

Unless certified public accountants approach tax engagements with full recognition of the responsibilities imposed on them by the AICPA code, by the preparer's declaration on the return, and by the *Statements on Responsibilities in Tax Practice,* they may quickly destroy public confidence in the profession. The interests of the taxpayer and of the government are directly opposed, and this conflict requires a most careful delineation of the CPA's responsibility. Because of public confidence in the CPA certificate and the reputation of the profession for integrity, any financial data to which the CPA lends his name gain in credibility even though no examination is made and no opinion is expressed. This level of public confidence and respect is an invaluable asset of the profession which deserves to be guarded with the greatest care.

Management advisory services and professional ethics

The rendering of management advisory services has in recent years represented a steadily rising proportion of the work performed by public accounting firms. CPAs serve management as systems analysts, data processing advisers, financial consultants, operations researchers, and budgetary experts.

Does the *Code of Professional Ethics* formulated by the AICPA for the field of auditing apply to the field of management advisory services as well? The answer, in the "Applicability of Rules" section of the Rules of Conduct, is "yes." If management advisory services are defined as part of public accounting, then clearly the code is applicable. Although the Rules of Conduct were devised primarily with reference to the expression of an opinion on financial statements, they have long been held applicable to income tax work by public accounting firms. In other words, income tax practice is regarded as part of public accounting and subject to the same code of ethics as auditing. It would be most confusing to the public and damaging to the prestige of a profession if its members were to adopt a double standard of ethics: a strict code for one segment of practice and a lenient code for another segment. For example, elaborate newspaper advertising by a certified public accountant describing in glowing terms his proficiency as a management consultant would surely have considerable impact upon his professional status as an auditor.

The field of management advisory services is, in fact, a part of public accounting, and an increasingly important part. Evidence supporting this conclusion includes the publication by the AICPA of the bimonthly journal *Management Adviser,* the establishment by the AICPA of a Committee on Management Advisory Services, and the issuance of Statements on Management Advisory Services (three to date) by that committee. The principal unanswered question in defining management advisory services is whether the range of activities which may reasonably be performed by public accounting firms shall be limited to those relating to accounting and financial matters or shall be unlimited in scope.

Does rendering of management advisory services threaten the auditor's independence?

A problem to be considered in rendering management advisory services is the possible threat to the auditor's independence when auditing and a variety of consulting services are performed for the same client. Can a public accounting firm which renders extensive management advisory services for a client still maintain the independent status so essential in an audit and in the expression of an opinion on the client's financial statements?

To begin with, it is clear that if the public accountant becomes in effect a part-time controller for a client and assumes a *decision-making* role in the client's affairs, he is not in a position to make an independent audit of the financial statements. On the other hand, abundant precedent exists showing that public accounting firms have long been rendering certain purely *advisory* services to management while continuing to perform audits in an independent manner which serves the public interest. Advisory services can generally be distinguished from management proper; the work of the consultant or adviser consists of such functions as conducting special studies and investigations, making suggestions to management, pointing out the existence of weaknesses, outlining various alternative corrective measures, and making recommendations. The new elements in the problem of maintaining independence appear to be the rendering of services relating to general management areas rather than accounting and financial management, and the extent of the services rendered.

If an auditor becomes deeply and continuously involved in rendering a great many management advisory services for a given client, the relationship could conceivably become so significant as to create doubt as to the auditor's independence in making periodic audits of the business. This threat is probably not a serious one, however; everyone is aware that many desirable activities if carried to an extreme will create difficulties. In the opinion of the authors, public accounting firms can render, and many are rendering, management advisory services of great value to their clients while maintaining the traditional status of independence vital to the role of an auditor.

The AICPA has long been concerned about the possible threat to the auditor's independence caused by his rendering management advisory services. In 1969 an AICPA Committee on Independence issued a report with recommendations to CPAs concerned that they might *appear* to lack independence because of rendering both audit and management advisory services to a client. The CPA was advised to consult with the members of the client's board of directors or audit committee to make certain they concurred as to the propriety of the rendering of management advisory services by the company's independent auditors. The report also recommended that the CPA report periodically to the board or audit committee on the nature of all important services being rendered for the client.

GROUP I
REVIEW QUESTIONS

2–1. Select the best answer choice for each of the following:
  a) A CPA should reject a management advisory services engagement if—
  (1) It would require him to make management decisions for an audit client.
  (2) His recommendations are to be subject to review by the client.
  (3) He audits the financial statements of a subsidiary of the prospective client.
  (4) The proposed engagement is not accounting-related.

  b) Printers, Inc., an audit client of James Frank, CPA, is contemplating the installation of an electronic data processing system. It would be inconsistent with Frank's independence as the auditor of Printers' financial statements for him to—
  (1) Recommend accounting controls to be exercised over the computer.
  (2) Recommend particular hardware and software packages to be used in the new computer center.
  (3) Prepare a study of the feasibility of computer installation.
  (4) Supervise operation of Printers' computer center on a part-time basis.

  c) The CPA should not undertake an engagement if his fee is to be based upon—
  (1) The findings of a tax authority.
  (2) A percentage of audited net income.
  (3) Per diem rates plus expenses.
  (4) Rates set by a city ordinance.

  d) The CPA ethically could—
  (1) Perform an examination for a financially distressed client at less than his customary fees.
  (2) Advertise only as to his expertise in preparing income tax returns.
  (3) Base his audit fee on a percentage of the proceeds of his client's stock issue.
  (4) Own preferred stock in a corporation which is an audit client.

  e) With respect to examination of the financial statements of the Third National Bank, a CPA's appearance of independence ordinarily would not be impaired by his—

(1) Obtaining a large loan for working capital purposes.
(2) Serving on the committee which approves the bank's loans.
(3) Utilizing the bank's time-sharing computer service.
(4) Owning a few inherited shares of Third National common stock.

f) Mercury Company, an audit client of Eric Jones, CPA, is considering acquiring Hermes, Inc. Jones' independence as Mercury's auditor would be impaired if he were to—

(1) Perform on behalf of Mercury a special examination of the financial affairs of Hermes.
(2) Render an opinion as to each party's compliance with financial covenants of the merger agreement.
(3) Arrange through mutual acquaintances the initial meeting between representatives of Mercury and Hermes.
(4) Negotiate the terms of the acquisition on behalf of Mercury.

g) The CPA who regularly examines Viola Corporation's financial statements has been asked to prepare pro forma income statements for the next five years. If the statements are to be based upon the corporation's operating assumptions and are for internal use only, the CPA should—

(1) Reject the engagement because the statements are to be based upon assumptions.
(2) Reject the engagement because the statements are for internal use.
(3) Accept the engagement provided full disclosure is made of the assumptions used and the extent of the CPA's responsibility.
(4) Accept the engagement provided Viola certifies in writing that the statements are for internal use only. (AICPA, adapted)

2–2. What are the ethical issues for a CPA in rendering a report containing a forecast of a client's future transactions? Discuss (AICPA, adapted)

2–3. Linda Murphy, CPA, is informed by Hollings, Inc., an audit client, that Hollings plans to process cash receipts, cash disbursements, and other original entry documents on its computer, then transmit these data to a service center for further processing into accounting records. The Hollings executive asks Miss Murphy to perform the service bureau function, using her firm's computer and software. Can Miss Murphy perform this service for Hollings, Inc.? Explain.

2–4. Mary Wilson, wife of Jack Wilson, CPA, plans to order personalized checks for the Wilsons' joint personal checking account at Eastern Bank. Can the checks be printed "Jack Wilson, CPA and Mary Wilson"? Explain.

2–5. Roger Hines, CPA, gave tax advice on a technical question to Hillard Company, a client of many years. Subsequently, Hillard Company, with the consent of Mr. Hines, submitted the same question to Gerard & Swank, CPAs, who, after consultation with Mr. Hines, concurred with Mr. Hines's advice on the tax question. Afterwards, Gerard & Swank mailed a general client memorandum on income taxes to Hillard Company. Was Gerard & Swank's action ethical? Explain.

2–6. Certified public accountants have imposed upon themselves a rigorous code of professional ethics. Discuss the underlying reasons for the accounting profession's adopting a code of professional ethics. (AICPA)

2–7. The attribute of independence has been traditionally associated with the CPA's function of auditing and expressing opinions on financial statements. What is meant by "independence" as applied to the CPA's function of auditing and expressing opinions on financial statements? Discuss. (AICPA)

2–8. Roy Mason, a member of the AICPA, was favorably impressed with a staff member of another CPA firm whom he met at a cocktail party. He called the staff man the next day and invited him to come to the office to discuss the possibility of joining Mason's staff. Did Mason's actions constitute a violation of the *Code of Professional Ethics?* Discuss.

2–9. A CPA who had reached retirement age arranged for the sale of his practice to another certified public accountant. Their agreement called for the transfer of all working papers and business correspondence to the accountant purchasing the practice. Comment on the propriety of this plan.

2–10. A firm of certified public accountants plans to reduce the routine work of an audit by retaining an outside mailing service to handle confirmations of the accounts receivable of clients upon whose financial statements the firm is to render an opinion. The work delegated to the mailing service would be to mail the requests, receive the replies, remove the replies from the envelopes, and return them to the accountants. Is this arrangement acceptable in terms of the professional ethics of the AICPA? Explain.

2–11. You receive a request to perform an audit of a newly formed corporation but are informed by the president that because of the weak cash position your fee would have to be paid in shares of the corporation's stock. He explains that the corporation has excellent prospects but that no established market price exists as yet for its stock. He proposes that in making payment of your fee, the stock should be valued at par of $10 per share, and explains that he and the other stockholders purchased shares at this price.

Required:

a) Would you consider this proposal to violate the AICPA rule with respect to contingent fees?

b) Would acceptance of this proposal take away the auditor's independence by reason of his prospective stock ownership?

2–12. Mrs. Arthur Hastings, wife of one of the partners of Evans, Bigelow, and Hastings, Certified Public Accountants, holds the position of vice president and treasurer of Adams Investments, Incorporated. Mrs. Hastings has worked for many years with this company, of which her father is president.

Should the public accounting firm of Evans, Bigelow, and Hastings be regarded as independent for the purpose of making an annual audit of Adams Investments, Incorporated? Explain.

2–13. A certified public accountant, now on the staff of a firm of certified public accountants but contemplating public practice in his own name, plans to send announcements of his establishment in practice to clients of the firm in which he is now employed, as well as to friends and acquaintances. Some such clients have indicated that they would like him to continue to supervise their work; they are not yet aware of his decision to enter practice for himself. Is this plan acceptable? (AICPA)

2–14. An announcement of the affiliation of Jasper Menske with the accounting firm of Kent and West was made in the *Denver Post*. Mr. Kent contends that this is entirely proper as the announcement was made in a very small conventional-type notice. Is he correct? (AICPA)

2–15. Wallace Company is indebted to a CPA for unpaid fees and has offered to issue to him unsecured interest-bearing notes. Would the CPA's acceptance of these notes have any bearing upon his independence in his relations with Wallace Company? Discuss. (AICPA, adapted)

GROUP II
QUESTIONS REQUIRING ANALYSIS

2–16. An auditor must not only appear to be independent; he must also be independent in fact.

Required:

    a) Explain the concept of an "auditor's independence" as it applies to third party reliance upon financial statements.

    b) (1) What determines whether or not an auditor is independent in fact?

        (2) What determines whether or not an auditor appears to be independent?

    c) Explain how an auditor may be independent in fact but not appear to be independent.

    d) Would a CPA be considered independent for an examination of the financial statements of a—

        (1) Church for which he is serving as treasurer without compensation? Explain.

        (2) Women's club for which his wife is serving as treasurer-bookkeeper if he is not to receive a fee for the examination? Explain. (AICPA)

2–17. With the approval of its board of directors, Thames Corporation made a sizable payment for advertising during the year being audited by Leslie Wade, CPA. The corporation deducted the full amount in its federal income tax return. The controller acknowledges that this deduction probably will be disallowed because it relates to political matters. He has not provided for this disallowance in his federal income tax provision and refuses to do so because he fears that this will cause the revenue agent to believe that the deduction is not valid. What is the CPA's responsibility in this situation? Explain. (AICPA, adapted)

2–18. William Ross, CPA, is requested by a director of his client, Third National Bank, to become a member of the bank's advisory committee. The director explains that the advisory committee serves in an advisory capacity only and is not involved in decision marking. Can Mr. Ross accept the director's request without impairing his audit independence? Explain.

2–19. Diane Reese, CPA, withdrew from the audit of Milligan Company after discovering irregularities in Milligan's income tax returns. One week later, Ms. Reese is telephoned by Richard West, CPA, who explains that he has just been retained by Milligan Company to replace Ms. Reese. Mr. West asks Ms. Reese why she withdrew from the Milligan engagement. What should she reply? Explain.

2–20. Carl Swift, CPA, is an alumnus of Wright College. Wright's alumni magazine publishes a section on recent promotions, and so forth, of alumni. Can Mr. Swift send a notice to the alumni magazine that he has just opened an office as "an accountant and tax consultant"? Explain.

2–21. A CPA is considering establishing a small-loan company, while continuing in the practice of public accounting. Is this permissible under the AICPA's *Code of Professional Ethics?* Why?

2–22. A CPA is approached by a prospective tax client who promises to pay the CPA a fee of "5 percent of whatever amount you save me in taxes." Can the CPA accept the tax engagement under this fee arrangement? Explain.

2–23. A client, without consulting its CPA, has changed its accounting so that it is not in accordance with generally accepted accounting principles. During the regular audit engagement the CPA discovers that the statements based on the accounts are so grossly misleading that they might be considered fraudulent.

Required:

a) Discuss the specific action to be taken by the CPA.
b) In this situation what obligation does the CPA have to outsiders if he is replaced? Discuss briefly.
c) In this situation what obligation does the CPA have to a new auditor if he is replaced? Discuss briefly. (AICPA)

2–24.   The CPAs' code of professional ethics prohibits the direct or indirect offer of employment by a CPA to an employee of another CPA without first informing the other CPA.

Required:

   a)   What are the justifications for this rule?
   b)   What action, if any, may the employee of a CPA take should he learn that another CPA firm has an open position for which he would like to apply? (AICPA)

2–25.   What effect, if any, does each of the following have upon the auditor's independence? Explain.
   a)   The auditor's acceptance of a fee from his client.
   b)   The client's preparation of working papers for the auditor's files.
   c)   The auditor's inquiries of client employees, in the course of his gathering of evidence.

2–26.   Donald Moss, a CPA and member of the American Institute of Certified Public Accountants, resigned from his position with a national firm of certified public accountants to establish his own practice in the field of management advisory services. Since Mr. Moss was well known for his skill and knowledge in the field of electronic data processing, he quickly acquired a considerable number of clients.

Mr. Moss deliberately avoided all auditing work because he felt his specialized abilities could be more profitably utilized in the area of management advisory services. To aid the growth of his practice he arranged with a newspaper to have an advertisement published once a week on the financial page. The advertisement consisted only of Mr. Moss's name, business address, and the phrase "Consulting Services in the Field of Data Processing." The advertisement did not indicate that Mr. Moss was a member of the AICPA nor did it identify him as a certified public accountant.

Did Donald Moss violate the AICPA *Code of Professional Ethics?* Explain fully.

GROUP III
PROBLEMS

2–27.   Fred Browning, CPA, has examined the financial statements of Grimm Company for several years. Grimm's president now has asked Mr. Browning to install an inventory control system for the company.

Required:

Discuss the factors that Mr. Browning should consider in determining whether to accept this engagement. (AICPA)

2–28,   Bell & Davis, CPAs, has been requested by the president of Worthmore, Inc. to audit the company's financial statements for the year ended November 30, 1974. Worthmore, Inc. has never before had an audit.

For each of the following cases, indicate whether Bell & Davis would be independent with respect to Worthmore, Inc. and explain why.

a) Two directors of Worthmore, Inc. became partners in Bell & Davis, CPAs on July 1, 1974, resigning their directorships on that date.

b) During 1974 the former controller of Worthmore, Inc., now a partner of Bell & Davis, was frequently called upon for assistance by Worthmore. He made decisions for Worthmore's management regarding plant and equipment acquisitions and the company's marketing mix. In addition, he conducted a computer feasibility study for Worthmore. (AICPA, adapted)

2–29.　You are approached by the president of Bates Mfg. Company to audit the company's financial statements. You have no knowledge of Bates Mfg. Company other than that it is a medium-sized company.

Required:

a) From an ethical standpoint, what should you learn about Bates Mfg. Company before you agree to accept the engagement? Discuss. (Since you have not yet been engaged, do not discuss the auditor's survey of the company's internal control to determine audit procedures.)

b) If you should find that Bates Mfg. Company has been the client of another CPA, is it ethical for you to discuss with the president the possibility of becoming the company's CPA? Discuss.

2–30.　Roland Company, a chain of retail stores, has utilized your services as independent auditor for several years. During the current year the company opened a new store; and in the course of your annual audit, you verify the cost of the fixtures installed in the new store by examining purchase orders, invoices, and other documents. This review brings to light an understated invoice nearly a year old in which a clerical error by the supplier, Western Showcase, Inc. caused the total of the invoice to read $4,893.62 when it should have been $8,493.62. The invoice was paid immediately upon receipt without any notice of the error, and subsequent statements and correspondence from Western Showcase, Inc. showed that the account with Roland Company had been "paid in full."

Required:

a) What action should you take in this situation?

b) If the client should decline to take any action in the matter, would you insist that the upaid amount of $3,600 be included in the liabilities shown on the balance sheet as a condition necessary to your issuance of an unqualified audit report?

c) Assuming that you were later retained to make an audit of Western Showcase, Inc., would you utilize the information gained in your examination of Roland Company to initiate a reopening of the account with that company?

2–31. Hillcrest Corporation was formed on October 1, 1974 and its fiscal year will end on September 30, 1975. You audited the corporation's opening balance sheet and rendered an unqualified opinion on it.

A month after issuing your report you are offered the position of secretary of the company because of the need for a complete set of officers and for convenience in signing various documents. You will have no financial interest in the company through stock ownership or otherwise, will receive no salary, will not maintain any corporate records, and will not have any influence on Hillcrest's financial matters other than occasional advice on income tax matters and similar advice normally given a client by a CPA.

Required:

a) Assume that you accept the offer but plan to resign the position prior to conducting your annual audit with the intention of again assuming the office after rendering an opinion on the statements. Can you render an independent opinion on the financial statements? Discuss.

b) Assume that you accept the offer on a temporary basis until the corporation has gotten under way and can elect a secretary. In any event you would permanently resign the position before conducting your annual audit. Can you render an independent opinion on the financial statements? Discuss. (AICPA, adapted)

2–32. During 1974 your client, March Corporation, requested that you conduct a feasibility study to advise management of the best way the corporation can utilize electronic data processing equipment and which computer, if any, best meets the corporation's requirements. You are technically competent in this area and accept the engagement. Upon completion of your study the corporation accepts your suggestions and installs the computer and related equipment that you recommended.

Required:

a) Discuss the effect acceptance of this management advisory services engagement would have upon your independence in expressing an opinion on the financial statements of March Corporation.

b) Instead of accepting the engagement, assume that you recommended Ike Mackey, of the CPA firm of Brown and Mackey, who is qualified in specialized services. Upon completion of the engagement your client requests that Mackey's partner, John Brown, perform services in other areas. Should Brown accept the engagement? Discuss.

c) A local printer of data processing forms customarily offers a commission for recommending him as supplier. The client is aware of the commission offer and suggests that Mackey accept it. Would it be proper for Mackey to accept the commission with the client's approval? Discuss. (AICPA, adapted)

3

Legal liability of auditors

THE RAPID growth of the public accounting profession during the past several years has been accompanied by a sharp increase in the number of court cases involving public accountants. The man or woman entering public accounting today should be aware of the legal liability inherent in the practice of public accounting. Thus, this chapter will describe briefly some aspects of common law and statutory law having a bearing on the work of the CPA, and some related court cases. It should be emphasized, however, that the court cases discussed in this chapter are isolated occurrences among the extensive services performed by certified public accountants.

The liability of the auditor to his client and to third parties

The question of legal liability of an auditor usually arises when someone sustains a loss as a result of relying upon financial statements which although covered by an auditor's report are later found to be misleading or to contain material errors. Is the auditor to be held financially responsible for any losses incurred by those who placed confidence in his professional skill and integrity? There is no simple, all-inclusive answer to this question. Before attempting even a tentative answer, we must take into consideration such factors as the following: Was the auditor guilty of fraud, of negligence, or merely of an honest error in judgment? Was the fraud localized and small in relation to the total operations, or was it so widespread and material as to make the financial statements false and misleading when viewed as a whole? Is the injured person who now seeks to recover damages the client who engaged the auditor, or is he a third party with whom the auditor had no contractual relationship? Was the audit made in connection with an issuance of securities and therefore subject to the rigorous rules of the Securities and Exchange Commission?

Before considering these various audit situations, we should emphasize one very basic point: *Auditors have often been held legally liable for losses caused by misleading financial statements.* Furthermore, for every case in which the courts have held auditors to be legally liable, there are probably many other cases in which public accounting firms have settled claims out of court to avoid unfavorable publicity. Consequently, we must not ignore the ever-present threat of legal liability overhanging every audit engagement as we make our appraisal of the standards and hazards of the public accounting profession.

Definition of terms

Discussion of auditor's liability is best prefaced by a definition of some of the common terms of business law. Among these are the following:

Breach of contract—failure of one or both parties to a contract to perform in accordance with the contract's provisions.

Fraud—misrepresentation by a person of a material fact, known by that person to be untrue or made with reckless indifference as to whether the fact is true, with the intention of deceiving the other party and with the result that the other party is injured.

Constructive fraud—not a misrepresentation of fact with intent to deceive but a violation of a legal duty or a relationship between the parties which requires the use of exceptional good faith.

Independent contractor—a party to a contract who undertakes according to terms of the contract to perform a specified task free of control of the other party to the contract except as provided in the agreement.

Negligence—violation of a legal duty to exercise a degree of care which an ordinarily prudent man would exercise under similar circumstances, with resultant damages to another party.

Ordinary negligence—lack of reasonable care.

Gross negligence—lack of even *slight* care, indicative of reckless disregard for fact.

Contributory negligence—negligence on the part of a party damaged by another's negligence.

Privity—the relationship between parties to a contract.

Proximate cause—damage to another directly attributable to a wrongdoer's act.

Third party beneficiary—a person, not the promisor or promisee, who is named in a contract with the intention he should have definite rights under the contract.

The auditor's functions and responsibilities

The auditor's relationship to his client is that of an independent contractor. In undertaking the customary audit engagement—the examination of and the expression of an opinion on the client's financial statements—the auditor is responsible for carrying out the assignment in accordance with the generally accepted standards of auditing and for complying with the *Code of Professional Ethics.* Since the auditor is rendering professional services, a higher level of care is required than that of the "ordinarily prudent man" of the *negligence* definition. This higher level of care is the "due professional care" of the third general standard.

Responsibility for detection of fraud

Let us assume that an auditor makes a first-time examination of a new client and submits an audit report indicating that the financial statements fairly reflect financial position and operating results. There is no mention by the auditor of any weakness in internal control or of the possibility of fraud. Some months later the client discovers that one of his long-time employees has been embezzling funds over a period of several years and has concealed his wrongdoing by making fictitious entries in the accounts. The client now charges the auditor with negligence, pointing out that a substantial portion of the total loss has occurred since the date of the auditor's examination, and that there recent losses could have been avoided had the auditor not failed to detect the existence of fraud. In brief, it is the contention of the client that the negligence of the auditor permitted the dishonest employee to continue his fraud and thereby cause further loss to the client.

Does failure to detect fraud constitute proof of negligence on the part of the auditor? The auditor does not guarantee the accuracy of financial statements; he merely expresses an opinion as to their fairness. Furthermore, the auditor does not make a complete and detailed examination of all records and all transactions. To do so would entail an almost prohibitive cost which would certainly not be warranted under ordinary business conditions. The auditor's examination is based upon a study and evaluation of the client's system of internal control; the extent and nature of specific auditing procedures will be determined by the strengths and weaknesses in the controls. If the scope and direction of the audit procedures have been well chosen, the conclusions of the auditor should generally be sound. However, there can never be any absolute assurance that fraud did not exist among the transactions not included in the auditor's tests. There is also the possibility that fraudulent documents have been so skillfully forged or other irregularities so expertly concealed that the application of generally accepted auditing techniques would not reveal the fraud.

When the auditor's examination has been made in accordance with generally accepted auditing standards, the auditor is not liable for failure to detect the existence of fraud. Throughout the course of the examination the auditor must exercise his professional judgment as to the procedures to be employed and the extent of the tests to be made. Because so many difficult, technical decisions must be made by the auditor, it is inevitable that some errors in judgment will occur. If the auditor acts in good faith and employs the same care and degree of skill commonly followed within the public accounting profession, an error in judgment is not regarded as negligence.

In summary, a client can ordinarily recover losses arising as a result of the auditor's failure to disclose the existence of localized fraud only if it can be shown that the auditor was guilty of negligence, or that he attempted to mislead the client. Nevertheless, every competent auditor is continuously alert to detect any evidence of the possible existence of fraud. If the auditor does discover evidence of possible material fraud, he should discuss his findings with the client's board of directors or the audit committee thereof to determine whether client personnel or the auditor himself should pursue the matter. Under no circumstances should the auditor abandon his customary examination to carry out a fraud investigation without obtaining the client's permission to do so.

Common law background of auditor's liability

The contract between the auditor and his client binds the auditor to a diligent performance of his work. Under contract law if the auditor does not carry out his obligations to the client and there is consequent harm to the client, the latter may sue the auditor for breach of contract or for torts such as negligence or fraud.

The responsibility of the auditor to third parties who may rely upon the audit report has evolved through four significant court cases. The principal aspects of these cases are discussed below.

In *Ultramares* v. *Touche & Co.,* 255 N.Y. 170 (1931), the defendant CPAs issued what was in essence an unqualified opinion on the balance sheet of a company engaged in the importation and sale of rubber. On the strength of the CPAs' opinion, the plaintiff, a factor, made a number of loans to the company. Shortly thereafter, the company was declared bankrupt.

The factor originally sued the CPAs for negligence; later, during trial, fraud was added to the complaint. The court found that the CPAs were grossly negligent in not discovering obvious material overstatements of sales and receivables, among other audit shortcomings; and that consequently the factor, though not a third party beneficiary in the case, could recover his losses from the auditors. As a result of the landmark *Ultramares* case, the defense of privity is invalid in the event of gross negligence.

In *State Street Trust Co.* v. *Ernst,* 278 N.Y. 104 (1938), and in *C.I.T. Financial Corp.* v. *Glover,* 224 F.2d 44 (1955), the doctrine established in the *Ultramares* case was strengthened and the defense of privity was further weakened. The relationship between gross negligence and constructive fraud was given added impetus by these two decisions. *Rusch Factors, Inc.* v. *Levin,* 284 F. Supp. 85 (1968), went even further; the court declared that an accountant who committed fraud in issuing a report is liable to all third parties he could *foresee* being injured, despite his lack of knowledge of actual third parties who might rely upon his report.

Thus, under common law, bankers, other creditors or investors who utilize financial statements covered by an audit report can recover from the auditor if it can be shown that the auditor was guilty of fraud or gross negligence in the performance of his professional duties. Fraud is obviously present if the auditor surrenders his independence and cooperates with the client to give outsiders a false impression of the financial position or operating results of the business. Gross negligence exists if the auditor has not conducted an examination of any real substance and consequently has no real basis for an opinion. To express an opinion in his role of independent expert when in fact he has no basis for an opinion is considered as gross negligence and provides a basis for legal action by injured third parties.

Auditor's liability under the securities acts

The preceding discussion of the auditor's legal liability to third parties is based on the common law and does not cover opinions expressed on financial statements included in registration statements filed with the SEC.

The Securities Act of 1933 and the Securities Exchange Act of 1934 place heavy responsibility on independent public accountants who prepare or examine any part of a registration statement or periodic report required under the acts. The inclusion of an untrue statement of material fact, or failure to state a material fact when such omission makes the statement misleading, opens the door to legal action against the public accountant by any person acquiring the security.

Securities Act of 1933

The auditor who expresses an opinion in a registration statement concerning a proposed offering of corporate securities has a very broad legal liability. The Securities Act of 1933 states that an accountant who expresses such an opinion may be held liable to third parties for their losses if the statements are later shown to include untrue statements of material fact or to omit material facts necessary to prevent the statements from being misleading. The wording of Section 11(a) of the act on this point is as follows:

In case any part of the registration statement, when such part became effective, contained an untrue statement of a material fact or omitted to state a material fact required to be stated therein or necessary to make the statements therein not misleading, any person acquiring such security (unless it is proved that at the time of such acquisition he knew of such untruth or omission) may, either at law or in equity, in any court of competent jurisdiction, sue. . . .

The third parties who have sustained losses may sue for recovery from the accountant and need not prove that they relied upon the statements or that the accountant was negligent. The burden of proof is placed upon the accountant to show that his audit work was adequate to support his opinion (the "due diligence" defense) or that the losses of third parties were not the result of errors or omissions in the statements.

The effect of the Securities Act of 1933 is therefore to give to third parties who purchase securities of registered companies the same rights against the auditor as are possessed by the client under the common law. In audits for registration statements, the auditor is liable not only for fraud and gross negligence but also for losses to third parties resulting from ordinary negligence. This legislation inaugurated a new era in the professional responsibilities of the independent public accountant.

Securities Exchange Act of 1934

In addition to the registration statements required in connection with new issues of securities, companies which are listed on the stock exchanges and certain companies whose stock is traded over the counter must file audited financial statements each year with the SEC, in accordance with provisions of the Securities Exchange Act of 1934. Section 18(a) of that act provides the following liability for misleading statements:

Any person who shall make or cause to be made any statement in any application, report, or document filed pursuant to this . . . (Act) or any rule or regulation thereunder . . . , which statement was at the time and in the light of the circumstances under which it was made false or misleading with respect to any material fact, shall be liable to any person (not knowing that such statement was false or misleading) who, in reliance upon such statement, shall have purchased or sold a security at a price which was affected by such statement, for damages caused by such reliance, unless the person sued shall prove that he acted in good faith and had no knowledge that such statement was false or misleading.

In addition, Rule 10b-5 promulgated by the SEC under the 1934 act reads as follows:

It shall be unlawful for any person, directly or indirectly, . . .
(1) to employ any device, scheme, or artifice to defraud,
(2) to make any untrue statement of a material fact or to omit to state a material fact necessary in order to make the statements made . . . not misleading, or
(3) to engage in any act, practice, or course of business which operates or would operate as a fraud or deceit upon any person, in connection with the purchase or sale of any security.

Certified public accountants have been sued under provisions of Section 11(a) of the 1933 act, and Section 18(a) and Rule 10b–5 of the 1934 act. Some of the most significant of these cases will be discussed in a later section of this chapter.

The SEC's regulation of accountants

The SEC has issued rules for the appearance and practice of CPAs, attorneys, and others before the Commission under the statutes which it administers. Rule of Practice 2(e), giving the SEC the power of suspension and disbarment, has the following wording:

The Commission may deny, temporarily on permanently, the privilege of appearing or practicing before it in any way to any person who is found by the Commission after notice of and opportunity for hearing in the matter (1) not to possess the requisite qualifications to represent others, or (2) to be lacking in character or integrity or to have engaged in unethical or improper professional conduct.

On several occasions the Commission has taken punitive action against public accounting firms when it has found the audit work deficient with regard to financial statements filed with the Commission. These actions against public accounting firms usually arise when a listed corporation encounters financial difficulties and it later appears that misleading financial statements had served to conceal for a time the losses being incurred by the company.

ILLUSTRATIVE CASE.   A case of this type, reported in *Accounting Series Release No. 78,* involved a commercial finance company (Seaboard Commercial Corporation) which after operating successfully for some years decided to concentrate its funds in advances to six companies. These six companies to which advances were made were all in poor condition and encountered further difficulties after receiving the advances from Seaboard. The end result was that the finance company sustained heavy losses on its receivables from the six debtor companies.

The SEC criticized the public accounting firm which audited the finance company's statements on several points, including the following:

1.   The allowance for uncollectible accounts on the audited balance sheet was materially inadequate.

2.   In reporting on financial statements including this inadequate allowance, the accountants "failed to follow generally accepted accounting and auditing standards and failed to exercise an independent and informed judgment."

3.   The public accountants had at one stage of the audit advised the client that a very much larger allowance for uncollectible accounts was needed. The audit working papers indicated that an audit report in draft form had been prepared early in the audit referring to the need for a much larger allowance. Later in the audit, however, the auditors modified their views and accepted as adequate an allowance which later proved to be far too small.

4.   The classification of certain receivables as current did not conform to good accounting practice because the debtor was not in a position to liquidate these debts currently.

5.   The income statement was misleading because the increase which was made in the allowance for uncollectible accounts was not charged against income.

In conclusion the Commission held that the financial statements and the audit report improperly minimized adverse disclosures and failed to give a realistic picture of the financial condition of the company. The Commission stressed that the independent public accountant has a responsibility not only to the client who pays his fee but also to other persons such as investors and creditors who rely upon the audited statements.

These findings by the Commission and the action taken against the public accounting firm (a 15-day suspension from practice before the Commission) were announced approximately 9 years after the audit in question. Four years had elapsed after the filing of the audited statements before the proceedings by the SEC were initiated. The case points up not only the extent to which the SEC may inquire into the auditor's work but also the long-continuing responsibility of the auditor after completion of an audit.

Some accountants have been critical of the Commission's reasoning in this case. These critics disagree with the inference that an auditor who modifies his original views on some aspect of the financial statements after listening to the arguments of the client may be regarded as having sacrificed his independence and improperly deferred to the client's wishes.

Cases of this type suggest that an auditor's own working papers may be a principal means of establishing charges against him. Such use of the auditor's working papers must be anticipated; in virtually every case in which the auditor's work is under attack in court, the attorneys for the plaintiff can be expected to obtain the auditor's working papers and search them for items which may be regarded as inconsistent with the conclusions finally reached by the auditor.

Other cases involving Rule 2(e) of the SEC's Rules of Practice are discussed in Chapter 14 on inventories and in Chapter 16 on intangible assets.

Having completed our discussion of auditor's liability under common law and under statutory law, we shall now consider recent court cases or other investigations which have had substantial impact on the public accounting profession. These cases are important for the lessons they provide to CPAs for avoiding similar unfortunate experiences.

Unaudited financial statements

Two significant cases have involved unaudited financial statements with which a CPA was associated as an *accountant* instead of as an *auditor*.

Investigation of U.S. Department of Agriculture.   In 1962 committees of the U.S. Senate and House of Representatives investigated the conduct of officials of the U.S. Department of Agriculture in their dealings with a prominent businessman engaged in storing surplus government-owned grain. The investigations brought out that the Agriculture Department officials had waived a proposed $300,000 increase in the businessman's bond, to $1,000,000. The waiver was granted because the businessman submitted to the department his personal balance sheet dated December 31, 1960, showing total assets of more than $20 million, including inventories of approximately $940,000, and total liabilities of nearly $6.4 million. A CPA's report accompanying the balance sheet read as follows:

We have examined the balance sheet presented in condensed form of . . . as of December 31, 1960. Our examination was made in accordance with generally accepted standards and accordingly included such tests of the accounting records and such other auditing procedures as we considered necessary in these circumstances, except that our examination did not include the generally accepted auditing procedure of observing and testing the methods used in determining inventory quantities, prices, and amounts.

By reason of the limitation of the scope of our examination as to inventories, no opinion may be expressed as to the fairness of the presentation in the accompanying balance sheet of the financial position of . . . as of December 31, 1960.

Agriculture Department officials testified they interpreted the CPA's report as lending credence to all balance sheet items except inventory, which was obviously immaterial. However, the CPA who issued the report admitted he had done no auditing whatsoever; he had merely reproduced on his firm's letterhead the balance sheet furnished him by the businessman and had attached the report to it.

The CPA's license was suspended for two years by his state's board of accountancy, and his membership in the AICPA was revoked.

1136 Tenants' Corporation v. Rothenberg. From November 1963 to March 1965, an incorporated apartment cooperative, owned by its share-holder-tenants and managed by a separate realty agent, orally retained a CPA firm to perform services leading to the preparation of financial statements for the cooperative and letters containing tax information to the shareholders. The CPAs' fee was to be $600 per year.

The CPAs submitted financial statements of the corporation for the year 1963 and for the first six months of 1964. The financial statements bore the notation "subject to comments in letter of transmittal." The referenced letter of transmittal read in part:

> Pursuant to our engagement, we have reviewed and summarized the statements of your managing agent and other data submitted to us by . . . (the agent), pertaining to 1136 Tenants' Corporation. . . .
> The following statements were prepared from the books and records of the Corporation. No independent verifications were undertaken thereon. . . .

The client corporation later sued the CPAs for damages totaling $174,000, for the CPAs' alleged failure to discover defalcations of the corporation's funds committed by the managing agent. The client contended that the CPAs had been retained to render all necessary accounting *and auditing* services for it. The CPAs maintained they had been engaged to do "write-up work" only, although a schedule they had prepared supporting accrued expenses payable in the balance sheet included an entry for "audit expense."

The New York state trial court ruled in favor of the plaintiff client, as did the appellate court of New York. The latter found that the CPAs' working papers indicated that the CPAs had examined the client's bank statements, invoices and bills, and had made notations concerning "missing invoices." The New York Court of Appeals (the state's highest court) affirmed the decision.

Influenced perhaps to some extent by the two preceding episodes, the AICPA in 1967 issued *Statement on Auditing Procedure No. 38,* "Unaudited Financial Statements." This *Statement* clarifies the CPA's responsibilities with respect to unaudited financial statements with which he is associated and recommends the following language for the CPA's report on unaudited financial statements:

The accompanying balance sheet of X Company as of December 31, 19____ and the related statements of income and retained earnings and of changes in financial position for the year then ended were not audited by us and accordingly we do not express an opinion on them.

In addition, each of the individual financial statements should be clearly and conspicuously marked as unaudited. Unaudited financial statements are considered further in Chapter 21, "Financial Statements and Audit Reports."

The "salad oil swindle"

The great "salad oil swindle" in 1963 arising out of the bankruptcy of Allied Crude Vegetable Oil Corporation has already been mentioned in Chapter 1. Allied was not audited, but the principal warehousing company whose warehouse receipts had been forged was a subsidiary of a publicly owned company subject to annual audits by independent CPAs. The parent's CPAs did not perform auditing procedures to determine the existence of stored goods of the warehousing subsidiary, reportedly because the stored goods were *not* the property of the warehouser. A "Special Report" issued in 1966 as *Statement on Auditing Procedure No. 37* by the AICPA's Committee on Auditing Procedure recommended that the independent auditor of a public warehouse apply extensive auditing procedures, including observation of physical counts, to goods stored but not owned by the warehouse.

The *BarChris* case

Escott v. *BarChris Construction Corporation,* 283 F. Supp. 643 (1968), was an action under Section 11 of the Securities Act of 1933 undertaken in 1962 by purchasers of BarChris's registered debentures against the directors, underwriters, and independent auditors of BarChris. Subsequent to issuance of the debentures, BarChris, a builder of bowling alleys, became bankrupt. The plaintiffs claimed that the registration statement for the debentures contained material false statements and material omissions; the defendants all countered with "due diligence" defenses. The court found that the registration statement was false and misleading, and that with a few exceptions none of the defendants had established their due diligence defenses. The court also found that the CPA firm had failed to comply with generally accepted auditing standards. The court was especially critical of the CPA firm's conduct of the "S-1 review," so-called because it is a special investigation carried out by a CPA just prior to the effective date of the "S-1" or similar registration statement filed with the SEC.

Subsequent to the decision of the court in BarChris, the AICPA's Committee on Auditing Procedure issued *Statement on Auditing Procedure No. 47,* "Subsequent Events," which clarified the auditing procedures required in an "S-1 review."

The *Continental Vending* case

In 1968 a federal district court jury found two partners and a manager of a national firm of certified public accountants guilty of criminal fraud in issuing an unqualified opinion on the September 30, 1962 financial statements of Continental Vending Machine Corporation, a publicly owned company required to report to the SEC. An earlier trial had ended in a "hung jury." The verdict of guilt was affirmed by a U.S. court of appeals in 1969, and the U.S. Supreme Court refused to review the case. The three CPAs were fined $7,000, $5,000, and $5,000, respectively. The president of Continental Vending, who had originally been indicted with the three CPAs and who subsequently pleaded guilty, received a six-month jail sentence. A $41 million civil suit which had been filed in 1965 by Continental's trustee in bankruptcy had been settled earlier by the CPA firm by the payment of $2 million to the trustee.

The principal facts of the Continental Vending case (*United States v. Simon*, 425, F. 2d 796 [1969]) are as follows. The U.S. government's case of fraud against the three CPAs hinged upon a footnote to Continental's September 30, 1962 financial statements which read:

The amount receivable from Valley Commercial Corp. (an affiliated company of which . . . (Continental's president) is an officer, director, and stockholder) bears interest at 12% a year. Such amount, less the balance of the notes payable to that company, is secured by the assignment to the Company of Valley's equity in certain marketable securities. As of February 15, 1963, the amount of such equity at current market quotations exceeded the net amount receivable.

The U.S. government charged the CPAs should have insisted that the note be worded as follows:

The amount receivable from Valley Commercial Corp. (an affiliated company of which . . . (Continental's president) is an officer, director and stockholder), which bears interest at 12% a year, was uncollectible at September 30, 1962, since Valley had loaned approximately the same amount to . . . (Continental's president) who was unable to pay. Since that date . . . (Continental's president) and others have pledged as security for the repayment of his obligation to Valley and its obligation to Continental (now $3,900,000, against which Continental's liability to Valley cannot be offset) securities which, as of February 15, 1963, had a market value of $2,978,000. Approximately 80% of such securities are stock and convertible debentures of the Company.

The receivable from Valley amounted to $3.5 million at September 30, 1962, of which more than $2.1 million was included in current assets (totaling $20.1 million) with the $1.4 million balance in other assets. The amount payable to Valley at September 30, 1962 was slightly more than $1 million, of which about one half was included in total current liabilities of $19 million and the remainder in long-term debt.

The CPA firm had been auditors for Continental since 1956. The court found that the CPAs had been concerned with the amounts receivable from and payable to Valley since at least 1958, especially as they involved loans to Continental's president; yet the CPAs had continued to issue opinions on Continental's financial statements despite the continued growth of the receivable from Valley. The court also found that the CPAs never were furnished audited financial statements for Valley during the 1962 audit, in spite of their repeated requests; and that the CPAs had never themselves been the auditors for Valley. In response to the defendant CPAs' claims that they had no motive for the alleged fraud, the U.S. government demonstrated to the appellate court's satisfaction that the CPAs were motivated to preserve their firm's reputation and to conceal the alleged derelictions of their predecessors and themselves in preceding years.

The Continental Vending case has significant implications for the public accounting profession. Not only is civil liability an ever-present hazard for public accountants but criminal charges may also be involved. It is worth noting that Rule 401 of the AICPA's Rules of Conduct (see Chapter 2) permits a CPA to insist upon auditing a component of combined or consolidated financial statements when the CPA considers the audit essential. This provision of the Rules was adopted subsequent to the Continental Vending case.

The *Yale Express* case

Early in 1964 a national CPA firm issued an unqualified opinion on the December 31, 1963 financial statements of Yale Express System, Inc., a trucking and freight forwarding concern. Three months later, the CPAs' opinion was included in the 1963 annual report filed with the SEC under provisions of the Securities Exchange Act of 1934. The 1963 audited income statement of Yale showed net income of $1.1 million on gross revenue of $65.9 million.

Sometime in 1964 (the CPA firm claimed *after* the 1963 audit report was issued), Yale retained the CPAs to perform a management advisory services engagement—a "special study" of Yale's past and current revenue and expenses. During the course of the special study, Yale issued unaudited quarterly earnings reports required by the New York Stock Exchange; for the nine months ended September 30, 1964 Yale reported net income of $904,000. However, in March 1965 Yale announced that its interim reported profits for 1964 were in error and that it estimated a net loss of $3.3 million for all of 1964. Then, in May 1965, Yale's CPAs reported a revised 1963 net loss for Yale of $1.3 million (later increased to $1.9 million) and a 1964 net loss of $2.9 million. The CPAs stated the previously reported audited 1963 net income of $1.1 million was in error because of omission of liabilities and overstatement of receivables.

Subsequently Yale went into bankruptcy and a number of shareholders and creditors filed suit against the CPA firm, charging the firm with deceit (deception) under the provisions of Section 18(a) of the Securities Exchange Act of 1934 and the SEC's Rule 10b-5. Basis of the plaintiff's deception claim was that the CPAs knew before the end of 1964 that the 1963 audited financial statements as well as the unaudited 1964 quarterly earnings reports were false and misleading, but they had not disclosed this knowledge until mid-1965. The CPAs filed a cross motion to have the case dismissed; the SEC as *amicus curiae* opposed the motion to dismiss. The court (*Fischer* v. *Kletz*, 266 F. Supp. 180 [1967]), denied the CPAs' motion for dismissal and held that there were no reasons for barring the action of deceit against the CPAs. The court also found that there were no reasons why a duty to disclose such knowledge is not imposed upon a CPA, despite the lack of privity of those interested in Yale's financial statements.

In a subsequent action in 1968, the former president and former administrative vice president of Yale were convicted of issuing fraudulent financial statements, fined, and given suspended prison sentences. In addition, the AICPA's Committee on Auditing Procedure in 1969 issued *Statement on Auditing Procedure No. 41*, "Subsequent Discovery of Facts Existing at the Date of the Auditor's Report." This *Statement* requires positive action by a CPA who becomes aware, subsequent to the date of his report on audited financial statements, of facts existing at the date of his report which might have affected his audit report if he had then known those facts.

The *Statement* calls for the CPA to investigate immediately such subsequently-discovered facts. If he ascertains that the facts are significant and that they existed at the date of his report, he should advise his client to make appropriate disclosure of the facts to anyone actually, or likely to be, relying upon the CPA's report and the related financial statements. If the client refuses to make appropriate disclosure, the CPA should inform each member of the client's board of directors of such refusal and should then notify regulatory agencies having jurisdiction over the client, as well as each person known by the auditor to be relying upon the financial statements, that the CPA's report can no longer be relied upon.

The CPA's posture in the "age of litigation"

In addition to the preceding court cases, several other actions against CPAs, under both common law and the securities acts, are pending trial. It is apparent that lawsuits will continue to plague the public accounting profession, as they have the legal and medical professions. The question thus is: What should be the CPA's reaction to this "age of litigation"?

In the opinion of the authors, positive actions helpful to CPAs in withstanding threats of possible lawsuits include the following:

1.   Greater emphasis upon compliance with the public accounting profession's generally accepted auditing standards and *Code of Professional Ethics.* Close analysis of the court cases and other actions described in this chapter discloses numerous instances in which the auditors appear not to have complied fully with one or more auditing standards and Rules of Conduct.

2.   Emphasis on professionalism rather than growth. Some CPA firms may have emphasized growth of their practices more than high quality of their work. Very rapid growth may bring excessive overtime work by overextended staff members and too heavy responsibilities for insufficiently "seasoned" accountants.

3.   Thorough investigation of prospective clients. As indicated in preceding sections of this chapter, many court cases involving CPAs have been accompanied by criminal charges against top management of the CPAs' clients. CPAs should use great care in screening prospective clients to avoid the risks involved in professional relationships with the criminally inclined.

4.   Use of engagement letters for all professional services. Controversies over what services are to be rendered by a CPA can be minimized by a clearly written contract describing the agreed-upon services and clearly pointing out that the ordinary audit is not designed to uncover fraud. Engagement letters are discussed in Chapter 4.

5.   Exercising extreme care in audits of clients in financial difficulties. Creditors and shareholders of companies which are insolvent or in bankruptcy are likely to seek scapegoats to blame for their losses. As the court cases described in this chapter demonstrate, litigation involving CPAs tends to center around auditing of clients which later become bankrupt.

6.   Avoidance of engagements involving unaudited financial statements and substantial client restrictions. The *1136 Tenants' Corporation* case indicates that CPAs preparing unaudited financial statements risk being charged with responsibility for carrying out *some* auditing procedures. The best interests of the public accounting profession dictate that CPAs avoid undertaking engagements involving financial statements which do not include examination of the statements in accordance with generally accepted auditing standards.

7.   Maintenance of adequate liability insurance coverage. Although liability insurance coverage should not be considered a substitute for the CPA's compliance with the six preceding recommendations, the pub-

lic accountant must protect himself against possible financial losses from lawsuits. Adequate liability insurance is essential.

GROUP I
REVIEW QUESTIONS

3–1. Select the best answer choice for the following and justify your selection.

On November 4, 1974, two months after completing field work and rendering an unqualified opinion as to the financial statements of Lambert Collieries for the year ended June 30, 1974, a CPA learns of four situations concerning this client which were not previously known to him. The CPA is required to determine that appropriate disclosure is made to persons relying upon the audited financial statements for the year ended June 30, 1974 in the situation of the—

a) Flooding of one of Lambert's two mines on October 15, 1974. This mine was acquired in 1970.

b) Discovery on October 25, 1974 of a defect in the title to the other mine, also acquired in 1970.

c) Settlement on November 3, 1974 of a damage suit against Lambert at an amount significantly lower than that reported in the audited balance sheet.

d) Decline in coal prices by $2 per ton on October 1, 1974. Net income for the coming year is expected to decrease 50 percent as a result. (AICPA, adapted)

3–2. Watts and Williams, a firm of certified public accountants, audited the balance sheet of Sampson Skins, Inc., a corporation that imports and deals in fine furs. Upon completion of the examination the auditors supplied Sampson Skins with 20 copies of the audited balance sheet. The firm knew in a general way that Sampson Skins wanted that number of copies of the auditor's report to furnish to banks and other potential lenders.

The balance sheet in question was in error by approximately $800,000. Instead of having a $600,000 net worth, the corporation was insolvent. The management of Sampson Skins had "doctored" the books to avoid bankruptcy. The assets had been overstated by $500,000 of fictitious and nonexisting accounts receivable and $300,000 of nonexisting skins listed as inventory when in fact there were only empty boxes. The audit failed to detect these fraudulent entries. Martinson, relying on the audited balance sheet, loaned Sampson Skins $200,000. He seeks to recover his loss from Watts and Williams.

Required:

State whether each of the following statements is true or false, and explain why.

a) If Martinson alleges and proves negligence on the part of Watts and Williams, he would be able to recover his loss.

b) If Martinson alleges and proves constructive fraud, that is, gross negligence on the part of Watts and Williams, he would be able to recover his loss.

c) Martinson is not in privity of contract with Watts and Williams.

d) Unless actual fraud on the part of Watts and Williams could be shown, Martinson could not recover.

e) Martinson is a third party beneficiary of the contract Watts and Williams made with Sampson Skins. (AICPA, adapted)

3–3. Compare the auditor's common law liability to clients with his common law liability to third parties.

3–4. What is *constructive fraud?*

3–5. Select the best answer choice for the following and justify your selection.

Subsequent to rendering an unqualified report on the financial statements of Rosenberg Company for the year ended December 31, 1974, a CPA learns that property taxes for the year 1974 have been significantly underaccrued. This resulted from the company's disregard of a taxing authority ruling that was made prior to completion of the CPA's examination but was not brought to his attention. Upon learning of the ruling the CPA's immediate responsibility is—

a) Advisory only since he did not learn of the ruling until after completion of his examination.

b) To make certain that the 1974 income statement is restated when the December 31, 1975 financial statements are prepared.

c) To immediately issue a disclaimer of opinion relative to the 1974 financial statements.

d) To ascertain that immediate steps are taken to inform all parties to whom this information would be important. (AICPA, adapted)

3–6. A certified public accounting firm was sued by a client for a large sum because of its failure to discover a large defalcation engineered by the treasurer of the client organization. In defense, the accounting firm argued that its examination had conformed to generally accepted auditing standards but admitted that it had accepted as authentic a number of documents which later were proved to be forgeries. Do you believe that the claim for damages against the CPA firm is a justifiable one? Explain.

3–7. Should an auditor who is engaged in the examination of a client's financial statements thoroughly investigate suspected material fraud? Explain.

3–8. Is privity a valid defense against third party charges of negligence against an auditor? Explain.

3–9. How does the SEC regulate CPAs who appear and practice before the Commission?

3–10. Dandy Container Corporation engaged the accounting firm of Adams and Adams to examine financial statements to be used in connection with a public offering of securities. The audit was completed, and an unqualified opinion was expressed on the financial statements which were submitted to the Securities and Exchange Commission along with the registration statement. Two hundred thousand shares of Dandy Container common stock were offered to the public at $11 a share. Eight months later the stock fell to $2 a share when it was disclosed that several large loans to two "paper" corporations owned by one of the directors were worthless. The loans were secured by the stock of the borrowing corporation which was owned by the director. These facts were not disclosed in the financial statements. The director involved and the two corporations are insolvent.

Required:

State whether each of the following statements is true or false, and explain why.

a) The Securities Act of 1933 applies to the above-described public offering of securities in interstate commerce.

b) The accounting firm has potential liability to any person who acquired the stock in reliance upon the registration statement.

c) An insider who had knowledge of all the facts regarding the loans to the two "paper" corporations could nevertheless recover from the accounting firm.

d) An investor who bought shares in Dandy Container would make a prima facie case if he alleges that the failure to explain the nature of the loans in question constituted a false statement or misleading omission in the financial statements.

e) The accountants could avoid liability if they could show they were neither negligent nor fraudulent.

f) The accountants could avoid or reduce the damages asserted against them if they could establish that the drop in price was due in whole or in part to other causes.

g) It would appear that the accountants were negligent in respect to the handling of the secured loans in question—if they discovered the facts regarding the loans to the "paper" corporations and failed to disclose them in their financial statements.

h) The Securities and Exchange Commission would defend any action brought against the accountants in that the SEC examined and approved the registration statement. (AICPA, adapted)

3–11. Select the best answer choice for the following and justify your selection.

Three months subsequent to the date of his report, a CPA becomes aware of facts which existed at the date of his report and affect the reliability of the financial statements of a client whose securities are widely held. If the client refuses to make appropriate disclosure, the CPA should notify

a) Regulatory agencies having jurisdiction over the client.

b) All stockholders.

c) All present and potential investors in the company.

d) Stockbrokers and the financial press. (AICPA, adapted)

3–12. What is the significance for the public accounting profession of the *1136 Tenants' Corporation* v. *Rothenberg* case?

3–13. What Rule of Conduct of the AICPA's *Code of Professional Ethics* was apparently a response to the *Continental Vending* case? Explain.

GROUP II
QUESTIONS REQUIRING ANALYSIS

3–14. The CPA firm of Winston & Mall was engaged by Fast Cargo Company, a retailer, to examine its financial statements for the year ended August 31, 1974. Winston & Mall followed generally accepted auditing standards and examined transactions on a test basis. A sample of 100 disbursements was used to test vouchers payable, cash disbursements, and receiving and purchasing procedures. An investigation of the sample disclosed several instances where purchases had been recorded and paid for without the required receiving report being included in the file of supporting documents. This was properly noted in the working papers by Martin, the staff assistant who did the sampling. Mall, the partner in charge, called these facts to the attention of Harris, Fast Cargo's chief accountant, who told him to not worry about it, that he would make certain that these receiving reports were properly included in the voucher file. Mall accepted this and did nothing further to investigate or follow-up on this situation.

Harris was engaged in a fraudulent scheme whereby he diverted the merchandise to a private warehouse where he leased space and sent the invoices to Fast Cargo for payment. The scheme was discovered later by a special investigation, and a preliminary estimate indicates that the loss to Fast Cargo will be in excess of $20,000.

Required:

a) What is the liability, if any, of Winston & Mall in this situation? Discuss.

b) What additional steps, if any, should have been taken by Mall? Explain. (AICPA, adapted)

3–15. The CPA firm of Bigelow, Barton, and Brown was expanding very rapidly. Consequently it hired several staff assistants, including a man named Small. Subsequently, the partners of the firm became dissatisfied with Small's production and warned him that they would be forced to discharge him unless his output increased significantly.

At that time Small was engaged in audits of several clients. He decided that to avoid being fired, he would reduce or omit entirely some of the required auditing procedures listed in audit programs prepared by the partners. One of the CPA firm's clients, Newell Corporation, was in serious financial difficulty and had adjusted several of its accounts being examined by Small to appear financially sound. Small prepared fictitious working papers in his home at night to support purported completion of auditing procedures assigned to him, although he in fact did not examine the Newell adjusting entries. The CPA firm rendered an unqualified opinion on Newell's financial statements, which were grossly misstated. Several creditors subsequently extended large sums of money to Newell Corporation relying upon the audited financial statements.

Required:

Would the CPA firm be liable to the creditors who extended the money in reliance on the erroneous financial statements if Newell Corporation should fail to pay the creditors? Explain. (AICPA, adapted)

3–16. On July 27, 1974, Arthur Ward, CPA, issued an unqualified audit report on the financial statements of Dexter Company for the year ended June 30, 1974. Two weeks later, Dexter Company mailed annual reports including the June 30, 1974 financial statements and Mr. Ward's audit report to 150 stockholders and to several creditors of Dexter Company. Dexter Company's stock is not actively traded on national exchanges or over the counter.

On September 5, 1974 the controller of Dexter Company informed Mr. Ward that an account payable for consulting services in the amount of $90,000 had inadvertently been omitted from Dexter's June 30, 1974 balance sheet. As a consequence, net income for the year ended June 30, 1974 was overstated $40,500, net of applicable federal and state income taxes. Both Mr. Ward and Dexter's controller agreed that the misstatements were material to Dexter's financial position at June 30, 1974 and operating results for the year then ended.

Required:

What should Mr. Ward's course of action be in this matter? Discuss.

3–17. Cragsmore & Company, a medium-sized partnership of CPAs, was engaged by Marlowe Manufacturing, Inc., a closely held corporation, to examine its financial statements for the year ended December 31, 1974.

Prior to preparing the auditor's report William Cragsmore, a partner, and Fred Willmore, a staff senior, reviewed the disclosures necessary in the footnotes to the financial statements. One footnote involved the terms, costs, and obligations of a lease between Marlowe and Acme Leasing Company.

Fred Willmore suggested that the footnote disclose the following: "The Acme Leasing Company is owned by persons who have a 35 percent interest in the capital stock and who are officers of Marlowe Manufacturing, Inc."

On Cragsmore's recommendation, this was revised by substituting "minority shareholders" for "persons who have a 35 percent interest in the capital stock and who are officers."

The auditor's report and financial statements were forwarded to Marlowe Manufacturing for review. The officer-shareholders of Marlowe who also owned Acme Leasing objected to the revised wording and insisted that the footnote be changed to describe the relationship between Acme and Marlowe as merely one of affiliation. Cragsmore acceded to this request.

The auditor's report was issued on this basis with an unqualified opinion. But the working papers included the drafts that showed the changes in the wording of the footnote.

Subsequent to delivery of the auditor's report, Marlowe suffered a substantial uninsured fire loss and has been forced into bankruptcy. The failure of Marlowe to carry any fire insurance coverage was not noted in the financial statements.

Required:

What legal problems are suggested by these facts for Cragsmore & Company? Discuss. (AICPA, adapted)

3–18. Williams, a CPA, was engaged by Jackson Financial Development Company to audit the financial statements of Apex Construction Company, a small closely held corporation. Williams was told when he was engaged that Jackson Financial needed reliable financial statements which would be used to determine whether or not to purchase a substantial amount of Apex Construction's convertible debentures at the price asked by the estate of one of Apex's former directors.

Williams performed his examination in a negligent manner. As a result of his negligence he failed to discover substantial defalcations by Brown, the Apex controller. Jackson Financial purchased the debentures but would not have if the defalcations had been discovered. After discovery of the fraud Jackson Financial promptly sold them for the highest price offered in the market at a $70,000 loss.

Required:

a) What liability does Williams have to Jackson Financial? Explain.
b) If Apex Construction also sues Williams for negligence, what are the probable legal defenses which Williams' attorney would raise? Explain.
c) Will the negligence of a CPA as described above prevent him from recovering on a liability insurance policy covering the practice of his profession? Explain. (AICPA)

3–19. Frequently questions have been raised ". . . regarding the responsibility of the independent auditor for the discovery of fraud (including defalcations and other similar irregularities), and concerning the proper course of conduct of the independent auditor when his examination discloses specific circumstances which arouse his suspicion as to the existence of fraud."

Required:

a) What are the (1) function and (2) responsibilities of the independent auditor in the examination of financial statements? Discuss fully, but in this part do not include fraud in the discussion.

b)   What are the responsibilities of the independent auditor for the detection of fraud? Discuss fully.

c)   What is the independent auditor's proper course of conduct when his examination discloses specific circumstances which arouse his suspicion as to the existence of fraud? (AICPA)

3–20.   Meglow Corporation manufactured ladies' dresses and blouses. Because its cash position was deteriorating, Meglow sought a loan from Busch Factors. Busch had previously extended $25,000 credit to Meglow but refused to lend any additional money without obtaining copies of Meglow's audited financial statements.

Meglow contacted the CPA firm of Watkins, Winslow & Watkins to perform the audit. In arranging for the examination, Meglow clearly indicated that its purpose was to satisfy Busch Factors as to the corporation's sound financial condition and thus to obtain an additional loan of $50,000. Watkins, Winslow & Watkins accepted the engagement, performed the examination in a negligent manner, and rendered an unqualified auditor's opinion. If an adequate examination had been performed, the financial statements would have been found to be misleading.

Meglow submitted the audited financial statements to Busch Factors and obtained an additional loan of $35,000. Busch refused to lend more than that amount. After several other factors also refused, Meglow finally was able to persuade Maxwell Department Stores, one of its customers, to lend the additional $15,000. Maxwell relied upon the financial statements examined by Watkins, Winslow & Watkins.

Meglow is now in bankruptcy, and Busch seeks to collect from Watkins, Winslow & Watkins the $60,000 it loaned Meglow. Maxwell seeks to recover from Watkins, Winslow & Watkins the $15,000 it loaned Meglow.

Required:

a)   Will Busch recover? Explain.

b)   Will Maxwell recover? Explain. (AICPA)

3–21.   Charles Worthington, the founding and senior partner of a successful and respected CPA firm, was a highly competent practitioner who always emphasized high professional standards. One of the policies of the firm was that all reports by members or staff be submitted to Worthington for review.

Recently, Arthur Craft, a junior partner in the firm, received a phone call from Herbert Flack, a close personal friend. Flack informed Craft that he, his family, and some friends were planning to create a corporation to engage in various land development ventures; that various members of the family are presently in a partnership (Flack Ventures) which holds some land and other assets; and that the partnership would contribute all of its assets to the new corporation and the corporation would assume the liabilities of the partnership.

Flack asked Craft to prepare a balance sheet of the partnership that he could show to members of his family, who were in the partnership, and friends to determine whether they might have an interest in joining in the formation and financing of the new corporation. Flack said he had the partnership general ledger in front of him and proceeded to read to Craft the names of the accounts and their balances at the end of the latest month. Craft took the notes he made during the telephone conversation with Flack, classified and organized the data into a conventional balance sheet, and had his secretary type the balance sheet and an accompanying letter on firm stationery. He did not consult Worthington on this matter or submit his work to him for review.

The transmittal letter stated: "We have reviewed the books and records of Flack Ventures, a partnership, and have prepared the attached balance sheet at March 31, 1974. We did not perform an examination in conformity with generally accepted auditing standards, and therefore do not express an opinion on the accompanying balance sheet." The balance sheet was prominently marked "unaudited." Craft signed the letter and instructed his secretary to send it to Flack.

Required:

What legal problems are suggested by these facts? Explain. (AICPA, adapted)

3–22. Risk Capital Limited, a Delaware corporation, was considering the purchase of a substantial amount of the treasury stock held by Florida Sunshine Corporation, a closely held corporation. Initial discussions with the Florida Sunshine Corporation began late in 1973.

Wilson and Wyatt, Florida Sunshine's independent public accountants, regularly prepared quarterly and annual unaudited financial statements. The most recently prepared financial statements were for the year ended September 30, 1974.

On November 15, 1974 after protracted negotiations, Risk Capital agreed to purchase 100,000 shares of no-par, Class A capital stock of Florida Sunshine at $12.50 per share. However, Risk Capital insisted upon audited statements for calendar year 1974. The contract specifically provided: "Risk Capital shall have the right to rescind the purchase of said stock if the audited financial statements of Florida Sunshine for calendar year 1974 show a material adverse change in the financial position of the Corporation."

The audited financial statements furnished to Florida Sunshine by Wilson and Wyatt showed no such material adverse change. Risk Capital relied upon the audited statements and purchased the treasury stock of Florida Sunshine. It was subsequently discovered that as of the balance sheet date, the audited statements were incorrect and that in fact there had been a material adverse change in the financial position of the corporation. Florida Sunshine is insolvent, and Risk Capital will lose virtually its entire investment.

Risk Capital seeks recovery against Wilson and Wyatt.

Required:

- a) Discuss each of the theories of liability that Risk Capital will probably assert as its basis for recovery.
- b) Assuming that only ordinary negligence is proven, will Risk Capital prevail? State "yes" or "no" and explain. (AICPA, adapted)

3–23. Barton and Company, CPAs, have been engaged to examine the financial statements for Mirror Manufacturing Corporation for the year ended September 30, 1974. Mirror Manufacturing needed additional cash to continue its operations. To raise funds it agreed to sell its common stock investment in a subsidiary. The buyers insisted upon having the proceeds placed in escrow because of the possibility of a major contingent tax liability. Carter, president of Mirror, explained this to Barton, the partner in charge of the Mirror audit. He indicated that he wished to show the proceeds from the sale of the subsidiary as an unrestricted current account receivable. He stated that in his opinion the government's claim was groundless and that he needed an "uncluttered" balance sheet and a "clean" auditor's opinion to obtain additional working capital. Barton acquiesced in this request. The government's claim proved to be valid and pursuant to the agreement with the buyers the purchase price of the subsidiary was reduced by $450,000. This coupled with other adverse developments caused Mirror to become insolvent with assets to cover only some of its liabilities. Barton and Company is being sued by several of Mirror's creditors who loaned money in reliance upon the financial statements upon which it rendered an unqualified opinion.

Required:

What is the liability, if any, of Barton and Company to the creditors of Mirror Manufacturing? Explain. (AICPA, adapted)

3–24. Chriswell Corporation decided to raise additional long-term capital by issuing $3,000,000 of 8 percent subordinated debentures to the public. May, Clark & Company, CPAs, the company's auditors, were engaged to examine the June 30, 1974 financial statements which were included in the registration statement for the debentures.

May, Clark & Company completed its examination and submitted an unqualified auditor's report dated July 15, 1974. The registration statement was filed and became effective on September 1, 1974. Two weeks prior to the effective date, one of the partners of May, Clark & Company called on Chriswell Corporation and had lunch with the financial vice president and the controller. He questioned both officials on the company's operations since June 30 and inquired whether there had been any material changes in the company's financial position since that date. Both officers assured him that everything had proceeded normally and that the financial position of the company had not changed materially.

Unfortunately the officers' representation was not true. On July

30, a substantial debtor of the company failed to pay the $400,000 due on its account receivable and indicated to Chriswell that it would probably be forced into bankruptcy. This receivable was shown as a collateralized loan on the June 30 financial statements. It was secured by stock of the debtor corporation which had a value in excess of the loan at the time the financial statements were prepared but was virtually worthless at the effective date of the registration statement. This $400,000 account receivable was material to the financial position of Chriswell Corporation, and the market price of the subordinated debentures decreased by nearly 50 percent after the foregoing facts were disclosed.

The debenture holders of Chriswell are seeking recovery of their loss against all parties connected with the debenture registration.

Required:

Is May, Clark & Company liable to the Chriswell debenture holders? Explain. (AICPA, adapted)

3–25. *Part* (*a*). Wells and White, the accountants for the Allie Corporation, provided various professional services for Allie over 15 years. The services included tax return preparation, special cost analyses, and the examination of the corporation's annual financial statements.

The relationship had been quite harmonious until the retirement of Roberts, the president and founder of Allie Corporation. His successor, Strong, was a very aggressive, expansion-oriented individual who lacked the competence and personal attraction of his predecessor. Two years after Roberts' retirement the unbroken record of increases in annual earnings was in jeopardy.

Strong realized that a decrease in earnings would have an unfavorable impact on his image and on his plans to merge with a well-known conglomerate. He called Wells, the senior partner of Wells and White, and demanded that the method of computing and reporting the current year's earnings be changed in a way that would preserve the upward trend in earnings.

Although the proposed method would be within the realm of generally accepted accounting principles, Wells subsequently told Strong that in the exercise of his professional judgment, there was no justification for such a change. Strong promptly dismissed the firm and refused to pay Wells and White's final billing of $1,750 for services rendered to the date of dismissal.

Wells and White have brought suit against Allie Corporation for the $1,750. Allie Corporation responded by denying liability on the ground that the firm's refusal to cooperate constituted a breach of contract which precluded recovery.

Required:

Is the Wells and White account receivable valid and enforceable against the Allie Corporation? State "yes" or "no" and explain.

Part (*b*). Continuing the situation described in Part (*a*) above: Strong was unable to find other accountants who approved of the proposed change in the method of computing and reporting earnings, so he abandoned this demand and then engaged new accountants, Bar & Cross. Income continued to decrease in the next two quarters, and Strong became convinced that the cause of this must be due to defalcations by some dishonest employee. Therefore, he engaged Bar & Cross to make a special study to discover the guilty person. After several months of intensive work Bar &. Cross were able to discover minor defalcations of $950. Of this amount, $600 was stolen during the last two years while Wells and White were Allie Corporation's accountants. Allie Corporation sues Wells and White for the loss.

Required:

Will Allie Corporation recover the loss from Wells and White? State "yes" or "no" and explain. (AICPA, adapted)

3–26.   In conducting the examination of the financial statements of Farber Corporation for the year ended September 30, 1974, Harper, a CPA, discovered that Nance, the president who was also one of the principal stockholders, had borrowed substantial amounts of money from the corporation. Nance indicated that he owned 51 percent of the corporation, that the money would be promptly repaid, and that the financial statements were being prepared for internal use only. He requested that these loans not be accounted for separately in the financial statements but be included in the other current accounts receivable. Harper acquiesed in this request. Nance was correct as to his stock ownership and the fact that the financial statements were for internal use only. However, he subsequently became insolvent and was unable to repay the loans.

Required:

What is Harper's liability? Explain. (AICPA, adapted)

GROUP III
PROBLEMS

3–27.   The CPA firm of Arnold and Bates was engaged by the trustee in bankruptcy for Martin & Co., a stockbrokerage firm which had incurred substantial embezzlement losses, to examine the financial statements of Martin & Co. for the nine years of its existence from July 1, 1965 through June 30, 1974. The U.S. bankruptcy court had authorized the engagement. The former owners of Martin & Co., who had perpetrated the embezzlement, were serving terms in federal prisons.

Roger Bates, a senior partner of Arnold and Bates, assumed charge of the Martin & Co. assignment. As the audit progressed, Mr.

Bates became aware of the irrefutable fact that the CPA who had examined the financial statements of Martin & Co. for the eight years ended June 30, 1973 had missed obviously material misstatements and omissions in Martin's financial statements for those years. Martin's trustee in bankruptcy had indicated he planned to seek recovery from the predecessor CPA if he had been guilty of gross negligence. To complicate Mr. Bates's problem, several other stockbrokerage clients of Arnold and Bates had filed with Martin's trustee substantial claims for unpaid amounts due them from transactions with Martin & Co.

Required:

Discuss the action, if any, that Mr. Bates should take in this situation with respect to the following:

a) Communication with the predecessor auditor.
b) Examination of the predecessor's working papers. ⤴
c) Communication with the AICPA and the state society of CPAs, if the predecessor is a member.
d) Communication with the state board of accountancy. ⤴
e) Disclosure of the predecessor's negligence in the audit report of Arnold and Bates.
f) Recommending establishing a receivable for damages from the predecessor CPA.
g) Notifying the other stockbrokerage clients of Arnold and Bates regarding their possibility of recovery from the predecessor CPA.

3–28. In a preliminary discussion, prior to beginning your audit of Mark Company, the president states that he would like to ascertain whether any key employees have interests which conflict with their duties at Mark Company. He asks that during your regular audit, you be watchful for signs of these conditions and report them to him.

Required:

Briefly discuss your professional position in this matter. Include the following aspects in your discussion:

a) The responsibility of the CPA for the discovery of conflicts of interest. Give reasons for your position.
b) The advisability of requesting that the client furnish you with a letter of representations which contains a statement that no conflict of interests is known to exist among the company's officers and employees. What action, if any, would you take if the client refused to provide the letter? How would his refusal affect your opinion?
c) At the same time that you are conducting the audit of Mark Company you are also conducting the audit of Timzin Company, a supplier of Mark Company. During your audit of Timzin Company you determine that an employee of Mark Company is receiving "kickbacks."

      (1)   Discuss your responsibility, if any, to reveal this practice to the president of Mark Company.

      (2)   Discuss your professional relationship with Timzin Company after discovering the "kickbacks." (AICPA, adapted)

GROUP IV
CASE STUDIES IN AUDITING

3–29.   MULTI-DIVERSIFIED INDUSTRIES, INC.

On March 15, 1974, the Beverly Hills, California, CPA firm of Lane, Reynolds & Co. was requested by Paul Morgan, chairman of the board and president of Multi-Diversified Industries, Inc., to examine the company's financial statements for the year ending March 31, 1974. In response to the inquiries of Martin Lane, senior partner of Lane, Reynolds & Co., Mr. Morgan stated that Multi-Diversified Industries, Inc. was a publicly owned company which had been organized April 1, 1973 through the statutory consolidation of Multi-Products Company and Diversified Industries Corporation. Multi-Products Company was a diversified manufacturing company with divisions in three Southern California cities, and Diversified Industries Corporation was also a varied-product manufacturer with divisions in four cities of northern California. Mr. Morgan also informed Mr. Lane that Multi-Diversified's board of directors had authorized Mr. Morgan to retain a new CPA firm because neither of the two CPA firms which had performed past audits of Multi-Products Company and Diversified Industries Corporation had offices in both northern and southern California. Mr. Morgan also stated that as a licensed attorney, he handled all of the legal matters of Multi-Diversified Industries, Inc.

Since only a short time remained before the March 31, 1974 close of Multi-Diversified's fiscal year, Mr. Lane made hurried telephone calls to John Oates, CPA, the predecessor auditor for Multi-Products Company, and to Robert Waddell, CPA, Diversified Industries Corporation's prior auditor. Learning that both CPA's had been amicably discharged by Mr. Morgan, Mr. Lane prepared an engagement letter for the March 31, 1974 audit of Multi-Diversified Industries, Inc. The engagement letter was immediately accepted by Mr. Morgan in his capacity of board chairman. Mr. Lane then began planning the audit, arranging for the staffing of the audit with personnel from the Lane, Reynolds & Co. offices nearest to the seven California locations of Multi-Diversified, and deciding upon appropriate auditing procedures for the seven divisions.

Throughout the audit of Multi-Diversified Industries, Inc., the staff accountants of Lane, Reynolds & Co. concentrated their auditing procedures on the transactions for the year ended March 31, 1974. Mr. Lane had decided upon this course of action because Mr. Morgan had provided Lane, Reynolds & Co. with copies of the audit reports of Multi-Diversified's two predecessor companies for the year ended March 31, 1973. These audit reports were used by Mr. Lane in determining that the April 1, 1973 combination of Multi-Products Company and Diversified Industries Corporation had been properly accounted for as a pooling of interests.

The field work of the audit proceeded uneventfully. On May 7, 1974, the final day of field work, Mr. Lane personally obtained a letter from Mr. Morgan addressed to Lane, Reynolds & Co., stating that to the best of Mr. Morgan's knowledge as legal counsel for Multi-Diversified Industries, Inc. there were no lawsuits or other matters pending as of March 31, 1974 which gave rise to contingent liabilities for Multi-Diversified at that date.

On May 18, 1974 Lane, Reynolds & Co. issued its unqualified audit report dated May 7, 1974 on the March 31, 1974 financial statements of Multi-Diversified Industries, Inc. The report was filed with the SEC under provisions of the Securities Exchange Act of 1934. Two weeks later, on June 1, 1974, Martin Lane read in his morning newspaper that a California appellate court had upheld a $1 million judgment against Multi-Diversified Industries, Inc., as successor to Diversified Industries Corporation, for patent infringement by the San Francisco division of Diversified Industries. According to the newspaper account, the suit had dragged on for five years. The newspaper also quoted Paul Morgan as stating that Multi-Diversified would be forced into bankruptcy by the judgment.

Mr. Lane hurried to his office to review the audit report of Robert Waddell on the March 31, 1973 financial statements of Diversified Industries Corporation but found no mention of the patent infringement suit in the financial statements or footnotes or in Mr. Waddell's report. Mr. Lane recalled that Mr. Morgan's May 18, 1974 letter to Lane, Reynolds & Co. stated there were no lawsuits pending at March 31, 1974. Mr. Lane telephoned Mr. Morgan, who told him that the patent infringement suit had been dormant for so long in the appeal process that Mr. Morgan had forgotten about it in both the 1974 audit and in the 1973 audit when he was president and legal counsel for Diversified Industries Corporation.

Thereupon, Mr. Lane requested Mr. Morgan to notify the SEC and any creditors or shareholders who might be currently relying upon the March 31, 1974 financial statements of Multi-Diversified Industries, Inc. that those statements and the accompanying audit report of Lane, Reynolds & Co. were no longer to be relied upon. Mr. Morgan refused, saying he was busy preparing the necessary papers and documents for the bankruptcy proceedings. Mr. Lane then wrote special delivery letters to all members of Multi-Diversified's board of directors, notifying them of Mr. Morgan's refusal. He also mailed a special delivery letter to the Washington, D.C. office of the SEC, informing the Commission that the March 31, 1974 financial statements of Multi-Diversified Industries, Inc. and the report of Lane, Reynolds & Co. thereon were no longer to be relied upon.

On July 7, 1974 several creditors and stockholders of Multi-Diversified Industries, Inc. filed suit under Section 18(a) of the Securities

Exchange Act of 1934 and Rule 10b-5 of the SEC against Multi-Diversified Industries, Inc. and its directors and officers; Lane, Reynolds & Co. and Martin Lane; and Robert Waddell. The plaintiffs charged the defendants with omitting to state a material fact necessary in order to make the March 31, 1973 financial statements of Diversified Industries Corporation and the March 31, 1974 statements of Multi-Diversified Industries, Inc. not misleading.

Required:

a) Do you think that the plaintiffs will prevail against the defendants? Explain.

b) Did the CPA firm of Lane, Reynolds & Co. comply with generally accepted auditing standards and the AICPA's *Code of Professional Ethics* in the audit of Multi-Diversified Industries, Inc.? Explain.

c) Is there a possibility for criminal charges to be filed by the U.S. government against any of the defendants in the civil suit? Explain.

4

The public accounting profession; planning the audit

THE PUBLIC accounting profession includes a large number of individual practitioners, but leaders of the profession have encouraged certified public accountants to operate under a partnership arrangement. When two or more accountants join forces, opportunity for specialization is increased; and the scope of services offered to clients may be expanded to include such areas as management advisory services, electronic data processing, and tax planning. Partnerships of certified public accountants are also able to develop and supervise an audit staff capable of handling audit engagements too large for the individual practitioner. A more intangible but significant advantage of the public accounting partnership is the stimulus toward professional development afforded by the interchange of ideas and frequent discussions among partners concerning auditing problems and objectives.

Partnerships of public accountants range in size from two-partner firms to organizations with scores of partners and thousands of employees, and with offices in principal cities throughout the world. Only a very large public accounting firm can conduct an audit of a business such as Sears, Roebuck and Company or United States Steel Corporation, with plants and branches spread throughout various countries.

Notice that this discussion speaks of the advantages gained when independent public accountants join forces in a partnership; no mention has been made of the use of a corporation for the practice of public accounting. Let us now consider the question of incorporation for a professional firm.

95

Why public accounting firms have begun to incorporate

In the past, two or more certified public accountants wishing to carry on a joint practice would organize a partnership, because the AICPA *Code of Professional Ethics* and most state laws prohibited public accounting practice by corporations. This prohibition was founded on the premise that CPAs using the traditional corporate form of organization might avoid personal responsibility for their professional acts by "hiding behind the corporate veil." A further objection to public accounting corporations was that a controlling interest might be acquired by someone other than a CPA—someone whose objective might be the earning of maximum profits without regard for professional ethics or auditing standards.

The partnership form of organization severely restricted the CPA's opportunities to minimize personal income tax liabilities and the exposure resulting from the recent wave of lawsuits described in Chapter 3. Consequently, a number of states have authorized the practice of public accounting by *professional* corporations, which differ from traditional corporations in a number of respects. Usually, all shareholders, directors, officers, and professional employees of a professional corporation must be licensed practitioners of the profession. Shares of a professional corporation may be transferred only to licensed practitioners or to the corporation itself. Professional corporations must maintain adequate insurance for potential claims of negligence.

In 1969 the membership of the AICPA, in recognition of the trend described in the preceding paragraph, amended the *Code of Professional Ethics* to make the professional corporation form of organization available to AICPA members. Presumably, many members of the AICPA will begin to practice in professional corporations as quickly as their state laws permit.

Organization of the public accounting firm

The organization of a typical public accounting firm includes partners, managers or supervisors, senior accountants, and staff assistants. Assistants to the senior accountants are sometimes divided into the categories of semiseniors and juniors, but these latter two terms appear to be falling into disuse. In addition to these various levels of professional accounting personnel, the firm will also necessarily employ typists, computer operators, receptionists, and other general office employees. Larger public accounting firms are often departmentalized into separate auditing, tax, and management advisory services sections, with perhaps a "small business" department integrating all three types of services for smaller clients.

Responsibilities of the partner. A partner maintains contacts with clients. These contacts include the arrangement of the objectives, scope, and time of examinations; consultations with clients over important issues; and the review and signing of audit reports. Recruitment of new staff members, professional development programs, establishment of the policies of the firm, and general supervision of staff members are other responsibilities of the partner.

Specialization by each partner in a different area of the firm's practice is often advantageous. One partner, for example, may become expert in tax matters and head the firm's tax department; another may specialize in SEC registrations; and a third may devote himself to design and installation of data processing systems.

The partnership level in a public accounting firm is comparable to that of top management in an industrial organization. Executives at this level are concerned with the long-run well-being of the organization and of the community it serves. They should and do contribute important amounts of time to civic, professional, and educational activities in the community. Participation in the state society of certified public accountants and in the AICPA is, of course, a requisite if the partner is to do his share in building the profession. Contribution of his specialized skills and professional judgment to leadership of civic organizations is equally necessary in developing the economic and social environment in which business and professional accomplishment is possible.

A secondary aspect of the partner's active participation in professional societies and in various business and civic organizations is the prestige and recognition which may come to his firm. The development of new business is an important responsibility of the partner. Since professional firms do not advertise for clients, the obtaining of new business may hinge to an important extent upon a wide acquaintance by partners in the business community. However, the obtaining of new business is not the motivating factor in the partner's participation in civic affairs. By the time he has reached the partnership level, he has usually acquired an appreciation of the ideals and basic values of a profession which enables him to contribute his services to the community without thought of direct personal gain. The partner who lends his professional talents to expanding and enriching college and university accounting courses, for example, may contribute greatly to the quality of accounting education; the possibility that his contribution may attract promising graduates to his firm is a secondary consideration, not the motivating reason for his assistance to educational institutions.

Responsibilities of the manager or supervisor. In large public accounting firms, managers or supervisors perform many of the duties which would be discharged by partners in smaller firms. The manager is often responsible for general supervision of two or more concurrent audit engagements. He reviews audit reports and working papers and arranges with the client for settlement of various accounting problems which may arise during the course of the engagement. The manager is responsible for determining the audit procedures applicable to specific audits and for maintaining uniform standards of field work. Familiarity with tax laws and with SEC regulations, as well as a broad and current knowledge of accounting theory and practice, are essential qualifications for a successful manager. Like the partner, the audit manager may specialize in specific industries or other areas of the firm's practice. Often the manager has the administrative duties of compiling and collecting the firm's billings to clients. In addition to the other duties mentioned, he may also assume responsibility for a program of staff training. In large CPA firms some managers may be assigned on a full-time basis to the function of staff training.

Responsibilities of the senior auditor.   The senior auditor is an individual competent to assume full responsibility for the planning and conducting of an audit and the writing of the audit report, subject to review and approval by the manager or partner. This requires that he delegate audit operations to his assistants based upon his appraisal of the ability and capacity of each assistant to perform particular phases of the work. A well-qualified university graduate with extensive formal education in accounting may progress from the position of a beginning assistant to that of a senior auditor within two or three years, or even less time.

One of the major responsibilities of the senior is on-the-job staff training. When assigning work to his assistants, he should make clear the end objectives of the particular audit operation. Constructive criticism of the work of assistants and judicious rotation of their duties in a manner that will provide diversified experience are important elements of the senior's work.

The review of working papers as rapidly as they are completed is another duty of the senior in charge of an audit. This enables him to control the progress of the work and to ascertain that each phase of the engagement is adequately covered. At the conclusion of the field work, he will make a final review, tracing all items from individual working papers to lead schedules or grouping sheets, and from the lead schedules to the financial statements.

The senior will also maintain a continuous record of the hours devoted by all members of the staff to the various phases of the examination. In addition to maintaining uniform professional standards of field work, he is responsible for preventing the accumulation of excessive man-hours on inconsequential matters and for completing the entire engagement within budgeted time, if possible.

Responsibilities of the staff assistant.   The first position of a college graduate entering the public accounting profession is that of a staff assistant. In the past, much was written about the routine nature of the duties of a beginning staff member. Although some factual basis existed for such statements a generation ago, the present-day staff assistant usually encounters a variety of assignments utilizing fully his capacity for analysis and growth. Of course some routine work must be done in every audit engagement, but the college graduate with thorough training in accounting need have no fear of being assigned for long to extensive routine procedures when he enters the field of public accounting. Most firms are anxious to assign more and more responsibility to younger staff members as rapidly as they are able to assume it. The demand for accounting services is so far beyond the available supply of competent individuals that every incentive exists for rapid development of promising assistants.

Many of the larger public accounting firms maintain well-organized training programs designed to integrate new staff members into the organization with maximum efficiency. One of the most attractive features of the public accounting profession is the richness and variety of experience acquired even by the beginning staff member. Because of the high quality of the experience gained by the certified public accountant as he moves from one audit engagement to another, many business concerns select individuals from the public accounting field to fill executive positions such as controller or treasurer.

The tax department

Most public accounting firms maintain separate tax departments, staffed by accountants who are experts in all aspects of federal and state income tax laws and regulations. Partners, managers, and seniors of the tax department review or prepare income tax returns for individuals, partnerships, estates, trusts, and corporations, as well as gift tax and inheritance tax returns. In addition, they assist clients in tax planning and consult with members of the audit department as to tax problems encountered during audits. Tax work, though not as significant as auditing in the production of fees for most firms, represents an increasingly important source of revenue in public accounting.

Management advisory services

Traditionally the services rendered by certified public accountants have centered about auditing and income tax work. Although these activities could reasonably be described as services to business management, the term "management advisory services" has acquired a specific meaning. "Management advisory services" describes advisory (consulting) services rendered by a CPA to improve a client's use of its capabilities and resources to achieve the objectives of the organization.

When firms of certified public accountants in the course of performing annual audits have discovered unsatisfactory situations in a client's business, it has been natural for them to offer suggestions for corrective action. Often the client has requested the accounting firm to undertake as a special assignment an extensive study of the problem, and to plan in detail the new procedures, policies, and organization required for a solution. In this evolutionary manner many public accounting firms found themselves gradually becoming involved in management consulting work. At first their engagements were mostly in the fields of accounting, finance, and office operations. Typical problems were the development of cost accounting systems, budgetary controls, improved general accounting procedures, and streamlined office operations. The prevalence in many companies of cumbersome, obsolete procedures, duplication of record keeping, and lack of information on product costs made consulting work a fertile field for public accounting firms. The certified public accountant's intimate knowledge of how things were done in the best-managed companies in the industry, plus his familiarity with his client's records and personnel, enabled him to devise highly effective recommendations for improved accounting methods and more efficient office operation.

After thus having extended their services from auditing and tax work to areas of systems design, costs, budgets, procedures, and office operations, public accounting firms found their field of work continuing to broaden. Up to this point the services being rendered were clearly related to accounting processes; these services could be rendered efficiently by persons with extensive experience in public accounting. Let us assume, however, that a CPA made an analytical study for a manufacturing client of the cost of certain products; assume further that the product cost information indicated that factory production costs were excessive in comparison with the costs of other firms in the industry or in relation to selling prices in a competitive market. Further progress in this situation called for study of factory production processes and physical facilities by industrial engineers. The public accounting firm then faced the alternatives of (*a*) employing as staff members industrial engineers who could handle the plant production aspects of consulting work, or (*b*) limiting the range of their management advisory services. Those firms which decided to take the step of employing industrial engineers soon faced the need of expanding further by adding staff men in such fields as personnel relations and marketing research. The advent of operations research created a further need for mathematicians and statisticians to be added to the staff.

The management advisory services department in the national
public accounting firm

Separate management advisory services divisions have been established in most of the national public accounting firms. The management
advisory services division in a national firm may have a hundred or
more full-time staff members, including cost accountants, industrial engineers, electronic engineers, mathematicians, statisticians, psychologists,
market analysts, and numerous other specialists.

In most cases the partners in charge of management advisory services
divisions have had extensive training and experience in fields other than
accounting. Some are qualified industrial engineers; others have had
extensive experience with management consulting firms. Every partner
in a public accounting firm must, of course, be a certified public accountant; the partners directing management advisory services departments must also be technically competent in other fields in order to
evaluate and supervise the specialists on their staffs.

A question is sometimes raised as to the ability of a public accounting
firm to attract a topflight engineer, statistician, or other specialist to
its staff; unless this individual is also a certified public accountant he
cannot hope to rise to the partnership level. The answer given by most
firms is that highly skilled specialists are attracted and retained by giving
them compensation and status equal or superior to that available in
industry. There is also the point that some people prefer the variety
and challenge of consulting work to continuous service in a single
organization.

In the management advisory services departments of some of the
national firms, the present staff has in large part been drawn from outside
the organization in order to develop rapidly a group with varied skills.
Some of the firms, however, look forward to a future policy of transferring young men and women from the auditing staff. Such a policy
would, of course, require extensive staff training programs as well as
continued professional study by the auditor moving into the management
advisory services field.

Management advisory services by small public accounting firms

The small public accounting firm has both an opportunity and a responsibility to render management advisory services to its clients. These
clients are for the most part small business concerns—too small to maintain a variety of specialists as full-time employees. Such concerns should
be able to call on their public accountants not only for auditing and
tax services but also for expert assistance on all problems relating to
accounting, finance, statistics, office methods and equipment, and data

processing. In some cases, counseling on general management problems may appropriately be added to the list.

Some small public accounting firms have been rendering such services to their clients for many years and have developed outstanding ability as management counselors. As the field of management advisory services gains greater recognition, the principal difficulty confronting small accounting firms of this caliber is how to deal with problems involving specialized skills quite apart from accounting.

Obviously the small public accounting firm cannot offer as broad a range of consulting services as a firm with a large management advisory services division including scores of specialists. When the rendering of management advisory services brings the accountant into contact with problems having engineering aspects or requiring other skills not possessed by his firm, he can suggest to clients the desirability of calling in other professional consultants. Perhaps, in time, standard practices for referral to other public accounting firms for specialized services may develop along the lines followed by the medical profession. At present most small public accounting firms are reluctant to make referrals to national firms for fear that the client may decide to utilize the larger firm for all his needs. In a few instances, however, accountants have referred their clients to other accounting firms for specialized services, and the arrangement has worked out well. Many leaders of the profession believe that the practice of referrals will eventually become much more common.

The certified public accountant serving a clientele of small businesses may appropriately ask himself the following questions: "Are tax services, bookkeeping services, systems work, and auditing the most important and valuable services which I can perform for my clients? Am I competent, or can I become competent, to aid clients in the solution of a wide range of management problems for which independent outside counsel is desirable?" Management is spending more each year for consulting services; if the certified public accountant does not expand the area of services he now renders, other consultants, perhaps less qualified, will surely move to meet this rising demand. Problems in general management, in production, industrial engineering, and marketing all demand skills other than accounting, yet often require a thorough accounting knowledge of the client's operations. No independent consultant other than the certified public accountant has this accounting background.

The CPA as an expert witness

As business affairs have grown more complex, the number of court cases involving accounting issues has increased greatly. The testimony of accountants and other experts is needed in order that the judge or jury gain the necessary understanding of the pertinent facts. An *expert witness* is one who has special knowledge, experience, or training in a given field or profession. He is able to analyze and evaluate matters within his specialized body of knowledge, on which the judge or jury lacking such specialized experience could not readily form an opinion. The CPA or other expert, by analyzing the facts of the case and forming an opinion, renders assistance to the court.

The role of the expert witness is sharply different from that of other witnesses. The lay witness is permitted to testify only as to facts he has seen or heard; he must usually leave the drawing of opinions or conclusions to the judge or jury. In some situations the lay witness may include an opinion in his testimony if that opinion is based on facts he personally has seen or heard. The expert witness, on the other hand, may draw opinions based on the testimony of others and upon information acquired by others and conveyed to him before or during the trial. For the expert's opinion to carry weight, the information on which it is based must of course come from a reliable source.

Hypothetical questions. The CPA called as an expert witness may in some cases be able to conduct his own investigation and give his opinion based on such firsthand knowledge of the situation. In other cases, the CPA may not have any direct knowledge of the facts and his expert knowledge is then utilized through hypothetical questions. Under this latter approach, the expert witness is asked to assume certain facts which have been previously presented as evidence in the case and to express his opinion on the basis of these assumptions.

During cross-examination the opposing counsel is likely to utilize other facts as the basis for additional hypothetical questions, hoping thereby to elicit a contradictory opinion, or at least force some modification of the expert's opinion as previously expressed. A danger inherent in the use of hypothetical questions is that the expert's opinion may not be based on *all* the material facts, or that some of the facts which he is required to assume may later be rejected by the jury.

Types of cases in which the CPA may testify

The CPA is retained as an expert witness by one of the parties to the litigation in the belief that the CPA's testimony will strengthen his case. Among the types of cases in which a CPA may appropriately serve as an expert witness are the following: (*a*) income tax cases, both criminal fraud cases and civil tax cases; (*b*) partnership dissolutions; (*c*) interpretations of contracts involving valuation of assets, bonuses, or determination of net income; (*d*) suits by minority stockholders who believe corporate officers and directors have been deficient in handling corporate affairs; (*e*) divorce cases involving disputes over separate property of the spouses; (f) probate proceedings; (g) rates and earnings of public utilities; and (h) other cases involving complex accounting measurements.

Tax litigation. The CPA may serve as an expert witness in behalf of the government in a tax case or more commonly in behalf of the taxpayer. In many tax cases, the government is charging an understatement of taxable income and a deficiency in the tax paid. In criminal fraud cases, an additional charge is made concerning the taxpayer's willful attempt to evade taxes. Tax litigation usually follows a revenue agent's examination of the taxpayer's records, which has disclosed serious discrepancies or controversial issues. To be of aid to the taxpayer, the expert witness may prepare schedules and analyses which summarize detailed records of numerous transactions. Review of the transactions and records of several years may be required. The CPA may also develop an opinion as to whether transactions have been interpreted and recorded in conformity with generally accepted accounting principles. If the CPA finds that he cannot agree with his client's position in the case, he should immediately make this clear; obviously a party to a lawsuit does not wish to retain an expert whose testimony would be damaging to his side of the case. Of course not all accountants will reach the same conclusion on any complex accounting issue; consequently, it is common to find that both sides in a lawsuit will have retained accounting experts to testify in support of their opposing positions.

In attempting to prove tax evasion, the government may rely on evidence that the taxpayer's net worth has increased during the year (apart from gifts or other nontaxable items) by an amount greater than the reported income. This approach requires that the government determine the taxpayer's net worth at the beginning and end of the year by assigning values to all his assets and liabilities. Since there are many alternative methods of accounting valuation, the CPA can function effectively as an expert witness in explaining and comparing these alternatives.

Partnership dissolutions. Partnership dissolutions occur for a variety of reasons, such as the death or retirement of a partner, or the reaching of an agreed termination date. A partner or his legal representative then has the right to an accounting for his interest. The CPA may be retained to prepare a report to the court on the dissolved partnership. This report must consider among other things any dissolution provisions in the partnership agreement, capital contributions, withdrawals, loans, the division of profits for the final period of operation, and the current market value of noncash assets.

The estimating of goodwill is often a controversial point in establishing the amount of a partner's equity. The CPA acting as an expert witness may develop his own estimate for goodwill and utilize accounting literature to support the methods he employs.

Interpretations of contracts involving accounting measurements. Many contracts call for payments which may vary in amount depending upon accounting measurements. For example, A and B organized a corporation, with A acquiring 25 percent of the stock and B, 75 percent. B also received an option to purchase the stock held by A at any time during the first five years of operation at a price equal to the book value of the shares at the date of exercising the option. The option was exercised, and B tendered his check in an amount based upon his accountant's calculations of book value. The minority stockholder, A, rejected the check, claiming that if proper accounting principles had been followed, the accounts would indicate a book value three times as high as that assumed by B. The result of the dispute was an extended court case in which certified public accountants appeared as expert witnesses in behalf of both parties to the litigation.

The CPA on the witness stand

The CPA will maximize his effectiveness as an expert witness if he responds to all questions from counsel on both sides clearly and in an impartial, courteous manner. He should speak slowly enough that the court reporter can record his statements, and he should bear in mind that his opinions will be of little value unless they are expressed in language which the judge or jury can understand.

A preliminary step when the CPA takes the witness stand is usually a series of questions designed to establish his qualifications and competence. His education, experience, publications, and professional affiliations are factors in qualifying him as an expert. Special knowledge of the field or industry involved in the case is particularly helpful.

As a result of pretrial conferences with the attorney, the CPA will be aware of most of the questions to be addressed to him during direct examination. In cross-examination by the opposing counsel, however, a great variety of questions may arise. The objective of the attorney conducting the cross-examination is to destroy the significance of the opinion expressed by the expert witness. This situation requires that the CPA consider each question carefully and answer it in a professional and deliberate manner. If he does not know the answer to a given question, it is usually best to say so. Thorough preparation and intimate knowledge of the issues are the best means by which the expert witness can uphold his position under rigorous cross-examination.

Obtaining clients

It is axiomatic that reputable members of a profession—whether it be law, architecture, medicine, public accounting, or any other similar field—do not advertise their services. New business is obtained through personal recommendations by present clients, by bankers, attorneys, and insurance agents and adjusters, and by other business and professional persons whose work brings them into contact with persons needing accounting services.

To the young accountant trying to establish a practice of his own, the bans against advertising and against solicitation of clients may seem at first glance to be barriers imposed by established public accountants to protect themselves from new competition. Such arguments are not well founded; if advertising were permissible for professional accountants, the larger, well-established firms would be able to outdo the new practitioner. Advertising would actually injure all certified public accountants because it is incompatible with the dignity and prestige of a professional practice. Nearly everyone prefers to engage an attorney, physician, or accountant who has been recommended by friends rather than to trust a professional man who speaks to the public in glowing terms of his own accomplishments.

But how does the young accountant attract clients and establish a practice? One answer is to buy an existing practice, or to enter partnership with an established, older practitioner who is contemplating retirement and wants to effect a gradual transition of his work to a younger man or woman. Another possibility is that the previous CPA firm employer of the young accountant may "cede" some of its smaller clients to the departed employee to help him establish a practice. Clients may also be obtained through a circle of friends and acquaintances. Participation in community activities, clubs, and organizations is an acceptable and proven method for the young professional person to obtain recognition. Speaking engagements before local groups is another useful step in becoming known to businessmen.

By far the most effective way of gaining new clients is the enthusiastic recommendation of a present client. It is not unusual for a satisfied client to go out of his way to recommend his independent accountant to business associates, with the result of generating new business in a short time. Consequently, the competent accountant, once he has established a nucleus of satisfied clients, often finds his practice snowballing suddenly into a demand for services that he is hard pressed to meet.

Background information for the audit

The CPA approached by a prospective client is well advised to investigate the prospect before undertaking the engagement. The names and backgrounds of the major stockholders, directors, and officers should be ascertained by the CPA. Credit ratings of the prospect should be obtained, and the identity and reputations of the company's legal counsel and banking affiliations should be determined. The CPA must not negotiate with the client of another CPA; the other CPA must first be discharged by the prospective client. The CPA should always obtain a prospective client's permission to consult with a predecessor CPA to ascertain the reasons for the predecessor's replacement. (Regulations of the SEC require companies subject to its jurisdiction to report changes in independent auditors, and the reasons therefor, to the Commission.)

It is always important for the auditor to discover why a new client wants an audit and what specific results he hopes for. Audit procedures are not the same for all types of engagements; the audit work to be done will depend to a considerable extent upon any special objectives such as (*a*) sale of the business, (*b*) change in a partnership agreement, or (*c*) obtaining of a bank loan. In some cases the accountant may find that the client is in need of services quite different from those he had in mind in engaging an independent accountant.

As background information, the auditor in charge should obtain through preliminary discussions with the new client a summary of the history, products, operations, financial structure, control, and personnel of the enterprise. This information is usually obtained through informal conversations with owners or executives and is recorded in a permanent file available for reference in repeat engagements.

Numerous other sources of information on new clients are available. Among these are previous audit reports, annual reports to shareholders, SEC filings, and prior years' income tax returns. The client's sales brochures and other advertising material furnish information on his products. Trade publications, as well as government agency publications, are useful in obtaining orientation in the client's industry. A company which has been audited in previous years will generally authorize the new auditor to request access to the working papers of the preceding CPA firm. Finally, as indicated in Chapter 1, the AICPA may have issued an "industry audit guide" for the client's industry.

Preliminary arrangements with clients

The auditor's approach to an engagement is not that of a detective looking for evidence of fraud; instead, the approach is the positive, constructive one of gathering evidence to prove the fairness and validity of the client's financial statements.

A conference with the client prior to beginning the engagement is a useful step in avoiding misunderstandings. This conference is especially important with new clients and for any others who are not well informed on auditing practices. The conference should include discussion of the auditing objectives and any matters which conceivably could produce friction. Since the fee is usually in the mind of both client and auditor, it should be frankly discussed, but without creating the impression that the auditor's chief interest is in the earning of a fee.

As a basis for a worthwhile conference prior to the engagement, the auditor may make a preliminary survey of the client's accounting records and monthly statements to help determine his needs and the existence of any special problems. The cost of the survey is usually not large; this cost is usually included in the total fee for the audit.

A clear understanding between the client and the auditor concerning the scope of the examination and the condition of the records at the starting date is a desirable first step in planning an audit. Otherwise the auditor may arrive to begin an examination only to find that transactions for the period to be examined have not yet been fully recorded. It is not the auditor's job to draft routine adjusting entries or to balance the subsidiary ledgers with the control accounts. For some clients the auditor may find it necessary to do this routine work, but it cannot be considered as economic use of audit manpower.

The new client should be informed as to the extent of investigation of the opening balances of such accounts as plant and equipment and capital stock. To determine the propriety of depreciation expense for the current year and the proper balances in plant and equipment accounts at the balance sheet date, it is obviously necessary to determine the validity of the property accounts at the beginning of the current period. In some cases, satisfactory audits of the business in preceding years by other reputable auditing firms may enable the auditor to accept the opening balances of the current year with a minimum of verification work; in other cases, in which no satisfactory recent audit has been made, an extensive analysis of transactions of prior years will be necessary to establish account balances as of the beginning of the current year. In these latter situations the client should be made to understand that the scope and cost of the initial audit may exceed that of repeat engagements, which will not require analysis of past years' transactions.

Use of client's staff to prepare working papers

Many audit working papers can be prepared for the auditor by the client's staff, thus reducing the cost of the audit and freeing the auditor from routine work. The auditor may set up the columnar headings for such working papers and give instructions to the client's staff as to the information to be gathered. These working papers should bear the label "Prepared By Client" or "P.B.C.," and also the initials of the auditor who verifies the work performed by the client's staff. Working papers prepared by the client should never be accepted at face value; they must be reviewed and tested by the auditor in order that he maintain his independent status.

Among the tasks which may be assigned to the client's employees are the preparation of a trial balance of the general ledger, preparation of an aged trial balance of accounts receivable, analyses of accounts receivable written off, lists of property additions and retirements during the year, and analyses of various revenue and expense accounts.

Fees

When a businessman engages the services of an independent public accountant, he will usually ask for an estimate of the cost of the audit. In supplying this estimate after being engaged, the accountant will give first consideration to the time probably required for the audit. Staff time is the basic unit of measurement for audit fees. Each public accounting firm develops a per hour or per diem fee schedule for each category of audit staff, based on direct salaries and such related costs as payroll taxes and insurance. The "direct" rate is then increased for allocated overhead costs and a profit element.

In addition to basic per diem or per hour fees, clients are charged for direct costs incurred by the public accounting firm for staff travel, report processing, and other "out-of-pocket" expenditures.

Estimating a fee for an audit thus usually involves the application of daily or hourly rates to the estimated time required. Since the exact number of days cannot be determined in advance, the auditor may merely give a rough estimate of the fee. Or he may multiply the rates by the estimated time, add an amount for unforeseen problems, and quote a range or bracket of amounts within which the total fee will fall. If a single estimate rather than a maximum-minimum range is given the client, it may be more expedient to quote a relatively high rather than a relatively low amount. Objections from clients are not likely if the actual fees turn out to be less than the estimated amount. Once the auditor has given an estimate of the fee to a client, he naturally feels some compulsion to keep his charges within this limit.

Per diem rates for audit work vary considerably in different sections of the country and even within a given community in accordance with the reputation and experience of the accounting firm. Of course the salaries paid to audit staff members are much less than the rates at which audit time is billed to clients. In many firms salaries represent about 40 percent of billing rates; the remainder is required to cover the cost of "nonbillable" time when auditors are not assigned, overhead expenses of the office, and a profit to the partners.

In addition to setting fees on the basis of daily or hourly rates, many CPA firms serve some clients under retainer contracts. An annual retainer fee (often payable in equal monthly amounts) is charged without regard to the amount of services rendered in a given month. The types of service covered by these retainer contracts may cover auditing, preparation of tax returns, tax planning, monthly statements, and management advisory services.

Engagement letters

These preliminary understandings with the client may desirably be recorded in an engagement letter by the auditor, making clear the nature of the engagement, any limitations on the scope of the audit, work to be performed by the client's staff, and the basis for computing the auditor's fee. Arrangements for an audit of a small or medium-sized business are often made with the owner, a partner, or an executive such as the president, treasurer, or controller. In large corporations, stockholders are often called upon to approve the directors' choice of auditors. The AICPA and the SEC have recommended that publicly owned corporations appoint committees composed of outside directors (those who are not officers or employees) to nominate independent auditors. Such audit committees should discuss with the auditors the scope of the examination and should invite recommendations on internal controls. This practice gives added assurance to the investing public that corporate financial statements are objectively prepared.

Engagement letters do not follow any standard form; an example of such a letter is presented in Figure 4–1.

Audit plans

After obtaining the client's acceptance of the engagement letter, the auditor begins the study and evaluation of the client's internal control. This operation is discussed in depth in Chapter 5. Once the internal control evaluation has been accomplished, the auditor should develop an appropriate plan of the audit. An audit plan provides essential background information for an audit assignment and outlines the objectives, timing, and other requirements of the engagement. Although audit plans differ in form and content among public accounting firms, an adequate plan should include details on the following:

1. Description of the client company—its structure, business, and organization.
2. Nature and extent of services to be performed for the client.
3. Timing and scheduling of the required work.
4. Summary of the internal control evaluation.
5. Description of special problems to be resolved in the audit.

The audit plan is usually drafted by the senior or manager, subject to review and approval by the partner in charge. A copy of the plan should be furnished to every auditor assigned to the engagement.

FIGURE 4–1
Engagement letter

Know

Adams, Barnes and Company

CERTIFIED PUBLIC ACCOUNTANTS

December 1, 1974

Mr. J. B. Barker, Chairman of the Board
Barker Tool Company
1825 LeMay Street
Chicago, Illinois 60642

Dear Mr. Barker:

This letter is written to confirm our understanding as to our examination of the financial statements of your company for the year ending December 31, 1974.

Our examination will be performed in accordance with generally accepted auditing standards and will include all procedures which we consider necessary to provide a basis for expression of our opinion on the fairness of the financial statements. The examination will include:

1. A study and evaluation of the system of internal control.
2. Tests of the accounting records and other evidence to the extent we consider necessary based on our evaluation of internal control.
3. Preparation of federal and state income tax returns.
4. Preparation of a short–form report, and a long–form report suitable for use in connection with the arrangement of bank loans.

If our investigation indicates the desirability of any changes in internal control procedures, we shall prepare a report on this subject for your consideration. The purpose of our examination is to enable us to express an opinion on the fairness of the financial statements; the examination is not designed to disclose fraud or defalcations, although if such irregularities exist, the examination may bring them to light.

Our fees for this examination will be based on the time spent by various members of our staff at our regular rates.

In order for us to work as efficiently as possible, it is understood that your staff will provide us with a year–end trial balance by January 15, 1975, and also certain working papers which we shall discuss with you in the next few days. Our examination will be completed and our report submitted by March 1, 1975.

Very truly yours,

Charles Adams

Accepted by _____
Date _____

Charles Adams
Adams, Barnes and Company

Audit programs

An audit program is a detailed outline of the auditing work to be performed, specifying the procedures to be followed in verification of each item in the financial statements and giving the estimated time required. As each step in the audit program is completed, the date, the auditor's initials, and the actual time consumed may be entered opposite the item. An audit program thus serves as a useful tool both in scheduling and in controlling audit work. It indicates the number of persons required and the relative proportions of senior and staff assistant hours needed, and it enables supervisors to keep currently informed on the progress being made.

The inclusion of detailed audit instructions in the program gives assurance that essential steps in verification will not be overlooked. These written instructions enable inexperienced auditors to work effectively with less personal supervision than would otherwise be required, and thus permit seniors and managers to concentrate upon those features of the examination which demand a high degree of analytical ability and the discriminating exercise of professional judgment.

Illustrative audit program. A typical example of the detailed audit procedures set forth in an audit program is the following partial list of procedures for audit of investments in marketable securities:

X COMPANY

PARTIAL AUDIT PROGRAM—SECURITIES
December 31, 1974

Working paper reference	*Date and initials*		*Time*	
			Estimated	*Actual*

1. Inspection of securities:
   a) Obtain or prepare list of securities owned as of balance sheet date.
   b) Compare list of securities with corresponding ledger account.
   c) Inspect securities on hand at or near date of balance sheet and compare with list of securities at balance sheet date. Reconcile securities to date of balance sheet and vouch transactions for intervening period. Maintain control of securities during this period.
   d) Compare serial numbers of securities inspected with serial numbers listed for these securities in prior year's audit.

Tailor-made audit programs. The conditions and problems encountered differ with every audit engagement; hence it is necessary for the auditor in charge of each examination to determine what procedures are appropriate in the circumstances. The audit program for a specific engagement should not be developed until the client's internal control has been studied and evaluated by the auditor. Weak internal control, as manifested by poor accounting records, incompetent personnel, or lack of internal auditing, necessitates much more extensive auditing than would be necessary for a well-staffed concern with strong internal controls, good accounting records, and an effective internal auditing department. Internal control is sometimes adequate for certain operations of the company but weak or absent in other areas. The amount of testing by the auditor should be increased in areas of operations for which internal controls are deficient and may properly be minimized in areas subject to strong internal controls. The great variation in quality of internal controls encountered, coupled with the variety of accounting methods and special problems peculiar to individual business concerns, requires that audit procedures be tailored to fit the circumstances of the individual audit engagement.

The value of the audit program as a means of giving coherence, order, and logical sequence to the investigation is beyond dispute. The audit program must not, however, be considered a substitute for an alert, resourceful attitude on the part of the auditor. He should be encouraged to explore fully any unusual transactions or questionable practices which come to his attention from any source and cautioned not to restrict himself to the investigative routines set forth in a prearranged audit program. As the examination progresses, the desirability of making certain modifications in the work contemplated by the audit program will usually become apparent. The selection of audit procedures appropriate to the circumstances requires professional judgment based on extensive auditing experience.

The ideal audit program should insure the application of minimum required audit operations in every engagement but be sufficiently flexible to encourage and require the accountant to use his own initiative in devising such additional audit operations as are indicated by facts developed during the course of the audit.

Time estimates for audit engagements

Public accounting firms usually charge clients on a time basis, and detailed time records must therefore be maintained on every audit engagement. A time estimate for an audit is constructed by estimating the time required for each step in the audit program for each of the various grades of auditors and totaling these estimated amounts. Time estimates serve other functions in addition to providing a basis for estimating fees. The time estimate is an important tool of the audit senior used to measure the efficiency of his assistants and to determine at each stage of the engagement whether the work is progressing at a satisfactory rate.

There is always pressure to complete an audit within the estimated time. The staff assistant who takes more than the normal time for a task is not likely to be popular with his supervisors or to win rapid advancement. Ability to do satisfactory work when given abundant time is not a sufficient qualification, *for time is never abundant in public accounting*.

The building of time estimates is facilitated in repeat engagements by reference to the preceding year's detailed time records. Sometimes time estimates prove quite unattainable because the client's records are not in satisfactory condition, or because of other special circumstances which arise. Even when time estimates are exceeded, there can be no compromise with qualitative standards in the performance of the field work. The auditor's professional reputation and his legal liability to clients and third parties do not permit any short-cutting or omission of audit procedures to meet a predetermined time estimate.

Audit manuals of public accounting firms

Audit manuals are considered by many accounting firms as a means of insuring that a uniformly high level of auditing technique is employed by staff members in the conduct of examinations. These manuals are in part a condensation of the literature of auditing and in part a condensation of the firm's own experience. The objective of the manual is to serve as a guide during the conduct of an examination. If all staff members of a CPA firm consistently apply the principles outlined in the manual, assurance is gained thereby of uniform compliance with generally accepted auditing standards. The firm may then properly use the standard short form of report, which contains the statement: "Our examination was made in accordance with generally accepted auditing standards and accordingly included such tests of the accounting records and such other auditing procedures as we considered necessary in the circumstances."

Contents of the audit manual. A comprehensive audit manual may contain:

a) General instruction on the conduct of examinations, such as—
   (1) Interim audit work.
   (2) Review of the system of internal control.
   (3) Relations with clients.
   (4) Duties of the auditor in charge of field work.
   (5) Use of permanent file and previous year's working papers.
b) An internal control questionnaire and instructions for its use.
c) A statement of policy on reports on internal control.

d)   An illustrative audit program.

e)   Instructions and illustrations for the preparation of audit working
papers.

f)   Instructions on report writing and questions of adequate disclosure
in financial statements.

Limitations of audit manuals.   An audit manual is no more than a
guide. It does not purport to take the place of professional judgment,
but it is often of practical aid to the auditor by suggesting procedures
which have been proved effective in many situations and may be capable
of application to the engagement at hand. The general audit manual
is applicable to all kinds and sizes of manufacturing and merchandising
enterprises. For the audit of some specialized types of business, such
as banks and stock brokerage firms, the general audit manual will require
extensive modification and the introduction of certain additional procedures. Some auditing firms have, therefore, developed specialized audit
manuals for use in audits of clients in such specialized types of business.

Auditing terminology

The terms used by the auditor to describe the various phases of
his work need to be precisely defined in order that audit programs,
working papers, and reports may be clearly understood. The following
terms are among those most commonly employed; others will be defined
as they are introduced in later chapters.

"Analyze" means the process of identifying and classifying for further
study all the debit and credit entries contained in a ledger account.
Accounts are analyzed in order to ascertain the nature of all the transactions which gave rise to the balance. An account such as Miscellaneous
Expense, for example, requires analysis before any real understanding
of its contents is possible.

"Compare" is usually used to mean the process of observing the similarity or variations of particular items in financial statements from one
period to the next. If the comparison of a given type of revenue or
expense for two successive years shows substantial change, further investigation to ascertain the cause of the change is necessary. The term
"compare" may also be used by the auditor to mean ascertaining the
agreement or lack of agreement between a journal entry and the corresponding entry in a ledger account, or between related documents
such as a purchase order and an invoice.

"Confirm" describes the process of proving the authenticity and accuracy of an account balance or entry by direct written communication
with the debtor, creditor, or other party to the transaction. Obtaining
proof from a source outside the client's records is thus a basic element
of confirmation. It is standard practice to confirm bank balances by

direct correspondence with the bank and to confirm accounts receivable by direct correspondence with customers. The letters or forms sent to outsiders for this purpose are called "confirmation requests."

"Count" has the same meaning in audit terminology as in everyday usage. As part of his verification work the auditor may count cash on hand, inventory, securities, and other assets. Counting is a specific step toward determination of quantities. The counting process may be in terms of dollars, pounds, physical units, or other denominators, and may vary from occasional test counts of small samples to complete counts of some types of property.

"Examine" means to review critically or to investigate. An "examination of the financial statements" has the same meaning as an "audit of the financial statements."

"Extend" means to compute by multiplication. To "extend" the client's physical inventory listing is to multiply the quantity in units by the cost per unit. The resultant product is the "extension."

"Footing" (or "down-footing") refers to the process of proving the totals of vertical columns of figures; "cross-footing" means the proving of totals of figures appearing in horizontal rows. By footing and cross-footing schedules and records the auditor derives positive assurance of their arithmetical accuracy.

"Inspect" implies a careful reading or point-by-point review of a document or record. Other terms frequently used by the auditor to convey the same or a similar meaning are "scrutinize" and "examine."

"Reconcile" means to establish agreement between two sets of independently maintained but related records. Thus, the ledger account for Cash in Bank is reconciled with the bank statement, and the home office record of shipments to a branch office is reconciled with the record of receipts maintained by the branch.

"Testing" or "test checking" means to select and examine a representative sample from a population of similar items. If the sample is properly chosen, the results of this limited test should reveal the same characteristics as would be disclosed by an examination of the entire lot of items.

"Trace" describes the process of following a transaction from one accounting record to another. The purchase of machinery, for example, might be verified by tracing the transaction from the voucher register to the check register.

"Verify" means to prove the validity and accuracy of records or to establish the existence and ownership of assets. Verification of plant and equipment, for example, might include analysis of ledger accounts, proof of footings, tracing of postings from journals, examination of documents authorizing acquisitions and retirements, and physical inspection of the assets.

"Voucher" is a term used to describe any document supporting a transaction. Examples are petty cash receipts, receiving memoranda, and paid checks.

"Vouching" means establishing the accuracy and authenticity of entries in ledger accounts or other records by examining such supporting evidence of the transactions as invoices, paid checks, and other original papers.

The use of the term "check" as a verb has fallen into disrepute because of its overuse and vagueness of meaning. There is little justification for the use of this term in lieu of more precise and descriptive terms such as "count," "compare," "reconcile," and "vouch."

Seasonal fluctuations in public accounting work

One of the traditional disadvantages of the public accounting profession has been the concentration of work during the "busy season" from December through March, followed by a period of slack demand during the summer months. This seasonal trend was caused by the fact that most concerns kept their records on a calendar-year basis and desired auditing services immediately after the December 31st closing of the books. Another important factor has been the spring deadline for filing of federal income tax returns. A generation ago it was customary, because of the seasonal concentration of work, for many audit firms to increase their staffs in December and to reduce them again a few months later. Such seasonal fluctuation in employment undoubtedly deterred many qualified persons from entering the field of public accounting.

In recent years the seasonal pattern of employment in public accounting has largely disappeared. A number of factors have contributed toward a more stable working force and more uniform distribution of work throughout the year. These factors include (a) the decision of many business concerns to adopt a fiscal year ending at a date of seasonal inactivity rather than a calendar year, and (b) recognition by the public accounting profession that much of the audit work traditionally performed after the annual closing of the books could just as effectively be performed on an interim basis throughout the year. Coupled with these changes has been a growing awareness of the need for personnel policies which tend to minimize overtime work and to provide stability of employment. Public accounting firms now offer the same stability of employment found in other professions.

GROUP I
REVIEW QUESTIONS

4–1. The following statements illustrate incorrect use of auditing terms. You are to substitute the proper terms for the italicized words.

a) We **checked** the cash on hand.

b) We **analyzed** the bank statement with the ledger balance for Cash in Bank.

c) We **confirmed** the ledger account for Miscellaneous Expense by classifying and reviewing the various kinds of debit and credit entries in the account.

d) We **vouched** the accounts receivable by direct written communication with customers.

e) We **reconciled** the minutes of directors' meetings for the entire period under audit.

4–2. Suggest some factors which might cause an audit engagement to exceed the original time estimate. Would the extra time be charged to the client?

4–3. What are "management advisory services"?

4–4. What information should a CPA seek in his investigation of a prospective client?

4–5. Describe the various levels or grades of accounting personnel in a large public accounting firm.

4–6. Distinguish between the responsibilities of a senior auditor and a staff assistant.

4–7. Explain the nature and general contents of the audit manuals used by many public accounting firms.

4–8. State the purpose and nature of an engagement letter.

4–9. Should a separate audit program be prepared for each audit engagement, or can a standard program be used for most engagements?

4–10. How does a professional corporation differ from the traditional corporation?

4–11. Is technical accounting ability or good judgment a more important qualification for a partner in a public accounting firm? For a staff assistant?

4–12. List three of the more important responsibilities of a partner in a public accounting firm.

4–13. Is an auditor justified in relying upon the accuracy of working papers prepared for him by employees of the client?

4–14. In recent years the work of public accounting firms has tended to be spread more uniformly over the year rather than being heavily concentrated in a few months. What are the principal reasons for this change?

4–15. Define and differentiate between an audit plan and an audit program.

4–16. Describe the preferred composition and role of the audit committee of a board of directors.

4–17. List four types of court cases in which the CPA may serve as an expert witness.

4–18. "An audit program is desirable when new staff members are assigned to an engagement, but an experienced auditor should be able to conduct an examination without reference to an audit program." Do you agree? Discuss.

GROUP II
QUESTIONS REQUIRING ANALYSIS

4–19. How can a CPA make the most effective use of the preceding year's audit program in a recurring examination? (AICPA, adapted)

4–20. The audit plan, the audit program, and the time budget are three important working papers prepared early in an audit. What functions do these working papers serve in the auditor's compliance with generally accepted auditing standards? Discuss.

4–21. Should a CPA accept a request to serve as an expert witness for the plaintiff in a case involving another CPA as defendant? Explain.

4–22. Jordan Finance Company opened four personal loan offices in neighboring cities on January 2, 1974. Small cash loans are made to borrowers who repay the principal with interest in monthly installments over a period not exceeding two years. Ralph Jordan, president of the company, uses one of the offices as a central office and visits the other offices periodically for supervision and internal auditing purposes.

Assume that you agreed to examine Jordan Finance Company's financial statements for the year ended December 31, 1974. No scope limitations were imposed.

a) How would you determine the scope necessary to satisfactorily complete your examination? Discuss.

b) Would you be responsible for the discovery of fraud in this examination? Discuss (AICPA, adapted)

4–23. Mr. Barton, president of the Bayview Corporation, has engaged you to make an audit of the corporation's financial statements. You are not familiar with the type of business of the corporation. Mr. Barton advises you that he would like to have an approximation of the cost of the examination. List the steps you would take to provide the requested estimate. (AICPA)

GROUP III
PROBLEMS

4–24. James Andrews, an experienced CPA and an officer of the Society of Certified Public Accountants in his state, was asked by the United States Attorney's office to serve as an expert witness in a case aimed at assessing additional income tax upon the McConnell Corporation.

Mr. Andrews had written several articles on inventory pricing. The publication of these articles in professional journals had been influential in causing the government to request his services in this case. Also considered important by the United States Attorney's office was the fact that Andrews' prior experience had included several years as a member of the accounting faculty in a large university. Since

Andrews had never served as an expert witness, he had some doubts as to whether he should accept the engagement. However, he decided to meet with the attorneys for the government and discuss the issues.

The conference indicated that the McConnell Corporation, a manufacturer of machinery and electronic equipment, had valued its inventories of work in process and finished goods on the basis of "prime costs" only. These "prime costs" included only raw materials and direct labor. All overhead had been deducted from revenue as incurred. The government's view was that this treatment violated generally accepted accounting principles and caused an undervaluation of inventories and an understatement of net income. The point was stressed that Mr. Andrews was not being asked to interpret tax laws but to express an expert opinion on generally accepted accounting principles with reference to inventory pricing. After some discussion, Andrews agreed to serve as an expert witness at the per diem rate he normally charged for consulting services. This rate was also applicable to time spent in preparing for his court appearance.

Prior to his appearance on the witness stand, Mr. Andrews spent most of a day in court while the taxpayer presented arguments supporting his position. Another CPA known to Andrews testified that he had designed McConnell Corporation's accounting system and that the omission of overhead from inventories was justified because of rapid change in product design, which made obsolescence of inventories a continuing problem. A well-known bank official also appeared as a defense witness. He testified that the bank made large loans to McConnell Corporation and regarded their financial statements as of excellent quality. He particularly approved the valuation of inventories at "prime cost" only and stated he would prefer to see all the bank's customers follow this practice.

When Mr. Andrews was called to the witness stand, his qualifications as an expert were established without difficulty. In the direct examination which followed, he was asked his opinion on a hypothetical question concerning the exclusion of factory overhead as part of inventory cost. Andrews replied that the exclusion of all overhead from inventory cost was not an acceptable accounting method. He stressed the point that the determination of net income required the matching of costs and revenue and that the cost of producing a manufactured article necessarily included a share of overhead as well as material and direct labor cost.

During cross-examination, the attorney for the defendant asked Mr. Andrews the following questions:

a) Have you discussed the issues in this case with anyone prior to your appearance in court?

b) Does accounting literature recognize the existence of a variety of methods for computing inventory costs?

c) In a business in which product obsolescence is a major threat, would you favor the valuation of inventories in a manner that would lead to a maximum or minimum valuation?

d)   Do you think a banker who daily makes loans on the basis of financial statements presented in support of loan applications is well-qualified to recognize good methods of financial reporting?

e)   If the production of a factory or a section thereof is shut down for a period of several months, would you include the continuing overhead expense as a part of inventory costs?

Required:

Draft the answers you think Andrews should give to each of the five questions. Give full explanations of the reasons underlying your answer. In choosing your language bear in mind that the judge is not a professional accountant. Try to answer the questions in a manner that will not destroy or weaken the value of the testimony previously given by Mr. Andrews.

4–25.   You are invited by the president of Westfield Corporation to discuss with him the possibility of your conducting an audit of the company. The corporation is a small, closely held manufacturing organization which appears to be expanding. No previous audit has been made by independent certified public accountants. Your discussions with the president include a review of the recent monthly financial statements, inspection of the accounting records, and review of policies with the chief accountant. You also are taken on a guided tour of the plant by the president. He then makes the following statement:

"Before making definite arrangements for an audit, I would like to know about how long it will take and about how much it will cost. I want quality work and expect to pay a fair price, but since this is our first experience with independent auditors, I would like a full explanation as to how the cost of the audit is determined. Will you please send me a memorandum covering these points?"

Write the memorandum requested by the president.

4–26.   Carlyle Company found its sales rising rapidly after the opening of a large military installation in its territory. To finance the increase in accounts receivable and the larger inventory required by the increased volume of sales, the company decided for the first time in its history to seek a bank loan. The president of the local bank informed Carlyle Company that an audit by a CPA would be a necessary prerequisite to approval of the loan application. Mr. Carlyle, sole proprietor of the business, engaged the newly formed CPA firm of Winston and Lowe to conduct the audit and provide the report requested by the bank. Carlyle Company had not previously been audited.

From the beginning of the audit engagement, nothing seemed to go well. Mr. Robert Corning, the staff accountant sent out by Winston and Lowe to begin the work, found that the books were not up to date and not in balance. He worked for a week assisting the Carlyle Company bookkeeper to get the books in shape. The problem was not reported to the partners until the following week because Mr. Winston was out of town and Mr. Lowe was suddenly taken ill.

In the meantime, the bookkeeper complained to Mr. Carlyle that the auditor was impeding his work.

After the audit work was well under way during the second week, Mr. Carlyle refused to permit the auditor to confirm accounts receivable, which were the largest current asset. He also stated that the pressure of current business prevented interrupting operations for the taking of a physical inventory. Mr. Corning protested that confirmation of accounts receivable and observation of a physical inventory were mandatory auditing procedures, but Mr. Carlyle rejected this protest.

Upon his return to town Mr. Winston was informed of the difficulties and went immediately to Mr. Carlyle's office. He explained to Mr. Carlyle that the omission of work on receivables and inventories would force the auditors to disclaim an opinion on the financial statements taken as a whole. Mr. Carlyle became quite angry; he asserted that he could borrow the money he needed from his mother-in-law and thereby eliminate any need for bankers or auditors in his business. Mr. Carlyle ordered Mr. Winston and Mr. Corning off the premises and asserted that he would pay them nothing. Mr. Winston replied that he had the Carlyle Company general ledger and other accounting records in his own office and that he would not return them until he received payment in full for all time expended, at the firm's regular per diem rates for Mr. Corning plus a charge for his own time.

Evaluate the actions taken by Winston and Lowe in this case and advise Mr. Winston on the action to be taken at this point.

5

Internal control

OUR CONSIDERATION of internal control has three major objectives: first, to explain the meaning and significance of internal control; second, to outline the steps required to create and maintain strong internal control; and third, to show how the auditor goes about his review of internal control.

No attempt is made in this chapter to present in detail the internal control procedures applicable to particular kinds of assets or to particular phase of operations, such as purchases or sales. Detailed information along these lines will be found in succeeding chapters as each phase of the auditor's examination is presented. Before studying internal controls designed for specific transactions, we need a clear understainding of the basic principles and objectives underlying all types of internal control. Both business managers and public accountants are concerned with this problem because the system of internal control is essential to both in meeting their respective responsibilities.

Business decisions of almost every kind are based at least in part on accounting data. These decisions range from such minor matters as authorizing overtime work or purchasing office supplies to such major issues as a shift from one product to another or making a choice between leasing or buying a new plant. Internal control provides assurance to management of the dependability of the accounting data used in making these decisions.

Decisions made by management become company policy. To be effective, this policy must be communicated throughout the company and consistently followed. Internal control aids in securing compliance with company policy. Management also has a direct responsibility of maintaining accounting records and producing financial statements which are adequate and reliable. Internal control provides assurance that this responsibility is being met.

To the independent public accountant, internal control is of equal significance. The quality of the internal controls in force, more than any other factor, determines the pattern of his examination. The independent auditor studies and evaluates the system of internal control in order to determine the extent and direction of the auditing work necessary to permit him to express an opinion as to the fairness of the financial statements.

The meaning of internal control

A system of internal control consists of all measures employed by a business for the purposes of (1) safeguarding its resources against waste, fraud, and inefficiency; (2) promoting accuracy and reliability in accounting and operating data; (3) encouraging and measuring compliance with company policy; and (4) judging the efficiency of operations in all divisions of the business.

The broad sweep of this definition indicates that internal control is much more than a device for the prevention of fraud or the detection of accidental errors in the accounting processes: it is an indispensable aid to efficient management, particularly in large-scale business enterprises. Internal control extends beyond accounting and financial functions; its scope is companywide and embraces such varied activities as employee training programs, internal auditing, statistical analyses, quality control, and production scheduling.

This broad sweeping concept of internal control is most significant when viewed against the backdrop of a large nationwide industrial organization, for internal control has developed into a technique of vital importance in enabling management of large complex enterprises to function efficiently. Since internal control has attained greatest significance in large-scale business organizations, the greater part of the discussion in this chapter is presented in terms of the large corporation. A separate section is presented at the end of the chapter, however, dealing with the problem of achieving internal control in a small business.

To summarize the preceding discussion of the meaning of internal control and the broadening of the concept in recent years, we may say that internal control in present-day usage embraces all departments and affects all activities of a business concern. It includes the methods by which top management delegates authority and assigns responsibility for such functions as selling, purchasing, accounting, and production.

It also includes the program for preparing, verifying, and distributing to various levels of supervision those current reports and analyses which enable executives to maintain control over the variety of activities and functions which constitute a large corporate enterprise. The use of budgetary techniques, production standards, inspection laboratories, time and motion studies, and employee training programs involve engineers and many other technicians far removed from accounting and financial activities; yet all of these devices are part of the mechanism now conceived as a system of internal control.

no Bearing on financial statements

Internal accounting controls versus internal administrative controls

The auditor is primarily interested in internal controls of an accounting nature—those controls which bear directly upon the dependability of the accounting records and the financial statements. For example, if the organization plan requires that monthly bank reconciliations be prepared by an employee not authorized to issue checks or handle cash, this division of duties constitutes an internal accounting control of importance to the auditor.

Some internal controls have no bearing on the financial statements and consequently are not of direct interest to the independent public accountant. Controls of this category are often referred to as internal administrative controls. Management is interested in maintaining strong internal control over factory operations and sales activities as well as over accounting and financial functions. Accordingly, management will establish "administrative controls" to provide operational efficiency and adherence to prescribed policies in all departments of the organization.

An example of an internal control device of an administrative nature is a written directive to the personnel department of a company establishing specific standards to be observed in the selection of new employees. Important though such a control device may be to successful operation of the company, it is not directly related to the dependability of the financial statements. Consequently, the independent public accountant in the course of his examination of the company's financial statements would probably not concern himself with the question of whether the personnel department was actually following the criteria stipulated by management for selection of new employees.

As another example of an administrative or nonfinancial type of internal control, the sales manager of a manufacturing company may require traveling salesmen to submit frequent reports showing the number of calls made on customers each day. Such a control device may be vital in maintaining the productivity of the sales force; however, it is probably not significant to the independent public accountant in verifying the company's financial statements.

Of course not all internal controls can be neatly classified and separated into mutually exclusive categories of "administrative" and "accounting." Neither can we say that the auditor will evaluate all accounting controls while ignoring all administrative controls. For example, let us assume that an auditor has reviewed the internal controls of an accounting nature relating to inventories, such as control accounts, detailed perpetual inventory cards, receiving reports, physical counts, and similar points. Assume also that the client in this case prepares extensive factory production reports with analyses of productive versus idle labor hours, unanticipated overtime, and other operating inefficiencies. In the usual examination, the auditor will not devote a great deal of time to these reports. However, if overtime or indirect labor costs appear excessive in relation to direct labor, the auditor may review the production reports more extensively to determine the propriety of the indirect costs charged to work-in-process inventories.

In recognition of the lack of a clear distinction between accounting controls and administrative controls, the AICPA's Committee on Auditing Procedure provided the following practical definitions in *Statement on Auditing Procedure No. 54,* "The Auditor's Study and Evaluation of Internal Control":

Administrative control includes, but is not limited to, the plan of organization and the procedures and records that are concerned with the decision processes leading to management's authorization of transactions. Such authorization is a management function directly associated with the responsibility for achieving the objectives of the organization and is the starting point for establishing accounting control of transactions.

Accounting control comprises the plan of organization and the procedures and records that are concerned with the safeguarding of assets and the reliability of financial records and consequently are designed to provide reasonable assurance that

a) Transactions are executed in accordance with management's general or specific authorization.

b) Transactions are recorded as necessary (1) to permit preparation of financial statements in conformity with generally accepted accounting principles or any other criteria applicable to such statements and (2) to maintain accountability for assets.

c) Access to assets is permitted only in accordance with management's authorization.

d) The recorded accountability for assets is compared with the existing assets at reasonable intervals and appropriate action is taken with respect to any differences.

In summary, an audit by a CPA includes the review of internal controls of an accounting nature. The review of internal controls of a purely administrative nature does not ordinarily fall within the responsibility of the auditor, whose objective is to express an opinion on the fairness of financial statements.

Public accounting firms often perform management advisory services for their clients in addition to making audits. In rendering management services the public accountant will frequently evaluate internal administrative controls and suggest modifications therein; such work, however, is not necessary to the expression of an opinion as to the fairness of financial statements. The internal auditing staff in most large corporations definitely *does* review internal administrative controls as well as those in the accounting areas. Internal auditing will be considered in another section of this chapter.

The need for internal control

The long-run trend for corporations to evolve into organizations of gigantic size and scope, including a great variety of specialized technical operations and numbering employees in thousands and tens of thousands, has made it impossible for corporate executives to exercise personal, firsthand supervision of operations. No longer able to rely upon personal observation as a means of appraising operating results and financial position, the corporate executive has, of necessity, come to depend upon a stream of accounting and statistical reports. These reports summarize current happenings and conditions throughout the enterprise; the units of measurement employed are not only dollars but man-hours, material weights, customer calls, employee terminations, and a host of other denominators.

The information carried by this stream of reports enables management to control and direct the enterprise. It keeps management informed as to whether company policy is being carried out, whether governmental regulations are being observed, and whether financial position is sound, operations profitable, and interdepartmental relations harmonious.

What assurance does management have of the reliability and completeness of the reports that are submitted for its guidance? An unfortunate tendency exists for many people to assume that an elaborate statistical report, replete with symbols, percentages, and footnotes, is inherently factual and free from bias or error. Business executives have learned from bitter experience that truth and logic are not inherent qualities of the reporting process. Only through a continuous process of verification and analysis of reports and the records from which they are derived can management place its confidence in the reliability of the data provided for its use.

Greater responsibility to governmental agencies

In recent years, business enterprises have been required to comply with a great variety of governmental regulations. Income, social security, and property taxes require accurate accounting data if compliance with the statutes and a minimum of tax liability are to be achieved. If a corporation is to offer its securities for public sale, the securities must qualify for registration with the Securities and Exchange Commission. Registration also requires full disclosure of the corporation's financial history and periodic reports of financial position and operating results so long as the securities are publicly traded.

Primary responsibility for the accuracy and completeness of information furnished investors lies with management, as evidenced by the Securities Act of 1933, which requires that signatures of officers and directors appear on registration statements and provides penalties for misstatements therein.

Other regulatory functions of government, such as the renegotiation or redetermination of government contracts, the extensive controls exercised over contractors operating under cost-plus-incentive-fee contracts, the supervision of airline and railroad rates, and many other points of contact between business and government make mandatory an adequate system of internal control if corporate management is to be prepared to face its present-day responsibilities to government. The size and scope of the corporate entity, coupled with the number and complexity of governmental regulations affecting business corporations, render it impossible for members of management to safeguard themselves from serious liability except through reliance upon strong internal controls as assurance of the accuracy of accounting data.

Responsibility of management for adequate informative disclosure

The growth of the large corporation as the dominant form of business organization has been accompanied by decreasing participation of owners in management. The diffusion of stock ownership and the concurrent relinquishment of control by stockholders have caused major corporate executives who constitute the top-management group to recognize a broader responsibility commensurate with the power and influence of the large corporation in the community.

The responsibility of corporate management extends not only to stockholders and governmental agencies but also to creditors, employees, potential investors, and the general public. Adequate informative disclosure of financial position, operating results, and changes in financial position has long been accepted as obligatory for corporations whose securities are offered for public sale; but in recent years, a policy of voluntary public reporting of such phases of operations as pension plans, profit-sharing agreements, wage scales, price policies, and scientific research has been adopted by many large corporations as an inevitable consequence of their expanding responsibilities to the public.

To discharge this responsibility for prompt reporting of corporate activities, top management must have reliable, informative reports depicting the operations of all segments of the enterprise. The system of internal control gives assurance to management that the data underlying corporate reports are accurate and authentic.

MEANS OF ACHIEVING INTERNAL CONTROL

Since every enterprise operates under conditions peculiar to its field of production, size, and location, no standard system of internal control can be prefabricated to fit the needs of all concerns; but certain factors can be stipulated as essential to satisfactory internal control in most large-scale organizations. These are:

1. A logical plan of organization, which establishes clear lines of authority and responsibility and segregates the operating, recording, and custodial functions.
2. An adequate accounting structure, including budgetary and cost accounting techniques, a chart and text of accounts, procedural manuals, and charts depicting the flow of transactions.
3. An internal auditing staff reporting to a member of the top-management group and charged with the responsibility of continuous survey, evaluation, and improvement of internal controls.
4. Personnel with the ability and experience required to perform satisfactorily the responsibilities assigned to them.

The organization plan

One of the maxims of internal control is that no one person should handle all phases of a transaction from beginning to end. When this principle is applied at the top-management level and on a companywide basis, it indicates the necessity of establishing separate and independent departments for such functions as purchasing, receiving, manufacturing, selling, accounting, and finance. The head of each department is responsible for efficient performance within his respective phase of the enterprise. His authority should be clearly defined in written statements of company policy and in organizational charts and should be commensurate with the responsibility assigned.

Organization of operations in a manner requiring two or more persons or departments to participate in each transaction causes the work of one employee to serve as a proof of the accuracy of the work of another. Internal control contemplates a segregation of responsibilities and division of labor that not only will add to the efficiency of operations but will produce a warning signal when an error, whether accidental or intentional, is introduced into the accounting process. The prevention and prompt detection of errors is essential if management is to be provided with reliable current information as a basis for intelligent direction of the enterprise. However, a satisfactory system of internal control must encompass more than the assurance of reliability in recording and reporting; it must also provide a means of informing supervisors and employees as to company policy and procedures and of disclosing to appropriate levels of management the extent of compliance with these directives.

ILLUSTRATIVE CASE. A manufacturer of golf clubs operated a large storeroom containing thousands of sets of golf clubs ready for shipment. Detailed perpetual inventory records were maintained by the employee in charge of the storeroom. A shortage of several sets of clubs developed as a result of theft by another employee who had acquired an unauthorized key to the storeroom. The employee responsible for the storeroom discovered the discrepancy between the clubs in stock and the quantities of clubs as shown by the records. Fearing criticism of his record keeping, he changed the inventory records to agree with the quantities on hand. The thefts continued, and large losses were sustained before the shortages were discovered. If the inventory records had been maintained by someone not responsible for physical custody of the merchandise, there would have been no incentive or opportunity to conceal a shortage by falsifying the records. The internal control principle involved is a simple and obvious one; separate the function of record keeping from that of custody of assets.

Organizational independence of departments. The participation by various independent departments in a purchase transaction is an example of the manner in which one department acts as a check upon the efficiency of another. If the purchasing department fails to place a purchase order promptly upon receipt of a purchase requisition from the material stores department, the latter department may find itself without materials required by production departments and subject to censure for inefficient storekeeping. The material stores department, therefore, has an incentive to follow up purchase requisitions and to demand prompt action by the purchasing agent. If through error the purchasing department ordered an excessive or insufficient quantity, the responsibility for the error could be definitely pinned down by reference to the purchase requisition, the purchase order, and the receiving report, each of which is prepared by an independent department. If errors are made by the receiving department in counting goods received, the discrepancy will normally be brought to light by the accounting department when it compares the receiving report with the vendor's invoice and the purchase order. If defective materials are accepted by the receiving department, responsibility for this oversight will be placed on the negligent department by personnel of the storekeeping or production departments, which must utilize the materials in question.

If it is assumed, on the other hand, that the various functional activities are not segregated by independent departments and that all aspects of a purchase transaction are handled by employees reporting to the purchasing agent, then top management has no convenient means of informing itself as to the efficiency of the purchasing activities. Duplication of orders, delays in shipment, acceptance of defective goods, and secret rebates ("kickbacks") to buyers could all be covered up. The possibilities of fraud would be greatly increased if a single department head were given the authority to place an order, receive the goods, approve the invoice for payment, and record the transaction. When these functions are assigned to independent departments, fraud becomes difficult, if not impossible, without the collusion of large numbers of key personnel.

ILLUSTRATIVE CASE. During an examination of the Foster Company, the auditor's study of organizational lines of authority and his use of an internal control questionnaire disclosed that receiving department personnel were under the direction of the purchasing agent. Accounts payable department employees had also been instructed to accept informal memoranda from the purchasing agent as evidence of the receipt of merchandise and propriety of invoices.

Because of this deficiency in internal control, the auditor made a very thorough examination of purchase invoices and came across a number of large December invoices from one supplier bearing the notation: "Subject to adjustment at time of delivery of merchandise." Investigation of these transactions disclosed that the merchandise had not yet been delivered, but the invoices had been paid. The purchasing agent explained that he had requested an advance billing in an effort to reduce taxable income for the year under audit, during which profits had been higher than usual. Further investigation revealed that the purchasing agent held a substantial personal interest in the supplier making the advance billings and that his actions had not been authorized by the management of the client company.

Internal control over branch offices. Companies operating branch offices in which the branch managers are not subject to direct supervision must give particular attention to the maintenance of strong internal control. One protective device is to establish a "one-way" bank account into which each day's cash receipts are deposited intact by the branch manager. However, the branch manager is not authorized to write checks on this account; only the home office can make withdrawals, and the bank is instructed that bank statements and paid checks are to be sent directly to the home office. The home office makes frequent transfers from this bank account into its general account so that the balance of the branch account is kept quite low.

Even better control over branch receipts is achieved by the "lockbox" system in which customers of the branch mail remittances to a post office box controlled by the bank. The bank records and processes the remittances, and reports collections periodically to the home office.

A separate bank account operated on an imprest basis may be maintained by the branch for its disbursements. As this account becomes depleted, the branch manager sends a list of the disbursements to the home office with a request for replenishment. The home office, and not the branch manager, is authorized to make deposits in this account. The bank statements and paid checks are sent to the home office for reconciliation. A variation of this procedure for controlling disbursements by the branch manager requires him to prepare each check in duplicate, with the carbon copy going immediately to the home office. The checks are serially numbered, and all numbers in the series are accounted for by the home office.

This complete separation of cash receipts and disbursements at the branch, coupled with the prompt deposit of receipts, daily reporting of transactions, and use of an imprest fund for disbursements, leaves little opportunity for fraudulent handling of cash or for accidental errors. It also tends to conserve working capital by holding to a minimum the amount of idle cash held at branch locations. Other internal control practices relating to branch operation include daily reporting of key operating figures, continuous compilation of ratios and percentages which will indicate any variation from budgeted performance, and surprise counts of branch inventories by home office personnel.

The accounting structure

If the accounting system is to produce strong internal control, it should include:

1. A chart of accounts classified in accordance with the responsibilities of individual supervisors and key employees.
2. A manual of accounting policies and procedures.
3. A budget or master operating plan consisting of a detailed forecast of operations with provision for prompt reporting and analysis of variations between actual performance and budgetary standards.
4. A manufacturing cost accounting system, if appropriate to the industry.
5. Well-designed documents and forms controlled by serial numbering.

Chart of accounts. A chart of accounts is a classified listing of all accounts to be used, accompanied by a detailed description of the purpose and content of each. Some concerns use both a chart of accounts and a text of accounts, the former being limited to a classification of ledger accounts and the latter consisting of explanatory material describing the transactions properly to be charged and credited to each account.

How many accounts are needed? The number will depend upon the extent to which a company uses the accounts as a means of holding individuals responsible for custody of assets, for earning revenue, and for incurring expenses. In too many cases the classification of accounts is looked upon as a mere listing of the items to be separately enumerated in the financial statements. A better approach is to view the chart of accounts as an internal control device consisting of separate accounts for recording the responsibilities of individual supervisors and employees.

For example, a petty cash fund should be in the custody of a single employee; a separate account for such fund is required if the accounts are to measure individual responsibility. The principle of relating accounts and personal responsibility is by no means limited to the custody of assets; it is equally applicable to revenue and expense control. For every executive charged with the obtaining of revenue or the incurring of expenses, separate revenue and expense accounts should be established to permit a clear measurement of his performance. Just as a machine operator may be held responsible for units of output, so should the department manager be held to account for the performance of the function entrusted to him. The development of an accounting plan on this basis is rendered difficult by any vagueness or inconsistency in the plan of organization and lines of responsibility. It is commonly found that for a given type of expense, such as repairs, several individuals have authority to make commitments; hence no one individual can be held responsible for excessive expenditures in this direction. Careful analysis of the chart of accounts, by applying the test of clear segregation of individual responsibilities, will often indicate a need of revision in lines of organizational responsibility. Even under the best of organization plans, certain expenses will probably not be clearly assignable to a single responsible individual. Obsolescence of plant and equipment, cost of performing work under product guarantees, and expenses associated with strikes or other industrial disputes are examples of such expenses. These expenses often result from policy decisions rather than from departmental operations and therefore should be segregated and clearly labeled.

Although classification of accounts along lines of individual responsibility is an essential step in achieving control of costs, it does not serve the purpose of providing management with cost figures for individual products. The techniques of cost accounting must be utilized for a reclassification, or distribution, of costs from the primary classification to a product basis.

Manual of accounting policies and procedures. Every business concern, large or small, has a body of established methods of initiating, recording, and summarizing transactions. These procedures should be stated in writing, perhaps in a loose-leaf manual, and should be revised as the pattern of operating routines changes. If accounting procedures are clearly stated in writing, the policies set by management can be enforced efficiently and consistently. Uniform handling of like transactions is essential to the production of reliable accounting records and reports, and uniformity in the handling of transactions is possible only when definite patterns for processing routine transactions are made known to all employees.

Budgetary control.   A budget is an operating and financial plan for a future period. It establishes definite goals, and thus provides management with a yardstick for evaluating actual performance. Budgeting is often associated with standard cost systems because both involve the setting of predetermined standards and continuing analysis of variations between these standards and actual operating figures. Although most concerns which employ standard costs also have well-developed financial and operating budgets, the use of budgets is by no means limited to businesses which utilize standard costs. On the contrary, nearly all concerns make use of budgets to some extent.

The simplest and most common application of budgeting is the cash budget in which the treasurer forecasts, for perhaps a year in advance, the flow of cash receipts and disbursements classified by source of receipt and object of disbursement. The principal aim of the cash budget, or "financial budget," as it is often called, is to insure that sufficient funds are available at all times to meet maturing liabilities. In addition, the scheduling of anticipated receipts from all sources makes fraud involving the withholding of receipts more susceptible of detection. Similarly, the detailed planning of cash disbursements discourages the potential embezzler from any attempt to falsify the records of cash disbursements.

A more comprehensive budget program would include:

1.   A sales budget, consisting of estimated sales by product and by territory, based on analysis of past sales performance, current trends of prices and business volume, and appraisal of new products, territories, and distribution methods.
2.   A production budget, specifying the quantities necessary to meet the sales budget, and detailing the quantity and cost of material, labor, and indirect expense for given levels of output.
3.   A distribution cost budget, consisting of estimates of costs of selling, advertising, delivery, credit and collection, and other expenses appropriate to the estimated sales volume, classified 'by product or territory, and as variable, semivariable, and fixed.
4.   A plant and equipment budget, consisting of estimates of amounts required for the acquisition of new equipment and the maintenance of presently-owned equipment.
5.   A financial budget, including an estimate of cash receipts and disbursements and of borrowing and repayments, and culminating in an estimated income statement and balance sheet.

The completed budget is summarized by preparing an estimated income statement for the coming year, supported by detailed analyses for territories, divisions, or branches. During the year, monthly income statements should be prepared comparing actual operating results with budgeted figures. These statements should be accompanied by explanations of all significant variations between budgeted and actual results with a definite fixing of responsibility for such variances.

In brief, a budget is a control device, involving the establishment of definite standards of performance throughout the business. Failure to attain these standards is promptly called to the attention of appropriate levels of management through variance reports.

Internal control through accounting techniques is most fully attained when a comprehensive budget program is combined with a classification of accounts that provides a separate account to record the commitments made by each individual responsible for initiating transactions.

Cost accounting system. Cost accounting systems have at least two separate basic objectives:

1. To provide information for management decision making, planning, and control over operations.
2. To develop historical data for determination of the inventory and cost of sales figures used in the balance sheet and income statement.

The information function of cost accounting provides reports to top management which will facilitate decisions on pricing of products, plant expansion, wage rates, and related issues. Reporting by the cost accountant also embraces reports to factory management on the details of operating performance, which should enable product supervisors to spot waste and inefficiency in the operations they direct. Cost data are most valuable for factory executives when classified by operation, stressing individual responsibilities. For the use of sales executives and general management, reclassification of costs to a product basis is necessary.

Much remains to be accomplished in the establishment of cost standards for selling and office work. Progress toward more effective control in these areas appears to lie in the extension of budgetary techniques, the development of more effective denominators for measuring output, and a sharper distinction between fixed and variable items of expense.

Serial numbering of documents. An internal control device of wide applicability is the use of serial numbers on documents. Checks, tickets, sales invoices, purchase orders, stock certificates, and many other business papers can be controlled in this manner. For some documents, such as checks, it may be desirable to account for every number of the series by a monthly or weekly inspection of the documents issued. For other situations, as in the case of serially numbered admission tickets, control may be achieved by noting the last serial number issued each day, and thereby computing the total value of tickets issued during the day.

Internal auditing—its relationship to internal control

Virtually every large corporation in the United States today maintains an internal auditing staff. The development of this staff function has been very rapid; prior to 1940 internal auditing departments were found in relatively few companies. The Institute of Internal Auditors was founded in 1941, with 24 members. Now the Institute is a worldwide organization with chapters in principal cities throughout much of the world. The growth of the Institute has paralleled the increase in acceptance of internal auditing as an essential control function in large corporations, governmental agencies, and large nonprofit organizations.

What is internal auditing?   The job of the internal auditor is to investigate and appraise the system of internal control and the efficiency with which the various units of the organization are carrying out their assigned functions. Internal auditing is associated principally with large organizations. In a small concern, the owner or manager can give personal attention to each phase of operations and thus become aware of any failure to protect assets or any wastefulness in operating routines. In a large corporation, however, top management usually creates a large number of departments, divisions, or other organizational units, and assigns a manager to each unit. The manager of each unit is guided by policies established by top management, but he enjoys a considerable amount of freedom within the limits of these policy directives. This decentralization of authority to a great number of organizational units sets the stage for the internal auditor. It is his assignment to visit and appraise the problems and performance of every department in the company. As a representative of top management, the internal auditor is interested in determining whether each branch or department has a clear understanding of its assignment, whether it is adequately staffed, maintains good records, protects cash, inventories, and other assets properly, cooperates harmoniously with other departments, and in general carries out effectively the function provided for in the overall plan and organization of the business.

Internal auditor contrasted with independent auditor.   The independent auditor's objective is the expression of an opinion on the client's financial statements; the internal auditor's objective is not to verify financial statements but to aid management in achieving the most efficient administration of the business. To this end he appraises the effectiveness of internal controls in various departments, branches, or other organizational units of the company. The internal auditor's work is not limited to accounting controls; he also monitors administrative controls.

The similarities between independent audits and internal auditing pertain to mechanics and techniques, not to objectives and end results. Both the internal auditor and the independent auditor examine accounting records and procedures and prepare working papers, but the reasons motivating the two lines of work and the end results obtained are entirely different.

For example, in the examination of accounts receivable, the independent auditor is primarily concerned with establishing that the receivables fairly reflect the amount likely to be collected. The internal auditor is concerned with studying the system of billing to see whether it provides for accumulation of all the information necessary and ensures that all the company's customers are properly billed for goods or services delivered. He is interested in seeing that the credit system is operated so that charges in excess of credit limits are not permitted, and in the collection system to see that working capital invested in receivables is realized in cash as quickly as possible. He is also interested in the effect of credit policies—do they provide adequate safeguards without being too restrictive?

A role of the internal auditor in some growth-through-acquisition companies which resembles that of the independent auditor is the acquisition investigation. In an acquisition audit, the internal auditor gathers evidence to substantiate or disprove the merger prospect's representations as to receivables collectibility, inventory valuation, contingent liabilities, sales volume, earnings trends, and other financial-statement oriented measures.

The internal auditor faces a most challenging assignment if he is to provide management with the information it needs for the most effective control of operations. The internal auditor in no way displaces or serves as a substitute for the services of the independent auditor; nor can the latter possibly perform the function of the internal auditor without abandoning the objectives which characterize the public accounting profession.

Internal audit reports.   When the internal auditor has completed the audit of an organizational unit, he drafts a report to the audit committee of the company's board of directors, or to the member of top management in direct charge of internal audits. The draft report is discussed with managers and employees of the unit involved so that they will be aware of the deficiencies reported by the internal auditor and can take corrective action. After submitting his final report, the internal auditor may later reinvestigate the affected unit to determine the nature and efficacy of corrective actions undertaken by the unit's management and employees.

Independence of the internal auditor.   Since the internal auditor is an employee of the company he serves, he obviously cannot achieve the CPA's independence in fact and in appearance. However, if the internal auditor reports direct to the audit committee of the board of directors, to the president, or other senior officer, he may achieve a greater degree of freedom and independence than if he reports to an official of lesser rank in the organization.

Limitations of internal control in preventing defalcations

Strong internal controls are a powerful deterrent to fraud but do not make fraud impossible. Even though a company has a good system of internal control and is audited each year by independent public accountants, defalcations may still occur. The extent of the internal controls adopted by a business is limited by cost considerations; to maintain a system of internal control so perfect as to make fraud "impossible" would usually cost more than was warranted by the threat of loss from fraud. Particularly in a small business, it is often impracticable to separate completely the custody of assets from the function of record keeping. When a business has only a few employees, the opportunities for subdivision of duties are obviously somewhat limited. Despite these limitations, however, many actual defalcations could have been prevented or disclosed at an early stage if even the most simple and inexpensive of internal control practices had been followed.

Fidelity bonds

The preceding discussion of the limitations of internal control as a means of preventing and disclosing fraud should make clear that strong internal control is not a guarantee against losses from dishonest employees. Neither is it possible to prevent fraud by emphasizing the selection of trustworthy employees. It is often the most trusted employee who engineers the biggest embezzlement. The fact that he is so highly trusted explains why he has access to cash, securities, and company records and is in a position which makes embezzlement possible. In short, embezzlers are usually the most trusted of employees.

To protect a business adequately from losses through embezzlement requires three things: (1) a strong system of internal control, (2) regular audits by independent public accountants, and (3) fidelity bonds guaranteeing the company up to an agreed amount against loss from employee dishonesty. Individual fidelity bonds may be obtained by concerns with only a few employees; larger concerns may prefer to obtain a blanket fidelity bond covering all employees. Before issuing fidelity bonds, underwriters investigate thoroughly the past records of the employees to be bonded. This service offers added protection by preventing the employment of persons with dubious records in positions of trust. Bonding companies are much more likely to prosecute fraud cases vigorously than are employers; general awareness of this fact is another deterrent against dishonesty of the part of bonded employees.

Fidelity bonds are not a substitute for internal control. If internal control is weak, losses may accumulate undiscovered until they exceed the fidelity coverage. Moreover, inadequate internal control often causes other losses, as when management places reliance on inaccurate and misleading accounting data. In connection with his evaluation of internal control, the auditor should give consideration to the fidelity bonds in force and may appropriately call the client's attention to any apparent inadequacies in fidelity insurance coverage.

THE AUDITOR'S REVIEW OF INTERNAL CONTROL

The generally accepted auditing standards set forth by the AICPA were presented in Chapter 1. One of these standards reads as follows: "There is to be a proper study and evaluation of the existing internal control as a basis for reliance thereon and for the determination of the resultant extent of the tests to which auditing procedures are to be restricted." In formulating this standard, the AICPA recognized that it is not possible for the auditor to verify all, or even a major portion, of the great number of transactions comprising a year's operations in a large enterprise. In order that the auditor make the most effective and searching investigation possible within reasonable time limits, he must determine whether the internal control in force is such as to insure the integrity of the financial statements. The decisions based on an analysis of internal control will govern the extent of test checking and will designate those areas which require most intensive examination.

Reliance by the auditor upon internal control

If the system of internal control appears to be adequate, the auditor's approach to the task of verifying the items in the financial statements is that of sampling and testing. This technique, which dominates modern auditing, is based on the assumption that the examination of a portion of the accounting entries or related data will reveal the same characteristics as would examination of all the items. Each category of transactions or accounts may be thought of as constituting a separate universe, from which a representative number of items is to be examined. Thus the auditor will examine a representative sample of cash receipts, of accounts receivable, of purchase and sale transactions, of journal entries, and of numerous other phases of the accounting records and procedures. The number and nature of errors discovered in these samples will indicate the effectiveness with which the internal control is functioning and will also determine whether more extensive investigation is warranted.

Since an adequate system of internal control is a major factor in the audit conducted by an independent public accountant, the question arises as to what action he should take when internal control is found to be seriously deficient. Can an auditor complete a satisfactory audit and properly express an opinion on the fairness of financial statements of a company which has little or no internal control over its transactions? Although in theory the auditor might compensate for the lack of internal control by making a detailed verification of all entries in the accounts and of all transactions, this approach would generally be beyond the realm of practicability unless the business were quite small. In the audit of a very small business with serious deficiencies in internal control, the auditor may rely upon detailed examination of accounting entries, business papers, and other supporting data. Such an auditing approach is relatively costly. In a large business the existence of adequate internal control over at least a considerable portion of the company's activities seems to be a prerequisite if the auditor is to establish that the company's statements reflect fairly its financial position and operating results.

Scope of the auditor's review of internal control

The auditor's review of internal control is in two phases—the *study* and the *evaluation.* In the study phase, the auditor gathers evidence as to the nature of the internal control system and the manner in which it is functioning. In his evaluation, the auditor critically appraises the weaknesses and strengths of the system. He then expands his audit program to compensate for internal control weaknesses. In areas where internal control is very strong, the auditor will limit auditing procedures to the minimum necessary in the circumstances.

Nature of the internal control system

How does the auditor gather evidence as to the nature of the system of internal control? The traditional approach to this phase of the audit is the filling in of a standardized internal control questionnaire. Many public accounting firms have developed their own questionnaires for this purpose. These usually consist of several separate sections devoted to topics such as petty cash, cash receipts, cash disbursements, notes receivable, etc. The questionnaire may thus conveniently be divided, completed in sections by different auditors, and later reassembled for review by the auditor in charge. Space is usually provided for explanatory comments for those questions which cannot be answered adequately without discussion.

Extensive experience with internal control questionnaires has led to the establishment of the following standards for an effective form of questionnaire:

1. Provision for indicating the source of information used in answering each question and the verification made, if any.
2. Provision for distinguishing between major and minor deficiencies in internal control.
3. Provision for a sufficiently detailed description of deficiencies in internal control to permit the writing of a report to the client regarding the weakness.

Most internal control questionnaires are designed so that a "no" answer to a question indicates a weakness in the system of internal control.

Written description of internal control

Some accountants have become so impressed with abuses associated with the questionnaire approach to internal control that they have curtailed or abandoned the use of this device. These abuses include:

1. Copying answers from the preceding year's questionnaire.
2. Mechanical filling in of "yes" and "no" answers without any real understanding or study of the problem.
3. Treating the questionnaire as an end instead of a means.

Some accounting firms which no longer use internal control questionnaires prepare, instead, a written description of the flow of transactions, records maintained, and division of responsibilities. For example, with respect to cash receipts, the auditor may investigate and describe such points as the following:

1. Opening and disposition of mail.
2. Preparation of independent record of cash and checks received for comparison with collections recorded by cashier.
3. Maintenance of cash receipts records and other duties assigned to person responsible for these records.
4. Prompt entry and deposit intact of cash receipts.
5. Use of prenumbered receipts for over-the-counter collections, with proper accounting for duplicate copies.
6. Control over C.O.D. sales, scrap sales, equipment sales, interest, dividends, and miscellaneous receipts.
7. Collections made by salesmen or others from customers.
8. Access by cashier to general or subsidiary ledgers.

The written description of these matters will usually include identification of the employee performing the function and may indicate in some detail the manner of performing the task. After preparing this written description of internal control procedures, the auditor may wish to summarize his appraisal by classifying each major section of the internal control system as "strong," "adequate," or "weak." A weak system of internal control usually exists when there is insufficient subdivision of duties—as, for example, when one employee is assigned all the functions of cashier, timekeeper, and bookkeeper. An adequate or strong system of internal control usually requires assignment to separate departments or employees of such functions as cash handling, accounts receivable bookkeeping, general accounting, accounts payable, and payroll.

Flowcharts of the internal control system

Another device for determining the nature of the internal control system is a *systems flowchart.* A flowchart is a symbolic representation of a system or a series of sequential processes. Preparation of a flowchart enables the auditor to quickly appraise the effectiveness of internal controls and avoids the detailed study of written descriptions of procedures or of lengthy questionnaires.

Figure 5–1 illustrates the standard systems flowcharting symbols adopted by the American National Standards Institute, Inc. A number of the specialized symbols presented in Figure 5–1 apply to electronic data processing systems, which will be discussed in Chapter 6.

Some basic concepts of systems flowcharting are:

1. The six basic symbols are adequate for preparing a complete systems flowchart, but the *document, off-line storage,* and *manual operation* symbols are also recommended for flowcharting a manual-type internal control system.
2. Every systems flowchart must begin with an input symbol and end with an output symbol. One or more processing symbols must intervene between an input symbol and an output symbol.
3. Arrowheads are not required to indicate the normal flow for a systems flowchart, which is top to bottom and left to right. Arrowheads must be used for bottom to top and right to left flows.
4. "Striping" may be used at the top of a processing symbol to indicate which department or employee performs the process.
5. The annotation symbol is used to amplify or elaborate upon any input/output or processing symbol.
6. The basic input/output symbol is used for accounting records such as journals and ledgers; the basic processing symbol is used for computer processing of data.

These concepts of systems flowcharting are illustrated in Figure 5–4.

Illustration of written description, questionnaire, and flowchart

The three methods of describing the system of internal control for cash receipts of a small company operating at only one location are

FIGURE 5–1
Standard systems flowcharting symbols adopted by American Standards
Institute, Inc.

BASIC SYMBOLS

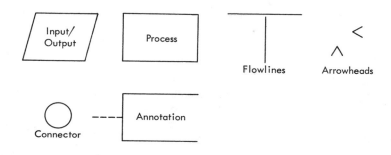

SPECIALIZED SYMBOLS

Specialized Input/Output Symbols

Specialized Processing Symbols

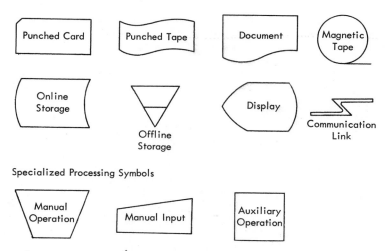

illustrated at Figures 5–2 (written description), 5–3 (questionnaire), and
5–4 (flowchart).

A review of the three illustrations brings to light the advantages
and disadvantages of each method for gathering evidence as to the
nature of the client's internal control system. The written description
is readily adaptable to unique internal control systems not covered by
standardized questionnaires. However, written descriptions are generally
practical for only small companies. The questionnaire has the advantage

FIGURE 5–2

Bennington Co, Inc.

Cash Receipts Procedures

December 31, 1974

Lorraine Martin is cashier, cash receipts journal, bookkeeper, and petty cash custodian. She picks up all mail at Bennington's post office box each workday morning. All cash receipts are received by mail in the form of current-dated checks, and are for trade accounts receivable remittances only. No securities or notes receivable are ever handled by Bennington Co, Inc.

Miss Martin gives the mail to Helen Ellis, the head bookkeeper, who opens all mail and distributes it as required. Customers' checks are given to Miss Martin at the adjacent desk, who immediately prepares bank deposit slips in duplicate and enters the remittances in the cash receipts journal. Miss Martin mails each day's deposit intact daily direct to First National Bank. The bank returns the validated duplicate deposit slips by mail, and Mrs. Ellis files them in chronological sequence. Mrs. Ellis posts the accounts receivable subsidiary ledger from the cash receipts journal. No other Bennington employee ever reviews or controls the bank deposits prepared by Miss Martin.

Any Bennington customer checks charged back by First National Bank are given by Mrs. Ellis to William Dale, controller, who follows up and redeposits the checks when appropriate. Mr. Dale also makes periodic reviews of the cash receipts journal for the propriety of sales discounts taken by customers.

Mrs. Ellis forwards monthly First National Bank statements and paid checks received in the mail to Mr. Dale. As part of his monthly bank reconciliation procedures, Mr. Dale compares dates and amounts of deposits recorded in the bank statement with the dates and amounts of entries in the cash receipts journal.

Miss Martin, Mrs. Ellis, and Mr. Dale are all bonded.

V.M.H.
12/6/74

FIGURE 5–3

INTERNAL CONTROL QUESTIONNAIRE
CASH RECEIPTS

Client _Bennington Co., Inc._   Audit Date _December 31, 1974_

Names and Positions of Client Personnel Interviewed:
Miss L. Martin–cashier; Mrs. H. Ellis–head bookkeeper; Mr. W. Dale–controller

QUESTION	NOT APPL.	YES	NO	MAJOR	MINOR	REMARKS
1. Are all persons receiving or disbursing cash bonded?		✔				
2. Is all incoming mail opened by a responsible employee who does not have access to accounting records and is not connected with the cashier's office?			✔	✔		H. Ellis is head bookkeeper
3. Does the employee assigned to the opening of incoming mail prepare a list of all checks and money received?			✔		✔	See mitigating control in #13
4. a) Is a copy of the listing of mail receipts forwarded to the accounts receivable department for comparison with the credits to customers' accounts?	✔					
b) Is a copy of this list turned over to an employee other than the cashier for comparison with the cash receipts book?	✔					
5. Are receipts from cash sales and other over–the–counter collections recorded by sales registers, cash registers, and serially numbered receipts?	✔					
6. Are the daily totals of cash registers or other mechanical devices verified by an employee not having access to cash?	✔					
7. Are physical facilities and mechanical equipment for receiving and recording cash adequate and conducive to good control?		✔				
8. Is revenue from investments, rent, concessions, and similar sources scheduled in advance so that nonreceipt on due date would be promptly investigated?	✔					
9. Do procedures for sale of scrap materials provide for direct reporting to accounting department concurrently with transfer of receipts to cashier?	✔					
10. Are securities and other negotiable assets in the custody of someone other that the cashier?	✔					
11. Are collections by branch offices deposited daily in a bank account subject to withdrawal only by home–office executives?	✔					
12. Are each day's receipts deposited intact and without delay by an employee other than the accounts receivable bookkeeper?		✔				
13. Are duplicate deposit tickets signed by the bank teller and compared with the cash receipts record and mailroom list of receipts by an employee other than the cashier or accounts receivable bookkeeper?		✔				W. Dale Controller
14. Are the duplicate deposit tickets properly filed and available for inspection by auditors?		✔				Chronological sequence
15. Are N.S.F. checks or other items returned by the bank delivered directly to an employee other than the cashier and promptly investigated?		✔				W. Dale Controller
16. Is the physical arrangement of offices and accounting records designed to prevent employees who handle cash from having access to accounting records?			✔		✔	Small Company logon't permit this.

Prepared By _V. M. Harris_   Date _12-6-74_   Manager Review _____ Date _____

Senior Review _____ Date _____   Partner Review _____ Date _____

of guiding the preparer through the investigation required for an adequate description of the internal control system. However, the fact that nearly one half of the questions are not applicable to a client as small as Bennington Company, Inc. implies a major weakness of the questionnaire—its inflexibility. The flowchart, like the written description, can be readily tailored to a specific client system; but more expertise is

FIGURE 5–4

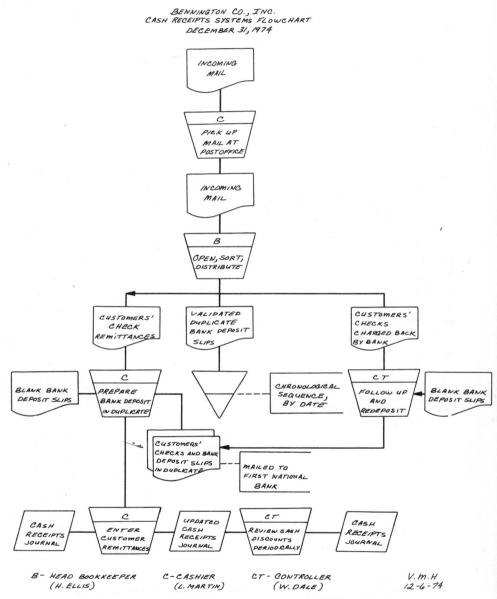

BENNINGTON CO., INC.
CASH RECEIPTS SYSTEMS FLOWCHART
DECEMBER 31, 1974

B– HEAD BOOKKEEPER   C–CASHIER   CT– CONTROLLER   V.m.H
   (H. ELLIS)   (L. MARTIN)   (W. DALE)   12-6-74

required to prepare a flowchart than to write a description or complete a questionnaire.

In the form of questionnaire illustrated in Figure 5–3 a "no" answer indicates a weakness, which is evaluated by the auditor as "major" or "minor," depending on his judgment as to the seriousness of the losses or misstatements which could conceivably result from this weakness. The "Remarks" column is used to explain the mitigating circumstances in the case of a "no" answer classified as a minor weakness. In the case of a "no" answer classified as a major weakness, the explanation should be sufficiently comprehensive to facilitate the writing of a report to the client regarding the weakness. The "Remarks" column is also used to identify employees performing the described functions.

Sources of information for description of internal control

Assistant auditors assigned the task of gathering evidence on a section of internal control are sometimes uncertain as to the appropriate method of obtaining information for the questionnaire, written description, or flowchart. The path of least resistance is to pose the questions to a well-informed officer or employee and accept his statements as to the internal control in use. If this approach is taken, verification of the answers supplied by the client's staff must be made as the audit progresses. Some auditors prefer to perform immediately the personal investigation and firsthand observation necessary to obtain dependable and conclusive answers to a questionnaire. To rely solely upon interrogation of the client's staff would be incompatible with the basic tenets of auditing.

The appropriate sources of information in studying the system of internal control include the following:

1. Organization charts, showing lines of authority and segregation of responsibilities. In large concerns, such charts are normally available not only for the organization as a whole but also for the detailed organization of individual departments, such as accounting, finance, sales, etc.
2. Chart and/or text of accounts showing the purpose and authorized usage and content of each account.
3. Methods and procedures manuals describing the approved practices to be followed in all phases of operations.
4. Job descriptions, detailing the scope of activities and responsibilities for specific occupational classifications, such as billing clerk, cashier, etc.
5. Interviews with officers and supervisors.
6. Discussions with operating personnel. The auditor must, of course, maintain an attitude of professional dignity and integrity. He should not encourage employees to criticize supervisors but may properly obtain valuable factual information concerning work being performed from operating personnel of all classifications.
7. Reports, working papers, and audit programs of the internal auditing staff. A critical review of the work done by internal audi-

tors is a major step in the study of internal control by the independent auditor.

8. Personal examination of accounting records, forms, documents, mechanical equipment, and all other media for recording transactions and processing operating and financial data.

9. Conducted tours throughout the offices and plant. The auditor needs to acquire through personal observation and contact a firsthand acquaintance with the physical facilities, the flow of operations, personnel, materials, and general organization of the enterprise. Such a tour is most valuable when conducted by an executive having an intimate knowledge of operations throughout the company.

10. Working papers, internal control reports, and audit reports from examinations made in prior years. When the auditor is engaged in repeat engagements, he of course utilizes all information concerning internal control contained in the audit working papers and permanent file. His investigation will then stress the areas shown as having questionable controls in prior years. It is imperative, however, that the auditor recognizes that the pattern of operations is an ever-changing one, that internal controls which were adequate last year may now be obsolete, and that the established use of a given control procedure is no assurance that it is currently being applied in an effective and intelligent manner.

Tests of transactions

The auditor must continually bear in mind in his study of internal control that the procedures described in accounting manuals or other management directives may not be in actual use. His evaluation of internal control must be based on firsthand observation whenever possible, rather than on statements by supervisors or employees. In many concerns it is customary to pay lip service to certain prescribed controls but to ignore them in the daily routine of operations.

ILLUSTRATIVE CASE. In his first examination of a radio and television manufacturing company, the auditor was informed by the controller that credit memoranda for merchandise returned by dealers were issued only after the returned merchandise had been inspected by receiving department personnel and an executive in the sales department had approved in writing the issuance of the credit.

The auditor wished to verify that this control procedure was being followed in practice. He therefore obtained a number of credit memoranda from the files. Several of these documents lacked any approval signature. Comparison of the dates on the credit memoranda with the dates on related receiving reports for the returned goods showed that the credits had been issued in some cases several weeks prior to the return of the goods, and that in other cases, merchandise for which credit had been granted had never been returned to the company. Discussions with various employees who prepared credit memoranda indicated disagreement as to the authorized procedures.

The auditor makes *tests of transactions* to determine whether the internal controls described in the questionnaire, the written description, or the flowchart are actually working as intended. In a test of transactions, the auditor traces specific transactions through the records from the point of initiation to that of completion. The tracing of a purchase transaction, for example, might begin with a request for purchase and be concluded with inspection of the article acquired and the check issued in payment. Or, the auditor might verify the propriety of a purchase transaction by examining the check issued to the vendor, then tracing the purchase back through the system to the originating requisition. For clearness of presentation in an auditing textbook, it seems preferable to describe in a single section all verification procedures pertaining to a particular balance sheet item, such as cash or accounts receivable; but the student of auditing should realize that the tests of cash or sales transactions must be made in conjunction with the study of internal control in advance of the balance sheet date.

Evaluation of internal control

After the auditor has carried out his study of internal control, he must evaluate the system. The study of internal control will have served to identify any weaknesses in the system. These weaknesses, as well as features of unusual strength, are summarized on a working paper which has space for listing additional auditing procedures to be performed in areas of weak controls and limitations on procedures in areas of unusually strong controls. The working paper may also contain a summary of recommendations to the client for strengthening weak points in the system.

A working paper used in evaluating internal control is illustrated in Figure 5–5. Notice that the extended auditing procedures and the limitations on procedures are thoroughly described in order to aid in the later preparation of a tailor-made audit program. Also note the conclusion of the auditor.

After completing his evaluation of internal control, the auditor should be prepared to draft the entire audit program for the engagement, as well as to write a report on internal control to the client.

Reports on internal control

When serious deficiencies in internal control are discovered, many accounting firms issue immediately a recommendation letter to the client containing suggestions for overcoming the weaknesses. This notification

FIGURE 5-5

Denver Manufacturing Company
Evaluation of Internal Control
December 31, 1974

Weakness in Internal Control	Extension of Auditing Procedures	Recommendation to Client
1. There is no established procedure for investigating and following up debit balances in accounts payable.	1. a. Obtain or prepare a listing of accounts payable debit balances at December 31, 1974. b. Mail confirmation requests to vendors having debit balances. c. Review credit standing of vendors having debit balances. d. Discuss with purchasing agent the prospects of additional purchases from debit balance vendors. e. Consider the need for an allowance for uncollectible debit balances.	1. The accounts payable departments should furnish a list of vendors with debit balances to the purchasing agent and the credit manager monthly. These individuals should follow up for procurement possibilities or collection of the debit balance.
2. The accounts receivable bookkeeper prepares and issues all credit memoranda for sales returns and allowances.	2. a. Inspect copies of all credit memos issued during the period. b. Review, with sales manager and controller, all credit memoranda issued during the period. c. Confirm accounts of all customers to whom credit memoranda were issued during the period.	2. The sales department should initiate all credit memoranda in excess of a stated minimum should be reviewed by the controller before being posted to the accounts receivable subsidiary ledger.

Unusual Strength in Internal Control	Limitation of Auditing Procedures	
1. The depository bank reconciles all of the clients bank accounts on the bank's data processing equipment.	1. Perform no independent bank reconciliations at December 31, 1974. Obtain and review the bank's reconciliations	

Conclusion:
Internal control of Denver Manufacturing Company is strong overall, and may be relied upon in completing the audit of Denver's financial statements.

V.M.H. 11/20/74

serves to minimize the liability of the auditor in the event that a major defalcation or other serious loss is later disclosed. If directed to the board of directors or to the audit committee of the board, the letter concerning internal control deficiencies creates a valuable contact not otherwise available and may also aid in building a better understanding and greater appreciation for the services rendered by the independent accountant. Since the appraisal of internal control is often made as part of the interim work preceding the audit date, the recommendation letter to management on major deficiencies in internal control may precede the formal audit report by several weeks.

In recent years, groups outside the client organization have become interested in independent auditors' internal control recommendations. Regulatory agencies may be interested in the letters because of their relevance to regulatory purposes or to the agencies' examination functions. For a client which retains different CPA firms to audit various subsidiaries or branches, each CPA firm will be interested in reports on internal control issued by the other auditors. In some cases, management or a regulatory agency may consider an independent auditor's recommendations useful to the general public.

Because of this increased interest in internal control recommendations, the AICPA's Committee on Auditing Porcedure issued *Statement on Auditing Procedure No. 49,* "Reports on Internal Control." One of the objectives of the *Statement* is to standardize the language of internal control reports issued by independent auditors to regulatory agencies or to the general public, so that the reports will not be misunderstood by the recipients. An illustration of such an internal control report follows.

Illustration of report on internal control

In studying the following internal control report, notice the detailed description of the objective and limitations of internal accounting control and the auditor's evaluation of it.

REPORT ON INTERNAL CONTROL

The Audit Committee
Board of Directors
Midwest Corporation
Chicago, Illinois

We have examined the financial statements of Midwest Corporation for the year ended December 31, 1974 and have issued our report thereon dated February 23, 1975. As a part of our examination, we reviewed and tested the Company's system of internal accounting control to the extent we considered necessary to evaluate the system as required by generally accepted auditing standards. Under these standards the purpose of such evaluation is to establish a basis for reliance thereon in determining the nature, timing, and extent of other auditing procedures that are necessary for expressing an opinion on the financial statements.

The objective of internal accounting control is to provide reasonable, but not absolute, assurance as to the safeguarding of assets against loss from unauthorized use or disposition, and the reliability of financial records for preparing financial statements and maintaining accountability for assets. The concept of reasonable assurance recognizes that the cost of a system of internal accounting control should not exceed the benefits derived and also recognizes that the evaluation of these factors necessarily requires estimates and judgments by management.

There are inherent limitations that should be recognized in considering the potential effectiveness of any system of internal accounting control. In the performance of most control procedures, errors can result from misunderstanding of instructions, mistakes of judgment, carelessness, or other personal factors. Control procedures whose effectiveness depends upon segregation of duties can be circumvented by collusion. Similarly, control procedures can be circumvented intentionally by management with respect either to the execution and recording of transactions or with respect to the estimates and judgments required in the preparation of financial statements. Further, projection of any evaluation of internal accounting control to future periods is subject to the risk that the procedures may become inadequate because of changes in conditions, and that the degree of compliance with the procedures may deteriorate.

Our study and evaluation of the Company's system of internal accounting control for the year ended December 31, 1974, which was made for the purpose set forth in the first paragraph above, was not designed for the purpose of expressing an opinion on internal accounting control and it would not necessarily disclose all weaknesses in the system. However, such study and evaluation disclosed the following conditions that we believe to be material weaknesses:

1. *The unit basis of depreciation and like rates for similar assets are not being used throughout the company.*

Because of your merger with Randall Company and Barnes Company in 1974, two different bases of depreciation have since been in effect in Midwest Corporation. The properties formerly owned by Randall Company are being depreciated on a unit basis, whereas the properties formerly owned by Barnes Company are being depreciated on composite rates. This difference in depreciation methods causes confusion when plant assets are transferred from one location to another and creates difficulties in computations which could be avoided. We recommend that consideration be given to changing to the unit basis of depreciation throughout the company and that like rates be used for similar assets. Since such a change would constitute a change of accounting method within the meaning of the Internal Revenue Code, application to the Commissioner of Internal Revenue within the first 90 days of the year in which the change is to be made is necessary. Before instituting this change, estimates should be developed of the effects on depreciation expense, net income, and income taxes.

2. *Serial number identification tags are not attached to each unit of plant equipment, and a detailed property ledger has not been established.*

The determination of original cost and accumulated depreciation applicable to plant assets being retired is becoming a greater problem yearly, as the length of time since purchase and the number of retirements increase. The difficulty is caused by equipment not being tagged to facilitate easy identification for either retirement accounting or physical inventory taking.

We suggest that a serial number identification tag be placed upon each item of equipment. At the same time, a record on punched cards should be started which will contain a description of the equipment, date of purchase, original cost, tag serial number, and department in which located.

3. *Annual vacations are not compulsory for financial and accounting personnel in positions of trust.*

Good internal accounting control requires that financial and accounting personnel in positions of trust take vacations annually, during which time their duties are handled by others. A compulsory vacations rule does not appear to exist at present, and certain key personnel have not been away from their duties except for brief intervals for several years.

4. *Doubtful accounts are being written off when turned over to a collection agency.*

The company's present policy is to write off doubtful accounts receivable at the time they are turned over to a collection agency. Further recoveries are made on many of these accounts, but since the amounts involved were previously written off, these recoveries are uncontrolled. We suggest a policy of transferring doubtful accounts to a suspense ledger at the time such accounts are sent to the collection agency. These accounts would be controlled through a separate general ledger account, and the company could keep track of an account a stipulated period of perhaps 90 days, or until the collection agency reported that no further recoveries were likely. Maintaining these accounts in a separate inactive ledger would not require any significant bookkeeping effort but would afford a measure of control over the recoveries which is presently lacking. If desired, a 100 percent valuation allowance could be carried against the suspense ledger so that the company's current assets would be valued on the same basis as at present.

❄   ❄   ❄   ❄   ❄

We have discussed these recommendations with affected personnel in the Company and have found general agreement on the desirability of studies and corrective action along the lines indicated. If the suggested studies are initiated, we shall, of course, be glad to lend any desired assistance.

Hill, Farnsworth & Co.
Certified Public Accountants
March 12, 1975

Electronic data processing—effect upon internal control

The generally accepted auditing standard which requires a study and evaluation of internal control applies to the audit of all companies, regardless of whether the record keeping is performed by an electronic computer or by manual methods.

In traditional manual accounting systems an important element of internal control consists of the division of duties among several persons in such a manner that the work of one employee verifies that of another and no one person handles a transaction in its entirety. When an electronic data processing system is installed, the work formerly done by numerous employees will be done by the machines. The employees operating the electronic machines do not have custody of assets nor do they handle transactions; their function is solely to process the data furnished by other departments.

Adequate internal control in this situation requires assurance that the employees operating the data processing machines do their work accurately and honestly. This assurance may be provided by creating a separate control group, whose function it is to verify the accuracy of the work of the data processing center. "Data processing center" is used to mean the electronic machines and the employees who operate them. The separate control group may carry out its verification function by maintaining memorandum records to accumulate key totals for comparison with totals produced by the machines.

For example, if payrolls are handled by the data processing center, the control group might compute independently such key figures as the total number of employees in selected departments and the total dollar amount of deductions authorized by these employees. These figures could be accumulated on adding machines for comparison with corresponding totals produced by the data processing center. If the volume of transactions is so great as to render the maintenance of such memoranda records burdensome, another approach is for the control group to make its tests by using the computer, at appropriate intervals, to process its own memoranda records. Internal control would not permit the control group to turn this task over to the employees of the data processing center, since the whole point is to prove the accuracy of the work of employees regularly operating the machines. Internal control over electronic data processing equipment is also strengthened by numerous controls built into the machines by the manufacturer and by other control devices included in the program by the user of the machines. These "automatic" controls guard against errors in computations, sequence of data, and various other types of errors.

Traditionally, accountants have felt that every accounting system, whether manual, mechanical, or electronic, should provide a trail of audit evidence. With the advent of more sophisticated electronic equipment, some relaxation of this view may be inevitable. This matter, together with the entire field of electronic data processing, is considered further in Chapter 6.

Internal control in the small company

The preceding discussion of the system of internal control and its evaluation by the auditor has been presented in terms of large corporations. In the large concern, excellent internal control may be achieved by extensive subdivision of duties, so that no one person handles a transaction completely from beginning to end. In the very small concern, however, with only one or two office employees, there is little or no opportunity for division of duties and responsibilities. Consequently internal control tends to be weak, if not completely absent, unless the owner-manager recognizes the importance of internal control and participates in key activities.

Because of the absence of adequate internal control in small concerns, the auditor must make a much more detailed examination of accounts, journal entries, and supporting documents than is required in larger organizations. Although it is well to recognize that internal control can never be adequate in a small business, this limitation is no justification for ignoring those forms of control which are available. There is seldom any excuse for failure to deposit cash receipts intact daily, but it is not uncommon to find this basic rule violated in small concerns. The violation is often defended on the grounds that internal control is not possible, anyway, so that cash receipts may as well be used for disbursements when convenient. The use of checks and invoices not controlled by serial numbers and the purchase of merchandise or materials without the issuance of formal purchase orders are other examples of negligence in operations sometimes encountered in small concerns. The auditor can make a valuable contribution to small business enterprises by encouraging the installation of such control procedures as are practicable in the circumstances. The following specific practices are almost always capable of use in even the smallest business:

1. Record all cash receipts immediately.
    a) For over-the-counter collections, utilize cash registers easily visible to customers. Record register readings daily.
    b) Prepare a list of all mail remittances immediately upon opening of the mail and retain this list for subsequent comparison with bank deposit tickets and entries in the cash receipts journal.
2. Deposit all cash receipts intact daily.
3. Make all payments by serially numbered checks, with the exception of small disbursements from petty cash.

4. Use an imprest petty cash fund entrusted to a single custodian for all payments other than by check.
5. Reconcile bank accounts monthly and retain copies of the reconciliations in the files.
6. Use serially numbered purchase orders for all purchase transactions.
7. Maintain a receiving record, preferably by means of serially numbered receiving reports.
8. Issue checks to vendors only in payment of approved invoices which have been matched with purchase orders and receiving reports.
9. Prepare serially numbered sales invoices for all shipments to customers.
10. Prepare and mail customers' statements monthly.
11. Balance subsidiary ledgers with control accounts at regular intervals.
12. Prepare comparative financial statements monthly in sufficient detail to disclose significant variations in any category of revenue or expense.
13. Retain a certified public accountant for an annual audit.

Conscientious enforcement of the practices listed above will significantly reduce the opportunity for substantial errors or major fraud to go undetected. If the size of the business permits a segregation of the duties of cash handling and record keeping, a fair degree of control can be achieved. If it is necessary that one employee serve as both bookkeeper and cashier, then active participation by the owner in certain key functions is necessary to guard against the concealment of fraud or errors. In a few minutes each day the owner, even though not trained in accounting, can create a significant amount of internal control by personally—

a) Reading cash registers daily and retaining possession of keys to registers.
b) Reconciling the bank account monthly.
c) Signing all checks and canceling the supporting documents.
d) Reviewing and canceling petty cash vouchers.
e) Approving all general journal entries.
f) Reviewing critically comparative monthly statements of revenue and expense.

GROUP I
REVIEW QUESTIONS

5–1. Normally the auditor does not rely upon his study and evaluation of the client's system of internal control to (select one):
    a) Evaluate the reliability of the system.

b)　Uncover embezzlements of the client's assets.

c)　Help determine the scope of other auditing procedures to be followed.

d)　Gain support for his opinion as to the accuracy and fairness of the financial statements. (AICPA, adapted)

5–2.　What is the purpose of the study and evaluation of internal control required by generally accepted auditing standards?

5–3.　Identify and describe the three basic methods utilized in the description of the internal control system.

5–4.　After completing the study of internal control, how does the auditor evaluate internal control?

5–5.　What dangers or abuses must be guarded against if a partner in a CPA firm instructs the auditing staff to rely largely upon the use of questionnaires as a basis for evaluation of internal control?

5–6.　The system of internal control for a particular business should be individually designed to meet the needs of that business, but a number of basic factors are usually considered as necessary to achieving satisfactory internal control in all large business organizations. List five of these common factors or characteristics necessary to a good system of internal control.

5–7.　"The principal distinction between independent audits and internal audits is that the latter activity is carried on by an organization's own salaried employees rather than by independent professional auditors." Criticize this quotation.

5–8.　Compare the objectives of the internal auditor with those of the independent auditor.

5–9.　Is a strong system of internal control of the same significance in both large and small companies? Is the adequacy of internal control likely to vary with the size of the organization?

5–10.　The owner of a medium-sized corporation asks you to state two or three principles to be followed in dividing responsibilities among employees in a manner that will produce strong internal control.

5–11.　What is meant by internal accounting controls as contrasted with internal administrative controls? Give examples of each and explain which category is of more importance to the CPA making an independent audit.

5–12.　Should an internal control questionnaire be used in the audit of all concerns, regardless of size? Explain.

5–13.　At what stage of an audit should the review of internal control be made? Why?

5–14.　Explain clearly the following:

a)　Study of internal control.

b)　Evaluation of internal control.

5–15.　A prospective client informs you that all officers and employees of his company are bonded, and he inquires whether under these circumstances you would forgo that part of the audit normally devoted to a review of the system of internal control. Construct a logical reply to this query. ~~,

5–16. Suggest a number of sources from which an auditor might obtain the information needed to fill in an internal control questionnaire.

5–17. During your first examination of a manufacturing company with approximately 100 production employees, you find that all aspects of factory payroll are handled by one employee and that none of the usual internal controls over payroll is observed. What action would you take?

5–18. In view of the reliance which the auditor places upon the system of internal control, how do you account for the fact that the standard short-form audit report makes no reference to internal control in describing the scope of the examination? *included in standard auditing procedures*

5–19. Name the three factors you consider of greatest importance in protecting a business against losses through embezzlement.

1) bonding
2) strong internal control
3) regular audit by CPA

GROUP II
QUESTIONS REQUIRING ANALYSIS

5–20. Adherence to generally accepted auditing standards requires, among other things, a proper study and evaluation of the existing internal control. The most common approaches to reviewing the system of internal control include the use of a questionnaire, preparation of a written description, preparation of a flowchart, and combinations of these methods.

Required:

a) What is a CPA's objective in reviewing internal control for an opinion audit?
b) Discuss the advantages to a CPA of reviewing internal control by using:
   (1) An internal control questionnaire.
   (2) The written description approach.
   (3) A flowchart.
c) If he is satisfied after completing his description of internal control for an opinion audit that no material weaknesses in the client's internal control system exist, is it necessary for the CPA to test transactions? Explain. (AICPA, adapted)

5–21. Internal auditing is a staff function found in virtually every large corporation. The internal audit function is also performed in many smaller companies as a part-time activity of individuals who may or may not be called internal auditors. The differences between the audits by independent auditors and the work of internal auditors are more basic than is generally recognized.

Required:

a) Briefly discuss the auditing work performed by the independent public accountant and the internal auditor with regard to—
   (1) Auditing objectives,
   (2) General nature of auditing work.

b) In conducting his audit, the independent auditor must evaluate the work of the internal auditor. Discuss briefly the reason for this evaluation.

c) List the auditing procedures used by an independent auditor in evaluating the work of the internal auditor. (AICPA, adapted)

5-22. During your first examination of a medium-sized manufacturing company, the owner explains that in order to establish clear-cut lines of responsibility for various aspects of the business, he has made one employee responsible for the purchasing, receiving, and storing of merchandise. A second employee has full responsibility for maintenance of accounts receivable records and collections from customers. A third employee is responsible for personnel records, timekeeping, preparation of payrolls, and distribution of payroll checks. The client asks your opinion concerning this plan of organization. Explain fully the reasons supporting your opinion.

5-23. At the Main Street Theatre the cashier, located in a box office at the entrance, receives cash from customers and operates a machine which ejects serially numbered tickets. To gain admission to the theater a customer hands the ticket to a doorman stationed some 50 feet from the box office at the entrance to the theater lobby. The doorman tears the ticket in half, opens the door for the customer, and returns the stub to him. The other half of the ticket is dropped by the doorman into a locked box.

Required:

a) What internal controls are present in this phase of handling cash receipts?

b) What steps should be taken regularly by the manager or other supervisor to give maximum effectiveness to these controls?

c) Assume that the cashier and the doorman decided to collaborate in an effort to abstract cash receipts. What action might they take?

d) Continuing the assumption made in (c) of collusion between the cashier and the doorman, what features of the control procedures would be likely to disclose the embezzlement?

5-24. The Carleton Company did not utilize the services of independent public accountants during the first several years of its existence. In the current year at the suggestion of its banker, the company decided to retain McTavish and Company, a CPA firm, to conduct an audit of its financial statements in order to qualify for a larger bank loan. The auditors found the system of internal control to be "extremely weak or nonexistent." Under these circumstances what kind of report, if any, could McTavish and Company issue? Explain fully. ⌐

5–25.   The Committee on Auditing Procedure of the AICPA has stated that an ordinary examination directed to the expression of an opinion on financial statements is not designed to disclose fraud, although discovery of defalcations or other fraud may sometimes result. How can this concept of an audit be reconciled with the standard practice which requires a CPA to expand the scope of his audit work when he finds weaknesses in internal control?

GROUP III
PROBLEMS

5–26.   You have been asked by the board of trustees of a local church to review its accounting procedures. As a part of this review you have prepared the following comments relating to the collections made at weekly services and record keeping for members' pledges and contributions:

(1)   The church's board of trustees has delegated responsibility for financial management and audit of the financial records to the finance committee. This group prepares the annual budget and approves major disbursements but is not involved in collections or recordkeeping. No audit has been considered necessary in recent years because the same trusted employee has kept church records and served as financial secretary for 15 years.

(2)   The collection at the weekly service is taken by a team of ushers. The head usher counts the collection in the church office following each service. He then places the collection and a notation of the amount counted in the church safe. Next morning the financial secretary opens the safe and recounts the collection. He withholds about $100 to meet cash expenditures during the coming week and deposits the remainder of the collection intact. In order to facilitate the deposit, members who contribute by check are asked to draw their checks to "cash."

(3)   At their request a few members are furnished prenumbered predated envelopes in which to insert their weekly contributions. The head usher removes the cash from the envelopes to be counted with the loose cash included in the collection and discards the envelopes. No record is maintained of issuance or return of the envelopes, and the envelope system is not encouraged.

(4)   Each member is asked to prepare a contribution pledge card annually. The pledge is regarded as a moral commitment by the member to contribute a stated weekly amount. Based upon the amounts shown on the pledge cards, the financial secretary furnishes a letter to requesting members to support the tax deductibility of their contributions.

Required:

Describe the weaknesses and recommend improvements in procedures for—

a)   Collections made at weekly services.

b)   Record keeping for members' pledges and contributions.

Organize your answer sheets as follows:

Weakness	Recommended improvement

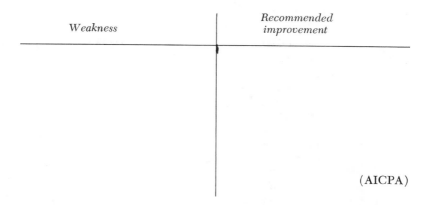

(AICPA)

5–27. The Richmond Company, a client of your firm, has come to you with the following problem: It has three clerical employees who must perform the following functions:

(1) Maintain general ledger.
(2) Maintain accounts payable ledger.
(3) Maintain accounts receivable ledger.
(4) Prepare checks for signature.
(5) Maintain disbursements journal.
(6) Issue credits on returns and allowances.
(7) Reconcile the bank account.
(8) Handle and deposit cash receipts.

Required:

   Assuming that there is no problem as to the ability of any of the employees, the company requests your advice on assigning the above functions to the three employees in such a manner as to achieve the highest degree of internal control. It may be assumed that these employees will perform no other accounting functions than the ones listed and that any accounting functions not listed will be performed by persons other than these three employees.

a)   State how you would recommend distributing the above functions among the three employees. Assume that, with the exception of the nominal jobs of the bank reconciliation and the issuance of credits on returns and allowances, all functions require an equal amount of time.

b)   List four possible unsatisfactory combinations of the above listed functions. (AICPA)

5–28. In early September the Downey Corporation retained you to make an examination of its financial statements for the current year ending December 31. Your appointment occurred shortly after the death of the CPA who had audited the company in prior years. Assume that you have completed your examination during the following February and have prepared a draft of your audit report containing an unqualified opinion on the financial statements. Your report, as required by your engagement letter, was addressed to the board of directors. You have also drafted a special report describing weaknesses in the system of internal control observed during your examination and setting forth your recommendations for the correction of these weaknesses.

During your review of the drafts of these reports with the president of Downey Corporation, he expressed his satisfaction with the unqualified report on the financial statements but indicated that the report on internal control was unnecessary. The president stated that he was aware of the weaknesses in internal control and that he would personally take steps to remedy them. Finally, the president instructed you not to render the internal control report. He explained that he felt the board of directors should deal with major policy decisions and not be burdened with day-to-day management problems.

Required:

a)   Enumerate at least five separate factors which should be considered before reaching a decision whether to render the internal control report.

b)   In the event that you decide to render the internal control report to Downey Corporation, would you render it to the board of directors or to the president? Explain fully. (AICPA, adapted)

5–29.   A description of some of the operating procedures of the Greystone Manufacturing Corporation is given in succeeding paragraphs. For each of the activities described, you are to point out (a) the deficiencies, if any, in internal control, including an explanation of the errors or manipulations which might occur; and (b) recommendations for changes in procedures which would correct the existing weakness.

(1)   When materials are ordered, a duplicate of the purchase order is sent to the receiving department. When the materials are received, the receiving clerk records the receipt on the copy of the order, which is then sent to the accounting department to support the entry to Accounts Payable and to Purchases. The materials are then taken to stores where the quantity is entered on bin records.

(2)   Timecards of employees are sent to a data processing department which prepares punched cards for use in the preparation of payrolls, payroll checks, and labor cost distribution records. The payroll checks are compared with the payrolls and signed by an official of the company who returns them to the supervisor of the data processing department for distribution to employees.

(3)   A sales branch of the company has an office force consisting of the manager and two assistants. The branch has a local bank account in which it deposits cash receipts. Checks drawn on this account require the manager's signature or the signature of the treasurer of the company. Bank statements and paid checks are returned by the bank to the manager, who retains them in his files after making the reconciliation. Reports of disbursements are prepared by the manager and submitted to the home office on scheduled dates. (AICPA, adapted)

5–30.   Taylor, Inc., your new audit client, processes its sales and cash receipts in the following manner:

1.   *Cash receipts.* The mail is opened each morning by a mail clerk in the sales department. The mail clerk prepares a remittance advice (showing customer and amount paid). The checks and remittance advices are then forwarded to the sales department supervisor, who reviews each check and forwards the checks and remittance advices to the accounting department supervisor.

The accounting department supervisor, who also functions as credit manager in approving new credit and all credit limits, reviews all checks for payments on past-due accounts and then forwards the checks and remittance advices to the accounts receivable clerk, who arranges the advices in alphabetical order. The remittance advices are posted directly to the accounts receivable ledger cards. The checks are endorsed by stamp and totaled. The total is posted to the cash receipts journal. The remittance advices are filed chronologically.

After receiving the cash from the previous day's cash sales, the accounts receivable clerk prepares the daily deposit slip in triplicate. The third copy of the deposit slip is filed by date, and the second copy and the original accompany the bank deposit.

2.   *Sales.* Salesclerks prepare sales invoices in triplicate. The original and second copy are presented to the cashier. The third copy is retained by the salesclerk in the sales book. When the sale is for cash, the customer pays the salesclerk, who presents the money to the cashier with the invoice copies.

A credit sale is approved by the cashier from an approved credit list after the salesclerk prepared the three-part invoice. After receiving the cash or approving the invoice, the cashier validates the original copy of the sales invoice and gives it to the customer. At the end of each day the cashier recaps the sales and cash received, files the recap by date, and forwards the cash and the second copy of all sales invoices to the accounts receivable clerk.

The accounts receivable clerk balances the cash received with cash sales invoices and prepares a daily sales summary. The credit sales invoices are posted to the accounts receivable ledger, and then all invoices are sent to the inventory control clerk in the sales department for posting to the inventory control cards. After posting, the inventory control clerk files all invoices numerically. The accounts receivable clerk posts the daily sales summary to the cash receipts journal and sales journal and files the sales summaries by date.

The cash from cash sales is combined with the cash received on account to comprise the daily bank deposit.

Required:

Prepare separate systems flowcharts for the cash receipts and sales procedures described above. (AICPA, adapted)

6

The audit of electronic data processing systems

THE RAPID growth of electronic data processing (EDP) for business use is having a greater impact upon public accounting than perhaps any other event in the history of this new profession. Although the computer has created some challenging problems for the professional accountant, it has also broadened his horizons and expanded the range and value of the services he offers. The computer is more than a new tool for performing familiar bookkeeping tasks with unprecedented speed and accuracy. It makes possible the development of information which could not have been gathered in the past because of time and cost limitations. When a client maintains his records with a complex and sophisticated EDP system, the auditor will find it helpful, and even necessary, to utilize the computer for performing many auditing procedures.[1]

This chapter will call attention to some of the most significant ways in which auditing work is being affected by EDP, but cannot impart extensive knowledge of technical computer skills. Many new terms and expressions will be introduced during the following discussions; for definitions, the reader should refer to the glossary in Appendix A at the end of the chapter. The auditor will find additional familiarity with

---

[1] Utilizing the computer in performing auditing procedures is often termed "auditing through the computer." This process differs from "auditing around the computer." This older approach called for the auditor to test computer output by manually processing a sample of the input transactions without making any use of the computer in the audit process.

the computer, including technical skills such as programming, to be of ever-increasing value in the accounting profession.

Nature of an electronic data processing system

Before considering the impact of electronic data processing systems on the work of the independent certified public accountant, some understanding of the nature of a computer and its capabilities is needed. A business EDP system usually consists of a digital computer and peripheral equipment known as *hardware;* and equally essential *software,* consisting of various programs and routines for operating the computer.

Hardware. The principal hardware component of a digital computer is the *central processing unit* (CPU). The CPU consists of a *control unit,* which processes a program of instructions for manipulating data; a *storage unit,* consisting of many tiny magnetic rings or cores, for storing the program of instructions and the data to be manipulated; and an *arthmetic unit* capable of addition, subtraction, multiplication, division, and comparison of data at speeds measured in *microseconds* or *nanoseconds.*

Peripheral to the central processing unit are devices for recording input and devices for auxiliary storage, output, and communications. Peripheral devices in direct communication with the CPU are said to be *on-line,* in contrast to *off-line* equipment not in direct communication with the CPU.

A first step in the functioning of an electronic data processing system is to convert the data to machine-sensible form. This is the role of recording and input devices such as card punches and readers, paper tape punches and readers, magnetic tape encoders, magnetic ink character readers, and optical scanners. Each of these devices either records data in some medium for later "reading into" the storage unit or communicates data direct to the CPU.

Auxiliary storage devices are utilized to augment the capacity of the storage unit of the CPU. Examples of auxiliary storage devices are magnetic tape, magnetic drums, and magnetic disk packs.

Computers use special codes called *machine language* to represent data being stored or processed within the computer. The purpose of a machine language is to permit all data to be expressed by combinations of only two symbols. Digital computer circuitry has two states in that any given circuit may be "on" or "off." By using an internal code capable of representing with two symbols any kind of data, the computer makes an "on" circuit represent one symbol and an "off" circuit represent the other. All data may then be expressed internally by the computer by a combination of "on" and "off" circuits. An example of a machine language is the *binary* number system.

The binary number system is similar to the more familiar decimal system. The decimal system is in the base 10. That is, any number can be stated as the sum of exponential powers of 10. Ones, the first digit to the left of the decimal point, are tens raised to the zero power (10^0). Tens, the second digit to the left of the decimal point, are tens raised to the first power (10^1). The number 25 really means 2 tens and 5 ones, and could be written in the decimal system as $(2 \times 10^1) + (5 \times 10^0)$.

Binary numbers are expressed in a similar manner, but working in base 2. All numbers are stated in terms of ones (2^0), twos (2^1), fours (2^2), eights (2^3), sixteens (2^4), etc. Only two digits are used in binary code: "1" and "0." These digits indicate whether or not specific exponential powers of 2 are included in a particular number.

For example, let us represent the number 25 in binary code. In terms of exponential powers of two, 25 is equal to $16 + 8 + 1$, or $2^4 + 2^3 + 2^0$. If an exponential power of two is included in a number, a "1" is placed in the position representing that exponential power. If an exponential power is not included (there is no 2 to the second power included in 25), a "0" is used to represent that power. Twenty-five, therefore, is considered to be $(1 \times 2^4) + (1 \times 2^3) + (0 \times 2^2) + (0 \times 2^1) + (1 \times 2^0)$. Since the declining exponential functions of 2 are understood in the binary system, binary code includes only the "1's" and "0's" indicating whether each function is to be included to arrive at the desired sum. The number 25 would be written in binary code as 11001.

Machines must also be used to translate the output of the computer back to a recognizable code or language. Output equipment includes card punches, paper tape punches, printers, cathode ray tubes, and console display panels.

Software. Manufacturers of computer hardware also provide software elements. Most important of the software components is the *program*—a series of instructions written in a language comprehensible to the computer. These instructions order the computer to process data. Early-day programs were laboriously written in machine language, but today, programming languages such as COBOL (common business-oriented language) are much like English. COBOL and similar languages are made possible by another software element called the *compiler*, which is a computer program utilized in *translating a programming language to machine binary codes.*

Another important software component is the prewritten utility program for recurring tasks of data processing such as sorting, sequencing, or merging data, language processing, and other routines closely related to the functioning of the computer. These prewritten utility programs are available from the computer manufacturer and do not generally pose any problem to the auditor, as they are not likely to be the source of errors in computer output. Furthermore, they are technically so complex as to make examination by the auditor impracticable in most cases.

This category of utility programs supplied by the computer manufacturer should be clearly distinguished from **user programs** developed by the client for his own accounting applications. The user programs developed by the client are a major source of errors in an EDP system. Consequently, the auditor must give close attention to the validity of user programs if he is to meet the auditing standard of obtaining sufficient competent evidence to provide a basis for his opinion on financial statements.

In concluding this brief discussion of the nature of an EDP system two points deserve emphasis. First, computer **hardware** is extremely reliable, but this machine precision does not assure that the computer output will be reliable. Secondly, the auditor has the same responsibility in auditing an EDP system as a manual system—which is to satisfy himself that the financial statements produced reflect the interpretation and processing of transactions in conformity with generally accepted accounting principles.

Internal control in the electronic data processing system

The discussion of internal control in Chapter 5 stressed the need for a proper division of duties among employees operating a manual or punched card accounting system. In such a system no one employee has the complete responsibility for a transaction, and the work of one person is verified by the work of another handling other aspects of the same transaction. This division of duties gives assurance of accuracy in records and reports, and protects the company against loss from fraud or carelessness.

When a company converts to an EDP system, however, the work formerly divided among many people is performed by the computer. Consolidation of activities and integration of functions are to be expected, since the computer can conveniently handle all related aspects of a transaction. For example, accounting for cash receipts may cease to be a separate accounting function but rather the final step of a related series of activities surrounding a sale. These activities consist of processing the customer's order, inventory control, accounts receivables, and cash receipts.

As another example, let us consider a payroll application. In the traditional manual accounting system, the principal step is getting out the paychecks. When payroll is handled by a computer, however, it is possible to carry out a variety of related tasks with only a single use of the master records. These tasks could include the maintenance of personnel files with information on seniority, rate of pay, insurance, etc.; a portion of the timekeeping function; distribution of labor costs; and preparation of payroll checks and payroll records.

Despite the integration of several functions in an EDP system, the importance of internal control is not in the least diminished. The essential factors described in Chapter 5 for satisfactory internal control in a large-scale organization are still relevant. Separation of duties and clearly defined responsibilities are still key ingredients despite the change in departmental boundaries, as will be explained in later sections of this chapter. These traditional control concepts are augmented however by controls written into the computer programs and controls built into the computer hardware.

Organizational controls in an electronic data processing system

The organization plan for a data processing department should provide definite lines of authority and responsibility, segregation of functions, and clear definition of duties for each employee in the department. An adequately staffed electronic data processing department should include the following positions:

Data processing manager.   A manager should be appointed to supervise the operations of the data processing department. He may report to the financial vice president, or perhaps to a vice president for data processing or information systems.

Systems analyst.   The systems analyst is responsible for designing the EDP system. After considering the objectives of the business and its data processing needs, he determines the goals of the system and the means of achieving these goals. Utilizing system flowcharts and detail instructions, he outlines the data processing system.

Programmer.   Guided by the specifications provided by the systems analyst, the programmer designs program flowcharts for computer programs required by the system. He then codes the required programs in computer language, generally making use of specialized programming languages such as COBOL and software elements such as assemblers, compilers, and utility programs. He tests the programs with "test decks" composed of genuine or dummy records and transactions, and performs the necessary debugging. Finally, the programmer prepares necessary documentation, such as the computer operator instructions.

Computer operator.   The computer operator manipulates the computer in accordance with the instructions developed by the programmer. On occasion the computer operator may have to intervene through the computer console during a run in order to correct an indicated error. All operator entries into the computer should be made through a console typewriter so that printed copies of the entries are available.

Key punch operator.   Source documents are converted by the key punch operator to data for computer processing. Card or tape punching equipment and verifying equipment are utilized by key punch operators.

Librarian.   The role of the librarian is to maintain protective custody of computer programs, master files, detail files, and other important records on magnetic tape or punched cards. To assure adequate control, the librarian maintains a formal "checkout" system for all records.

Control group.   The control group of a data processing department reviews and tests all input procedures; monitors computer processing; handles the reprocessing of errors detected by the computer; and reviews and distributes all computer output.

The history of computer-centered fraud shows that the persons responsible for frauds typically "set up the system and run the whole show" as programmer and operator.

ILLUSTRATIVE CASE.   A programmer for a large bank wrote a program for identifying and listing all overdrawn accounts. Later, as operator of the bank's computer, he was able to insert a "patch" in the program to cause the computer to ignore overdrafts in his own account. The programmer-operator was then able to overdraw his bank account at will, without the overdraft coming to management's attention. The fraud was not discovered until the computer broke down and the listing of overdrawn accounts had to be prepared manually.

The number of personnel and the organizational structure will of course determine the extent to which segregation of duties is possible. As a minimum, the function of programming should be separated from the functions controlling input to the computer program, and the function of the computer operator should be segregated from functions requiring detailed knowledge or custody of the computer program.

If one person is permitted to perform duties in several of these functions, internal control is weakened and the opportunity exists for fraudulent data to be inserted in the system. Separation of duties does not always appear efficient or convenient when nearly all aspects of a transaction are handled by the computer. However, cases of large-scale fraud have already appeared in EDP systems, and the threat may increase if emphasis upon separation of duties is lessened.

In addition to segregation of functions, the data processing organization plan should provide for rotation of programmer assignments, rotation of operator assignments, mandatory vacations, and adequate fidelity bonds for employees. At least two of the qualified data processing personnel should be present whenever the computer facility is in use. Further, the reporting responsibility of the data processing manager should provide for his independence from the controller, treasurer, and other managers who initiate the transactions which he processes.

Documentation

Internal control in an EDP department requires not only subdivision of duties but also the maintenance of adequate documentation describing the system and procedures used in all data processing tasks. Although several **runs** through the computer may be necessary to perform all of the elements of a specific data processing task, the run is usually the basic unit of computer documentation. Documentation of each computer run is included in a **run manual.**

A run manual is prepared by either the systems analyst or programmer and contains a complete description of the program used for the run. As a minimum, run documentation should include:

1. A statement of the problems to be solved by elements of the system.
2. System flowcharts showing sources and nature of input, operations, and output.
3. Detailed instructions and explanations for the system.
4. Record layouts showing the placement of data on punched cards, magnetic tape and print-outs.
5. Program flowcharts showing the major steps and logic of each computer program.
6. Program listings showing the detailed assembler and compiler printouts.
7. Program approval and change sheets showing proper authorization for all initial programs and subsequent changes.
8. Operator instructions for processing the programs.
9. Test decks utilized in testing and debugging programs.

Complete run manuals may be utilized by systems analysts and programmers for making authorized changes in programs. Computer operators, on the other hand, should have access only to the instructions for processing the programs. If operators have access to the complete run manual, the opportunities for an operator changing or patching a program are increased.

Documentation is helpful to the auditor in reviewing the controls over program changes, evaluating controls written into programs, and determining the program logic. The auditor must also refer to format and layout information in the documentation in order to prepare test decks or special audit programs for testing the clients' processing programs and computerized files. In other words, the auditor's study of internal control and his planning of audit programs to test the client's system require him to utilize the client's documentation.

File and record maintenance.   All magnetic tape and punched card files should be properly identified by external labels and machine-readable internal **header** labels. The librarian should maintain a log recording all files checked out and returned to the library, and the signature of the authorized person responsible for the file during the check-out period.

Generally, three "generations" of master files should be retained to enable reproduction of files lost or destroyed. Under this **grandfather-**

father-son principle of file retention, the current updated master file is the "son"; the master file utilized in the updating run which produced the son is the "father"; and the previous father is the "grandfather." Tapes of transactions for the current period and for the prior period should also be retained to facilitate updating the older master tapes in the event that the current master tape was accidentally destroyed. The three generations should be stored in separate sections of the library, or in separate locations, to minimize the risk of losing all three generations at once. Adequate insurance coverage for the files is essential.

Processing controls in an electronic data processing system

Equipment controls. Modern electronic data processing equipment is highly accurate and reliable. Most errors in computer output result from erroneous input or an error in the program. The auditor, however, should be familiar with the equipment controls within a given system in order to appraise the reliability of the hardware, either for evaluating output, or for searching for probable causes of erroneous output. Equipment controls are built into the computer by the computer manufacturer. Among the more common equipment or hardware controls are the following:

1. *Read after write.* The computer reads back the data after they have been recorded in storage and verifies their accuracy.
2. *Dual read or read after punch.* Data on magnetic tape or punched cards are read twice during the input phase, and the two readings are compared.
3. *Parity check.* Data are processed by the computer in arrays of *bits* (binary digits). In addition to bits necessary to represent the numeric or alphabetic character, a *parity* bit is added when necessary to make the sum of all the "1" bits always odd or even, depending upon the make of the computer. As data are transferred at rapid speeds between computer components, the parity check is applied by the computer to assure that bits are not lost during the transfer process.
4. *Echo check.* The echo check involves transmitting data received by an output device back to the source unit for comparison with the original data.
5. *Reverse multiplication.* In reverse multiplication, the roles of the original multiplicand and multiplier are reversed and the resultant product is compared to the original product.

A program of preventive maintenance is essential to assure the proper functioning of the equipment controls.

Program controls. A variety of program controls may be incorporated into computer programs to assure reliability and accuracy of data processing. Common program controls include:

1. *Item (or record) count.* A count of number of items or transactions to be processed in a given batch.
2. *Control total.* The predetermined total of one field of information for all items in a batch. An example would be total sales for a batch of sales orders. This control protects against missing amounts, duplication, and transposition errors in input or processing.
3. *Hash total.* A total of one field of information for all items in a batch, used in much the same manner as a control total. The difference between a hash total and a control total is that a hash total has no intrinsic meaning. An example of a hash total would be the sum of the employee numbers in a payroll application.
4. *Validity (code validity) test.* A comparison of employee, vendor, and other codes against a master file for authenticity.
5. *Limit test.* A test of the reasonableness of a field of data, given a predetermined upper and/or lower limit.
6. *Character mode.* A test to verify that all characters within a field are alphabetic, numeric, or alphanumeric, as required.
7. *Self-checking number.* A number containing redundant information, such as the sum of digits in another number, permitting a check for accuracy after the number has been transmitted from one device to another.
8. *File labels.* Labels used to insure that the proper transaction file or master file is being used on a specific run. A *header label* is a machine readable message at the beginning of a tape file, identifying the file and its release date. A *trailer label* is the last record in a file and contains such control devices as an item count and/or control totals.

In cases of exceptions or errors disclosed by program controls, the computer processing will halt, or the errors will be printed out. Error print-outs should be transmitted direct to the control group for follow-up. The control group's responsibility includes ascertaining that corrections of errors are properly entered into the appropriate batches and that duplicate corrections are avoided.

Controls over input and output. A number of controls over input and output are necessary for adequate internal control in an EDP system. One of these is the *batch* procedure for processing source documents. In most off-line computer systems, transaction documents are collected into batches for processing in sequence as one lot. The sequence of serial numbers in each batch should be accounted for. In addition, key totals such as item counts, control totals, and hash totals should be developed for each batch; these totals may then be verified during each stage of the processing of the batch.

In converting source documents to machine-readable media, provision should be made for verifying the accuracy of the conversion, at least on a test basis. For key punch operations, a verifier punch should test the accuracy of the mechanical key stroke, or as an alternative, the punched cards may be interpreted and visually compared to the source documents. A self-checking number may also be utilized.

Departments external to the data processing center contribute to internal control by maintaining independent control totals of input and by reviewing the output returned by the data processing department. The EDP control group should have the responsibility for distributing the computer output to the appropriate recipients and for following up on exceptions and errors reported by the recipients.

The control group also monitors the operator's activities. A log maintained by the operator should be available to the control group. The log records the description of each run, the elapsed time for the run, operator console interventions, machine halts, master files utilized, etc.

An internal auditing function may exist separate and distinct from the work of the control group in the data processing department. The control group is primarily concerned with day-to-day maintenance of the internal accounting controls for data processing, whereas the internal auditors are interested in both administrative controls and accounting controls.

The auditor's study and evaluation of internal control for an EDP system

The auditor may use several techniques to test and evaluate the internal control of an EDP system. Among the techniques commonly employed are:

1. Internal control questionnaires for EDP systems.
2. Flowchart analysis.
3. Test decks.
4. Controlled (duplicate) programs.
5. Generalized (computer) audit programs.

Internal control questionnaire for EDP systems

The auditor will generally use a specially-designed questionnaire in his study of internal control for an EDP system. In obtaining answers to the questionnaire, he will make inquiries, observe operations, inspect records and documents, study flowcharts, and test transactions. An internal control questionnaire designed for EDP systems by Laventhol

Krekstein Horwath & Horwath, a national CPA firm, is illustrated by special permission in Appendix B of this chapter.

Questionnaires are best suited for a study of organizational controls and controls over input and output. The questionnaire approach is not well suited to studying the effectiveness of program controls because neither the auditor nor the respondent is usually aware of situations in which program controls are inadequate.

Flowchart analysis

As illustrated in Chapter 5, a systems flowchart may be a useful tool in the study and evaluation of internal control. An EDP department should have systems flowcharts available for all computer applications as part of the standard documentation. Systems flowcharts may be used by the auditor for essentially the same types of evaluation as may be conducted through the questionnaire approach.

An illustration of a system flowchart for sales, accounts receivable, and cash receipts appears in Figure 6–1. The following description of the illustrated procedures and processing steps should be helpful in studying the illustrated flowchart.

1. Orders are received from salesmen, and sales invoices are mechanically produced by a posting machine. A punched paper tape is a by-product of the writing of the sales invoice. Two copies of the invoice are mailed to the customer, one copy is sent to the shipping department, and one copy is filed off-line. The punched paper tape of sales invoice transactions is converted to magnetic tape. The items on the magnetic tape are then sorted into the proper sequence on another magnetic tape.

2. Individual cash remittance advices from customers are received from the mail room and verified to a batch total which is also received from the mail room. These remittances are keypunched on cards, and the cards are verified. The deck of punched cards is then converted to magnetic tape. The items on the magnetic tape are in turn sorted into proper sequence on another magnetic tape.

3. The accounts receivable master file is updated by processing both the sales transactions tape and the cash receipts transactions tape. A by-product of the updating of the accounts receivable master file is an *error report* for the run and a print-out (on an on-line typewriter) of any job messages.

Program flowcharts. Standard documentation should include program flowcharts as well as systems flowcharts. Program flowcharts illustrate the detailed logic of specific computer programs. The auditor capable of interpreting program flowcharts may evaluate the program controls

FIGURE 6–1
System flowchart

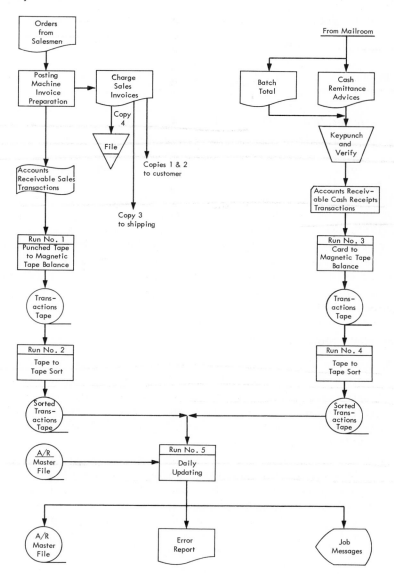

contained in specific computer applications and draw inferences regarding the computer output. Many computers will accept software routines which generate computer-made flowcharts of the programs in use. The auditor may use such routines to insure that the program flowcharts contained in the documentation actually describe the programs in use.

A shortcoming of this method is that even a trained auditor may overlook a major deficiency within a program unless he knows what type of problem he should be looking for.

Test decks

In the audit of a manual accounting system, the auditor traces sample transactions through the records from their inception to their final disposition. In the audit of an EDP system, a comparable approach is the use of a test deck. The test decks developed by the client's programmers may be utilized by the independent auditor once he has satisfied himself by study of flowcharts and print-outs that the tests are valid. Less desirably in terms of audit effort, the auditor may develop his own test decks.

Test decks should include all conceivable types of exceptions and errors in a process. Among these would be missing transactions, erroneous transactions, illogical transactions, out-of-balance batches, and out-of-sequence records. The auditor will carefully appraise the program controls and control group functions with respect to the test deck errors and exceptions. Dummy transactions and records used in test decks can be specially coded to avoid contamination of the client's genuine records and files.

Controlled programs

As an alternative or supplement to the test deck approach, the auditor may monitor the processing of current data by a duplicate program which has been under his control. He then compares the output to that developed by the client's copy of the program. He may also request the reprocessing of historical data with his controlled program for comparison with the original output.

Controlled programs are advantageous because the auditor may test the client's program with both "live" (genuine) and test data. A problem arises in testing historical data, however, since the client may not retain tape files beyond three generations.

Through controlled programs, the auditor may test program controls without risk of contaminating the client's files. Also, the testing may be conducted at an independent computer facility without utilizing the client's computer or data processing personnel.

Generalized (computer) audit programs

Many large CPA firms have developed *generalized audit programs* (computer programs) which may be used to test the reliability of the client's programs as well as to perform many specific auditing functions.

FIGURE 6–2
Flowchart of parallel simulation process

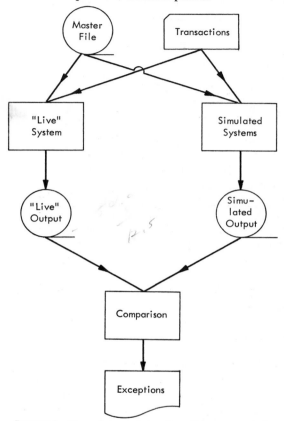

Reprinted with special permission from *Tempo*, a quarterly
journal published by Touche Ross & Co. Winter, 1971–72, p. 14.

Generalized computer audit programs verify the reliability of the
client's programs through a process which has been termed "parallel
simulation." The generalized audit program is designed so that it can
perform processing functions essentially equivalent to those of the client's
programs. The generalized audit program uses the same files (transaction
files and master files) as do the client's programs and should ideally
produce the same results as were produced by the client's programs.
Thus, the generalized audit program "simulates" the client's processing
of live data.

Although the generalized audit program is likely to be less efficient
than the client's programs, the output should be comparable in all material respects. The generalized audit program compares the simulated
output to the client's records and prepares a listing of discrepancies.
These discrepancies, of course, should be followed up and reconciled

by the auditor. A flowchart of the parallel simulation process is illustrated in Figure 6–2.

The value of generalized audit programs lies in the fact that the auditor is able to conduct independent processing of live data. Often, the verification of the client's output would be too large a task to be undertaken manually but can be done efficiently through a parallel computer program. Even when manual verification would be possible, the use of a parallel program allows the auditor to expand greatly the size of the sample of transactions to be tested. An extensive examination of the client's files may become a feasible and economic undertaking. It is not necessary, however, to duplicate all of the client's data processing. Testing should only be performed to the extent necessary to determine the reliability of the client's financial reporting systems.

The auditor does not need extensive technical EDP knowledge in order to make use of generalized computer audit programs. He will find it necessary to perform only a modest amount of programming. In fact, many CPA firms have found that they can train audit staff members to code specification sheets and operate a generalized audit program within a time span of a week or two. Because of the simplified procedures which have been developed, the auditor can, after limited training, program and operate the generalized audit program independently—that is, without assistance from the client's EDP personnel.

Parallel simulation is only one use of generalized audit programs. Other common applications include:

1. Stratification of populations for sampling.
2. Selection of random samples of transactions for testing.
3. Selection of accounts receivable for confirmation.
4. Identification of slow-moving inventory.
5. Identification of past-due receivables.
6. Comparison of budgeted and actual data.
7. Comparison of inventory test counts and perpetual inventory records.
8. Comparison of sales prices in master files to sales prices on invoices.
9. Verification of inventory extensions and footings.

As previously mentioned, a number of the larger CPA firms have developed their own generalized audit programs. Similar programs are available to other members of the profession through the AICPA. These programs are sometimes referred to as *generalized audit packages.*

Implications of on-line, real-time systems

An on-line, real-time system is one in which users have direct (on-line) access to the computer and the recording of transactions causes instantaneous updating of all relevant files. An example of an on-line, real-time (OLRT) system is frequently encountered in savings and loan associations. These systems allow a teller at any branch to update a customer's account immediately by recording his deposit or withdrawal on a computer terminal. On-line, real-time systems may have a significant impact upon the traditional *audit trail.*

When an OLRT system is in use, input need not be entered to the computer in batch runs. Elimination of the batch concept poses several problems for the auditor. For example:

1. Original source documents may not be available to support input to the computer.
2. A grandfather-father-son system of historical master files and transaction files may not exist.
3. Batch controls, such as control totals, item counts, and hash totals may not be applicable.
4. Conventional print-outs of journals and ledgers may not be available.
5. The overall amount of hard copy included in the audit trail may be substantially reduced.

In an OLRT system there is a greater degree of reliance upon the computer for internal control. Input and output errors are detected primarily through program controls. Control must be exercised to prevent manipulation of the system as a whole, since periodic hard copy and possibilities for output verification are substantially reduced.

The following controls relating to input of information should be in effect in an on-line, real-time system:

1. A self-checking digit should be used with account numbers to prevent input into the wrong accounts.
2. A daily record of transactions from each input terminal should be provided by the computer. Transaction records in an OLRT system list transactions in the order received by the computer rather than in batches of similar transactions. The transactions may, however, be segregated by terminal. If specified terminals are used for certain types of transactions, the transaction records will be grouped by types of transactions.
3. A log of all input should be maintained at each input terminal. These logs should be reconciled with the daily record of transactions maintained by the computer.
4. Security should be provided at each terminal to assure that certain operations are initiated only by authorized personnel. A validity check of an identification number should be made before a terminal user gains access to the files.

5. EDP personnel should not initiate input to the computer except for testing purposes; thus a segregation of duties is maintained. Any testing should be done after regular processing is completed and should be recorded in the computer log.
6. The internal auditors should not initiate input to the computer in order that they not be in the position of reviewing their own work.
7. Computer file security should be provided to assure that entries are not made to the accounts except during regular processing hours.

In addition to these controls over the input of information to an on-line, real-time system, other controls of special significance include the following:

1. Account balances should be printed out periodically. These print-outs should be stored with the transaction records in a separate location from the computer files so they can be used to reconstruct the files if necessary.
2. There should be provision for continued operations in the event of a computer failure, for example, each terminal should have mechanical registers in addition to the computer's electronic registers.
3. Mechanical equipment should be kept available, whenever feasible, to permit the continuance of operations in the event of a breakdown of computer facilities.
4. The work of the internal audit staff should include the testing of computer-created records and review of error reports followed by written recommendations for corrective action to an appropriate official.

Computer service centers

Computer service centers provide data processing services to customers who do not do enough data processing to justify having their own computers. The customer delivers the input to the computer service center, and the service center processes the data and returns the output to the customer.

Computer service centers actually strengthen internal control because of increased subdivision of duties. Deliberate manipulation of a company's records is less likely because the persons doing the data processing do not have access to the company's assets. Also, since the service center processes input in small batches and provides hard-copy output to the customer, the independent auditor will have an adequate audit trail for evaluation of the processing conducted by the computer service center. Control totals, hash totals, and item counts may also be used effectively to insure the reliability of the batch processing.

While the applications performed for customers by a computer service center are usually relatively simple (such as payroll preparation), the operations of the computer service center may be quite complex. The auditor, therefore, will usually evaluate the reliability of the data processing by examination of the hard-copy output and possibly by testing the computer service center's programs with test decks. A complete evaluation of the internal control of the computer service center is usually not practical or necessary.

Time-sharing systems

Time-sharing systems consist of a large, fast central computer which may be used simultaneously by a number of independent users at remote locations. Communication devices related to the computer permit translation of computer input into codes which are transmitted over telephone lines. Each user (subscriber) has on-line access to the central computer through a terminal in his office. To use this terminal, either to enter input or receive output, the user merely dials a telephone number and is automatically connected to the computer. The user's files are maintained at the central computer facility. To prevent access to these files or other use of the computer by an unauthorized person, each user is required to type an identification code into his terminal.

The subscriber to a commercial time-sharing system can, through his terminal, run programs, store these programs in the computer for subsequent use, use the programs developed by the time-sharing company and store files of data in the computer for subsequent use. In brief, the user of a time-sharing system has available most of the services which would be available through ownership of a computer.

The central computer center should maintain controls to prevent unauthorized use of each customer's proprietary programs, loss or destruction of customers' data files, and alteration of customers' programs. Provision should also be made for file reconstruction. The internal controls most important to the auditor of a company having a time-sharing terminal are the user's control over input data and the program controls such as item counts and control totals. Substantial hard-copy output is usually generated at the user's access terminal; thus an adequate audit trail usually exists for verifying the reliability of data processing.

In most cases it is not feasible or necessary for the auditor to test or evaluate the internal control for the central computer; however, he may test the client's proprietary programs. Care must be taken so that test data do not permanently contaminate the client's files.

Some large CPA firms have terminals in their offices across the country, all linked to national time-sharing networks. These terminals are used for such projects as forecasting financial statements with numerous input variables, preparation of tax returns, selection of random samples for testing, staff training in computer skills, and also for administrative processes within the firm.

Auditing EDP Systems—a look to the future

The computer was once viewed by some as a potential menace to the auditor—a black box which threatened to make his task impossible by eliminating the audit trail. However, the public accounting profession has responded impressively to the challenges posed by the computer. Auditors have modified their procedures to fit electronic data processing systems and have harnessed the power of the computer to assist in the performance of many audit functions. Generalized computer audit programs have been developed which not only test the client's files and programs but also perform simulations, capital budgeting applications, and other functions useful to both auditor and client. No longer is the auditor dependent upon programmers in communicating with the computer. He is acquiring a new independent capacity to utilize the computer in achieving his goals.

As the routine clerical aspects of auditing are increasingly being delegated to the computer, the auditor is able to broaden the scope of his activities and to emphasize the testing of management plans and policies. The use of computerized audit techniques may pave the way to the audit of quarterly financial statements as well as annual statements. Since interim financial statements are used as a basis for investment decisions, adding to their credibility through extension of the auditor's role seems to deserve consideration.

The challenges of EDP are continuing to grow, and the auditor will have to become increasingly familiar with EDP systems if he is to meet these challenges. In a study cosponsored by the AICPA,[2] it was suggested that the beginning CPA should have the following computer-oriented capabilities:

1. A basic knowledge of one computer system.
2. The ability to chart or diagram an information system of modest complexity.
3. A working knowledge of at least one computer language and information system.
4. The ability to design a simple information system, program the system, and test and debug the program.

To carry on the audit of a variety of clients having EDP systems and to comply with generally accepted auditing standards, it appears

[2] *Horizons for a Profession: The common body of knowledge for certified public accountants.* A study sponsored by the Carnegie Corporation of New York and the American Institute of Certified Public Accountants (New York, 1967).

probable that the CPA will need more extensive capabilities than those listed above. The scope of this more extensive knowledge might reasonably include:

1. Familiarity with EDP terminology.
2. Knowledge of hardware, programs, and EDP controls.
3. Familiarity with main and peripheral computer components.
4. Ability to develop test decks and special-purpose computer audit programs.
5. Familiarity with a wide range of and uses for generalized audit programs.
6. Ability to determine the reliability of computer processing by study of the logic of processing flowcharts.

The audit team of the future may well include specialists in electronic data processing and specialists in statistical sampling. These specialists may work with an auditing "generalist," who is well versed in these specialized fields as well as in general audit practice.

Computer audit programs for use with an on-line, real-time system may eventually be designed as part of the client's EDP system. These programs and related special-purpose hardware might select random samples of the data processed for subsequent review by the auditors. Other audit functions made part of the system might be to insure that all transactions processed meet stipulated criteria.

The painstaking work of developing input for a computer by use of punched cards or tape may be solved by improvements in optical scanning devices. A typewriter may be a sufficient input device if optical scanners capable of reading ordinary printed or typed material are available. In fact, auditors may type the evidence they gather on working papers which will be read by optical scanners, automatically recorded on magnetic tape, and made available for processing by the computer.

APPENDIX A

GLOSSARY OF SELECTED EDP TERMS

address. A name, label, or number identifying a location in storage.

ADP. Automatic data processing: data processing carried out by electronic or electrical equipment requiring a minimum of human assistance.

alphanumeric. A character set which includes alphabetic characters and numeric characters.

assembler. A computer program which assembles, item by item, programs written in symbolic language to create machine-language coding.

auditing around the computer. An auditing technique which does not utilize the computer to perform tests and select samples.

auditing through the computer. An audit technique which utilizes the computer to perform tests and select samples.

audit trail. Documentation or other evidence created to facilitate tracing source documents to machine-produced output, and vice versa.

auxiliary storage (mass storage, secondary storage). Storage devices which supplement a computer's main storage.

batch. A group of transactions processed in sequence as one lot.

binary. Pertaining to the number system of base two, which includes only the digits 0 and 1. Generally used in digital computers since they have only two stable states.

bit. A binary digit—0 or 1—in a binary number.

block. A group of words, characters, or digits held or processed as a unit by the computer.

boundary protection. Protection against unauthorized entry (read or write) to a tape, disk, or other storage device.

bug. A mistake in the design of a computer system or program, or an equipment malfunction.

byte. A group of eight adjacent bits that can represent one alphanumeric character or two decimal digits.

central processing unit (CPU, main frame). The component of a computer system which contains the main storage, arithmetic, and control units.

character mode test. A programmed test for determining that all characters in a field are of the prescribed mode—alphabetic, numeric, or alphanumeric.

check digit. A redundant digit added to a normal number for the purpose of detecting errors in transcribing numbers. Numbers with check digits are called *self-checking numbers* and may be useful for various types of identification numbers such as employee payroll numbers and bank checking account numbers.

COBOL (Common Business Oriented Language). A near-English programming language for business data processing; it is translated by a computer program into a machine code.

compiler. A computer program which prepares a machine-language program from a program written in a procedure-oriented language such as COBOL.

completeness test. A programmed test for determining that all necessary fields of information are present for a transaction.

console. A computer component used for communication between operators or maintenance engineers and the computer by means of displays and manual controls such as a typewriter.

console run book. A book of computer operator instructions for a run.

control group. Persons who control and review all data processed by the computer and all computer output before its distribution.

control total. A total of one information field for all the records of a batch, such as the total sales dollars for a batch of sales invoices.

converter. A device that converts data from one form, such as punched cards, to another, such as magnetic tape, to facilitate processing the data by high-speed computer equipment.

CPU. The central processing unit or principal hardware component of a digital computer containing an arithmetic unit, the primary storage, and a control unit.

debug. To locate and eliminate errors in a computer program or malfunctions of the computer itself.

detail file. A file containing relatively transient data, such as the checks written in one day.

digital computer. A computer which processes discrete or discontinuous data, usually in sequences of arithmetic or logical operations.

disk. A random access storage device consisting of a circular metal plate with magnetic material on both sides.

dual read. The reading of one record by two separate reading stations, with the results compared to detect reading errors.

dummy record. A record containing fictitious data inserted into a file for testing purposes.

dummy transaction. A fictitious transaction entered into a data processing system for testing purposes.

dump. The listing of all or part of contents of storage.

echo check. A hardware control which involves transmitting data received by an output device back to the source unit for comparison with original data.

edit. To rearrange or modify the form or format of data, such as inserting dollar signs and decimal points, suppressing leading zeros, providing headings and page numbers.

emulator. A device enabling one computer to execute untranslated machine programs written for a dissimilar computer.

error listing. A supplement to a computer program, which lists all of the types and probable causes of errors which the program has been designed to detect, and the likely necessary corrective action.

error report. A report which lists only the file records or batch transactions which fall outside a normal or expected range.

error routine. A routine initiating corrective action when errors occur.

external label. An identifying label affixed to the outside of a file holder, such as a magnetic tape file.

field. A subdivision of a record, such as a group of columns in a punched card earmarked for one item, or a subdivision of a computer word or instruction.

field validity test (limit test). A programmed test for determining whether the value of a field exceeds fixed or reasonable limits; for example, a month of the year less than 1 or greater than 12.

file. An organized collection of related records, such as a customer file, which is usually arranged in sequence according to a key contained in each record.

file label. An internal machine-readable record identifying a file, or an external label attached to a file holder.

file protection ring. A removable plastic or metal ring designed to prevent improper usage of a magnetic tape file.

format. A predetermined arrangement of characters, fields, lines, and so forth in a file or on a single sheet.

FORTRAN (Formula Translator). A programming language for problems involving mathematical computations.

generalized audit programs. Computer programs developed by CPA firms for the purpose of auditing; such programs enable the auditor to verify the client's programs by simulating the client's processing of live data and identifying exceptions.

grandfather-father-son. The principle of record retention which provides for maintaining three generations of magnetic tape master files: the "son," or current updated file; the "father," or master file used as input in the current updating; and the "grandfather," or master file used in the immediately preceding updating.

hard copy. Computer output in printed form, such as printed listings, reports, and summaries.

hardware. Physical equipment and devices comprising an electronic data processing system.

hash total. A meaningless control total, such as the total of all invoice numbers in a batch of sales invoices, utilized to determine whether data are lost between operations.

header label. A machine-readable record at the beginning of a file which identifies the file.

hole count. A control in punched card equipment providing for disclosure of read errors by counting the holes in punched cards at each of two read stations and comparing the results.

input. Data transferred from an external storage medium to internal storage of the computer.

interpret. To print on a punched card data or information punched in the card.

item count. A count of the number of transactions or items in a batch.

key punch. A device to record data in machine-readable form as holes punched in cards or paper tape.

library. A collection of magnetic tape files and records.

log. A record of computer operations containing for each run the elapsed time, errors detected and printed out, operator actions in response to machine halts, and identification of magnetic tape files used.

loop. A sequence of instructions in a program that are performed repetitively. Each repetition is called a cycle. Repetition continues for a predetermined number of cycles, or until all data have been processed.

machine language (code) program. A computer program in the form used by the computer.

master file. A file of relatively permanent data or information which is generally updated periodically.

merge. To form a single sequenced file by combining two or more similarly sequenced files.

microsecond. One millionth of a second (10^{-6} seconds).

millisecond. One thousandth of a second (10^{-3} seconds).

monitor. To supervise and verify the correct operation of a program during its execution.

nanosecond. One billionth of a second (10^{-9} seconds).

off-line. Pertaining to peripheral devices or equipment which are not in direct communication with the central processing unit of the computer.

on-line. Pertaining to peripheral devices or equipment which are in direct communication with the central processing unit of the computer.

operator. The person who manipulates computer controls, places information media into input devices, removes output, and performs related functions.

output. Data transferred from internal storage of the computer to auxiliary storage or to any device outside the computer.

overflow. A condition arising when the result of an arithmetic operation exceeds the capacity of the allotted storage space in the computer.

parallel simulation. A technique of program verification consisting of using one program to simulate the processing functions of another program and comparing the results.

parity bit. A redundant bit added to an array of bits to make the sum of the "1" bits in the array either odd or even, depending on the make of the computer.

parity check. A hardware control designed to disclose the loss of data in transmission by verifying the proper odd or even "1" bit configuration of each array of bits.

pass. One complete cycle of input, processing, and output in the execution of a computer program.

patch. A new section of coding added in a rough or expedient way to modify a program.

peripheral equipment. Components of an electronic data processing system other than the central processing unit.

preventive maintenance. Maintenance designed to keep computer equipment in proper operating condition.

program. The entire sequence of machine instructions and routines required to process data.

program control. A test that is initiated by a series of instructions in a program.

program flowchart. A graphic representation of the major steps and logic of a computer program.

programmer. A person who prepares programs, program flowcharts, and debugging routines.

random access. Pertaining to a storage technique in which the time required to gain access to data is not significantly affected by the location of the data in storage. A disk is a random access device.

random number generator. A special routine designed to produce one or more random numbers in accordance with specific limitations.

real-time processing. Data processing of a transaction performed concurrently with the occurrence of the transaction, providing output immediately useful.

record. A group of related items or fields of data handled as a unit.

record count. A program control providing for the count of records processed during the various phases of operation of a program.

record layout. A diagram showing all the fields of data in a record and their arrangement in the record.

routine. A set of sequenced instructions that causes a computer to perform a particular process.

run. The performance of a specific computer program, with little or no operator intervention. A run serves as the basic unit of computer operation.

run manual. A manual documenting the processing system, program, controls, and operating instructions of a specific computer run.

self-checking number. A number which contains a redundant suffixed digit (check digit) permitting the number to be verified for accuracy after it has been transferred from one device or medium to another.

sequential access. Pertaining to a storage technique in which the time required to gain access to data is related to the location of the data in storage. Magnetic tape is a sequential storage device.

sentinel. A character that signals the end of a file.

serial access. Pertaining to a storage technique in which the time required to gain access to data is affected by the necessity for waiting while non-desired storage locations are processed in turn.

software. Programs and routines, including assemblers and compilers, furnished by a computer manufacturer to facilitate the operation of a computer.

solid state components. Transistors, diodes, and other electronic components which control or convey electrons within solid materials.

sort. To arrange data or records in sequence or in groups according to a key or field contained in the data or records.

source document. A document from which data are extracted for input to a computer.

storage. A device into which data may be entered and from which data may be retrieved as desired.

system flowchart. A graphic representation of the flow of documents and operations in a data processing application.

systems analyst. The person who examines a business activity to determine what must be accomplished and how it is to be accomplished.

test deck. A set of dummy records and transactions developed to test the adequacy of a computer program or system.

time sharing. A technique or system designed to furnish computing services simultaneously to a number of users, providing rapid responses to each user.

update. To bring a master file up to date by posting recent transactions, adding new records, and deleting obsolete records.

utility program (or routine). A standard program for performing a commonly required process such as sorting, merging, and file maintenance.

validity check. A check to determine whether a particular code is a legitimate member of a particular set. Used, for example, to test employee numbers in a payroll application.

verify. To determine the accuracy of a data transcription or data transfer operation.

word. A group of bits or characters treated as a unit and stored in one storage location.

APPENDIX B

EDP INTERNAL CONTROL QUESTIONNAIRE

CLIENT_____

Prepared by

Date

_____   _____

_____   _____

_____   _____

Client personnel consulted

Position

_____   _____

_____   _____

_____   _____

Reviewed by

Date

_____   _____

This questionnaire is to be used to evaluate the controls over the electronic data processing segment of the company's accounting system. It is to supplement the internal control questionnaire used for manual and semiautomatic systems. The conventional questionnaire will continue to be used to evaluate the controls over assets and data before and after data processing by the computer.

The answer to each question should be checked in the appropriate column: Yes, No or N/A (Not Applicable). If the question is applicable, an affirmative answer indicates adequate internal control. However, a negative answer must be completely investigated to see whether alternative procedures provide the desired control.

Some of the questions refer to the controls over the operation of the EDP department, while others refer to processing controls incorporated into specific applications. When considering the questions which relate to specific applications, insert the name of each application at the top of a column and check the blocks in the proper columns. Consider the controls over each application individually; a processing control may be present in one application but not in another.

-1-

APPENDIX B continued

Section A -- General Information

A - 1 Where is the computer located? _____

A - 2 Give a brief description of equipment _____

   (a) Manufacturer and model number of computer (this can be obtained from a copy
        of the manufacturer's invoice) _____

   (b) Internal memory size _____

   (c) File storage devices

        Magnetic tape (no. units _____)   _____
        Disk (no. drives _____)   _____
        Other (describe)   _____
        _____

   (d) Input/output devices

        Card reader   _____
        Card punch   _____
        Printer   _____
        Other (list)   _____
        _____

A - 3 Applications

        Cash   _____
        Receivables   _____
        Inventory   _____
        Property, plant and equipment   _____
        Payables   _____
        Sales   _____
        Payroll   _____
        Cost and expenses   _____
        Other (list major ones below)   _____
        _____

Section B -- Organization of the EDP Function *Organizational controls*

   An important factor in internal control is the organization of the EDP department. It must be so designed to give maximum service to other departments,
   yet be independent of them. The procedures in the EDP department must be
   documented, with a minimum of oral instructions. <u>Obtain or prepare an
   organization chart of the EDP organization.</u>

-2-

APPENDIX B continued

		Yes	No	N/A
B-1	Is there a segregation of duties such that:			
	(a) The functions and duties of system design and programming are separate from computer operation?	____	____	____
	(b) Programmers do not operate the computer for regular processing runs?	____	____	____
	(c) Computer operators are restricted from access to data and program information not necessary for performing their assigned task?	____	____	____
	(d) The employees in data processing are separated from all duties relating to the initiation of requests for changes to the master files?	____	____	____
B-2	Are the operators assigned to individual application runs rotated periodically?	____	____	____
B-3	Are the computer operators required to take vacations?	____	____	____
B-4	Is supervision of operators sufficient to verify operator's adherence to prescribed operating procedures?	____	____	____
B-5	Is access to the computer center limited to persons having a legitimate reason for being there?	____	____	____
B-6	Is there a person or group charged with responsibility for the control function in the data processing department? Obtain description of duties. These duties will normally include:	____	____	____
	(a) Control over receipt of input data and recording of control information.	____	____	____
	(b) Reconciliation of control information (batch control with computer control totals, run-to-run controls, etc.).	____	____	____
	(c) Control over distribution of output.	____	____	____
	(d) Control over errors to ensure that they are reported, corrected and reprocessed.	____	____	____
	(e) Review of console logs, error listings and other evidence of error detection and control.	____	____	____
B-7	Is the person or group responsible for control over processing by the data processing department independent from the person or group responsible for the operation of the equipment?	____	____	____
B-8	If there is an internal auditing group, does it perform EDP control activities related to:			
	(a) Review or audit?	____	____	____

-3-

APPENDIX B continued

	Yes	No	N/A
(b) Day-to-day control activities?	___	___	___

If "Yes", note the nature and extent of these activities. _____

_____

	Yes	No	N/A
B-9 Are master file changes authorized in writing by initiating departments?	___	___	___
B-10 Are departments that initiate changes in master file data furnished with notices or a register showing changes actually made? (Examples of such changes are changes in pay rates, selling prices, credit limits and commission tables.)	___	___	___
B-11 Is the EDP department independent of all operating units for which it performs data processing functions?	___	___	___
B-12 Are there provisions for the use of alternative facilities in the event of fire or other lengthy interruption?	___	___	___
B-13 Is there adequate data processing insurance (other than fire coverage)?	___	___	___
B-14 Are data processing personnel covered by fidelity insurance?	___	___	___

Section C -- Input Controls

Application
(if additional columns are required, use additional pages)

	#1			#2		
	Yes	No	N/A	Yes	No	N/A
C-1 Are initiating departments required to establish control over data submitted for processing (through the use of batch totals, document counts or other)?	___	___	___	___	___	___
C-2 Are there adequate controls over the creation of data and its conversion to machine-readable form?	___	___	___	___	___	___
(a) Procedural controls	___	___	___	___	___	___
(b) Mechanical or visual verification	___	___	___	___	___	___
(c) Check digit	___	___	___	___	___	___
C-3 Is there adequate control over transmittal and input of data to detect loss or nonprocessing?	___	___	___	___	___	___
(a) Financial control totals	___	___	___	___	___	___
(b) Hash control totals	___	___	___	___	___	___
(c) Document counts	___	___	___	___	___	___
(d) Sequential numbering of input documents	___	___	___	___	___	___

APPENDIX B continued

	#1			#2		
	Yes	No	N/A	Yes	No	N/A

(e) Other (describe) _____

C-4 Are the input control totals and run-to-run control totals for each application checked by someone other than the equipment operator? ___ ___ ___ ___ ___ ___
By whom?_____

C-5 If data transmission is used, are controls adequate to determine that transmission is correct and no messages are lost? ___ ___ ___ ___ ___ ___

(a) Message counts ___ ___ ___ ___ ___ ___

(b) Character counts ___ ___ ___ ___ ___ ___

(c) Dual transmission ___ ___ ___ ___ ___ ___

(d) Other (describe) _____

C-6 Is input data adequately tested for validity, correctness and sequence? ___ ___ ___ ___ ___ ___
Note: Questions may have to be applied to each important data field of the input being reviewed by the auditor. Consider the following criteria and evaluate:

(a) Validity tests:
    (1) Valid code_____
    (2) Valid character_____
    (3) Valid field _____
    (4) Valid transaction _____
    (5) Valid combinations _____
    (6) Missing data_____

(b) Sequence _____

(c) Limit _____

(d) Reasonableness _____

(e) Other_____

C-7 Are all source documents identified by batch number and cancelled to prevent reprocessing? ___ ___ ___ ___ ___ ___

Section D -- Output Controls

D-1 Do initiating departments maintain schedules of the reports and documents they are to receive from the EDP department? ___ ___ ___ ___ ___ ___

APPENDIX B continued

	#1			#2		
	Yes	No	N/A	Yes	No	N/A
D-2 Are output reports and documents reviewed before distribution to ascertain the reasonableness of the output?	___	___	___	___	___	___
D-3 Are there adequate procedures for control over the distribution of reports?	___	___	___	___	___	___
D-4 Describe the control function, if any, for evaluating quality of output.	___	___	___	___	___	___

Section E -- Programmed Controls

E-1 Do the program loading routines include tests to verify that the individual programs are completely and accurately read into inventory? (Card counts, hash totals, record counts, sequence checks, etc.)

E-2 Are control totals used to check for completeness of processing? These may include trailer file labels, run-to-run totals, etc.

E-3 Are programmed controls used to test processing of significant items?
For instance,

  (a) Limit and reasonableness test

  (b) Crossfooting test

E-4 Does the program check for improper switch settings (if sense switches are used)?

E-5 Does the program provide an adequate console printout of control information (switch settings, control violations, operator intervention, etc.)?

E-6 When a program is interrupted, are there adequate provisions for re-start?

E-7 Are there adequate controls over the process of identifying, correcting and reprocessing data rejected by the program?

E-8 Inquire into handling of unmatched transactions (no master record corresponding to transaction record).
Is it adequate?

  (a) Reject and note on error log

  (b) Reject and write on suspense record

  (c) Other (describe)_____

0 who's responsible for this   -6-

APPENDIX B continued

	#1			#2		
	Yes	No	N/A	Yes	No	N/A

<u>Section F -- Master File Controls</u>

F-1 Are control total and other techniques (card counts, sequence checks), being utilized to assure that the master card file being processed is complete and accurate?

F-2 Are controls over master file changes adequate?

   (a) Written request for change from outside data processing

   (b) Register of all changes reviewed by initiating department

   (c) Supervisory or other review of changes

F-3 Are there adequate provisions for periodically checking master file contents?

   (a) Periodic printout and review

   (b) Periodic test against physical count

   (c) Other_____

F-4 Are the back-up and reconstruction provisions adequate? Describe _____
_____

<u>Section G -- Data and Master File Protection</u>

G-1 Are important computer programs, essential documentation, records and files kept in fireproof storage?

G-2 Are copies of important programs, essential documentation, records and files stored in off-premises locations?

G-3 Are external labels used on all files?

G-4 Are internal labels used on all magnetic tape files?

G-5 Are file header labels checked by programs using the files?

G-6 Are file protection rings used on all magnetic tape files to be preserved?

G-7 Is the responsibility for issuing and storing magnetic tape or portable disk packs assigned to a tape librarian, either as a full-time or part-time duty?

APPENDIX B continued

	Yes	No	N/A

Section H -- Management of the EDP Department

H-1 Is a run manual prepared for each computer run?

H-2 Are operator instructions prepared for each run?

H-3 Are documentation practices adequate?
Does the normal documentation for an application include the following?

    Problem statement
    System flowchart
    Record layouts
    Program flowcharts
    Program listing
    Test data
    Operator instructions
    Summary of controls
    Approval and change record

H-4 Is there supervisory review of documentation to ensure that it is adequate?

H-5 Is documentation kept up to date?

H-6 Is each program revision authorized by a request for change properly approved by management or supervisory personnel?

    (a) Who authorizes? _____

    (b) How evidenced? _____

H-7 Are program changes, together with their effective dates, documented in a manner which preserves an accurate chronological record of the system?

H-8 Are provisions adequate to prevent unauthorized entry of program changes and/or data through the console? The following questions reflect the types of controls which may be used.

    (a) Are adequate machine operation logs being maintained? For each run, these should include information covering the run identification, operator, start and stop time, error halts and delays, and details of reruns. Idle time, down time, program testing, etc., should also be logged.

    (b) Is there an independent examination of computer logs to check the operator performance and machine efficiency?
    If "Yes",

        (1) How often _____ (2) By whom _____
        (3) How carried out _____

    (c) If the computer has a typewriter console, is there an independent examination

APPENDIX B concluded

of the console printouts to detect operator problems and unauthorized intervention?   _____ _____ _____

    (1) How often _____ (2) By whom _____
    (3) How performed_____

H – 9 Are records maintained of errors occurring in the EDP system?   _____ _____ _____

H–10 Are these error records periodically reviewed by someone independent of data processing? _____ _____ _____

H–11 Do the records or references provide the means to adequately:

    (a) Trace any transaction forward to a final total?   _____ _____ _____

    (b) Trace any transaction back to the original source document or input?   _____ _____ _____

    (c) Trace any final total back to the component transactions?   _____ _____ _____

    When ledgers (general or subsidiary) are maintained on computer media, does the system
    of processing provide:

    (a) An historical record of activity in the accounts?   _____ _____ _____

    (b) A periodic trial balance of the accounts?   _____ _____ _____

H–12 Are source documents retained for an adequate period of time in a manner which allows
       identification with related output records and documents?   _____ _____ _____

Section I -- EDP Planning

I – 1 Is there a written plan for future changes to be made to the system?   _____ _____ _____

I – 2 Is approval for each application supported by a study of cost and benefit?   _____ _____ _____

I – 3 Is a schedule of implementation prepared showing actual versus planned progress?   _____ _____ _____

I – 4 Is there a systems and procedures manual for the activities of the installation?   _____ _____ _____

GROUP I
REVIEW QUESTIONS

6–1.   Distinguish between the terms "programming language" and "binary code." What is the function of the "compiler" in relation to the two preceding terms?

6–2.   A computer component can be in one of two possible states: "on" or "off." One state is designated as "1" and the other as "0," which are the symbols comprising a **binary** number system. The binary number system expresses any quantity in powers of the base 2 in contrast to the decimal system which uses the base 10. How would the quantity 43 be expressed in binary code?

6–3.   Auxiliary storage devices used to augment the capacity of the storage unit of a computer include which of the following: (*a*) cathode ray tubes, (*b*) magnetic drums, (*c*) card punches, (*d*) magnetic tape, (*e*) magnetic disk packs, (*f*) console display panels, (*g*) compilers, and (*h*) magnetic tape encoders?

6–4.   Distinguish between a "utility program" and a "user program." Which is of greater concern to the auditor in establishing the validity of the financial statements of a client using an EDP system?

6–5.   What are the principal responsibilities of the "control group" in an electronic data processing department?

6–6.   The first requirement of an effective system of internal control is a satisfactory plan of organization. List the characteristics of a satisfactory plan of organization for an EDP department, including the relationship between the department and the rest of the organization. (AICPA)

6–7.   Explain briefly the meaning of the terms "documentation" and "run manual" as used in an EDP department. How might a client's "documentation" be used by the auditor?

6–8.   The number of personnel in an EDP department may limit the extent to which subdivision of duties is feasible. What is the minimum amount of segregation of duties that will permit satisfactory internal control?

6–9.   Define and give the purpose of each of the following program or hardware controls:
   a)   Record counts.
   b)   Limit test.
   c)   Reverse multiplication.
   d)   Hash totals. (AICPA, adapted)

6–10. Most electronic data processing equipment manufacturers have built-in controls to ensure that information is correctly read, processed, transferred within the system, and recorded. One of these built-in controls is the parity bit.
   a)   What is the parity bit?
   b)   When would the parity bit control be used? (AICPA)

6–11.   Distinguish equipment controls from program controls and give examples of each.

6–12.   Explain briefly the term "print-out" with respect to the audit of a client performing accounting work on a computer.

6–13.   In auditing "through" the computer, the CPA may use a "test deck."
  a)   What is a "test deck?"
  b)   Why does the CPA use a "test deck?" (AICPA)

6–14.   Apart from the use of an internal control questionnaire, what other approaches may the auditor take to test and evaluate the internal control of an EDP system?

6–15.   Differentiate between a system flowchart and a program flowchart.

6–16.   An auditor should be familiar with the terminology employed in electronic data processing even though he may not utilize an electronic computer in conducting an examination. The following statements contain some of the term nology so employed. Indicate whether each statement is true or false.
  a)   An error report will not be produced as a byproduct of processing by a computer unless provision was made for such a report in the program.
  b)   An internal label is one of the controls built into the hardware by the manufacturer of a magnetic tape system.
  c)   The term "grandfather-father-son" refers to a method of computer record security rather than to generations in the evolution of computer hardware.
  d)   A control total is an example of a self-checking number within a batch control.
  e)   Most accounting applications would be processed on a digital computer rather than on an analog computer.
  f)   An assembler print-out would be required to audit around the computer.
  g)   A test deck can be contained on magnetic or paper tape as well as on punched cards.
  h)   Field validity tests are employed to determine whether or not a computer word has the proper parity. (AICPA, adapted)

6–17.   Explain the fundamental difference between the use of a test deck and the use of a generalized audit program.

6–18.   Is the term "parallel simulation" associated with auditing "around the computer" or "through the computer"?

6–19.   Explain briefly the term "on-line, real-time system."

6–20.   What is a "computer service center"? Does the use of a computer service center tend to strengthen or weaken a client's internal control? Explain.

6–21.   Does a time-sharing system require the user to deliver batches of data to a center for processing?

GROUP II
QUESTIONS REQUIRING ANALYSIS

6–22. What are the essential characteristics of an on-line, real-time system? Do you think these characteristics would make such a system appropriate for a major airline in handling ticket reservations by customers? Explain fully.

6–23. Student A in an auditing class made the following comment on the impact of computers on auditing.

"A few years ago, auditors were inclined to audit 'around the computer.' They were anxious to have clients preserve an adequate 'audit trail' by creating hard-copy print-outs which in effect provided the auditor with the records and documents he was accustomed to using in a manual system. Now auditors are using test decks to audit 'through the computer' and test the system. This seems to be moving away from a verification of amounts on financial statements toward an evaluation of the system that produces financial statements and other information."

Student B responded as follows:

"You are overemphasizing test decks as a means of auditing 'through the computer.' Generalized audit programs developed by CPA firms are a far more efficient way to use the computer as an audit tool. However, I would agree that emphasis is shifting from the verification of amounts on annual financial statements to an analysis of the EDP system as a whole."

Evaluate the opinions expressed by the two students.

6–24. After reading an article on the use of computers for processing accounting data, a student of auditing commented as follows: "Auditing standards require the CPA to evaluate the system of internal control as a basis for determining an appropriate audit program for a given business. The system of internal control means principally the division of work among numerous employees and departments so that the work of one serves to verify that of another. However, if a business uses a computer for its accounting work, the computer will take the place of the numerous individuals who formerly handled these operations. Consequently, there will be no system of internal control for the CPA to review, and it will not be possible for him to follow the auditing standards required for expression of an unqualified opinion on the fairness of financial statements." Evaluate the quoted comments, indicating with reasons your agreement or disagreement with the principal points set forth.

6–25. "The auditor should not attempt to review complex computer programs but should rely solely on the use of test decks to review the performance of a computer." Do you agree? Discuss.

6–26. An effective system of internal control also requires a sound system of records control, of operations and transactions (source data and their flow), and of classification of data within the accounts. For an EDP system, these controls include input controls, processing controls, and output controls. List the characteristics of a satisfactory system of input controls. (Confine your comments to a batch-controlled system employing punched cards and to the steps that occur prior to the processing of the input cards in the computer.) (AICPA, adapted)

6–27. (1) An extract from a problem statement reads:

"Persons who are 60 years of age or over when commencing employment are not eligible for the pension plan. All other employees automatically become members during the 37th month of continuous employment, and each employee's pension fund contribution will be deducted on the employee's payroll check each <u>month thereafter</u>."

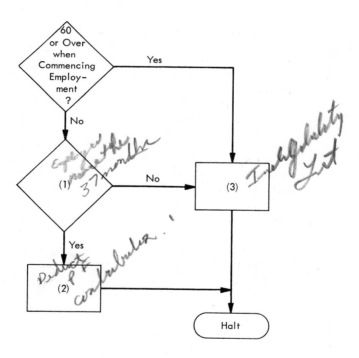

Numbered symbol (1) in the above flowchart should be replaced by which of the following statements?

a)   Deduct pension fund contribution.
b)   Print ineligibility list.
c)   Employed more than 36 months?
d)   Employed more than 37 months?

(2)   Numbered symbol (2) should be replaced by which of the following statements?

a)   Deduct pension fund contribution.
b)   Print ineligibility list.
c)   Employed more than 36 months?
d)   Employed more than 37 months?

(3) Numbered symbol (3) should be replaced by which of the following statements?

a) Deduct pension fund contribution.

(*b*)) Print ineligibility list.

c) Employed more than 36 months?

d) Employed more than 37 months? (AICPA, adapted)

6–28. The three following items contain examples of internal control deficiencies observed by a CPA in his client's computer data processing system. For each of these conditions or situations, select from the list of control features or procedures the one which if properly utilized would have been *most* useful in either preventing the error or in ensuring its immediate and prompt correction.

a) A customer payment recorded legibly on the remittance advice as $13.01 was entered into the computer from punched cards as $1,301. The best control procedure would be:

(1) A limit test.   (3) Keypunch verification.

(2) A valid field test.   (4) A check digit.

b) A program for the analysis of sales provided questionable results and data processing personnel were unable to explain how the program operated. The programmer who wrote the program no longer works for the company. The best control procedure would be:

(1) A run manual.   (3) Layouts.

(2) Operator instructions. (4) Assembly run checking.

c) The master inventory file, contained on a removable magnetic disk, was destroyed by a small fire next to the area where it was stored. The company had to take a special complete inventory in order to reestablish the file. The best control procedure would be:

(1) Fire insurance.   (3) A copy of the disk.

(2) Data processing insurance. (4) Remote storage of a copy of the disk and the transactions since the disk was copied.

(AICPA, adapted)

GROUP III
PROBLEMS

6–29. Robert Miller, CPA, is examining the financial statements of the Limestone Sales Corporation, which recently installed an off-line electronic computer. The following comments have been extracted from Mr. Miller's notes on computer operations and the processing and control of shipping notices and customer invoices:

To minimize inconvenience Limestone converted without change its existing data processing system, which utilized tabulating equipment. The computer company supervised the conversion and has provided training to all computer department employees (except key punch operators) in systems design, operations, and programming.

Each computer run is assigned to a specific employee, who is responsible for making program changes, running the program, and answering questions. This procedure has the advantage of eliminating the need for records of computer operations because each employee is responsible for his own computer runs.

At least one computer department employee remains in the computer room during office hours, and only computer department employees have keys to the computer room.

System documentation consists of those materials furnished by the computer company—a set of record formats and program listings. These and the tape library are kept in a corner of the computer department.

The corporation considered the desirability of program controls but decided to retain the manual controls from its existing system.

Company products are shipped directly from public warehouses which forward shipping notices to general accounting. There a billing clerk enters the price of the item and accounts for the numerical sequence of shipping notices from each warehouse. The billing clerk also prepares daily adding machine tapes ("control tapes") of the units shipped and the unit prices.

Shipping notices and control tapes are forwarded to the computer department for key punching and processing. Extensions are made on the computer. Output consists of invoices (in six copies) and a daily sales register. The daily sales register shows the aggregate totals of units shipped and unit prices which the computer operator compares to the control tapes.

All copies of the invoice are returned to the billing clerk. The clerk mails three copies to the customer, forwards one copy to the warehouse, maintains one copy in a numerical file, and retains one copy in an open invoice file that serves as a detail accounts receivable record.

Required:

Describe weaknesses in internal control over information and data flows and the procedures for processing shipping notices and customer invoices, and recommend improvements in these controls and processing procedures. Organize your answer sheets as follows:

Weakness	Recommended improvement

(AICPA, adapted)

6–30.   Robert Hill, CPA, has examined the financial statements of Bell Products Company for several years and is making preliminary plans for
the audit of the year ended June 30, 1975. For this examination
Mr. Hill plans to use a set of generalized computer audit programs.
The EDP manager for Bell Products Company has agreed to prepare
special tapes of data from company records for the CPA's use with
the generalized programs.

   The following information is applicable to Mr. Hill's examination
of Bell's accounts payable and related procedures:

(1)   The formats of pertinent tapes appear on page 205.
(2)   The following monthly runs are prepared:
    a)   Cash disbursements by check number.
    b)   Outstanding payables.
    c)   Purchase journals arranged (1) by account charged and
        (2) by vendor.
(3)   Vouchers and supporting invoices, receiving reports and purchase
order copies are filed by vendor code. Purchase orders and checks
are filed numerically.
(4)   Company records are maintained on magnetic tapes. All tapes
are stored in a restricted area within the computer room. A
grandfather-father-son policy is followed for retaining and safeguarding tape files.

Required:

a)   Explain the grandfather-father-son policy. Describe how files could
be reconstructed when this policy is used.
b)   Discuss whether company policies for retaining and safeguarding
the tape files provide adequate protection against losses of data.
c)   Describe the controls that the CPA should maintain over:
    (1)   Preparing the special tape.
    (2)   Processing the special tape with the generalized computer
        audit programs.
d)   Prepare a schedule for the EDP manager outlining the data that
should be included on the special tape for the CPA's examination
of accounts payable and related procedures. This schedule should
show the:
    (1)   Client tape from which the item should be extracted.
    (2)   Name of the item of data.
    (Note: The schedule may be headed as shown below; preliminary
work in completing the schedule is also shown.)

BELL PRODUCTS COMPANY

SCHEDULE OF DATA TO BE RETAINED ON THE SPECIAL TAPE

Source—client tape	Item of data
Master file—vendor name	Vendor code
	Vendor name
Transaction file—expense detail	

(AICPA, adapted)

MASTER FILE — VENDOR NAME

Vendor Code	Rec'd Type	Space	Blank	Vendor Name	Blank	Card Code 100

MASTER FILE — VENDOR ADDRESS

Vendor Code	Rec'd Type	Space	Blank	Address—Line 1	Address—Line 2	Address—Line 3	Blank	Card Code 120

TRANSACTION FILE — EXPENSE DETAIL

Vendor Code	Rec'd Type	Voucher Number	Batch	Block	Voucher Number	Voucher Date	Vendor Code	Invoice Date	Due Date	Invoice Number	Purchase Order Number	Debit Account	Pd Type	Product Code	Blank	Amount	Quantity	Card Code 160

TRANSACTION FILE — PAYMENT DETAIL

Vendor Code	Rec'd Type	Voucher Number	Batch	Block	Voucher Number	Voucher Date	Vendor Code	Invoice Date	Due Date	Invoice Number	Purchase Order Number	Check Number	Check Date	Blank	Amount	Blank	Card Code 170

6–31.   You will be examining for the first time the financial statements of Central Savings and Loan Association for the year ending December 31. The CPA firm which examined the association's financial statements for the prior year issued an unqualified audit report.

At the beginning of the current year, the association installed an on-line, real-time computer system. Each teller in the association's main office and seven branch offices has an on-line input-output terminal. Customers' mortgage payments and savings account deposits and withdrawals are recorded in the accounts by the computer from data input by the teller at the time of the transaction. The teller keys the proper account by account number and enters the information in the terminal keyboard to record the transaction. The accounting department at the main office has both punched card and typewriter input-output devices. The computer is housed at the main office.

Required:

You would expect the association to have certain internal controls in effect because an on-line real-time computer system is employed. List the internal controls which should be in effect solely because this system is employed, classifying them as:

a)   Those controls pertaining to input of information.

b)   All other types of computer controls. (AICPA, adapted)

6–32.   Home Products Company, a drug manufacturer, has the following system for billing and recording accounts receivable:

(1)   An incoming customer's purchase order is received in the order department by a clerk who prepares a prenumbered company sales order form in which is inserted the pertinent information, such as the customer's name and address, customer's account number, quantity, and items ordered. After the sales order has been prepared, the customer's purchase order is stapled to it.

(2)   The sales order form is then passed to the credit department for credit approval. Rough approximations of the billing values of the orders are made in the credit department for those accounts on which credit limitations are imposed. After investigation, approval of credit is noted on the form.

(3)   Next the sales order form is passed to the billing department, where a clerk types the customer's invoice on a billing machine that cross-multiplies the number of items and the unit price, then adds the automatically extended amounts for the total amount of the invoice. The billing clerk determines the unit prices for the items from a list of billing prices.

The billing machine has registers that automatically accumulate daily totals of customer account numbers and invoice amounts to provide "hash" totals and control amounts. These totals, which are inserted in a daily record book, serve as predetermined batch totals for verification of computer inputs.

The billing is done on prenumbered, continuous, carbon-interleaved forms having the following designations:

a)   "Customer's copy."

b)   "Sales department copy," for information purposes.

c)   "File copy."

d) "Shipping department copy," which serves as a shipping order. Bills of lading are also prepared as carbon copy by-products of the invoicing procedure.

(4) The shipping department copy of the invoice and the bills of lading are then sent to the shipping department. After the order has been shipped, copies of the bill of lading are returned to the billing department. The shipping department copy of the invoice is filed in the shipping department.

(5) In the billing department, one copy of the bill of lading is attached to the customer's copy of the invoice and both are mailed to the customer. The other copy of the bill of lading, together with the sales order form, is then stapled to the invoice file copy and filed in invoice numerical order.

(6) A key punch machine is connected to the billing machine so that punched cards are created during the preparation of the invoices. The punched cards then become the means by which the sales data are transmitted to a computer.

The punched cards are fed to the computer in batches. One day's accumulation of cards comprises a batch. After the punched cards have been processed by the computer, they are placed in files and held for about two years.

Required:

List the procedures that a CPA would employ in his examination of his selected audit samples of the company's:

a) Typed invoices, including the source documents.

b) Punched cards.

(The listed procedures should be limited to the verification of the sales data being fed into the computer. Do not carry the procedures beyond the point at which the cards are ready to be fed to the computer.) (AICPA)

7

Evidence—what kind and how much?

THE FINANCIAL STATEMENTS of a business constitute representations by management as to the financial position, operating results and changes in financial position of the business. An audit report, on the other hand, is an expression of opinion by an independent expert on the fairness of the client's financial statements. Although in some engagements the auditor may participate in the preparation of the financial statements, the completed statements are nonetheless the statements of the client. The role of the auditor is that of an independent professional critic who investigates, analyzes, and evaluates the information underlying the statements as a means of reaching a conclusion as to their fairness.

Auditor's opinion based on evidence

Before an auditor can express an opinion on financial statements, he must have evidence that—

a) The items in the financial statements are supported by the balances in the ledger accounts.

b) The balances in the ledger accounts summarize correctly the numerous debit and credit entries.

c) These debit and credit entries in the accounts represent proper accounting interpretation of all the transactions entered into by the business.

In the audit of a company using a traditional manual accounting

208

system, this chain of evidence extends from documents describing individual transactions through the books of original entry to ledger accounts, and from ledger accounts to financial statements. For a company using electronic data processing, the form of the records will differ, but the chain of evidence linking business transactions to financial statements is still essential to permit verification by the auditor. The making of an audit may be thought of as the process of gathering and evaluating sufficient evidence to provide an adequate basis for expression of an opinion on financial statements.

Auditing procedures—a means of gathering evidence

The scope paragraph of the short-form audit report tells in very concise language what the auditor has done to develop a basis for his opinion:

Our examination was made in accordance with generally accepted auditing standards, and accordingly included such tests of the accounting records and such other auditing procedures as we considered necessary in the circumstances.

Why does the auditor make "tests of the accounting records"? The purpose is to gather evidence. We need evidence that transactions have been properly analyzed and recorded, evidence of arithmetical accuracy in the records, and evidence that the work of summarizing the accounts and preparing the statements has been performed accurately in accordance with generally accepted accounting principles.

Why does the auditor carry out "other auditing procedures"? Again, the purpose is to gather evidence. We need evidence by physical inspection that the assets listed on the balance sheet actually exist and are owned by the client, evidence that all liabilities owed by the client are included in the financial statements, and evidence from banks, customers, and other sources outside the business that will tend to substantiate the evidence gathered from the accounting records.

Evidence needed for material items

The purpose of an audit is to enable the auditor to express an opinion on the financial statements *as a whole.* It follows that the auditor should gather evidence on the material items in the statements—those items of sufficient size and importance to have a significant bearing on the statements viewed as a whole. The more material an item, the greater the need for evidence of its validity. The concept of materiality was defined in Chapter 1 as a state of relative importance, and the point made that an asset of $5,000 might be a material item in a small company but quite immaterial on the statements of a large corporation.

If an item is definitely not material, the auditor may be quite undisturbed over the fact that its treatment in the accounts violates accounting principles. As a somewhat extreme example, consider the audit of a motion-picture theater: the inventory of popcorn on hand would probably not be of material amount, and the auditor would not care whether this inventory was listed as an asset or charged directly to expense when purchased. The experienced auditor is always careful to avoid making an issue of an inconsequential matter.

Quantity and quality of evidence

The AICPA Committee on Auditing Procedure in defining standards of field work has stated:

> **Sufficient competent evidential matter** is to be obtained through inspection, observation, inquiries and confirmations to afford a reasonable basis for an opinion regarding the financial statements under examination.

This standard goes further than a mere requirement that the auditor gather evidence as a basis for his opinion; the evidence gathered must be **sufficient** and **competent**. The term "sufficient" relates to the quantity or amount of evidence to be gathered; the word "competent" signifies the quality, the dependability, and the conclusiveness of the evidence. "How much evidence is sufficient" and "what evidence is competent" are questions to be answered by the auditor. This standard of field work can be applied only through the exercise of his professional judgment. The necessity of continuous exercise of judgment by auditors is one of the factors that make auditing a profession comparable to the older professional callings of law and medicine.

Some types of evidence are far superior to other types. A count of currency and coins on hand, for example, is stronger evidence of the existence of a petty cash fund than is the mere statement by an employee of the client that the fund exists and is intact. A small quantity of evidence of excellent quality may form a better basis for an opinion than a large quantity of evidence of lesser quality. To reach a decision on the quantity of evidence needed will usually require an evaluation of the quality of the various types of available evidence. The source of evidence is an important consideration to the auditor in evaluating its quality; therefore it is helpful to classify the various types of evidence according to source.

Types of evidence

A fuller understanding of audit field work may be gained by a brief consideration of the more important types of evidence gathered by the auditor as a basis for his opinion. The types of evidence to be discussed are as follows:

1. Internal control.
2. Physical evidence.
3. Documentary evidence.
   a) Documentary evidence created outside the organization and transmitted directly to the auditor.
   b) Documentary evidence created outside the organization and held by the client.
   c) Documentary evidence created within the organization.
4. Ledgers and journals.
5. Comparisons and ratios.
6. Computations.
7. Oral evidence.

Internal control as evidence

An adequate system of internal control promotes accuracy and reliability in accounting data. Errors are quickly and automatically brought to light by the built-in proofs and cross-checks inherent in the system. Consequently, if the auditor finds that the business has a carefully devised system of internal control and that practices prescribed by management are being consistently followed in day-to-day operations, he will regard the existence of this system of internal control as strong evidence of the validity of the amounts in the financial statements.

In verifying the financial statements by working back through the accounting records, it is not practicable for the auditor to examine every invoice, check, or other piece of documentary evidence. The solution lies in a study of the methods and procedures by which the company carries on its accounting processes. If these procedures are well designed and consistently followed, the end results in the form of financial statements will be valid. The auditor's approach is, therefore, to study and evaluate the system of internal control, including in his study a series of tests to satisfy himself that the company's accounting procedures are actually working as intended. Much of the auditor's professional skill lies in his ability to evaluate the effectiveness of various control devices and to select the appropriate tests to prove the agreement of the financial statements with the underlying accounting records.

The adequacy of the system of internal control is a major factor in determining how much evidence the auditor will need to gather from documents, records, inquiries, and other sources. The stronger the internal control, the less evidence of other nature that will be required as a basis for the auditor's opinion. When internal control is weak, the auditor must gather a correspondingly greater amount of evidence of other kinds.

Physical evidence

Actual inspection or count of certain types of assets is the best evidence of their physical existence. The amount of cash on hand is verified by counting; notes receivable, marketable securities, and inventories are also examined and counted. The existence of property and equipment such as automobiles, buildings, office equipment, and factory machinery may also be established by physical inspection.

At first thought, it might seem that physical examination of an asset would be conclusive verification, but this is often not true. For example, if the cash on hand to be counted by the auditor includes checks received from customers, the making of a count provides no assurance that all of the checks will prove to be collectible when deposited. There is also the possibility that one or more worthless checks may have been created deliberately by a dishonest employee as a means of concealing from the auditor the existence of a cash shortage.

The physical inspection of inventory may also leave some important questions unanswered. The quality and condition of merchandise or of work in process are vital in determining salability. If the goods counted by the auditor contain hidden defects or are obsolete, a mere counting of units does not substantiate the dollar value shown on the balance sheet.

ILLUSTRATIVE CASE. During his observation of the physical inventory of a company manufacturing costly aircraft instruments, an auditor counted more than a hundred instruments of a given type, each of which had cost several hundred dollars to manufacture. After the inventory taking had been completed, the auditor was informed by the client that these instruments were defective and could not be sold. The defective instruments were identical in appearance with other satisfactory instruments.

There are many similar situations in which a physical inspection and count by the auditor verifies the quantity but not the quality of an asset. The auditor does not claim to be an expert in judging the quality of materials. His responsibility for the detection of shortcomings in quality of goods is much less than his responsibility for accuracy in quantities. Since he examines such widely differing businesses as breweries, mines, and jewelry stores, it is not possible for him to become expert in appraising the products of all his clients. However, he should be alert to any clues which raise a doubt as to the quality or condition of inventories.

In the case of plant and equipment, physical inspection establishes the existence of the asset but gives no proof of ownership. A fleet of automobiles used by salesmen and company executives, for example, might be leased rather than owned—or if owned might be subject to a mortgage.

In summary, the physical examination of an asset implies identification of the thing being examined, determination of quantity, and at least an effort to determine the quality or genuineness of the article. It does not establish ownership. Physical evidence is available only for the asset elements in the financial statements. Although physical evidence is important in the verification of a number of assets, it must generally be supplemented by other types of evidence. For some types of assets such as accounts receivable or intangible assets, there may be no opportunity to gather physical evidence.

Documentary evidence

The most important type of evidence relied upon by auditors consists of documents. The worth of a document as evidence depends in part upon whether it was created within the company (for example, a sales invoice) or came from outside the company, as in the case of a vendor's invoice. Some documents created within the company (checks, for example) are sent outside the organization for endorsement and processing; because of this critical review by outsiders these documents are regarded as very reliable evidence.

In appraising the reliability of documentary evidence, the auditor should consider whether the document is of a type which could easily be forged or created in its entirety by a dishonest employee. A stock certificate evidencing an investment in marketable securities is usually elaborately engraved and would be most difficult to falsify. On the other hand, a note receivable may be created by anyone in a moment merely by filling in the blank spaces in one of the standard note forms available at any bank.

Documentary evidence created outside the organization and transmitted directly to the auditor. The best quality of documentary evidence consists of documents created by independent agencies outside the client's organization and transmitted directly to the auditor without passing through the client's hands. For example, in the verification of accounts receivable, the customer is requested by the client to write directly to the auditor to confirm the amount owed to the auditor's client. To assure that the customer's reply comes directly to the auditor and not to the client, the auditor will enclose with the confirmation request a return envelope addressed to his (the auditor's) office. If the replies were addressed to the auditor at the client's place of business, an opportunity would exist for someone in the client's organization to intercept the customer's letter and alter the amount of indebtedness reported, or even destroy the letter.

Similar precautions are taken in the verification of cash in bank. The client will arrange for the bank to advise the auditor directly in writing of the amount the client has on deposit.

Other types of documents created outside the client's organization and transmitted directly to the auditor include letters from the client's attorneys describing any pending litigation; listings of insurance in force provided by the client's insurance broker; and representations from the client's actuaries concerning the propriety of the client's pension cost. In each case, the client requests the outsider to furnish the information directly to the auditor in an envelope addressed to the auditor's office.

Documentary evidence created outside the organization and held by the client.   Many of the externally created documents referred to by the auditor will, however, be in the client's possession. Examples include bank statements, vendors' invoices and statements, notes receivable, contracts, customers' purchase orders, and stock and bond certificates. In deciding how much reliance to place upon this type of evidence, the auditor should consider whether the document is of a type that could be easily created or altered by someone in the client's employ. The auditor should be particularly cautious in accepting as evidence any documents which have been altered in any way. Of course an alteration may have been made by the company originating the document to correct an accidental error. In general, however, business concerns do not send out documents marred by errors and corrections. The auditor cannot afford to overlook the possibility that an alteration on a document may have been made deliberately to misstate the facts and to mislead auditors or others who relied upon the document.

In pointing out the possibility that externally created documents in the client's possession *might* have been forged or altered, it is not intended to discredit this type of evidence. Externally created documents in the possession of the client are used extensively by auditors and are considered, in general, as a stronger type of evidence than documents created by the client.

Documentary evidence created within the organization.   No doubt the most dependable single piece of documentary evidence created within the client's organization is a paid check. The check bears the endorsement of the payee and a perforation or stamp indicating payment by the bank. Because of this review and processing of a check by outsiders, the auditor will usually look upon a paid check as a strong type of evidence. He may rely upon the paid check as evidence that an asset was acquired at a given cost, or as a proof that a liability was paid, or an expense incurred. Of course the amount of the check might have been raised by an alteration subsequent to its payment, but protection against this possibility is afforded through the preparation of bank reconciliations and also through comparison of paid checks with the entries on the bank statement and in the cash payment records.

Most companies place great emphasis on proper internal control of cash disbursements by such devices as the use of serial numbers on checks, signature (or two signatures) by responsible officials, and separation of the check-writing function from the accounting function. This emphasis on internal control over cash payments lends additional assurance that a paid check is a valid document.

Most documents created within the business represent a lower quality of evidence than a paid check because they circulate within the company only and do not receive critical review by an outsider. Examples of internally created documents which do not leave the client's possession are sales invoices and sales summaries, shipping notices, purchase orders, receiving reports, credit memoranda, trial balances, and a variety of operating and financial reports prepared for use by management. Of course the original copy of a sales invoice or purchase order is sent to the customer or supplier, but the carbon copy available for the auditor's inspection has not left the client's possession.

The degree of reliance to be placed on documents created and used only within the organization depends on the adequacy of the system of internal control. If the accounting procedures are so designed that a document prepared by one person must be critically reviewed by another, and if all documents are serially numbered and all numbers in the series accounted for, these documents may represent reasonably good evidence. Adequate internal control will also provide for extensive subdivision of duties so that no one employee handles a transaction from beginning to end. An employee who maintains records or creates documents such as credit memoranda should not have access to cash. Under these conditions there is no incentive for an employee to falsify a document since the employee creating documents does not have custody of assets.

On the other hand, if internal control is weak, the auditor cannot place much reliance on documentary evidence created within the organization and not reviewed by outsiders. There is the danger not only of fictitious documents created to cover theft by an employee but also the possibility, however remote, that management is purposely presenting misleading financial statements and has prepared false supporting documents for the purpose of deceiving the auditor.

One important type of internally created document is the letter of representations prepared by an officer of the client company at the auditor's request setting forth certain facts about the company's financial position or operations. For example, the controller of the company under audit may be asked to write a letter stating that to the best of his knowledge all liabilities of the company are reflected in the accounts. The auditor's purpose in requesting such a formal written statement is to bring to light any unrecorded liabilities, and also to impress upon management its primary responsibility for the financial statements. A document of this nature may serve a useful function, but it does not relieve the auditor of his duty to verify management's representations. The financial statements themselves constitute a representation by management; a letter signed by management as to the inclusiveness of the liability figure shown in the balance sheet is merely a further representation. Consequently, a letter of representations by management does not rank very high in our scale for evaluation of various types of evidence.

Ledgers and journals as evidence

When an auditor attempts to verify an amount in the financial statements by tracing it back through the accounting records, he will ordinarily carry this tracing process through the ledgers to the journals and on back to such basic documentary evidence as a paid check, invoice, or other original papers. To some extent, however, the ledger accounts and the journals constitute worthwhile evidence in themselves.

The dependability of ledgers and journals as evidence is indicated by the extent of internal control covering their preparation. Whenever possible, subsidiary ledgers for receivables, payables, and plant equipment should be maintained by persons not responsible for the general ledger. All general journal entries should be approved in writing by the controller or other official. If ledgers and journals are produced by an electronic data processing system, the safeguards described in Chapter 6 should be in effect. When controls of this type exist and the records appear to be well maintained, the auditor may regard the ledgers and journals as affording considerable support for the financial statements.

As a specific example, an auditor wishes to determine that the sale of certain old factory machinery during the year under audit was properly recorded. By reference to the subsidiary ledger for plant and equipment, he might ascertain that the depreciation accumulated during the years the machine was owned agreed with the amount cleared out of the Accumulated Depreciation account at the time of sale. He might also note that the original cost of the machine as shown on the plant ledger card agreed with the credit to the Plant and Equipment control account when the machine was sold, and that the proceeds from sale were entered in the cash receipts journal. Assuming that the plant ledger, general ledger, and the cash receipts journal are independently maintained by three different employees, or are produced by an electronic data processing department with effective internal control, the agreement of these records offers considerable evidence that the sale of the machine was a legitimate transaction and properly recorded. Whether the auditor should go beyond this evidence and examine original documents such as the bill of sale or a work order authorizing the sale would depend upon the relative importance of the amount involved and upon other circumstances of the audit.

Comparisons and ratios as evidence

Comparison of the amount of each asset, liability, revenue, and expense with the corresponding balance for the preceding period is a simple means of spotting any significant changes. Any unusual changes from year to year should be explored until the auditor is satisfied that a valid reason exists for the variation in amount.

In addition to comparing dollar amounts from year to year, the auditor will also study the percentage relationships of various items on the statements. For example, an auditor noticed that uncollectible accounts expense which had been running about 1 percent of net sales for several years had increased in the current year to 8 percent of net sales. This significant variation caused him to make a very careful investigation of all accounts written off during the year and those presently past due. Most of the "uncollectible" accounts examined were found to be fictitious, and the cashier–bookkeeper then admitted that he had created these accounts to cover up his abstraction of cash receipts.

Comparison of the gross profit on sales percentages from year to year affords a means of verifying the overall reasonableness of the cost of sales and of the ending inventory. The relative proportions of the various types of inventory (raw materials, work in process, and finished goods) should also be related to the rate of production and the trend of sales. Other useful comparisons are the relationship of accounts receivable changes to sales trends, actual revenue and expenses versus budgeted amounts, and the comparison of accounts payable changes to cost of sales trends. These overall tests and comparisons supplement the detailed verification of individual accounts and provide assurance that the auditor will not "fail to see the forest because of the trees."

Computations as evidence

A form of evidence closely related to the comparisons and ratios described above consists of calculations made independently by the auditor to prove the arithmetical accuracy of the client's records. In its simplest form, this evidence might consist of footing a column of figures in a journal or ledger to prove the accuracy of the column total.

Calculations also provide evidence when the auditor tests the computation of the depreciation expense for the year, using rates adopted by the client, and thus proves the arithmetical accuracy of the depreciation expense entered in the accounts. If the company determines uncollectible accounts expense as a percentage of sales, or takes up profits on long-term contracts on the basis of percentage of completion, the results obtained by the client should be verified by means of independent calculations by the auditor. Other familiar examples in which the auditor's calculations provide important evidence are bonus plans and profit-sharing agreements with executives, rental agreements based on a percentage of sales, and provisions for federal and state income taxes.

Oral evidence

Throughout his examination the auditor will ask a great many questions of the officers and employees of the client's organization. A novice auditor is sometimes afraid to ask questions for fear that he will seem uninformed and inexperienced. Such an attitude is quite illogical; even the most experienced and competent auditor will ask a great many questions. These questions cover an endless range of topics—the location of records and documents, the reasons underlying an unusual accounting procedure, the probabilities of collecting a long past-due account receivable.

The answers which an auditor receives to these questions constitute another type of evidence. Generally, oral evidence is not sufficient in itself, but it may be useful in disclosing situations that require investigation or in corroborating other forms of evidence. For example, an auditor after making a careful analysis of all past-due accounts receivable will normally sit down with the credit manager and get his views on the prospects for collection of accounts considered doubtful. If the opinions of the credit manager are in accordance with the estimates of uncollectible accounts losses made independently by the auditor, this oral evidence will constitute significant support of the conclusions reached. In repeat examinations of a business, the auditor will be in a better position to evaluate the opinions of the credit manager based on how well his estimates in prior years have worked out.

In asking questions the auditor should be neither apologetic nor authoritarian. He is conducting the audit at the request of the client; consequently, it is in the client's own interest that all employees cooperate in providing any information they have which is needed by the auditor. On the other hand, the auditor should avoid a "police" attitude; he does not cross-examine employees or demand information. A deficiency in tact and courtesy will spell failure in public accounting work even faster than a deficiency in technical skill.

The cost of obtaining evidence

An auditor can no more disregard the cost of alternative auditing procedures than a store manager can disregard a difference in the costs of competing brands of merchandise. Cost is not the primary factor influencing the auditor in deciding what evidence should be obtained, but cost is always an important consideration.

The cost factor may preclude the gathering of the "ideal" form of evidence and necessitate the substitution of other forms of evidence which are of lesser quality yet still satisfactory. For example, assume that an auditor finds that his client has a large note receivable from a customer. What evidence should the auditor obtain to satisfy himself that the note is authentic and will be paid at maturity? One alternative is for the auditor to correspond directly with the customer and obtain written confirmation of the amount, maturity date, and other terms of the note. This confirmation is evidence that the customer issued the note and regards it as a valid obligation. Secondly, the auditor might test the collectibility of the note by obtaining a credit report on the customer from Dun & Bradstreet, Inc., or from a local credit association. He might also obtain copies of the customer's most recent financial statements, accompanied, if possible, by the opinion of an independent CPA. To carry our illustration to an extreme, the auditor might obtain permission to make an audit of the financial statements of the customer. The cost of conducting this separate audit could conceivably amount to more than the note receivable which the auditor wished to verify.

The point of this illustration is that the auditor does not always insist upon obtaining the strongest possible evidence. He does insist upon obtaining evidence which is adequate under the circumstances. The more material the item to be verified, the stronger the evidence required by the auditor, and the greater the cost he may be willing to incur in obtaining it.

Calculated risk

An auditor must be reasonably certain before he expresses an opinion; he is never completely certain. Every audit report he signs represents the taking of a calculated risk. However the existence and growth of worldwide, long-established public accounting firms is evidence that this factor of calculated risk can be accurately estimated and held within reasonable bounds. At the same time, the history of public accounting contains numerous cases in which accounting firms were forced to pay heavy damages because of the lack of adequate evidence to support the opinions they expressed. In some instances these losses and the attendant bad publicity brought an end to the firm's existence.

The independent public accountant who goes to an extreme in gathering evidence to support his opinion will price himself out of the market; the accountant who relies upon inferior or insufficient evidence as a basis for his opinion will as surely be eliminated from the scene through lawsuits filed by those who use his services and sustain losses thereby. For an auditor to steer a course between these two extremes requires the continued exercise of professional judgment.

Relative risk

Is the risk of misstatement, or of fraud, or of violation of accounting principles about the same in all audits? Certainly not. In certain situations, which the auditor must learn to recognize, the risk of substantial error and misstatement in the accounts and in the financial statements is far greater than in other audits. When relative risk is above normal, the auditor should demand more and better evidence than he would normally require as a basis for his opinion. The following examples illustrate some relatively high-risk auditing situations:

1. *Unsound financial condition.* A business operating at a loss or hard pressed to pay its creditors is more likely to postpone writing off worthless receivables or obsolete inventories of merchandise, or perhaps to "forget" to record a liability, than is a strong, well-financed, profitable company.
2. *Weak internal control.* The system of internal control is itself one of the more important types of evidence utilized by the auditor. Internal control may be weak or absent in certain areas of the client's affairs or throughout the business. In this situation the auditor is on notice to exercise added caution and to gather other forms of detailed evidence to compensate for the weakness in internal control. This topic has already received attention in the chapter devoted to internal control.
3. *Revision of income tax rates or regulations.* When income tax rates are suddenly raised significantly, the reaction of some businesses may be to look harder than ever for ways to minimize taxable income. The pressure of a heavy tax burden sometimes leads to the twisting of accounting principles and to interpretations of business transactions in a manner inconsistent with that of prior years. When any sharp change in tax rates or regulations is anticipated for the following year, an incentive exists for the client to shift income from one period to another.

The concept of relative risk may also be applied to the gathering of evidence on particular items in the financial statements. The very nature of some assets makes the risk of misstatement greater than for others. Assume that in a given business the asset of cash amounts to only half as much as the Buildings account. Does this relationship indicate that the auditor should spend only half as much time in the verification of cash as in the verification of the buildings? Cash is much more susceptible to theft than are plant and equipment, and the great number of cash transactions affords an opportunity for errors to be well hidden. The amount of audit time devoted to the verification of cash balances and of cash transactions during the year will generally be much greater in proportion to the dollar amounts involved than will be necessary for such assets as plant and equipment.

In some special audit engagements the auditor is aware in advance that fraud is suspected and that the records may include fictitious or altered entries. Perhaps the auditor has been engaged because of a dispute between partners, or because of dissatisfaction on the part of stockholders with the existing management. The risks involved in such engagements will cause the auditor to assign different weights to various types of evidence than he otherwise would.

ILLUSTRATIVE CASE. Bruce Henry, a resident of New York, owned a 90 percent stock interest in a California automobile agency. The other 10 percent of the stock was owned by James Barr, who also had a contract to act as general manager of the business. As compensation for his managerial services, Mr. Barr received a percentage of net income rather than a fixed salary. The reported net income in recent years had been large and increasing each year, with correspondingly larger payments to Mr. Barr as manager. However, during this period of reported rising income, the cash position of the business as shown by the balance sheet had been deteriorating rapidly. Working capital had been adequate when Mr. Barr took over as manager but was now critically low.

Mr. Henry, the majority stockholder in New York, was quite concerned over these trends. He was further disturbed by reports that Mr. Barr was spending a great deal of time in Las Vegas and that he had placed several relatives on the payroll of the automobile agency. Mr. Henry decided to engage a CPA to make an audit of the business. He explained fully to the CPA his doubts as to the fairness of the reported net income and his misgivings as to Mr. Barr's personal integrity. Mr. Henry added that he wished to buy Mr. Barr's stockholdings but first needed some basis for valuing the stock.

An audit initiated under these circumstances obviously called for a greater amount of evidence and a greater degree of caution by the auditor than would normally be required. Oral evidence from Mr. Barr could not be given much weight. Documents created within the business might very possibly have been falsified. In brief, the degree of risk was great, and the auditor's approach was modified to fit the circumstances. More evidence and more conclusive evidence was called for than in a more routine audit of an automobile agency.

The outcome of the audit in question was a disclosure of a gross overstatement of inventories and the reporting of numerous fictitious sales. Commission payments were also found to have been made to persons not participating in the business.

Evidence provided by subsequent events

The auditor's opinion about items in the financial statements may be considerably changed by subsequent events—those events occurring after the date of the balance sheet but prior to completion of the audit and issuance of the report. Evidence not available at the close of the period under audit often becomes available before the auditor finishes his field work and writes his report.

As an example let us assume that a client's accounts receivable at December 31 included one large account and numerous small ones. The large amount due from the major customer was regarded as good and collectible at the year-end, but during the course of the audit engagement the customer entered bankruptcy. As a result of this information, the auditor might have found it necessary to insist on an increase in the allowance for uncollectible accounts. The fact that the receivable from this customer was believed to be collectible at December 31 is no reason to ignore a change in the prospects for collection during the course of the audit.

Other examples of evidence coming into existence subsequent to the period under audit include the following:

1. Customers' checks included in the cash receipts of the last day of the year prove to be uncollectible and are charged back to the client's account by the bank. If the checks were material in amount, an adjustment of the December 31 cash balance may be necessary to exclude the checks now known to be uncollectible.
2. Rejection by inspectors of manufactured units. If inspectors reject an unusually large number of completed units leaving the client's assembly line in January, this situation indicates that a considerable part of the work-in-process inventory at December 31 consisted of defective units. Reduction of the year-end figure for work in process may be necessary.
3. A six-month note receivable held by the client which matured two weeks after the balance sheet date was dishonored by the maker. This evidence may justify a reduction in the carrying value of notes receivable as of the balance sheet date.
4. Settlement of a pending lawsuit during the course of the audit caused a large and unexpected cash payment by the client to become necessary. The settlement of the lawsuit constitutes evidence that a *real,* rather than a *contingent,* liability may have existed as of December 31, although there had been no admission of the obligation by the client nor any entry in the accounts to reflect such a liability.

The first three of the preceding examples may be regarded as falling into one specific class: events directly affecting amounts shown in the balance sheet. If the amounts involved in this category of subsequent events are material, the client should include them in the year-end financial statements.

The fourth example, that of a pending lawsuit settled after the balance sheet date by a ruling against the client, is essentially of the same category. The existence of a contingent liability in the form of a pending lawsuit was known at the balance sheet date; if the outcome of the suit becomes known during the course of the audit, disclosure is called for, and probably the most useful method of disclosure is to insert the liability in the balance sheet.

In summary, the first class of subsequent events includes those which provide additional evidence with respect to conditions that existed at the date of the balance sheet and affect the estimates inherent in the process of preparing financial statements. The effects of these subsequent events should be reflected in the financial statements for the period under audit.

Footnote disclosure of subsequent events

Having considered examples of subsequent events which should be included in the financial statements by revising dollar amounts, let us turn next to a second class of subsequent events which do not necessarily alter the financial position of the company as of the balance sheet date but may be significant in any appraisal of future prospects. In considering the following examples, assume that the event occurred after the balance sheet date but prior to completion of the audit field work and issuance of the report.

1. Plant and equipment seriously damaged by flood or earthquake.
2. Acquisition of competing company.
3. Loss on receivables resulting from a customer's major casualty.
4. Death of company treasurer in airplane crash.
5. Introduction of a new line of products.
6. Plant closed by a strike.
7. New labor contract.
8. Newspaper story that a large stockholder may launch a proxy fight to secure control of company.

Although these events may be significant in the future operations of the company and of interest to many who read the audited financial statements, none of these occurrences has any bearing on the results of the year under audit, and their bearing on future results is not easily determinable. The AICPA *Code of Professional Ethics* prohibits members from attesting to estimates of future earnings. Prophecies as to the effect of specific events on future operations may be equally inappropriate. The question facing the independent auditor is: Which, if any, of these events should be reflected in footnotes to the financial statements in order to achieve adequate informative disclosure?

It is generally agreed that substantial casualty losses, mergers and acquisitions, and other significant changes in a company's financial position or financial structure should be disclosed in footnotes. Otherwise the financial statements might be misleading rather than informative. Consequently, the first three of the preceding examples (major property loss, acquisition of a competing company, and significant loss on receivables resulting from customer's casualty) should be disclosed in notes to the financial statements. Ocassionally, such events may be so significant that supplementary pro forma financial data should be provided, giving effect to the events as though they had occurred as of the date of the balance sheet. On the other hand, nonaccounting matters such as management changes, product line changes, strikes, new labor contracts, and rumors of an impending proxy fight are not disclosed in footnotes unless particular circumstances make such information essential to the proper interpretation of the financial statements.

Footnotes are an integral part of the financial statements. Disclosure in a footnote of any events not essential to proper interpretation of the financial statements raises questions as to the reason for disclosure and creates a possibility that misleading inferences may be drawn. Some subsequent events may be regarded as "favorable" and others as "unfavorable," but not all readers of the statements will agree as to these qualities. Conceivably, the financial statements might be made misleading rather than more informative if disclosure were made of "favorable" events but not of other "unfavorable" events, or vice versa. Primary responsibility for disclosure of significant subsequent events rests with management, just as primary responsibility for the financial statements rests with management. Management has other means of disclosure apart from the financial statements, such as the president's letter to stockholders which usually appears in the annual report, or in unaudited quarterly statements and news releases.

The auditor's responsibility for subsequent events

In *Statement on Auditing Procedure No. 47* the AICPA's Committee on Auditing Procedure outlined the auditor's responsibility for subsequent events. During the period subsequent to the balance sheet date the auditor should always determine that proper "cutoffs" of cash receipts and disbursements, sales and purchases have been made, and should examine data to aid in the evaluation of assets and liabilities as of the balance sheet date. In addition, the auditor should—

1. Review the latest available interim financial statements, and minutes of directors', stockholders', and appropriate committees' meetings.
2. Inquire about matters dealt with at meetings for which minutes are not available.

3. Inquire of appropriate client officials as to contingent liabilities, changes in capital stock, debt or working capital, changes in the current status of items estimated in the financial statements under audit, or any unusual adjustments made subsequent to the balance sheet date.

4. Obtain a letter from the client's attorney describing pending litigation and other contingent liabilities.

5. Obtain a letter of representations from the client.

Throughout the course of his field work, the auditor should maintain an alert attitude as to the impact of current happenings on the financial position of the client at the balance sheet date.

Generally, the independent auditor's responsibility for evidence as to subsequent events extends only to the date he completes the audit field work. However, even after completing normal audit procedures, the auditor has the responsibility to evaluate subsequent events which come to his attention. Specific rules have been established with respect to audits relating to registration statements for the issuance of securities; these rules impose a greater degree of responsibility on the auditor for disclosure of subsequent events than is generally recognized for annual audits. The provisions of the Securities Act of 1933 extend the period of responsibility to the effective date of the registration statement—a date often many weeks after the normal audit field work has been completed. Accordingly, for SEC registrations, the auditor should conduct an additional review of subsequent events on a date reasonably close to the effective date of the registration statement. *Statement on Auditing Procedure No. 47* provides guidelines for this review.

TESTS AND SAMPLES

Reliance by the auditor upon tests and samples

For the auditor to examine every entry in the accounting records and every document supporting those entries would be tremendously costly—so expensive in fact that probably very few companies would feel that they could afford to be audited. Fortunately, such an item-by-item type of examination is quite unnecessary. The auditor's objective is to obtain sufficient evidence to support his opinion as to the fairness of the financial statements. The accepted approach in obtaining this evidence includes the two following steps:

a) An evaluation of the system of internal control.
b) Tests of the data supporting the financial statements.

Recognition of these two distinct steps is helpful in planning and administering an audit program; however, we must also recognize that in practice an audit consists of an intermixture of these two phases of work rather than of two neatly divided compartments. Although the evaluation of internal control will in general precede the verification of the amounts in the financial statements and will indicate the necessary scope of that verification, much of the work done by the auditor serves the dual purpose of indicating the adequacy of internal control and at the same time of verifying amounts shown in the statements. Sampling procedures are useful in both areas.

To test accounting data means to examine a portion or sample of the financial transactions to determine quality, genuineness, and freedom from error. By examining a representative sample of a large homogeneous group of transactions, the auditor may draw conclusions concerning the entire group. The sampling process signifies more than examination of a portion of the available data; it indicates that a portion of a group of transactions is examined for the purpose of estimating the characteristics of the entire group. For example, assume that 5,000 sales invoices were issued during the period under audit. These 5,000 invoices may be called the universe or population to be tested. Let us assume further that the auditor decides to test these invoices by examining carefully a sample of 200. The 5,000 invoices are serially numbered, and the auditor selects every 25th invoice in the series to comprise the 200-unit sample. It is highly probable that the proportion of errors found in the 200 units selected will correspond closely to the proportion of errors present in the population of 5,000 invoices; the auditor can therefore form an opinion as to the reliability of the sales invoices in their entirety. The cost of examining the sample is, of course, much less than the cost of examining the entire population.

The terms "universe" and "population" as used in auditing may deserve further illustration. All items of one type constitute a universe or population. All checks issued during the year comprise a universe; and all entries in the sales journal form another universe.

The theory of probability tells us that a sample selected from a large series of similar items will tend to show the same characteristics that would be found in an examination of the entire series. The larger the sample, the greater the tendency for the characteristics to correspond to those of the universe. For example, a sample of 200 drawn from a universe of 1,000 will give a more accurate picture than will a sample of only 100. It is erroneous to assume, however, the correspondence between the sample and the universe follows the percentage relationship of the items tested to the universe. As an illustration of this point, assume that we have two identical populations: one consisting of 5,000 items and the other of 50,000 items. If a sample of 500 is adequate for the small population, it may also be adequate for the larger population. A sample of 500 (1 percent) drawn from the 50,000 population may give approximately as accurate a picture as does the sample of 500 (10 percent) drawn from the population of 5,000.

Typical examples of the use of sampling procedures in verifying amounts in the financial statements include the verification of accounts receivable and inventories. The validity of accounts receivable may be determined by direct written communication with a selected group of customers. Inventories may be verified by test counting a portion of the goods, and by test checking a number of prices, extensions, and footings.

Selecting audit samples

In present-day practice the determination of which transactions are to be tested and the extent of the testing is primarily the responsibility of the accountant in charge of each engagement. There are no generally accepted percentages, tables, or rules for selecting audit samples; rather, the transactions to be examined are selected by the auditor based upon his knowledge of the client's system of internal control, the relative materiality of the transactions, and the types of errors found on the previous or the current engagement.

Two basic methods for selecting samples of a client's transactions are used by independent auditors. These techniques, known as *judgment sampling* and *statistical sampling,* have both been approved by the AICPA, but the choice of which method to apply in a specific audit has been left to the independent auditor. When properly applied, both methods are in accordance with generally accepted auditing standards. In judgment sampling, the size and composition of each audit sample is predetermined by the auditor without reference to other sources. In statistical sampling, the auditor selects desired levels of risk and precision and estimates the expected number of exceptions for each sample. He then refers to statistical sampling tables for the appropriate sample size and, in some cases, for the specific transactions to be included in the sample. The following sections of this chapter discuss judgment sampling in detail; statistical sampling is considered further in Chapter 8.

Judgment block samples

A block sample usually includes all items in a selected time period, numerical sequence, or alphabetical sequence. For example, in verifying cash disbursements, the auditor might decide to examine all checks issued for the months of April and December, or all checks numbered 3,581 through 3,880. In the audit of accounts receivable, all accounts with customers in the alphabetical section from L to N might be examined.

The same months or alphabetical sections should not be chosen for sampling in successive audits, and the auditor should be careful not to indicate in advance the blocks to be sampled. On the other hand, many auditors feel that the last month of the audit period requires testing to a greater extent than other months because of the likelihood of irregularities being introduced just prior to the closing of the books.

A weakness of the block sample is that it ignores changes in the client's accounting personnel during the period under audit. A bookkeeper or cashier who worked for three or four months during the year may have made numerous errors which will not be disclosed if the block sample happens to be taken from other months. However, block samples are especially effective in detecting lapping activities (fraud involving delay in entering cash receipts) by persons handling cash and cash records; in addition, block sampling is a convenient process and is widely used by auditors. From a statistical sampling viewpoint, block sampling is deficient in that all items in the population do not stand an equal chance of being chosen.

Judgment random samples

When a random sample is used, every item in the universe has an equal chance of being selected. Let us say, for example, that the auditor wishes to select a random sample of 100 paid checks from a universe of 2,000. A convenient method of selecting the sample would be to draw every 20th check in the series; this process is known as *systematic selection*. Audit instructions such as "verify the footings on every 10th ledger account" or "test computation of pay for every 20th employee on the payroll" are common examples of systematic sampling. Although these methods are usually satisfactory, they will not produce random samples if the population being tested is not in a random sequence.

Judgment stratified sampling

Stratified sampling means classifying the population into strata or subgroups, with each subgroup to be samples independently. The stratification principle is often applied to block sampling. For example, the audit instruction for a stratified block sample might be worded as follows: "Examine all April sales invoices for amounts of $100 or more, plus 5 percent of April invoices under $100." This method of sampling has the advantage of assuring that all material items are accurate. In many cases the auditor, by selecting the large items, can account for perhaps 70 percent or 80 percent of the dollar balance in an account by examining 10 percent or less of the total items comprising the account.

If the client's staff is aware that the auditor makes a habit of looking only at items of large dollar amount, carelessness or fraud in the handling of small transactions may be encouraged. There is also the danger that what appears to be a small item may actually be an incorrectly recorded large item. It is often desirable for the auditor to supplement his examination of all large items by a random sampling of small items.

Evaluation of errors found by sampling

Regardless of the method of choosing a sample, every item included in the sample should be examined with the greatest care. In determining the number of erroneous items in a sample, a definition of an error is necessary. For example, in the examination of a sample of 100 sales invoices, one invoice was found to be priced at $1 per unit of product instead of the correct price of $10 per unit. On another invoice the customer's name appeared as "B. E. Brown" rather than the correct name of "B. D. Brown." Obviously these two "errors" are not of the same significance, although both raise a question as to the adequacy of the internal review of invoices. The error in pricing may even indicate the presence of fraud. No matter how errors are defined, the auditor must exercise professional judgment in evaluating the significance and cause of each error found in the sampling process. He must constantly raise such questions as:

1. Does this error indicate a lack of important internal controls?
2. Does this error indicate that internal controls prescribed by management are not being followed in actual practice?
3. Does this error suggest fraudulent intent?

If the errors disclosed by the sample are numerous, serious in nature, or suggestive of fraud, the auditor may decide to extend the scope of his testing, or even to make a 100 percent verification of the class of transactions in question. The sampling technique does not replace the need for judgment and experience on the part of the auditor.

Size of judgment audit samples

When internal control is strong and the accounting records and procedures are well designed and maintained, audit samples can reasonably be much smaller than in less favorable situations. Today's better kept records are more conducive to sampling that those of yesterday. Large corporations with a great volume of transactions typically have good systems of internal control, machine-kept records, extensive subdivision of duties among employees, and a competent internal auditing staff. Under these circumstances, the sampling of many classes of transactions is often limited to less than 1 percent of the items. Incidentally, sampling is standard practice for the internal auditor as well as for the independent auditor.

It is not possible to suggest the proper size of judgment samples for various parts of an audit. The proper size for a sample depends upon all the circumstances of the individual audit.

Sampling and the detection of fraud

As indicated in Chapter 3, one consequence of relying upon tests rather than making a complete examination of all transactions is that fraudulent transactions may not be disclosed by the audit. However, this argument does not invalidate the testing process. If fraud is widespread in the accounts or material in amount, it is probable that the samples examined by the auditor will disclose the irregularities because samples are chosen with a view to materiality of amounts and to the strength of internal control. Minor isolated instances of fraud may not be disclosed by tests, but the discovery of small infrequent irregularities is not a primary objective of an audit.

Working rules for audit tests   *Know for test.*

For the purpose of emphasis, certain points covered in the preceding discussion of audit tests may be restated in the form of guidelines, as follows:

Important (Summary)

1. The extent of testing and the size of samples depend upon the system of internal control. When internal control is weak, larger samples are required than under strong systems of internal control.

2. The extent of testing is also influenced by the relative risk considered to exist in a particular audit engagement. Suspected fraud and weak financial condition, for example, indicate need for an increased amount of testing.

3. A desirable quality in a sample is representativeness; representative samples will give an accurate picture of the population from which they are drawn.

4. By including all large transactions in the sample, the auditor is able to verify most of the dollar amounts shown on the financial statements in comparatively short time. This purposeful selection of large items, however, does not lead to representative samples.

5. Every item in the sample should be studied intensively. When audit decisions are based upon a small proportion of the total transactions, great care must be taken to interpret correctly any irregularities in the sample.

6. Audits based on test checks will not necessarily detect isolated cases

of fraud. However, widespread or continued falsification of the accounts will probably be detected.

7. Drawing conclusions based on samples involves a degree of risk; the conclusion reached may be erroneous if the sample is not representative, or if the items comprising the entire population are not of a homogeneous nature.

8. The efficiency and cost-saving advantages inherent in sampling make this approach the only practicable one in the examination of most organizations.

Criticism of judgment approach to audit test checking

With the adoption of the test-check method of auditing, the public accounting profession has been faced with the problem of how to select samples which will be representative of the transactions to be tested and also with the question of determining the point at which the sampling process should cease. Stated in other words, the questions become:

1. How should the auditor select the transactions to be tested?
2. How much test checking is enough?

The traditional answer to these questions has stressed the use of professional judgment by the auditor. It is argued that the experienced auditor, skilled in reviewing accounting records and in detecting weaknesses in internal control, can determine in the light of all the circumstances of a given engagement the appropriate extent of the tests required. To many people this answer has not seemed satisfactory. Critics of judgment methods of audit test checking argue that the auditor relies too heavily upon intuition, that he uses no objective method of measuring the adequacy of samples, that no system of logic underlies his testing program, and that different auditors confronted with identical sets of circumstances would not employ the same types or amounts of testing.

Statistical sampling

The solution generally proposed by these critics of traditional judgment sampling is to apply the principles of statistical sampling to auditing, with the aim of imparting a greater degree of objectivity to the testing process. In using test checks the auditor has of course been relying upon the theory of probability, but he has made only limited use of statistical techniques in selecting and interpreting samples. In the sciences and in many professional fields dealing with quantitative data, statistical techniques have become tremendously important. The "judgment sample" traditionally used by auditors is influenced by many subjective factors not easily measured; these factors may include, for example, the auditor's personal reactions to the client's employees, his recent exposure to fraud cases, the condition of his health, and sometimes, unfortunately, the time and personnel available to complete the engagement.

Statisticians have long studied the problem of selecting samples. Statistical procedures have been used quite successfully in the field of industrial quality control, whereby goods purchased or coming off an assembly line have been subjected to sampling tests to determine their compliance with standards of quality. Rather than inspect every item for conformity to standards, many manufacturers have resorted to the less costly method of sampling the produced goods and either accepting or rejecting entire groups based upon the relationship of the actual number of defectives found in each sample to a predetermined acceptable number of defectives.

The first efforts to carry over to the field of auditing the sampling techniques developed in quality control work in industry were not overly successful. The data being examined by the auditor are different in many respects from manufactured goods flowing from an assembly line. The manufacturer reaches a decision to accept or reject products solely on the basis of a sample; however, the auditor's decision that financial statements constitute a fair presentation rests upon a great variety of interrelated tests and upon many phases of the examination other than the study of samples.

After these early efforts by auditors to apply acceptance sampling methods, the opportunities for use of other statistical sampling techniques, such as sampling for attributes and sampling for variables, became apparent. Today statistical sampling constitutes an important part of auditing practice. Within a few years, a professional statistician may be a member of the audit "team" on most large engagements. The application of statistical concepts to audit work is presented in some detail in Chapter 8.

evidence: 1. quality
2. materiality
3. risk

GROUP I
REVIEW QUESTIONS

7–1. A principal purpose of a letter of representations from management is to (select one):

  a) Serve as an introduction to company personnel and an authorization to examine the records.

  b) Discharge the auditor from legal liability for his examination.

  c) Affirm in writing management's approval of limitations on the scope of the audit.

  d) Remind management of its primary responsibility for financial statements. (AICPA, adapted)

7-2.   *a)*   What is a letter of representations? *That financial stmt. responsibility of client.*
      b)   What information should a letter of representations contain? *title to assets, loans recorded*
      c)   What effect does a letter of representations have on a CPA's examination of a client's financial statements? (AICPA, adapted)

7-3.   Define, and differentiate between, judgment sampling and statistical sampling.

7-4.   Compare the advantages and disadvantages of judgment block sampling and judgment random sampling.

7-5.   "In deciding upon the type of evidence to be gathered in support of a given item on the financial statements, the auditor should not permit himself to be influenced by the differences in cost of obtaining alternative forms of evidence." Do you agree? Explain.

7-6.   Identify and explain the considerations that guide the auditor in deciding how much evidence he must examine as a basis for expressing an opinion on a client's financial statements.

7-7.   List several general types of evidence relied upon by auditors and give an example of each type.

7-8.   "The best means of verification of cash, inventory, office equipment, and nearly all other assets is a physical count of the units; only a physical count gives the auditor complete assurance as to the accuracy of the amounts listed on the balance sheet." Evaluate this statement.

7-9.   What are "subsequent events"? *occurring after balance sheet date but prior to report. (goes further)*

7-10.   Give three examples of subsequent events which might influence the auditor's opinion as to one or more items on the balance sheet.

7-11.   In verifying the asset accounts Notes Receivable and Marketable Securities, the auditor examined all notes receivable and all stock certificates. Which of these documents represents the stronger type of evidence? Why?

7-12.   As part of the verification of accounts receivable as of the balance sheet date, the auditor might inspect copies of sales invoices. Similarly, as part of the verification of accounts payable, the auditor might examine purchase invoices. Which of these two types of invoices do you think represents the stronger type of evidence? Why?

7-13.   Explain how comparisons and ratios may be used by the auditor as evidence to support his opinion on the fairness of the financial statements. *p.222*

1. events that cause a adjustment to the amt. on bal. sh. or inc. stmt.

2 events requiring disclosure by footnote.

GROUP II
QUESTIONS REQUIRING ANALYSIS

7-14.   An example of a subsequent event which normally would not require disclosure in the financial statements would be (select one; justify your selection):
      a)   Decreased sales volume resulting from a general business recession.
      b)   Serious damage to the company's plant from a widespread flood.

3. do not require footnote.

c)   Issuance of a widely advertised capital stock issue with restrictive covenants.

d)   Settlement of a large liability for considerably less than the amount recorded. (AICPA, adapted)

7–15.   Rate each of the following examples of audit evidence on the basis of *competence*. Arrange your answer in the form of a separate paragraph for each item. As a first step in each paragraph, identify the item as belonging in one of the following two arbitrary classifications: Class A—highly competent evidence; Class B—less competent evidence. In addition to this classification, explain fully the reasoning employed in judging the competence of each item.

a)   Copies of client's sales invoices.

b)   Auditor's independent computation of earnings per share.

c)   Paid checks returned with bank statement.

d)   Response from customer of client addressed to auditor's office confirming amount owed to client at balance sheet date.

e)   Letter of representations by treasurer of client company stating that all liabilities of which he has knowledge are reflected in the company's accounts.

7–16.   The financial statements of the Yale Company show sales of $10 million for the year. What evidence might the auditor utilize in verifying this amount?

7–17.   In evaluating evidence concerning accounts receivable, it is customary to give considerable weight to confirmations from customers, acknowledging the indebtedness. Would you attach comparable weight to a statement by the custodian of a petty cash fund that the fund was intact? What significant difference, if any, exists between these two examples of evidence?

7–18.   In auditing the financial statements of a manufacturing company that were prepared from data processed by electronic data processing equipment, the CPA has found that his traditional "audit trail" has been obscured. As a result the CPA may place increased emphasis upon overall tests of the data under audit. These overall tests, which are also applied in auditing manual accounting systems, include the computation of ratios, which are compared to prior year ratios or to industrywide norms. Examples of such overall ratios are the computation of the rate of inventory turnover and computation of the number of days' sales in receivables.

Required:

a)   Discuss the advantages to the CPA of the use of ratios as overall tests in an audit.

b)   In addition to the computations given above, list the ratios that a CPA may compute during an audit as overall tests on balance sheet accounts and related income statement accounts. For each ratio listed name the two (or more) accounts used in its computation.

c) When a CPA discovers that there has been a significant change in a ratio when compared to the prior year's ratio, he considers the possible reasons for the change. Give the possible reasons for the following significant changes in ratios:

    (1) The rate of the inventory turnover (ratio of cost of sales and average inventory) has decreased from the prior year's rate.

    (2) The number of days' sales in receivables (ratio of average daily accounts receivable and sales) has increased over the prior year. (AICPA, adapted)

7–19. The Marshall Land Company owns substantial amounts of farm and timberlands, and consequently property taxes represent one of the more important types of expense. What specific documents or other evidence should the auditor examine in verifying the Property Taxes Expense account?

7–20. The Coldstream Corporation has large investments in marketable securities. What documentary evidence should the auditor examine in verifying (*a*) the Marketable Securities account, and (*b*) interest and dividends revenue?

7–21. Shortly after completing his field work but before writing his report on the financial statements of Field Electronics, a manufacturer of components for television sets, William Baxter, CPA, learned the following facts from a newspaper story. A major electronics firm had introduced a line of products that would compete directly with Field's primary line, now being produced in a specially designed new plant. Because of manufacturing innovations, the competitor's line of products will be of comparable quality but priced 50 percent below Field's line. Mr. Baxter discussed this news with Field executives and was informed that Field would meet the lower prices, which are high enough to cover variable manufacturing and selling expenses but will permit recovery of only a portion of fixed costs.

Required:

What additional disclosure, if any, in the financial statements and footnotes should Mr. Baxter recommend to his client because of this subsequent event? (AICPA, adapted)

GROUP III
PROBLEMS

7–22. The Robertson Company had accounts receivable of $100,000 at December 31, 1974 and had provided an allowance for uncollectible accounts of $3,000. After performing all normal auditing procedures relating to the receivables and to the valuation allowance, the independent auditor was satisfied that this asset was fairly stated and that the allowance for uncollectible accounts was adequate. Just before completion of the audit field work late in February, however, the auditor learned that the entire plant of the Thompson Corporation, a major customer, had been destroyed by a flood early in February, and that as a result the Thompson Corporation was hopelessly insolvent.

The account receivable from the Thompson Corporation in the amount of $22,000 originated on December 28; terms of payment were "net 60 days." The receivable had been regarded as entirely collectible at December 31, and the auditor had so considered it in reaching his conclusion as to the adequacy of the allowance for uncollectible accounts. In discussing the news concerning the flood, the controller of the Robertson Company emphasized to the auditor that the probable loss of $22,000 should be regarded as a loss of the year 1975 and not of 1974, the year under audit.

What action, if any, should the auditor recommend with respect to the receivable from the Thompson Corporation?

7–23. What would you accept as satisfactory documentary evidence in support of entries in the following:

a)   Sales register.
b)   Sales returns register.
c)   Voucher or invoice register.
d)   Payroll register.
e)   Check register. (AICPA, adapted)

7–24. In connection with your examination of the financial statements of Hollis Mfg. Corporation for the year ended December 31, 1974, your subsequent events review disclosed the following items:

(1)   January 3, 1975: The state government approved a plan for the construction of an express highway. The plan will result in the appropriation of a portion of the land area owned by Hollis Mfg. Corporation. Construction will begin in late 1975. No estimate of the condemnation award is available.

(2)   January 7, 1975: The mineral content of a shipment of ore en route to Hollis Mfg. Corporation on December 31, 1974 was determined to be 72 percent. The shipment was recorded at year-end at an estimated content of 50 percent by a debt to Raw Material Inventory and a credit to Accounts Payable in the amount of $20,600. The final liability to the vendor is based on the actual mineral content of the shipment.

(3)   January 15, 1975: Culminating a series of personal disagreements between Mr. Hollis, the president, and his brother-in-law, the treasurer, the latter resigned, effective immediately, under an agreement whereby the corporation would purchase his 10 percent stock ownership at book value as of December 31, 1974. Payment is to be made in two equal amounts in cash on April 1 and October 1. 1975. In December the treasurer had obtained a divorce from his wife, who was Mr. Hollis's sister.

(4)   January 31, 1975: As a result of reduced sales, production was curtailed in mid-January and some workers were laid off. On February 5, 1975, all the remaining workers went on strike. To date the strike is unsettled.

Required:

Assume that the above items came to your attention prior to completion of your audit work on February 15, 1975 and that you will render a short-form report. For each of the above items, discuss the disclosure that you would recommend for the item, listing all details that you would suggest should be disclosed. Indicate those items or details, if any, that should not be disclosed. Give your reasons for recommending or not recommending disclosure of the items or details. (AICPA, adapted)

7–25. In his examination of financial statements the CPA is concerned with the accumulation of audit evidence.

Required:

a) What is the objective of the CPA's accumulation of audit evidence during the course of his examination?

b) The source of the audit evidence is of primary importance in the CPA's evaluation of its quality. Audit evidence may be classified according to source. For example, one class originates within the client's organization, passes through the hands of third parties, and returns to the client, where it may be examined by the auditor. List the classification of audit evidence according to source, briefly discussing the effect of the source on the reliability of the evidence. (AICPA, adapted)

7–26. The financial statements of your client indicate that large amounts of notes payable to banks were retired during the period under audit. Evaluate the reliability of each of the following types of evidence supporting these transactions:

a) Debit entries in the Notes Payable account.

b) Entries in the check register.

c) Paid checks.

d) Notes payable bearing bank perforation stamp "PAID" and the date of payment.

e) Statement by client's treasurer that notes had been paid at maturity.

f) Letter received by auditor directly from bank stating that no indebtness on part of client existed as of the balance sheet date.

7–27. During your examination of the accounts receivable of a new client, you notice that one account is much larger than the rest, and you therefore decide to examine the evidence supporting this customer's account. Comment on the relative reliability and adequacy of the following types of evidence:

a) Ledger card from accounts receivable subsidiary ledger.

b) Copies of sales invoices in amount of the receivable.

c) Purchase order received from customer.

d) Shipping document describing the articles sold.

e) Letter received by client from customer acknowledging the correctness of the receivable in the amount shown on client's books.

f) Letter received by auditor directly from customer acknowledging the correctness of the amount shown as receivable on client's books.

8

Statistical sampling[*]

STATISTICAL SAMPLING is the same general process as the judgment sampling method traditionally used by the auditor but involves certain refinements. The key to an understanding of statistical sampling and its many advantages to the auditor is a knowledge of these refinements. Statistical sampling is a tool which permits the auditor to determine sample reliability and the risk of his accepting it. The method requires the auditor to define clearly the standards used in arriving at sample size, and it results in a sample which is representative of the entire group. Statistical sampling methods are not new; they have been used extensively for many years in a number of areas, including industrial product quality control, public opinion polls, marketing studies, analyses of census data, biological and physical sciences, medicine, and psychology.

Statistical sampling techniques are not a substitute for the auditor's judgment, nor should it be assumed that they are always superior to traditional judgment sampling. The adoption of statistical sampling by an auditor does not constitute an admission on his part that his traditional techniques were improper. In the history of public accounting, there are relatively few cases in which the application of judgment sampling techniques did not result in an acceptable sample. Further, the use of statistical sampling techniques does not require the auditor to forfeit his right to exercise judgment.

* The authors are greatly indebted to Edwin M. Lamb, CPA, partner, Arthur Young & Company. Mr. Lamb provided expert guidance on current developments in the application of statistical sampling to auditing problems.

238

Sampling, whether statistical or judgmental, is the process of selecting a sample from a larger field of items (called the *population*) and using the characteristics of the sample to draw inferences about the characteristics of the entire field of items. The underlying assumption is that the sample is *representative of the population*, meaning that the sample will possess essentially the same characteristics as the population. Inherent in the technique of sampling is the risk of "sampling error"—the possibility of selecting a sample which, purely by chance, *is not* representative of the population. Due to the ever-present risk of sampling error, there is always some degree of risk that sampling will lead to incorrect conclusions concerning the population.

As a general rule, the risk of sampling error is reduced by increasing the sample size. When the sample size is increased to 100 percent of the population, the sample is by definition representative of the population and the risk of sampling error is eliminated. Larger samples, however, are more costly and time consuming. A key element in utilizing sampling effectively is to balance the risk of material error resulting from sampling error against the cost of increasing the sample size.

An advantage of statistical sampling is that the risk of material errors resulting from sampling error may be measured. The auditor may determine the probability that his conclusions regarding the population are valid, and thereby become informed of the risk he takes in accepting the sample results. Judgment sampling, on the other hand, provides the auditor with no means of determining the risk of material error. Often, judgment sampling results in the costly practice of taking far larger samples than are justified by the materiality of potential errors, "just to be on the safe side."

Statistical sampling versus random sampling

A common misinterpretation of statistical sampling is that which equates statistical sampling with random sampling. The emphasis upon drawing "representative" samples is frequently overdone, leading the auditor to the conclusion that all statistical sampling has to offer is the obtaining of samples that are representative of the population. Statistical sampling is much more than that. The application of any statistical sampling plan has five distinct phases in which the auditor must—

1. Define the objectives and nature of the test.
2. Determine the method of sampling to be used.
3. Calculate the sample size.
4. Select the sample.
5. Interpret the sample results.

This entire process is described as statistical sampling. Random sampling relates only to the fourth item listed above, that of selecting the sample. In statistical sampling, if the sample has been selected on a random or "probability" basis, it is a *random sample.* Random sampling, therefore, is only part of the statistical sampling procedure and not the entire process. In applying statistical sampling, the auditor has at his command a powerful tool capable of more than merely drawing samples on a random basis.

Statistical selection and statistical measurement

Generally, statistical sampling may be separated into two distinct phases: statistical selection and statistical measurement. Statistical selection refers to the method of drawing the sample, whereas statistical measurement involves the calculation of the sample size and the interpretation of sample results. For example, assume that an auditor desires to examine a sample of payroll checks to determine the effectiveness of the system of internal control over the payment of payrolls. To accomplish this purpose, he obtains a number of checks and examines them for signatures and endorsements, compares them with the payroll records for payee and amount, traces the pay rates to the payroll records, and calculates the gross pay and the various deductions. Upon completion, he decides the extent to which he may rely upon the system in determining his audit procedures. The method of selecting the sample (that is, determining which payroll checks are to be drawn from the files for examination) is *statistical selection. Statistical measurement* techniques are used to calculate the sample size and interpret the sample results.

The distinction between statistical selection and statistical measurement is significant in practice. Statistical selection may be used independently from statistical measurement. The independent auditor may apply statistical selection techniques in determining the items to be drawn for the sample but may rely on his subjective judgment in determining the sample size and interpreting the sample results. As between statistical selection and statistical measurement, the auditor will find the former easier to understand. If he utilizes statistical selection techniques alone, he will make substantial progress towards solving the problems of audit sampling.

In this chapter we will first consider statistical selection techniques, and secondly statistical measurement. The reader should realize that a brief presentation in simple language of this rather complicated subject requires some simplifications and generalizations. The chapter does not purport to cover statistical sampling in its entirety.

STATISTICAL SELECTION

Four statistical methods of selecting items for examination are available to the auditor: random number table selection, systematic selection, stratified selection, and cluster selection. If properly applied, each of these methods permits the auditor to select a sample from the group of items to be examined (usually described as the "population," "universe," or "field") in such a manner that each item in the group has the same chance of being chosen for examination as every other item. The general process is known statistically as "random sampling" and is sometimes described as "probability sampling." Except in unusual circumstances, statistical measurement techniques cannot be applied unless the sample is drawn on a random basis.

Of the four statistical selection techniques, the random number table selection method has the greatest application in normal auditing situations. Systematic selection is useful but must be applied with more care. Stratified selection is particularly valuable when the population includes large and small items. Successful use of the cluster selection method, however, usually requires the guidance of an expert. The auditor needs some acquaintance with all of these methods; they are described below with emphasis placed upon the random number table selection method.

Random number table selection

Perhaps the easiest method of selecting items to be tested on a random basis is the use of the random number table. One page from a well-known random number table is reproduced in Figure 8–1.

The random numbers appearing in the illustrative table are arranged into columns of five digits. Except that the columnar arrangement permits the reader of the table to select numbers easily, the columns are purely arbitrary and otherwise meaningless. Each digit on the table is a random digit; the table does not represent a listing of random five-digit numbers. The columnar arrangement is for convenience only.

To illustrate a common misinterpretation of random number tables, assume that the auditor wishes to select a sample from a group of items which are numbered from 1 to 999. After a glance at the table, he may conclude that not one number in the table fulfills the requirement to select numbers in the low range between 001 and 009. Because he interprets the table as a listing of five-digit random numbers, he looks for numbers between 00001 to 00009 and cannot find them any place. This interpretation is not proper. When the auditor realizes that he can form the digits on the table into any columnar arrangement (in this case, columns of three digits), on the single page illustrated he

FIGURE 8–1
Table of random numbers

Line	(1)	(2)	(3)	(4)	(5)	(6)	(7)	(8)	(9)	(10)	(11)	(12)	(13)	(14)
1	10480	15011	01536	02011	81647	91646	69179	14194	62590	36207	20969	99570	91291	90700
2	22368	46573	25595	85393	30995	89198	27982	53402	93965	34095	52666	19174	39615	99505
3	24130	48360	22527	97265	76393	64809	15179	24830	49340	32081	30680	19655	63348	58629
4	42167	93093	06243	61680	07856	16376	39440	53537	71341	57004	00849	74917	97758	16379
5	37570	39975	81837	16656	06121	91782	60468	81305	49684	60672	14110	06927	01263	54613
6	77921	06907	11008	42751	27756	53498	18602	70659	90655	15053	21916	81825	44394	42880
7	99562	72905	56420	69994	98872	31016	71194	18738	44013	48840	63213	21069	10634	12952
8	96301	91977	05463	07972	18876	20922	94595	56869	69014	60045	18425	84903	42508	32307
9	89579	14342	63661	10281	17453	18103	57740	84378	25331	12566	58678	44947	05585	56941
10	85475	36857	53342	53988	53060	59533	38867	62300	08158	17983	16439	11458	18593	64952
11	28918	69578	88231	33276	70997	79936	56865	05859	90106	31595	01547	85590	91610	78188
12	63553	40961	48235	03427	49626	69445	18663	72695	52180	20847	12234	90511	33703	90322
13	09429	93969	52636	92737	88974	33488	36320	17617	30015	08272	84115	27156	30613	74952
14	10365	61129	87529	85689	48237	52267	67689	93394	01511	26358	85104	20285	29975	89868
15	07119	97336	71048	08178	77233	13916	47564	81056	97735	85977	29372	74461	28551	90707
16	51085	12765	51821	51259	77452	16308	60756	92144	49442	53900	70960	63990	75601	40719
17	02368	21382	52404	60268	89368	19885	55322	44819	01188	65255	64835	44919	05944	55157
18	01011	54092	33362	94904	31273	04146	18594	29852	71585	85030	51132	01915	92747	64951
19	52162	53916	46369	58586	23216	14513	83149	98736	23495	64350	94738	17752	35156	35749
20	07056	97628	33787	09998	42698	06691	76988	13602	51851	46104	88916	19509	25625	58104
21	48663	91245	85828	14346	09172	30168	90229	04734	59193	22178	30421	61666	99904	32812
22	54164	58492	22421	74103	47070	25306	76468	26384	58151	06646	21524	15227	96909	44592
23	32639	32363	05597	24200	13363	38005	94342	28728	35806	06912	17012	64161	18296	22851
24	29334	27001	87637	87308	58731	00256	45834	15398	46557	94970	25280	99066	02910	77775
25	02488	33062	28834	07351	19731	92420	60952	61280	50001	67658	32586	86679	50720	94953
26	81525	72295	04839	96423	24878	82651	66566	14778	76797	14780	13300	87074	79666	95725
27	29676	20591	68086	26432	46901	20849	89768	81536	86645	12659	92259	57102	80428	25280
28	00742	57392	39064	66432	84673	40027	32832	61362	98947	96067	64760	64584	96096	98253
29	05366	04213	25669	26422	44407	44048	37937	63904	45766	66134	75470	66520	34693	90449
30	91921	26418	64117	94305	26766	25940	39972	22209	71500	64568	91402	42416	07844	69618
31	00582	04711	87917	77341	42206	35126	74087	99547	81817	42607	43808	76655	62028	76630
32	00725	69884	62797	56170	86324	88072	76222	36086	84637	93161	76038	65855	77919	88006
33	69011	65795	95876	55293	18988	27354	26575	08625	40801	59920	29841	80150	12777	48501
34	25976	57948	29888	88604	67917	48708	18912	82271	65424	69774	33611	54262	85963	03547
35	09763	83473	73577	12908	30883	18317	28290	35797	05998	41688	34952	37888	38917	88050
36	91567	42595	27958	30134	04024	86385	29880	99730	55536	84855	29080	09250	79656	73211
37	17955	56349	90999	49127	20044	59931	06115	20542	18059	02008	73708	83517	36103	42791
38	46503	18584	18845	49618	02304	51038	20655	58727	28168	15475	56942	53389	20562	87338
39	92157	89634	94824	78171	84610	82834	09922	25417	44137	48413	25555	21246	35509	20468
40	14577	62765	35605	81263	39667	47358	56873	56307	61607	49518	89656	20103	77490	18062
41	98427	07523	33362	64270	01638	92477	66969	98420	04880	45585	46565	04102	46880	45709
42	34914	63976	88720	82765	34476	17032	87589	40836	32427	70002	70663	88863	77775	69348
43	70060	28277	39475	46473	23219	53416	94970	25832	69975	94884	19661	72828	00102	66794
44	53976	54914	06990	67245	68350	82948	11398	42878	80287	88267	47363	46634	06541	97809
45	76072	29515	40980	07391	58745	25774	22987	80059	39911	96189	41151	14222	60697	59583
46	90725	52210	83974	29992	65831	38857	50490	83765	55657	14361	31720	57375	56228	41546
47	64364	67412	33339	31926	14883	24413	59744	92351	97473	89286	35931	04110	23726	51900
48	08962	00358	31662	25388	61642	34072	81249	35648	56891	69352	48373	45578	78547	81788
49	95012	68379	93526	70765	10592	04542	76463	54328	02349	17247	28865	14777	62730	92277
50	15664	10493	20492	38391	91132	21999	59516	81652	27195	48223	46751	22923	32261	85653

Source: Interstate Commerce Commission, *Table of 105,000 Random Decimal Digits* (Washington, D.C.: Bureau of Transport, Economics and Statistics, 1949).

will find many instances in which he will be able to draw numbers between 001 and 009.

Using the random number table

A random number table may be read in many different ways. We may begin at any starting point on the table and follow any route from that point to select additional numbers. Once the route is selected, however, it should be followed consistently throughout the table.

Assume, for example, that a client's accounts receivable are numbered from 0001 to 5,000 and that we want to select a random sample of 300 for confirmation. Using the random number table in Figure 8–1, we decide to start at the top of column 2 and to proceed from top to bottom. Reading only the first four digits of the numbers in column 2, we would select 1501, 4657, and 4836 as three of the account numbers to be sampled. The next number, 9309, would be ignored, since there is no account with that number. The next numbers to be included in our sample would be 3997, 0690, 1434, etc. Once we reach the bottom of column 2, we could continue to the next page of the random number table, or go to the top of column 3. Any route is permissible, so long as it is followed consistently.

Transactions numbered in blocks. Frequently, the auditor will find it necessary to select a sample from a group of items numbered in blocks. For example, certain transactions may be numbered in such a way that the first digit, or digits, of the number correspond with the month in which the transaction took place and the remaining digits represent the number of the transaction in the particular month. A series of vouchers may be numbered as follows:

Month	Inclusive transaction numbers
January...............	1–1 to 1–1000
February.............	2–1 to 2–700
March...............	3–1 to 3–1020

In this situation the auditor has at least two choices: he may either mentally renumber the transactions into a consecutive sequence or he may assign the first part of each random number drawn to a month involved and the latter part to the number of the transaction. Assuming he follows the first procedure, the results will be as follows:

Month	Inclusive transaction numbers	Assigned number
January...............	1–1 to 1–1000	1 to 1000
February...............	2–1 to 2–700	1001 to 1700
March...............	3–1 to 3–1020	1701 to 2720

If the auditor then draws from the random number table the numbers 0490, 1715, and 0102, he may rapidly translate these random numbers into the following voucher numbers respectively: 1–490, 3–015, and 1–102.

In the above illustration, the auditor was able to use a series of four-digit random numbers. Another method consists of assigning the first digits of the random numbers selected to designate the month of the year and the remaining digits to the particular voucher number. Applying this method to the above illustration, the auditor finds he must use a series of five-digit random numbers since one digit will be needed for the month designation and four for the transaction numbers. For example, under this method, if he drew from the table the number 10480, he would interpret the result as the 480th voucher in the month of January; number 31002 would be the 1002d voucher in March, and so forth. Obviously, if the group of items to be sampled involves all months of the year and if the voucher numbers in any one month contain four or more digits, a larger number of digits must be used in selecting numbers from the table. This will create inefficiency both through the use of larger numbers and because many numbers appearing in the random number table will be unusable to the extent that the transaction numbers for any month do not run high enough. The previously illustrated process of renumbering the items to form a sequence, although it does not appear most economical at the beginning, may prove to be the best method in the long run.

Alphanumerically numbered items or unnumbered items. The same procedures outlined above may be applied when the auditor desires to select a sample from an alphanumerically numbered group. For example, transactions are frequently numbered A–001, B–001, etc. The alphabetics may be translated into numbers: 1 representing A, 2 representing B, etc., or the entire population may be assigned consecutive numbers.

When the population is not prenumbered, the auditor may mentally assign a number to each item in the group to be examined. A common illustration is the test of items on a group of inventory sheets. Assume that the auditor is presented with a series of inventory sheets numbered from 001 to 205 with approximately 25 to 40 items on each page. To select the items to be examined, he may use the random number table with series of five digits. Referring to the illustrative table, starting on the first line of column 1, he would draw the number 10480. This could be interpreted as page 104, item 80. However, there are not 80 items on the page; thus, the auditor must proceed down the column until he finds a number which applies. On line 18, he finds 01011 which he may interpret as page 10, item 11, which he will select for examination. This procedure is obviously time consuming, and the auditor may wish to assign consecutive numbers as follows:

Page No.	Number of items on page	Random number equivalent
1........................	40	1 to 40
2........................	35	41 to 75
3........................	38	76 to 113
etc........................	etc.	etc.

Thus, if the auditor draws the number 044, he may interpret it as the fourth item on the second page. In many instances the number of items listed on each page is uniform except at the end of the listing. When this situation prevails, the assignment of consecutive numbers is clearly the more economical technique.

Duplicate numbers. In using a random number table, it is possible that the auditor will draw the same number more than once. If the auditor ignores a number that is drawn a second time and goes on to the next number, he is "*sampling without replacement.*" This term means that an item once selected is not "replaced" into the population of eligible items, and consequently it cannot be drawn for inclusion in the sample a second time.

The alternative to sampling without replacement is "*sampling with replacement.*" This method requires that if a particular number is drawn two or more times, the number must be included two or more times in the sample. Sampling with replacement means that once an item has been selected, it is immediately "replaced" into the population of eligible items and may be selected a second time.

Statistical measurement techniques assume sampling with replacement. As a practical matter, however, samples are often selected without replacement. Sampling without replacement is more conservative, since samples are likely to include more items. For example, assume that we select a sample of 100 items sampling without replacement. When we finish selecting the sample we will have exactly 100 different items. If we sampled with replacement, however, we could end up with less than 100 different items, since the same item could be counted two or more times in our sample.

Random number generator

Even when items are assigned consecutive numbers, the selection of a large sample from a random number table may be a very time-consuming process. Computer programs called *random number generators* may be used to provide any length list of random numbers applicable to a given population. Random number generators may be programmed to select random numbers with specific characteristics, so that the list of random numbers provided to the auditor includes only numbers present in the population. Generalized computer audit programs include a random number generator.

Systematic selection

The systematic selection of items from a group for examination is a method commonly used by auditors. It involves the drawing of every *n*th item from the group of items to be sampled. For example, if the auditor wishes to select 200 paid checks for examination out of a total of 10,000 checks, he may specify that every 50th item be examined. With certain refinements and careful application, this traditional method may be converted into the statistical method of systematic selection.

When the auditor decides that every *n*th item in the population is to be examined, he has no assurance that his sample will be random because the population may not be arranged in a random sequence. If, during an audit of inventory prices, the auditor was not aware that all expensive parts were assigned identification numbers ending in zero, it would be quite possible that application of the systematic technique would result in his examining only items which were inexpensive or only items which were expensive. If the auditor decided to examine every 10th item and started with the 4th item, his examination would cover only the inexpensive parts; if he started with the 10th item, he would cover only the expensive parts.

Other possibilities exist of obtaining a nonrandom sample through the use of the systematic selection technique. If all transactions of a particular type are processed all at one time during each month or accounting period, the systematic selection method may result in a sample which does not contain these items.

To prevent drawing a nonrandom or "biased" sample when the systematic selection technique is used, the auditor should first determine that the population is arranged in random order. This may be done by inspecting it on a judgment basis, by comparing it with another population known to be random, or by use of statistical formulae. If he determines that certain elements of the group are not arranged in random order, he may stratify the population (as explained on page 247) into segments, each of which is in random order, and apply the procedure to each segment.

Two or more random starting points. Another method by which the auditor may guard against a nonrandom sample is to use two or more random starting points. Assume that the auditor wishes to examine 200 sales invoices out of a group of invoices numbered between 1 and 3,000. From his inspection of the population, he may decide, for example, that four random starts are necessary. Fifty items (200 ÷ 4) will be selected following each of the four random starts. Therefore, the auditor will select every 60th item (3000 ÷ 50) after each of the random starts. In order that 50 items be selected from each of the random starts, the auditor must move both upward and downward from each of the random starting points. For example, if 141 were a random starting point, both 81 (141 − 60) and 21 (81 − 60) would be included in the sample, as well as every 60th number after 141.

The systematic selection technique has the obvious advantage of enabling the auditor to obtain a sample from a population of unnumbered documents or transactions. If the documents to be examined are unnumbered, there is no necessity under this method to number them either physically or mentally, as required under the random number table selection technique. Rather, the auditor merely counts off the sampling interval to select the documents, or he may use a ruler to measure the interval.

Systematic selection may also be less time consuming than the use of a random number table. It is often easier to select every nth item than to select numbers from a random number table, sort them into order, and draw the necessary documents for examination.

Stratified selection

There is no requirement that only one method of statistical sample selection be applied to the entire group of items to be examined. Rather, the population may be stratified and different techniques applied to each stratum, if desired. Stratified selection is not by itself a technique of drawing samples. However, it is useful for two purposes: to arrange the population into various strata of significance and to utilize different sample selection techniques. The auditor is usually concerned with the materiality of transactions, as well as with the type of transactions. To examine a population composed of items having varying dollar values, or which represent different types of transactions, the auditor may stratify it and apply different procedures to the various strata. For example, if the auditor wishes to use statistical sampling techniques to confirm accounts receivable, he might stratify and test as follows:

Stratum	*Composition of stratum*	*Method of selection used*
1	All accounts of $10,000 and over	100% examination
2	Wholesale accounts receivable (under $10,000), all numbered with numbers ending in zero.	Random number table selection
3	All other accounts (under $10,000) in random order	Systematic selection

The above illustrates the stratification of a population not only by dollar values but also by transaction type. In addition to stratifying the population on these bases, the auditor may also stratify by transaction frequency. For instance, in a test of internal control, the auditor may wish to stratify the population into high and low volume transactions when he knows that the controls are more likely to be violated during the processing of low volume transactions.

Stratified sampling has at least two major advantages to the auditor. It enables the auditor to relate sample selection to the materiality, turnover, or other characteristics of items and to apply different auditing procedures to each stratum. The method is also favored by statisticians since it improves the reliability of the sample. Whenever items of extremely high or low values, or of unusual characteristics, are segregated into separate populations, each population becomes more homogeneous. The more homogeneous a population is, the more probable that a sample will be representative of that population. Thus, stratified selection may increase sample reliability.

Cluster selection

A fourth method of selecting items to be examined is the cluster selection technique. Frequently, the auditor will encounter a group of items to be examined which may conveniently be broken down into subgroups. Each of these subgroups may be described as a "cluster." For example, the accounts receivable of a department store may be contained in a number of trays. If there were 10,000 accounts receivable cards in 50 trays, each tray of cards may be considered as a cluster. Under this method, the auditor may select on a random basis (perhaps by using a random number table) a few trays of cards to be examined.

This method of sampling would appear at first glance to be simple as compared with either the random number table or systematic selection methods. However, in cluster sampling, the auditor must evaluate each cluster as if it were a single observation. If this cluster consists of 500 cards, the evaluation becomes a formidable task. Because of these statistical requirements, the auditor will normally find that the apparent saving in time proves to be an illusion because of the need for a larger sample size to achieve the desired results. This method calls for the assistance of a specialist in statistical sampling.

STATISTICAL MEASUREMENT

Statistical selection techniques are limited to helping the auditor select items to be sampled; he may wish to take a further step and avail himself of statistical measurement methods to determine sample sizes and to interpret sample results. If the auditor plans to use statistical measurement techniques, he will usually employ statistical selection in drawing the sample. However, there are occasions when statistical measurement is used to evaluate a sample, the size of which was determined on a judgment basis.

Four statistical measurement techniques (or "statistical sampling plans") have been much discussed in auditing literature. These are:

1. *Acceptance sampling.* This method permits the auditor to reject or accept a population in accordance with a stipulated allowable error rate at a predetermined confidence level.
2. *Estimation sampling for attributes.* This method permits the auditor to determine the rate of occurrence of certain characteristics (for example, exceptions) in a population within prescribed ranges of precision and levels of confidence.
3. *Discovery sampling.* This method is used to locate at least one error item, provided that the error occurs within the population with at least a specified occurrence rate.
4. *Estimation sampling for variables.* This method permits the auditor to estimate a total dollar amount of a population within prescribed ranges of precision and levels of confidence.

In order to understand any of these statistical sampling plans, the auditor must first be familiar with the meanings and interrelationships among certain statistical concepts, such as *occurrence rate, precision, confidence level,* and *sample size. Occurrence rate* is the frequency with which a given characteristic occurs in the population being studied. Since the characteristic the auditor is interested in is frequently some type of error, an occurrence rate is often referred to as an *error rate.*

Precision

In any sampling process, whether it be statistical or judgment, the sample results may not be *exactly* representative of the characteristics of the population. The possibility of sampling error is always present. In utilizing statistical sampling techniques, the auditor *measures the possibility of sampling error* by calculating precision and confidence level.

Precision is the range, set by + and − limits from the sample results, within which the true value of the population characteristic being measured is likely to lie. For example, assume a sample is taken to determine the occurrence rate of a certain type of error in the preparation of invoices. The sample indicates an error rate of 2.1 percent. We have little assurance that the error rate in the population is exactly 2.1 percent, but we know that the sample result probably approximates the population error rate. Therefore, we may set a *range* from the sample result within which we expect the population error rate to be.

A precision of ±1 percent would mean we expect the population error rate to be between 1.1 percent and 3.1 percent. The less precision we require (meaning the wider the range we allow), the more confident we may be that the true population characteristic lies within the range. In this example, a precision of ±2 percent would mean we assume the population error rate to be between 0.1 percent and 4.1 percent. Obviously, it is more probable that the true population error rate will lie within this larger precision range than within the smaller precision range at ±1 percent. Remember, less precision means a wider range; more precision means a narrower range because the true population characteristic is assumed to be closer to the sample results.

Precision may also be stated as a dollar value range. For example, we may attempt to estimate the total dollar value of receivables with a precision of ±$10,000. Precision may be viewed as the allowable margin of error. The precision required by the auditor should be determined in the light of the materiality of this allowable margin of error.

Confidence level

The true population characteristic may not always lie within our specified range of precision. Our confidence level is the percentage of the time we can expect the sample results to represent the true population characteristic within the specified range of precision. Confidence level measures the reliability of the sample, and the risk that the true population characteristic value lies outside the range of precision of the sample.

A 95 percent confidence level means we can expect that 95 percent of the time the sample results will represent the true population characteristic value. Conversely, there is a 5 percent risk that the true population characteristic value is not within the range of precision of our sample result.

Given a specific sample, the less precision we require, the greater our level of confidence that the true population value lies within the range of precision. The greater the required precision, the lower will be our confidence level that the sample represents the population within the desired range of precision.

Sample size

The size of our sample has a direct effect upon both precision and confidence level. With a very small sample, we cannot have a high confidence level unless we allow a very great range of precision. On the other hand, a sample of 100 percent of the population allows us a 100 percent confidence level with maximum precision (±0 percent).

In general, both confidence level and the degree of precision can be increased by increasing sample size. In other words, the greater the desired precision and/or the higher the desired confidence level, the larger the sample that will be required. Finally, required sample size increases as the expected occurrence rate becomes larger. Although the occurrence rate has an effect on sample size, the effect is usually not as great as that of precision and confidence level.

Tables similar to those illustrated later in this chapter are available to the auditor for determining the required sample size. To make use of tables, the auditor must use his judgment to establish his requirements concerning precision and confidence level and must make an estimate of the occurrence rate. Usually, the occurrence rate is estimated from past experience. If the auditor is examining a field for the first time, he may use a *pilot sample* to estimate the occurrence rate. A pilot sample of 50 items is usually adequate.

After determining the required sample size, the auditor uses statistical selection techniques to select the sample items. If his examination of the sample items confirms his approximation of occurrence rate, his work is completed. If, however, the occurrence rate determined from the examination of the sample is larger than the expected or acceptable rate, the auditor may conclude that his original estimation of the sample size was too low and that he must draw a larger sample. Infrequently, he may reevaluate the required precision and confidence level. He may also stop the entire statistical sampling process and adopt other auditing procedures.

Why sample size need not increase proportionately with population

Every sample represents a specific population within an established confidence level and degree of precision. As the population increases in size, the sample size necessary to represent the population with the same confidence level and degree of precision will increase, but not proportionately to the increase in the population.

Let us look at a hypothetical example of the above general statement. Suppose an auditor finds that a sample of 100 items will represent a population of 5,000 with a 95 percent confidence level and ±2 percent precision. How large a sample will he need to provide equally reliable information about a population of 10,000 with similar characteristics? If the sample size increased proportionately to population size, the auditor would need to draw a sample of 200 items, but this is unnecessary. Consider that 100 sample items represent a population of 5,000 with a ±2 percent precision. Now, consider that 5,000 group as if it were itself a sample from the population of 10,000. This large a sample (50 percent) would represent this 10,000 population with a very high degree of precision at the 95 percent confidence level. Let us assume the degree of precision to be as low as ±0.1 percent. The original sample of 100 items then represents the 10,000 population at a 95 percent confidence level with the *sum of the precision allowances,* that is, to a 2.1 percent degree of precision (2 percent + 0.1 percent). However, since we desire slightly greater precision (2 percent) in our sampling of the 10,000 population, the 100-item sample should be increased slightly. Mathematical formulae can supply the exact sample size necessary, but logically we can see that a very small increase (say from 100 to 115) in the sample size should easily reduce the precision allowance from 2.1 to 2, and a sample size of 200 is clearly unnecessary.

Acceptance sampling

While early writings recommended acceptance sampling for auditing, this method does not appear to have as much utility for audit purposes as originally contemplated. The essence of acceptance sampling is a decision whether to accept or to reject an entire population in reliance upon the information derived from the sample. Acceptance sampling requires the auditor to make a "yes" or "no" decision. It is not easy for the auditor to make a decision which rejects a population, because the alternatives may be a 100 percent examination of the population or the qualification of the audit report. Both these alternatives are likely to be impracticable in many normal auditing situations.

In using acceptance sampling the auditor must specify the maximum error rate acceptable to him and the confidence level he deems appropriate. As a practical matter, setting a maximum tolerable percentage of erroneous items is so difficult as to leave the auditor in a very vulnerable position. If, for example, we are testing for required approval signatures on vouchers payable, there is little logical basis for specifying what proportion of items lacking the prescribed approval signature might cause financial statement amounts for inventory or payables to be significantly affected.

Acceptance sampling was developed to assist the quality control expert in determining the physical characteristics of manufactured products, and it is questionable whether the characteristics of the normal types of accounting data are similar to those of manufactured products. Acceptance sampling formulae also provide for a lesser degree of risk in rejecting an acceptable population than in accepting a population that should be rejected. The result is the possibility under these plans that populations containing rates of error less than the specified acceptable level will be rejected. All of these conditions indicate that acceptance sampling is less valuable to the auditor than estimation and discovery techniques, although much attention has been given to this topic in auditing literature.

Estimation sampling for attributes

Estimation sampling for attributes (sometimes called frequency sampling) is a useful statistical method available to the auditor, especially for evaluating the effectiveness of internal control. This method enables the auditor to determine, within prescribed limits of precision and confidence, the frequency of occurrence of certain characteristics in a population; that is, it furnishes a description of the field in terms of the rate of occurrence of the characteristics in which he is interested. Generally, the auditor will use this method to determine exception (error) rates. For example, he may use it to determine the frequency with which sales invoices are not properly priced, purchase invoices not adequately supported, checks not prepared in conformity with the client's policies, or inventory prices not properly calculated. This method of sampling is performed on a unit basis; it produces a result in terms of the number of exceptions or the number of documents examined. The application of the method does not result in dollar value information. However, through the application of a more sophisticated technique (estimation sampling for variables), the results obtained through the use of estimation sampling for attributes may be converted into dollar measurements.

Tables for estimating error rates. To enable the auditor to use estimation sampling for attributes without resorting to complicated mathematical formulae, tables such as the one in Figure 8–2 have been prepared. This illustration is a reproduction of one page from a book containing 212 pages of tables for estimating error rates. This particular page has been prepared for a confidence level of 95 percent and a population size of 50,000. Columns are provided for various ranges of precision. The column heading "p in %" means expected occurrence rate. The table shows, for the stipulated confidence level and population size, sample sizes for various expected occurrence rates and ranges of precision. The full set of tables from which this page has been reproduced contains series of tables for each of the 90 percent, 95 percent, 99 percent, and 99.7 percent confidence levels. For each confidence level, separate tables are provided for population sizes ranging from 200 to 999,999.[1]

Procedures for applying estimation sampling for attributes. The following auditing procedures for applying estimation sampling for attributes are predicated upon the use of the table presented in Figure

---

[1] Another set of tables suitable for the auditor's use in applying estimation sampling for attributes appears in Henry P. Hill, Joseph L. Roth, and Herbert Arkin, *Sampling in Auditing—A Simplified Guide and Statistical Tables* (New York: The Ronald Press Co., 1962). The AICPA's *Sampling for Attributes* (New York, 1967) includes tables for estimation sampling for attributes which require no knowledge of population size.

FIGURE 8–2
Sampling table for estimating error rates (confidence level = 95%; population size = 50,000)

p in %	.005	.010	.015	.020	.025	.030	.035	.040	.045	.050	.060	.080	.100
1	1476	377	168	95	61								
2	2841	742	332	188	120	84	61						
3	4105	1093	492	278	178	124	91	70	55				
4	5278	1433	647	366	235	163	120	92	73	59			
5	6369	1761	798	452	290	202	149	114	90	73	51		
6	7386	2077	945	536	344	240	176	135	107	87	60		
7	8336	2382	1087	617	397	276	203	156	123	100	69		
8	9224	2676	1226	697	448	312	230	176	139	113	78		
9	10055	2960	1360	774	498	347	256	196	155	126	87	.4	
10	10834	3234	1491	850	547	381	281	215	170	138	96		
11	11564	3498	1617	923	595	414	305	234	185	150	104	59	
12	12251	3752	1740	994	641	447	329	252	200	162	112	63	
13	12897	3997	1859	1063	686	478	352	270	214	173	120	68	
14	13504	4234	1975	1130	729	509	375	287	227	184	128	72	
15	14076	4461	2086	1195	772	538	397	304	241	195	136	76	
16	14616	4680	2194	1258	813	567	418	321	254	206	143	81	52
17	15124	4890	2298	1319	852	595	439	337	266	216	150	85	54
18	15603	5093	2399	1378	891	622	459	352	278	226	157	88	57
19	16055	5287	2496	1436	928	648	478	367	290	235	164	92	59
20	16481	5474	2590	1491	964	674	497	381	302	245	170	96	61
21	16884	5653	2681	1544	999	698	515	395	313	254	176	99	64
22	17264	5824	2768	1595	1033	722	532	409	323	262	182	103	66
23	17623	5989	2851	1645	1065	745	549	422	334	271	188	106	68
24	17960	6146	2932	1692	1097	767	566	434	344	279	194	109	70
25	18279	6296	3009	1738	1127	788	581	446	353	286	199	112	72
30	19612	6947	3346	1939	1258	881	650	499	395	321	223	126	81
35	20574	7439	3604	2093	1360	953	703	540	428	347	242	136	87
40	21224	7784	3787	2203	1433	1004	741	570	451	366	255	144	92
45	21601	7989	3896	2269	1476	1035	764	587	465	377	263	148	95
50	21725	8057	3933	2291	1491	1045	772	593	470	381	265	150	96

Precision

Source: R. Gene Brown and Lawrence L. Vance, *Sampling Tables for Estimating Error Rates or Other Proportions.* Public Accounting Research Project, Institute of Business and Economic Research, University of California, Berkeley, California, 1961.

8–2; however, only slight modifications are necessary if other tables are used.

1. *Determine the field to be sampled.* This involves a clear definition of the group of items to be examined and determination of the approximate size of the field. The population may be stratified at this time if desired; all subsequent procedures would apply separately to each stratum.

2. *Define the nature of the tests to be made.* The auditor must determine the objectives of his examination. For example, the objective may be an evaluation of internal control or a verification of the balance appearing in a specific account or accounts. Having made this determination, the auditor must next define what he means by an "exception." The audit personnel performing the examination must understand clearly what is to be considered an exception. The nature of an exception will vary with the objectives of the test. Finally, the auditor must determine the testing procedures to be followed. These comprise the typical audit steps of observation, inspection, comparison, confirmation, and calculation.

3. *Determine the expected occurrence rate.* The expected occurrence rate will be established in the light of the auditor's knowledge of the client's business, the type of transactions involved, and the system of internal control. If necessary, a pilot sample may be taken.

4. *Stipulate precision (reliability) and confidence level (risk) desired.* The determination of precision and confidence level required will be based primarily upon the auditor's judgment and is considered in detail below.

5. *Determine the preliminary sample size from the table.* This process is illustrated in a case study appearing below.

6. *Draw the sample.* In drawing sample items, the auditor should apply appropriate statistical selection techniques previously explained.

7. *Inspect the sample by applying the auditing procedures previously determined.*

8. *Interpret the results of the examination.* The auditor may either be satisfied with the results of the examination or he may decide to expand the scope of the examination through the drawing of additional sample items or through the application of other auditing procedures. He may sometimes reevaluate his requirements as to confidence level and precision.

9. *Resume auditing as required by the interpretation of the sample results.*

Determining precision and confidence level. Perhaps the most difficult of the auditor's decisions is his determination of precision and confidence level. Although auditors have been making reliability and risk judgments ever since the auditing profession came into being, it is unusual for the auditor to assign quantitative values in making these decisions. How does the auditor determine, for example, that he wishes a precision of ±2 percent at a confidence level of 95 percent? The answer depends primarily upon the acceptability of the results to him. He should consider factors such as the following in making his decision: prior experience on the engagement; quality of the internal control system; expected occurrence rate; purpose of the test; effect of the transactions being examined on the financial statements or other products of the audit; and the defensibility of his decision.

The auditor's prior experience on the engagement and the quality of the internal control system are the major factors influencing his determination of precision and confidence level. When internal controls are strong and prior experience indicates reliable processing of accounting data, the auditor may select less stringent values for precision and assume a greater degree of risk.

Consideration must also be given to the maximum acceptable occurrence rate in determining precision. Assume, for example, that the auditor expects an occurrence rate of 2 percent and stipulates a precision ±1 percent; the expected occurrence rate, when added to the upper range of precision, results in the maximum acceptable occurrence rate, which, in this case, would be 3 percent. The auditor then faces the question: "Can I accept an upper range of error of 3 percent?" (The auditor is usually concerned with the upper rather than the lower range of precision.) Further, the acceptable occurrence rate may have some influence on the auditor's determination of confidence level or risk. Should the occurrence rate be uncomfortably high, he may wish to take less risk of being wrong and stipulate a higher confidence level. The converse may also be true.

The purpose of the test and the type of transaction being examined also have a bearing on the determination of precision and confidence level. In a review of internal controls, the auditor may separate the types of exceptions he is looking for into two major categories: (1) exceptions of a procedural nature that have no direct effect on the financial statements and (2) exceptions which may directly affect account balances and, therefore, the financial statements. If the exceptions of a procedural nature (such as the failure to obtain two signatures on checks) are compensated for by other internal controls, the auditor should be able to stipulate a fairly wide range of precision coupled with a relatively high degree of risk. On the other hand, if the exception is of the type which may directly affect the financial statements (such as the incorrect pricing of inventory items), the auditor must generally stipulate a narrow range of precision and a low risk. *When he is stipulating precision, in these instances, the auditor will be guided primarily by the effect of the exceptions on the financial statements.* If he is attempting to determine the accuracy of the inventory counts of items having a known small value, he may be willing to accept a less stringent range of precision than if the items were material. On the other hand, if the auditor were to use a sampling technique to determine the existence of unrecorded liabilities, he should stipulate stringent precision ranges and take a very small risk, since the major objective of his examination is to determine the existence of unrecorded amounts as opposed to recorded amounts.

[Although precision and confidence level are not independent of one another, the auditor may view precision as the allowable margin of error, and the confidence level as establishing the risk of being wrong. Precision, then, should be determined by the materiality of the characteristic being tested. Confidence level should be determined in the light of the amount of supporting evidence the auditor requires for rendering an opinion.

Illustration of estimation sampling for attributes

The following sections illustrate the application of the auditing procedures mentioned on page 255 and the sampling table appearing in Figure 8–2.

Determine the field to be sampled. Assume that the auditor wishes to examine a field consisting of 49,500 vouchers for the purchase of materials during the first 11 months of the year being audited. He determines that the field is homogeneous and need not be stratified; in other words, there are no unusually large vouchers and only an insignificant number of small purchases.

Define the nature of the tests to be made. The auditor wishes to evaluate the effectiveness of the system of internal control for the matching of receiving documents with purchase invoices for materials. He is, therefore, interested in the clerical accuracy of the matching process and in determining whether the internal control system which requires the matching of invoices with receiving documents is working. In this simplified illustration, the auditor defines an exception as any one or more of the following with respect to each invoice and the related receiver:

1. Any invoice not supported by a receiving document.
2. Any invoice supported by a receiving document which is applicable to another invoice.
3. Any differences between the invoice and the receiving document as to quantities shipped.
4. Any irregularities in the documents which were not subsequently corrected.

5. Any evidence of deliberate manipulation or circumvention of the internal control system.

For this elementary type of test, the only testing procedure needed is inspection of the documents and matching of receivers with invoices.

✲ **Determine the expected occurrence rate.** In the audits of the previous three years, the auditor observed that exceptions of the type described above produced occurrence rates of 0.5 percent, 0.9 percent, and 0.7 percent in the respective years. No positive trend can be discerned from the figures for these three years; the auditor, therefore, selects an expected occurrence rate of 1 percent, knowing that this rate is higher than any prior observed rates and that he can defend it on the basis of conservatism and reasonableness. The rate, however, is not so high as to result in an unreasonably large sample size.

✲ **Stipulate precision and confidence level.** From his prior experience and his preliminary survey of the company's internal controls, the auditor concludes that the system of control over the matching of receiving documents with purchase orders, although not weak, is susceptible to improvement. He also realizes that mistakes in matching receiving documents with purchase orders can affect the financial statements through overpayment of vendors and overstatement of inventories. On the other hand, he knows that certain recommendations he made during the prior audit for improvement of the internal control system in this area have been adopted. Based upon these considerations, and others mentioned above, he decides upon a precision of ±1 percent and a confidence level of 95 percent.

Determine the preliminary sample size from the table. Since the size of the population is 49,500 items and the confidence level selected is 95 percent, the table presented in Figure 8–2 is applicable. Opposite the expected error rate of 1 percent in the "*p* in %" column and under the column for a precision of ±1 percent, the auditor finds a preliminary sample size of 377 items.

Draw and inspect the sample. The auditor proceeds to draw 377 purchase invoices by using a random number table. He then examines the documents for each of the types of exceptions previously defined.

Interpret the results of the examination. In interpreting the sample results, the auditor must consider not only the actual percentage of exceptions observed but also the nature of the exceptions. There are three possibilities to be considered: (1) the actual occurrence rate is equal to, or less than, the expected rate; (2) the actual occurrence rate is more than the expected rate; and (3) one or more of the exceptions observed contain evidence of a deliberate manipulation or circumvention of the internal control system.

If the actual occurrence rate observed in the sample items examined is equal to or less than 1 percent and there is no evidence of a deliberate manipulation or circumvention of the internal control system, the auditor may cease his sampling at this point. He has assurance that if he continues sampling, the observed occurrence rate will fall between 0 percent and 2 percent in 95 out of 100 times.

Assume, however, that the actual occurrence rate observed is 2 percent and that none of the exceptions observed indicate a deliberate manipulation or circumvention of the internal control system. In this situation, the auditor had the following alternatives: expand the size of his sample; resort to other auditing procedures to protect himself against the indicated occurrence rate; reevaluate precision; or reevaluate risk.

His first alternative is to expand the size of his sample to 742 items (the sample size for 2 percent expected occurrence rate at a required precision of ±1 percent for a confidence level of 95 percent). If he adopts this course, he is not required to examine 742 additional items but only 365 items, which represent the difference between 742 and the original sample of 377. The additional sample items would be drawn on the same method of random selection used for the original sample. The auditor may decide to expand his sample for two reasons: (1) he may feel that the increased sample will produce an overall occurrence rate approximating the originally estimated rate, or (2) he may wish to verify that the occurrence rate is 2 percent ±1 percent precision at the 95 percent confidence level. In this particular case, the expansion of the sampling in the hope of obtaining the originally estimated occurrence rate is hazardous, since the auditor would have to expect no exceptions in the additional 365 items to be examined. However, in other situations, he may have good reason to follow this course.

There is no requirement that the auditor continue to use statistical sampling techniques after his preliminary sample has indicated that the characteristics of the population are not acceptable. He may well stipulate the application of other auditing procedures to protect himself against the indicated occurrence rate or to develop the required adjustment. For example, if he decides that the indicated exception rate in matching purchase invoices with receiving documents is too high, he may request that a thorough examination be performed in this area by the client's employees under his supervision. Or, he may be able to isolate the exceptions noted to a particular time period. Most of the exceptions may have been caused, for instance, by a replacement employee when the regular employee was on sick leave. If that is the case, the auditor may select auditing procedures to detect the materiality of the deficiencies in internal controls during the period indicated.

During his tests of internal control, the auditor may observe occurrence rates in excess of acceptable limits, yet not expand his work on internal control. For example, if his tests of internal control over accounts receivable indicate error rates in excess of acceptable limits, he may decide not to continue his tests of internal control but to expand his confirmation and other work on accounts receivable at the year-end date.

Two other alternatives, both of which are risky, are available to the auditor when the observed occurrence rate exceeds the expected rate. He may reevaluate his requirements as to precision or confidence level. Such a reevaluation can be made only after a careful consideration of all circumstances and the factors entering into the auditor's original determination of precision and confidence level. In the case presented here, the observed occurrence rate of 2 percent on a sample size of 377 items would indicate to the auditor that the precision he may expect would be approximately 1.5 percent. He arrives at this observation by reading the table horizontally on the 2 percent "p in %" line until he finds a sample size that approximates the size of the sample drawn. In this case, 332 sample items for a 2 percent error rate would indicate a precision of 1.5 percent. Interpolating, he may conclude that with a sample size of 377, his precision is slightly less than 1.5 percent. He must then ask himself whether an observed error rate of 2 percent ± 1.5 percent (an indicated maximum acceptable occurrence rate of 3.5 percent) can be accepted. Further, by using other tables in the book from which Figure 8–2 is reproduced, the auditor may reevaluate the confidence level by referring to tables of a lower confidence level which indicate the approximate size of the sample that he originally drew for the precision stipulated. If the auditor has considered all pertinent factors in his original stipulation of precision and confidence level, he will normally find it difficult to make a reevaluation.

Regardless of the occurrence rate observed, if one or more of the exceptions discovered by the auditor indicates fraud or circumvention of the internal control system, other auditing procedures become necessary. The auditor must evaluate the effect of the exceptions on the financial statements and adopt auditing procedures which are specifically designed to protect against the type of exception observed. The nature of the exception may be more important than its rate of occurrence.

Definition of audit exceptions

In the foregoing illustration of the application of estimation sampling for attributes, the auditor's problem in defining the nature of audit exceptions was simplified because the illustration was limited to only one phase of the evaluation of internal controls over purchasing and receiving. In practice, the auditor has many objectives for each of his tests, and his definition of audit exceptions must accordingly be expanded.

Each test for each type of exception may be treated as a separate observation. The auditor may stipulate differing ranges of precision and, if desired, varying confidence levels for each type of exception. Therefore, the sample sizes for the examination of each type of exception could also vary.

Discovery sampling

Discovery sampling is actually a modified case of acceptance sampling. The purpose of a discovery sample is to detect at least *one exception,* with a predetermined level of confidence, providing the exception exists with a specified occurrence rate in the population. One important use of discovery sampling is to locate examples of a suspected fraud.

Although discovery sampling is designed to locate relatively rare items, it cannot locate "a needle in a haystack." If an exception exists within a population but has an insignificant occurrence rate (0.5 percent or less), no sampling plan can provide adequate assurance that an example of the exception will be encountered. Still, discovery sampling can (with a very high degree of confidence) insure detection of exceptions occurring at a rate as low as 0.5 to 1 percent.

If the auditor wishes to avoid the use of complicated mathematical formulae, tables such as Figure 8–3 are available for discovery sampling. In using this table the auditor must determine the confidence level required and the size of the population and must estimate the frequency of occurrence of the exception. The table may best be explained by reference to the upper extremes. For example, if the size of the population (field) is 500 and the auditor anticipates a 5 percent rate of occurrence of the particular exception, it will be necessary for him to examine 200 sample items in order to be 100 percent confident that he will find at least one occurrence of the exception. Again assuming a field size of 500 and an estimated rate of occurrence of 5 percent, he may be 93.3 percent confident of discovering at least one exception from the examination of 50 sample items.

Discovery sampling is easy to understand. Although the auditor traditionally prefers to obtain an occurrence rate from his sampling, there are many situations in which he may apply the discovery sampling technique. This technique is applicable primarily in those situations in which the auditor can define an exception as either "critical" or "noncritical." When an exception is "critical," such as the discovery of fraud, any occurrence rate may be intolerable. Consequently, if such an exception is discovered, the auditor may abandon his sampling procedures and undertake a thorough examination of the population.

As an illustration, let us assume that there is reason to suspect that someone has been preparing fraudulent purchase orders, receiving

FIGURE 8–3
Probabilities of including at least one occurrence in a sample (for random samples only)

When Sample Size Is:	.05%	.1%	.5%	1%	2%	5%	10%
				When Occurrence Rate Is:			
			Probability of Finding at Least One Occurrence Is:				
Field Size Is 200							
10				9.8%	18.7%	40.9%	66.0%
25				23.5	41.6	74.6	94.0
40				36.1	59.4	89.9	99.1
50				43.8	68.7	94.8	99.8
60				51.1	76.3	97.4	99.9
80				64.1	87.3	99.5	100.0
Field Size Is 500							
10			5.9%	9.6%	18.4%	40.4%	65.5%
25			14.3	22.7	40.4	73.2	93.3
50			27.1	41.1	65.5	93.3	99.6
75			38.7	55.8	80.6	98.5	100.0
100			48.9	67.4	89.5	99.7	100.0
200			78.5	92.3	99.4	100.0	100.0
Field Size Is 1000							
10		1.0%	4.9%	9.6%	18.4%	40.3%	65.3%
25		2.5	11.9	22.5	40.0	72.7	93.1
50		5.0	22.7	40.3	64.5	92.8	99.6
100		10.0	41.0	65.3	88.1	99.6	100.0
200		20.0	67.3	89.4	98.9	100.0	100.0
400		40.0	92.3	99.4	100.0	100.0	100.0
Field Size Is 2000							
10	0.5%	1.0%	4.9%	9.6%	18.3%	40.2%	65.2%
50	2.5	4.9	22.4	39.9	64.0	92.6	99.5
100	5.0	9.8	40.2	64.3	87.4	99.5	100.0
200	10.0	19.0	65.2	88.0	98.6	100.0	100.0
400	20.0	36.0	89.3	98.9	100.0	100.0	100.0
600	30.0	51.0	97.2	99.9	100.0	100.0	100.0
Field Size Is 3000							
10	0.5%	1.0%	4.9%	9.6%	18.3%	40.2%	65.2%
100	5.0	9.7	39.3	64.0	87.2	99.5	100.0
200	9.8	18.7	64.6	87.5	98.5	100.0	100.0
400	19.3	34.9	88.4	98.7	100.0	100.0	100.0
600	28.4	48.8	96.5	99.9	100.0	100.0	100.0
800	37.2	60.6	99.1	100.0	100.0	100.0	100.0
1000	45.6	70.4	99.8	100.0	100.0	100.0	100.0
Field Size Is 10,000							
100	4.9%	9.6%	39.6%	63.6%	86.9%		
200	9.6	18.3	63.7	86.9	98.3		
500	22.6	40.1	92.4	99.4	100.0		
1000	41.0	65.1	99.5	100.0	100.0		
Field Size Is 15,000							
100	4.9%	9.6%	39.5%	63.5%	86.8%		
200	9.6	18.2	63.4	86.8	98.3		
500	22.4	39.9	92.2	99.4	100.0		
1000	40.4	64.5	99.4	100.0	100.0		

From Henry P. Hill, Joseph L. Roth, and Herbert Arkin, *Sampling in Auditing—A Simplified Guide and Statistical Tables* (New York: The Ronald Press Co., 1962).

reports, and purchase invoices. In order to determine whether or not this has occurred, it will be necessary to locate only one set of the fraudulent documents in the file of paid vouchers. If the accounting department has recorded 3,000 purchase invoices and we desire to locate at least one fraudulent invoice, we could effectively employ discovery sampling.

Assume that we wish to be at least 95 percent certain that our sample will bring to light a fraudulent invoice, if the population of 3,000 invoices contains 0.5 percent or more fraudulent items. The table illustrated in Figure 8–3 indicates that we would need to select a sample of 600 purchase invoices to meet the testing requirements we have prescribed. If no fraudulent invoices were discovered in this sample, we would be 96.5 percent certain that fraudulent invoices were not present in the population to the extent of 0.5 percent (1 in every 200 items). We have not, however, ruled out the possibility that one or more of the 3,000 purchase invoices is fraudulent.

Estimation sampling for variables

Although both sampling for attributes and discovery sampling are techniques of great use to the auditor, they do not provide him with results stated in dollars. Estimation sampling for variables, often called "dollar value estimation," permits the auditor to estimate dollar amounts. This technique is designed to estimate the *average dollar value of items in a population,* within a specified precision and confidence level, by determining the *average* dollar value of the sample items. If an estimate of the *total* dollar value of a population is desired, the estimated average value and the limits of precision must be multiplied by the number of items in the population.

Sampling for variables is very useful to the auditor in such functions as estimating the dollar value of inventories or accounts receivable, or the aggregate dollar amount of each age classification in an aging schedule of accounts receivable.

Theory of sampling for variables

The assumption underlying sampling for variables is that the mean of a sample will, within a certain precision and confidence level, represent the mean of the population. Sampling for variables is a more sophisticated statistical process than attribute or discovery sampling. Even if tables are used to determine the required sample size, the auditor needs some familiarity with statistical theory and terminology. Of particular importance are the concepts of *normal distribution, standard deviation,* and *standard error of the sample means.*

Normal distribution. Many populations, such as the heights of all men, may be described as normal distributions. A normal distribution is illustrated by the familiar bell-shaped curve, illustrated in Figure 8–4, in which the values of the individual items tend to congregate around the population *mean.* Notice that the distribution of individual item values is symmetrical on both sides of the mean. There is no tendency

FIGURE 8–4
Normal distribution

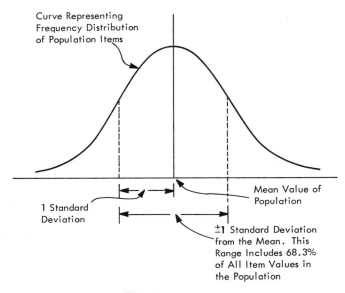

Curve Representing
Frequency Distribution
of Population Items

Mean Value of
Population

1 Standard
Deviation

±1 Standard Deviation
from the Mean. This
Range Includes 68.3%
of All Item Values in
the Population

for deviations to be to one side rather than the other. Although not all populations are normally distributed, it is often useful to assume normal distribution. In cases where the normal distribution assumption is clearly inappropriate, the auditor should enlist the services of an expert statistician.

Standard deviation. In a normal distribution, the dispersion of individual item values about the population mean may be described by the *standard deviation* of the population. It is inherent in the definitions of normal distribution and standard deviation that 68.3 percent of the item values in a normal distribution fall within ±1 standard deviation of the population mean, 95.4 percent fall within ±2 standard deviations, and 99.7 percent fall within ±3 standard deviations. These percentage relationships hold true by definition; however, the dollar amount of the standard deviation will vary from population to population.[2]

---

[2] The standard deviation is the square root of the following quotient: the sum of the squares of the deviation of each item value from the mean, divided by one less than the number of items in the population.

Standard error of the sample means. If a series of samples of a given size are taken from a normal population, the means of these samples should vary from the population (true) mean because of sampling error. The sample means should, however, be normally distributed about the true mean. The standard deviation of this normal distribution of sample means is called the *standard error of the sample means.* The words "standard error" are used in place of "standard deviation" to stress that deviation of sample means from the true mean is caused by *sampling error.*

Standard errors are another way of *stating the precision* with which a sample mean represents the true mean at a given confidence level. Since the standard error is the standard deviation of a distribution of sample means, we know that 68.3 percent of the possible sample means fall within ±1 standard error of the true mean, 95.4 percent fall within ±2 standard errors, and 99.7 percent fall within ±3 standard errors. Thus, a given sample mean represents the true mean with a precision of ±1 standard error at a 68.3 percent level of confidence, a precision of ±2 standard errors at a 95 (actually 95.4) percent confidence level, and a precision of ±3 standard errors at the 99 (99.7) percent confidence level.

The standard error of the sample means is caused by sampling error. Just as larger sample size will usually reduce sampling error, a distribution of means of larger size samples will usually have a smaller standard error. The relationship of the standard error to sample size is expressed by the following formula:[3]

$$\text{Standard error of the sample means} = \frac{\text{Standard deviation of population}}{\text{Square root of sample size}}$$

Determination of sample size

Sampling for variables is like other sampling plans in that the auditor must predetermine the precision and confidence level with which his sample should represent the population. Since the range of precision in sampling for variables is a dollar amount, the materiality of the tolerable margin of error should be the criterion used to establish precision. The confidence level used by the auditor will depend upon the evidential support he requires for rendering his opinion.

Since our specified range of precision may also be stated in terms of standard errors, we may use the relationship of standard errors to sample size to determine the sample size required to give our specified

---

[3] This formula is based upon an infinite population. The effect on the standard error when the population is finite but of significant size is not material.

precision and confidence level. The formula relating standard errors to sample size on page 265 may be rearranged to read:

$$\text{Sample size} = \left(\frac{\text{Standard deviation of population}}{\text{Standard error of the sample means}}\right)^2$$

To determine the required sample size, we must (1) estimate the standard deviation of the population, (2) use our specified dollar range of precision to find the dollar value of the permissible standard error, and (3) solve the formula for sample size. The following procedure may be used to estimate the standard deviation of a population:

1. Select a random sample of 49 items.
2. Group the selected items into seven groups of seven items each, based upon the order in which the items were selected.
3. Find the range (difference) between the highest and lowest item in each group.
4. Compute the average of the seven ranges.
5. Divide this average range by 2.704 to obtain an estimate of the standard deviation of the population.

2.326 - GRoups of 5   2.534 - Groups of 6   2.847 Groups of 8

To find the dollar value of the permissible standard error, we need only to:

1. State our specified sample precision in terms of standard errors.
2. Divide the dollar range of precision by the range of precision in standard errors. The resulting amount is the dollar value of one standard error.

Illustration of estimation sampling for variables

Assume a client has an inventory of 10,000 head of beef cattle (steers) located in feed lots. The steers were purchased at various dates and at varying prices. The client's records show a value for the inventory equal to his purchase cost of the cattle plus the cumulative costs of feeding these cattle. Assume that the current price quotation for beef cattle of this grade is 40 cents per pound. As auditors, we wish to estimate the market value of the inventory to determine that the carrying value of the cattle on the books does not exceed current market value.

In view of the dollar amounts involved, we wish our estimate of the market value of the cattle to have a precision of ±$50,000 at a 95 percent level of confidence. Since sampling for variables deals with average amounts, we must actually estimate the average market value per steer and multiply this estimate by the number of cattle in the inventory. If the estimate of total market value is to have a precision of ±$50,000 at the 95 percent confidence level, the estimate of average market value per steer must have a precision of ±$5 $\left(\dfrac{\$50,000}{10,000}\right)$.

The standard deviation of the population of cattle values may be estimated by selecting a random sample of 49 steers, weighing each one to determine its market value, and following the procedures described on page 266. Let us assume that this process results in an estimated standard deviation of $30.

To determine the dollar value of the allowable standard error of the sample means, we recall that we may expect a given sample mean to fall within ±2 standard errors of the true mean with a confidence level of 95 percent. (Tables are available to find precision measured in standard errors at other confidence levels.) If our sample mean is to fall within both ±$5 and ±2 standard errors of the true mean, the maximum allowable standard error must be $2.50 $\left(\dfrac{\pm \$5}{\pm 2 \text{ standard errors}}\right)$.

Using the sample size formula we may now compute our necessary sample size:

$$\text{Sample size} = \left(\frac{\text{Standard deviation of population}}{\text{Standard error of the sample means}}\right)^2$$
$$= \left(\frac{30}{2.50}\right)^2 = \frac{900}{6.25} = 144 \text{ steers}$$

Since we have already sampled 49 steers, we need only to select on a random basis another 95 to complete our required sample of 144. Assuming our sample mean indicated an average market value of $280 per steer, we could be 95 percent confident that the current market value of the inventory is $2,800,000 ± $50,000.

Combined use of sampling for attributes, sampling for variables, and discovery sampling

After gaining a thorough knowledge of the various techniques of statistical measurement, the auditor will find occasions in which he uses two or more of the techniques concurrently. For example, assume that the auditor wishes to establish the validity of perpetual inventory cards by making cycle counts. He may select items for physical observation and comparison with the perpetual inventory cards through the application of estimation sampling for attributes. If he is satisfied with the results, he may stop. However, there may be situations when he must interpret the results of the examination in dollars. He may convert the attribute sampling to the dollar value method and use the latter to assist him in the evaluation of sample results. Further, if he finds any evidence of deliberate manipulation or circumvention of the internal control system, he may use discovery sampling techniques to assist him in evaluating the possible presence of exceptions of this nature.

Advantages of statistical sampling

The principal advantages of statistical sampling may be summarized as follows. Statistical sampling—

1. Permits the auditor to calculate sample reliability (precision) and the risk of reliance on the sample (confidence level). He must make an objective definition of the quality required in his sample and measure the reliability and degree of assurance which can be placed upon the sample results.

2. Requires the auditor to plan his approach in a more orderly manner than is common when judgment sampling is employed. He must establish in advance the objectives of his test and the nature of audit exceptions and must make estimates as to certain characteristics of the field to be examined.

3. Permits the auditor to interpret the results of the sampling process on a more objective basis than is traditionally employed. He has a clearer understanding of the characteristics of the field and the types of exceptions observed. Further, he is provided with values representing precision and confidence levels which are easier to evaluate than an entire series of often unrelated events.

4. Permits the auditor to employ a smaller sample size than he would use in judgment sampling, especially when the population is relatively large. As the population size increases, the ratio of increase in sample size diminishes; thus, if the auditor adopts the traditional judgment sampling technique of drawing a sample which represents a flat percentage of the population, he usually draws a larger sample than is necessary under statistical techniques.

5. Permits a more intensive examination of the sample items. Because smaller sample sizes are possible and justifiable, the auditor is able to scrutinize thoroughly each item drawn for examination. He realizes the effect of each exception on his calculations of precision and confidence levels and, therefore, tends to make a closer inspection.

Statistical sampling does not change the decisions which the auditor must make. It helps him to obtain a more efficient sample than under judgment techniques and gives him a means to measure reliability and risk. The auditor should avail himself of this effective tool for use in the many areas in which it will help him perform more effectively than will traditional judgment sampling.

GROUP I
REVIEW QUESTIONS

8–1. Do statistical sampling techniques preclude the need for the auditor to exercise judgment in evaluating a client's records? Explain.

8–2. Explain why a random stratified sample is superior to a judgment sample. (AICPA)

8–3. Would it be acceptable practice for the auditor to use both statistical sampling and judgment sampling in the same audit engagement? Explain.

8–4. Distinguish between statistical selection and statistical measurement. May each be used independently?

8–5. Explain the meaning of "sampling without replacement" and "sampling with replacement." Which method of sampling is assumed in most statistical formulae? What is the effect upon sample results if the other method is used?

8–6. In selecting items for examination an auditor considered four alternatives: (*a*) random number table selection, (*b*) systematic selection, (*c*) stratified selection, and (*d*) cluster selection. Which, if any, of the four methods would lead to a random sample if properly applied?

8–7. Explain briefly the term "systematic selection" as used in auditing and indicate the precautions to be taken if a random sample is to be obtained. Is systematic selection applicable to unnumbered documents? Explain.

8–8. Explain briefly how the auditor using statistical sampling techniques may measure the possibility that the sample drawn has characteristics not representative of the population.

8–9. What relationships exist between confidence level, precision, and sample size? (AICPA)

8–10. Identify the three statistical sampling plans that are most useful to the auditor.

8–11. Assume population item values are randomly distributed between $0 and $10,000. Do these item values form a normal distribution?

8–12. When using an acceptance sampling plan, what three conclusions may the auditor reach? Explain.

8–13. Why is discovery sampling well suited to the detection of fraud?

8–14. What would be the difference in an estimation sampling for attributes plan and an estimation sampling for variables plan in a test of inventory extensions?

8–15. What is meant by the term "standard error of the sample means"? Why is this measurement of significance to the auditor?

8–16. If a sample of 100 items indicates an error rate of 3 percent, should the auditor conclude that the entire population also has approximately a 3 percent error rate?

8–17. What relationship exists between the expected occurrence rate and sample size?

8–18. Explain what is meant by a precision of ±1 percent at a confidence level of 90 percent. (AICPA, adapted)

8–19. The 12 following statements apply to unrestricted random sampling with replacement. Indicate whether each statement is true or false.

a) The auditor's prior knowledge of the materiality of the items to be tested may negate the need for random selection. *Exp. If 10 items com 5% of rec. Julywice*

b) A rigid definition of the population of accounts receivable must specify that only active accounts with balances be included.

c) If a population consists mostly of accounts with large balances, it is acceptable to exclude accounts with small balances from the population to be sampled because the error in a small balance could not be material.

d) Excluding extremely large items from the definition of the population and evaluating them separately so that they have no chance of being included in the sample would violate the definition of unrestricted random sampling. *we have the opportunity to define the popula*

e) To be random a sample must be completely unbiased and its selection governed completely by chance.

f) If there is great variability in the number of entries on each item to be sampled, the population could be defined first to select a random sample of items (such as invoices) and then to select a random sample of one entry (quantity and/or price and/or amount) from each item selected.

g) The precision of an estimate of a population mean from a sample mean increases as the degree of confidence in the estimate increases.

h) It is likely that five different random samples from the same population would produce five different estimates of the true population mean.

i) A 100 percent sample would have to be taken to attain a precision range of ±$0 with 100 percent reliability. *confidence*

j) The effect of the inclusion by chance of a very large or very small item in a random sample can be lessened by increasing the size of the sample.

k) The standard deviation is a measure of the variability of items in a population.

l) The standard error of the means will usually be less than the estimated standard deviation computed from a sample estimate. (AICPA, adapted)

8–20. A client wishes to conduct his physical inventory on a sampling basis. Many items will not be counted. Under what general conditions will this method of taking inventory be acceptable to the auditors?

GROUP II
QUESTIONS REQUIRING ANALYSIS

8-21. Increasing attention is being given by CPAs to the application of statistical sampling techniques to audit testing.

Required:

a) List and explain the advantages of applying statistical sampling techniques to audit testing.

b) List and discuss the decisions involving professional judgment that must be made by the CPA in applying statistical sampling techniques to audit testing.

c) You have applied probability sampling techniques to the client's pricing of the inventory and discovered from your sampling that the occurrence rate exceeded your predetermined maximum acceptable occurrence rate. Discuss the courses of action you can take. (AICPA, adapted)

8-22. An auditor has reason to suspect that fraud has occurred through forgery of the treasurer's signature on company checks. The population under consideration consists of 3,000 checks. Can discovery sampling be used to rule out the possibility that any forged signatures exist among the 3,000 checks? Explain.

8-23. In connection with his examination of the financial statements of the Hilltop Corporation, an auditor is making a rough estimate of the total value of an inventory of 2,000 items. Assume that his estimate of the total, based upon the mean of the unrestricted random sample, is to be within precision limits of ±$18,000. With what precision must his sample mean represent the true population mean? Explain. (AICPA, adapted)

8-24. During an audit of Potter Company, an auditor needs to estimate the average gross value of the 5,000 invoices processed during June. The auditor estimates the standard deviation of the population to be $8. Determine the size sample the auditor should select to achieve a precision of ±$1 with a 95 percent level of confidence. (AICPA, adapted)

8-25. Bock Company had two billing clerks during the year. Clerk A worked nine months, and Clerk B worked three months. Assume the quantity of bills per month is constant. If the same maximum tolerable occurrence rate and confidence level are specified for each population, should the ratio of the size of the sample drawn from Clerk A's bills to the size of the sample drawn from Clerk B's bills be 3:1? Discuss. (AICPA, adapted)

8-26. For his test of the pricing and mathematical accuracy of sales invoices, an auditor selected a sample of 500 sales invoices from a total of 100,000 invoices that were issued during the year under examination. The 500 invoices represented total recorded sales of $22,500. Total sales for the year amounted to $5,000,000. The examination disclosed that of the 500 invoices audited, 15 were not properly priced or contained errors in extensions and footings. The 15 incorrect invoices represented $720 of the total recorded sales, and the errors found resulted in a net understatement of these invoices by $30.

What may the auditor conclude from the above information (*a*) if the sample was drawn on a judgment basis, and (*b*) if the sample was drawn by a statistical method?

GROUP III
PROBLEMS

8–27.   The following questions relate to the use of the random number table presented in Figure 8–1 of this chapter. In using the table, read from the left-hand side of each column, starting at the top and proceeding to the bottom. When you reach the end of the column, skip to the next full column on the right.

a)   You wish to select a sample of 100 vouchers for examination. The vouchers for the year being audited are numbered with two series of digits, the first representing the month in which the voucher is prepared and the second, the number of the voucher within each month, as follows:

January	1–1	to	1–296
February	2–1	to	2–227
March	3–1	to	3–301
April	4–1	to	4–325
May	5–1	to	5–289
June	6–1	to	6–311
July	7–1	to	7–352
August	8–1	to	8–271
September	9–1	to	9–309
October	10–1	to	10–243
November	11–1	to	11–295
December	12–1	to	12–338

Starting at the top of column 1 of the random number table, what would be the voucher numbers of the first 10 items you would select for examination? Explain fully the method or methods to be used.

b)   You wish to test the pricing of a company's physical inventory. The inventory listing presented to you consists of 52 pages. There are 36 items on each page except the following:

Page number   *Number of items*

2	40
10	32
18	35
29	40
43	31
52	26

Starting at the top of column 7 of the random number table, explain fully two alternative methods which could be used to identify the first five items to be selected for your price test.

8–28. The use of statistical sampling techniques in an examination of financial statements does not eliminate judgmental decisions.

Required:

a) Identify and explain four areas where judgment may be exercised by a CPA in planning a statistical test.

b) Assume that an auditor's sample shows an unacceptable error rate. Discuss the various actions that he may take based upon this finding.

c) A nonstratified sample of 80 accounts payable vouchers is to be selected from a population of 3,200. The vouchers are numbered consecutively from 1 to 3,200 and are listed, 40 to a page, in the voucher register. Describe four different techniques for selecting a random sample of vouchers for review. (AICPA, adapted)

8–29. During your examination of the financial statements of Southwest Oil Company, you confirm accounts receivable from credit card customers. At the date of your examination, June 30, there are approximately 30,000 accounts with balances ranging from $5 to $200 and averaging about $40. You select a sample of 500 accounts on a random basis; and after all accounts have been confirmed or otherwise examined through alternative procedures, your assistant shows you a working paper containing the following exceptions he has noted in the examination:

Number of sample item drawn	Nature of exception
10	Customer claims that he made his payment on June 29. Our investigation discloses that the check was received from the customer on June 30, but it was not processed because of the large volume of cash receipts on that date. However, the check was deposited and recorded as a receipt on July 1.
25	The customer had purchased a set of tires which were found to be defective and returned them to one of the company's service stations in June. The service station issued a credit memo on July 2 which was received and recorded by the accounting office the following day.
30	The customer paid one of the company's branches for his account on July 1. Investigation discloses that the branch held its cashbook open to pick up all July 1 cash receipts as June 30 business.
31	Confirmation was returned by the customer's trustee in bankruptcy. The trustee states that the customer will be unable to pay; however, the credit manager feels that in the long run a partial collection is possible.
40	Customer claims that he paid his account in full before the middle of June. Investigation discloses that all open charges to this customer's account should have been charged to another account. There was a transposition in customer account numbers. Account 99026 was charged instead of account 99062.
45	Customer claimed he mailed his payment on June 29. Investigation shows that the payment was received and recorded on July 2.
47	Customer refuses to pay for delinquent charges on an installment plan

[Handwritten annotations:] ERROR – Any over – or – understatement of Account. Cutoff wrong. Terrible F/C – not recorded deposited. Cash AR. Sales Ret A/R. AR Card. No Error. Just a misclassification. No Problem. We had goods at June 30.

purchase of automobile tires. For policy reasons, the client will not press for collection and the amount will be charged off in July. *NO*

50   Customer claims he paid on June 25. Investigation discloses that the payment was received on June 29 but was not accompanied by the payment slip. The company was unable to identify the payment and credited it to a suspense account pending identification. *NP*

55   Customer reported that the balance of his account should be $129.62 instead of $119.62 as shown by his statement. Investigation disclosed that the detail credit card slips were improperly footed. *Yes A/R are undere*

60   Customer claims he returned a bulk purchase container for credit several months previously. Investigation discloses that a credit memo for the container was inadvertently not issued. *ERROR*

Sales Return A/R

What error rate (in numbers of accounts) has your sample disclosed? What analysis should you make of the above exceptions noted by your assistant?

9

Audit working papers

WORKING PAPERS are vitally important instruments of the auditing profession. The need for the auditor to acquire skill and judgment in the design and use of these basic tools is scarcely less than the need for a surgeon to master the use of operating instruments. Working papers are the connecting link between the client's records and the auditor's report. In fact, the work of an audit centers around the systematic preparation of a series of working papers in such form, and with such content, that the auditor may prepare therefrom a report on the financial position and operations of the client. If a client's records were in ideal condition, that is, free from error and completely current without reflecting any transactions which overlapped between accounting periods, the need for working papers would be greatly reduced. Under such hypothetical circumstances the client's financial statements could be compared directly to the accounting records with a minimum of working papers to record the auditor's activities. However, actual accounting records are never so perfect. During the course of his verification of the financial statements, the auditor finds it necessary to analyze, to draft adjustments for errors in amount and errors in accounting principles, and to gather supplementary information to support the records. It is this analyzing, adjusting, and compiling of auditing evidence that necessitates the use of extensive working papers.

Definition of working papers

The Committee on Auditing Procedure of the AICPA, in discussing standards of field work, has pointed out that "sufficient competent evidential matter is to be obtained through inspection, observation, inquiries and confirmations to afford a reasonable basis for an opinion regarding the financial statements under examination." In building up this evidence the auditor prepares working papers. Some of these may take the form of bank reconciliations or analyses of ledger accounts; others may consist of copies of correspondence, copies of minutes of directors' and stockholders' meetings, and lists of stockholders; still others might be organization charts or graphical presentations of plant layout. Working trial balances, audit programs, internal control questionnaires, a letter of representations obtained from the client, returned confirmation forms—all these various schedules, analyses, lists, notes, and documents form parts of the auditor's working papers.

✱   The term "working papers" is thus a comprehensive one; it includes all the evidence gathered by the auditor to show the work he has done, the methods and procedures he has followed, and the conclusions he has developed. In his working papers the auditor has the basis for his report to the client, evidence of the extent of his examination, and proof of the professional care exercised in his investigation.

Confidential nature of working papers

To conduct a satisfactory audit the auditor must be given unrestricted access to all information about the client's business. Much of this information is confidential, such as the profit margins on individual products and the salaries of officers and key employees. The client would not be willing to make available to the auditor information which is carefully guarded from competitors and employees unless he could rely on the auditor maintaining a professional silence on these matters.

✱   Much of the information gained in confidence by the auditor is recorded in his working papers; consequently, the working papers are confidential in nature. The *Code of Professional Ethics* developed by the AICPA includes the rule that: "A member shall not disclose any confidential information obtained in the course of a professional engagement except with the consent of the client." In interpreting this rule the Division of Professional Ethics has expressed the opinion that when one CPA sells his practice to another, he should not give the purchaser access to working papers without first obtaining permission from the client.

Ownership and control of working papers

Since audit working papers are highly confidential, they must be safeguarded at all times. Safeguarding working papers usually means keeping them locked in a briefcase during lunch and after working hours.

If the client wishes to keep some of his employees uninformed on executive salaries, mergers, or other aspects of the business, the auditor obviously should not defeat this policy by exposing his working papers to unauthorized employees of the client. The policy of close control of audit working papers is also necessary because if employees were seeking to conceal fraud or to mislead the auditor for any reason, they might make alterations in the papers. The working papers may identify particular accounts, branches, or time periods to be tested; to permit the client's employees to learn of these in advance would weaken the significance of the tests.

Audit working papers are prepared on the client's premises, from the client's records, and at the client's expense, yet these papers are the exclusive property of the auditor. This ownership of working papers follows logically from the relationship between the auditor and the client and has been supported in the courts. The auditor is not an employee or agent of the client; rather he is an independent contractor free to determine the methods and procedures necessary to the carrying out of his professional duties.

Purposes of audit working papers

Audit working papers, being the compilation of all evidence gathered by the auditor, serve several purposes. The most important purposes are:

1. To coordinate and organize all phases of the audit engagement.
2. To facilitate preparation of the audit report.
3. To substantiate and explain in detail the opinions and findings summarized in the report.

A supplementary purpose of working papers is to provide information for preparation of income tax returns and registration documents with the SEC and other governmental agencies. Of course each annual set of working papers also serves as a useful guide in subsequent engagements. Although clients may sometimes find it helpful to request information from the auditor's working papers of prior years, these working papers should not be regarded as a substitute for the client's own accounting records.[1]

Working papers and auditing standards

The three major purposes listed in the preceding section are applicable to the working papers prepared for recurring annual audits and

---

[1] *Statement on Auditing Procedure No. 39*, issued by the Committee on Auditing Procedure, AICPA, September, 1967.

apply to most nonrecurring special investigations as well. Each of these three major purposes of audit working papers will now be considered individually and related to the three generally accepted standards of field work.

To coordinate and organize audit work.   Coordination of all phases of the audit work is achieved through the working papers. As each step of verification and analysis is performed, significant facts and relationships come to the attention of the auditor. Unless these matters are set down in writing when observed, they are likely to be forgotten before they can be properly appraised in the light of information disclosed by other phases of the audit. By carefully planning the assignment of assistants to work on different papers, a senior auditor may efficiently coordinate and organize many phases of the examination work at one time. Thus the working papers show that the first standard of field work (adequate planning of the work and proper supervision of assistants) has been met.

The senior auditor may instruct each assistant to prepare a separate working paper on different items under examination, and then proceed from one assistant to another, supervising the work done. Frequently the senior may prepare working paper headings and enter a few sample transactions, requesting assistants to complete the papers; in this manner, he initiates the examination of several items simultaneously and follows each project to completion. It is often not feasible for the auditor to carry out all verification work on a particular account at one time. For example, cash on hand may be counted on the first day of the investigation, but confirmation of bank balances not completed until several days later. As each phase is completed, the working papers are filed, to be expanded and added to as additional information is obtained. Thus the audit file on a given account may be begun early in the engagement but may not be completed until after other phases of the audit have been fully carried out.

When an audit covers several scattered branches of a company, working papers are of great assistance in organizing and coordinating the work. Each branch's records may be examined by different staff members, perhaps by individuals from different offices of the auditing firm. Working papers will then be prepared at each place of examination and sent to a central location, where they can be assembled and reviewed prior to the writing of the report. Working papers of uniformly high quality are obviously of basic importance in audits of this type.

An audit does not end when the accountant leaves the client's office. The report must be completed, or in some cases written in its entirety, tax returns prepared, and the entire engagement reviewed by a manager or partner. These last stages of the audit are made possible by the working papers. The manager or partner, with the working papers before him, has a view of the entire audit as an organized and coordinated whole; only then can he judge whether the audit meets professional auditing standards.

To facilitate preparation of the report. Working papers facilitate the preparation of the auditor's report to the client because they are the source from which the report writer draws material. This report may assume a variety of forms, depending upon the purpose and scope of the engagement. A summary of the principal findings and recommendations constitutes the most essential part of the report for most special investigations and also for most long-form reports used for credit purposes. The scope of the work performed and other general background information may accompany the findings and recommendations. For nearly all types of audit situations, the end product of the auditor's work is a report; this report and any related financial statements or schedules will be drawn from the audit working papers.

To substantiate the report. Since audit reports are prepared from the working papers, it follows that audit working papers substantiate and explain the conclusions reached in the report. The auditor may on occasion be called upon to testify in court concerning the financial affairs of a client, or he may be required to defend in court the accuracy and reasonableness of his report. In all such cases, working papers are the principal means of substantiating the audit report. After completion of the audit, the auditor may draft a report on internal control to the client. In identifying existing weaknesses in internal control and in developing recommendations to correct these weaknesses, the auditor will use the working papers as a principal source of information.

To clearly substantiate the auditor's report, audit working papers must provide evidence of the auditor's compliance with the generally accepted auditing standards. The working papers should especially demonstrate adequate planning of the audit and proper supervision of all staff members; a comprehensive study and evaluation of the client's system of internal control and the relation of the internal control evaluation to the audit program; and the accumulation of sufficient competent evidence to support the auditor's opinion on the client's financial statements. Other essential contents of working papers in order to substantiate the report include the actions taken to resolve exceptions or other unusual matters discovered during the audit, and the auditor's conclusions on specific aspects of the engagement.

Working papers and accountants' liability

In the discussion of the auditor's legal liability in Chapter 3, an illustrative case was presented in which the auditor's own working papers were used against him by the SEC to support charges of improper professional conduct. The working papers showed that the auditor early in the engagement had formed the opinion that the allowance for uncollectible accounts was inadequate; later in the engagement (perhaps because of pressure from the client, perhaps for other reasons) he had modified his position.

The significant point is that working papers, if not properly prepared, are as likely to injure the auditor as to protect him. *To look over a set of working papers for supporting information is one thing; to look over these same papers for details which may be used to attack the auditor's conclusions is quite another.* This latter possibility suggests the need for public accounting firms to make a critical review of working papers at the end of each engagement, and to give thought to the possibility that any contradictory statements, or evidence inconsistent with the conclusions finally reached, may be used to support charges of negligence at a later date.

Part of the difficulty in avoiding inconsistent and conflicting evidence in working papers is that the papers are prepared in large part by less experienced staff members. When the papers are reviewed by a supervisor, he will give careful consideration to any questionable points. In studying these points the supervisor often gives consideration to many other aspects of the audit and of the client's records with which he is familiar; these other factors may lead him to the conclusion that an issue raised in the working papers does not warrant any corrective action. In some instances he may conclude that the assistant who prepared the paper has misinterpreted the situation. Years later if a dispute arises and the working papers are being subjected to critical study by attorneys representing an "injured" client or third party, these questionable points in the papers may appear in a different light. The supervisor who cleared the issue based on his personal knowledge of the client's business may not be available to explain the reasoning involved, or the other special considerations present at the time of the audit. This long-range responsibility suggests that the supervisor should, at the time of deciding upon disposition of a troublesome point, insert an adequate explanation of his action in the working papers.

From time to time a public accounting firm should make a critical evaluation of its policies for preparation, review, and preservation of working papers. Recent experience in cases involving legal liability may lead some firms to considerable modification in the traditional handling of working papers.

Essentials of good working papers

The technical ability and the professional skill of the public accountant are reflected in the working papers which he prepares. To achieve recognition as a competent auditor capable of performing field work in accordance with generally accepted auditing standards, the auditor must attach real importance to the creation of working papers of maximum usefulness. To accomplish this end, he must, first, make his work complete but free of nonessential data; and, second, organize and arrange the papers in a manner that will facilitate rapid reference and will make them readily understandable to others.

Audit working papers are complete when they clearly reflect full information regarding the composition of all significant data in the records, together with the methods of verification employed and such other evidence as is necessary for the preparation of an opinion and report.

The mark of the experienced auditor is his ability to produce papers which contain all essential information but do not include any superfluous material. Verification work usually involves the examination of numerous documents. Does it follow that each document examined should be transcribed into the working papers? Or, as a compromise, should the date, serial number, and similar key points of each document be recorded by the auditor? Not at all; there are many instances in which the only appropriate entry in the working papers is a notation by the auditor indicating that certain supporting documents have been inspected. This notation may consist merely of the auditor's initials and the date placed in the audit program to indicate that a specific procedure has been completed.

An auditor is an investigator trained to distinguish sharply between facts and opinions. An audit report may properly include both facts and opinions but should not confuse or intermingle the two. Consequently, the working papers must also clearly identify factual statements and matters of judgment. Every factural statement and every figure in the report should be supported and explained in the working papers. As the examination progresses, the auditor should think ahead to the problems of report writing and include in the working papers comments and explanations which will later become part of the report. There should be no hesitancy in adding full explanatory remarks to any schedule or analysis prepared during any part of the audit. Working papers are not limited to quantitative data; they should include notes and explanations which record fully what was done by the auditor, his reasons for following certain audit procedures and omitting others, and his reactions and opinions concerning the quality of the data examined, the adequacy of the internal controls in force, and the competence of the persons responsible for the operations or records under review.

In addition to the possible examination of working papers by outsiders, working papers are reviewed by seniors and managers or supervisors to determine the adequacy and efficiency of the audit work performed by staff members under their supervision. In such reviews the working papers must speak for themselves; they must be complete, legible, and systematically arranged so that no supplementary explanations or interpretations by the author are necessary.

It is inevitable that errors of judgment will be made in the design and preparation of working papers. Occasionally an inexperienced auditor will become absorbed in a line of investigation altogether irrelevant to the objectives of the audit. He may create extensive working papers before the misdirection of his energies is detected. If these working papers have no bearing on the audit, they should not be preserved. There is a very natural reluctance to destroy papers which embody many hours of labor, but to retain such superfluous papers does not serve to regain the time wasted. On the contrary, inclusion of unnecessary working papers in the file detracts from the quality of the papers as a whole and may lead to further wasted effort during subsequent reviews of the work performed. In all cases the ultimate purpose of the papers should be considered the guiding criterion as to what material is included and what is omitted as unnecessary.

Planning working papers

The development of adequate working papers requires careful planning before and during the course of the audit. As each phase in the verification process develops, the auditor should review the material to be covered and try to visualize the type of working paper that will most effectively present the evidence. Unplanned papers, prepared hastily and without foresight, seldom serve the desired purpose, and repetition of investigative work may be necessary to remedy the deficiencies in the working papers.

Form of schedules and analyses. There are always alternative ways of preparing any given type of working paper. It is usually advantageous to study the similar schedule or analysis form used in the preceding audit. In some cases, the old form may be copied without change; in other cases, opportunity for improvements will be readily apparent; and in still other instances, the old form may be regarded as no longer appropriate. It is usually preferred practice to use a separate sheet for each item or account to be analyzed or scheduled. However, occasions arise when working papers covering different but related accounts may well be combined. For example, it is sometimes convenient to analyze notes payable together with accrued interest payable and prepaid interest. Accumulated depreciation and depreciation expense accounts are commonly analyzed on a single working paper.

The auditor should always bear in mind the possible need for expansion of a working paper. New information may appear at any time during the course of an audit. Since pasting sheets together horizontally is generally undesirable, it is well to plan working papers with a view to vertical expansion. It is obviously more practicable to carry totals forward to a second page than to extend the width of a sheet. In this manner, working papers may be kept to a standard size, a prerequisite for efficient filing or binding.

The content of working papers

Since audit working papers include all information gathered by the auditor, there are innumerable varieties and types of papers. However, there are certain general categories into which most of these may be grouped; these are: (1) audit plans, audit programs, questionnaires, flowcharts and agenda sheets; (2) working trial balances or grouping sheets; (3) adjusting journal entries; (4) supporting schedules, analyses, and computational working papers; (5) copies of minutes and other records or documents; and (6) clients' letters of representations. The original draft of the auditor's report, including financial statements, is also considered part of the audit working papers.

Audit plans, audit programs, agenda sheets, flowcharts, and questionnaires. Audit plans and audit programs were discussed in Chapter 4, and questionnaires and flowcharts in Chapter 5. Closely allied to the audit program is the agenda sheet. This is little more than a note sheet upon which questionable points, comments on unfinished items, and matters to be referred to the client for discussion are recorded for "clearing." The agenda sheet will contain not only these comments and notes but the initials of the persons who investigated them and full explanations as to their disposition or adequate cross-references to other working papers showing their final treatment.

Working trial balance. The working trial balance is a schedule listing the balances of the accounts in the general ledger for the current and the previous year, and also providing columns for the auditor's adjustments and reclassifications and for the final amounts which will appear in the financial statements. A working trial balance is the "backbone" of the entire set of audit working papers; it is the key schedule which controls and summarizes all supporting papers.

Each page of a working trial balance will usually include the following column headings:

Working Paper Reference	Account Title	Final Balance Dec. 31, 19— (Last Year)	Balance per Books Dec. 31, 19— (This Year)	Adjustments and Reclassifications		Final Balance Dec. 31, 19— (This Year)
				Dr.	Cr.	

Although most of these column headings are self-explanatory, a brief discussion of the third and fourth columns is appropriate. In the third column, the final adjusted balances from the previous year's audit are listed. Inclusion of the previous year's figures facilitates comparison with the corresponding amounts for the current year and focuses attention upon any unusual changes.

The fourth column provides for the account balances at the close of the year under audit; these balances are usually taken directly from the general ledger. The balances of the revenue and expense accounts should be included even though these accounts have been closed into the Retained Earnings account prior to the auditor's arrival. The amount to be listed for the Retained Earnings account is the balance at the beginning of the year under audit. Dividends declared during the year are listed as a separate item, as is the computed Net Income for the year.

In many audits, the client furnishes the auditor with a working trial balance after all normal end-of-period journal entries have been posted. Before accepting the trial balance for his working papers, the auditor should trace the amounts to the general ledger and satisfy himself that all ledger accounts have been included in the client-prepared trial balance.

If the auditor finds that the ledger is out of balance, he should ordinarily request that the client's staff locate the error or errors and correct the accounts. If the client prefers that the auditor do the routine work to put the ledger in balance, he should be made to understand that such work is outside the scope of an audit and must be charged for as an additional service. It is generally uneconomical for the auditor's time to be devoted to detailed bookkeeping which could be performed by the client's employees.

Grouping sheets. A working trial balance is appropriate for the audit of a small client having relatively few general ledger accounts. For larger clients with numerous ledger accounts, the working trial balance method is unwieldy. Many general ledger accounts must be combined into a single figure in the audit report balance sheet and statement of income.

The grouping-sheet technique was designed to overcome this disadvantage of the working trial balance. *Grouping sheets* are working papers with columnar headings similar to those for the working trial balance. Separate grouping sheets (also called *lead schedules* or *summary schedules*) are set up to combine similar general ledger accounts, the total of which will appear in the client's balance sheet or statement of income as a single amount. For example, a Cash grouping sheet might combine the following hypothetical general ledger accounts: Petty Cash, $500; General Bank Account, $348,216; Office Payroll Bank Account, $1,500;

Factory Payroll Bank Account, $2,000; and Dividend Bank Account, $500. Similar grouping sheets would be set up for Accounts Receivable, Inventories, Stockholders' Equity, Net Sales, and for any other balance sheet or income statement caption.

Adjusting journal entries and reclassification entries accepted by the client are posted to the appropriate grouping sheets. All columns of the grouping sheets are totaled; then the columnar totals are recapitulated in a *working balance sheet* or *working statement of income*, as appropriate. These two working statements also have columnar headings identical to those for the working trial balance. The working balance sheet, which summarizes all grouping sheets for assets, liabilities, and owners' equity, and the working statement of income, which summarizes all grouping sheets for revenue and expenses, thus constitute the basic working papers supporting the balance sheet and statement of income appearing in the audit report.

The use of grouping sheets facilitates the review of working papers by supervisors. Minor details are eliminated from the working balance sheet and the working statement of income, and the major issues stand forth more clearly.

Adjusting journal entries and reclassification entries

During the course of an audit, the auditor discovers errors of omission or commission in the client's financial statements and accounting records. To correct these errors, the auditor drafts *adjusting journal entries* for later discussion with the client. In addition, the auditor develops *reclassification entries* for items which, although not incorrectly recorded in the accounting records, must be reclassified for fair presentation in the client's financial statements.

Proposed adjusting entries are typically identified by numbers, and reclassification entries are assigned letters. The critical component of each type of entry is the *explanation*; without a complete, lucid explanation, an adjusting or reclassification entry is nearly worthless.

Examples of adjusting and reclassification entries are presented in Figure 9–1. The working paper formats for adjusting and reclassification entries are similar, with columns provided for working paper references and account numbers, as well as for account titles and dollar amounts.

Distinction between adjusting entries and reclassification entries

A distinction must be made between reclassification entries used solely in the auditor's working papers for the purpose of obtaining proper grouping in the financial statements and adjusting entries intended for recording in the client's accounts. A reclassification entry serves to transfer or reclassify an amount on the auditor's working papers; it is not turned over to the client for entry in the books. Typical of the reclassification entries is the one made to reclassify customers' accounts with credit balances so that they will appear on the balance sheet as liabilities rather than being offset against accounts receivable with debit balances. Such an account will ordinarily regain its normal debit balance within a short time and should therefore be continued in the client's records as part of accounts receivable. A similar reclassification entry is made for debit balances in accounts payable, as shown in Figure 9–1.

Adjusting entries for material items only

A legend has long persisted in business folklore and popular fiction that an auditor is a person busily engaged in making minute adjustments

FIGURE 9–1

The Berkeley Corporation
Proposed Adjusting Journal Entries — D-1
December 31, 1974

Working Paper Reference	Account No.	Account Title and Explanation	Dr.	Cr.
		①		
K-1-1	151	Buildings	8 400.00	
R-1-1	509	Depreciation Expense-Buildings	210.00	
R-1-3	531	Repairs and Maintenance Expense		8 400.00
K-2-1	155	Accumulated Depreciation-Bldgs.		210.00
		To correct distribution of Lehnberg Co. invoice dated 6/30/74 for construction of new shipping room and overhead doors. Depreciation based on remaining 20-year life of building		
		②		
K-1-3	153	Office Equipment	760.00	
M-2	218	Federal Income Tax Payable	53.20	
R-2-6	522	Sales Supplies		760.00
N-3	241	Unamortized Investment Credit		53.20
		To correct distribution of Reese Office Supplies invoice dated 12/26/74 for a calculator, and to set up related 7% investment credit		
			V.M.H.	1-19-7

FIGURE 9–1 (continued)

The Berkeley Corporation
Proposed Reclassification Entry   *D–2*
December 31, 1974

Working Paper Reference	Account No.	Account Title and Explanation Ⓐ	Dr.	Cv.
G–1	121	Accounts Receivable	12 000 00	
M–1	200	Accounts Payable		12 000 00
		To transfer debit balance in Accounts Payable to asset classification. (Advance to McQuay Company in connection with purchase order No. 12-73.)		
				U.M.H. 1-19-75

to correct accounting records to a state of precise accuracy. This misconception has perhaps been bolstered by textbook illustrations which, as a matter of convenience, have used very small dollar amounts to illustrate the principle of the adjusting entry.

In the examination of some small companies which lack competent accounting personnel, an auditor may in fact assume the burden of making routine adjusting entries for depreciation, expired insurance, and accrued expenses, as well as entries to correct numerous errors. In such situations, however, the auditor's role is really a combination of auditor and part-time accountant. In the examination of larger concerns with well-qualified accounting personnel, the auditor will find that all normal year-end adjustments for depreciation, prepayments, accruals, and similar items have been completed; the books may have been closed and transactions recorded for the subsequent period before the audit work is performed. Adjusting entries by the auditor will then be few in number and limited to matters which have an important bearing on the financial statements. In other words, the auditor's purpose in proposing an adjusting entry is not to secure greater accuracy of details in the accounting records but to modify financial statements so that they will "present fairly" the financial position and operating results of the company. The adjustments must, however, be entered in the books so that the accounts will agree with the financial statements.

No quantitative rule can be employed to indicate whether a proposed adjustment is sufficiently material to warrant its being made. In reaching a decision the auditor may consider whether the adjustment is of a type that would cause a change in the net income for the year, and the amount of the change expressed as a percentage of net sales and net income. If the proposed adjustment affects balance sheet accounts only, the significance of the amount may be appraised by expressing it as a percentage of total assets, or as a percentage of current assets. However, the qualitative aspects of the adjustment must be considered along with its quantitative importance. An error relating to the Cash account might warrant correction even though an error of comparable size in the Plant account was considered not to require adjustment. Some "errors" are definite violations of accounting principles; others are borderline cases in which room for difference of opinion as to propriety may reasonably exist.

If the reaction of the reader of· the statement is likely to be influenced by reason of a proposed correction of an error, then surely the error may be considered material. For many adjustments, however, the impact on the financial statements is not sufficiently great that one can say with assurance that the user of the statements will be influenced by the change. In making decisions as to whether an adjustment should be made or "passed," there is no satisfactory substitute for the judgment of the partner or manager supervising the examination, since he is in a position consider all the special circumstances of the engagement. In all cases, he will consider the *cumulative* materiality of proposed adjustments which appear to be immaterial when considered individually.

Auditor's adjusting entries recorded by client

Prior to the conclusion of the audit the proposed adjusting journal entries drafted by the auditor will be discussed with the client's controller or chief accountant. In most cases the controller will approve the entries and authorize their recording in the company's accounting records. The auditor records the approved entries on his working trial balance or grouping sheets and extends the adjusted balances to the "Final" column.

The auditor does not personally make entries in the client's accounts: to do so would be to abandon at least temporarily his role of independent auditor. Some of the adjusting journal entries worked out by the auditor may relate to transactions already recorded by the client in the following period. In such cases the auditor should provide the client with a list of the reversing entries which should be made to offset the adjusting journal entries. The auditor must always verify that the adjusting and reversing entries are recorded in the accounts; otherwise, the financial statements appearing in his report will not agree with the client's ledger.

ILLUSTRATIVE CASE.   An auditor found that an unrecorded liability in the amount of $10,000 existed at the balance sheet date for repair to buildings completed during December of the year under audit. The client had recorded the liability as though it were a January transaction of the following year. Since the amount was quite material for this company, the auditor insisted that the repair expense should be reflected in the year in which the work was done and the liability incurred. He therefore drafted an adjusting entry and a reversing entry, both to be recorded by the client in the accounts.

Another practical difficulty sometimes encountered when the auditor does not begin his examination until some time after the end of the period to be audited is that the client may have closed his books and begun entering revenue and expense items in the accounts for the succeeding year. The only alternative open to the auditor in this situation is to make adjustments affecting revenue or expense directly to the Retained Earnings account. Of course the prior closing of the books affects *only* the entries to be entered in the books—and not the entries on the working papers leading to the statement amounts.

Supporting schedules

As the auditor verifies the individual items in the working trial balance, he prepares a variety of working papers in substantiation of the financial and operating data under review. As previously stated, extensive transcribing of company records should be avoided. If such documents are needed in the working papers, copies should be secured. If the purpose of each working paper is clearly defined before it is begun, much pointless work can be avoided. Time spent in construction of working papers is well invested when the papers aid in determining financial status or provide a record of verification. If the auditor plunges into the examination of records without first deciding upon definite objectives, his working papers will usually be recognized by the experienced reviewer as the result of a "make-work" project.

Although all types of working papers may loosely be called "schedules," the auditor prefers to use this term to describe a listing of the elements or details comprising the balance in an asset or liability account as a specific date. No historical review is involved—simply a listing. Thus, a list of securities owned making up the balance in the Marketable Securities account without regard to the changes during the period is properly described as a "schedule."

Working paper for analysis of a ledger account

An analysis of a ledger account is another common type of audit working paper. To analyze a ledger account the auditor first lists the beginning balance and indicates the nature of the items comprising this balance. Next, the auditor lists and investigates the nature of all debits and credits to the account during the period. These entries when combined with the beginning balance produce a figure representing the balance in the account as of the audit date. If any errors or omissions of importance are detected during this analysis of the account, the necessary debit or credit adjustment approved by the client is entered on the working paper to produce the adjusted balance required for the financial statements.

In preparing schedules and analyses, it is usually desirable for the auditor to arrive at a figure equal to the general ledger account balance before he makes any adjustments to correct such balance. In this manner he accounts for the balance of the ledger account as it stands; and at the same time, by scheduling or analyzing the account, he discloses any items improperly included therein. In other words, the auditor first records in his working paper all of the current year's entries in the account, even though some of these entries are improper. Then, after having accounted for the balance of the account and having analyzed the activity therein, he proceeds to make any necessary additions, deletions, or other corrections and arrives at an adjusted balance. Among the various errors which the analysis of a ledger account might disclose are errors in addition of items, the entering of debits as credits and vice versa, posting of erroneous amounts, misclassification of entries, and duplication of entries. The omission of entries belonging in the account is less easily detected, although comparison of the account with a corresponding analysis for the prior year may sometimes suggest the omission of items.

Computational working papers

Another type of supporting working paper is the computational working paper. The auditor's approach to verifying certain types of accounts and other figures is to make an independent computation and compare his results with the amounts shown by the client's records. Examples of amounts which might be verified by computation are the bonuses paid to executives, pension accruals, royalty expense, interest on notes, and accrued taxes. Bonuses, pensions, and royalties are ordinarily specified in contracts; by making computations based on the terms of the contracts, the auditor determines whether these items are stated in accordance with contractual requirements. Social security taxes are based on the amount of wages and salaries paid; the auditor's verification in this case consists of applying the tax rates to the taxable wages and salaries for the period.

Copies of minutes and other records or documents

Auditing is not limited to the examination of financial records, and working papers are not confined to schedules and analyses. During the course of an audit the auditor may gather much purely expository material to substantiate his report. One common example is copies of minutes of directors' and stockholders' meetings. Other examples include copies of articles of incorporation and bylaws; copies of important contracts, bond indentures, and mortgages; and memoranda pertaining to examination of records, confirmations of accounts receivable, and bank deposits.

Letters of representations provided by clients

It is customary for the auditor to obtain letters of representations from clients regarding inventories, liabilities, and other matters. These generally take the form of letters addressed to the auditing firm, signed by the client, and containing statements as to the correctness and authenticity of inventory quantities and prices; the completeness and correctness of liabilities recorded on the books; and any other matter concerning which the auditor may see fit to obtain such representation. Although representations by the client do not excuse the auditor from any necessary auditing procedures, they do have the effect of reminding the client that he is primarily responsible for the correctness of the accounts and the financial statements.

The permanent file

The auditor usually maintains two files of working papers for each client: (1) annual audit files for every completed examination, and (2) a permanent file of relatively unchanging data. The annual file (as for the 1974 audit) pertains solely to that year's examination; the permanent file contains such things as copies of the articles of incorporation which need not be duplicated in subsequent examinations. The permanent file serves three purposes: (1) to refresh the auditor's memory on items applicable over a period of many years; (2) to provide for new staff members a quick summary of the policies and organization of the client; and (3) to preserve working papers on items which show relatively few or no changes, thus eliminating the necessity for their preparation year after year.

Much of the information contained in the permanent file is gathered during the course of the first audit of a client's records. A considerable portion of the time spent on a first audit is devoted to gathering and appraising background information such as the following:

1. Copies of articles of incorporation and bylaws.
2. Charts of accounts, procedure manuals, accounting manuals, and other data concerning internal control.

3. Terms of stock issue permits and bond indentures.
4. Copies of leases, patent agreements, pension plans, labor contracts, profit-sharing and bonus plans, long-term contracts, and guarantee agreements.
5. Organization charts and scope of authority and responsibility of officers.
6. Plant layout, manufacturing processes, and principal products.
7. Copies of minutes of directors', stockholders', and committees' meetings.
8. Analyses of such "permanent" accounts as land, capital stock, long-term debt, retained earnings, and paid-in capital in excess of par or stated value.
9. Copies of income tax returns for prior years.
10. Statistical sampling data.
11. Summary of accounting principles employed by client.

This information should be carefully preserved by the auditor in a permanent file so that he may avoid any unnecessary repetition of work during subsequent examinations. Most business executives are quite willing to spend considerable time with representatives of an auditing firm during the first audit in order to make them conversant with the history, policies, and key personnel of the business. They do not, however, expect to repeat this indoctrination process in full each year. To fulfill its function, the permanent file must be brought up to date during each examination. Copies of new minutes, recent contracts and agreements, any changes in bylaws, and similar developments should be added each year to the file. In each repeat engagement the system of internal control should be reexamined and any changes or improvements recorded. The permanent file should be properly indexed to provide ready reference and adequately bound so that it may be carried to each engagement.

Analyses of accounts which show few or no changes over a period of years are also included in the permanent file. These accounts may include land, buildings, accumulated depreciation, long-term investments, long-term liabilities, capital stock, and other owners' equity accounts. The initial investigation of these accounts must often include the transactions of many years. But once these historical analyses have been brought up to date, the work required in subsequent examinations will be limited to a review of the current year's transactions in these accounts. In this respect, the permanent file is a timesaving device because current changes in such accounts need only be added to the permanent papers without reappearing in the current working papers. Adequate cross-indexing in the working papers should, of course, be provided to show where in the permanent file such information is to be found.

Indexing and preserving working papers

Audit working papers should be indexed either during the audit or upon its completion. There are many alternative methods of indexing; the following tabulation illustrates one such method:

A. Draft of audit report and financial statements.
    A–1. Audit report.
    A–2. Statement of financial position.
    A–3. Statement of income and retained earnings.
    A–4. Statement of changes in financial position.
    A–5. Notes to financial statements.
B. Planning working papers.
    B–1. Engagement letter.
    B–2. Audit plan.
    B–3. Study and evaluation of internal control.
    B–4. Audit program.
    B–5. Time budget.
    B–6. Agenda sheets.
C. Working balance sheet and working statement of income.
D. Adjusting journal entries and reclassification entries.
E. Cash grouping sheet.
    E–1. Petty cash.
    E–2. Bank reconciliations.
        E–2–1. Bank confirmations.
F. Marketable securities.
G. Receivables grouping sheet.
    G–1. Trial balance of accounts receivable.
        G–1–1. Accounts receivable confirmations.
    G–2. Notes receivable analysis.
        G–2–2. Notes receivable confirmations.
    G–3. Analysis of allowance for uncollectible accounts and notes.
H. Inventories grouping sheet.
    H–1. Raw materials physical inventory.
    H–2. Work in process physical inventory.
    H–3. Finished goods physical inventory.
    H–4. Observation of phyiscal inventory.
    H–5. Tests of inventory pricing.
J. Prepaid expenses grouping sheet.
K. Property, plant, and equipment grouping sheet.
    K–1. Summary analysis of plant and equipment.
    K–2. Tests of depreciation.
L. Other assets.
M. Current liabilities grouping sheet.

M–1.   Accounts payable trial balance.
M–2.   Analyses of federal and state income taxes payable.
M–3.   Accrued liabilities.
N.   Long-term liabilities.
P.   Stockholders' equity grouping sheet.
Q.   Revenue grouping sheet.
Q–1.   Analysis of sales.
Q–2.   Analysis of other revenue.
R.   Costs and expenses grouping sheet. *(Lead sceduales)*
R–1.   Analysis of cost of sales.
R–2.   Analysis of selling expenses.
R–3.   Analysis of administrative expenses.
R–4.   Analysis of other expenses. *Unusual Items   Non-Recurring Items*
S.   Extraordinary gains and losses.
T.   Consolidating working papers.
U.   Permanent file.

Index references should be marked in colored pencil on the upper or lower right-hand corner of each working paper, where they will be most conspicuous. Whenever reference is made in one working paper to another, there should be adequate cross-indexing. The index itself should be filed with the working papers, and the index symbols marked alongside the captions in the working trial balance or grouping sheets. Supporting schedules and analyses should always be referenced in some way to the working trial balance.

After being indexed, the working papers are ready for filing. A satisfactory filing procedure is one that gives protection against such hazards as fire and theft and insures that the working papers may be readily found and referred to when needed. Working papers that are inaccessible are obviously of little use. Public accountants may keep current working papers in their offices for three to five years and place the older papers in public storage. Permanent files, of course, are all kept on hand. It is sometimes advantageous to develop separate files for tax returns and reports to governmental agencies. This is particularly useful when the accounting firm maintains separate departments specializing in income tax and SEC registration work.

The question of how long working papers should be retained is a controversial one. The statute of limitations restricting the time within which legal action may be brought varies by state and by the type of action but does not often extend beyond six years. The occasions are few and far between, however, when an auditor can say with assurance that certain working papers have no possible future value.

Indefinite retention of working papers creates a serious storage problem; many CPA firms microfilm working papers for economy of storage.

Standards for preparation of working papers

An auditor is often judged by his working papers. When working papers are prepared in good form with proper attention to layout, design, and legibility, with complete headings, explanations of sources, and verification work performed, they create in supervisors and reviewers a feeling of confidence in the auditor on the job. Working papers should convey an impression of system and order and of conscientious attention to detail, coupled with a clear distinction between the important and the trivial.

The following list of rules to be observed in preparing working papers reflects current professional practice.

1. Every working paper must be properly identified. The heading should include the name of the company (this may be inserted with a rubber stamp for the entire set of papers), a description of the information presented, and the period covered or applicable date.

2. A separate working paper should be used for each topic. Any information of sufficient value to warrant inclusion in the working papers merits a complete sheet of paper with descriptive heading. Only one side of a sheet is used; this prevents the overlooking of material recorded on the back of a paper.

3. Every working paper should contain the name or initials of the accountant preparing it, the date prepared, and the name or initials of the senior, manager, or partner reviewing it. These may be conveniently placed in the upper or lower right-hand corner of each paper. Frequently, special spaces are printed on working papers for this purpose.

4. Complete and specific identification of accounts analyzed, employees interviewed, and documents examined is a requisite of good audit practice. There is often a temptation to omit such details as the full name or title of an employee mentioned in the working papers, or the date and source of a document reviewed. Such omissions often rise to embarrass the auditor in subsequent review of the audit findings. They are hallmarks of hurried inefficiency, which, in the long run, waste substantial amounts of time.

5. All working papers should be indexed to the working trial balance or grouping sheets. Where reference is necessary between working papers, there must be adequate cross-indexing.

6. The source of the data presented on each working paper should be clearly stated. There should be no room for doubt in the mind of the reviewer as to whether information was obtained from a ledger account, a financial report, an invoice, or other source.

7. The nature of verification work performed by the auditor should be indicated on each working paper. A review of paid invoices, for example, might be supplemented by the testing of related purchase

orders to substantiate the authenticity of the invoices examined; a description of this verification procedure should be included on the working paper. As previously stated, copying figures from the records is not, in itself, verification. The working papers should describe the verification procedures followed rather than being devoted to the detail of the amounts examined.

Extensive use of colored tick marks may aid in identifying the procedures followed in preparing a working paper and avoid lengthy explanation. For example, a red tick mark placed beside figures on a working trial balance may mean that the account balance concerned was verified by footing debit and credit columns; or the letter "E" placed beside figures representing investments in stocks and bonds may designate that the certificates were examined. Whenever tick marks are employed, they must be accompanied by a legend explaining their significance. Tick marks should never be recorded until the procedures which they signify have actually been executed.

8. The extent and scope of test checking should be clearly stated on every phase of the audit in which this procedure is applied. In the examination of repair expense, for example, the auditor might, by examining 10 percent of all invoices, account for 90 percent of the total charges involved. Reliance upon sampling typifies present audit practice; the working papers should disclose the character and extent of all tests made.

9. The purpose of each working paper and its relation to the audit objectives should be clear. Any data compiled which prove irrelevant should be destroyed, not permitted to clutter up the working papers.

10. A separate agenda or note sheet listing points to be investigated should be developed as the audit proceeds. In the course of the investigation, many questions will arise which cannot be answered or settled immediately. By listing these points on a working paper designed for that purpose, the auditor can avoid interrupting the work at hand but make sure that the question will not be forgotten. Before the audit is finished, the agenda sheet must be reviewed and each question satisfactorily settled.

11. The working papers should include comments by the auditor indicating his conclusions on each aspect of the work. In other words, the auditor should take a stand on all findings.

12. Working papers should be placed in the completed file as rapidly as they are finished. As each schedule, analysis, or memorandum is completed, it should be brought together with other completed papers in a file, binder, or folder. It is usually advisable to keep these papers in the order in which they will appear when permanently filed.

13. The rewriting of working papers should be considered evidence of inefficiency and inadequate planning. There is little or no justification

for the practice of recording audit data on a type of paper or in a manner which will necessitate rewriting. The old maxim of "write it once and write it right" is just as applicable to the production of audit working papers as it is to the recording phases of accounting.

GROUP I
REVIEW QUESTIONS

9–1. Audit working papers should not (select one):

    a)   Include any client-prepared papers or documents other than those prepared by the CPA or his assistant(s).

    b)   Be kept by the CPA after review and completion of the audit except for items required for the income tax return or the permanent file.

    c)   Be submitted to the client to support the financial statements and to provide evidence of the audit work performed.

    d)   By themselves be expected to provide sufficient support for the auditor's opinion. (AICPA, adapted)

9–2.   List several rules to be observed in the preparation of working papers which will reflect current professional practice. *p. 295*

9–3.   What advantages do grouping sheets offer in contrast to the working trial balance?

9–4.   List the major types of audit working papers and give a brief explanation of each. For example, one type of audit working paper is an account analysis. This working paper shows the changes which occurred in a given account during the period under audit. By analyzing an account the auditor determines its nature and content. *p. 283*

9–5.   When a file of audit working papers for a given engagement is viewed as a whole, what are the major purposes served by preparing and preserving the papers? *p. 277*

9–6.   "A well-prepared set of audit working papers should include a listing of the name and serial number of every document examined during the course of the audit in order to provide a complete record of the audit work performed." Do you agree? Explain.

9–7.   Explain the meaning of the term "permanent file" as used in connection with audit working papers. What kinds of information are usually included in the permanent file? *p. 291*

9–8.   To what extent, if at all, should an auditor rely upon statements or explanations by the client in the preparation of the audit working papers? Explain.

9–9.   Thomas Walsh, CPA, found that his office was becoming crowded with files of audit working papers from completed audit engagements and considered the possibility of throwing away some of the papers. What uses to be made of audit working papers after the audit engagement has been completed should be considered by Walsh in reaching a decision on his problem?

9-10.   "Audit working papers are the property of the auditor and he may destroy them, sell them, or give them away." Criticize this quotation.

9-11.   Describe a situation in which a set of audit working papers might be used by third parties to support a charge of gross negligence against the auditor.

9-12.   "I have finished my testing of footings of the cash journals," said the assistant auditor to the senior. "Shall I state in the working papers the period for which I verified footings, or should I just list the totals of the receipts and disbursements I have proved to be correct?" Prepare an answer to the assistant's question, stressing the reasoning involved.

9-13.   Do generally accepted auditing standards permit the auditor to utilize the services of the client's employees in the preparation of audit working papers? Explain fully.

GROUP II
QUESTIONS REQUIRING ANALYSIS

9-14.   The preparation of working papers is an integral part of a CPA's examination of financial statements. On a recurring engagement a CPA reviews the working papers from his prior examination while planning his current examination to determine their usefulness for the current engagement.

Required:

a)   (1)   What are the purposes or functions of aduit working papers?
     (2)   What records may be included in audit working papers?

b)   What factors affect the CPA's judgment of the type and content of the working papers for a particular engagement?

c)   To comply with generally accepted auditing standards a CPA includes certain evidence in his working papers, for example, "evidence that the engagement was planned and work of assistants was supervised and reviewed." What other evidence should a CPA include in audit working papers to comply with generally accepted auditing standards? (AICPA, adapted)

9-15.   An important part of every examination of financial statements is the preparation of audit working papers.

Required:

a)   Discuss the relationship of audit working papers to each of the standards of field work.

b)   You are instructing an inexperienced staffman on his first auditing assignment. He is to examine an account. An analysis of the account has been prepared by the client for inclusion in the audit working papers. Prepare a list of the comments, commentaries, and notations that the staffman should make or have made on the account analysis to provide an adequate working paper as evidence of his examination (Do not include a description of auditing procedures applicable to the account.) (AICPA)

9–16. An auditor discovered the existence of errors in the client's records during his analysis of the Office Equipment account in the general ledger. He turned his working paper over to a clerical employee of the client with the comment: "You would probably like the opportunity to reconcile your figures with the amounts I have found to be correct. Let me know what you find out about these discrepancies." Was this action by the auditor justifiable? Explain fully.

9–17. "Working papers should contain facts and nothing but facts," said student A. "Not at all," replied student B. "The audit working papers may also include expressions of opinion. Facts are not always available to settle all issues." "In my opinion," said student C, "a mixture of facts and opinions in the audit working papers would be most confusing if the papers were produced as a means of supporting the auditor's position when his report has been challenged." Evaluate the issues underlying these arguments.

9–18. At twelve o'clock when the plant whistle sounded, the assistant auditor had his desk completely covered with various types of working papers. He stopped work immediately, but not wanting to leave the desk with such a disorderly appearance took a few minutes to sort the papers into proper order, place them in a neat pile, and weigh them down with a heavy ash tray. He then departed for lunch. The auditor in charge, who had been observing what was going on, was critical of the assistant's actions. What do you think was the basis for criticism by the auditor in charge?

9–19. An assistant auditor spent the greater part of a day in transcribing sales invoices into the working papers as the result of a misunderstanding of audit procedures to be followed. There was no apparent use for the working papers he produced. Under these circumstances, do you believe that the working papers in question should be destroyed or placed in the file with an explanation of the misunderstanding? Give reasons for your answer.

9–20. You have been assigned by your firm to complete the examination of the 1974 financial statements of Hamilton Manufacturing Corporation because the senior accountant and his inexperienced assistant who began the engagement were hospitalized as the result of an accident. The engagement is about one-half completed. Your auditor's report must be delivered in three weeks as agreed when your firm accepted the engagement. You estimate that by utilizing the client's staff to the greatest possible extent you can complete the engagement in five weeks. Your firm cannot assign an assistant to you.

The working papers show the status of work on the examination as follows:

(1) *Completed*—Cash, property and equipment, depreciation, mortgage payable and stockholders' equity.

(2) *Completed except as noted later*—Inventories, accounts payable, tests of purchase transactions, and payrolls.

(3) *Nothing done*—Trade accounts receivable, inventory receiving cutoff and price testing, accrued expenses payable, unrecorded liability test, tests of sales transactions, payroll deductions test and observation of payroll check distribution, analysis of other expenses, analytic review of operations, vouching of December purchase transactions, auditor's report, internal control investigation, internal control report, minutes, preparation of tax returns, subsequent events, supervision and review.

Your review discloses that the assistant's working papers are incomplete and were not reviewed by the senior accountant. For example, the inventory working papers present incomplete notations, incomplete explanations, and no cross-referencing.

Required:

a) What field work standards have been violated by the senior accountant who preceded you on this assignment? Explain why you feel the standards you list have been violated.

b) In planning your work to complete this engagement you should scan working papers and schedule certain work as soon as possible and also identify work which may be postponed until after the report is rendered to the client.

(1) List the areas on which you should plan to work first, say in your first week of work, and for each item explain why it deserves early attention.

(2) State which work you believe could be postponed until after the report is rendered to the client and give reasons why the work may be postponed. (AICPA, adapted)

GROUP III
PROBLEMS

9–21. Criticize the working paper on page 301, which you are reviewing as senior in charge of the November 30, 1974 audit of Pratt Company.

9–22. One of the practical problems confronting the auditor is that of determining whether adjusting entries or other corrective actions are warranted by errors, omissions, and inconsistencies. The following items were noted by the auditor during his year-end examination of a small manufacturing partnership having net sales of approximately $1,600,000; net income of approximately $20,000; total assets of nearly $2,000,000; and total partners' capital of $300,000.

(1) Proceeds of $250 from the sale of fully depreciated office equipment were credited to Miscellaneous Revenue rather than to Gain and Loss on Sale of Equipment, a ledger account which had not been used for several years.

(2) The Accounts Receivable control account showed a balance of $79,600. The individual accounts comprising this balance included three with credit balances of $320, $19, and $250, respectively.

Pratt Company
Cash
Date   E-2   (above + to the right)

                                                    ref from Bank conf.

Balance Per bank   11-30-74   44,874.50 ✓

      Deposit in transit   837.50 ×

      Bank charges   2.80 A
                                         45,714.80 T

   Outstanding checks:
                    46.40   need
                    10.00   check
                    30.00   #'s
                 1,013.60 ✓
                 1,200.00 ✓
                    10.00
                    25.00 ×
                    15.00 ×
                    50.00 ×
                 1,002.00 ✓   3,402.00
Balance Per books   T   42,312.80 ✓ ₦
                                                   T

   × Traced to 12-31-74 bank statement
   Ø - Trace to check register cof.
   V - Verified Traced to bank statement cof.
   T Footed
        R.J.H.
       12-3-74
   A Examined for propriety   A Determine what Bank
   Ø Agree to cash receipts journal   charge is
      Disb.
   ₦ Agreed to cash balance in general ledger

(3) Several debits and credits to general ledger accounts had been made
    directly without use of journal entries. The amounts involved did not
    exceed $500.
(4) Credit memoranda were not serially numbered or signed, but a file of
    duplicates was maintained.
(5) General journal entries did not include explanations for any but un-
    usual transactions.
(6) Posting references were occasionally omitted from entries in general
    ledger accounts.
(7) An expenditure of $200 for automobile repairs was recorded as a De-

cember expense, although shown by the invoice to be a November charge.

(8) The auditor's count of petty cash disclosed a shortage of $20.

(9) Expenditures for advertising amounting to $8,000 were charged to the Advertising Expense account; other advertising expenses amounting to $3,000 had been charged to Miscellaneous Expense.

(10) On a bank loan of $300,000, negotiated September 5, for a period of four months at an annual interest rate of 6 percent, the entire amount of interest had been deducted in advance. The client's bookkeeper had charged the full amount of interest to expense. He stated that he did not consider an entry to defer a part of the expense to the following year to be warranted by the amount involved.

Required:

You are to state clearly the position which you as an auditor would take with respect to each of the above items during the course of an annual audit. If adjusting journal entries are necessary, include them in your solution.

9–23. The following audit working papers from an audit still in process are listed in alphabetical order. You are to rearrange them in logical order and assign an index reference to each.

(1) Accounts Receivable Grouping Sheet.
(2) Allowance for Uncollectible Accounts.
(3) Analysis of Accumulated Depreciation.
(4) Analysis of Capital Stock.
(5) Analysis of Cost of Sales.
(6) Analysis of Miscellaneous Expense.
(7) Analysis of Repairs and Maintenance.
(8) Audit Plan.
(9) Audit Program.
(10) Automobiles.
(11) Buildings.
(12) Confirmation from First National Bank.
(13) Confirmations of Accounts Receivable.
(14) Copies of Minutes.
(15) Count of Petty Cash.
(16) Draft of Audit Report.
(17) Federal Income Tax Payable.
(18) Financial Statements Prepared by Client.
(19) Internal Control Evaluation.
(20) Internal Control Questionnaire.
(21) Inventory Grouping Sheet.
(22) Inventory—Tests of Pricing.
(23) Land.
(24) Letter of Representations from Client.
(25) List of Stockholders.
(26) Mortgage Payable.
(27) Notes on Observation of Physical Inventory.
(28) Notes Payable.
(29) Prepaid Insurance.
(30) Property Tax Expense.
(31) Proposed Adjusting Journal Entries.
(32) Reconciliation of Bank Account.
(33) Reserve for Contingencies.

(34) Retained Earnings Analysis.
(35) Summary of Administrative and General Expenses.
(36) Summary of Property and Equipment.
(37) Summary of Sales.
(38) Summary of Selling Expenses.
(39) Working Trial Balance.

GROUP IV
CASE STUDIES IN AUDITING

9–24.   BRYAN INSTRUMENT MANUFACTURING COMPANY
Audit Working Papers and Legal Liability of Auditors

During the examination of Bryan Instrument Manufacturing Company, Dwight Bond, an assistant auditor, was assigned by the auditor in charge to the verification of the accounts receivable. The receivables totaled more than $2 million and included accounts with governmental agencies, national mail-order houses, manufacturers, wholesalers, and retailers. Dwight Bond had recently read a study of credit losses in this industry covering the past 10 years; and as a preliminary step, he computed an allowance for uncollectible accounts by applying to the total accounts receivable a percentage mentioned in the 10-year study as the average rate of uncollectible account losses for the sales of the entire industry. Application of this percentage to the Bryan Company's receivables indicated an uncollectible account loss of $90,000; the allowance provided by the management was $25,000. The working paper showing the computation of the $90,000 estimate of uncollectible account losses was placed in the file of working papers by Mr. Bond.

After making this preliminary calculation, Bond undertook a careful study of the receivables; as a first step he obtained from the client a classification of the accounts by type of customer and by age. He made a careful analysis of individual accounts which appeared in any way doubtful, discussed all past-due accounts with the credit manager, and reviewed the company's prior history of uncollectible account losses. He then reviewed his findings with the auditor in charge, who after further investigation and discussion with the client took the position that the allowance for uncollectible accounts must be increased from $25,000 to $40,000 or an unqualified opinion could not be given. The client was not convinced of the need for the increase but finally agreed to make the change.

While Dwight Bond was working on the accounts receivable, another staff assistant, Charles Roberts, was engaged in verification of inventory. Mr. Roberts overheard a stock clerk remark that the finished goods inventory was full of obsolete products that could never be sold. As a result of this chance remark, Mr. Roberts made tests of a number of items in the inventory, comparing the quantities on hand with the amount of recent sales. These tests indicated the quantities in inventory were reasonable and that the items were moving out to customers. Because of the technical nature of the instruments manufactured by the company, Mr. Roberts was not able to determine by inspection whether the articles in stock were obsolete or unsalable for any other reason. He made a point of questioning officials of the company on the possibility of obsolescence in the inventory and was assured that no serious problem of obsolescence existed.

In preparing the working papers covering his investigation, Mr. Roberts included a separate memorandum quoting the remark he had overheard concerning the obsolescence of the inventory, and added a suggestion of his own that this question of obsolescence be given special attention in succeeding examinations. He prepared a detailed description of certain portions of the inventory and suggested that in the succeeding examination the auditors determine whether these specific units were still on hand. During the review of the working papers, the auditor in charge questioned Charles Roberts at length about the tests for obsolescence. He interviewed the employee who had made the remark about the impossibility of disposing of the finished goods inventory; the employee denied having made any such statement. The auditor in charge then discussed the issue with company officials and came to the conclusion that the inventory was properly valued and readily salable. In completing his review of the working papers, he added the following comment to the memorandum prepared by Mr. Roberts: "Question of obsolescence investigated and passed, but we should give consideration to this issue in succeeding examinations."

After all adjustments recommended by the auditors had been made, the financial statements of the company indicated a considerably weaker financial position than in prior years. The president complained that the adjustments insisted on by the auditors made the company's position look so bad that it would be difficult to obtain private long-term financing for which he had been negotiating. An unqualified audit report was issued.

Two months later the Bryan Instrument Manufacturing Company became insolvent. Principal causes of the failure, according to the president, were unexpectedly large credit losses and inability to dispose of inventories which had become obsolete because of newly designed products being offered by competitors in recent years. He acknowledged that the company had made sales to customers of questionable credit standing because of the need for disposing of inventories threatened by obsolescence. Creditors of the company attempted to recover their losses from the auditors, charging them with gross negligence and lack of independence in reviewing the valuation of the accounts receivable and inventory. Attention was directed to the working papers prepared by Mr. Bond and Mr. Roberts; it was charged that these papers showed the auditors had knowledge of the overvaluation of receivables and inventory but under pressure from the client had failed to disclose the facts.

Required:

a) Should the working paper showing the percentage calculation of a $90,000 allowance for uncollectible accounts have been prepared and retained? Explain. Comment on the industry rate of loss.

b) Should the working paper quoting the stock clerk's remark about obsolescence have been prepared and retained? Explain.

c) Did the auditor in charge handle his duties satisfactorily?

d) Do you think the working papers tended to support or injure the auditors' defense against the charges of the creditors? Explain.

e) Do you consider the creditors' charges to be well founded? Give reasons for your answer.

10

Beginning the audit: Examination of general records

Relationships with clients

IN FICTION and in folklore the auditor has sometimes been depicted as aloof, cold, and impersonal. There may have been a degree of truth in this image of the auditor a half-century or more ago when the detection of fraud was a major objective of many audits. Such traits are not at all descriptive of the auditor in today's world. The wide-ranging scope of the CPA's activities today demands that he be interested and well informed on economic trends, political developments, sports events, and the many other topics that play a significant part in business and social contacts. Although an in-depth knowledge of accounting is a most important qualification of the CPA, an ability to meet people easily and to gain their confidence and goodwill may be no less important in achieving success in the profession of public accounting. The ability to work effectively with clients will be enhanced by a sincere interest in their problems and by a relaxed and cordial manner.

The question of the auditor's independence inevitably arises in considering the advisability of social activities with clients. The partner in today's public accounting firm typically does play golf with the executives of client companies and other businessmen. These relationships may actually make it easier to resolve differences of opinions which arise during the audit, if the client has learned to know and respect the CPA partner. This mutual understanding need not prevent the CPA from standing firm on matters of accounting principle. This is perhaps the "moment of truth" for the practitioners of a profession.

Many CPA firms tend to distinguish between the desirability of social ties between clients and CPA partners as contrasted with friendships of audit staff members with client employees. However, this tendency to limit contacts at the staff level to a business setting does not restrict the policy of encouraging a relaxed and cordial manner on the part of every member of the CPA's organization. The staff auditor will be most successful if he is known for unfailing courtesy and good humor. In other words, he is cordial and approachable, yet maintains an independence in mental attitude. He observes the client's rules as to working hours, smoking, use of telephone and other facilities. His manner, tone of voice, and interest in minimizing any inconvenience to the client's employees should make clear that his professional objective is not the detection of fraud or errors but the substantiation of financial statements as valid reports on the client's affairs.

Beginning the audit

In the preceding chapters considerable attention has been given to the preliminary work of an audit. For repeat engagements a review of the audit working papers constituting the permanent file will refresh the auditor's memory as to the client's policies, organization, and internal controls. For an initial examination, much can be gained by discussing with the new client the purposes of the examination, the basis of the auditor's fee, and the use of the client's staff for preparation of working papers or other clerical operations designed to reduce the cost of the audit. Another useful preliminary step for the auditor is to become familiar with the physical facilities of the company.

Inspection tour of plant and offices

interim basis

Before beginning an examination of the client's financial statements, the auditor should arrange for an inspection tour of the plant and offices of the company. This tour will give the auditor some understanding of the plant layout, the manufacturing processes, the principal products, and the physical safeguards surrounding inventories. A background knowledge of the physical facilities for receiving, storing, and issuing of materials will be helpful later in the examination when the auditor is evaluating the internal controls relating to inventories. In addition the tour will afford him an opportunity to meet the key personnel whose names he may have noted on the organization chart. In going through the offices the auditor will learn the location of various accounting records and will become aware of the number of office employees and the extent to which accounting activities are subdivided. The auditor will also make a thorough inspection of a client's electronic data processing department.

Review of general records

Before beginning the verification and analysis of specific transactions and accounts, it is appropriate for the auditor to review the *general records.* This review should provide him with a concise picture of the policies and plans of owners and managers, thus making it possible, as the examination progresses, to determine whether the transactions reflected in the accounts were properly authorized and executed in accordance with the directives of the owners or their appointed representatives. In addition, the preliminary review of general records provides a fund of background information that is most helpful in the interpretation of the accounts and statements. If the auditor is thoroughly familiar with the history and problems of the business, the duties and responsibilities of key officials, and the nature and quality of the accounting records and procedures, then he is prepared to carry out each phase of the audit with confidence and understanding. If he does not acquire this background information before beginning the work of verifying assets and analyzing transactions, he is almost certain to proceed in a mechanical and routine manner, unaware of the real significance of much of the evidence examined.

The term "general records" is used to include the following categories:

1. Nonfinancial records.
   a) Corporate charter and bylaws.
   b) Partnership agreement.
   c) Minutes of directors' and stockholders' meetings.
   d) Contracts with customers and suppliers.
   e) Contracts with officers and employees, including union agreements, stock option, profit-sharing, bonus, and pension plans.
   f) Governmental regulations directly affecting the enterprise.
   g) Correspondence files.
2. Financial records.
   a) Income tax returns of prior years.
   b) Financial statements and annual reports of prior years.
   c) Registration statements and periodic reports filed with the SEC.
3. Accounting records.
   a) General ledger.
   b) General journal.

REVIEW OF NONFINANCIAL RECORDS

Corporate charter and bylaws

In the first audit of a client's financial statement, a senior auditor will obtain copies of the articles of incorporation and bylaws, reviewing them for such information as the exact name of the corporation, the date and state of incorporation, the authorized capital structure, and the number of directors authorized.

The articles of incorporation is the basic document evidencing the existence of a corporate entity and is, therefore, the most appropriate source of information for the above listed items. Accuracy is of paramount importance in compiling this information—even for the most minute points. The name of the corporation will appear prominently in the heading of the auditor's formal report, and there is no excuse for error in its statement. For example, "The Blank Manufacturing Company, Inc." must not be called "Blank Manufacturing Corporation" or "The Blank Manufacturing Company, Incorporated." In reorganizations the corporate name is sometimes changed in only the slightest degree, and care is required to avoid confusing the new corporate entity with its predecessor. Apart from any practical consequences, an auditor, by virtue of his traditional reputation for accuracy and precision, cannot afford to allow minor irregularities as to names and dates to creep into his reports, because such slips are sure to lessen the confidence and respect of clients. The articles of incorporation contain information on the corporate structure, powers, and restrictions conferred upon the company by the state. The bylaws, on the other hand, indicate the administrative organization, rules, and procedures adopted by the corporate stockholders. For example, the bylaws may stipulate the frequency of stockholders' meetings and the date and method for election of directors and selection of officers.

Copies of both the corporate charter and the bylaws will, as previously mentioned, be obtained during the first audit engagement with a client and will be preserved in the auditor's permanent file for convenient reference during repeat engagements. Although repetition of this original investigative work is to be avoided in subsequent audits, the auditor must be alert to recognize and review any amendments or additions to these documents. Copies of such revisions should be entered in the permanent file so that the usefulness of that record may be maintained.

Partnership agreement

In an audit of a business organized as a partnership, the auditor reviews the partnership agreement in much the same manner as he examines the charter and bylaws of corporate clients. The articles of partnership represent a contractural agreement by owners on the rules to be followed in the operation of the enterprise. The information available in a copy of the partnership agreement obtained from the permanent file during the first audit includes:

1. The name and address of the firm.
2. The names and addresses of the individual partners.
3. The amount, date, and nature of the investment made by each member.
4. The profit-sharing ratio, partners' salaries, interest on partners' capital, and restrictions on withdrawals.
5. The duties, responsibilities, and authority of each member.
6. The provision for insurance on lives of partners.
7. The provisions concerning dissolution of the firm and distribution of assets.

In repeat examinations the auditor must ascertain whether any modification of the partnership agreement has been made and obtain copies of the modifications for the permanent file. If no change has occurred since the preceding audit, a notation to that effect should be made.

Corporate minutes book

The corporate minutes book is an official record of the actions taken at meetings of directors and stockholders. Typical of the actions taken at meetings of stockholders is the extension of authority to management to issue or to reacquire securities, to acquire or dispose of subsidiaries or other important properties, and to adopt or modify plans for participation in profits by officers and employees. The stockholders customarily select or approve the selection of a firm of independent auditors and often request the auditors to attend the stockholders' meeting for the purpose of answering any questions that may arise concerning the operations or financial position of the business.

Minutes of the directors' meetings usually contain a record of authorizations for important transactions and contractual arrangements such as the establishment of bank accounts, setting of officers' salaries, declaration of dividends, and formation of long-term agreements with vendors, customers, and lessors. In large corporations the board of directors often finds it necessary to work throught committees appointed to deal with special phases of operations and bearing descriptive titles such as "Audit Committee" or "Investment Committee." Minutes of the meetings of such committees are, of course, just as essential to the auditor's investigation as are the minutes covering meetings of the entire board.

Procedure for review of minutes.   In the first audit of a client, it may be necessary to review minutes recorded in prior years. Copies of these minutes will be preserved in the permanent file; and as succeeding annual audits are made, the file will be appropriately expanded.

The auditor in charge will obtain from the secretary or other corporate officer copies of all minutes, including those of board committees, directors, and stockholders, for both regular and special meetings. These copies should be certified by a corporate officer and should be compared with the official minutes book to an extent sufficient to establish their completeness and authenticity. The recent trend toward spreading audit work uniformly over the year is reflected in the practice of some public accounting firms which request their regular clients to forward copies of the minutes immediately after each meeting. Verification of these copies at year-end is an essential part of such practices.

The senior reviewing the minutes will (1) note the date of the meeting and whether a quorum was present, and (2) underscore or otherwise highlight in the permanent file copies of the minutes such actions and decisions as, in his judgment, have a significant effect on the company's financial position or operations or should influence the conduct of the audit. Nonessential material can be scanned rapidly, and highlighting can be limited to issues which warrant investigation during the course of the audit. For this phase of the audit work, there is no substitute for breadth of experience and maturity of judgment; for these factors make possible a sharp distinction between matters of real import to the audit and those which may safely be passed by.

Relationship of corporate minutes to verification procedures.   The nature of the information to be highlighted in the minutes copies and the uses to be made of this information as the audit progresses can be made clear by a few examples. The following list shows several audit procedures and indicates for each such phase of the audit certain transactions which require authorization by the board of directors.

1. Verification of cash in bank.
    a) The opening and closing of corporate bank accounts are acts requiring authorization by the board of directors.
    b) The authority to sign checks is delegated to specific officers by the board.
    c) The obtaining of loans from banks requires approval in advance by directors.
2. Verification of investments.
    a) Purchases, sales, and exchanges of securities should be authorized in advance by the board of directors or a committee thereof.

  b) Designation of two officers to have dual custody of securities is customarily made by the board

  c) The location of securities, whether in the company's own safe, a bank safe-deposit box, or elsewhere should conform to instructions by the board.

  d) Pledging of securities as a basis for obtaining credit or guaranteeing performance of a contract requires board approval.

3. Proof of liabilities.

  a) Authority for declaration of dividends rests exclusively with the board of directors.

  b) Liabilities for pending lawsuits, tax disputes, accommodation endorsements, guarantees, and other contingencies should receive approval of directors when entered in the accounts.

  c) The assumption of long-term debt by issuance of bonds or mortgages should be supported by the approval of stockholders and should also be covered in the minutes of directors' meetings.

  d) Unusual purchase commitments and contracts for extensive future deliveries are often referred to the board for approval.

This list does not purport to show all the various areas of an audit in which reference to authorizations by the board would be appropriate. On the contrary, it is safe to say that in virtually every area of an audit, the auditor may need to refer to actions by the board of directors.

The review of the minutes, including those for directors' and stockholders' meetings taking place subsequent to the balance sheet date but prior to completion of the audit field work, is a mandatory step. Corporate management generally is aware of the significance of this record in the auditor's investigation. In rare instances, however, the auditor may encounter reluctance on the part of management to make the minutes available for his review, or he may find that the minutes book has not been properly maintained. In these cases the auditor must make it clear that if he is to express an independent opinion concerning the financial statements, he must have unlimited access to all documents and records having any bearing on the integrity of the financial statements. Any other position taken by the auditor would be in violation of generally accepted auditing standards. If the minutes book has not been kept up to date, the auditor should explain to the client the importance of this record and urge that the missing data be promptly recorded. Lack of complete minutes warrants comment in the auditor's report to the client on internal control.

Contracts held or issued by client

Early in the audit engagement a senior auditor should obtain copies of the major contracts to which the client is a party. Information obtained from an analysis of contracts may be helpful in interpreting such accounts as Advances from Suppliers, Progress Payments under Government Contracts, and Stock Options. In addition to production contracts with governmental agencies and other companies, the auditor may review contracts with suppliers for future delivery of materials, royalty agreements for use of patents, union labor contracts, leases, pension plans, stock options, and bonus contracts with officers.

The terms of existing contracts are often material factors in the measurement of debt-paying ability and in the estimating of future earnings. When examinations are being made in behalf of prospective investors, creditors, or purchasers of a business, the nature of contracts with customers may outweigh all other considerations in determining a market value for the business.

The procedure for examination of contracts will depend upon the length and nature of the contract in question. A contract from the federal government to an aircraft manufacturer may be a sizable volume with hundreds of pages of exhibits and specifications. Such contracts are generally accompanied by large numbers of change orders issued at frequent intervals throughout the life of the contract. When contracts are extremely long and technical, the auditor may find it necessary to rely upon summaries prepared by the client's staff or legal counsel. Data obtained in this manner should, of course, be verified by comparison with the basic contract to an extent considered reasonable in the circumstances.

The auditor may at times require the assistance of engineers, attorneys, and other specialists in the interpretation of important contracts. Most contracts include accounting concepts such as net income or working capital, but unfortunately those who draft the contracts may not in all cases understand the true meaning of the accounting terminology they employ. Skill in analyzing and interpreting the financial aspects of contracts appears to be a qualification of increasing importance to the independent auditor.

In revieweing a contract the auditor will usually note the following items, among others:

1. Exact title of the contract.
2. Names and addresses of the parties.
3. Date effective, duration, and schedule for performance, if any.
4. Type of contract (fixed price, cost reimbursement, incentive); and provisions for such matters as price redetermination, cost-of-living adjustments, progress payments, and cancellation.
5. Provision for settlement of disputes.
6. Provision for audit of records to determine amount owing under contract.

7. General impact of the contract upon financial position and operations.

The points listed above should be considered as suggestive of the information sought rather than as a comprehensive list. The great variety of contracts coming under the auditor's review makes it difficult to formulate any uniform rules as to the information which should be highlighted. When the auditor has completed his review of a contract, all pertinent points should be traced to the accounts, to determine that contractual obligations are being observed and that all rights and obligations are fully reflected in the accounts.

Government regulations

Although the independent auditor is not licensed to give legal advice or to interpret federal or state laws, he must be familiar with laws and regulations that affect his client's financial statements. The auditor should consult with the client's legal counsel—and his own attorney, if necessary—when he believes a legal problem affects performance of the audit or requires disclosure in the financial statements.

Among the laws and regulations with which the auditor should be familiar are the following:

State corporations codes. Laws governing the formation and operation of corporations vary among the states. The auditor should obtain a copy of the corporations code of each client's state of incorporation and become familiar with provisions of the code which affect the client's financial statements.

Uniform Partnership Act. This act, in effect in most states, governs the operations of partnerships in areas not covered by the partnership agreement.

State and federal corporate securities laws. Most states have "blue sky" laws regulating the issuance of corporate securities within their jurisdictions. In addition, the federal Securities Act of 1933 governs the interstate issuance of corporate securities, while the Securities Exchange Act of 1934 deals with the trading of securities on national exchanges and over the counter.

Uniform Commercial Code. This code, recently adopted by most of the states, regulates sales of goods, commercial paper such as checks, bank collections and letters of credit, warehouse receipts, bills of lading, investment securities, and secured transactions in personal property.

Antitrust laws. The federal Robinson-Patman Act of 1936, which forbids price discrimination in interstate commerce, is an antitrust act of direct concern to many audit clients.

Labor laws.   Federal laws regulating labor include the Fair Labor Standards Act of 1938 and 1939, the Walsh-Healy Act of 1936, the Social Security Act of 1935, and the Welfare and Pension Plans Disclosure Act of 1959. The Fair Labor Standards Act provides for a minimum wage, overtime premiums, and equal pay for men and women for equal work. The Walsh-Healy Act governs wages, hours, and working conditions of contractors having contracts with U.S. government agencies. The Social Security Act provides for payroll taxes on employers and employees to finance retirement and medical benefits for retired persons over specified ages. The Welfare and Pension Plans Disclosure Act requires administrators of employee welfare and pension plans to submit to the Secretary of Labor a description and an annual report for each plan.

Regulations for specific industries.   Clients in regulated industries, such as insurance companies, banks, savings and loan associations, public utilities, airlines, truck lines, and railroads, are subject to additional specific controls often administered by federal and state regulatory commissions. The auditor with clients in these regulated areas will need to be familiar with the special laws and regulations that directly affect operation of these companies.

"Temporary" controls.   In addition to the seemingly permanent statutes listed above, various "temporary" regulations are occasionally imposed by government which affect the transactions subject to review by the auditor. Examples include controls over wages, prices, and dividends. If apparent violations come to the auditor's attention, he should inform both management and legal counsel of the client company and consider the possible existence of unrecorded liabilities in the form of fines or penalties.

Correspondence files

The general correspondence files of the client may contain much information of importance to the auditor, but it would be quite out of the question for him to plow through the great mass of general correspondence on file in search of pertinent letters. When the reading of corporate minutes, contract files, or other data indicates the existence of significant correspondence on matters of concern to the auditor, he should request the client to provide him with copies of such letters. In addition, the auditor will usually review the client's correspondence with banks and other lending institutions, attorneys, and governmental agencies. Correspondence may generally be accepted as authentic; but if reason for doubt exists, the auditor may wish to confirm the contents of letters directly with the responsible persons.

REVIEW OF FINANCIAL RECORDS

Income tax returns of prior years

A review of income tax returns of prior years will aid the auditor in planning any tax services required by the terms of his engagement. The possibility of assessment of additional income taxes exists with respect to the returns of recent years not yet cleared by tax authorities. By reviewing tax returns and revenue agents' reports the auditor may become aware of any matters which pose a threat of additional assessments; he may also find a basis for filing a claim for a tax refund.

Other information which the auditor can obtain from reviewing the prior-year tax returns of a new client includes the accounting principles used by the client for uncollectible accounts, inventory valuation, and depreciation, as well as the compensation and stock ownership of officers and the existence of affiliated organizations.

Financial statements and annual reports of prior years

Study of the financial statements and annual reports of prior years and of any available monthly or quarterly statements for the current year is a convenient way for the auditor to gain a general background knowledge of the financial history and problems of the business. If independent auditors have submitted audit reports in prior years, these documents may also be useful in drawing the auditor's attention to matters requiring special consideration.

Reports to the SEC

Registration statements and periodic reports filed by the client with the SEC contain valuable information for the auditor—especially in a first audit. Included in this information will be the client's capital structure, a summary of earnings for the past five years, identity of affiliated companies, descriptions of the business and property of the client, pending legal proceedings, names of directors and executive officers of the client and their remuneration, stock option plans, and principal shareholders of the client.

REVIEW OF ACCOUNTING RECORDS

Soon after beginning the examination, the auditor should undertake a review of the journals and the general ledger as part of the study of the client's internal control. The objectives of this review are: (1) to verify the mechanical accuracy of the records, and (2) to determine the overall propriety and adequacy of the journal entries and ledger accounts. The auditor should make sufficient tests to satisfy himself that all entries in the general ledger were posted from authentic sources. This procedure is important because the financial statements are drawn from general ledger balances, and these balances conceivably could be falsified through the recording of unsupported debits or credits in the general ledger.

In addition to proving the mechanical accuracy of the journals and ledgers, the auditor should consider journal entries in terms of their general reasonableness. If he has already reviewed the articles of incorporation or partnership agreement, the minutes book, important contracts, and prior years' financial statements, he has acquired considerable background information useful in determining the propriety and reasonableness of entries in the accounts.

The general ledger

One of the tests of internal control for the general ledger consists of verifying the footings of some or all of the ledger accounts. The term "footings" is used among practicing accountants to designate column totals. "To foot," on the other hand, means to verify the total by adding the column. Precision in the use of auditing terminology is necessary to avoid misunderstanding when verification work is divided among a number of staff members.

The extent to which accounts are footed depends upon two factors: (1) the auditor's preliminary appraisal of the client's system of internal control, developed from the questionnaire, written description, or flow-charts; and (2) the frequency and relative importance of any errors discovered during the actual footing tests. If the client's accounting records and procedures are well designed and efficiently maintained, it is obviously possible to devote less audit time to verifying the mechanical accuracy of the records than would be required in audits where less satisfactory conditions prevail. In short, the emphasis placed upon the verification of footings may justifiably vary widely from one audit to the next.

As another test of internal control for the general ledger, the auditor may verify postings by comparing journal entries and ledger accounts. The principles governing the extent of the auditor's test of footings were explained in the preceding paragraph. The same principles are utilized in determining the extent to which postings should be verified; that is, the scope of verification is dependent upon the auditor's preliminary appraisal of the system of internal control and the number and kinds of errors discovered during the actual verification of postings. Statistical sampling techniques may also be utilized in this test.

There are two commonly used methods of testing postings: (1) by tracing transactions from the ledger to the books of original entry, and (2) by tracing entries from the journals to the ledger. Some auditors advocate the former method on the grounds that the objective is to verify the source of the entries; others prefer to use the second procedure so that all entries for a given period may be verified with the least expenditure of effort. In some audit situations a combination of the two methods may be desirable; that is, the entries for one accounting period may be verified by tracing journal entries to ledger accounts, and transactions selected at random from the remainder of the year's work may be traced from the ledger accounts to the journals. This combination of procedures may compensate to some extent for deficiencies inherent in each method.

A client utilizing electronic data processing may not maintain a traditional general ledger. Instead, an updated daily trial balance, showing beginning account balances, debit and credit transactions entries, and ending balances, is printed out by the computer. The auditor may test footings for selected daily trial balances; in addition, he should trace beginning account balances in the selected trial balances to the ending account balances of the previous day.

Errors disclosed by the test of the general ledger should be summarized on a separate working paper. Each error listed should be carefully investigated to determine its significance and probable cause. Although most errors are the result of clerical inaccuracy, the possibility of fraud as a motive must always be considered. In many cases the chief significance of an error lies in the direction of the auditor's attention to inadequate internal control.

The general journal

The general journal is a book of original entry used to record all transactions for which special journals have not been provided. In its simplest form, the general journal has only a single pair of columns for the recording of debit and credit entries, but many variations from this basic design are encountered. A third column may be added to provide for entries to subsidiary ledgers, or various multicolumn forms may be used. The addition of a number of debit and credit columns is intended to facilitate the recording of transactions which occur so frequently as to make individual postings undesirable but are not sufficiently numerous to warrant the establishment of a special journal.

Some concerns maintain a system of "journal vouchers." These are serially numbered documents, each containing a single general journal entry, with full supporting details, and bearing the signature of an officer authorized to approve the entry. A general journal in traditional form may be prepared from the journal vouchers, or that series of documents may be utilized in lieu of a general journal. Companies having electronic data processing equipment generally keypunch journal vouchers to serve as one of the transaction sources for the computer printed-out trial balance described in the preceding section.

Suggested procedures for testing the general journal follow:

1. *Foot column totals of the journal.*   .

The testing of footings in the general journal follows the pattern previously described for verification of ledger balances. A representative period for testing is selected, and all journal columns falling within that period are footed. Errors disclosed should be summarized on a working paper, investigated, and appropriate disposition made. With respect to the multi-column form of general journal, it is necessary to cross-foot (add horizontally) the column totals and prove the equality of debits and credits. Discrepancies between the total of the debit columns and the total of the credit columns indicate either faulty addition or errors in individual entries. Analysis of the entire page may sometimes be necessary to locate the error or errors.

2. *Vouch selected entries to original documents.*

"To vouch" a journal entry means to examine the original papers and documents supporting the entry. The term "voucher" is used to describe any type of supporting documentary evidence. For example, a journal entry recording the trade-in of a machine would be vouched by comparing it with an invoice, purchase order, sales contract, receiving report, and paid check—the vouchers for this entry. The auditor might not consider it necessary to examine all these documents if the evidence first examined appeared to provide adequate support for the entry. All general journal entries selected for testing should be vouched.

Entries in the general journal should include clear informative explanations; but, unfortunately, deviations from this principle are frequently encountered. The auditor should determine whether (1) the explanation is in agreement with the supporting documentation, and (2) the entry reflects the transaction properly in the light of generally accepted accounting principles.

The supporting evidence to be examined during the review of general journal entries may include purchase orders, invoices, receiving records, sales contracts, correspondence, the minutes book, and articles of partnership. Journal vouchers represent an internal control device; they should not be considered as evidence supporting entries in the general journal. Verification of journal entries requires that the auditor refer to original invoices and other evidence previously described.

3. *Scan the general journal for unusual entries.*

The importance of certain types of transactions which are recorded in the general journal makes it desirable for the auditor to scan this record for the entire period under audit, in addition to vouching all entries selected for testing. The following list is illustrative of the type of significant transactions for which the auditor should look in this scanning process:

a) The write-off of assets, particularly notes and accounts receivable. Collections from customers abstracted by employees and not recorded in the accounts may be permanently concealed if the accounts in question are written off as uncollectible. General journal entries containing credits to accounts and loans receivable from officers and employees require full investigation to provide assurance that such transactions are proper and have been authorized.

b) Assumption of liabilities. Transactions which create liabilities, such as the purchase of merchandise, materials, or equipment, or the receipt of cash, are normally recorded in special journals. General journal entries which serve to bring liabilities into the record warrant close investigation to determine that they have received proper authorization and are adequately supported.

c) Unexplained or fragmentary transactions, the purpose and nature of which are not apparent from the journal entry. General journal entries with inadequate or unintelligible explanations suggest that the person making the entry did not understand the issues involved or was unwilling to state the facts clearly. Entries of this type and entries which affect seemingly unrelated accounts should be fully investigated.

d) Any debits or credits to cash accounts, other than for bank charges and other bank reconciliation items. Most transactions affecting cash are recorded in special journals.

4.   Determine that all general journal entries have received the approval of an officer.

An adequate system of internal control includes procedures for regular review and written approval of all general journal entries by the controller or other appropriate executive. The auditor should determine that such procedures have been consistently followed. In those cases in which the client does not regularly review and approve journal entries, the auditor may deem it desirable to review the general journal with the client and request his signature on each page as approval thereof. The internal control report to the client should include a suggestion that the client undertake the review and approval of journal entries.

5.   Trace selected transactions to general and subsidiary ledgers.

This procedure will usually be combined with the verification of postings to general ledger accounts. It is listed here for the purpose of emphasizing that a review of postings from the general journal should include the tracing of entries to subsidiary ledgers as well as to general ledger control accounts.

In tracing general journal entries to the ledgers, inspection of the posting reference in the folio column is not sufficient; the entry should be traced directly into the account. The tracing of postings should be preceded by sufficient study of the client's chart of accounts to minimize the work required in locating accounts. In addition to tracing the posting of selected transactions, the auditor should ascertain that the column totals of a multicolumn general journal have been posted to the appropriate accounts.

Auditor's description of his examination of accounting records

Upon completion of the review of accounting records, the auditor should summarize the work performed in a working paper describing the records in use, the verification procedures followed, the nature and significance of errors discovered, and any suggestions for revision of the accounting system. This working paper serves as part of the auditor's record of his study and evaluation of the client's internal control. The development of a complete written description of this phase of the audit is not a difficult task if it is undertaken while the details of the work are fresh in the auditor's mind. At the beginning of the next annual audit, a review of this working paper will enable the auditor to concentrate immediately upon the most significant aspects of the accounting records and avoid the repetition of any mistakes or waste motion characterizing the previous engagement.

Interim examination of general records

The review of general records and the evaluation of the system of internal control are examples of investigative work that need not await the closing of the books, for the quality of the records and the adequacy of the client's internal control can be appraised during the fiscal year as well as at the end of the period. The spreading of the auditor's work load more uniformly throughout the year has numerous advantages. It permits more efficient utilization of audit manpower, minimizes interference with the client's accounting staff while the books are being closed, and adds to the quality of auditing services by freeing the auditor from the more mechanical phases of his work during the time when he is concentrating on correlation of audit findings and preparation of the audit report. In addition, the evaluation of internal control and the review of important contracts and other records well in advance of the balance sheet date will often reveal information necessary in devising the most effective audit program.

Organization of succeeding chapters

The pattern of work in most audits is organized in terms of balance sheet topics such as cash, marketable securities, inventories, and plant and equipment. Perhaps in part this method of organizing the work is a carry-over from the days when the auditor's objective was the verification of the balance sheet alone. Even though the present-day auditor is very much concerned with the verification of the income statement, he still finds it convenient to use a balance sheet approach in laying out the plan of the audit work.

The verification of a balance sheet item will ordinarily involve closely related income statement accounts. For example, the verification of notes receivable is inseparably linked with interest earned, and it is convenient for the auditor to verify both at the same time. Similarly, depreciation expense will be verified in conjunction with the examination of plant and equipment; uncollectible accounts expense will be verified together with accounts receivable; and the verification of bonds payable will include review of bond interest expense and the amortization of bond discount or bond premium.

In the next 9 chapters of this book we shall consider the audit work to be done on the major balance sheet topics, beginning with cash and concluding with owners' equity. In each chapter we shall also consider any closely related revenue and expense accounts. Then we shall round out our study of revenue and expense transactions with a chapter devoted exclusively to the auditor's further work in verifying the income statement. In brief the organization of the next 10 chapters is similar to the organizational plan followed in most audit engagements.

GROUP I
REVIEW QUESTIONS

10–1. With respect to proceedings of the meetings of the board of directors of a client corporation, the normal auditing procedure is to (select one):

a) Obtain from the company secretary a minutes representation letter which summarizes actions pertinent to the financial statements.

b) Discuss proceedings of the board with its chairman or his designated representative.

c) Review the minutes of all meetings.

d) Obtain tapes or written transcripts of all meetings or attend all meetings.

10–2.   During the first audit of a corporate client, the auditor will probably obtain a copy of the bylaws and review them carefully.

       Required:

       a)   What are bylaws of a corporation?

       b)   What provisions of the bylaws are of interest to the independent auditor? Explain.

10–3.   Should the CPA expect to find a traditional type of general ledger in his audit of a client utilizing electronic data processing equipment? Explain.

10–4.   Identify several federal laws with the independent auditor should be familiar.

10–5.   List three types of general journal entries for which the auditor would search in his scanning of the general journal for unusual entries, and explain why the journal entries you list are unusual.

10–6.   Charles Halstead, CPA, has a number of clients who desire audits at the end of the calendar year. In an effort to spread his work load more uniformly throughout the year, he is preparing a list of audit procedures which could be performed satisfactorily prior to the year-end balance sheet date. What work, if any, might be done on the general records in advance of the balance sheet date?

10–7.   State five significant provisions for which an auditor should particularly look in examining the articles of incorporation of a company and any amendments thereto. (AICPA)

10–8.   In connection with an annual audit of a corporation engaged in manufacturing operations, the auditors have regularly reviewed the minutes of the meetings of stockholders and of the board of directors. Name 10 important items that might be found in the minutes of the meetings held during the period under review which would be of interest and significance to the auditor. (AICPA)

10–9.   What should be the scope of an auditor's review of the corporate minutes book during the first audit of a client? During a repeat engagement?

10–10.   Should the auditor make a complete review of all correspondence in the client's files? Explain.

10–11.   What is the nature of the working papers used by the auditor to summarize the audit work performed on the accounting records?

10–12.   Is it feasible for the auditor to combine his examination of the general journal and general ledger with his review of special journals and original papers such as sales invoices and purchase invoices? Explain.

GROUP II
QUESTIONS REQUIRING ANALYSIS

10–13.   In a discussion between Adams and Barnes, two auditing students, Adams made the following statement:

"A CPA is a professional person who is licensed by the state for the purpose of providing an independent expert opinion on the fairness of financial statements. To maintain an attitude of mental independence and objectivity in all phases of his audit work, it is advisable that he not fraternize with client personnel. He should be courteous but reserved and dignified at all times. If he indulges in social contacts with clients outside of business hours, this will make it more difficult for him to be firm and objective if he finds evidence of fraud or of unsound accounting practices."

Barnes replied as follows:

"You are 50 years behind the times, Adams. An auditor and a client are both human beings. The auditor needs the cooperation of the client to do a good job; he's much more likely to get cooperation if he's relaxed and friendly rather than being cold and impersonal. Having a few beers or going to a football game with a client won't keep the CPA from being independent. It will make the working relationship a lot more comfortable and will probably cause the client to recommend the CPA to other business people who need auditing services. In other words, the approach you're recommending should be called "How to Avoid Friends and Alienate Clients." I will admit though that with so many women entering public accounting and other women holding executive positions in business, a few complications may arise when auditor-client relations get pretty relaxed."

Evaluate the opposing views expressed by Adams and Barnes.

10–14. In a recent court case, the presiding judge criticized the work of a senior in charge of an audit in approximately the following language: "As to minutes, the senior read only what the secretary (of the company) gave him, which consisted only of the board of directors' minutes. He did not read such minutes as there were of the executive committee of the board. He did not know that there was an executive committee, hence he did not discover that the treasurer had notes of executive committee minutes which had not been written up."

Required:

How can the independent auditor be certain the client has provided him with minutes of all meetings of the board and committees thereof? Explain.

10–15. James Russell, CPA, agreed to perform an audit of a new client engaged in the manufacture of power tools. After some preliminary discussion of the purposes of the audit and the basis for determination of the audit fee, Russell asked that he be taken on a comprehensive guided tour of the client's plant facilities. Explain specific ways that the knowledge gained by Russell during the plant tour may help him in planning and conducting the audit.

10–16. A normal procedure in the audit of a corporate client consists of a careful reading of the minutes of meetings of the board of directors. One of the CPA's objectives in reading the minutes is to determine whether the transactions recorded in the accounting records are in agreement with actions approved by the board of directors.

Required:

a) What is the reasoning underlying this objective of reconciling transactions in the corporate accounting records with actions approved by the board of directors? Describe fully how the CPA achieves the stated objective after he had read the minutes of directors' meetings.

b) Discuss the effect each of the following situations would have on specific audit steps in a CPA's examination and on his auditor's opinion:

(1) The minutes book does not show approval for the sale of an important manufacturing division which was consummated during the year.

(2) Some details of a contract negotiated during the year with the labor union are different from the outline of the contract included in the minutes of the board of directors.

(3) The minutes of a meeting of directors held after the balance sheet date have not yet been written, but the corporation's secretary shows the CPA notes from which the minutes are to be prepared when the secretary has time.

c) What corporate actions should be approved by stockholders and recorded in the minutes of the stockholders' meetings? (AICPA, adapted)

GROUP III
PROBLEMS

10–17. Martin George, CPA, is engaged in his first examination of the financial statements of Chapman Mfg. Company, Inc., for the year ended December 31, 1974. In scanning the client's general journal, Mr. George noted the following entry dated June 30, 1974:

Cost of Sales	186,453	
Raw Materials		84,916
Work in Process		24,518
Finished Goods		77,019

To adjust book inventories to amounts of physical inventory taken this date.

The client-prepared income statement shows net sales and net income of approximately $5,500,000 and $600,000, respectively.

Required:

Do you think Mr. George should investigate the above entry? Explain fully.

10–18. Summarize, in good form for the audit working papers, those contents of the following minutes of directors' meetings which you consider to be of significance in the conduct of an annual audit.

MEETING OF FEBRUARY 15, 1974

The meeting was called to order at 2:15 P.M. by Mr. H. R. Jensen, chairman of the board. The following directors were present:

John J. Savage	Harold Bruce Smith
Henry R. King	Lee McCormick
W. B. Andrews	Dale H. Lindberg
H. R. Coleman	Ralph Barker
George Anderson	H. R. Jensen
	Kenneth J. Bryan

Absent was Director J. B. Adams, who was in New York City on company business in connection with the opening of a sales office.

The minutes of the preceding meeting, December 15, 1973, were read by the secretary and duly approved as read.

Upon a motion by Mr. King, seconded by Mr. Savage, and unanimously carried, the secretary was instructed to notify the firm of Black, Bryson and MacDougal, Certified Public Accountants, of their selection to conduct an annual audit of the company's financial statements as of March 31, 1974.

President John J. Savage outlined the current status of negotiations leading toward the acquisition of a new factory site in San Diego, California, and recommended to the board the purchase of said property at a price not to exceed $80,000.

Mr. King offered the following resolution, which was seconded by Mr. Smith, and unanimously carried:

Resolved: That Mr. Savage hereby is authorized to acquire in behalf of the company the factory site located at Exmont and Donaldson Avenues, San Diego, California, at a price not in excess of $80,000, to be paid for in cash from the general funds of the corporation.

Upon a motion by Mr. Savage, seconded by Mr. King and carried unanimously, the secretary was instructed to arrange for the purchase from the estate of J. B. Williams, former director, 100 shares of the company's own stock at a price not in excess of $110 per share.

Mr. Savage, after discussing the progress of the company in recent months and its current financial condition, submitted the following resolution, which was seconded by Mr. King and unanimously passed:

Resolved: That the following cash dividends are hereby declared, payable April 10, 1974, to stockholders of record on March 31, 1974.

a)   The regular quarterly dividend of $1 per share of capital stock.

b)   A special dividend of $0.50 per share of capital stock.

There being no further business brought before the meeting, the meeting was adjourned at 4:00 P.M.

Kenneth J. Bryan
Secretary

MEETING OF MARCH 15, 1974

The meeting was called to order at 2:15 P.M. by Mr. H. R. Jensen, chairman of the board. The following directors were present:

John J. Savage	Harold Bruce Smith
Henry R. King	Lee McCormick
W. B. Andrews	Dale H. Lindberg
H. R. Coleman	J. B. Adams
George Anderson	H. R. Jensen
	Kenneth J. Bryan

Absent was Director Ralph Barker.

The minutes of the preceding meeting, February 15, 1974, were read by the secretary and duly approved as read.

Chairman H. R. Jensen stated that nominations for the coming year were in order for the positions of president, vice president in charge of sales, vice president in charge of manufacturing, treasurer, controller, and secretary.

The following nominations were made by Mr. King, and there being no further nominations the nominations were declared closed:

President	John J. Savage
Vice president—sales	Otis Widener
Vice president—manufacturing	Henry Pendleton
Treasurer	W. B. Andrews
Controller	Roger Dunn
Secretary	Kenneth J. Bryan

The above nominees were duly elected.

Mr. McCormick then offered the following resolution, which was seconded by Mr. Coleman and unanimously carried:

Resolved: That the salaries of all officers be continued for the next year at the same rates currently in effect. These rates are as follows:

John J. Savage—president	$60,000
Otis Widener—vice president—sales	35,000
Henry Pendleton—vice president—manufacturing	25,000
W. B. Andrews—treasurer	25,000
Roger Dunn—controller	25,000
Kenneth J. Bryan—secretary	18,000

Mr. Bryan offered the following resolution, which was seconded by Mr. Andrews and unanimously carried:

Resolved: That the company establish a bank account at the United National Bank, San Diego, California, to be subject to check by either John J. Savage or W. B. Andrews.

There being no further business to come before the meeting, the meeting was adjourned at 4:00 P.M.

Kenneth J. Bryan
Secretary

10–19.   The partnership of Wheat Brothers operated successfully for many years until the death of one of the brothers. The business was reorganized as a corporation at the beginning of the current year with John Wheat, the surviving brother, elected to serve as president of the new entity, Wheat Corporation. Mr. Wheat was also the largest stockholder.

To permit a cash settlement with the estate of the deceased partner, the organization of the corporation involved obtaining outside capital. This was readily accomplished by sale of capital stock to local residents who were familiar with the success and reputation of the business conducted by Wheat Brothers.

Near the close of the first year of operation as a corporation, John Wheat, president of the company, retained you to perform a year-end audit. Prior to the balance sheet date you requested the secretary of Wheat Corporation to provide you with the minutes books covering all meetings of the stockholders, the board of directors, and any committees of the board. The secretary had held a responsible position in the company throughout its years of operations as a partnership during which time the company had never been audited. He expressed some reluctance to making available information which he regarded as highly confidential, but finally he offered to provide you with a certified copy of all resolutions relating to accounting matters which had been passed by the stockholders, the board of directors, and committees of the board. The secretary explained that some nonaccounting matters of a highly confidential nature had been discussed in some of the board meetings and that he considered it unwise for this confidential information to be made available to anyone other than directors of the company.

The secretary also informed you that he had discussed your request for the minutes books with Mr. Wheat and that the president had suggested that you might be elected to the board of directors at an upcoming meeting. After such election, all records of the board and its committees would automatically be available to you.

Required:

a) What is the most likely explanation of the secretary's response to your request?

b) How would you respond to the statements by the secretary? Explain fully.

11

Cash

What is the auditor looking for?

IN AUDIT work on cash (and other assets), the auditor is on guard against *overstatement of asset values.* Assume, for example, that the client's balance sheet shows "Cash . . . . . $50,000." There is little chance that the business has more cash than shown; the real danger is that the actual cash is less than $50,000. If a cash shortage exists, it may have been concealed merely by inserting a fictitious check in the year-end cash receipts, or by omitting an outstanding check from the year-end bank reconciliation. In this case the amount of cash on hand and on deposit is actually less than the $50,000 amount shown in the balance sheet.

Another way of summarizing the auditor's approach to verification of cash is to say that he is alert for any understatement of cash receipts or overstatement of cash disbursements. Either of these misstatements can conceal a theft of cash by reducing the book figure for cash to the amount remaining after the theft.

The auditor's objectives in examination of cash

In the examination of cash, the auditor's principal objectives are: (a) to study and evaluate the internal controls over cash transactions, and (b) to determine that cash is fairly presented in the client's financial statements.

329

After determining the nature of the internal controls relating to cash, the auditor then examines a portion of the individual cash transactions, setting the size of the sample to be tested and the areas to be sampled according to the relative quality of internal control over the various phases of cash receiving, cash disbursement, and cash budgeting. As a result of the tests of cash transactions, the auditor knows the extent to which the controls purportedly in use are actually functioning in practice. These tests permit the auditor to satisfy himself as to the validity of the recorded cash transactions, the soundness of the methods used in handling and recording cash, and the general credibility of the accounting records.

The second objective—that of determining the fairness with which cash is presented as part of the client's overall financial position—is relatively simple, because cash, unlike other assets, poses virtually no problems of valuation. To substantiate the amount of cash shown on the balance sheet, the auditor will employ such audit procedures as confirming the amounts on deposit by direct communication with banks, and possibly by counting any cash on hand. Other important procedures to achieve the objective of fair presentation of cash include a review of the year-end cutoff of cash receipts and payments and consideration of the reasonableness of the year-end cash balance in relation to the company's needs and any available cash forecasts. Ascertaining the existence of any restrictions on certain cash balances (such as foreign deposits) is also an essential step in determining the fairness of the balance sheet presentation of cash.

This discussion of major audit objectives has purposely omitted the detection of fraud. Regardless of whether the asset under consideration is cash, inventory, plant and equipment, or some other category, the detection of fraud is relevant to overall fairness of the client's financial statements only if such fraud is material in amount. If fraud is material and widespread, normal auditing practices should lead to its disclosure.

How much audit time for cash?

The factor of materiality applies to audit work on cash as well as to other sections of the examination. The counting of a small petty cash fund, which is inconsequential in relation to the company's overall financial position, makes little contribution to achievement of the auditor's basic objective of expressing his professional opinion on the financial statements. Nevertheless, many auditors do devote a much larger proportion of the total audit hours to cash than is indicated by the relative amount of cash shown on the balance sheet. For example, it is not uncommon to find that cash represents only 5 percent of total assets but that the auditor has spent 15 percent of his total time in the verification of cash. This inconsistency is heightened by the fact that scarcely any valuation problem exists for cash, whereas considerable audit time is expended on valuation problems in the work on inventories and accounts receivable.

Several reasons exist to explain this traditional emphasis by auditors on cash transactions. Cash is the most liquid of assets and offers the greatest temptation to officers or employees whose moral standards may crumble during personal financial crises or succumb to the urge for quick financial gain. Relative risk is high for liquid assets, and auditors tend to respond to high risk situations with more detailed investigation.

In some audit engagements (especially of small companies), the client may have specific reason to suspect the existence of fraud and may ask the auditor to stress the examination of cash transactions. Or if the auditor's study and evaluation of internal control over cash disclose significant weaknesses, he may take the initiative in extending the scope of his work on cash. In the area of small business enterprises, some clients still cling to the outmoded notion that failure of the auditor to detect a defalcation, even a small one, is evidence of incompetence. Such reasoning shows a lack of understanding of the objectives of an audit; but as long as clients react this way, the auditor may feel compelled to do extensive work on cash merely to protect himself. The long-run answer is of course to educate clients as to the real values to be gained from an audit.

Another reason contributing to "excessive" auditing of cash is the benefit of verifying other accounts in connection with investigation of cash transactions. Liabilities, revenue, and expenses as well as most other asset accounts involve a cash transaction. The examination of cash thus assists in the verification of many other components of the financial statements.

Internal control over cash transactions

Know

Ideally the system of internal control should provide assurance that—

1. All cash which should have been received *was* in fact received and recorded promptly and accurately.
2. Cash disbursements have been made only for authorized business purposes and have been properly recorded.
3. Cash on hand and in bank is accurately stated and subject to appropriate safeguards.
4. Cash balances are maintained at adequate but not excessive levels by budgeting expected cash receipts and payments related to normal operations. The need for obtaining loans or for investing excess cash is thus made known on a timely basis.

The auditor is often able to suggest changes in operating procedures which will strengthen controls over cash receipts and disbursements without imposing additional operating costs. Although a detailed study of the operating routines of the individual client is a necessary prelude to the development of the most efficient control procedures, there are some general guidelines useful to the auditor in appraising the cash-handling practices of all types of business. These universal rules for achieving internal control over cash may be summarized as follows:

1. Do not permit any one employee to handle a transaction from beginning to end.
2. Separate cash handling from record keeping.
3. Centralize receiving of cash as much as possible.
4. Locate cash registers so that customers can observe amounts recorded.
5. Record cash receipts immediately.
6. Deposit each day's cash receipts intact.
7. Make all disbursements by check, with the exception of expenditures from petty cash.
8. Have bank reconciliations performed by employees not responsible for the issuance of checks or handling of cash.

Several good reasons exist for the rule that each day's cash receipts should be deposited intact. Daily deposits mean that less cash will be on hand to invite "borrowing"; moreover the deposit of each day's receipts as a unit tends to prevent the substituting of later cash receipts to cover a shortage. If company policy permits the paying of expenses out of cash receipts, fictitious disbursements and overstatement of actual payments are much more easily concealed than when liabilities are paid by check after proper verification. Any delay in depositing checks increases the risk that the checks will be uncollectible. Further, undeposited receipts represent idle cash, which is not a revenue-producing asset.

Internal control over cash sales

Control over cash sales is strongest when two or more employees (usually a salesclerk and a cashier) participate in each transaction with a customer. Restaurants and cafeterias often use a centrally located cashier who receives cash from the customer along with a sales ticket prepared by another employee. Theaters generally have a cashier selling prenumbered tickets which are collected by a doorman when the customer is admitted. If tickets or sales checks are serially numbered and all numbers accounted for, this separation of responsibility for the transaction is an effective means of preventing fraud.

Control features of cash registers. In many retail establishments the nature of the business is such that one employee must make over-the-counter sales, deliver the merchandise, receive cash, and record the transaction. In this situation dishonesty may be discouraged by proper use of cash registers and form-writing machines with locked-in copies. The protective features of the cash register include (*a*) the ringing of a bell to call attention to the opening of the cash drawer, (*b*) the flashing of the amount of the sale at the top of the register in full view of the customer, (*c*) the printing of a receipt which the customer is urged to take with the merchandise, and (*d*) the accumulation of a locked-in total of the day's sales. At the end of the day the salesperson counts the cash in the drawer and turns in this amount without knowing the total sales recorded on the register. A supervisor inserts a key in the cash register which permits a reading of the total sales for the day to be taken. Overages and shortages will inevitably occur from time to time, but a careful record of cash turned in and sales recorded by each salesperson will quickly disclose any unreasonable variations.

Control features of form-writing machines. Many businesses making sales over the counter find that internal control is strengthened by use of a machine containing triplicate sales tickets. As each sales check is written, two copies are ejected by the machine and a third copy is retained in a locked compartment. The retention of the third copy which is not available to the salesclerk tends to prevent a dishonest employee from reducing the store's copy of the sales check to an amount less than that shown on the customer's copy.

Internal control over collections from customers

In many manufacturing and wholesale businesses, cash receipts consist principally of checks received through the mail. This situation poses little threat of defalcation unless one employee is permitted to receive and deposit these checks and also to record the credits to the customers' accounts. Under these circumstances considerable protection can be gained if the manager or another employee will open the mail and prepare a list of all checks received. This list can later be compared with the daily deposits and the credits to accounts receivable. The listing of incoming checks in the mailroom is also practiced in some companies having extensive subdivision of cash-handling and accounting procedures.

When the nature of operations permits, different employees should be assigned responsibility for (*a*) preparation of sales invoices, (*b*) maintenance of customers' accounts, (*c*) balancing of customers' ledgers with control accounts, (*d*) collection acitivty on past-due accounts, and (*e*) the receiving and depositing of collections from customers. Credits to customers' accounts should be posted from customers' remittance advices rather than from the checks themselves.

Internal control over cash disbursements

The dangers inherent in making disbursements out of cash receipts have already been discussed. To state the issue in positive terms, all disbursements should be made by check, except for payment of minor items from petty cash funds. Although the issuance of checks is somewhat more costly than making payments in cash, the advantages gained by use of checks usually justify the expense involved. A principal advantage is the obtaining of a receipt from the payee in the form of an endorsement on the check. Other advantages include (*a*) the centralization of disbursement authority in the hands of a few designated officials—the only persons authorized to sign checks, (*b*) a permanent record of disbursements, and (*c*) a reduction in the amount of cash kept on hand.

To secure in full the internal control benefits implicit in the use of checks, it is essential that all checks be prenumbered and all numbers in the series accounted for. Voided checks should be defaced to eliminate any possibility of further use, and filed in the regular sequence of paid checks. Dollar amounts should be printed on all checks with a check-protecting machine. This practice prevents anyone from altering a check by raising its amount.

Two signatures may be required on each check, or on all checks in excess of a minimum amount. This safeguard appears to be falling into disuse, probably because the second signature is apt to be a perfunctory gesture. For example, an executive before leaving for a business trip may sign a number of blank checks and leave them for use of the officials authorized to countersign.

Officials authorized to sign checks should review the documents supporting the payment and perforate these documents at the time of signing the check to prevent them from being submitted a second time. The official signing checks should maintain control of the checks until they are placed in the mail. Typically the check comes to the official complete except for signature. It is imperative that the signed checks not be returned to the custody of the employee who prepared them for signature.

The reconciliation of bank statements should be assigned to an employee having no part in handling cash receipts or disbursements, and the statements from the bank should come unopened to this employee.

Internal control aspects of petty cash funds

An *imprest* system for petty cash requires that the checks issued periodically to replenish the fund agree with the amount of disbursements from the fund. Consequently, an imprest petty cash fund remains at a fixed balance.

Payment of minor items can more conveniently be made in cash from an imprest fund than by going through the formal verification procedures required for issuance of a check. Internal control over payments from an imprest petty cash fund is achieved at the time the fund is replenished to its fixed balance rather than at the time of handing out small amounts of cash. When the custodian of a petty cash fund requests replenishment of the fund, the documents supporting each disbursement should be reviewed for completeness and authenticity, and perforated to prevent reuse. Since the types and amounts of disbursements to be made from the fund are usually specifically limited, the opportunities for fraud of significant amount are not great.

Petty cash funds are sometimes kept in the form of separate bank accounts. The bank should be instructed in writing not to accept for deposit in such an account any checks payable to the company. The deposits will be limited to checks to replenish the fund and drawn payable to the bank or to the custodian of the fund. The prohibition against deposit of checks payable to the company is designed to prevent the routing of cash receipts into petty cash, since this would violate the basic assumption of limited disbursements and review at time of replenishing the fund.

Many companies permit the cashier to cash personal checks for employees and customers out of the petty cash. Check cashing may be kept within bounds by creating a list of persons for whom checks may be cashed and by establishing maximum dollar amounts for such checks.

Petty cash funds should normally be of sufficient amount that replenishment will be required no more frequently than every two to four weeks. Too large a petty cash fund encourages abuses such as unauthorized "borrowing" and payment for costly items that should be handled through issuance of checks. Too small a fund requires excessive work through very frequent replenishment.

The petty cash fund should always be replenished at the end of the fiscal year so that expenses will be reflected in the proper accounting period. If the auditor finds that the fund was not replenished at year-end, he may draft an adjusting entry for the unrecorded expenditures or he may decide against proposing an adjustment on the grounds that the amounts involved are not material.

Internal control and the computer

The computer can contribute substantially to strong internal control for cash. Remittance advices or lists prepared by mail clerks for customers' payments can be keypunched for processing by the computer. Many companies also issue checks in the form of punched cards. The daily computer processing of the punched cards for cash receipts and checks provides a cash receipts journal, a check register, an updated cash balance, and current information for cash planning and forecasting. In addition, the monthly bank reconciliation can be processed by the computer.

Audit working papers for cash

The auditor's working papers should include a written description, questionnaire, or flowchart describing the client's system of internal control for cash; working papers evidencing tests of cash transactions; and an evaluation of internal control for cash. Additional cash working papers include a grouping sheet, cash counts, bank reconciliations, bank confirmations, outstanding check lists, lists of checks investigated, and written conclusions of the auditor regarding the fairness of cash presented in the client's balance sheet.

Audit program for cash

The following list of procedures indicates the general pattern of work performed by the auditor in the verification of cash. Selection of the most appropriate procedures for a particular audit will of course be guided by the nature of the internal controls in force and by other circumstances of the engagement.

Study and evaluation of internal control for cash:

1. Obtain a description of the internal control for cash.
2. Test cash transactions:
   a) Prove footings of cash journals and trace postings to ledger accounts.
   b) Compare details of bank deposits with client's record of cash receipts.
   c) Reconcile bank activity for one or more months with cash activity per books.
   d) Verify cash transactions in one or more selected expense accounts.
3. Evaluate internal control for cash.

Procedures for cash at balance sheet date:

4. Count and list all cash on hand. Verify cutoff of cash receipts and cash disbursements.
5. Send confirmation letters to banks to verify amounts on deposit.
6. Obtain or prepare a reconciliation of the bank account as of the balance sheet date.
   a) Investigate any checks payable to cash or to bearer.
   b) Investigate any checks representing large or unusual payments to directors, officers, employees, or affiliates.

c) Investigate N.S.F. checks and other items charged back by bank.

d) Investigate any checks outstanding for more than 30 days.

7. Obtain a cutoff bank statement containing transactions of at least seven business days subsequent to balance sheet date.

8. Trace all bank transfers for last week of audit year and first week of following year.

9. Determine proper balance sheet presentation of cash.

1. *Obtain a description of the internal control for cash.*

In his study of the internal controls over cash in a small enterprise, the auditor may prepare a written description of the controls in force, based on the questioning of owners and employees and on firsthand observation. In the review of internal controls in larger concerns, the auditor will usually employ a flowchart or an internal control questionnaire. An internal control questionnaire for cash receipts was illustrated in Chapter 5; questions for cash disbursements might include the following:

1. Are all disbursements, except those from petty cash, made by pre-numbered checks?

2. Are voided checks preserved and filed after appropriate mutilation?

3. Is there definite written prohibition against—

    a) Drawing checks payable to "cash" or "bearer"?

    b) Signing checks in advance?

4. If a check-signing machine is in use, is the signature plate properly controlled?

5. Is the check-signing authority restricted to executives who do not have access to accounting records or to negotiable assets?

6. *a*) Are vouchers or other supporting documents presented with checks submitted for signature?

    b) Are these documents stamped or perforated to prevent a second presentation?

7. Are checks mailed directly after being signed, without the employees responsible for their preparation having further access to them?

Other sections of the internal control questionnaire, flowchart, or written description for cash would cover cash disbursements for payroll and dividends, and bank reconciliation procedures. All questions of the internal control questionnaire are designed to require affirmative answers when satisfactory controls exist.

2a. *Prove footings of cash journals and trace postings to ledger accounts.*

The purpose of proving footings of the cash receipts and cash disbursements journals is to verify the mechanical accuracy of the journals. The extent of the footings tests should be based upon the internal controls for cash described in the flowchart, questionnaire, or written description. For example, if one employee serves as both cashier and bookkeeper, the auditor will generally test footings of most, if not all, of the journals. Cash embezzlements have been concealed by an understatement of the cash receipts journal "Cash-Debit" column or an overstatement of the "Cash-Credit" column of the cash disbursements journal. Generally, the "Sales Discounts" column total of the cash receipts journal will be overstated in the same amount as the cash column understatement, so that the journal will be in balance. In like manner, the "Purchase Discounts" column total of the cash disbursements journal would be understated to offset an overstatement of the Cash column total.

Closely associated with the proof of cashbook footings is the tracing of postings to the general ledger. Since there is usually only one posting per month from the cash receipts journal to the Cash account and one per month to the control accounts for receivables, it requires very little time to trace the posting of the cash and accounts receivable columns for the entire year. Similar verification may readily be made for the totals posted from the cash payments journal to the Cash account and Accounts Payable account in the general ledger. With respect to other columns in the cashbooks, particularly the "Miscellaneous" column, verification of postings for a judgment or statistical sample is usually deemed sufficient. If the testing of postings and footings discloses sloppy bookkeeping work, with numerous errors and corrections, indistinct figures and ambiguous totals, the scope of the auditor's work should be increased, for these are often the hallmarks of fraudulent manipulation of the records.

2b.   Compare details of bank deposits with client's record of cash receipts.

Satisfactory internal control over cash receipts demands that each day's collections be deposited intact no later than the next banking day. Businesses that operate on weekends and holidays should segregate each day's receipts and prepare separate deposit tickets for each day. Thus, on Tuesday morning following a Labor Day weekend, three separate deposits should be made, each of which will consist of a single day's receipts. Rigid adherence to the rule of depositing each day's receipts intact will minimize the opportunity for employees handling cash to "borrow" from the funds in their custody. Moreover, this practice facilitates comparison by the auditor of the cash receipts record with the deposits per the bank.

In making a comparison of receipts and deposits the auditor should emphasize the detailed examination of daily deposits rather than relying on monthly or yearly totals. Agreement of total receipts and deposits for a period gives no assurance that receipts have not been withheld for a portion of the period and the shortage made good by subsequent deposits. To detect delays in the making of deposits or the substitution of checks or cash from receipts of previous days, it is necessary to compare the details shown on the individual deposit tickets with the details of the cash receipts record. The period to be covered by the test will depend upon the circumstances of each examination.

The auditor's comparison of bank deposits with the cash receipts journal may uncover fraud known as "lapping." **Lapping** may be defined as "the concealment of a shortage by delaying the recording of cash receipts." If cash collected from customer A is withheld by the cashier, a subsequent collection from customer B may be entered as a credit to A's account. B's account will not be shown as paid until a collection from customer C is recorded as a credit to B. Unless the money abstracted by the cashier is replaced, the accounts receivable as a group remain overstated; but judicious shifting of the overstatement from one account receivable to another may avert protests from customers receiving monthly statements. In companies in which the cashier has access to the general accounting records, shortages created in this manner have sometimes been transferred to inventory accounts or elsewhere in the records for temporary concealment.

An analysis of lapping activities indicates that three distinct elements are generally involved. The first of these is failure to record all cash receipts; the second is abstraction of the unrecorded receipts, which are at least partly currency; and the third is the crediting of subsequent receipts to the wrong account.

If an employee who receives collections from cutomers is responsible for the posting of customers' accounts, lapping is most easily carried on. Familiarity with customers' accounts makes it relatively easy to lodge a shortage in an account that will not be currently questioned.

If the cashier and the accounts receivable bookkeeper are different persons but the bookkeeper is called upon to handle the cash-receiving function during the lunch hour or in emergencies, the opportunity for lapping still exists.

In many organizations, efficient operating routines appear to require that the record of cash receipts be prepared by the person receiving cash from customers and preparing the bank deposit. The cash receipts journal as prepared by the cashier may then be turned over to the bookkeeper, or remittance advices corresponding to the cash receipts journal may be used as a posting medium. The possibility of lapping is inherent in these situations because even though the cashier does not maintain the customers' ledgers he creates the record from which such ledgers are posted.

Duplicate deposit tickets in the possession of the client may be subject to alteration. If the auditor suspects that the duplicate slips have been altered, he should compare them with the originals on file at the bank.

Most banks are willing to furnish the auditor with copies of deposit tickets for comparison with the client's record of cash receipts.

2c. *Reconcile bank activity for one or more months with cash activity per books.*

This audit procedure (called a "proof of cash") is particularly appropriate when internal controls for cash appear weak or the client has requested a thorough investigation of cash transactions. It may be omitted when internal controls are strong and the principal purpose of the audit is the expression of an opinion on the fairness of the financial statements. The procedure requires the selection of a test period (the month of December in the illustration) and detailed study of cash transactions during this period. The starting point for this study is preparation of a four-column bank reconciliation covering the test period, as illustrated in Figure 11–1.

Notice the following points in the illustrated four-column bank reconciliation:

a) The balance per bank is reconciled with the balance per books at the beginning of the test period (column 1) and at the end of this period (column 4).

b) Deposits per the bank during December are reconciled with receipts per the books (column 2).

c) Checks paid by the bank during December are reconciled with the payments per the books (column 3).

Next let us consider the source of the figures used in this reconciliation. The amounts in column 1 (Balance, November 30) were taken by the auditor from the client's bank reconciliation as of November 30. Similarly, the figures for column 4 (Balance, December 31) were taken from the client's bank reconciliation as of December 31. For column 2 (Deposits) the auditor arrived at the $46,001 of deposits per the bank by listing on an adding machine the deposits appearing on the December bank statement. He obtained the $45,338.50 of receipts per the books by referring to the Cash in Bank account in the general ledger. In column 3 the auditor computed the $40,362.90 of checks paid by the bank as the amount required to balance out the top line of the reconciliation. The bottom figure in column 3 represents the disbursements per the books during December and was taken from the general ledger account. The reconciling items listed in columns 2 and 3 were computed by the auditor by comparing the reconciling items at the beginning and end of December.

After completing the four-column bank reconciliation form, the auditor should prove the footings of all four columns and make a detailed verification of the figures used in the reconciliation. The balances taken

FIGURE 11-1

The Fairview Corporation

Acct. No. 101   Proof of Cash for December, 1975   E-4

12/31/75

	Balance 11/30/75	+ Receipts Deposits	− Disburse = Checks	Balance 12/31/75
Per bank statement	39 236 40= (34 1-0 40)	46 001 00 #	40 362 90	44 874 50= (44 774 50)
Deposits in transit:				
at 11/30/75	600 00=	(600 00)		
at 12/31/75		837 50		837 50
Outstanding checks:	1 141 00			
at 11/30/75	(1 241 00) x		(1 241 00)	
at 12/31/75			3 402 00	(3 402 00) v
Bank service charge:				
November	4 60		4 60	
December			(2 80)	2 80
Check of customer A. G. Speeler charged back by bank 12/12/75, redeposited 12/15/75		(900 00)	(900 00)	
Per books	38 600 00 n	45 338 50 n	41 625 70 n (41 725 70)	42 312 80 n E-1

z- Traced to client's 11/30/75 bank reconciliation and/or to December, 1975, bank statement.
#- Per adding machine tape at E-4-1.
x- Per adding machine tape at E-4-2.
v- Per adding machine tape at E-4-3.
n- Traced to general ledger.

Obtained authenticated duplicate deposit slips for December, 1975, from bank and compared with cash receipts record. Footed cash receipts journal and check register for December, 1975. Accounted for numerical sequence of all checks issued December, 1975 - nos. 610-792. Vouched all December, 1975, disbursements to vendors' invoices or statements and other supporting documents. No exceptions.

V. M. H.
1/10/76

Have to eliminate multiple receipts

from the client's bank reconciliations as of November 30 and December 31 should be traced to the bank statements and to the Cash in Bank account in the general ledger.

VERIFICATION OF RECEIPTS AND DEPOSITS DURING THE TEST PERIOD. To verify receipts and deposits for the month being tested, an adding machine tape of deposits listed on the bank statement should be compared with the client's cash receipts record. This step will include not only a comparison of the total receipts with the total deposits but also a comparison of the date of each deposit with the date such funds were received by the company. Any failure to deposit each day's receipts intact should be investigated. For a few days of the period it may be desirable to obtain authenticated duplicate deposit tickets and to trace each item on the tickets to individual entries in the cash receipts records and to supporting documents such as customers' remittance advices and cash register tapes showing total cash sales for the day. Sales discounts taken by customers during the test period may also be verified by computing the discounts and noting the dates of invoices and customers' payments.

VERIFICATION OF DISBURSEMENTS DURING THE TEST PERIOD. An audit of disbursements during the test period may include the following steps:

a)   Prove the figure for checks paid by the bank ($40,362.90 in the illustrated bank reconciliation form) by preparing an adding machine tape of the paid checks.

b)   Prove that all of the checks listed were actually paid during the test period by noting the perforated payment date on each check.

c)   Determine that every check listed as outstanding at November 30 was either paid during December or is included in the list of outstanding checks at December 31.

d)   Trace each check to the cash disbursements records, noting agreement as to check number, date, payee, and amount. Place a distinctive tick mark opposite each disbursement verified in this way and determine that all disbursements not ticked off are included in the outstanding check list at December 31. The total of outstanding checks verified by this step should be traced to the four-column bank reconciliation.

e)   Examine any checks voided during the month and account for all check numbers. Determine the last check number used in November and the last check number used in December. All intervening check numbers must have been paid, voided, or listed as outstanding at December 31.

f)   Vouch a representative number of the cash disbursements for December to supporting evidence such as properly approved vendors' invoices and payroll records. Normally done in A/P exam.

Satisfactory completion of the four-column bank reconciliation and the related steps of verifying cash activity for the test period will usually provide a clear indication as to whether cash receipts and disbursements are being properly handled and cash balances are accurately stated. In addition, this work will enable the auditor to learn whether prescribed internal controls are being effectively carried out in actual practice.

2d. **Verify cash transactions in one or more selected expense accounts.**

In companies with strong internal controls over cash disbursements, checks are issued only in payment of approved liabilities. A voucher system, for example, usually provides that a check may be issued only after a voucher has been prepared and the transaction verified and recorded as a liability. Many companies with weak internal control over cash disbursements do, however, permits checks to be issued in payment of expenses without first verifying that a liability was properly incurred. In these situations analysis of the cash transactions in one or more selected accounts is a desirable auditing procedure—one which may shed considerable light on the adequacy of the internal control over cash.

If cash is paid out without authorization or for any improper purpose, the person responsible for the irregular payment must arrange for some account to be debited to offset the credit to Cash. For example, assume that an official of the company being audited had arranged for a company check to be sent to a department store in payment for his personal expenditures. What account would probably be charged with this cash transaction? Experience shows that such accounts as Miscellaneous Expense, Entertainment Expense, and Sales Promotion Expense are among the most "likely" accounts to be charged with improper disbursements. If the auditor finds that personal expenses of employees or officials have been treated as business expense, the appropriate adjusting entry is usually a transfer of the charge to a drawing account or account receivable.

The extent to which cash disbursements are tested will, of course, be influenced by the number and nature of errors found. This procedure represents one specific example of the sampling techniques used by auditors, and of the part played by tests of transactions in evaluating internal control.

3. **Evaluate internal control for cash.**

When the auditor has completed the procedures described in the preceding sections, he should evaluate the client's internal control for cash. As illustrated in Chapter 5, the internal control evaluation describes weaknesses and unusual strengths in internal control, related extensions or limitations of auditing procedures, and recommendations for inclusion in the internal control report to the client. The auditor then drafts the portion of the audit program devoted to the verification of cash as of the balance sheet date.

4. *Count and list all cash on hand. Verify cutoff of cash receipts and cash disbursements.*

One of the objectives of the auditor's work on cash is to substantiate the amount shown on the balance sheet. A direct approach to this objective is to count the cash on hand at year-end, verify the amount on deposit and prepare a reconciliation between the bank statement and the books.

Cash on hand ordinarily consists of undeposited cash receipts, petty cash funds, and change funds. The petty cash funds and change funds may be counted at any time before or after the balance sheet date; many auditors prefer to make a surprise count of these funds. If the client's internal audit staff regularly performs surprise counts of petty cash and change funds, the CPA may review the internal auditor's working papers for these counts and conclude that it is unnecessary to include a count of petty cash and change funds among the procedures of the annual independent audit. If undeposited cash receipts constitute a material factor, a count at the balance sheet date is desirable; otherwise the auditor may verify the deposit in transit at year-end by referring to the date of deposit shown on the "cutoff" bank statement.

Whenever the auditor makes a cash count, he should insist that the *custodian of the funds be present throughout the count.* At the completion of the count, the auditor should obtain from the custodian a signed and dated acknowledgement that the funds were counted in his presence and were returned to him intact. Such procedures avoid the possibility of an employee trying to explain a cash shortage by claiming that the funds were intact when turned over to the auditor. In some situations, the independent auditor may arrange for the client's internal auditing staff to assist under the CPA's supervision in the count of large amounts of cash on hand.

A first step in the verification of cash on hand is to establish control over all negotiable assets, such as cash funds, marketable securities, notes receivable, and warehouse receipts. Unless all negotiable assets are verified at one time, an opportunity exists for a dishonest officer or employee to conceal a shortage by transferring it from one asset category to another.

ILLUSTRATIVE CASE.   John Sidell, a key office employee in a small business, misappropriated $10,000 by withholding cash collections and postponing the required credits to accounts receivable from customers. The books were in balance, but Mr. Sidell was aware that when the independent auditors confirmed the balances due from customers, the shortage would be disclosed. He therefore "borrowed" negotiable securities from the office safe shortly before the annual audit and used them as collateral to obtain a short-term loan of $10,000. He intermingled the proceeds of this loan with the cash receipts on hand and credited the customers' accounts with all payments received to date. Mr. Sidell knew that unless the auditors insisted on verifying the securities owned by the business concurrently with their verification of cash, he would be able to abstract funds again after the cash had been counted, use these funds to pay off his loan, and return the "borrowed" securities to the safe before the auditors began their verification of investments. The defalcation was discovered when the auditors insisted on a simultaneous verification of all negotiable assets.

The balance sheet figure for cash should include all cash received on the final day of the year and none received subsequently. In other words, an accurate cutoff of cash receipts (and of cash disbursements) at year-end is essential to a proper statement of cash on the balance sheet. If the auditor can arrange to be present at the client's office at the close of business on the last day of the fiscal year, he will be able to verify the cutoff by counting the undeposited cash receipts. It will then be impossible for the client to include in the records any cash received after this cutoff point, without the auditor being aware of such actions.

All customers' checks included in cash on hand should have been entered in the cash receipts journal before the auditor's count. The auditor should compare these checks, both as to name and amount, with the cashbook entries. If checks have been credited to accounts other than those of the drawers of the checks, a likelihood of lapping or other fraudulent activity is indicated.

It is not uncommon to find included in cash on hand personal checks cashed for the convenience of officers, employees, or representatives of the customers and the suppliers. Such checks will, of course, not be entered in the cash receipts journal. The auditor's primary concern is to determine whether these checks are valid and collectible. This is best established by direct confirmation with the drawers of the checks or by observing the presentation of the checks at the bank for deposit or cashing, coupled with subsequent examination of unpaid checks returned by the bank. The auditor's verification should include a review of the client's policy as to check cashing.

Noncash items disclosed by the count should receive the auditor's close attention. Such items as N.S.F. checks held for redeposit, postdated checks, I.O.U.'s from employees, or expense vouchers included in the balance of cash per the books should be reviewed with a member of management, and definite disposition agreed upon. Adjusting entries will normally be necessary to exclude such items from the cash classification if the amounts are significant.

The principal audit objective in connection with undeposited receipts is to prove that the checks and cash items *counted and listed* by the auditor are valid and collectible, thus qualifying for inclusion in the balance sheet figure for cash. Accomplishment of this objective may usually be achieved through the following steps:

a) Supervise preparation of the deposit by the client and obtain a duplicate copy of the deposit slip. Currency, coins, checks, and other
cash items may be included in the deposit; but no collections received subsequent to the auditor's count may be included. In brief,
the deposit must contain only the items counted by the auditor.

b) Maintain control over the deposit until it is delivered to the bank in
the auditor's presence. A confirmation request should be submitted
with the deposit asking the bank to advise the auditor directly as to
the correctness of the deposit slip.

c) Obtain cutoff bank statement directly from the bank (see Procedure
7) and determine whether any of the checks counted and listed by
the auditor were charged back to the client's account as uncollectible. This is the final step in determining the validity of checks
presented to the auditor as part of cash on hand at the time of the
cash count.

d) Investigate fully any returned items disclosed by step (*c*). If customers' checks are returned, these should be redeposited or charged
to the customers' accounts by the client. Returned checks of employees or others cashed by the client as an accommodation should
be reviewed with an appropriate executive and recorded as a special receivable or written off as worthless.

The action to be taken upon discovery of a shortage during the count
of cash cannot be prescribed by any set of rules, but certain general
considerations are of wide applicability. These are:

a) Be reasonably assured that an irregularity exists before taking any
action. Errors in the process of counting or reconciling must be completely ruled out before suspicion is directed at any employee.

b) Give the employee responsible for the funds in question an opportunity to explain any discrepancy between the total per the count
and the amount with which he is charged. Small discrepancies may
be disposed of by transfer to an over and short account.

c) Communicate with the supervising auditor before entering into any
discussion of an apparent shortage with the officers or employees of
the client.

The foregoing suggestions are obviously little more than an elabora-
tion of the commonsense policy of securing and appraising all available
information before making a decision. The work of an experienced auditor is methodical and thorough; he is never guilty of impetuous accusa-
tions or loose talk concerning unproved irregularities.

Of course an auditor cannot visit every client's place of business
on the last day of the fiscal year, nor is his presence at this time essential
to a satisfactory verification of cash. As an alternative to a count on

the balance sheet date, the auditor can verify the cutoff of cash receipts by observing that deposits in transit as shown on the year-end bank reconciliation appear as credits on the bank statement on the first business day of the new year. Failure to make *immediate* deposit of the closing day's cash receipts would suggest that cash received at a later time might have been included in the deposit, thus overstating the cash balance at the statement date.

To insure an accurate cutoff of cash disbursements, the auditor should determine the serial number of the last check written on each bank account on the final day of the year and should inquire whether all checks up to this number have been placed in the mail. Some companies, in an effort to improve the current ratio, will prepare checks *Important* payable to creditors and enter these checks as cash disbursements on the last day of the fiscal year, although there is no intention of mailing the checks until several days or weeks later. When the auditor makes a note of the number of the last check issued for the period, he will be in a position to detect at once any additional checks which the client might later issue and seek to show as disbursements of the year under audit.

An alternative means of verifying the accuracy of the cutoff of cash disbursements when the auditor is not on hand at the year-end consists of giving particular attention to the time period before checks outstanding at year-end are presented to the bank for payment. This step is more fully considered in Procedure 7.

5. *Send confirmation letters to banks to verify amounts on deposit.*

Confirmation of amounts on deposit as of the balance sheet date is necessary in all cases, even when unopened bank statements are made available to the auditor. The confirmation letters must be mailed personally by the auditor, with return envelopes bearing the auditor's office address enclosed.

A standard form of bank confirmation request agreed upon by the AICPA and the Bank Administration Institute is widely used by the public accounting profession. This form is prepared in duplicate, the orginal to be retained by the bank and the duplicate to be returned to the auditor. An illustration of this form appears in Figure 11–2.

An important element of the confirmation letter is the request for disclosure of all indebtedness of the client to the bank. This request thus serves to bring to light any unrecorded liabilities to banks, as well as to confirm the existence of assets. The auditor should send confirmation letters to all banks in which the client has had deposits during the year, even though the deposit account may have been closed out during the period. It is entirely possible that a bank loan may continue after the closing of the deposit account. The same line of reasoning leads to the conclusion that confirmation letters are necessary even when the

FIGURE 11–2

STANDARD BANK CONFIRMATION INQUIRY

Approved 1966 by
AMERICAN INSTITUTE OF CERTIFIED PUBLIC ACCOUNTANTS
NABAC, THE ASSOCIATION FOR BANK AUDIT, CONTROL
AND OPERATION

E–1–1

DUPLICATE
To be mailed to accountant

January 16, 19 75

Dear Sirs:

Your completion of the following report will be sincerely appreciated. **IF THE ANSWER TO ANY ITEM IS "NONE", PLEASE SO STATE.** Kindly mail it in the enclosed stamped, addressed envelope direct to the accountant named below.

Report from

Yours truly,

The Fairview Corporation
(ACCOUNT NAME PER BANK RECORDS)

(Bank) Security National Bank

1000 Wilshire Boulevard

Los Angeles, California 90017

By *Carl G. Frazier*
Authorized Signature

Bank customer should check here if confirmation of bank balances only (item 1) is desired. ☐

Name of Accountant
Douglas and Troon, CPAs
800 Hill Street
Los Angeles, California 90014

NOTE—If the space provided is inadequate, please enter totals hereon and attach a statement giving full details as called for by the columnar headings below.

Dear Sirs:

1. At the close of business on December 31, 19 74 our records showed the following balance(s) to the *credit* of the above named customer. In the event that we could readily ascertain whether there were any balances to the credit of the customer not designated in this request, the appropriate information is given below.

AMOUNT	ACCOUNT NAME	ACCOUNT NUMBER	SUBJECT TO WITHDRAWAL BY CHECK?	INTEREST BEARING? GIVE RATE
E–1 $ 44,874.50	General Account	123-5828	Yes	No
E–2 3,215.89	Payroll Account	123-6451	Yes	No

2. The customer was directly liable to us in respect of loans, acceptances, etc., at the close of business on that date in the total amount of $ 20,000.00 , as follows:

AMOUNT	DATE OF LOAN OR DISCOUNT	DUE DATE	INTEREST RATE	INTEREST PAID TO	DESCRIPTION OF LIABILITY, COLLATERAL, SECURITY INTERESTS, LIENS, ENDORSERS, ETC.
M–1 $ 20,000.00	10/1/74	4/1/75	6%	–	Unsecured

3. The customer was contingently liable as endorser of notes discounted and/or as guarantor at the close of business on that date in the total amount of $ None , as below:

AMOUNT	NAME OF MAKER	DATE OF NOTE	DUE DATE	REMARKS
$				

4. Other direct or contingent liabilities, open letters of credit, and relative collateral, were None

5. Security agreements under the Uniform Commercial Code or any other agreements providing for restrictions, not noted above, were as follows (if officially recorded, indicate date and office in which filed): None

Date January 12, 19 75

Yours truly, (Bank) Security National Bank
By *Jonathan Richard*
Authorized Signature

Additional copies of this form are available from the American Institute of CPAs, 666 Fifth Avenue, New York, N. Y. 10019

auditor obtains the bank statements and paid checks directly from the bank.

6. *Obtain or prepare a reconciliation of the bank account as of the balance sheet date.*

Determination of a company's cash position at the close of the period requires a reconciliation of the balance per the bank statement at that date with the balance per the company's books. Even though the auditor may not be able to begin his work for some time after the close of the year, he will prepare a bank reconciliation as of the balance sheet date or review the one prepared by the client.

If the year-end reconciliation has been made by the client prior to arrival of the auditor, there is no need for duplicating the work. However, the auditor should examine the reconciliation in detail to satisfy himself that it has been properly prepared. His inspection of a reconciliation made by the client will include proof of the arithmetical accuracy of the reconciliation, tracing of balances to the bank statement and ledger account, and investigation of the reconciling items. The total checks drawn during the month according to the cash disbursements book should be equal to the total of the paid checks returned by the bank plus the outstanding checks at the end of the period and minus the outstanding checks at the beginning of the period. The importance of a careful review of the client's reconciliation is indicated by the fact that a cash shortage may be concealed merely by omitting a check from the outstanding list, or by purposely making an error in addition on the reconciliation.

There are many satisfactory forms of bank reconciliations. The most appropriate form for the auditor begins with balance per bank and ends with unadjusted balance per books. This format permits posting adjusting entries affecting cash directly to the bank reconciliation working paper, so that the final balance can be cross-indexed to the grouping sheet for cash or to the working trial balance.

In the audit of clients with questionable internal controls over cash, the auditor's work on the bank reconciliation takes on special importance. A comparison of the paid checks with the client's records will achieve several objectives, such as:

a) Determining that paid checks agree as to amount, number, date, and payee with the entry in the cash records.

b) Ascertaining whether any checks paid in the current period were issued in the preceding period but omitted from the preceding reconciliation.

c) Obtaining assurance that all paid checks were properly endorsed by the payee.

d) Determining whether the practice of using only prenumbered checks is consistently followed.

e) Observing the treatment by the client of any checks spoiled in the course of preparation.

In addition to these specific objectives, the review of checks, if carried on in an alert and intelligent manner, may disclose other irregularities of a nature not normally anticipated. All check numbers should be accounted for. For each check examined, a tick mark should be placed opposite the cashbook entry or on the list of oustanding checks in the preceding reconciliation. Checks spoiled in preparation should have been mutilated by the client by tearing off the signature space. The check should then have been filed in proper numercial sequence with the paid checks. A missing number in a series of checks always carries the possibility that a cash shortage has been concealed by issuing an unrecorded check which is currently outstanding.

The mechanics of balancing the ledger account with the bank statement by no means complete the auditor's verification of cash on deposit. The authenticity of the individual items making up the reconciliation must be established by reference to their respective sources. The balance per the bank statement, for example, is not accepted at face value but is verified by direct confirmation with the bank, as described in the preceding pages. Other verification procedures associated with the reconciliation of the bank statement will now be discussed.

6a.   *Investigate any checks payable to cash or to bearer.*

The drawing of checks payable to cash or bearer is a common practice, but one which violates the fundamental principles of internal control. Such checks do not require endorsement, hence there is no evidence as to who received the funds. Checks payable to cash or bearer are often used to replenish petty cash, to make expense advances to traveling employees, to reimburse officers for expenditures made in furtherance of company interests, to provide cash for personal drawings by officers, and to permit payment of wages in cash. In all of these cases, it is usually practicable for the check to be drawn payable to the individual authorized to receive the money; hence the auditor should exert his influence against the issuance of checks payable to cash.

Investigation of this category of checks usually consists of an examination of supporting vouchers, analysis of the accounts to which the charges were made, and interrogation of officers. In some concerns, checks drawn to cash or bearer have been used to provide funds for unethical commissions to buyers or to others who bestow favors on the concern. Such transactions are not usually explained or identified in the accounts or by supporting vouchers. The extent of the auditor's investigation of these disbursements must be determined tactfully and with professional judgment. One ever-present danger of such practices is that employees or officers familiar with the situation will abstract funds by drawing checks. payable to cash and utilizing the tradition of inadequate support for similar checks as a cloak to avoid detection.

6b.   *Investigate any checks representing large or unusual payments to directors, officers, employees, or affiliates.*

All checks payable to directors, officers, employees (other than payroll checks and nominal expense reimbursements), or affiliates should be carefully reviewed by the auditor for the purpose of determining (*a*) whether the funds were received by the individual named as payee, and (*b*) whether the disbursement was properly supported and authorized.

Endorsement of a check is evidence of the receipt of funds. In examining endorsements the auditor should be alert to detect and investigate any irregularity. Extra endorsements or missing endorsements warrant inquiry. Checks processed in a routine manner will show on the reverse side the endorsement of the payee, the stamp of the bank in which deposited, and the cancellation mark of the bank on which the check was drawn. When checks other than for payroll or fee purposes are drawn to the order of directors, officers, or employees, the possibility exists that the check may never reach the person named as payee but may be fraudulently endorsed and negotiated by the person issuing the check. Dishonest treasurers have been known to obtain funds through the use of checks which purported to represent reimbursement of traveling expenses of fellow officers or employees but which were, in fact, never delivered to the named payees.

In addition to satisfying himself that any large or unusual checks drawn in favor of directors, officers, employees, or affiliates represent actual disbursements to the indicated payees, the auditor should ascertain that each such transaction has been charged to the proper account, is supported by adequate vouchers or other records, and was specifically approved prior to payment by an officer other than the one receiving the funds. A check representing an advance to an officer but charged to miscellaneous expense will serve as an effective means of obtaining funds without the creation of a record to require repayment. Misclassification of checks issued to reimburse officers or employees for expenditures made in behalf of the company may open the door to duplicate reimbursement or to the concealment of improper expenditures. Most executives are anxious to have all payments to them supported and documented in a manner that will leave no room for doubt as to the propriety of the disbursement.

6c. Investigate N.S.F. checks and other items charged back by bank.

One of the traditional methods of attempting to conceal a cash shortage from the auditor consists of the insertion of a fictitious check in the cash receipts, petty cash, or other cash on hand. If the auditor supervises the deposit of all checks included in the cash count, the fictitious check will of course fail to clear the bank on which it is drawn and will be returned by the client's bank marked "N.S.F." (not sufficient funds), or "No such account," or with some similar term indicating its uncollectibility.

In addition to the problem of N.S.F. checks included in cash at the audit date, there is often a weakness in the procedures for handling customers' checks which have been deposited but returned by the bank as uncollectible. These should be immediately redeposited or charged back to the customer's account in the subsidiary ledger for accounts receivable. Often the returned check will be paid if deposited a second time; this creates the danger of misuse of these checks and concealment of such misuse by writing off the customer's account as worthless. The auditor should ascertain whether definite instructions have been issued to employees concerning the treatment of N.S.F. checks and whether these items receive the prompt attention of executives.

6d.   *Investigate any checks outstanding for more than 30 days.*

If checks are permitted to remain outstanding for long periods, internal control over cash disbursements is weakened. Employees who become aware that certain checks have long been outstanding and may never be presented have an opportunity to conceal a cash shortage merely by omitting the old oustanding check from the bank reconciliation. Such omissions will serve to increase the apparent balance of cash on deposit and may thus induce an employee to abstract a corresponding amount of cash on hand.

The auditor's investigation of old outstanding checks will include examination of the voucher and other documents supporting the payment. Checks outstanding for long periods should be called to the attention of the client, who will customarily contact the payee to ascertain the reason for nonpresentation. Payroll and dividend checks are the types most commonly misplaced or lost. It is good practice for the client to eliminate long-outstanding checks of this nature by an entry debiting the Cash account and crediting Unclaimed Wages or another special liability account. This will reduce the work required in bank reconciliations, as well as lessen the opportunity for irregularities. Wherever outstanding checks are reported as lost, a stop-payment order should be entered with the bank and a duplicate check then issued. Use of the stop-payment order will make the bank responsible if both the original and replacement checks are subsequently paid.

7.   *Obtain a cutoff bank statement containing transactions of at least seven business days subsequent to balance sheet date.*

A cutoff bank statement is a statement covering a specified number of business days (usually 7 to 10) following the end of the client's fiscal year. The client will request the bank to prepare such a statement and deliver it to the auditor. Most auditors do not actually prepare a second bank reconciliaton but merely examine the cutoff statement closely to see that the year-end reconciling items such as deposits in transit and outstanding checks have cleared the bank in the interval between the two statements.

As previously mentioned, the verification of an accurate cutoff of cash disbursements is facilitated by observing the serial number of the last check issued on the final day of the year. Another approach to reviewing the accuracy of the cutoff involves examination of the checks included in the cutoff bank statement. With respect to checks which were shown as outstanding at year-end, the auditor should determine the dates on which these checks were paid by the bank. By noting the dates of payment of these checks, the auditor can determine whether the time intervals between the dates of the check and the time of payment by the bank were unreasonably long. Unreasonable delay in the presentation of these checks for payment constitutes a strong implication that the checks were not mailed by the client until some time after the close of the year. The appropriate adjusting entry in such cases consists of a debit to Cash and a credit to a liability account.

8. *Trace all bank transfers for last week of audit year and first week of following year.*

Many concerns carry accounts with a number of banks and often find it necessary to transfer funds from one bank to another. If a check drawn on the last day of the period on the X Bank is not entered as a cash disbursement but is immediately deposited with the Y Bank, the amount of the check will form part of the balance on deposit in both banks as of the balance sheet date. Such a maneuver requires, of course, that the Cash debit and credit sides of the transaction be recorded on different dates. Detection of this irregularity, which is a form of "kiting," is not difficult. Examination of the details of the deposit tickets for a short period before and after the end of the client's fiscal year and comparison of the dates of issuance and deposit for checks of this type will disclose any delay in recording the disbursement. A regular routine in the reconciliation of bank accounts should be the preparation of a working paper listing all bank transfers and showing date of check, date of payment by bank, and date of entry in the cashbook both as a disbursement and as a deposit.

Kiting between banks is sometimes resorted to as a device for meeting temporary financial crises. If a Los Angeles businessman maintains checking accounts in both Los Angeles and New York, he may draw a check on the New York bank, deposit it to his account in Los Angeles, and rely upon subsequent deposits being made in New York before the check has traveled through the banking system to the bank on which drawn. This reliance on "float" to avoid overdrafts is discouraged by most banks because, although it may not involve fraud, it is often associated with other irregularities and should be viewed with suspicion.

9. *Determine proper balance sheet presentation of cash.*

The balance sheet figure for cash should include only those amounts which are available for use in current operations. Most users of the balance sheet are not interested in the breakdown of cash by various bank accounts or in the distinction between cash on hand and on deposit. Consequently, all cash on hand and in banks which is available for general use is presented as a single amount on the balance sheet. Change funds and petty cash funds, although somewhat lacking in the "general availability" test, are usually not material in amount, and are included in the balance sheet figure for cash.

A bank deposit which is restricted to use in paying long-term debt should not be included in cash. Other types of restricted bank deposits, if material, are also generally excluded from cash and shown separately, perhaps as current assets. An acceptable alternative for certificates of deposit or time deposits is to include these amounts in the figure for cash but to add a parenthetical note disclosing the amount of such deposits. For example, in a recent annual report, Scott Paper Company shows:

Cash (including time deposits of $4,830,000). $14,310,000

WINDOW DRESSING.   The term *window dressing* refers to actions taken shortly before the balance sheet date to improve the cash position or in other ways to create an improved financial picture of the company. For example, if the cash receipts book is "held open" for a few days after the close of the year, the balance sheet figure for cash is improperly increased to include cash collections actually received after the balance sheet date. Another approach to window dressing is found when a corporate officer who has borrowed money from the corporation repays the loan just before the end of the year and then promptly obtains the loan again after the balance sheet has been prepared. This second example is not an outright misrepresentation of the cash position (as in the case of holding the cashbook open) but nevertheless creates misleading financial statements which fail to portray the underlying economic position and operations of the company.

Not all forms of window dressing require action by the auditor. Many companies make strenuous efforts at year-end to achieve an improved financial picture by rushing shipments to customers, by pressing for collection of receivables, and sometimes by paying liabilities down to an unusually low level. Such efforts to improve the financial picture to be reported are not improper. Before giving approval to the balance sheet presentation of cash, the auditor should use his professional judgment to determine whether the client has engaged in window dressing of a nature which causes the financial statements to be misleading.

COMPENSATING BANK BALANCES.   Long-term loan agreements or lines of credit with banks carried by the client may require him to maintain a minimum bank balance of perhaps 20 percent or so of the loan or the loan commitment. This compensating balance, by limiting the amount of usable cash available to the borrowing corporation, results in increasing the effective interest rate on the loan. Disclosure of compensating balances, parenthetically or by footnote, appears desirable as a means of portraying the economic realities about a company. The SEC is currently considering a requirement that such disclosures be made in SEC filings.

COMBINING CASH AND MARKETABLE SECURITIES. A recent edition of the AICPA's *Accounting Trends & Techniques* points out that a steadily increasing number of published balance sheets are presenting cash and marketable securities under a single caption. To be aware of such innovative trends in financial statement presentation and disclosure is a continuing responsibility of the certified public accountant.

Interim audit work on cash

In public accounting firms a question under continuous study is this: "How can we perform a larger share of our auditing work before the year-end?" In order to avoid a concentration of audit work within a few months of the year, public accountants sometimes divide an audit program into two portions: (*a*) procedures which can be performed on an interim basis during the year, and (*b*) procedures which cannot be carried out until the end of the year. The audit procedures illustrated in this chapter can be subdivided in this manner because the study and evaluation of internal control is ideally completed on an interim basis.

The extent to which other audit work can be performed prior to the balance sheet date will depend in large part upon the adequacy of internal control. The stronger the system of internal control, the larger the amount of audit work which can be satisfactorily performed in advance of the balance sheet date. If we assume an audit of a company having excellent internal control over cash transactions, the greater part of the audit program we have discussed in this chapter could be done prior to the year-end. Such procedures as the testing of cash transactions, the reconciliation of bank activity with cash activity per books, and the counting of petty cash funds could be performed at any convenient time during the year.

At year-end the audit work on cash might be limited to a review of the client's bank reconciliation, confirmation of year-end bank balances, procedures associated with the bank cutoff statement, and a general review of cash transactions and changes in cash position during the interval between the interim work on cash and the end of the period.

The point to emphasize is that much of the work suggested by the audit procedures discussed in this chapter could be done before the balance sheet date.

GROUP I
REVIEW QUESTIONS

11–1.   Select the best answer for each of the following.

  a)   The cashier of Baker Company of Denver covered a shortage in his petty cash fund with cash obtained on December 31 from a local bank by cashing an unrecorded check drawn on the company's New York bank. The auditor would discover this manipulation by—

  (1)   Preparing independent bank reconciliations as of December 31.
  (2)   Counting the cash working fund at the close of business on December 31.
  (3)   Investigating items returned with the bank cutoff statements.
  (4)   Confirming the December 31 bank balances.

  b)   Kiting most likely would be detected by—

  (1)   Tracing the amounts of daily deposits from the cash receipts journal to bank statements.
  (2)   Confirming accounts receivable by direct communication with debtors.
  (3)   Preparing a four-column proof of cash.
  (4)   Preparing a schedule of interbank transfers.

  c)   To minimize the opportunity for fraud, unclaimed salary checks should be—

  (1)   Deposited in a special bank account.
  (2)   Kept in the payroll department.
  (3)   Left with the employee's supervisor.
  (4)   Held for the employee in the personnel department.

  d)   A responsibility that should be assigned to a specific employee and not shared jointly is that of—

  (1)   Access to the company's safe-deposit box.
  (2)   Placing orders and maintaining relationships with a prime supplier.
  (3)   Attempting to collect a particular delinquent account.
  (4)   Custodianship of the petty cash fund. (AICPA, adapted)

11–2.   List the information a CPA should solicit in a standard bank confirmation inquiry sent to an audit client's bank. (AICPA)

11–3.   Explain the objectives of each of the following audit procedures for cash:

  a)   Verify the cutoff of cash receipts and cash disbursements.
  b)   Compare paid checks returned with bank statement to list of outstanding checks in previous reconciliation.

    c)   Trace all bank transfers during the last week of the audit year and the first week of the following year.

11–4.   An internal control questionnaire includes the following items. For each item, explain what is accomplished by the existence of the controls involved:

    a)   Are each day's cash receipts deposited intact and without delay?

    b)   If an imprest fund is represented by a bank account, has the bank been notified that no checks payable to the company should be accepted for deposit?

    c)   Are payroll disbursements made from an imprest bank account restricted to that purpose? (AICPA)

11–5.   What is the purpose of obtaining a cutoff bank statement subsequent to the date of the balance sheet?

11–6.   Should an internal control questionnaire concerning cash receipts and disbursements be filled out for all audits? At what stage of an audit would you recommend use of the questionnaire?

11–7.   An assistant auditor received the following instructions from his supervisor: "Here is a cutoff bank statement covering the first seven business days of January. Compare the paid checks returned with the statement and dated December 31 or earlier with the list of checks outstanding at December 31." What type of irregularity might this audit procedure bring to light? Explain.

11–8.   During your reconciliation of bank accounts in a balance sheet audit, you find that a number of checks of <u>small</u> amount have been outstanding for more than a year. Does this situation call for any action by the auditor? Explain.

11–9.   During your audit of a small manufacturing firm you find numerous checks of large amount drawn payable to the treasurer and charged to the Miscellaneous Expense account. Does this require any action by the auditor? Explain.

11–10.   During the early months of the year, the cashier in a small company engaged in lapping operations, but he was able to restore the amount of cash borrowed by March 31 and refrained from any fraudulent acts after that date. Will the year-end audit probably disclose his lapping activities? Explain.

11–11.   What is the auditor's primary objective in tracing transfers between banks?

11–12.   What action should be taken by the auditor when his count of cash on hand discloses a shortage?

11–13.   In the examination of paid checks returned by the bank to the drawer, state the features of the check to be examined and the recorded data with which the check would be compared. Give a reason for each operation.

11–14.   In what ways can the use of cash registers contribute to the effectiveness of internal control over receipts from cash sales? Explain. (AICPA)

11–15.   Prepare a simple illustration of "lapping" of cash receipts showing actual transactions and the cashbook entries. (AICPA)

11–16.   "The auditor should send confirmation requests to all banks with which the client has had deposits during the year, even though some of these accounts have been closed prior to the balance sheet date." Do you agree? Explain.

11–17.   What is the meaning of the term "window dressing" when used in connection with year-end financial statements? How might the term be related to the making of loans by a corporation to one or more of its executives?

GROUP II
QUESTIONS REQUIRING ANALYSIS

11–18.   You are retained on October 1 by Wilson Manufacturing Company to perform an audit for the year ended December 31. Prior to the year-end you undertake a study of the new client's internal control over cash.

Virtually all of the cash receipts consist of checks received through the mail, but there is no prelisting of cash receipts before they are recorded in the accounts. You find that the incoming mail is opened either by the cashier or by the employee maintaining customers' individual accounts, depending on which employee has time available. The controller stresses the necessity of flexibility in assignment of duties to the 20 employees comprising the office staff in order to keep all employees busy and achieve maximum economy of operation.

Required:

a)   Explain how prelisting of cash receipts strengthens internal control over cash.

b)   List specific duties that should not be performed by an employee assigned to prelist the cash receipts in order to avoid any opportunity for him to conceal embezzlement of cash receipts. (AICPA, adapted)

11–19.   The CPA obtains a July 10, 1975 bank statement directly from the bank. Explain how he will use this cutoff bank statement:

a)   In his review of the June 30, 1975 bank reconciliation.

b)   To obtain other audit information. (AICPA, adapted)

11–20.   Palmer Company is a nationwide corporation with clearly defined regional sales divisions. Each sales division is responsible for the collection of its own accounts receivable. A separate local bank account is maintained by each division in which all cash receipts are deposited intact on a daily basis. Each Wednesday and Saturday these collections are transferred by check to the home office. No other checks are drawn on these bank accounts. The sales division offices maintain no accounting records other than for accounts receivable, cash receipts, and cash disbursements. However, all cash records such as paid checks, bank statements, and remittance lists are retained in the sales division offices. In planning your annual audit of Palmer Company you decide that members of your audit staff will visit the sales division offices in all regions and examine the cash transfers between the sales divisions and the home office.

Required:

a) List the specific purposes of the audit of cash transfers.
b) Design the specific audit steps your assistants should follow in auditing the cash transfers from the sales divisions to the home office. (Do not list other audit procedures relating to cash or receivables, as it is assumed that your assistants have adequate knowledge of such audit procedures.)

11–21. A new assistant on an audit staff asked why it was necessary to make any audit of petty cash when both the size of the fund and the total petty cash expenditures for the audit period appeared to be immaterial.

How would you answer the assistant's question? Give the reasons for your answer. (AICPA)

11–22. Although the primary objective of an independent audit is not the discovery of fraud, the auditor in his work on cash takes into consideration the high relative risk associated with this asset. One evidence of this attitude is evidenced by the CPA's alertness for signs of "lapping."

Required:

a) Define "lapping." *concealment of shortage by delaying recording of cash receipts.*
b) Prepare a list of audit procedures that a CPA might utilize to uncover "lapping." *1) Confirm A/R 2) make surprise of cash & checks on hand 3) compare details of remittance list with duplicate deposit slips. return to see if deposits. 4) check remittance slips with checks*

11–23. During the examination of cash, the CPA is alert for any indications of "kiting." *follow up*

Required:

a) Define "kiting." *writing check on one bank unrecorded & depositing in another bank.*
b) Prepare a list of audit procedures that the CPA could employ to uncover "kiting."

11–24. In reviewing the cutoff of cash receipts at the balance sheet date, the auditor found that the Devlin Company had held the cashbook open to include payments from customers which were dated and mailed December 31 or earlier but were not received until early

January. Presuming that the amounts involved were material, what action, if any, should the auditor take? Does the practice described cause any misstatement in the income statement or balance sheet? Explain.

11–25. In planning your examination of a large manufacturing company, you decide that it will not be practicable to have members of your audit staff present at each of the many branch offices of the client to count the substantial undeposited cash receipts on the last day of the fiscal year.

As an alternative means of verifying the year-end cutoff of cash receipts you observed that deposits in transit as shown on the year-end bank reconciliation appeared as credits on the bank statement on the first business day of the new year. You were satisfied as to the cutoff of cash receipts by the use of the alternative procedure.

Required:

From the following alternatives, select the one which best explains the effect of the above on your audit report. Defend the selection you make.

a) The limitation of scope resulting from the omission of a generally accepted auditing procedure (cash count) would require disclosure in the scope paragraph of the use of the alternative auditing procedures even though the auditor was able to satisfy himself by their application.

b) When an auditor is able to satisfy himself concerning cash by the application of any alternative auditing procedures, reference to the alternative procedures is not required anywhere in the auditor's report.

c) The limitation of scope caused by the necessity to apply alternative auditing procedures would require the issuance of either a qualified opinion or a disclaimer of opinion depending upon the materiality of the amount involved.

d) Generally accepted auditing standards would permit only the issuance of a piecemeal opinion in those cases where an auditor omitted making a cash count. (AICPA, adapted)

11–26. Leeward Company obtained a three-year, 6 percent loan of $5,000,000 from its bank in order to finance its expanding volume of inventory and receivables. Terms of the borrowing agreement provided that Leeward Company must maintain a compensating balance equal to 15 percent of the amount of the loan throughout the period of the indebtedness.

a) What effect if any does the provision for a compensating balance have upon the effective rate of interest on the loan? Explain.

b) What disclosure, if any, is appropriate in the financial statements with respect to the compensating balance provision of the loan? Give reasons.

GROUP III
PROBLEMS

11–27. The general ledger of Alexandria Corporation, after all audit adjustments were posted, included the following balances at October 31, 1975:

Petty cash......................................	$ 500
Change funds...................................	1,500
Cash in bank—checking–regular account.............	321,452
Cash in bank—checking–payroll account.............	2,000
Cash in bank—checking–dividend account............	1,500
Cash in bank—bond sinking fund...................	127,840
Cash in bank—loan repayment account..............	100,000
6% certificate of deposit, due May 1, 1976...........	250,000

Your audit working papers contain information showing that the sinking fund is held by a trustee and is being accumulated in accordance with the terms of a bond issue maturing March 1, 1987. The only other loan payable is a bank loan due May 1, 1976. The bank loan does not require maintenance of a compensating balance.

Required:

a) A partial balance sheet for Alexandria Corporation at October 31, 1975, reflecting the general ledger accounts listed above. Make any appropriate combinations.

b) A brief explanation supporting your presentation in (a) and describing any alternative presentation you would consider acceptable for the certificate of deposit.

11–28. When you arrive at Norwood Company's office on January 11, 1975 to begin the December 31, 1974 audit, you discover the client had been drawing checks as creditors' invoices became due but not necessarily mailing them. Because of a working capital shortage, some checks have been held for two or three weeks.

The client informs you that unmailed checks totaling $48,500 were on hand at December 31, 1974. He states these December-dated checks had been entered in the cash disbursements book and charged to the respective creditors' accounts in December because the checks were prenumbered. Heavy collections permitted him to mail the checks before your arrival. The client wants to adjust the cash balance and accounts payable at December 31 by $48,500 because the Cash account had a credit balance. He objects to submitting to his bank your audit report showing an overdraft of cash.

Required:

a) Submit a detailed audit program indicating the procedures you would use to satisfy yourself of the accuracy of the cash balance on the client's statements.

b) Discuss the propriety of reversing the indicated amount of outstanding checks. (AICPA, adapted)

11–29. In connection with an audit of Elmwood Company you are given the following working paper prepared by the client:

ELMWOOD COMPANY

BANK RECONCILIATION
December 31, 1974

Balance per ledger 12-31-1974		$17,174.86
Add:		
Collections received on the last day of December and charged to "Cash in Bank" on books but not deposited		2,662.25
Debit memo for customer's check returned unpaid (check is on hand but no entry has been made on the books)		200.00
Debit memo for bank service charge for December		5.50
		$20,142.61
		20,842.61
Deduct:		
Checks drawn but not paid by bank (see detailed list below)	$2,267.75	
Credit memo for proceeds of a note receivable which had been left at the bank for collection but which has not been recorded as collected per books	400.00	
Check for an account payable entered on books as $240.90 but drawn by company and paid by bank as $419.00	178.10	845
		2,945.85
Computed balance		$17,196.76
Unlocated difference		200.00
Balance per bank (agreed to confirmation)		$16,996.76

CHECKS DRAWN BUT NOT PAID BY BANK

No.	Amount
573	$ 67.27
724	9.90
903	456.67
907	305.50
911	482.75
913	550.00
914	366.76
916	10.00
917	218.90
	$2,267.75

Required:

a) Prepare a corrected reconciliation for your working papers.
b) Prepare a journal entry for items which should be adjusted prior to closing the books. (AICPA, adapted)

11–30. Mr. William Green recently acquired the financial controlling interest of Importers and Wholesalers, Inc., importers and distributors of cutlery. In his review of the duties of employees, Mr. Green became aware of loose practices in the signing of checks and the operation of the petty cash fund.

You have been engaged as the company's CPA, and Mr. Green's first request is that you suggest a system of sound practices for the signing of checks and the operation of the petty cash fund. Mr. Green prefers not to acquire a check-signing machine.

In addition to Mr. Green, who is the company president, the company has 20 employees including four corporate officers. About 200 checks are drawn each month. The petty cash fund has a working balance of about $200 and about $500 is expended by the fund each month.

Required:

Prepare a letter to Mr. Green containing your recommendations for good internal control procedures for:

a) Signing checks. (Mr. Green is unwilling to be drawn into routine check-signing duties.. Assume that you decided to recommend two signatures on each check.)

b) Operation of the petty cash fund. (Where the effect of the control procedure is not evident, give the reason for the procedure.) (AICPA)

11–31. You are auditing the Hawaii Branch of Ellis Distributing Company. This branch has substantial annual sales which are billed and collected locally. As a part of your audit you find that the procedures for handling cash receipts are as follows:

Cash collections on over-the-counter sales and C.O.D. sales are received by the cashier from the customer or delivery service. Upon receipt of cash the cashier stamps the sales ticket "paid" and files a copy for future reference. The only record of C.O.D. sales is a copy of the sales ticket which is given to the cashier to hold until the cash is received from the delivery service.

Mail is opened by the secretary to the credit manager and remittances are given to the credit manager for his review. The credit manager then places the remittances in a tray on the cashier's desk. At the daily deposit cutoff time, the cashier delivers the checks and cash on hand to the assistant credit manager, who prepares remittance lists and makes up the bank deposit which he also takes to the bank. The assistant credit manager also posts remittances to the accounts receivable ledger cards and verifies the cash discount allowable.

You ascertain that the credit manager obtains approval from the executive office of Ellis Distributing Company, located in Chicago, to write off uncollectible accounts, and that he has retained in his custody as of the end of the fiscal year some remittances that were received on various days during the last month.

Required:

a)   Describe the irregularities that might occur under the procedures now in effect for handling cash collections and remittances.

b)   Give procedures that you would recommend to strengthen internal control over cash collections and remittances.

11–32.   The Westminster Company had poor internal control over its cash transactions. Facts about its cash position at November 30, 1974 were as follows:

The cashbooks showed a balance of $18,901.62, which included undeposited receipts. A credit of $100 on the bank's records did not appear on the books of the company. The balance per bank statement was $15,550. Outstanding checks were: No. 62 for $116.25, No. 183 for $150, No. 284 for $253.25, No. 8621 for $190.71, No. 8623 for $206.80, and No. 8632 for $145.28.

The cashier abstracted all undeposited receipts in excess of $3,794.41 and prepared the following reconciliation:

Balance per books, November 30, 1974.............		$18,901.62
Add: Outstanding checks:		
8621...............................	$190.71	
8623...............................	206.80	
8632...............................	145.28	442.79
		$19,344.41
Less: Undeposited receipts...................		3,794.41
Balance per bank, November 30, 1974.............		$15,550.00
Deduct: Unrecorded credit......................		100.00
True cash, November 30, 1974..................		$15,450.00

Required

a)   Prepare a working paper showing how much the cashier abstracted.

b)   How did he attempt to conceal his theft?

c)   Using only the information given, name two specific features of internal control which were apparently lacking.

11–33.   Discuss briefly what you regard as the more important deficiencies in the system of internal control in the following situation and in addition include what you consider a proper remedy for each deficiency:

The cashier of the Edgemont Company intercepted customer A's check, payable to the company in the amount of $500, and deposited it in a bank account which was part of the company petty cash fund, of which he was custodian. He then drew a $500 check on the petty cash fund bank account payable to himself, signed it, and cashed it. At the end of the month, while processing the monthly statements to customers, he was able to change the statement to customer A so as to show that A had received credit for the $500 check that had been intercepted. Ten days later he made an entry in the cash received book which purported to record receipt of a remittance of $500 from customer A, thus restoring A's account to its proper balance but overstating cash in bank. He covered the overstatement by omitting from the list of outstanding checks in the bank reconciliation two checks, the aggregate amount of which was $500. (AICPA)

11–34.   You are the senior in charge of the July 31, 1974 audit of Fairbanks Company, Inc. Your newly hired staff assistant reports to you that she is unable to complete the four-column "proof of cash" for the month of April 1974, which you instructed her to do as part of the study of internal control for cash.

Your assistant shows you the following working paper which she has prepared:

FAIRBANKS COMPANY, INC.
PROOF OF CASH FOR APRIL 1974
July 31, 1974

	Balance 3/31/74	Deposits	Checks	Balance 4/30/74
Per bank statement	71,682.84	61,488.19	68,119.40	65,051.63
Deposits in transit:				
At 3-31-74......	2,118.18			(2,118.18)
At 4-30-74......		4,918.16		4,918.16
Outstanding checks:				
At 3-31-74......	(14,888.16)		14,888.16	
At 4-30-74......			(22,914.70)	22,914.70
Bank service charges:				
March 1974.....	(22.18)		22.18	
April 1974......			(19.14)	19.14
Note receivable collected by bank 4-30-74........		18,180.00		18,180.00
N.S.F. check of customer L. G. Waite, charged back by bank 3-31-74, redeposited and cleared 4-3-74........	(418.19)	418.19		
Balances as computed.....	58,472.49	85,004.54	60,095.90	108,965.45
Balances per books	59,353.23	45,689.98	76,148.98	28,894.23
Unlocated difference	(880.74)	39,314.56	(16,053.08)	80,071.22

Your review of your assistant's work reveals that the dollar amounts of all of the items in her working paper are correct. You learn that the accountant for Fairbanks Company, Inc. makes no journal entries for bank services charges or note collections until the month following the bank's recording of the item, and that he makes no journal entries whatsoever for N.S.F. checks which are redeposited and cleared.

Required:

Prepare a corrected four-column proof of cash in good form for Fairbanks Company, Inc. for the month of April 1974.

GROUP IV
CASE STUDIES IN AUDITING

Environmental Protection Corporation

11–35.   On October 21, Rand & Brink, a CPA firm, was retained by Environmental Protection Corporation to perform an audit for the year ended December 31. A month later James Minor, president of the corporation, invited Mr. Rand and Mr. Brink to attend a meeting of all officers of the corporation. Mr. Minor opened the meeting with the following statement:

"All of you know that we are not in a very liquid position and our October 31 balance sheet shows it. We need to raise some outside capital in January and our December 31 financial statements (both balance sheet and income statement) must look reasonably good if we're going to make a favorable impression upon lenders or investors. I want every officer of this company to do everything possible during the next month to insure that at December 31, our financial statements look as strong as possible, especially our current position, and our earnings."

"I have invited our auditors to attend this meeting so they will understand the reason for some year-end transactions which might be a little unusual. It is essential that our financial statements carry the auditor's approval, or we'll never be able to get the financing we need. Now what suggestions can you offer?"

The vice president for sales was first to offer suggestions: "I can talk some of our large customers into placing some orders in December that they wouldn't ordinarily place until the first part of next year. If we get those extra orders shipped, it will increase this year's earnings and also increase our current assets."

The vice president in charge of production commented: "We can ship every order we have now and every order we get during December before the close of business on December 31. We'll have to pay some overtime in our shipping department, but we'll try not to have a single unshipped order on hand at year-end. Also we could overship some orders and the customers wouldn't make returns until January."

The controller spoke next: "If there are late December orders from customers which we can't actually ship, we can just label the merchandise as sold and bill the customers with December 31 sales invoices. Also, there are always some checks from customers dated December 31 which don't reach us until January—some as late as

January 10. We can record all those customers' checks bearing dates of late December as part of our December 31 cash balance."

The treasurer offered the following suggestions: "I owe the company $50,000 on a call note I issued to buy some of our stock. I can borrow $50,000 from my mother-in-law about Christmas time and repay my note to the company. However, I'll have to borrow the money from the company again early in January, because my mother-in-law is buying an apartment building and will need the $50,000 back by January 15."

"Another thing we can do to improve our current ratio is to write checks on December 31 to pay most of our current liabilities. We might even wait to mail the checks for a few days or mail them to the wrong addresses. That will give time for the January cash receipts to cover the December 31 checks."

The vice president for research and development made the final suggestion: "Some of our research expenditures which were treated as expense this year may lead to some commercial production later. Those expenses might be transferred to a Deferred Research and Development account and written off next year. That will cause this year's net income to be quite a bit higher. Also some of our inventory which we had tentatively identified as obsolete does not represent an open and shut case of being unsalable. We could defer any write down until next year."

"Another item is some machinery we have ordered for delivery in December. We could instruct the manufacturer not to ship the machines and not to bill us before January."

After listening to these suggestions, the president, James Minor, spoke directly to Rand and Brink, the auditors. "You can see I'm doing my best to give you full information and cooperation. If any of these suggested actions would prevent you from giving a clean bill of health to our year-end statements, I want to know about it now so we can avoid doing anything that would keep you from issuing an unqualified audit report. I know you'll be doing a lot of preliminary work here before December 31, but I'd like for you not to bill us before January. Will you please give us your reactions to what has been said in this meeting?"

Required:

a) Put yourself in the role of Rand & Brink, CPAs, and evaluate **separately** each suggestion made in the meeting. What general term is applicable to most of the suggested actions?

b) Could you assure the client that an unqualified audit report would be issued if your recommendations were followed on all the matters discussed? Explain.

c) Would the discussions in this meeting cause you to withdraw from the engagement? Your answer on this point should be included as part of a statement to Mr. Minor summarizing your position as independent auditors.

12

Securities and other investments, and investment revenue

FROM THE viewpoint of the auditor, stocks and bonds are the most important category of investments because they are found more frequently and are usually of greater dollar value than other kinds of investment holdings. Bank certificates of deposit, commercial paper issued by corporations, and the cash surrender value of life insurance policies are other types of investments often encountered. The greater part of this chapter is devoted to an audit program for securities; a brief discussion of audit procedures appropriate for other types of investments is presented in the latter part of the chapter.

Investments in securities are made by business concerns for a variety of reasons. In some lines of business, operations are highly seasonal and the cash required at the peak of operations would be idle and unproductive were it not invested during the slack season. Other concerns maintain semipermanent holdings of marketable securities which will be sold or used as collateral for loans in case of emergency. Such holdings are regarded as a secondary cash reserve, capable of quick conversion to cash at any time, although producing a steady, but modest, rate of return. The length of time such investments are held may be determined by the trend of the securities markets and by the company's income tax position, as well as by its cash requirements.

Investments in securities may also exist for the purpose of maintaining control over affiliated companies. Although investment in common stock is the basic means of maintaining control over subsidiaries, the auditor often finds that loans are extended by one affiliated company to another through the acquisition of bonds or notes.

The auditor's objectives in examination of securities

In the examination of investments in securities the auditor attempts to determine that adequate control exists over the securities and the revenue from these investments. Other objectives include determining that the securities actually exist and are the property of the client; are fairly valued in accordance with generally accepted accounting principles; and are properly classified on the balance sheet. In addition to these objectives, the auditor's work is intended to determine that all revenue arising from the investments has been promptly collected and recorded. The verification of securities may, therefore, be considered as including the analysis of such related accounts as dividend revenue, interest earned, accrued interest, dividends receivable, and gain and loss on sale of securities. If the audit engagement includes the preparation of income tax returns, the procedures may be extended to obtain all necessary information such as the dates of transactions and the tax basis of securities.

Internal control for securities

Since most securities are readily negotiable, the problem of physical protection has an importance similar to that of safeguarding cash and notes receivable. The auditor's review of internal control will indicate the extent and direction of the auditing procedures required in a particular engagement. The review may also enable him to suggest changes in records and procedures which will reduce the risk of loss through fraud or accidental error.

The major elements of an adequate system of internal control over securities include the following:

1. Separation of duties between the custodian of the securities and the person maintaining the record of investments.
2. Complete detailed records of all securities owned and the related revenue from interest and dividends.
3. Authorization of all purchase and sale transactions by responsible officials.
4. Registration of securities in the name of the company.
5. Periodic physical inspection of securities by an official having no responsibility for the custody or record keeping of investments.

In many concerns, segregation of the functions of custody and record keeping is achieved by the use of an independent safekeeping agent, such as a broker, bank, or trust company. Since the agent has no direct contact with the employee responsible for the securities ledger, the possibilities of concealing fraud through falsification of the accounts are greatly reduced. The risks of physical loss or destruction are also minimized because the independent agent generally has fireproof vaults and other facilities especially designed to safeguard valuable documents. If securities are not placed in the custody of an independent agent, they should be kept in a safe-deposit box under the joint control of two or more officers. "Joint control" means that neither of the two custodians may have access to the securities except in the presence of the other. This is accomplished through the use of two separate locks. A tally card or list of securities in the box should be maintained, and the deposit or withdrawal of securities should be recorded on this list along with the date and signatures of all persons present. The safe-deposit box should be in the name of the company, not in the name of an officer having custody of securities.

Complete detailed records of all securities owned and of any securities held for others are essential to a satisfactory system of internal control. These records frequently consist of a subsidiary record for each security, with such identifying data as the exact name, face amount, certificate number, number of shares, date of acquisition, name of broker, cost, and interest or dividends payments received. For securities providing regularly scheduled revenue, it may be feasible to schedule in advance the payments to be received, thus providing a means for calling attention to delay in receipt of revenue. Securities written off as worthless should be transferred to a separate account and periodically reviewed for possible recovery of value.

All purchases and sales of securities should be made only upon written authorization of an officer or committee of directors. The system of authorizations must not be so inflexible or cumbersome as to prevent the prompt action necessary to take advantage of security market movements and to minimize income tax liability. It is often convenient to entrust the purchase and sale of securities to a responsible financial executive, subject to frequent review by an investment committee of the board of directors.

The auditor may occasionally find that securities owned by the client are registered in the name of an officer or other individual rather than in the name of the company. Immediate registration in the company's name at date of purchase is the preferred practice, since this reduces the likelihood of fraudulent transfer or unauthorized use of the securities as collateral. Some bonds are payable to bearer and cannot be registered in the name of the owner. The registration of securities should not be considered as a substitute for the other control procedures described.

An internal auditor or other responsible employee should at frequent intervals inspect the securities on hand, compare the serial numbers and other identifying data of the securities examined with the accounting records, and reconcile the securities subsidiary record with the control account. This procedure supplements the control inherent in the segregation of the functions of record keeping and custodianship.

Internal control questionnaire

The following questionnaire is indicative of the matters to be reviewed by the auditor in studying the internal controls relating to securities:

1. Are securities and similar instruments under the control of a responsible official?
2. Are all persons having access to securities properly bonded?
3. Is an independent safekeeping agent employed?
4. Are securities kept in a safe-deposit box?
    a) Does access to the safe-deposit box require the presence of two or more officials?
    b) Is a detailed record kept of all visits to the safe-deposit box?
5. Is a record maintained of all securities placed in and removed from the box?
6. Does the accounting department maintain a record of each security, its cost, description, and identifying certificate number?
7. Are all securities in the name of the company?
8. Are securities held for others as collateral, for safekeeping, or for other purposes properly segregated and kept under accounting control?
9. Are all purchases and sales of securities authorized by a financial executive or by a committee of the board of directors?
10. Are brokers' advices and other original papers evidencing purchases and sales of securities properly filed and available for inspection by auditors?
11. Is a satisfactory record of investment revenue maintained?
12. Are securities which have been written off recorded in a separate ledger and periodically reviewed as to possibility of recoveries?
13. Do internal auditors or other employees not responsible for custody of securities or record keeping periodically inspect the securities, confirm those held by outsiders, and reconcile the documents inspected or confirmed with the records?

Audit working papers for securities

Grouping sheets are rarely required for securities, because a single ledger account, supported by subsidiary records, generally suffices for each balance sheet classification of securities. For marketable securities, the principal working paper is an analysis of the type illustrated in Figure 12–1.

FIGURE 12-1

Acct. No. 112

Fairfield Corporation
Marketable Securities
12/31/74

F-1

	Balance 12/31/73		Purchases (Sales)			Balance 12/31/74		Item (Loss) on sale Acct. 744	Net Sales Proceeds Acct. 744	Interest and Dividends Received	Market Value Per Share	Total 12/31/74
	Shares or Face Amount	Cost	Date	Shares or Face Amount	Cost	Shares or Face Amount	Cost					
Bonds:												
A.T.&T. 4⅞s 95 #8356-85 ~	30,000.00	28,600.00				30,000.00	28,600.00			1,312.50 xx	83¾	25,250.00√
Gen. Tobacco 5⅞s 1974 #6145-547 ᴺ	10,000.00	9,850.00				10,000.00	9,850.00			587.50 xx	94½	9,850.00√
Lucago 7¾s 2001 #376-475	100,000.00	94,600.00	7/15/74	(100,000.00)ᴰ	(94,600.00)				102,500.00 K	7,900.00√	232.00 x	87⅛	—
U.S. Treasury 4s 80 #240-339 ᴺ			10/1/74	100,000.00	99,900.00	100,000.00	99,900.00			—	87.75000	87,750.00√
		244,250.00√		18,560.00√			259,910.00√					
Stocks:												
Gen. Motors Com. 20069 ᴺ	1,000	33,700.00				1,000	33,700.00			5,000.00 x	84	86,000.00√
Lyons Rubber Com. 4583ᴺ	500	30,100.00	9/21/74	(1,000)	(27,200.00)	500	27,200.00	45,000.00 K	17,800.00√	1,500.00 x	110¾	55,375.00√
Everett Electric Com. 10267ᴺ	2,000	57,400.00	12/1/74	800	40,560.00	1,000	40,560.00			2,000.00 x	57¾	57,750.00√
Vernon Carbide Com. E9485ᴺ						800					51	40,800.00√
							259,910.00√	147,500.00√	25,700.00√	12,700.00√		364,175.00√

Loss: Accrued at 12/31/73 ...... (1,485.00)√
Plus: Accrued at 12/31/74 ...... 1,870.00√
                                  12,887.00√
A.G.E.7 – Gen. Motors special div.
Acct. No. 407 ...... 1,200.00
                     14,087.00√
                                  Ⓑ

A.G.E.7
Dividends Receivable:
   Interest and Dividends 1,200.00
   To accrue special Gen. Motors dividend
   of $1.20 per share declared 12/1/74
   payable 1/15/75 to stockholders of
   record 12/15/74

Above securities inspected in my
presence and returned to me
intact.   J. B. Clark 1/2/75

J.M.H.
1/2/75

√ – Footed and cross-footed
ᴺ – Inspected certificate 1/2/75 at Pacific National Bank. Bank records
      show no access to safe deposit box since 12/1/74.
C – Computation verified.
x – Traced to cash receipts record.
4 – Details agreed to 12/31/73 audit working paper.
F – Per 1/2/75 Wall Street Journal.
A – Compared with Ditchie Stock Record.
g – Examined broker's advices and authorizations for purchase and sale
      by investment committee of Board of Directors.

Fairfield's policy is to accrue dividends, and the
stockholders record state. A.G.E.7 was prepared in
conformity with this policy.
   Mr. J. B. Clark, Treasurer, stated that Fairfield
marketable securities are regarded as a secondary
cash reserve and would at any time the company's
cash position make such action advisable. Accordingly,
Fairfield does not amortize premium or discount on
bonds, and classifies these investments as
current assets.

Audit program for securities

The following list of procedures is typical of work performed by the auditor to achieve the objectives described earlier in this chapter. The procedures most appropriate for a particular engagement depend upon the auditor's study and evaluation of internal control for securities.

1. Obtain or prepare analyses of security investment accounts and related revenue accounts.
2. Examine securities on hand and compare serial numbers with those shown on previous examination.
3. Obtain confirmation of securities in the custody of others.
4. Verify purchases and sales of securities during the year and for a short period subsequent to the balance sheet date.
5. Verify gain or loss on security transactions and obtain information for income tax returns.
6. Make an independent computation of revenue from securities by reference to dividend record books or other primary sources.
7. Investigate method of accounting for investments in subsidiary companies.
8. Investigate valuation of investments in common stock of affiliates other than subsidiaries.
9. Determine market value of securities at date of balance sheet.
10. Determine proper balance sheet presentation for securities.

1. *Obtain or prepare analyses of security investment accounts and related revenue accounts.*

The working paper in Figure 12–1 shows a client-prepared analysis of changes in the Marketable Securities account during the year and the steps the auditor has taken to verify these changes and the closing balances. Comparable analyses would be obtained or prepared for securities classified in the Investments section of the balance sheet. The starting point in the analysis is the beginning balance for each security; this balance is expressed in terms of cost, and also as a number of shares of stock or face value of bonds. The beginning balances are verified by comparison with the ending balances shown in the preceding year's audit working papers. The figures for purchases and sales of securities during the year are verified by examination of brokers' advices and authorizations by the board of directors. Interest on bonds may be verified by independent computation of the amounts earned, and dividends on stock investments may be verified by reference to published dividend record books.

In proving the accuracy of the analysis the auditor foots and cross-foots the cost columns for beginning balances, purchases or sales, and ending balances. The column total for cost of securities sold plus the column total for gain or loss equals the column total showing the net proceeds of sale. The total cost of all securities on hand at year-end should, of course, agree with the figure for marketable securities in the working trial balance or grouping sheet.

Revenue accounts showing interest and dividends earned on securities may occasionally reveal revenue from securities not recorded in the asset accounts. For this reason the analysis of these related revenue accounts is an integral part of the verification of securities: the revenue from securities is usually included in the working paper analyzing the Marketable Securities account as illustrated in Figure 12–1. Any reversing entries should be fully investigated, since the abstraction of dividend or interest checks is sometimes camouflaged by fictitious reversing entries. Standard procedure for the analysis of all types of revenue accounts includes particular attention to any debit entries.

Notice the tick marks and the explanatory legend used in the working paper to show the verification steps performed by the auditor. In this illustration the analysis of the Marketable Securities account has also been used in making an inspection of securities on hand and includes the receipt from the custodian acknowledging return of the securities. If the company held a large number of securities, a separate "count sheet" would be more convenient.

The bonds held by the Fairfield Corporation are shown at cost. This is a common practice among investors and in general an acceptable one, although amortization of discount or premium is theoretically preferable if the bonds are to be held to maturity.

2. *Examine securities on hand and compare serial numbers with those shown on previous examination.*

The inspection of securities on hand should be made at or near the balance sheet date whenever possible, and as pointed out in the preceding chapter should be made concurrently with the count of cash and the verification of other negotiable assets. If the inspection cannot be made until a later date, the count must first be reconciled with the books at that later date and then an investigation made of any intervening security transactions. When securities are kept in a safe-deposit box, it is sometimes feasible for the client to instruct the bank on the balance sheet date that no one is to have access to the safe-deposit box unless accompanied by the auditor. A letter may then be obtained from the bank stating that the client's safe-deposit box was not opened between the balance sheet date and the auditor's arrival. Under this procedure the securities found in the box may be considered as having been on hand at the close of the period. These precautions are, of course, intended to prevent the concealment of a shortage or other irregularity by substitution of one type of asset for another. The auditor should insist that a representative of the client be present throughout the count of securities.

The data to be noted when inspecting securities include:

a)   Serial numbers.
b)   Name of issuer.
c)   Face value of bonds, par value of stock, and number of shares represented by each certificate.
d)   Name in which registered.
e)   Maturity dates of bonds.
f)   Interest and dividend dates and rates.
g)   Maturity date of next succeeding coupon attached to bond.

The auditor may not be able to detect forged securities, but he should be alert for any obvious alterations on the face of the documents. Any irregularities observed, including deviations between the securities counted and the analysis prepared from the books, should be recorded on the working paper, which must be rigidly controlled by the auditor throughout the examination.

Case histories of frauds involving securities often show that securities have been removed by a dishonest officer or employee and other securities of the same issue and denomination placed in the vault or safe-deposit box before the audit date. The requirement that two persons be present at each opening of the safe-deposit box has already been mentioned as a control procedure designed to prevent unauthorized removal of securities. Substitution of similar securities can best be detected by a careful comparison of serial numbers of the securities inspected with those on the security detail records and also with the serial numbers listed on the auditor's working papers for the preceding examination.

3.   *Obtain confirmation of securities in the custody of others.*

Securities belonging to the client may be in the possession of other parties for safekeeping, for transfer, or as collateral for loans. Confirmation of the latter group should include confirmation of the amount of the notes or loans payable. Securities may also have been deposited in escrow for assurance of faithful performance under certain contracts or court orders. A client-prepared letter of confirmation should be sent by the auditor direct to the holder of such securities, requesting verification of all details of the securities held and the reason for which they are held. This letter should request that the reply be mailed direct to the auditor's office. Second and third confirmation requests may sometimes be necessary. If irregularities are indicated, the auditor may deem it desirable to visit the outside custodian. Careful investigation should be made of all instances where securities are not on hand and not in the custody of properly authorized persons. When such a condition exists, the auditor should not be satisfied with a confirmation; he should insist that the certificates be presented for his inspection and should point out to the client the risks involved in such uncontrolled handling of negotiable assets.

Auditors are not held responsible for the genuineness of stock and bond certificates; hence it is not common practice to obtain confirmation from the corporations issuing the securities. This type of confirmation might be desirable, however, if evidence of fraud in the handling of securities were disclosed.

4. Verify purchases and sales of securities during the year and for a short period subsequent to the balance sheet date.

The auditor must determine that securities purchased during the period have been recorded at cost, determined in accordance with generally accepted accounting principles, and that the investment accounts have been credited with the cost or other carrying value of securities sold. The recording of the proceeds of sale must also be reviewed. By vouching all changes in the investment accounts during the year under audit, the auditor is assured of the validity of the ledger balances at the audit date.

The process of verifying purchases and sales during the year emphasizes the vouching of entries in the accounts to original documents, principally broker's advices and statements. A typical form of broker's advice is illustrated in Figure 12–2. Examination of these documents may be supplemented by inspection, on a test basis, of paid checks issued in payment for securities purchased. Sales of securities may be vouched to brokers' advices of sale and receipts for delivery of securities. The proceeds may also be traced to the cash receipts journal. All transactions for the period may then be traced to the minutes of the board of directors for approval authorizations. The ending balances computed as a result of these transactions should be compared with the general ledger and subsidiary records analysis.

The cost of a marketable security includes commissions, taxes on the transaction, and shipping charges. If securities are purchased on margin, the full cost should be charged to the investment account and a liability established for that portion of the cost not paid in cash. In recording a sale it is customary to enter the net proceeds—that is, the sale price reduced by the broker's commission and any miscellaneous charges incurred. The cost of a bond does not include any accrued interest purchased; this element should be recorded in a separate account or charged to the Interest Earned account.

Transactions occurring during a period of two or three weeks following the balance sheet date should be reviewed. The purpose of this procedure is to determine that a correct cutoff of transactions was made

FIGURE 12–2
Broker's advice covering sale of securities

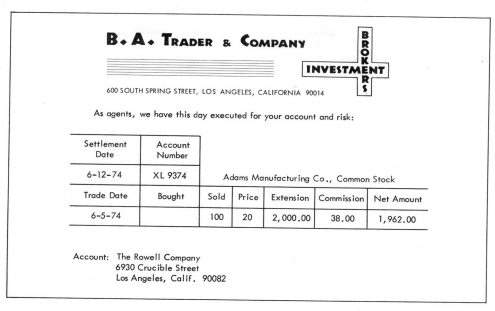

B. A. TRADER & COMPANY

INVESTMENT

BROKERS

600 SOUTH SPRING STREET, LOS ANGELES, CALIFORNIA 90014

As agents, we have this day executed for your account and risk:

Settlement Date	Account Number						
6–12–74	XL 9374	Adams Manufacturing Co., Common Stock					
Trade Date	Bought	Sold	Price	Extension	Commission	Net Amount	
6–5–74		100	20	2,000.00	38.00	1,962.00	

Account: The Rowell Company
6930 Crucible Street
Los Angeles, Calif. 90082

on the balance sheet date and that there have been no irregular transactions subsequent to this date which affect the audited period. Occasionally securities may be sold before the cutoff date but not recorded as sales until they are actually delivered some time early in the next period. Errors of this type are likely to go undiscovered unless the auditor examines transactions after the cutoff date, comparing so-called "trade dates" on the brokers' advices with settlement dates. This review of transactions may be integrated with the reconciliation of the auditor's count of securities and the ledger balances in those engagements in which the count cannot be made until some time after the balance sheet date.

5. Verify gain or loss on security transactions and obtain information for income tax returns.

The gain or loss on sales or exchanges of securities may be computed on the same working paper used to analyze security transactions. This working paper already contains information as to cost of securities sold, and columns may conveniently be added to show net proceeds and gain or loss.

Some accountants also add the necessary columns to show capital gains and losses under federal and state income tax rules, although this may not be considered part of the work of verifying securities.

Preferably a separate working paper should be used for income and franchise tax purposes. The dates of transactions are of prime importance because these will determine the percentage of gain or loss to be used on the return. Care should be given also to the basis of the securities sold, since the tax authorities recognize only identified cost or first-in, first-out cost. The investment accounts, however, are sometimes maintained on an average-cost basis.

6. **Make an independent computation of revenue from securities by reference to dividend record books and other primary sources.**

Dividend declarations, amounts, and payment dates on all listed stocks may be obtained from dividend record books published by various investment advisory services. The interest earned and collected on investments in bonds can be computed from the interest rates and payment dates shown on the bond certificates. From these sources the auditor can compute independently the revenue from investments for the year under audit. The total revenue as computed should be compared with the ledger balances for dividend and interest revenue, and any material discrepancies investigated.

The most frequent errors encountered in verifying revenue from investments include:

a) Charging accrued interest purchased to the Bond Investment account and crediting Interest Earned with the full amount of bond interest collected.

b) Recording ordinary stock dividends as revenue.

c) Recording liquidating dividends, representing return of invested capital, as revenue.

d) Inaccuracies in accruing bond interest at the balance sheet date.

The first three types of errors misstate the carrying value of the investment as well as the revenue for the period. Because of the misstatement of the cost basis, subsequently recorded gains and losses on sale of securities will be incorrect.

The auditor's work in verification of revenue from bonds should include analysis of the interest accrual accounts. Accrued revenue at the beginning of the period may be proved by comparison with the previous year's audit working papers. The computation of accrued interest on bond investments sold between interest dates should then be verified, along with the computation of accrued interest at the close of the year. Verification of accruals and tracing of interest collected to the cash receipts record will generally disclose the cause of any discrepancy between the year's interest earned as computed by the auditor and as reflected by the accounts.

The auditor should also review the propriety of any amortization of bond premium or discount. Many investors do not amortize the premium or the discount on bond investments, on the grounds that bonds are often sold prior to maturity and that the sales price is apt to be more influenced by other market considerations than by the approach of the maturity date. Auditors do not, as a rule, object to such practices.

The auditor's independent computation of revenue from securities may reveal that dividends declared and paid according to published dividend record books have not been received. This suggests the diversion of cash receipts and warrants detailed investigation. The fact that dividends are often not set up as receivables prior to collection may suggest to a dishonest employee the possibility of abstracting a dividend check without the need for concurrent falsification of the accounts.

7. *Investigate method of accounting for investments in subsidiary companies.*

A business combination which results in a parent-subsidiary relationship requires an Investment in Subsidiary account in the ledger of the parent company. The independent auditor must ascertain that the client's accounting for investments in subsidiary companies is in accordance with the requirements of *Accounting Principles Board Opinion No. 16,* "Business Combinations." If the subsidiary was acquired in a *pooling of interests,* the investment account should reflect at the date of the combination the parent's equity in the net assets of the subsidiary at their values recorded in the subsidiary's financial statements. To verify the propriety of the parent company's accounting for an investment in the pooled subsidiary, the auditor will usually perform the following procedures:

1. Review all aspects of the business combination to ascertain if it met the criteria set forth in *APB Opinion No. 16* for a pooling of interests.
2. Examine audited financial statements of the pooled subsidiary as of the date of pooling, to determine that the Investment in Subsidiary account reflected the client's equity in the net assets of the subsidiary at the date of pooling.
3. Make certain all direct expenses incurred in arranging the pooling combination were treated as expense in the period incurred.
4. Review audited financial statements of the pooled subsidiary subsequent to the date of the business combination to ascertain whether a client using the equity method of accounting for investments in subsidiaries has correctly applied this method.

The auditor must also carefully review all facets of a business combination recorded as a *purchase* under the provisions of *APB Opinion*

No. 16. Investments in purchased subsidiaries must be recorded at **cost at the date of acquisition.** Cost is measured by the amount of cash paid, or by the fair value of the subsidiary's net assets acquired or the stock or debt issued by the acquiring company, whichever is more clearly evident. Cost of a purchased subsidiary also includes the direct costs of acquisition, such as legal fees and "finder's fees."

A parent company is required by current AICPA standards[1] to use the equity method of accounting for investments in purchased subsidiaries which are **not** consolidated with the parent. In investigating the client's accounting for an investment in a purchased subsidiary, the auditor should vouch all cost computations to supporting documents (including minutes of directors' meetings), and examine subsequent audited financial statements of purchased subsidiaries for which the parent company uses the equity method of accounting.

Generally, the auditor of the parent company will have examined the financial statements of the subsidiaries, both at the date of the business combination and for subsequent fiscal years. The reporting problems involved when another independent auditor has examined the subsidiaries are discussed in Chapter 21.

Working papers showing all adjustments of the accounts reflecting investments in subsidiaries should be maintained in the auditor's permanent file to facilitate quick review of the past handling of such investments.

8. *Investigate valuation of investments in common stock of affiliates other than subsidiaries.*

The AICPA, in *APB Opinion No. 18,* "The Equity Method of Accounting for Investments in Common Stock," required use of the equity method of accounting for investments in corporate joint ventures. This method is also required for investments in common stock which give the investor the ability to exercise significant influence over operating and financial policies of the investee even though the investor owns 50 percent or less of the voting stock. Recognizing that the ability of an investor to exercise influence over the investee is not always clearly demonstrable, the board set a voting stock ownership cutoff of 20 percent as a practical measure of influence, in the absence of evidence to the contrary.

To ascertain whether the client has used the appropriate method of accounting for an investment in common stock of an investee, the auditor should question the client as to the extent of its influence over the investee. Then the auditor must make an independent determination of the propriety of the client's position on its accounting for the investee. *APB Opinion No. 18* suggests that an investor's ability to influence an

---

[1] "The Equity Method of Accounting for Investments in Common Stock," *Opinion No. 18* of the Accounting Principles Board, AICPA (New York, 1971).

investee's operating and financial policies may be demonstrated by the following:

1. Investor representation on the investee's board of directors.
2. Investor participation in policy-making processes of the investee.
3. Material intercompany transactions between investor and investee.
4. Interchange of managerial personnel between investor and investee.
5. Technological dependency of investee on investor.

If the auditor concludes that the equity method of accounting is appropriate for the client's investment in an investee, he should examine audited financial statements of the investee to determine the propriety of the amounts recorded by the client. In applying the equity method, the client must make adjustments to its share of the investee's reported income similar to those required for preparing consolidated financial statements.

If audited financial statements of an investee are not available for the period covered by the independent auditor's report on the investor, the auditor should apply auditing procedures to the investee's financial statements sufficient to determine the fairness of amounts recorded by the investee. In determining the extent of these auditing procedures, the auditor should consider the materiality of the client's investment in the investee.

9. *Determine market value of securities at date of balance sheet.*

Marketable securities are usually shown on the balance sheet at cost; however, many accountants believe valuation at current market value would be more useful. In all cases, the market value of marketable security holdings should be *disclosed* on the balance sheet. It is, therefore, standard practice for the auditor to obtain current market quotations for all marketable securities owned. The current sales prices for actively traded listed and over-the-counter securities can readily be obtained from the financial pages of daily newspapers; for less active securities, quotations are often obtainable from investment brokers. Closing sales prices should be used whenever available. If there were no sales on the last day of the period, the closing bid price may be used.

The current market price per share should be listed and extended on the basic working paper described in the first section of this audit program. The column showing total market value for each security should then be footed, so that the present market value of all marketable securities owned is available for comparison with the cost figures and for use in the balance sheet.

10. *Determine proper balance sheet presentation for securities.*

Only readily marketable securities should be included in current assets. Some accounting textbooks draw a sharp distinction between temporary and permanent investments in marketable securities, classifying short-time holdings as current assets and permanent holdings as noncurrent. Under this line of reasoning, qualification as a current asset depends primarily upon the expressed intent of management to hold or to dispose of the investment during the next accounting period, rather than upon the nature of the asset. Experienced auditors are well aware of the practical difficulty of basing balance sheet classification upon such an indeterminate and subjective rule.

In a great many cases, management holds listed stocks and bonds without any definite plans for their sale, but stands ready to sell them at any time if the company's cash position should be weakened or if the trend of the securities market, coupled with the company's income tax position, appears to render sale advantageous. Accounting theorists have been inclined to oversimplify the situation by assuming that investments in the marketable securities were either (*a*) very short-term holdings purchased as an alternative to excessive cash balances during the slack months of a highly seasonal business, or (*b*) long-term, permanent holdings acquired with a view toward control of the issuing company. It is not surprising that rules for balance sheet classification developed from such unrealistic assumptions should be incapable of effective use. Attempts to classify marketable securities on the basis of management's intent to sell or not to sell may result, in some cases, in shifting marketable securities back and forth between current and noncurrent classifications in successive balance sheets depending upon the prevailing current ratio and working capital position. The end result of such shifting may be to conceal significant changes in debt-paying ability.

From the viewpoint of both bankers and other creditors engaged in analyzing the balance sheet of a prospective borrower or customer, marketable securities are definitely current assets of the first rank. They are superior to both receivables and inventory because they can be instantly converted into cash at any time without disturbing the normal routine of operations. To exclude U.S. government bonds from the current asset section on the grounds that management does not propose to sell them during the ensuing period detracts from the usefulness of the balance sheet as a means of portraying short-run, debt-paying ability.

Other considerations in determining the most useful balance sheet presentation include the following:

1. Investments in unconsolidated subsidiaries, joint ventures, and other affiliates should be presented in an Investments section of the balance sheet.
2. The basis used by the client in valuation of securities should be stated in the balance sheet and followed consistently from year to year. An exception to the consistency rule occurs when the client

no longer owns voting stock in an investee in an amount sufficient to influence the investee.

3. A note to financial statements should disclose the principles underlying consolidation of subsidiaries, or exclusion of subsidiaries from the consolidation. Wholly owned or wholly controlled companies are often omitted from consolidation for various reasons. The AICPA has recommended that investments in subsidiaries not consolidated should be accounted for under the equity method.

4. The name of each investee and percentage of common stock owned should be disclosed in the balance sheet or a note.

5. A material and apparently permanent loss in value of a marketable security or an investment should be recognized in the financial statements.

6. If a substantial decline in market value has occurred subsequent to the date of the balance sheet, this price movement should be disclosed.

7. If the client's own securities are included in a sinking fund or otherwise shown as an asset in the balance sheet, this fact should be disclosed.

8. Securities pledged to secure indebtedness should be identified and cross-referenced to the related liability.

OTHER INVESTMENTS

A bank certificate of deposit is a receipt given by a bank for the deposit of funds for a specified period of time. Certificates of deposit are usually negotiable and bear an interest rate greater than that for ordinary bank savings accounts.

To verify a client's certificates of deposit, the auditor will use the standard bank confirmation form described and illustrated in Chapter 11, and will inspect the certificate in his examination and count of cash and other negotiable assets. The Federal Deposit Insurance Corporation provides limited insurance for certificates of deposit. If the client has a certificate in excess of the insured amount issued by a bank having financial difficulties, the auditor must consider the possible need for an allowance for loss on the certificate.

The term *commercial paper* describes unsecured promissory notes issued by corporations at a discount for periods generally less than one year. The auditor should inspect the client's commercial paper and confirm it with the issuer. If the auditor has any doubt concerning the collectibility of the commercial paper, he should investigate the financial status of the issuer.

The use of life insurance policies by business concerns to compensate for the losses arising from the death of key members of the organization and to provide cash for settlement with the estate of a deceased partner or stockholder is described in most advanced accounting textbooks. When the business is named as a beneficiary of a life insurance policy, an asset element is created in the form of the cash surrender value, which requires verification by the auditor during his examination of investments. Concurrently with the verification of cash surrender values, the auditor customarily reviews other aspects of agreements and transactions relating to life insurance policies which name the client company as beneficiary. These related matters include premiums paid, dividends received, loans on policies, and agreements for disposition of insurance proceeds.

The auditing procedures for verification of this form of investment may include the following:

1. Prepare or obtain a schedule of life insurance policies.
2. Obtain confirmation from insurance companies of cash surrender values, policy loans, and accumulated dividends. A "Standard Confirmation Inquiry for Life Insurance Policies" is available from the AICPA.
3. Verify computation of insurance expense and prepaid insurance.
4. Review agreements for use of proceeds of policies.

Balance sheet presentation of other investments

As pointed out in Chapter 11, certificates of deposit which are material in amount are shown separately in the current assets section of the balance sheet, or sometimes combined with cash (with a parenthetical disclosure). Commercial paper may also be shown as a separate current asset or may be combined with marketable securities included as current assets.

Although the cash surrender value of life insurance policies represents a source of immediately available funds, the AICPA has specifically recommended that cash surrender values not be included in current assets. Exclusion of cash surrender values from the current asset classification may be supported by the argument that the funds are obtainable through cancellation of the policy; and cancellation might violate collateral agreements with partners, stockholders, or others, and is generally not contemplated by management. The balance sheet classification of the cash surrender value of the policy is not altered by its use as collateral. Loans are sometimes obtained from insurance companies with the intention not of repayment but of ultimate liquidation by offset against the proceeds of the policy upon the death of the insured. Since there is no risk of loss, insurance companies are willing to carry such loans on a permanent basis. Under these circumstances the loan may be excluded from current liabilities, and offset against the related cash surrender value in the investments section of the balance sheet.

GROUP I
REVIEW QUESTIONS

12–1.   Is a bank certificate of deposit the same as a bank savings account? Explain.

12–2.   How are cost, market value, and the equity method used in valuing securities?

12–3.   Under what conditions would the CPA accept a confirmation of the securities on hand from the custodian in lieu of inspecting the securities himself? (AICPA)

12–4.   What are some of the kinds of errors sometimes encountered by auditors in examining revenue recorded on security investments?

12–5.   Should the auditor communicate directly with the issuing corporation to establish the authenticity of securities held as investments by his client? Explain.

12–6.   Accountants have sometimes tried to apply different methods of balance sheet classification for so-called "permanent" and "temporary" investments in marketable securities. What difficulties may the auditor encounter if he attempts to make this distinction?

12–7.   What documents should be examined in verifying the purchases and sales of securities made during the year under audit?

12–8.   A company which you are auditing carries $3 million of insurance on the lives of its officers. List the principal steps required in the verification of these policies and state how the transactions for the year and balances at the end of the year should be reflected in the financial statements. (AICPA)

12–9.   Should the inspection of securities on hand be correlated with any other specific phase of the audit? Explain.

12–10.   Should marketable securities generally be included in the current asset section of the balance sheet? Explain.

12–11.   How can the auditor determine that all dividends applicable to marketable securities owned by the client have been received and recorded?

12–12.   What are the main objectives of the auditor in the examination of investments in securities?

12–13.   What information should be noted by the auditor during his inspection of securities on hand?

12–14.   What are the major considerations that induce manufacturing and merchandising concerns to invest in securities?

12–15.   Under what circumstances may securities owned by the client not be on hand at the balance sheet date?

12–16.   Is the auditor concerned with security transactions subsequent to the balance sheet date? Explain.

12–17.   During your examination of a client's investments in corporate bonds you note that premiums and discounts on these investments are not being amortized. Would you take exception to this practice? Explain.

12–18.   Assume that it is not possible for you to be present on the balance sheet date to inspect the securities owned by the client. What variation in audit procedures is appropriate if the count is not made until two weeks after the balance sheet date?

12–19.   One of your clients which has never before invested in securities recently acquired more than a million dollars in cash from the sale of real estate no longer used in operations. The president intends to invest this money in marketable securities until such time as the opportunity arises for advantageous acquisition of a new plant site. He asks you to enumerate the principal factors you would recommend to create a strong system of internal control over marketable securities.

GROUP II
QUESTIONS REQUIRING ANALYSIS

12–20.   Your new client, Harding Company, has $10 million total assets in its November 30, 1974 balance sheet, including the following:

25% interest in Suppliers, Inc., at cost................ $2,000,000

You have examined a Suppliers, Inc. stock certificate for 400 shares, dated April 1, 1974, in the name of Harding Company, and a paid Harding check for $2,000,000, dated March 31, 1974, payable to and endorsed by Suppliers, Inc.

Required:

Have you accumulated sufficient competent evidence for Harding Company's investment in Suppliers, Inc.? Explain.

12–21.   During your audit of the Quigley Company for the year ended December 31, 1974, you find in the ledger a new account entitled "Investment in Bonds" with a debit balance of $45,100. Reference to the underlying documents and discussion with officers of the company disclosed that the amount represented the total cost including brokerage and accrued interest on $40,000 par value of the 6 percent, first-mortgage bonds of the Harlow Corporation. The maturity date of the bonds is June 1, 1981; interest payment dates are December 1 and June 1. The bonds were purchased by the Quigley Company on July 1, 1974; the only entry made since that time was to credit to Interest Revenue the interest received for the six months ended December 1. The company expects to hold the bonds until maturity.

Draft the adjusting entry or entries that you would propose. Include full details of any computations supporting the adjusting entry or entries.

12–22.   The cashier of a bank is also treasurer of a local charity. He is authorized to purchase $10,000 U.S. Treasury bonds for the bank and a similar amount for the charity. He makes both purchases but misappropriates the bonds belonging to the charity. When an audit is made of the charity, the treasurer borrows the bonds from the bank and places them in the charity's safe-deposit box.

What internal controls would you recommend for the charity to prevent the occurrence of this manipulation? (AICPA)

12–23.   You have been retained to make an examination of the financial statements of James Hunt, an individual with large investments in marinas, motels, and apartments. In your review of the general ledger you notice an account entitled "Hill and Miller" which has a debit balance of $50,000. Your investigation shows this to be the name of a local stockbrokerage firm with which your client had made a deposit for purchase of securities on margin. The only security transaction to date had been the purchase on December 10 of 1,000 shares of National Environmental Products at a price per share of $80. The brokerage fee on the transaction had been $522. No entry had been made for this purchase.

Give the adjusting entry or entries that you consider necessary for a proper presentation of these facts in the balance sheet at December 31.

GROUP III
PROBLEMS

12–24.   A new client, Midtown Corporation, has retained you to audit its financial statements for the year ended June 30, 1975. On May 1, 1975, Midtown Corporation had borrowed $500,000 from Valley National Bank to finance plant expansion. The long-term note agreement provided for the annual payment of principal and interest over five years. The existing plant was pledged as security for the loan.

Because of unexpected difficulties in acquiring the building site, the plant expansion had not begun at June 30, 1975. To derive some revenue from the borrowed funds, management had decided to invest in stocks and bonds; and on May 16, 1975, the $500,000 had been invested in marketable securities.

Required:

a)   How could you verify the securities owned by Midtown at June 30, 1975?

b)   In your audit of marketable securities, how would you:
     (1)   Verify the dividend and interest revenue recorded?
     (2)   Determine market value?
     (3)   Establish the authority for security purchases? (AICPA, adapted)

12–25.   In an audit at December 31, 1974 of a new client, Samson Corporation, you find that the company owns only one security but that this investment is quite material in relation to other assets. The investment consists of $200,000 face value of a 6 percent bond issue listed on the New York Stock Exchange. The bonds were issued by one of the world's largest corporations, and you find by referring to published security manuals that the entire bond issue totaled $100,000,000 and carried a very high rating.

The only entry in your client's accounting records pertaining to the investment was a debit to the general ledger account, Investment in Securities, and a credit to Cash, in the amount of $225,800. The journal entry for the investment was dated November 1, 1974 and carried an explanation that the $225,800 payment included a broker's commission of $1,000 and accrued interest of $2,000. The maturity date of the bonds was September 1, 1994. The treasurer of Samson made the following comment to you. "We have no plans for selling these bonds in the forseeable future; they are top quality, and we may hold them until maturity."

Required:

a) The monthly balance sheets prepared by the company included the bond investment among the current assets. Would this classification be acceptable for the year-end audited financial statements? Give reasons for your answer.

b) What audit evidence would you need for verification of this investment apart from examination of the ledger account and journal entry?

c) Draft the adjusting entry relating to the bond investment which Samson Corporation should make at December 31. What alternative adjusting entry, if any, would you consider acceptable?

12–26. You have been retained to make an examination of Oroville Company for the year ended December 31, 1974. The company carries on a wholesale and retail business in lumber and building supplies; total assets amount to $1 million and stockholders' equity to $500,000.

The company's records show an investment of $100,000 for 100 shares of common stock of one of its customers, the Home Building Corporation. You learn that Home Building Corporation is closely held and that its capital stock, consisting of 1,000 shares of issued and outstanding common stock, has no published or quoted market value.

Examination of your client's cash disbursements record reveals an entry of a check for $100,000 drawn on January 23, 1974, to Mr. Felix Wolfe, who is said to be the former holder of the 100 shares of stock. Mr. Wolfe is president of the Oroville Company. Oroville Company has no other investments.

Required:

a) List the auditing procedures you would employ in connection with the $100,000 investment of your client in the capital stock of the Home Building Corporation.

b) Discuss the presentation of the investment on the balance sheet, including its valuation.

12–27. You are in charge of the audit of the financial statements of the Maitland Corporation for the year ended December 31, 1974. The corporation has had the policy of investing its surplus cash in marketable securities. Its stock and bond certificates are kept in a safe-deposit box in a local bank. Only the president or the treasurer of the corporation has access to the box.

You were unable to obtain access to the safe-deposit box on December 31 because neither the president nor the treasurer was available. Arrangements were made for your assistant to accompany the treasurer to the bank on January 11 to examine the securities. Your assistant has never examined securities that were being kept in a safe-deposit box and requires instructions. He should be able to inspect all securities on hand in an hour.

Required:

a) List the instructions that you would give to your assistant regarding the examination of the stock and bond certificates kept in the safe-deposit box. Include in your instructions the details of the securities to be examined and the reasons for examining these details.

b) When he returned from the bank your assistant reported that the treasurer had entered the box on January 4. The treasurer stated that he had removed an old photograph of the corporation's original building. The photograph was loaned to the local chamber of commerce for display purposes. List the additional audit procedures that are required because of the treasurer's action. (AICPA)

13

Accounts and notes receivable; and sales transactions

SALES TRANSACTIONS and receivables from customers are so closely related that the two can best be considered jointly in a discussion of auditing objectives and procedures. Receivables from customers of course include both accounts receivable and the various types of notes receivable. One of the traditional objectives of the auditor in the verification of receivables has been to determine the genuineness of customers' accounts and notes. What better approach to this objective can be found than a study of the internal control procedures governing the issuance of sales invoices, shipping documents, and other evidences of claims against customers? Before examining the problem of internal control over sales and receivables, however, it is desirable, first, to consider the nature of the various claims which may be grouped under the classification of accounts and notes receivable and, second, to state the major objectives of the auditor in this phase of his examination.

Meaning of accounts receivable

Accounts receivable in a broad sense include not only claims against customers arising from the sale of goods or services but also a great variety of miscellaneous claims, such as advances to officers or employees, loans to subsidiaries, uncollected stock subscriptions, claims against railroads or other public carriers, claims for tax refunds, and advances to suppliers. Similar audit procedures are used in the verification of

390

all these various types of receivables, although additional investigation may be required with respect to transactions which do not involve arm's-length bargaining—for example, loans to officers.

Meaning of notes receivable

Typically, notes and acceptances receivable are used for handling transactions of substantial amount; these negotiable documents are widely used by both industrial and commercial concerns. In banks and finance companies, of course, notes receivable usually constitute the most important single asset.

Notes receivable may be acquired in a variety of ways. In some lines of business, particularly the marketing of durable equipment of high unit cost, it is common practice to accept notes from customers in payment for the sale of merchandise. Installment notes are very widely used in the sale of industrial machinery, farm equipment, tractors, and automobiles. An installment note or contract is a negotiable instrument which grants possession of the goods to the purchaser but permits the seller to retain title as security until the final installment under the note has been received. Other transactions which may lead to the acquisition of notes receivable include: the disposal of equipment; the sale of divisions or subsidiary companies; the issuance of capital stock; and the making of loans to officers, employees, and affiliated companies. Another common transaction leading to the acquisition of notes of somewhat dubious value is encountered when a past-due account receivable is converted to a note in an effort to strengthen the position of the creditor.

Mortgage notes and trust deed notes receivable are another important category of notes receivable. A real estate mortgage is a lien upon real property and is usually given by a debtor to a creditor, to secure the payment of an obligation. In some states, trust deeds are used in lieu of mortgages. The trust deed is quite similar to a mortgage in that it is given to secure an obligation and creates a specific lien on real property. It is not, however, issued directly to the creditor but is given instead to a third party, usually a bank or trust company, who acts as a trustee for the benefit of the creditor.

Mortgage notes and trust deeds receivable are usually carried at cost adjusted by amortization of premium or discount and reduced by any payments collected applicable to the principal. To establish the propriety of such valuation, the auditor must consider collectibility of the note. Pertinent evidence to be reviewed includes authorization for acquisition of the note, the paid check, the title insurance policy or abstract of title, appraisal report, property tax receipts, and fire insurance policies. Since most mortgage notes are collected in regular monthly or quarterly payments, the regularity of past payments by the debtor is an important indicator of the degree of risk involved. Confirmation of the current balance of the mortgage note is an important step in proving that all payments received have been properly entered in the accounts.

Real estate mortgages and trust deeds are important asset categories for banks, savings and loan associations, and insurance companies. They originate in these concerns through the lending of money to the owner of real property, or at the time of sale of real property, through a loan to the buyer to enable him to finance the purchase. Existing mortgages and trust deeds may also be acquired through outright purchase. Financial institutions also invest in installment contracts, or liens on personal property such as automobiles, furniture, and appliances.

Regardless of the type or source of the notes on hand, however, the auditor's objectives and the procedures he employs to attain those objectives are sufficiently uniform that the following discussion may be considered applicable to virtually all types of notes receivables and to trade acceptances as well. The ***trade acceptance*** is a form of draft, defined as a "bill of exchange drawn by the seller on the purchaser, of goods sold, and accepted by such purchaser." The purchaser or acceptor becomes primarily liable on the instrument, thus occupying a position similar to that of the maker of a note. The drawer of an acceptance is secondarily liable, as is an endorser on a note.

Printed note forms are readily available at any bank; an unscrupulous officer or employee desiring to create a fictitious note could do so by obtaining a blank note form and filling in the amount, date, maturity, and signature. The relative ease of creating a forged or fictitious note suggests that physical inspection by the auditor represents a less significant and conclusive audit procedure in verification of notes receivable than for cash or marketable securities.

The auditor's objectives in examination of receivables and sales

The principal objectives of the auditor in his examination of receivables and sales are to determine (*a*) the adequacy of internal control for sales transactions and receivables, (*b*) the validity or genuineness of the recorded receivables, (*c*) the approximate realizable value of this group of assets, and (*d*) the propriety of the amounts recorded as sales and as interest revenue.

The most significant factor in selecting the audit procedures required for a particular engagement is the adequacy of the system of internal control. It is, therefore, appropriate to consider at this point the nature of internal control as applied to sales and receivable accounts and the audit techniques for testing and appraising these controls.

Internal control of sales transactions and accounts receivable

It is not practicable within the space limitations of this chapter to describe the various types of sales organizations found in such diverse fields as retailing, mining, banking, and manufacturing. The following discussion will, for the sake of simplicity and brevity, be developed primarily in terms of the sales activities of manufacturing concerns.

When internal controls over sales on account are inadequate, large credit losses are almost inevitable. Merchandise may be shipped to customers whose credit standing has not been approved. Shipments may be made to customers without notice being given to the billing department—consequently no sales invoice is prepared. Sales invoices may contain errors in prices and quantities; and if sales invoices are not controlled by serial numbers, some may be lost and never recorded as accounts receivable. To avoid such difficulties, strong internal controls over credit sales are necessary. Usually internal control is best achieved by a division of duties so that different departments or individuals are responsible for (1) preparation of the sales order, (2) credit approval, (3) issuance of merchandise from stock, (4) shipment, (5) billing, (6) invoice verification, (7) maintenance of control accounts, (8) maintenance of customers' ledgers, (9) approval of sales returns and allowances, and (10) authorization of write-offs of uncollectible accounts. When this degree of subdivision of duties is feasible, accidental errors are likely to be detected quickly through the comparison of documents and amounts emerging from independent units of the company, and the opportunity for fraud is reduced to a minimum.

Controlling customers' orders. The controlling and processing of orders received from customers requires carefully designed operating procedures and numerous control devices if costly errors are to be avoided. Important initial steps include: the registering of the customer's order, a review of items and quantities to determine whether the order can be filled within a reasonable time, and the preparation of a sales order. The sales order is a translation of the terms of the customer's order into a set of specific instructions for the guidance of the factory, the shipping department, and the billing department. The action to be taken by the factory upon receipt of the sales order will depend upon whether the goods are standard products carried in stock or are to be produced to specifications set by the customer.

The shipping function. When the goods are transmitted by the factory to the shipping department, this group must arrange for space in railroad cars, aircraft, or motor freight carriers. Shipping documents are created at the time of loading the goods into cars or trucks. The shipping documents are numerically controlled and are entered in a shipping register before being forwarded to the billing department. When shipments are made by truck, some type of gate control is also needed to insure that all goods leaving the plant have been recorded as shipments. This may require the surrender to the gatekeeper of special copies of shipping documents.

The billing function.   Billing should be performed by a department not under the control of sales executives. The function is generally assigned to a separate section within the accounting or finance departments. The billing section has the responsibility of (a) accounting for the serially numbered shipping documents, (b) comparing shipping documents with sales orders and customers' original orders and change notices, (c) entering pertinent data from these documents on the sales invoice, (d) applying prices and discounts from price lists to the invoice, (e) making the necessary extensions and footings, and (f) accumulating the total amounts billed. In the case of government contracts, the formal contract usually specifies prices, delivery procedures, inspection and acceptance routines, method of liquidating advances, and numerous other details, so that the contract is a most important source of information for preparation of the sales invoice.

Before invoices are mailed to customers, they should be reviewed to determine the propriety and accuracy of prices, credit terms, transportation charges, extensions, and footings. Daily totals of amounts invoiced should be transmitted directly to the general ledger accounting section for entry in control accounts. Copies of individual invoices should be transmitted to the accounts receivable section under control of transmittal letters, with a listing by serial number of all invoices being submitted.

Collection of receivables.   As receivables are collected, the cashier will retain customers' remittance advices or prepare a comparable form, listing the credit to each customer's account. These remittance advices will then be forwarded to the accounts receivable section, which will post them to the appropriate accounts in the customers' ledger. The total reduction in accounts receivable will be posted periodically to the general ledger control account from the total of the accounts receivable column in the cashbook. Credit memoranda will be handled in a parallel manner. An aged trial balance of customers' accounts should be prepared at regular intervals for use by the credit department in carrying out its collection program. Under this system the general ledger and the subsidiary ledger for accounts receivable are developed from separate data by employees working independently of each other, thus assuring detection of nearly all accidental errors. Fraud becomes unlikely except in the event of collusion of two or more employees. The subsidiary ledger should be balanced periodically with the control account by an employee not responsible for maintenance of the records.

Write-off of receivables. Receivables judged by management to be uncollectible should be written off and transferred to a separate ledger and control account. This record may be of a memorandum nature rather than part of the regular accounting structure, but it is essential that the accounts which are written off be properly controlled. Otherwise any subsequent collections may be abstracted by employees without the necessity of any falsification of the records to conceal the theft.

Internal audit of receivables. Some large companies operate internal auditing departments which periodically take over the mailing of monthly statements to customers and investigate any discrepancies reported; or they may make extensive reviews of shipping reports, invoices, credit memoranda, and aged trial balances of receivables to determine whether authorized procedures are being consistently carried out.

Internal control of notes receivable

As previously stated, a basic element of internal control consists of the subdivision of duties. As applied to notes receivable, this principle requires that—

1. The custodian of notes receivable not have access to cash or to the general accounting records.
2. The acceptance and renewal of notes be authorized in writing by a responsible official who does not have custody of the notes.
3. The write-off of defaulted notes be approved in writing by responsible officials, and effective procedures adopted for subsequent follow-up of such defaulted notes.

These rules are obviously corollaries of the general proposition that the recording function should be entirely separate from the custodial function, especially for cash and receivables.

If the acceptance of a note from a customer requires written approval of a responsible official, the likelihood of fictitious notes being created to offset a theft of cash is materially reduced. The same review and approval should be required for renewal of a note; otherwise an opportunity is created for the withholding of cash when a note is collected and the concealment of the shortage by unauthorized "renewal" of the paid note. The protection given by this procedure for executive approval of the acceptance and renewal of notes will be greatly augmented if notes receivable are periodically confirmed directly with the makers by the internal auditing department.

The abstraction of cash receipts is sometimes concealed by failing to make any entry to record receipt of a partial payment on a note. Satisfactory control procedures for recording partial payments require that the date and amount of the payment and the new unpaid balance should be entered on the back of the instrument, with proper credit being given the debtor in the note register. Any notes written off as uncollectible should be kept under accounting control, for occasionally debtors may attempt to reestablish their credit in later years by paying old dishonored notes. Any credit memoranda or journal vouchers for partial payments, write-offs, or adjustment of disputed notes should be authorized by proper officials and kept under numerical control.

Postdated checks are sometimes found among notes receivable; these require separate treatment, since they are especially susceptible to mishandling. Proper accounting control over postdated checks may be attained in two ways: (1) by using a debit account in the general ledger to record the checks with a contra credit account, or (2) by using a memorandum record. In any case, these checks should not be in the custody of the cashier or accounts receivable employees.

Financial institutions and other investors holding numerous notes secured by mortgages or trust deeds maintain general ledger control accounts for these investments, supported by subsidiary ledgers consisting of a separate ledger card for each individual mortgage or trust deed note. This ledger card contains the names, addresses, dates, amounts, and other data necessary for proper servicing of the loan. The term "servicing" includes a continuous follow-up to determine that interest and principal installments are received when due, that taxes and insurance premiums are paid, and that all necessary action is taken to protect the interests of the creditor. In addition to the ledger cards, the original notes obtained by the creditors will be on file and controlled by the general ledger control account. Payments received for interest and principal installments may be recorded on both the notes and subsidiary ledger cards. Another important part of the accounting records for mortgages consists of a file of large envelopes or jackets, one for each mortgage. Each envelope contains the documents supporting an individual mortgage note. The principal documents include the mortgage or trust deed, title insurance policy giving protection against losses arising from any defect in the title to the mortgaged property, fire insurance policies, receipts or other evidence of tax payments, and the appraisal report on the property in question.

Adequate internal controls over notes receivable secured by mortgages and trust deeds must include follow-up procedures that assure prompt action on delinquent taxes and insurance premiums, as well as for nonpayment of interest and principal installments.

In many companies internal control is strengthened by the preparation of monthly reports summarizing note receivable transactions during the month and the details of notes owned at the end of the reporting period. These reports are often designed to focus executive attention immediately upon any delinquent notes, and to require advance approval for renewals of maturing notes. In addition a monthly report on notes receivable will ordinarily show the amounts collected during the month, the new notes accepted, notes discounted, and interest earned. The person responsible for reporting on note transactions should be someone other than the custodian of the notes.

Internal control and the computer

The auditor whose client uses a computer may find sales and accounts receivable transactions processed by either a batch or an on-line, real-time system. Batch system print-outs usually include a daily sales journal (including sales returns and allowances) and a daily updated accounts receivable trial balance which reflects cash receipts and other accounts receivable transactions as well as sales.

The principal on-line, real-time print-outs are a log of sales transactions in order of acceptance by the computer and a daily transactions journal for each computer terminal. In either situation, the traditional segregation of employee functions for sales and receivables is absent, and the auditor must study the internal control system for the computer itself in appraising the internal control for sales transactions and receivables.

Audit working papers for receivables and sales

In addition to preparing grouping sheets for receivables and net sales, the auditor obtains or prepares the following working papers, among others:

1. Aged trial balance of trade accounts receivable.
2. Analyses of other accounts receivable.
3. Analysis of notes receivable and related interest.
4. Analysis of allowance for uncollectible accounts and notes.
5. Comparative analyses of sales transactions by month, by product or territory, or relating budgeted to actual sales.

Figure 13–1, on page 405, illustrates an aged trial balance of trade accounts receivable, and Figure 13–2, on page 407, is an example of an analysis of notes receivable and related interest.

Audit program for receivables and sales transactions

The following audit procedures are typical of the work done in the verification of notes and accounts receivable and sales transactions.

Study and evaluation of internal control for receivables and sales:

1. Obtain description of internal control for receivables and sales.
2. Test sales and receivables transactions:
   a) Examine all aspects of a sample of sales transactions.
   b) Compare a sample of shipping documents to related sales invoices.
   c) Review the use and authorization of credit memoranda.
   d) Review cash discounts and freight allowances.
   e) Review accounting for sales taxes and proceeds from disposals of plant and equipment.
   f) Reconcile selected cash register tapes and sales tickets with sales journals.
   g) Review the basis for recognizing profit on installment sales.
3. Evaluate internal control for receivables and sales.

Procedures for receivables and sales at balance sheet date:

4. Obtain or prepare an aged trial balance of trade accounts receivable and analyses of other accounts receivable.
5. Obtain or prepare an analysis of notes receivable and related interest.
6. Inspect notes on hand and confirm those not on hand by direct communication with holders.
7. Confirm notes and accounts receivable by direct communication with debtors.
8. Determine whether shipments on consignment have been included in sales and receivables.
9. Review and confirm notes and accounts written off as uncollectible.
10. Enter in the working papers any collections of notes and accounts receivable subsequent to the balance sheet date.
11. Determine adequacy of allowance for uncollectible accounts and notes.
12. Review the year-end cutoff of sales transactions. *(extent)*
13. Ascertain whether notes or accounts of "insiders" paid prior to the balance sheet date have since been renewed.
14. Ascertain whether any receivables have been pledged and determine the contingent liability for notes receivable discounted.
15. Obtain or prepare a comparative analysis of sales and cost of sales.
16. Review the accounting for intercompany or interbranch transfers of merchandise.
17. Verify interest earned on notes and accrued interest receivable.
18. Determine proper balance sheet presentation of notes and accounts receivable and proper income statement presentation of sales.
19. Obtain from client a letter of representations concerning notes and accounts receivable and sales.

1. *Obtain description of internal control for receivables and sales.*

The auditor's study and evaluation of internal controls over receivables and sales may begin with the preparation of a written description or flowchart or the filling in of an internal control questionnaire. The abridged internal control questionnaire which follows should be looked upon as an enumeration of matters to be investigated rather than as questions to be disposed of with "yes" or "no" answers.

1. Are orders from customers recorded and reviewed by a sales order department?
2. Are numerically controlled sales orders prepared for all orders received from customers?
3. Are all sales orders approved by the credit department before shipment?
4. Are the following functions performed by employees other than accounts receivable personnel:
   a) Handling cash and maintaining cash records?
   b) Opening incoming mail?
   c) Credit and collection?
   d) Review and mailing of statements to customers?
   e) Approval of adjustment credits, and write-off of uncollectible accounts?
5. Are prenumbered shipping advices prepared for all goods shipped?
6. Are sales invoices prenumbered and all numbers accounted for?
7. Are sales invoices verified before mailing—
   a) As to prices?
   b) As to quantities?
   c) As to extensions and footings?
   d) As to credit terms?
   e) By comparison with customers' orders?
   f) By comparison with shipping advices?
8. Are receiving reports prepared for all merchandise returned by customers?
9. Are credit memoranda prenumbered and all numbers accounted for?
10. Do credit memoranda include the approval signature of an appropriate official? Do credit memoranda for returned goods carry the number of the related receiving report?
11. Are aged trial balances of accounts receivable regularly prepared and submitted for executive approval?
12. Is the acceptance or renewal of notes receivable subject to approval by a responsible official?
13. Are notes receivable and related collateral kept under dual custody in a safe-deposit box or other fireproof, locked container?

14. Does the write-off of an uncollectible note or account receivable require prior authorization by a responsible official?
15. Are notes and accounts receivable, after being written off as uncollectible, carried in a separate ledger and collection efforts thereon regularly reviewed by an executive?
16. Are paid notes returned to the makers?

2a. Examine all aspects of a sample of sales transactions.

To determine that the internal control procedures for sales are being applied properly, the auditor selects a sample of sales transactions for detailed testing. The size of the sample and the transactions included therein may be determined by either statistical sampling or judgment sampling techniques. A generalized computer audit program is often used to select the invoices to be tested. To prove the extent of compliance with internal controls supposedly in force, the auditor should examine every aspect of the selected group of sales transactions.

In manufacturing companies the audit procedure for verification of a sales transaction which has been selected for testing may begin with a comparison of the customer's purchase order, the client's sales order, and the duplicate copy of the sales invoice. The descriptions of items and the quantities are compared on these three documents and traced to the duplicate copy of the related shipping document. A signature denoting approval of the customer's credit should appear on the sales order. If the customer's purchase order included items not presently in stock, these items were probably back ordered and should be traced to the invoice and shipping document used in filling the back order.

ILLUSTRATIVE CASE. In a discussion with the president of the Raytown Manufacturing Company, a new client, the independent auditor was informed that credit losses were heavy in the industry at present but that the company had taken every precaution to minimize uncollectible accounts expense. In discussing the internal controls in force, the president explained that every customer's order was routed to the office of the credit manager, Mr. William Baylor, for written approval before the goods were shipped.

After completing his description of indicated internal controls, the auditor selected a number of sales transactions for detailed testing. This testing consisted of tracing these selected transactions through the records, from the receipt of the customer's order to the collection of the account receivable. In several cases the auditor found that the date of credit approval written on the customer's order was several days after the shipment of the merchandise. A discussion with the credit manager, who was also general office manager, revealed that in order to speed up this phase of his duties, he devoted an hour each Friday afternoon to reviewing the credit record of customers to whom shipments had been made during the week. Mr. Baylor explained that he had arranged with the shipping department to ship the orders and then send the documents to him for credit approval. He agreed that this practice permitted shipments to be made to customers of unsatisfactory credit rating, but explained that his work load as office manager was so great that it was impossible for him to review each order from a customer prior to shipment. When the president learned of the breakdown of this control procedure, he made extensive changes in the assignments of office personnel.

The extensions and footings on the invoice should be proved and the date of the invoice compared with the date on the shipping document and with the date of entry in the accounts receivable subsidiary ledger. Prices on the invoice may be compared with price lists, catalogs, or other official sources used in preparing invoices. If a block sample of invoices covering transactions of a week or a month has been selected, the sequence of invoice serial numbers should also be reviewed for any missing numbers. Bills of lading and freight bills may also be compared with invoices as a further test of validity.

After proving the accuracy of selected individual invoices, the auditor next traces the invoices to the sales journal. The footing of the sales journal is proven, and the total is traced to the general ledger account for sales.

In summary, this process of testing selected sales transactions consists of tracing each transaction through the system from the receipt of the customer's order to the shipment of the goods and the subsequent collection of the account receivable. A converse technique may be used; entries in the sales journal may be selected for vouching to supporting invoices, customer purchase orders, and shipping documents. By these tests, the auditor should satisfy himself that all sales are being accurately and promptly billed, that billings do not include any anticipated sales or extraneous transactions, and that the amounts billed are accurately and promptly recorded in customers' ledgers and in control accounts. If these conditions prevail, the auditor is entitled to rely upon the charges appearing in customers' accounts.

2b. Compare a sample of shipping documents to related sales invoices.

The preceding step in the audit program called for an examination of selected invoices and a comparison of such invoices with sales records and shipping documents. That procedure would not, however, disclose orders which had been shipped but not billed. To assure that all shipments are billed, it is necessary for the auditor to obtain a sample of shipping documents issued during the year and to compare these to sales invoices. In making this test, particular emphasis should be placed upon accounting for all shipping tickets by serial number. Any voided tickets should have been mutilated and retained in the files. The purposeful or accidental destruction of shipping documents prior to the creation of a sales invoice might go undetected if this type of test were not made. Correlation of serial numbers of sales orders, shipping advices, and sales invoices is highly desirable. In some concerns, shipping advices and sales invoices are created simultaneously.

2c.   *Review the use and authorization of credit memoranda.*

All allowances to customers for returned or defective merchandise should be supported by serially numbered credit memoranda signed by an officer or responsible employee having no duties relating to cash handling or to the maintenance of customers' ledgers. Good internal control over credits for returned merchandise usually includes a requirement that the returned goods be received and examined before credit is given. The credit memoranda should then bear the date and serial number of the receiving report on the return shipment.

The auditor's test of internal control for credit memoranda follows a pattern similar to that employed in the test of sales invoices. Credit memoranda, however, are normally issued in minor volume, as compared with invoices, and are more susceptible to fraudulent manipulation. It may, therefore, be both practicable and desirable to examine a larger proportion of credit memoranda than is appropriate in testing sales invoices.

In addition to establishing that credit memoranda were properly authorized, the auditor should make tests of these documents similar to those suggested for sales invoices. Prices, extensions, and footings should be verified, and postings traced from the sales return journal or other book of original entry to the customers' accounts in the subsidiary receivable ledgers.

2d.   *Review cash discounts and freight allowances.*

The auditor's review of internal control for cash discounts allowed should begin with a study of the client's established policy as to the rates of discounts for various classes of customers. He will then scan the discounts column of the cash receipts journal, noting any deviations from the prescribed rates. This test should be supplemented by selecting a number of customers' accounts in the accounts receivable subsidiary ledger, comparing the collections recorded therein with the credit terms shown on the duplicate sales invoices and tracing the entries to the cash records. Discounts allowed on payments beyond the discount period and any other variations should be reviewed with an appropriate executive.

Another approach in reviewing the propriety of recorded cash discounts is to analyze by months the dollar amount of collections on receivables, the dollar amount of cash discounts allowed, and the percentage relationship of discounts to collections. Any significant variations should be fully investigated. Comparison, period by period, of the ratio of cash discounts to net sales is also a useful step in bringing to light variations of substantial amount.

The review of freight allowances, trade discounts, and other reductions from invoice list prices may be begun by inquiry into the client's policies for such deductions from sales. It is customary for any such items to be deducted at the time of billing. The procedures employed should be investigated in detail and described in the audit working papers.

2e. Review accounting for sales taxes and proceeds from disposals of plant and equipment.

Some companies responsible for collecting state sales taxes on their products credit tax collections to the Sales account. This is especially true for companies having substantial cash sales. The auditor should test the client's sales tax accounting procedures to ascertain that a liability account is credited for sales taxes payable, either at the time of sale or by adjusting entry at the end of the accounting period.

In testing sales transactions the auditor should be alert to detect any credits to sales representing the proceeds from disposal of items of plant and equipment. This type of error is most likely to occur when detailed subsidiary records are not maintained for plant and equipment. A similar type of error is crediting the Sales account for deposits on containers and for miscellaneous receipts, such as rental revenue, refunds of overpayments to vendors, and return of deposits. If the client sells products in returnable containers, the auditor should investigate the possibility that deposits on containers may have been treated as sales.

2f. Reconcile selected cash register tapes and sales tickets with sales journals.

In auditing concerns making a substantial amount of sales for cash, the auditor may compare selected daily totals in the sales journal with cash register readings or tapes. The serial numbers of all sales tickets used during the selected periods should be accounted for, and the individual tickets examined for accuracy of calculations and traced to the sale summary or journal.

2g. Review the basis of recognizing profit on installment sales.

If the client makes sales on the installment plan, the auditor should determine the basis used in recognizing profit on these transactions and should prepare a memorandum for the working papers describing the method in use. The AICPA, in *Accounting Principles Board Opinion No. 10*, stated that the installment method of accounting for installment sales is acceptable only if collection of the sales price is not reasonably assured. In other words, revenue should ordinarily be recognized at the time of the sale, with appropriate provision for uncollectible receivables.

The company's method of accounting for repossessed merchandise should also be covered in a memorandum, with particular attention being given to the procedures employed in placing valuations on repossessed goods.

3. *Evaluate internal control for receivables and sales.*

When the auditor has completed his description of internal control for receivables and sales and his tests of sales transactions, he will have accumulated sufficient evidence to evaluate internal control for receivables and sales. In his evaluation, the auditor will identify weaknesses which require extension of auditing procedures and strengths which permit curtailment of procedures. The evaluation is thus closely integrated with the audit program for receivables and sales as of the balance sheet date.

4. *Obtain or prepare an aged trial balance of trade accounts receivable and analyses of other accounts receivable.*

An aged trial balance of trade accounts receivable at the audit date is commonly prepared for the auditor by employees of the client, often in the form of a computer print-out. Accounts receivable trial balances of smaller clients may be prepared by hand or may take the form of accounting machine "proof tapes," or adding machine tapes, with the names of customers written in. The client-prepared schedule illustrated in Figure 13–1 is a multipurpose form designed for the aging of customers' accounts, the estimating of probable credit losses, and the controlling of confirmation requests. The inclusion of so many phases of the examination of receivables in a single working paper is practicable only for small concerns with a limited number of customers.

The auditor should also obtain from the client analyses of all types of accounts receivable other than trade accounts. Analyses of such accounts receivables are required because the transactions creating the receivables are often not at arm's length. Transactions not conducted at arm's length require more than ordinary attention from the auditor. Accounts with officers, directors, employees, stockholders, and affiliated enterprises are sometimes paid near the close of the year to avoid disclosure in the financial statements but are reopened early in the succeeding period. Expense advances and various other types of receivable accounts have at times been used to disguise loans made to officers in violation of state corporation laws or the client's bylaws. The nature of the transactions and the propriety of credits to the accounts should be studied. Any write-offs of receivables from insiders are naturally of questionable propriety.

Analyses of accounts receivable from branches or affiliated companies often disclose debit entries for transactions other than the sale of merchandise. The auditor should determine that the receivable balance agrees with the payable balance in the affiliate's books. The elimination of intercompany accounts is, of course, essential to the preparation of consolidated statements and constitutes another reason for detailed analysis of such receivable accounts by the auditor.

When trial balances or analyses of accounts receivable are furnished

The Coast Company
Accounts Receivable - Trade
December 31, 1974

Acct. No. 121

G-1

Confirmation No.	Customer	Balance 12/31/74	Billed In December	November	October	Prior Months	Credit Balance	Collections subsequent to 12/31/74	Estimated Loss Acct. No. 185
1	Adams Lime	c⊔ 8,255.60√	7,921.60⌐		334.00⌐			7,921.60	334.00
2	Barber Company, Inc.	c 205.00⌐		205.00⌐				205.00	
3	Case Mfg. Co., Inc.	c 7,310.20⌐	1,500.20⌐	1,210.00⌐	500.00⌐	4,100.00⌐		4,100.00	
	Douglas Supply Co.	22.00⌐				22.00⌐			22.00
4	Electric Mfg. Co., Inc.	c 1,250.00⌐	1,250.00⌐					1,250.00	
	J. R. Farkes	3,000.00⌐	3,000.00⌐						
64	Young Industries	c⊔ 1,625.00⌐	1,575.00⌐			250.00⌐			125.00
	Zenith Co.	47.19⌐	47.19√					47.19	
		78,629.62	48,801.67	21,245.60	2,875.20	6,302.15	(600.00)		3,320.00⊔
	A.J.E.2—Errout J.R. Farkes 62	(3,000.00)	(3,000.00)						
		75,629.62⊔	45,801.67⊔	21,245.60⊔	2,875.20⊔	6,302.15⊔	(600.00)⊔		G-5
		G	G						

A.J.E.2
Accounts Receivable - Officers
  Accounts Receivable - Trade   3,000.00
    Correct classification of account
    receivable from J. R. Farkes,
    President.

Prepared 14
B.R. White

⊔ — Footed and cross footed. √—Agreed to general ledger.
⌐ — Traced to accounts receivable subsidiary ledger. } no differences noted
√ — Verified aging
c — Confirmed; no exceptions.
c⊔ — Confirmed with exceptions. See G-1-1

See audit program (B-2) for extent of confirmation
and other auditing procedures.

J.M.H.
1/20/75

to the auditor by the client's employees, some independent verification of the listing is essential. Determination of the proper extent of testing should be made in relation to the adequacy of the internal controls over receivables. The auditor should test footings, cross-footings and agings; compare totals with related control accounts; and trace selected individual accounts to the appropriate subsidiary ledger balances. In addition, the balances of the subsidiary ledger cards should be verified by footing the debit and credit columns on a test basis. Generalized computer audit programs may be used to perform these tests when the client's accounts receivable are processed by an electronic data processing system.

5.   Obtain or prepare an analysis of notes receivable and related interest.

An analysis of notes receivable supporting the general ledger control account may be prepared for the auditor by the client's staff. The information to be included in the analysis will normally include the name of the maker, date, maturity, amount, and interest rate. Additional data concerning interest earned are often added, as shown by the columnar headings in Figure 13–2.

If the analysis is prepared by the client, it will be necessary for the auditor to verify its accuracy and completeness by footing and cross-footing the analysis, comparing the ending balance of notes receivable to the general ledger control account, and tracing selected items to the detailed records and to the notes themselves.

6.   Inspect notes on hand and confirm those not on hand by direct communication with holders.

The inspection of notes receivable on hand should be performed concurrently with the count of cash and securities to prevent the concealment of a shortage by substitution of cash for misappropriated negotiable instruments, or vice versa. Any collateral held by the client as security for notes receivable should be examined and listed at the same time. Complete control over all negotiable instruments should be maintained by the auditor until the count and inspection are completed.

The information to be gathered by the auditor in his inspection of notes receivable has already been described in connection with the form of analysis to be prepared. If the analysis was prepared from the note register or from the control account, the notes should be compared in detail with the analysis. If, on the other hand, the auditor prepares the analysis from his examination of the notes, he should compare the analysis with the notes receivable subsidiary ledger.

Practical considerations prevent the auditor from inspecting notes receivable owned by the client but held by others at the time of the examination. Confirmation in writing from the holder of the note is considered as an acceptable alternative to inspection; it does not, how-

FIGURE 13-2

The Coast Company
Notes Receivable and Interest
December 31, 1974

Acct. Nos. 124, 125, 433   G-4

Confirmation No.	Maker	Date Made	Date Due	Interest Rate	Interest Paid to	Face Amount	Acct. No. 124 — Notes Balance 12/31/73	Additions	Payments	Balance 12/31/74	Interest Receivable 12/31/73	Interest Earned Acct. No. 433	Received	Receivable 12/31/74 Acct. No. 125
✓	Brandline, Inc.	7/1/73	4/30/74	6%	6/30/74	10,000.00	10,000.00	-0-	10,000.00 ✓	-0-	300.00	300.00 ✓	600.00 ✓	-0-
	Brandview Hotel	4/15/74	10/15/74	5%	10/15/74	4,000.00	-0-	4,000.00	4,000.00 ✓	-0-	-0-	100.00 ✓	100.00 ✓	-0-
1	Miners Plate Co.	2/1/74	7/1/75	6%	-c	5,000.00	-0-	5,000.00	-0-	5,000.00 c	-0-	150.00 ✓	-0-	150.00
2	J. Blackburn & Co.	7/1/74	Demand	6%	-c	4,800.00	-0-	4,800.00	-0-	4,800.00 c	-0-	144.00 ✓	-0-	144.00
3	C. A. Lockett, Inc.	9/1/74	9/1/75	6%	-c	8,000.00	-0-	8,000.00	-0-	8,000.00 c	-0-	160.00 ✓	-0-	160.00
							10,000.00 ✓	21,800.00 ✓	14,000.00 ✓	17,800.00 ✓ G	300.00 ✓	854.00 ✓ G	700.00 ✓	454.00 G

✓ – Foot and cross foot.   ✓ – Agreed to general ledger.

✓ – Details of Brandline Inc note agreed to 12/31/73 work paper G-5.

✓ – Examined note 12/31/74 during cash count and inspection of marketable securities.

c – Confirmed with maker, no exceptions.

✓ – Traced to cash receipts.

u – Computation verified.

V.M.H.
1/20/75

ever, eliminate the need for securing confirmation from the maker of the note. The confirmation letter sent to a bank, collection agency, secured creditor, or other holder should contain a request to verify the name of the maker, the balance of the note, the interest rate, and the due date. An illustration of a note receivable confirmation letter of this type is presented in Figure 13–3.

Confirmation of notes receivable discounted or pledged as collateral with banks will be obtained in connection with the verification of cash on deposit, since the standard form of bank confirmation request includes specific inquiry on these matters.

7.   Confirm notes and accounts receivable by direct communication with debtors.

Direct communication with debtors is generally considered to be the most essential and conclusive step in the verification of notes and accounts receivable. Written acknowledgment of the debt by the maker or customer serves the dual purposes of (*a*) establishing the existence and validity of the asset, and (*b*) providing some assurance that no lapping or other manipulations affecting receivables exists at the balance sheet date.

A better understanding of the emphasis placed on confirmation of receivables can be gained by a brief review of auditing history. Audit objectives and procedures were drastically revised in the late 1930s. Prior to that time the usual audit did not include procedures to assure that the receivables were genuine claims against existing companies, or that inventories actually existed and had been accurately counted. For the auditor to confirm receivables (or to observe the taking of physical inventory) was considered too expensive and not particularly important. Auditors generally relied in that early era upon a written statement by management concerning the validity of receivables and the existence of inventories.

Wide publicity given in 1938 to the spectacular McKesson & Robbins fraud case involving millions of dollars in fictitious receivables and inventories led to a thorough reconsideration of the auditor's responsibility for receivables and inventories. In October 1939, the membership of the AICPA voted that henceforth an examination must include both the confirmation of receivables and the observation of inventories if an unqualified audit report were to be issued. That 1939 document, known as "Extensions of Auditing Procedure," was truly an important milestone in the movement toward enhancing the importance and value of an independent auditor's report on financial statements.

Some modifications of the requirements established in 1939 were made in *Statement on Auditing Procedure No. 43* issued in 1970 by the AICPA Committee on Auditing Procedure. In this publication the Committee reaffirmed the importance of confirming receivables but deleted the re-

FIGURE 13–3
Confirmation request for notes receivable in possession of bank or collection agency

TORINO CORPORATION

218 VISTA AVENUE, SAN FRANCISCO, CALIFORNIA 94110

July 5, 1975

Pacific Collection Agency
1001 Main Street
Los Angeles, California 90010

Dear Sirs:

Our auditors Payne, Welch and Co., are now making their annual examination of our financial statements as of the close of business June 30, 1975. In connection with this examination, will you please confirm the correctness of the following list of notes which you were holding for collection for our account on June 30, 1975:

Maker	Date Made	Date Due	Unpaid Balance	Interest Rate
Smith's Market	9-1-74	6-11-75	$3,769	6%
Jones' Stores	1-28-75	6-28-75	2,000	7%

Please return this letter to our auditors in the enclosed envelope, which requires no postage. Report any exceptions direct to the auditors.

Torino Corporation

By_____
(Controller)

Payne, Welch and Co.
Certified Public Accountants
San Francisco, California 94115

The above information is correct, except as follows:

_____
_____
_____

Date_____   By_____

quirement of disclosure in the audit report of omission of the confirmation procedure in some circumstances. The following quotations from *Statement on Auditing Procedure No. 43* summarize the current status of the confirmation procedure.

The Committee believes that if the independent auditor has been unable to apply the customary auditing procedures of confirming receivables or observing inventories because it was impracticable or impossible to do so but nevertheless has satisfied himself by means of other auditing procedures, it is unlikely that disclosure of that fact in the auditor's report has any significance to the reader. Further, there is a possibility that the disclosure may be misinterpreted by the reader to be a qualification of the auditor's opinion.

The Committee, therefore, has concluded that if the independent auditor has been unable to confirm receivables or observe the client's taking of physical inventories solely because it was impracticable or impossible to do so but has satisfied himself as to receivables or inventories by means of other auditing procedures, no comment need be made in his report, although he may wish to disclose the circumstances of the engagement and describe the other procedures. The auditor should consider carefully his decision that confirmation of receivables or observation of inventories is impracticable or impossible.

When the independent auditor is unable to satisfy himself by the application of other auditing procedures, depending on the degree of materiality of the amounts involved, he should indicate clearly in the scope paragraph (or in a middle paragraph) the limitations on his work and either qualify his opinion on the financial statements taken as a whole or disclaim an opinion on them.

If either confirmation of receivables or observation of inventories is omitted because of a restriction imposed by the client, and such inventories or receivables are material, the auditor should indicate clearly in the scope paragraph (or in a middle paragraph) the limitations on his work and, generally, should disclaim an opinion on the financial statements taken as a whole.

Perhaps the most common example of a situation in which it is impracticable or impossible to confirm receivables arises when sales are made to governmental agencies. The operating records and procedures of these agencies will not ordinarily enable them to confirm the amounts payable under government contracts and purchase orders. The auditor will, therefore, resort to alternative methods of verification—such as the examination of contracts, purchase orders, shipping documents, sales invoices, subsequent payments, and other similar evidence—to satisfy himself that the receivable resulted from an actual order and shipment.

Occasionally during the process of confirming receivables from commercial concerns the auditor may receive a reply from a customer stating that a voucher system is in use in place of an accounts payable ledger and that consequently no record is available of the total liability to an individual supplier. When such replies are received, the auditor must resort to the alternative procedures for verification described above. In some cases, it may be possible to confirm one or more selected unpaid invoices comprising the major portion of the total receivable from the customer using a voucher system. It has sometimes been said that the best proof available to an auditor as to the validity of an account receivable is its collection during the course of his examination. But this statement requires qualification, as indicated by the following situation:

ILLUSTRATIVE CASE. During the first audit of a small manufacturing company the auditor sent confirmation requests to all customers whose accounts showed balances in excess of $100. Satisfactory replies were received from all but one account, which had a balance of approximately $10,000. A second confirmation request sent to this customer produced no response; but before the auditor could investigate further, he was informed by the cashier—bookkeeper that the account has been paid in full. The auditor asked to examine the customer's check and the accompanying remittance advice but was told that the check had been deposited and the remittance letter destroyed. Further questioning concerning transactions with this customer evoked such vague responses from the cashier—bookkeeper that the auditor decided to discuss the account with the officers of the company. At this point the cashier—bookkeeper confessed that the account in question was a fictitious one created to conceal a shortage and that he had "collected" the account to satisfy the auditor by diverting current collections from other customers whose accounts had already been confirmed.

All requests for confirmation of notes and accounts receivable should be mailed in envelopes bearing the return address of the auditor. A stamped or "business reply" envelope addressed to the office of the auditor should be enclosed with the request. The confirmation requests should be deposited personally by the auditor at the post office or in a government mailbox. These procedures are designed to prevent the client's employees from having any opportunity to alter or intercept a confirmation request or the customer's reply thereto. The entire process of confirming receivables will obviously contribute nothing toward the detection of overstated or fictitious accounts if the confirmation requests or replies from customers pass through the hands of the client. Requests returned as undeliverable by the post office may be of prime significance to the auditor and hence should be returned directly to his office.

There are two methods of confirming receivables by direct communication with the debtor. In each type of communication, the **client** makes the formal request for confirmation.

1. The "positive" method consists of a communication addressed to the debtor asking him to confirm **to the auditor** the accuracy of the balance shown. Thus, the essential characteristic of the positive method is that it calls for a reply in every case. An illustration of this form of request for an account receivable is shown in Figure 13–4. The form of positive confirmation request to be sent to the maker of a note is similar to that illustrated in Figure 13–3 for confirmation by the **holder** of the client's notes.

FIGURE 13–4
Positive form of confirmation request

Smith & Co.

♦♦♦♦♦

1416 EIGHTEENTH STREET, LOS ANGELES, CALIFORNIA 90035

December 31, 1974

Dear Sirs:

    Please advise our auditors, Adams and Barnes, Certified Public Accountants, of the correctness of the balance in your account as shown on the enclosed statement dated December 31, 1974; or state any exception you may take thereto.

    The prompt return of the bottom portion of this form in the enclosed stamped envelope is essential to the completion of the auditors' examination of our financial statements and will be greatly appreciated.

Smith & Co.

By _M. J. Crowley_
(Controller)

THIS IS NOT A REQUEST FOR PAYMENT, BUT MERELY FOR
CONFIRMATION OF YOUR ACCOUNT.

— —

Confirmation Request No. _83_

Adams and Barnes
Certified Public Accountants
1000 Spring Street
Los Angeles, California 90014

Dear Sirs:

    The statement of our account showing a balance of $ _8,640.00_   as of
_12/31/74_   is correct with the exceptions noted below.

Very truly yours,

Benson Brothers

Date_ January 16, 1975_   By_ R. J. Benson_

Exceptions:

None

Balance Large

2. The "negative" method consists of a communication addressed to the debtor asking him to advise the independent public accountant only if the balance shown is incorrect. This type of request may be made by applying a rubber stamp to the customer's regular monthly statement or by affixing thereto a gummed label bearing the words shown in Figure 13–5.

FIGURE 13–5
Negative form of confirmation request

> Please examine this statement carefully and advise our auditors
>
>   Adams and Barnes
>   Certified Public Accountants
>   1000 Spring Street, Los Angeles, California 90014
>
> As to any exceptions.
>
> A business reply envelope requiring no postage is enclosed for your convenience.
>
> THIS IS NOT A REQUEST FOR PAYMENT

← Balance Small + many of them [handwritten margin note]

The AICPA in *Statement on Auditing Procedure No. 43* has commented as follows on the methods of confirming receivables:

Because the use of the positive form results in either (*a*) the receipt of a response from the debtor constituting evidence regarding the debt or (*b*) the use of other procedures to provide evidence as to the validity and accuracy of significant nonresponding accounts, the use of the positive form is preferable when individual account balances are relatively large or when there is reason to believe that there may be a substantial number of accounts in dispute or with inaccuracies or irregularities. The negative form is useful particularly when internal control surrounding accounts receivable is considered to be effective, when a large number of small balances are involved, and when the auditor has no reason to believe the persons receiving the requests are unlikely to give them consideration. If the negative rather than the positive form of confirmation is used, the number of requests sent or the extent of the other auditing procedures applied to the receivable balance should normally be greater in order for the independent auditor to obtain the same degree of satisfaction with respect to the accounts receivable balance.

Very dnylor [?] fund [handwritten margin note]

In many situations a combination of the two forms may be appropriate, with the positive form used for large balances and the negative form for small balances.

In the audit of concerns with adequate systems of internal control, it is customary to limit the confirmation procedure to a representative sample of the accounts receivable. In selecting the sample to be confirmed, the auditor will ordinarily include the following types of accounts:

a) All accounts with large balances, whether current or past due. This increases the significance of the confirmation procedure by accounting for a major part of the total dollar value of receivables.

b) Accounts with customers who are bankrupt, in receivership, or in other stages of financial difficulty.

c) Accounts in the hands of attorneys or collection agencies.

d) Accounts in dispute, as evidenced by correspondence with customer or other sources.

e) Past-due or inactive accounts. If such accounts are to be accepted as valid assets, it is essential that an acknowledgment of the existence of the debt be obtained directly from the customer.

f) A representative sample of accounts with small balances.

Generalized computer audit programs are useful in stratifying computer-processed accounts receivable to facilitate the selection process described above.

It is not unusual for a client to request that certain accounts or notes not be confirmed. The auditor will generally honor legitimate client requests of this nature. A list of such accounts should be submitted to the client for written approval and made part of the audit working papers. Amounts receivable from officers, employees, directors, and stockholders should be confirmed in all cases.

The auditor should resolve unusual or significant differences reported by customers; other exceptions may be turned over to employees of the client with the request that investigation be made and explanations furnished to the auditor. The majority of such reported discrepancies arise because of normal lags in the recording of transactions or because of misunderstanding on the part of the customer as to the date of the balance he is asked to confirm. Some replies may state that the balance listed is incorrect because it does not reflect recent cash payments; in such instances the auditor may wish to trace the reported payments to the cash records.

The percentage of replies to be regarded as satisfactory when the positive form of confirmation request is used is a difficult point on which to generalize; however, it is safe to say that replies to less than 50 or 60 percent of the dollar amount of confirmations requested would seldom, if ever, be considered satisfactory. The percentage of replies to be expected will vary greatly according to the type of debtor. Second and third requests, the latter usually by registered mail or telegram, are often found necessary to produce replies. When replies are not received on notes or accounts with substantial balances, the auditor should verify the existence, location, and credit standing of the debtor by reference to credit agencies or other sources independent of the client, as well as establish the authenticity of the underlying transactions by examination of supporting documents. The auditor may also wish to review with a responsible official of the company the list of debtors not replying to confirmation requests.

When all expected replies to confirmation requests have been received, a summary should be prepared outlining the extent and nature of the confirmation program and the overall results obtained. Such a summary is a highly important part of the audit working papers.

In any audit in which receivables are material but are not confirmed when it is practicable and possible to do so, the CPA should disclose in the scope paragraph of his report the omission of this generally accepted procedure. Generally, the CPA must disclaim an opinion when confirmation would have been practicable and possible but was not carried out. Whether or not he can express an unqualified opinion when confirmation was not practicable or possible will depend upon the ability of the CPA to satisfy himself concerning the receivables by audit procedures other than confirmation.

8. *Determine whether shipments on consignment have been included in sales and receivables.*

Many concerns which dispose of only a small portion of their total output by consignment shipments fail to make any distinction between consignment shipments and regular sales. The same shipping documents are used to control outward movement of consigned goods, and regular sales invoices are prepared and used as a medium for posting to the accounts receivable ledger.

Accounts containing large debit entries and more numerous small credit entries should suggest to the auditor that goods have been shipped on consignment and that payments are being received only as the consignee makes sales. Notations such as "Consignment shipment" or "On approval" are sometimes found on customer ledger cards or on the duplicate copies of sales invoices. Numerous large returns of merchandise are also suggestive of consignment shipments.

When the auditor finds that consignment shipments have been recorded as sales, he should examine consignment contracts, reports from consignees, and shipping records to ascertain the total amount of consigned goods remaining unsold at the balance sheet date. This amount should be eliminated from sales by an adjusting entry debiting Sales and crediting Accounts Receivable. The unsold consigned goods should be removed from cost of sales and included in inventory at cost plus freight, cartage, and insurance charges incurred in shipping the goods to consignees. It is common practice for the auditor to obtain from the client a written representation that consignment shipments have been identified as such in the accounts.

9. *Review and confirm notes and accounts written off as uncollectible.*

The auditor should determine that proper authorization was obtained for all notes and accounts of significant amount written off as uncollectible during the year. A systematic review of the notes and accounts written off can conveniently be made by obtaining or preparing an analysis of the Allowance for Uncollectible Accounts and Notes. Debits to the allowance may be traced to the authorizing documents and to the control record of accounts and notes written off; confirmation requests should be mailed to these debtors. Credit entries should be compared with the charges to Uncollectible Accounts and Notes Expense. Any write-off which appears unreasonable on its face should be fully investigated. Charge-off of a note or account receivable from an officer, stockholder, or director is unreasonable on its face and warrants the most searching investigation by the auditor. Documentary evidence of aggressive collection efforts will normally be available to support the classification of a note or an account receivable as uncollectible. In the absence of proper authorization procedures, it is obvious that a dishonest employee could permanently conceal a shortage by a charge to notes or accounts receivable and subsequent write-off.

The disposition of any collateral held on written-off notes or accounts should be ascertained; and in the case of installment notes receivable written off, the disposition of any repossessed merchandise should be reviewed. The preparation of percentages relating the year's write-offs to net credit sales, to the provision for uncollectible accounts and notes, and to the allowance for uncollectible accounts and notes may be useful in bringing to light any abnormal write-offs and also in judging the adequacy of the provision for credit losses. A tabulation of these percentages year by year may conveniently be maintained in the permanent file.

10. *Enter in the working papers any collections of notes and accounts receivable subsequent to the balance sheet date.*

The auditor's best evidence of collectibility of accounts and notes receivable is payment in full by the debtors subsequent to the balance sheet date. The auditor should note in the working papers any such amounts paid; in the illustrated trial balance of trade accounts receivable (Figure 13–1) a special column has been provided for this purpose. Since one of the auditor's objectives in the examination of notes and accounts receivable is the determination of their collectibility, it is highly important for the auditor to be aware of any collections on past-due accounts or matured notes during the period subsequent to the balance sheet date.

11. *Determine adequacy of allowance for uncollectible accounts and notes.*

If the balance sheet is to reflect fairly the financial position of the business, the receivables must be stated at net realizable value, that is, face value less an adequate allowance for uncollectible notes and accounts. Accurate measurement of income requires an impartial matching of costs and revenue. Since one of the costs involved is the charge for uncollectible notes and accounts, the auditor's review of doubtful receivables should be looked upon as the verification of both income statement and balance sheet accounts.

In judging the adequacy of the allowance for doubtful notes receivable, the auditor should bear in mind that his inspection of a note and confirmation of the note with the maker do not establish collectibility. A note receivable, especially one obtained in settlement of a past-due account receivable, may involve as much—or more—credit risk as an account receivable. Provision for loss may reasonably be made for notes which have been repeatedly renewed, for installment notes on which payments have been late and irregular, for notes received in consequence of past-due accounts receivable, for dishonored notes, and for notes of concerns known to be financial difficulties. When a note receivable proves to be uncollectible at maturity, it is customary to eliminate the dishonored note from the Notes Receivable account by charging the amount due to an account receivable.

To appraise the collectibility of notes receivable, the auditor may investigate the credit standing of the makers of any large or doubtful notes. Reports from credit-rating agencies and financial statements from the makers of notes should be available in the client's credit department. The source of nontrade notes should be investigated because the extension of credit to persons outside the trade is not a normal business function. The auditor will sometimes find that notes receivable have been turned over to attorneys or collection agencies: in this case he should request the holders to furnish estimates, if possible, of the probable recovery. Evaluation of any collateral supplied by the makers is another step in determining the collectibility of notes receivable. The auditor should determine current market value of securities held as collateral by the client by reference to market quotations or by inquiry from brokers. Attention of the client should be called to any cases in which the market value of the collateral is less than the note; the deficiency might have to be considered uncollectible.

A somewhat different problem arises in the examination of installment notes receivable secured by mortgages, trust deeds, or other collateral. These notes often form an important asset category in banks, savings and loan associations, and finance companies. Delinquent payments are considered a major factor in estimating probable losses on these loans.

Each note or contract receivable is customarily filed in a separate envelope or loan jacket, the entire file of notes (or contracts) representing a subsidiary ledger controlled by a general ledger account. In his examination of these files, the auditor in addition to verifying the amount of delinquencies will ascertain that the mortgage, trust deed, or other evidence of title such as an automobile registration certificate shows the client's interest in the property. Insurance policies of appropriate amount with a loss-payable clause drawn in favor of the client should also be on hand for all collateral securing this category of notes receivable. The auditor will also examine evidence of current appraisal reports to determine whether the resale value of property securing delinquent installment notes receivable is sufficient to cover the client's interest.

A lender sometimes attempts to reduce the risk inherent in a large note receivable by insertion of restrictive provisions; for example, he may insist that the debtor agree not to pay dividends, not to purchase plant and equipment, and not to raise managerial salaries during the life of the note. Often the agreement permits these actions by the borrower, provided a specified amount of working capital and specified ratios are maintained. The auditor should ascertain if these restrictions have been observed by debtors of the client. Violations of the restrictions may indicate that a debtor will be unable to pay a note when it matures.

To provide a basis for estimating the necessary size of the allowance for uncollectible accounts receivable, the auditor may take the following steps:

a) Examine in detail the past-due accounts listed in the aging schedule which have not been paid subsequent to the balance sheet date, noting such factors as the size and recency of payments, receipt of notes, settlement of old balances, and whether recent sales are on a cash or a credit basis. The client's correspondence file may furnish much of this information.

b) Investigate the credit ratings for delinquent and unusually large accounts. An account with a single customer may represent a major portion of the total receivables.

c) Review confirmation exceptions for indication of amounts in dispute or other clues as to possible uncollectible accounts.

d) Request the opinion of collection agents or attorneys as to prospects for collection of accounts which they are following up for the client.

e) Summarize in a working paper accounts considered to be doubtful of collection based on the preceding procedures. List customer names, doubtful amounts, and reasons considered doubtful.

f) Review with the credit manager the current status of each doubtful account, ascertaining the collection action taken and the opinion of the credit manager as to ultimate collectibility. Indicate on the doubtful accounts working paper the credit manager's opinion as to

collectible portion of each account listed, and provide for the estimated losses on accounts considered uncollectible.

g) Compute ratios expressing the relationship of the valuation allowance to (1) accounts receivable, (2) net credit sales, and (3) accounts written off during the year and compare to comparable ratios
for prior years.

Closely related to the allowance for uncollectible receivables is the
allowance for sales discounts. Although most auditors would probably
agree on the theoretical justification of this allowance, it is seldom material and hence it is not customary to propose any adjusting entries
to create this account if the client's policy does not include it. The
auditor's function therefore is limited to a review of the methods and
computations used by clients employing such an account.

12. *Review the year-end cutoff of sales transactions.*

One of the more common methods of falsifying accounting records
is to inflate the sales for the year by holding open the sales journal
beyond the balance sheet date. Shipments made in the first part of
January may be covered by sales invoices bearing a December date
and included in December sales. The purpose of such misleading entries
is to present a more favorable financial picture than actually exists.
Since sales are frequently used as the base for computation of bonuses
and commissions, an additional incentive for padding the Sales account
is often present.

The recording as part of the current year's business of sales not actually made until the following period is sometimes accompanied by
an entry charging cost of sales and reducing inventory. If this entry
is made, the overstatement of the year's profit is limited to the excess
of the selling price of the goods over their cost. In many instances,
however, when sales are inflated the inventory balance is not reduced,
and consequently the year's profit is overstated by the full amount of
the recorded sale. Unfortunately, some businessmen who would never
consider falsification of accounts in other respects seem to regard the
predating of invoices for shipments made shortly after the balance sheet
date as a minor infraction of honest reporting.

In addition to the intentional inflation of sales described above, the
auditor often encounters accidental errors in the cutoff of the sales
records. Auditing procedures for the review of sales transactions for
several days before and after the balance sheet date should, however,
reveal errors in the year-end cutoff, whether purposeful or accidental.
A related abuse affecting accounts receivable is the practice of holding
the cashbook open beyond the closing date; auditing procedures designed to detect this practice were described in connection with the
audit of cash transactions in Chapter 11.

The auditor's review of the cutoff of sales transactions consists principally of a comparison of shipping and receiving records with duplicate sales invoices and credit memoranda for several days spanning the balance sheet date. The effectiveness of this step is largely dependent upon the degree of segregation of duties between the shipping, receiving, and billing functions. If warehousing, shipping, billing, and receiving are independently controlled, it is most unlikely that records in all these departments will be manipulated to disguise shipments of one period as sales of the preceding period. On the other hand, if one individual controls both shipping records and billing documents, he will presumably manipulate both sets of records if overstatement of the year's sales is attempted. Confirmation of balances by direct communication with customers will aid in disclosing any irregularities in the record of shipping and invoicing dates. In addition, the auditor's cutoff review in connection with the observation of physical inventory, described in Chapter 14, aids in the determination of an accurate sales cutoff.

Fictitious sales, as well as predated shipments, are occasionally recorded at year-end as a means of "window dressing" the financial statements. The merchandise in question may even be shipped to a customer without his prior knowledge, and subsequently returned. In this case, comparison of the shipping record with the duplicate invoices may not indicate any irregularity. To complete this type of fraudulent manipulation, however, issuance of a credit memorandum in the month following the balance sheet date is necessary to dispose of the fictitious account receivable. To guard against such manipulation, the auditor should review carefully all substantial sales returns following the balance sheet date which may apply to receivables originating in the year under audit. Consideration should be given to reflecting these returns in the current year's business by means of adjusting entries. Confirmation of accounts receivable, if made at the balance sheet date, should also serve to bring any large unauthorized shipments to the attention of the auditor.

An exception to the rule that goods must be shipped before a sale is recorded may be found in government contracts. Goods ready for shipment under "fixed-price" contracts with U.S. government agencies may be accepted by government "source inspectors" on the client's premises. This acceptance constitutes passage of title to the goods to the government agency, despite the fact that the goods have not been shipped.

The importance of the auditor's review of the sales cutoff cannot be stressed too greatly. This procedure is vital for determining if sales are fairly presented in the income statement. It is also essential for the verification of accounts receivable and inventories in the balance sheet.

13. *Ascertain whether notes or accounts of "insiders" paid prior to the balance sheet date have since been renewed.*

Loans by a corporation to its officers, directors, stockholders, or affiliates require particular attention from the auditor because these transactions are not the result of arm's-length bargaining by parties of opposing interests. Furthermore, such loans are often prohibited by state law or by the corporation's bylaws. It is somewhat difficult to reconcile substantial loans to insiders by a nonfinancial corporation with the avowed operating objectives of such an organization. The independent auditor has an obligation to stockholders, creditors, and others who rely upon audited statements to disclose any self-dealing on the part of the management. It seems apparent that most loans to officers, directors, and stockholders are made for the convenience of the borrower rather than for the profit of the corporation. Because of the somewhat questionable character of such loans, they are sometimes paid off just prior to the balance sheet date and renewed shortly thereafter, in an effort to avoid disclosure in financial statements. Under these circumstances the renewed borrowing may be detected by the auditor by the scanning of notes and accounts receivable transactions subsequent to the balance sheet date.

14. *Ascertain whether any receivables have been pledged and determine the contingent liability for notes receivable discounted.*

The auditor should inquire directly whether any notes or accounts receivable have been pledged or assigned. Evidence of the pledging of receivables may also be disclosed through the medium of bank confirmation requests which specifically call for description of collateral securing bank loans. Analysis of the interest expense accounts may reflect charges from the pledging of receivables to finance companies or factors.

Accounts receivable which have been pledged should, of course, be plainly labeled by stamping on the ledger card a notice such as "Pledged to First National Bank under loan agreement of December 31, 1974." Accounts labeled in this manner would be separately classified by the auditor in his initial review of receivables and confirmed by direct correspondence with the bank or other concerns to which pledged. The auditor cannot, however, proceed on the assumption that all pledged receivables have been labeled to that effect, and he must be alert to detect any suggestions of an unrecorded pledging of accounts.

When the payee of a note discounts it at a bank, he guarantees that he will pay the note if the maker fails to do so. This contingent liability should be reflected in the accounting records, and, if material, in a note to the financial statements. Some concerns, however, do not use a Notes Receivable Discounted account; they record the discounting transaction by debiting Cash for the amount received, crediting the Notes Receivable account for the face of the note, and entering the difference as a debit or credit to Interest Earned or Interest Expense, thus ignoring the contingent liability altogether.

In determining the contingent liability which should be disclosed in the balance sheet, the auditor should supplement the information obtainable from his analysis of the accounts involved by inquiry of the client's bank. The standard form of bank confirmation request approved by the AICPA and illustrated in Chapter 11, "Cash," contains a section requesting the bank to state the amount of any contingent liability of the client and to identify the notes involved. The auditor may also ask the client for a written representation that all known contingent liabilities have been disclosed.

15. *Obtain or prepare a comparative analysis of sales and cost of sales.*

A key step used by the auditor to determine that all sales have been recorded and classified on a consistent basis is the comparison of monthly and annual sales of the current fiscal year with those of the prior period.

If the comparison of total sales for the current and the preceding year shows a significant variation, the auditor should determine the cause or causes. Perhaps the variation is the result of an error in recording sales invoices, or in making an accurate cutoff; perhaps it is the result of fraud involving purposeful omission of sales transactions from the records. In most cases the variation is easily accounted for as the result of price changes, strikes, new products, or other factors already known to management. The point to be stressed is that the auditor should be aware of any significant variation in sales and should determine the causes.

Even though annual sales figures are uniform from year to year, a comparison of monthly sales figures may disclose startling variations. If sales for April this year are far above or below the sales of April a year ago, the auditor must search for the reason. The opening of a new territory, the closing of a branch, the introduction of new models—these are typical examples of factors that may cause monthly sales totals to show sudden variations. On the other hand, errors in classification or calculation and outright fraud are also possible explanations. If no apparent reason is found for a sharp change in monthly sales, the auditor's next step is to trace the monthly total back to daily sales totals and, if necessary, to individual sales invoices.

In manufacturing companies the comparison of monthly sales figures is most meaningful when the figures are classified by type of product. An expanding volume of sales for a new product may be offset by accidental or purposeful understatement of the sales of other products, with the net result that total sales for the month are unchanged from total sales of the same month a year ago. Unless the summary of monthly sales is classified by product, such irregularities may go unnoticed. In retail businesses, the classification of sales is often more conveniently made by department than by product.

Similar reasoning indicates the desirability of making a comparative study of the relationship between sales and sales returns. In a first examination, some auditors will prepare for the permanent file of audit working papers an analysis of sales and sales returns for several prior years. This analysis will show the ratio of sales returns to sales and may be brought up to date in each succeeding examination. Any sudden or substantial change in the ratio of sales returns to sales is a matter to be investigated and discussed with officials of the company.

Comparative summaries of sales are most useful when the related figures for cost of sales are included. The comparison may then show for each product the percentage of gross profit to sales. Any variation in profit margin is of course reason for more detailed investigation. Another comparative device available in the audit of some manufacturing companies is to calculate the pounds of product sold each month. By applying established prices to the pounds of material sold, the auditor may test the validity of the dollar amounts of sales.

16. *Review the accounting for intercompany or interbranch transfers of merchandise.*

Effective control over intercompany or interbranch transfers of merchandise often requires the same kind of formal procedures for billing, shipping, and collection functions as for sales to outsiders; hence these movements of merchandise are often invoiced and recorded as sales. When the operations of the several organizational units are consolidated into one income statement, however, it is apparent that any transactions not representing sales to outsiders should be eliminated from the Sales account. In the examination of companies which operate subsidiaries or branches, the auditor should investigate the procedures for recording movements of merchandise between the various units of the company.

17. *Verify interest earned on notes and accrued interest receivable.*

Before beginning a review of interest earned, the auditor should become familiar with the client's policy for the computation, accrual, and recording of interest. Variations in accounting policy relating to interest are often found, such as recording interest at time of receiving the note, entries on a monthly basis, or at time of collection only. As long as the method used by the client gives reasonable results in the determination of income, most auditors raise no objections. Interest revenue is seldom material enough to justify an adjustment, even though the method used has some theoretical deficiencies.

The most effective verification of the Interest Earned account consists of an independent computation by the auditor of the interest earned during the year on notes receivable. To compute the total interest earned for the year, it is necessary to take into account the interest which has been earned but not collected as of the balance sheet date, and also the accrued interest receivable as of the beginning of the year. In large companies with well-organized accounting departments, the interest accrued on each note receivable as of the year-end will have been computed and the total amount of accrued interest will have been recorded by a journal entry debiting Accrued Interest Receivable and crediting Interest Earned. In some small companies without well-qualified accounting personnel, the responsibility may be shifted to the auditor for drafting the year-end entry for accrued interest. In either situation the auditor will need to make an independent computation of interest earned during the year and of accrued interest receivable as of the balance sheet date.

The independent computation of interest by the auditor may conveniently be handled on the same working paper (Figure 13–2) used to analyze notes receivable, since this working paper shows the interest rate and date of issuance of each note. The interest section of this working paper consists of four columns which show for each note receivable owned during the year the following information:

a) Accrued interest receivable at the beginning of the year (taken from the preceding year's audit working papers).

b) Interest earned during the year (computed from the terms of the notes).

c) Interest collected during the year (traced to cash receipts records).

d) Accrued interest receivable at the end of the year (computed by the auditor).

These four columns comprise a self-balancing set. The beginning balance of accrued interest receivable (first column) plus the interest earned during the year (second column) and minus the interest collected (third column) should equal the accrued interest receivable at the end of the year (fourth column). The totals of the four columns should be cross-footed to insure that they are in balance; in addition the individual column totals should be traced to the balances in the ledger.

If the interest earned for the year as computed by the auditor does not agree with interest earned as shown in the books, the next step is an analysis of the ledger account. Any unaccounted-for credits in the Interest Earned account deserve particular attention because these credits may represent interest received on notes which have never been recorded.

ILLUSTRATIVE CASE.   In an examination of a company which held numerous notes receivable, the auditor made an independent computation of the interest earned during the year. The amount of interest earned shown by the books was somewhat larger than the amount computed by the auditor. Careful analysis of entries in the Interest Earned account revealed one credit entry not related to any of the notes shown in the Notes Receivable account. Further investigation of this entry disclosed that a note had been obtained from a customer who was delinquent in paying his account receivable. The note receivable had not been recorded as an asset, but the account receivable which was replaced by the note had been written off as uncollectible.

Because of this situation the auditor made a thorough investigation of all accounts written off in recent years. Several of the former customers when contacted stated that they had been asked to sign demand notes for the balances owed and had been assured there would be no pressure for collection as long as interest was paid regularly. The existence of notes receivable totaling many thousands of dollars was brought to light; these notes were not recorded as assets and were not known to the officers. The note transactions had been arranged by a trusted employee who admitted having abstracted the interest payments received with the exception of one payment which, through oversight, he had permitted to be deposited and recorded as interest earned.

For financial institutions or other clients having numerous notes receivable, the auditor may verify interest computations on only a sample of the notes. In addition, he should test the reasonableness of total interest earned for the year by applying a weighted average rate of interest to the average balance of the Notes Receivable ledger account during the year.

18. *Determine proper balance sheet presentation of notes and accounts receivable and proper income statement presentation of sales.*

The principal objective in presenting notes and accounts receivable in the current assets section of the balance sheet is adequate informative disclosure of the kinds or sources of the receivables, their estimated realizable value, their liquidity, and their availability. In more detailed specific terms, good statement presentation requires that trade notes and accounts receivable be shown as a separate item and that other receivables be itemized if the amounts are material. Examples of these other kinds of receivables which may require separate listings include: accounts with affiliated companies; loans to officers and employees; claims for refund of federal income taxes; receivables from U.S. government agencies, including unbilled amounts under "cost-reimbursement" contracts and termination claims; uncollected stock subscriptions; amounts collectible in foreign currencies; claims against public carriers and insurance companies; advances to suppliers; miscellaneous deposits; charges for returnable containers; dividends receivable; and other items of accrued revenue. Receivables from consolidated subsidiaries are eliminated in consolidation.

Installment notes receivable frequently have collection schedules extending more than a year in the future; these may be segregated into current and noncurrent portions, or, as indicated in *APB Accounting*

Principles, may be included in current assets if they conform to normal trade practices and terms within the business. Unearned discount should be deducted from the face amount of the installment notes.

Accounts receivable with credit balances, if material in amount, should be reclassified as current liabilities. Charges for returnable containers represent equipment temporarily in the hands of customers and should not ordinarily be included in current assets.

Some types of receivables do not qualify as current assets. Prominent among these are advances to officers, directors, and affiliated companies; such extensions of credit are more commonly made for the convenience of the borrower rather than in the interest of the lending company, and presumably will be collected only at the convenience of the borrower. It is a basic tenet of statement presentation that transactions not characterized by arm's-length bargaining be fully publicized.

Inclusion of receivables in the category of current assets also requires that the time to maturity not exceed one year or one operating cycle (whichever is longer) from the balance sheet date. For noncurrent receivables, any implicit or imputed interest, computed in accordance with *APB Opinion No. 21,* should be treated as discount or premium and shown as a deduction from or addition to the face amount of the note. Such noncurrent receivables are properly included in the Other Assets section of the balance sheet.

Identification of pledged receivables is, of course, a first essential of proper statement presentation. When receivables are divided into several classifications, a question arises as to the position of the valuation allowance. If a valuation allowance relates exclusively to a given type of receivable, it should be deducted therefrom; otherwise, it should appear as a deduction from the group total.

The collateral for any secured notes or accounts receivable should be described in the balance sheet or in an appended note. Notes receivable discounted have been presented on statements in a variety of ways. However, the most generally accepted procedure is to omit notes receivable discounted from the body of the balance sheet and to mention the contingent liability, if any, in a balance sheet footnote.

In the Revenue section of the income statement, sales should be listed first at the gross amount, with deductions for sales returns and allowances and for sales discounts. Intercompany sales must be excluded, regardless of whether they arose from transactions with consolidated subsidiaries, unconsolidated subsidiaries, corporate joint ventures, or affiliates for which operating and financing policies were influenced by the client.

19.   *Obtain from client a letter of representations concerning notes and accounts receivable and sales.*

Many accounting firms obtain from their clients written representations concerning accounts receivable, notes receivable, and sales, as well as various other items. A single letter of representations may be obtained with sections for inventories, receivables, etc.; or separate ones may be obtained for different financial statement categories. The client's letter of representations is not a substitute for any auditing procedure and does not reduce the auditor's responsibility. It may, however, have a valuable psychological effect on management by emphasizing to executives that primary responsibility for accurate financial statements rests with them rather than with the auditor. A typical letter of representations covering receivables follows:

> With respect to your examination of our financial statements, we hereby make the following representations concerning accounts and notes receivable shown in the balance sheet at December 31, 19___, in the aggregate gross amount of $_____.
> 1. All accounts and notes receivable represent valid claims against debtors for sales or other charges arising on or before December 31, 19___.
> 2. The accounts and notes receivable are unencumbered assets of the company.
> 3. Merchandise shipped on consignment has been identified as such in the records and is not included in accounts receivable.
> 4. All known uncollectible accounts and notes receivable have been written off.
> 5. The amount of $_____ provided for doubtful receivables is, in our judgment, sufficient to cover losses which may be sustained in realization of the notes and accounts receivable.

Signature of officer

Client company

Interim audit work on receivables and sales

Much of the audit work on receivables and sales can be performed one or two months before the balance sheet date. This interim work may include the confirmation of accounts receivable as well as evaluation of the internal controls.

If interim audit work has been done on receivables and sales, the year-end audit work may be modified considerably. For example, if the confirmation of accounts receivable was performed at October 31, the year-end audit program would include preparation of a summary analysis of postings to the Accounts Receivable control account for the period from November 1 through December 31. This analysis would list the postings by month, showing the journal source of each. These postings would be traced to the respective journals, such as sales journal and cash receipts journal. The amounts of the postings would be compared with the amounts in preceding months and with the corresponding months in prior years. The purpose of this work is to bring to light any significant variations in receivables during the months between the interim audit work and the balance sheet date.

In addition to this analysis of the entries to the receivable account for the intervening period, the audit work at year-end would include obtaining the aging of the accounts receivable at December 31, confirmation of any large accounts in the year-end trial balance that are new or delinquent, and the usual investigation of the year-end cutoff of sales and cash receipts.

The comparison of current period sales with those for prior periods may be carried out in November for the first 10 months of the year and later completed by entering figures for the final 2 months. Investigation of such problems as the handling of consignments, and interbranch shipments can also largely be completed as preliminary work.

GROUP I
REVIEW QUESTIONS

13–1. Select the best answer choice for each of the following:

   a) Maria Nolan, CPA, in examining the financial statements of the Quinn Helicopter Corporation for the year ended September 30, 1974, found a material amount of receivables from the federal government. The governmental agencies replied neither to the first nor second confirmation requests nor to a third request made by telephone. Miss Nolan satisfied herself as to the proper statement of these receivables by means of other auditing procedures. The auditor's report on Quinn's September 30, 1974 financial statements requires—

   (1) Neither a comment on the use of other procedures nor an opinion qualification.

   (2) Both a scope qualification and an opinion qualification.

   (3) No reference to the use of other auditing procedures but does require an opinion qualification.

   (4) A description of the limitation on the scope and the other auditing procedures used but does not require an opinion qualification.

   b) The auditor is most likely to learn of the pledging of accounts receivable from—

   (1) An analysis of the Accounts Receivable account.

   (2) An analysis of the Sales account.

   (3) An analysis of the Interest Expense account.

   (4) Direct confirmation with debtors.

   c) Negative accounts receivable confirmations would be most appropriate in confirming the balances of—

   (1) Large over-due accounts.

   (2) Small accounts which have been written off.

   (3) Customers whose large balances represent many small purchases.

   (4) Accounts due from governmental subdivisions. (AICPA, adapted)

13–2. A CPA wishes to test his client's sales cutoff at June 30, 1974. Describe the steps that he should include in this test. (AICPA, adapted)

13–3. Several accounts receivable confirmations have been returned with the notation that "verifications of vendors' statements are no longer possible because of our data processing system." What alternative auditing procedures could be used to verify these accounts receivable? (AICPA, adapted) *trace to source document*

13–4. *a)* What is an audit confirmation?

    b) What characteristics should an audit confirmation possess if a CPA is to consider it as valid evidence?

    c) Distinguish between a positive confirmation and a negative confirmation in the auditor's examination of accounts receivable.

    d) In confirming an audit client's accounts receivable, what characteristics should be present in the accounts if the CPA is to use negative confirmations? (AICPA, adapted) *a lot of small accounts; internal control good.*

13–5. The confirmation of accounts receivable is an important auditing procedure. Should the formal request for confirmation be made by the client or by the auditor? Should the return envelope be addressed to the client, to the auditor in care of the client, or to the auditor's office? Explain.

13–6. In his audit of the client's allowance for uncollectible accounts, how does the auditor identify accounts of dubious collectibility?

13–7. A new client operating a medium-sized manufacturing business complains to you that he believes his business has sustained significant losses on several occasions because certain sales invoices were misplaced and never recorded as accounts receivable. What internal control procedure can you suggest to guard against such problems?

13–8. In determining the propriety of cash discounts allowed, what overall test can the auditor make to determine the reasonableness of cash discounts taken by customers? *% relationship of discounts to collections.*

13–9. In the examination of credit memoranda covering allowances to customers for goods returned, how can the auditor ascertain whether the customer actually did return merchandise in each case in which accounts receivable were reduced? *Receiving reports. receiving department separate from purchase dept.*

13–10. Does the letter of representations obtained by the auditor from the client concerning accounts receivable usually include any representation as to collectibility? Explain. *no*

13–11. What auditing procedures, if any, are necessary for notes receivable but are not required for accounts receivable?

13–12. During preliminary conversations with a new staff assistant you instruct him to send out confirmation requests for both accounts receivable and notes receivable. He asks whether the confirmation requests should go to the makers of the notes or to the holders of the notes in the case of notes which have been discounted or sold. Give reasons for your answer.

13–13. In the examination of an automobile agency, you find that installment notes received from the purchasers of automobiles are promptly discounted with a bank. Would you consider it necessary to confirm these notes by a communication with the bank? With the makers? Explain.

13–14. Your review of notes receivable from officers, directors, stockholders, and affiliated companies discloses that several notes of small amount were written off to the allowance for uncollectible notes during the year. Have these transactions any special significance? Explain.

13–15. Worthington Corporation has requested you to conduct an audit so that it may support its application for a bank loan with audited financial statements. The client agrees that you shall have access to all records of the company and shall employ any audit procedures you deem necessary except that you are not to communicate with customers. Under these circumstances will it be possible for you to issue an unqualified audit report? Explain.

13–16. Good presentation of receivables in the balance sheet is achieved through observing a number of specific points such as the segregation of material trade receivables, deposits, amounts due from officers, and any other special classes of receivables. List several other specific points to be observed.

13–17. Among the accounts receivable of the Toland Manufacturing Company are two large accounts receivable from mail-order concerns. When you attempt to confirm these balances, you receive replies stating that because of the voucher system used for handling payables it is not possible to verify the amount owing to a particular supplier. What effect would these replies have upon your verification of receivables?

13–18. Among specific procedures which contribute to good internal control over accounts receivable are (*a*) the approval of uncollectible account write-offs and credit memoranda by an executive, and (*b*) the sending of monthly statements to all customers. State three other procedures conducive to strong internal control. (AICPA)

13–19. What additional auditing procedures should, or might, be undertaken in connection with the confirmation of accounts receivable where customers having substantial balances fail to reply after second request forms have been mailed directly to them? (AICPA)

13–20. In your review of sales transactions and records of the Manchester Manufacturing Company, you find that goods are occasionally shipped on consignment to certain dealers, but that these shipments are recorded as sales. How would this discovery affect the pattern of your audit work?

13–21. Would an auditor be concerned with sales invoices or shipping documents dated subsequent to the close of the period under audit? Explain.

13–22. In your first examination of the Hydro Manufacturing Company, a manufacturer of outboard motors, you discover that an unusually large number of sales transactions were recorded just prior to the end of the fiscal year. What significance would you attach to this unusual volume?

13–23.   In connection with a regular annual audit, what are the purposes
of a review of sales returns and allowances subsequent to the balance
sheet date? (AICPA, adapted)

13–24.   An inexperienced clerk assigned to the preparation of sales invoices
in a manufacturing company became confused as to the nature of
certain articles being shipped, with the result that the prices used
on the invoices were far less than called for in the company's price
lists. What internal control procedures could be established to guard
against such errors? Would errors of this type be disclosed in the
normal audit by an independent public accountant? Explain.

13–25.   The accounts receivable section of the accounting department in the
Annandale Products Company maintains subsidiary ledgers which
are posted from carbon copies of the sales invoices transmitted daily
from the billing department. How may the accounts receivable section
be sure that it receives promptly a copy of each sales invoice
prepared?

13–26.   The Edendale Company, a dealer in new automobiles, had approximately the same volume of sales and earned approximately the same
gross profit and the same net income for the years 1973 and 1974.
The gross profit on new cars decreased in 1974 as compared with
the preceding year, but this decrease was offset by increased gross
profit from the sale of accessories attached to the new cars, particularly air-conditioning units. Would the normal examination by an
independent auditor disclose these changes in the sources of gross
profit? Explain.

13–27.   Every business that ships goods to its customers must establish procedures to insure that a sales invoice is prepared for every shipment.
Describe procedures to meet this requirement.

GROUP II
QUESTIONS REQUIRING ANALYSIS

13–28.   Select the best answer choice for each of the following and defend
your selection.

a)   In connection with his examination of the Beke Supply Company
for the year ended August 31, 1974, Derek Lowe, CPA, has
mailed accounts receivable confirmations to three groups as
follows:

Group number	Type of customer	Type of confirmation
1.........	Wholesale	Positive
2.........	Current retail	Negative
3.........	Past-due retail	Positive

The confirmation responses from each group vary from 10 percent to 90 percent. The most likely response percentages are:

(1)   Group 1, 90%; Group 2, 50%; Group 3, 10%.
(2)   Group 1, 90%; Group 2, 10%; Group 3, 50%.
(3)   Group 1, 50%; Group 2, 90%; Group 3, 10%.
(4)   Group 1, 10%; Group 2, 50%; Group 3, 90%.

b)   A CPA is examining the financial statements of a small telephone company and wishes to test whether customers are being billed. One procedure that he might use is to—

(1)   Compare a sample of listings in the telephone directory to the billing control.
(2)   Trace a sample of postings from the billing control to the subsidiary accounts receivable ledger.
(3)   Balance the subsidiary accounts receivable ledger to the general ledger control account.
(4)   Confirm a representative number of accounts receivable. (AICPA, adapted)

13–29.   a)   What are the implications to a CPA, if, during his examination of accounts receivable some of a client's trade customers do not respond to his request for positive confirmation of their accounts?
b)   Should the CPA send second requests? Why?
c)   What auditing steps should a CPA perform if there is no response to a second request for a positive confirmation? (AICPA)

13–30.   The vice president for finance of a client company, Topeka Corporation, operating a chain of retail stores, provides you with the following information concerning three short-term notes receivable due in the near future. The three notes have recently been discounted by the corporation with its bank.

(1)   A $40,000 note received from an unconsolidated subsidiary, Wichita Inc., which operates a dude ranch. The subsidiary is operating profitably but is in a weak cash position as a result of having made extensive capital additions. The parent company intends in the near future to make a $60,000 advance to Wichita, Inc., with a five-year maturity. This proposed advance will enable the subsidiary to pay the present $40,000 loan at maturity and meet certain other obligations.
(2)   A $10,000 60-day 6 percent note from a customer of unquestioned financial standing.
(3)   A $5,000 note from a former key executive of the Topeka Corporation who was released because of excessive gambling. The maker of the note is presently unemployed and without personal resources.

What is the appropriate presentation of this information on the balance sheet? State any assumptions which you consider necessary.

13–31.   You are conducting an audit of a wholesaler for which accounts receivable constitute a material part of current assets. Early in the engagement you mailed positive confirmations to 250 of the 1,000 accounts receivable on the books, accounting for more than three fourths of the dollar amount of receivables. After a follow-up of those accounts which did not reply to the first request, you found that you had a reasonable number of replies. Thirty-five of the replies showed differences.

Required:

a) Give a detailed list of possible reasons for the differences.
b) Why would you investigate these differences?
c) In general terms, describe the procedures to be followed in an investigation of the differences.
d) What should be done about the accounts of the customers who did not reply to either the first request or the follow-up? (AICPA, adapted)

13–32. You are considering using the services of a reputable outside mailing service for the confirmation of accounts receivable balances. The service would prepare and mail the confirmation requests and remove the returned confirmations from the envelopes and give them directly to you.

What reliance, if any, could you place on the services of the outside mailing service? Discuss and state the reasons in support of your answer. (AICPA)

13–33. An assistant auditor was instructed to "test the aging of accounts receivable as shown on the trial balance prepared by the client." In making this test, the assistant traced all past-due accounts shown on the trial balance to the ledger cards in the accounts receivable subsidiary ledger and recomputed the aging of these accounts. He found no discrepancies and reported to the senior auditor that the aging work performed by the client was satisfactory.

Comment on the logic and adequacy of this test of the aging of accounts receivable.

13–34. A student of auditing wrote the following comment on physical inspection and count as a means of verification by the auditor:

"The most conclusive of all audit procedures is that of physical inspection and count. This procedure is appropriate to the verification of cash, notes receivable, and marketable securities. When physical inspection and count show cash, notes receivable, and marketable securities to be on hand in the amounts indicated by the financial statements, the auditor has established beyond any reasonable doubt the validity of this portion of the assets." Do you agree? Explain.

13–35. During your annual examination of the financial statements of Wilshire Corporation, you undertake the confirmation of accounts receivable, using the positive form of confirmation request. Satisfactory replies are received for all but one of the large accounts. You sent a second and third request to this customer but received no reply. At this point an employee of the client informed you that a check had been received for the full amount of the receivable. Would you regard this as a satisfactory disposition of the matter? Explain.

13–36.   Milton Chambers, CPA, was retained by Wall Corporation to perform an audit of its financial statements for the year ending December 31. In a preliminary meeting with company officials, Chambers learned that the corporation customarily accepted numerous notes receivable from its customers. At December 31 the client provided Chambers with a list of the individual notes receivable owned at that date. The list showed for each note the date of origin, amount, interest rate, maturity date, and name and address of the maker. Chambers proved the footing of the list and determined that the total agreed with the general ledger control account for notes receivable and also with the amount shown in the balance sheet. Next he selected 20 of the larger amounts on the list of notes receivable for detailed investigation. This investigation consisted of confirming the amount, date, maturity, interest rate, and collateral pledged, if any, by direct communication with the makers of the notes. By selection of the larger amounts, Chambers was able to verify 75 percent of the dollar amount of notes receivable by confirming only 20 percent of the notes. In addition, however, he selected a random sample of another 20 percent of the smaller notes on the list for confirmation with the makers. Satisfactory replies were received to all confirmation requests.

The president of Wall Corporation informed Chambers that the company never required any collateral in support of the notes receivable; the replies to confirmation requests indicated no collateral had been pledged.

No notes were past due at the balance sheet date, and the credit manager stated that no losses were anticipated. Chambers verified the credit status of the makers of all the notes he had confirmed by reference to audited financial statements and Dun & Bradstreet, Inc. credit ratings.

By independent computation of the interest accrued on the notes receivable at the balance sheet date, Chambers determined that the accrued interest receivable as shown on the balance sheet was correct.

Since Chambers found no deficiencies in any part of his examination, he issued an unqualified audit report. Some months later, the Wall Corporation became insolvent and the president fled the country. Chambers was sued by creditors of the company who charged that his audit was inadequate and failed to meet minimum professional standards. You are to comment on the audit program followed by Chambers with respect to notes receivable *only.*

GROUP III
PROBLEMS

13–37.   Lawrence Company maintains its accounts on the basis of a fiscal year ending October 31. Assume that you were retained by the company in August 1974 to perform an audit for the fiscal year ending October 31, 1974. You decide to perform certain auditing procedures in advance of the balance sheet date. Among these interim procedures is the confirmation of accounts receivable, which you perform at September 30, 1974.

The accounts receivable at September 30, 1974 consisted of approximately 200 accounts with balances totaling $956,750. Seventy-five of these accounts with balances totaling $650,725 were selected for circularization. All but 20 of the confirmation requests have been returned; 30 were signed without comments, 14 had minor differences which have been cleared satisfactorily, while 11 confirmations had the following comments:

(1) We are sorry but we cannot answer your request for confirmation of our account as the PDQ Company uses an accounts payable voucher system.

(2) The balance of $1,050 was paid on September 23, 1974.

(3) The above balance of $7,750 was paid on October 5, 1974.

(4) The above balance has been paid.

(5) We do not owe you anything at September 30, 1974, as the goods represented by your invoice dated September 30, 1974, number 25,050, in the amount of $11,550, were received on October 5, 1974, on f.o.b. destination terms.

(6) An advance payment of $2,500 made by us in August 1974 should cover the two invoices totaling $1,350 shown on the statement attached.

(7) We never received these goods.

(8) We are contesting the propriety of the $12,525 charge. We think the charge is excessive.

(9) Amount okay. As the goods have been shipped to us on consignment we will remit payment upon selling the goods.

(10) The $10,000, representing a deposit under a lease, will be applied against the rent due to us during 1977, the last year of the lease.

(11) Your credit dated September 5, 1974 in the amount of $440 cancels the above balance.

Required:

What steps would you take to clear satisfactorily each of the above 11 comments? (AICPA, adapted)

13–38. You are performing your first examination of the financial statements of Havers Company, Inc., a closely-held corporation. The balance sheet at June 30, 1974 as drafted by the controller of Havers shows total assets of $9,500,000 and stockholders' equity of $4,000,000.

During the course of your examination of notes receivable you discover that the corporation had loaned $1,200,000 on March 31, 1974 to the majority shareholder, on a 6 percent, unsecured note payable on demand. On June 30, 1974, Havers Company, Inc. sold this note without recourse to its depository bank. On July 1, 1974, Havers reacquired this note from the bank without recourse. The standard bank confirmation form returned to you by the bank shows no contingent liability at June 30, 1974 in connection with the $1,200,000 note.

Required:

Discuss the implications of the above transactions as they affect your audit report.

13–39. The July 31, 1974 general ledger trial balance of Aerospace Contractors, Inc. reflects the following accounts associated with receivables. Balances of the accounts are after all adjusting journal entries proposed by the auditor and accepted by the client.

Accounts receivable—commercial...............	$ 595,000
Accounts receivable—U.S. government..........	3,182,000
Allowance for doubtful accounts and notes......	75,000 cr.
Claims receivable—public carriers..............	7,000
Claims receivable—U.S. government terminated contracts........................	320,000
Due from Harwood Co., affiliate...............	480,000
Notes receivable—trade.......................	15,000

Required:

a) Draft a partial balance sheet for Aerospace Contractors at July 31, 1974. In deciding upon which items deserve separate listing, consider materiality as well as the nature of the accounts.

b) Write an explanation of the reasoning employed in your balance sheet presentation of these accounts.

13–40. During your examination of the financial statements of Martin Mfg. Co., a new client, for the year ended March 31, 1974, you note the following entry in the general journal dated March 31, 1974:

Notes Receivable............................	550,000	
Land.................................		500,000
Gain on Sale of Land.................		50,000

To record sale of excess plant-site land to Ardmore Corp. for 4 percent note due March 31, 1979. No interest payment required until maturity of note.

Your review of the contract for sale between Martin and Ardmore, your inquiries of Martin executives, and your study of minutes of Martin's directors' meetings develop the following facts:

(1) The land has been carried on your client's books at its cost of $500,000.

(2) Ardmore Corp. is a land developer and plans to subdivide and resell the land acquired from Martin Mfg. Co.

(3) Martin had originally negotiated with Ardmore on the basis of an 8 percent interest rate on the note. This interest rate was established by Martin after a careful analysis of Ardmore's credit standing and current money market conditions.

(4) Ardmore had rejected the 8 percent interest rate because the total outlay on an 8 percent note for $550,000 would amount to $770,000 at the end of five years; and Ardmore felt a total outlay of this amount would leave it with an inadequate return on the subdivision. Ardmore held out for a total cash outlay of $660,000, and Martin Mfg. Co. finally agreed to this position.

Required:

Ignoring income tax considerations, is the journal entry recording Martin's sale of the land to Ardmore acceptable? Explain fully and draft an adjusting entry if you consider one to be necessary.

GROUP IV
CASE STUDIES IN AUDITING

STAR FINANCE COMPANY

13–41.   The Star Finance Company was in the business of making small loans and investing in installment sales contracts purchased from dealers in automobiles, appliances, and other durable goods. Early in 1975, the company retained McGregor and Company, CPAs, to make an examination of the financial statements for the fiscal year ended February 28, 1975. Mr. James Smith, one of the partners in the CPA firm, went to the office of Star Finance to begin the audit. He took with him a senior auditor, Charles Brown, and spent some time explaining to Mr. Brown some of the differences between the handling of receivables in a finance company and in a merchandising concern. He stressed to Brown the importance in this business of obtaining bank loans and other capital and of lending these funds to customers at higher interest rates. He added that a finance company was usually not anxious to have a customer pay an account in full because the company might then lose contact with him. On the contrary, Mr. Smith pointed out, the finance company would probably encourage its small-loan customers to obtain a new loan before the original one was paid off. If the customer could be developed into a more or less permanent borrower, the finance company would benefit from this relationship even though it never collected a loan in full. The important element, Mr. Smith commented, was to keep the customer in debt and paying interest charges.

One of the first steps taken by Mr. Smith and Mr. Brown was to obtain a trial balance of the general ledger. This trial balance showed installment notes receivable of $615,428.24. The allowance for losses on collection of these receivables was $6,473.26.

Early in the audit Mr. Brown made tests to determine that the detail of the receivables was in agreement with the control account and sent out requests for confirmation of the balances due from the borrowers. In addition he made inquiries into the collectibility of the receivables. He found that the installment receivables consisted of 1,706 accounts, of which 18 were classified by the company as delinquent; these 18 accounts had aggregate uncollected balances of $5,167.25. However, in reviewing the receivables Mr. Brown noticed quite a number of accounts that were rather slow in collection; as a matter of fact, some of them showed no recent collections of principal.

After having developed this information, Mr. Brown made inquiries of the president of Star Finance Company as to the company's basis of considering an account as delinquent. He was informed that the company defined a delinquent account as one upon which no collection had been received on either principal or interest within the last 60 days, or generally, therefore, 30 days from the due date; conversely, accounts on which collections of principal or interest were being received currently (although not necessarily the full monthly payment) were considered as current. Furthermore, the president pointed out, all accounts defined by the company as delinquent 90 days or more (and which aggregated approximately $25,000) had been written off at February 28, 1975 by a charge against operations.

The number of accounts which seemed to be slow in collection continued to disturb Mr. Brown, and he made a further study of receivables and the recent payments thereon. This study covered 169 other accounts classified by the company as current and indicated the following status:

	Number	*Amount*
Paying interest only..............................	29	$ 12,556.68
All other (including some accounts on which all interest had been waived).........................	140	88,112.53
	169	$100,669.21

After comparing the results of this test with the amount of the allowance for losses, which amounted to only $6,473.26, Mr. Brown became further concerned as to the adequacy of the provision for collection losses. He decided that he should make some further inquiries into the status of these accounts, and so he requested the Star Finance Company to compile the following information as to the 169 accounts (which he then tested):

	Total	*Paying interest only*	*All others*
Balance, February 28, 1974.....	$106,298.52	$12,312.72	$ 93,985.80
Add additional loans made.....	9,907.94	249.55	9,658.39
Total...................	$116,206.46	$12,562.27	$103,644.19
Deduct collection received:			
Total collections............	$ 34,180.42	$ 1,471.34	$ 32,709.08
Less amount applied to interest.................	18,643.17	1,465.75	17,177.42
Remainder—applied to principal................	$ 15,537.25	$ 5.59	$ 15,531.66
Balance, February 28, 1975 (representing 169 accounts)	$100,669.21	$12,556.68	$ 88,112.53

Mr. Brown conferred with Mr. Smith, and they agreed that the allowance was insufficient. Both Mr. Smith and Mr. Brown then discussed the matter with the president of the Star Finance Company, and it was decided that further studies should be made by the company. At the conclusion of these studies, the company increased its allowance from $6,473.26 to $34,182.10. This allowance, the company insisted, was sufficient to cover losses on collections of the receivables.

Mr. Brown was inclined first to think that the allowance of $34,182.10 would be sufficient; after all it did represent better than 5 percent of the receivables and, furthermore, the company would be receiving interest in the future on all of its loans, out of which further provision could be made if necessary; Mr. Smith, however, did not agree. On the other hand, Mr. Smith was not sure that he could indicate in his report the amount of allowance which should be necessary because (1) he did not regard himself as being qualified as an appraiser to evaluate the accounts, and (2) the company had been in existence only a few years and hence did not have an extended background of credit experience.

The report, as finally issued by Mr. Smith, set forth much of the information given above and indicated that the company was of the opinion its allowance was sufficient. In his report Mr. Smith broke down the installment notes receivable as follows:

Notes being collected in substantial accordance with contract
   terms, $509,591.78 (less allowance for losses, $16,182.10)... $493,409.68
Notes not being collected in substantial accordance with
   contract terms, $105,836.46 (less allowance for losses,
   $18,000.00)..   87,836.46
      Total.. $581,246.14

His report also contained the following:

As to the allowances for losses carried by the company against its notes receivable, we are of the opinion, based largely on the company's collection experience and in the light of present conditions, that—
(1)   The allowance of $16,182.10 carried against notes collected in substantial accordance with contract terms should be sufficient.
(2)   The allowance of $18,000 carried against notes not being collected in substantial accordance with contract terms is insufficient and losses substantially in excess of $18,000 may be expected thereon. However, inasmuch as the company has been in existence only a relatively short period of years and consequently does not have extensive experience as to losses and collections, and, further, since the ascertainment of adequate loss allowance in the absence of extensive loss experience is a technical matter for persons trained in small-loan operations and credits, we are not in a position to express an opinion as to the amount of loss allowance which we believe should be required.

In his opinion paragraph he said "in our opinion, except that the allowance for loss carried against installment notes receivable not being collected in substantial accordance with contract terms is inadequate, the aforementioned financial statements present fairly the financial position of the company at February 28, 1975, and the results of its operations and the changes in its financial position for the year then ended, in conformity with generally accepted accounting principles applied on a basis consistent with that of the preceding year."

On review of the report, the president of the Star Finance Company claimed Mr. Smith was putting him out of business and that his report would result in the bank (extending credit to the company) calling its line of credit; the president demanded that Mr. Smith change the report.

Required:

a) Do you agree with Mr. Smith's opinion that the allowance for losses on installment receivables was insufficient?

b) Do you think that Mr. Smith should have specified the amount of allowance he deemed to be sufficient?

c) Do you think that Mr. Smith should have been swayed by the statement of the president of the Star Finance Company that this report would put him out of business, and if so, what else should Mr. Smith have done?

d) Was there anything else which Mr. Smith could have done that he did not do?

14

Invent●ries and cost of sales

auditor concerned with overstatement.
most important thing is to determine
that it exists. (be there &
observe Taking
of inventory))

THE RESPONSIBILITIES of the auditor with respect to inventories can best be understood by turning back to the time of the spectacular McKesson & Robbins fraud case. As mentioned in Chapter 13, the hearings conducted by the SEC in 1939 disclosed that the audited financial statements of McKesson & Robbins, Inc., a drug company listed on the New York Stock Exchange, contained $19,000,000 of fictitious assets, about one fourth of the total assets shown on the balance sheet. The fictitious assets included $10,000,000 of nonexistent inventories. How was it possible for the independent auditors to have conducted an audit and to have issued an unqualified report without discovering the gigantic fraud? The audit program followed for inventories in this case was in accordance with customary auditing practice of the 1930s. The significant point is that in this period it was customary to limit the audit work on inventories to an examination of records only; the standards of that era did not require any physical count, observation, inspection, or other actual contact with the inventory. *Important*

Up to the time of the McKesson & Robbins case, auditors had avoided taking responsibility for verifying the accuracy of inventory quantities and the physical existence of the goods. With questionable logic, many auditors had argued that they were experts in handling figures and analyzing accounting records but were not qualified to identify and measure the great variety of raw materials and manufactured goods found in the factories, warehouses, and store buildings of their clients.

The McKesson & Robbins case brought a quick end to such limited views of the auditor's responsibility. The public accounting profession was faced with the necessity of accepting responsibility for verifying the physical existence of inventories or of confessing that its audit function offered no real protection to investors or other users of financial statements. The profession met the challenge by adopting new standards requiring the auditor to observe the taking of the physical inventory and to confirm accounts receivable. In any audit in which the observation of inventories is practicable and possible to carry out but is omitted, disclosure of this omission must be made in the audit report. Ordinarily, the expression of an opinion on the overall fairness of the statements will then not be possible. These new requirements were approved by the membership of the AICPA at the 1939 annual meeting and remained as an unchanging standard for over 30 years.

In 1970 the AICPA issued *Statement on Auditing Procedure No. 43*, which reaffirmed the importance of the auditor's observation of physical inventories but authorized the substitution of other auditing procedures under certain circumstances. *SAP No. 43* made a distinction between companies which determine inventory quantities solely by an annual physical count and companies with well-kept perpetual inventory records. The latter companies often have strong internal control over inventories and may employ statistical sampling techniques to verify the records by occasional test counts rather than by a complete annual count of the entire inventory. For these latter clients the auditor's observation of physical inventory may be limited to such counts as he considers appropriate and may occur during or after the end of the period being audited.

The most difficult part of *SAP No. 43* to interpret is the provision which permits the auditor to substitute other audit procedures for the observation of inventories because it was *impracticable* or *impossible* for him to observe the physical inventory. The difficulty lies in defining the circumstances which make it *impracticable* or *impossible* to observe physical inventory. When observation of the physical inventory is determined to be impracticable or impossible but the auditor is able to satisfy himself through the use of other auditing procedures, he may issue an unqualified report without making any disclosure (as previously required) of the omission of an observation of the physical inventory. Continued recognition of the importance of contact with items of inventory, as well as records and documents, is stressed by *SAP No. 43* in stipulating that the use of alternative auditing procedures must always include observing or making some physical counts of inventory even though this occurs after the balance sheet date.

Critical importance of inventories to the auditor

Inventories have probably received more attention in auditing literature and in discussions among professional accountants than any other classification to be found on financial statements. The reasons for the special significance attached to the verification of inventories are readily apparent:

1. Inventories usually constitute the largest current asset of an enterprise and are more susceptible to major errors and manipulation than any other asset category.

2. Numerous alternative methods for valuation of inventory are sanctioned by the accounting profession, the SEC, and the Internal Revenue Service—principally because of inflationary price changes over many years.

3. The determination of inventory value directly affects the cost of sales and has a major impact upon income for the year.

4. The verification of inventory quantity, condition, and value is inherently a more complex and difficult task than is the verification of most elements of financial position.

The interrelationship of inventories and cost of sales makes it logical for the two topics to be considered together in an auditing textbook. In this chapter the term "inventories" is used to include: (1) goods on hand ready for sale, either the merchandise of a trading concern or the finished goods of a manufacturer; (2) goods in the process of production, commonly referred to as "work in process"; and (3) goods to be consumed directly or indirectly in production, consisting of raw materials, purchased parts, and supplies.

The auditor's objectives in examination of inventories and cost of sales

The principal objectives of the auditor in the examination of inventories and cost of sales are to determine (a) the adequacy of internal controls for inventories and cost of sales; (b) the existence and ownership of the inventories; (c) the quality or condition of the inventories; (d) the propriety of the valuation of inventories, including pricing, extensions, and footings; and (e) the fairness of the amount presented as cost of sales in the income statement.

The auditor's approach to the verification of inventories and cost of sales should be one of awareness to the possibility of intentional misstatement, as well as to the prevalence of accidental error in the determination of inventory quantities and amounts. Purposeful misstatement of inventory has often been employed to evade income taxes, to conceal shortages arising from various irregularities, and to mislead stockholders or other inactive owners as to profits and financial position.

The very nature of entries in the Cost of Sales ledger account makes it susceptible to misstatements, especially when perpetual inventories are maintained. For example, consider the variety of charges or credits that may be determinants of cost of sales for a manufacturing concern using perpetual inventories:

1. Amounts transferred from work-in-process or finished goods inventory accounts.
2. Proceeds from sales of scrap.
3. Charges for idle plant and equipment.
4. Underabsorbed or overabsorbed factory overhead.
5. Standard cost variances.
6. Inventory write-downs for shortages, obsolescence, etc.
7. Losses on firm fixed-price contracts.

For a trading concern using the periodic method of determining inventories, the Cost of Sales account is much less active. It is generally utilized only at the end of an accounting period when the ending inventory has been compiled. Nevertheless, a trading concern's cost of sales should be carefully examined to determine whether any significant inventory shrinkages are "buried" therein.

Internal control of inventories and cost of sales

The importance of adequate internal control over inventories and cost of sales from the viewpoint of both management and the auditor can scarcely be overemphasized. In some companies, management stresses internal controls over cash and securities but ignores the problem of control over inventories. This attitude may be based on the outmoded notion that the primary purpose of internal control is to prevent and detect fraud. Since many types of inventory are composed of items not particularly susceptible to theft, management may consider internal controls to be unnecessary in this area. Such thinking ignores the fact that internal control performs other functions more important than fraud prevention.

Efficient utilization of the capital invested in inventories requires that management have a continuous, detailed knowledge of the kinds and quantities of goods on hand. Losses from excessive stockpiling and from deterioration of goods long in storage may result from poor control procedures which permit materials to accumulate unreasonably in storerooms while new purchases are made for current needs. If management is not currently and accurately informed of the quantities and locations of goods on hand, the waste and inefficiency from this situation may be far greater than losses from theft.

Good internal control is a means of providing accurate cost data for inventories and cost of sales as well as accuracy in reporting physical quantities. Inadequate internal controls may cause losses by permitting erroneous cost data to be used by management in setting prices and in making other decisions based on reported profit margins. If the accounts do not furnish a realistic picture of the cost of inventories on hand, the cost of goods manufactured, and the cost of goods sold, the financial statements may be grossly misleading both as to earnings and as to financial position. A number of spectacular cases have demonstrated the disastrous consequences to management and to independent public accountants of ignoring weaknesses in internal control over inventories.

ILLUSTRATIVE CASE.   The work-in-process inventory of Drayer-Hanson, Incorporated, per the audited statements, amounted to approximately $244,000; but during an investigation by the Securities and Exchange Commission, reported in *Accounting Series Releases No. 64* and *No. 67,* an overstatement of $85,000 in this asset was established. This overstatement amounted to one third of the owners' equity of the firm and had enabled the company to obtain financing which otherwise would have been denied.

How could such a gross overstatement of work in process arise and go undetected by the auditors? The answer must be that internal controls over inventory were seriously deficient and that the public accountants were negligent in their review of internal control. Among the specific shortcomings in internal control which led to the misleading financial statements were the following:
1. Job cost sheets did not reflect the quantity or cost of completed units transferred to finished goods or shipped to customers.
2. Requisitions were not prepared for all materials withdrawn from stores, and "balancing" requisitions were prepared retroactively.
3. The general ledger account for inventory of raw material was not supported by a detailed stores record in dollars.
4. There was no tie-in between physical units in the plant and the dollar amount of inventories.

Despite these shortcomings, the company represented that a controlled job cost system was in operation and the auditors in their report indicated that the company had a dependable system of internal control. The SEC censured the auditing firm severely for the inadequacy of its procedures and indicated that the auditors had every reason to be aware of the lack of internal control. Shortly thereafter the auditing firm passed out of existence, possibly because of the adverse publicity arising from the Drayer-Hanson case.

Good internal control procedures for inventories and cost of sales affect nearly all the functions involved in producing and disposing of the company's products. Purchasing, receiving, storing, issuing, processing, and shipping are the physical functions directly connected with inventories; the cost accounting system and the perpetual inventory records comprise the recording functions. Since the auditor is interested in the final products of the recording functions, it is necessary for him to appraise and understand the cost accounting system and the perpetual inventory records, as well as the various procedures and original documents underlying the preparation of final data.

Physical control

The purchasing function. Adequate internal control over purchases requires, first of all, an organizational structure which delegates to a separate department of the company exclusive authority to make all purchases of materials and services. The purchasing, receiving, and recording functions should be clearly separated and lodged in separate departments. In small concerns, this type of departmentalized operation may not be possible; but even in very small enterprises, it is usually feasible to make one person responsible for all purchase transactions.

Serially numbered formal purchase orders should be prepared for all purchases, and copies forwarded to the accounting and receiving departments. The copy sent to receiving should have the quantities ordered and unit prices blacked out to assure that receiving personnel make independent counts of the merchandise received. Even though the buyer may actually place an order by telephone, the formal purchase order should be prepared and forwarded. In many large organizations, purchase orders are issued only after compliance with extensive procedures for (*a*) determining the need for the item, (*b*) obtaining of competitive bids, and (*c*) obtaining approval of the financial aspect of the commitment.

The receiving function. All goods received by the company—without exception—should be cleared through a receiving department which is independent of purchasing, storing, and shipping departments. This department is responsible for (1) the determination of quantities of goods received, (2) the determination that quality of goods received is in accordance with the purchase order, (3) the detection of damaged or defective merchandise, (4) the preparation of a receiving report, and (5) the prompt transmittal of goods received to the stores department.

The storing function. As goods are delivered to stores, they are counted, inspected, and receipted for. The stores department will then notify the accounting department of the amount received and placed in stock. In performing these functions, the storeskeeper makes an important contribution to overall control of inventories: by signing for the goods, he fixes his own responsibility; and by notifying the accounting department of actual goods stored, he provides verification of the receiving department's work.

The issuing function. The storeskeeper, being responsible for all goods under his control, has reason to insist that for all items passing out of his hands he be given a prenumbered requisition accompanied by a signed receipt from the department accepting the goods. Requisitions are usually prepared in triplicate. One copy is retained by the department making the request; another acts as the storeskeeper's receipt; and the third is a notice to the accounting or cost department for cost distribution. To prevent the indiscriminate writing of requisitions for questionable purposes, some organizations establish policies requiring that requisitions be drawn only upon the authority of a bill of materials, an engineering order, or a sales order. In mercantile concerns, shipping orders rather than factory requisitions serve to authorize withdrawals from stores.

The processing function. Practices governing the control of goods in the process of production vary with the type of manufacturing operation. In all cases, however, responsibility for the goods must be fixed, usually on foremen or superintendents. Thus, from the time materials are delivered to the factory until they are completed and routed to a finished goods storeroom, a designated supervisor should be in control and prepared to answer for their location and disposition.

The system of internal control over work in process may include regular inspection procedures to reveal defective work. This aids in disclosing inefficiencies in the productive system and also tends to prevent inflation of the work-in-process inventory by the accumulation of costs for work which will eventually be scrapped.

Control procedures should also assure that goods scrapped during the process of production are promptly reported to the accounting department so that the decrease in value of work-in-process inventories may be recorded. Scrapped materials may have substantial salvage value, and this calls for segregation and control of scrap inventories.

The shipping function. Shipments of goods should be made only after proper authorization has been received. This authorization will normally be an order from the sales department, although the shipping function also includes the returning of defective goods to suppliers. In this latter case the authorization may take the form of a shipping advice from a purchasing department executive.

One copy of the shipping authorization will go to the storeroom; a second copy will be retained by the shipping department as evidence of shipment; and a third copy will be enclosed as a packing slip with the goods when they are shipped. These forms should be prenumbered and kept under accounting control. The control aspect of this procedure is strengthened by the fact that an outsider, the customer, will inspect the packing slip and notify the company of any discrepancy between this list, the goods ordered, and the goods actually received.

When the goods have been shipped, the shipping department will attach to a fourth copy of each shipping order the related evidence of shipment: bills of lading, trucking bills, carriers' receipts, freight bills, etc. This facilitates subsequent audit by grouping together the vouchers showing that shipments were properly authorized and carried out. The shipping advice, with vouchers attached, is then sent to the billing department, where it is used as the basis for invoicing the customer.

Established shipping routines should be followed for all types of shipments, including the sale of scrap, return of defective goods, and forwarding of materials and parts to subcontractors.

Record control

The cost accounting system. To account for the usage of raw materials and supplies, to determine the content and value of work-in-process inventories, and to compute the finished goods inventory, an adequate cost accounting system is necessary. This system comprises all the records, orders, requisitions, time tickets, etc., needed in a proper accounting for the disposition of materials as they enter the flow of production and as they continue through the factory in the process of becoming finished goods. The cost accounting system also serves to accumulate labor costs and indirect costs which contribute to the work-in-process and finished goods inventories. The cost accounting system thus forms an integral part of the internal control for inventories.

The figures produced by the cost system should be controlled by general ledger accounts. Two general types of systems are widely used. Under one, all transactions in a factory are passed through a "factory ledger." The net balance of this ledger is represented by a "factory ledger control" in the general ledger. The other system records the cost of materials, labor, and factory overhead in individual work-in-process accounts for each production order or process. These work-in-process accounts are controlled by a single general ledger work-in-process inventory account. In effect, a subsidiary work-in-process ledger is produced by the cost system, which must at all times be represented in the general records.

Underlying this upper level of control between the factory records and the general ledger is found a system of production orders, material requisitions, job tickets or other labor distributions, and factory overhead distributions. Control is effected by having each order properly authorized, recorded, and followed up. Payroll records are compiled only after all time tickets have been verified for accuracy. Indirect costs are distributed to the various job orders or processes through predetermined rates, which are adjusted to actual cost at the period's end. In addition, many cost systems have introduced methods of determining spoilage, idle labor, and idle machine time. These systems, known as "standard costing," provide for the prompt pricing of inventories and for a control over operations through a study of variances between actual and standard figures. All these various types of cost accounting systems are alike in that all are designed to contribute to effective internal control by tracing the execution of managerial directives in the factory, by providing reliable and accurate inventory figures, and by safeguarding company assets.

Companies having significant supply contracts with certain U.S. Government agencies are subject to the pronouncements of the Cost Accounting Standards Board. This five-member board, chaired by the U.S. Comptroller General, was established by Congress to narrow the options in cost accounting which are available under generally accepted accounting principles. Cost accounting standards adopted by the board are published in the *Federal Register* (the daily publication of the U.S. National Archives and Records Service). Unless Congress objects to a proposed standard, the standard becomes effective shortly after its final publication in the *Federal Register*.

The perpetual inventory system. Perpetual inventory records constitute a most important part of the system of internal control. These records, by showing at all times the quantity of goods on hand, provide information essential to intelligent purchasing, sales, and production-planning policies. With such a record it is possible to guide procurement by establishing points of minimum and maximum quantities for each standard item stocked.

The use of maximum–minimum stock quantities as a guide to reordering does not warrant placement of the ordering function in the hands of one employee and does not eliminate the need for review of decisions to order goods. Good internal control requires a regular review of prospective purchases before final authority is given for placing the order.

ILLUSTRATIVE CASE. A large aircraft manufacturer planned to adopt the practice of an annual "Family Day," on which the families and friends of employees would be invited to visit the plant, go through the latest-model airplanes, and view movies concerning aircraft of the future. In anticipation of a crowd of more than 100,000 people, the plant protection department decided to erect numerous rope lanes to guide the crowds along a designated route. The plan required enormous quantities of rope, so a supervisor called the material stores department to see how much rope was in stock and whether additional amounts might be borrowed from neighboring plants. He was informed that through error the company had recently purchased 100,000 feet of rope when it had intended to buy only 10,000 feet. The plant protection department obtained the rope and used it in handling the Family Day crowds with the intention of returning it to the stockroom in the next day or so. In the interim a stock clerk noticed that 100,000 feet of rope had been withdrawn from stores within the past week and that only a small quantity remained in stock. The stock clerk was accustomed to dealing in large quantities of various materials. Assuming that the withdrawal of 100,000 feet of rope during the past week was normal usage and that the company should have 10 weeks' supply on hand, the stock clerk prepared a "Rush" request for an order of 1,000,000 feet of rope.

This colossal mistake was corrected through an internal control practice of requiring a supervisor to review and give written approval to all requests for orders of material before a purchase order was issued. The supervisor was puzzled as to why such quantities of rope were needed and insisted upon a full investigation of the facts of the situation before he signed the request.

If perpetual inventory records are to produce the control implicit in their nature, it is desirable that the subsidiary records be maintained both in quantities and dollars for all stock, that the subsidiary records be controlled by the general ledger, that trial balances be taken at reasonable intervals, and that both the detailed records and the general ledger control accounts be adjusted to agree with physical counts whenever taken.

Perpetual inventory records discourage inventory theft and waste, since storeskeepers and other employees are aware of the accountability over goods established by this continuous record of goods received, issued, and on hand. The records, however, must be periodically verified through the physical counting of goods. There is no other adequate means of assurance that the book figures are accurate. Good internal control usually requires at least one annual count of all stock on hand. The counting process may be performed (1) at the end of the accounting period; (2) periodically throughout the year, a few items being counted every day or week; or (3) by a combination of these methods. One highly desirable method calls for periodic physical counts of various items combined with an annual inventory of all stock. This assures good control during the year, as well as an accurate ending inventory figure. Upon completion of each verification, it is necessary to adjust the book inventory to the quantities on hand per the physical count. All differences should be thoroughly investigated if the system is to accomplish the purpose of providing control.

Because physical inventory taking is a costly process, efforts have been made to apply statistical sampling techniques in the periodic counting process. If the sampling is appropriately planned and executed, the entire inventory need not be counted more frequently than every two or three years.

Internal control and the computer

Computers may be used for a number of inventory processes. Computer programs often provide for routine ordering of inventory items falling below established minimum quantities. The computer may also be programmed to periodically print out such information as slow-moving inventory items. An updated perpetual inventory ˙ sting can be provided by the computer as frequently as management requires it.

Audit working papers for inventories and cost of sales

A great variety of working papers may be prepared by the auditor in his verification of inventories and cost of sales. These papers will range in form from written comments on the manner in which the physical inventory was taken to elaborate analyses of production costs of finished goods and work in process. Selected working papers will be illustrated in connection with the audit procedures to be described in succeeding sections of this chapter.

Audit program for inventories and cost of sales

The following audit procedures for the verification of inventories and cost of sales will be discussed in detail in the succeeding pages:

1. Prepare a description of internal controls for inventories and cost of sales.
2. Test inventory and cost of sales transactions:
    2a.   Examine a sample of purchase orders.
    2b.   Test the cost accounting system.
3. Evaluate internal controls for inventories and cost of sales.
4. Participate in advance planning of physical inventory.
5. Observe the taking of physical inventory.
    5a.   Make test counts and compare the counts with final summaries of inventories.
    5b.   Review the handling of goods held on consignment and determine that inventories do not include any items owned by others or properly chargeable to other asset accounts.
    5c.   Verify existence of goods held by public warehouses and goods out on consignment.
    5d.   Review the cutoff of purchases and sales.
    5e.   Determine inventory quality and condition.
6. Review the bases and methods of inventory pricing.
7. Test pricing of raw materials or purchased merchandise.
8. Determine reasonableness and accuracy of the pricing of finished goods and work in process.
9. Apply "lower of cost or market" test to inventory prices.
10. Obtain copy of the completed physical inventory and determine its clerical accuracy.
11. Compare the completed physical inventory to perpetual inventory records.
12. Test the reasonableness of inventories by comparison with prior years, by application of the gross profit percentage method, by computing the rate of turnover, and by reference to capacity of storage facilities.
13. Determine whether any inventories have been pledged and review purchase and sales commitments.
14. Obtain and review an analysis of cost of sales.
15. Determine proper balance sheet presentation of inventories.
16. In the first audit of a new client, investigate the beginning inventory.
17. Obtain from client a letter of representations on inventories.

1. *Prepare a description of internal controls for inventories and cost of sales.*

As previously indicated, the study of internal controls may involve the filling out of a questionnaire, the writing of descriptive memoranda, and the preparation of flowcharts depicting organizational structure and the flow of materials and documents. All these approaches utilize the same basic investigative techniques of interview, study of reports and records, and the first-hand observation of employees' work.

During the course of his review of internal controls over inventory, the auditor should become thoroughly conversant with the procedures for purchasing, receiving, storing, and issuing goods and for controlling production, as well as acquiring understanding of the cost accounting system and the perpetual inventory records.

The auditor may also give consideration to the physical protection given inventories. Any deficiencies in storage facilities, in guard service, or in physical handling which may lead to losses from weather, fire, flood, or theft may appropriately be called to the attention of management.

Should the auditor's study of internal control over inventories (or plant and equipment) include consideration of the client's insurance coverage? Management's policy as to the extent of insuring assets against fire, flood, earthquake, and other hazards will vary greatly from one company to another. The auditor's responsibility does not include a determination of what constitutes "adequate" insurance coverage. Consequently the auditor's report on financial statements need not contain any disclosure on the client's policies with respect to insurance coverage.

Certain clients may wish to obtain comments from the auditor in his role of impartial and experienced observer as to the adequacy of the insurance coverage. If such advice is provided in a report on internal control, it represents a service to the client quite apart from attesting to the fairness of financial statements.

The matters to be investigated in the auditor's review of internal controls over inventory and cost of sales are fairly well indicated by the following questionnaire:

1. Are perpetual inventory records maintained both in quantities and dollars for each of the following classes of inventory:
   a) Raw materials?
   b) Purchased parts?
   c) Work in process?
   d) Finished goods?
   e) Supplies?
2. Are trial balances of perpetual inventory records taken at regular intervals and balanced with the general ledger control accounts?

3. Are the perpetual inventory records maintained by employees who have no access to materials stored?

4. Are the perpetual inventory records verified by physical inventories at least once each year?

5. Has full responsibility for all phases of taking and compiling the physical inventory been lodged in a responsible employee other than the storeskeeper?

6. Are physical inventories taken by employees other than storeskeepers?

7. Do the procedures for taking physical inventories require:
    a) Written instructions to all participating employees?
    b) Use of prenumbered tags?
    c) Accounting for all inventory tags whether used or not?
    d) Effective cutoff of receipts and shipments?
    e) Identification of obsolete and damaged goods?
    f) Segregation of goods held on consignment, customers' goods, and any other items owned by outsiders?
    g) Comparison of original detail listings with final summary of inventories?
    h) Independent verification of prices, extensions, and footings?

8. Are discrepancies between the perpetual inventory records and the physical count promptly investigated and appropriate adjustments of the records made?

9. Do adjustments of the perpetual inventory records require executive approval?

10. Are there effective accounting procedures and controls over the following types of material:
    a) Goods stored in public warehouses?
    b) Materials held by mills or other processors or suppliers?
    c) Goods shipped on consignment?

11. Does the company have a separate purchasing department responsible for the purchasing of all material, supplies, and equipment?

12. Are serially numbered purchase orders used for all purchase transactions?

13. Are purchase orders sent to the accounting department and used in the verification of invoices?

14. Does the accounting department account for the serial number sequence of purchase orders?

15. Do purchases in excess of specified amounts require approval of major executives?

16. Are price files maintained for items purchased frequently?

17. Are prices established at the time of placing orders for goods to be manufactured to order, rather than placing such orders on an "advise price" basis?

18. Are all incoming shipments, including returns by customers, processed by a separate receiving department?

19. Are prenumbered receiving reports used and copies thereof forwarded to the accounting department?

20. Are returned purchases recorded by the shipping department on shipping

documents and are these documents reconciled with credit memoranda received from vendors?

21. Are materials and supplies of all types held in central stores under custody of storekeepers and issued only on properly approved requisitions?

22. Are shipping and billing procedures so designed and correlated as to insure the billing of all materials leaving the plant?

23. Are there "gate controls" to assure that all outgoing shipments are legitimate and supported by adequate shipping documents?

24. Are the procedures for sale of scrap materials conducive to good internal control?

25. If a cost accounting system is being used:
    a) Is it controlled through the general ledger?
    b) Does it provide reasonably accurate inventory values for the balance sheet?
    c) Is it regularly used in costing sales?

2a.   Examine a sample of purchase orders.

As part of the study of internal controls for inventories and cost of sales, the auditor should trace specific transactions through the entire system, observing the use of authorizations, transfers of responsibility, adequacy of documents and records, and degree of understanding by employees of the control procedures prescribed by management.

In most businesses, the purchasing function is inherently susceptible to fraud. Purchasing agents are beleaguered by salesmen of prospective vendors, and the possibility of conflicts of interest through "kickbacks" and other fraudulent activities is often present. Although the auditor is not ordinarily responsible for discovering conflicts of interest, he should carefully test the purchasing procedures and make recommendations to the client for strengthening weak internal controls in the purchasing department.

The following procedures are typical of the audit activities relating to purchase transactions. The principal objective is to ascertain whether the internal control procedures stated to be in use are actually functioning, and thereby to determine the degree of reliance to be placed upon purchases recorded in ledger accounts.

1. Select a sample of purchase orders from purchasing department files.

2. Examine the purchase requisition or other authorization for each purchase order in the sample.

3. Examine the related invoice, receiving report, and paid check copy for each purchase order in the sample. Trace invoices to the voucher register and checks to the check register.

4. Review invoices for approval of prices, extensions, footings, freight and credit terms, and account distribution.

5. Compare quantities and prices in invoice, purchase order, and receiving report.

6. Foot and cross-foot voucher register on a test basis.
7. Trace postings from voucher register to general ledger and any applicable subsidiary ledgers.
8. Select a sample of debit memoranda and perform procedures comparable to above. Also inspect shipping reports for goods returned to vendors.

The auditor's review of purchases will often include a comparison of the volume of transactions from period to period. In this study the purchase transactions may be classified by vendor and also by type of product; comparisons made in this manner sometimes disclose unusual variations of quantities purchased or unusual concentration of purchases with particular vendors.

2b. Test the cost accounting system.

For a client in the manufacturing field, the auditor must become familiar with the cost accounting system in use, as a part of his study and evaluation of internal control. A wide variety of practices will be encountered for the costing of finished units. The cost accounting records may be controlled by general ledger accounts or operated independently of the general accounting system. In the latter case, the cost of completed units may be difficult or impossible to verify and may represent nothing more than a well-reasoned guess. Because cost accounting methods vary so widely, even among manufacturing concerns in the same industry, audit procedures for a cost accounting system must be designed to fit the specific circumstances encountered in each case.

In any cost accounting system, the three elements of manufacturing cost are direct materials costs, direct labor costs, and manufacturing overhead. Cost accounting systems may accumulate either actual costs or standard costs according to *processes* or *jobs.* The auditor's tests of the client's cost accounting system must be designed to determine that costs allocated to specific jobs or processes are appropriately compiled.

To achieve this objective, the auditor must test the propriety of direct materials quantities and unit costs, direct labor hours and hourly rates, and overhead rates and allocation bases. Quantities of direct materials charged to jobs or processes are vouched to materials requisition forms, while unit materials costs are traced to the raw materials perpetual inventory records. The auditor should examine job tickets or time summaries supporting direct labor hours accumulations and should trace direct labor hourly rates to union contracts or individual employee personnel files.

The auditor must recognize that a variety of methods are generally accepted for the application of manufacturing overhead to inventories. A predetermined rate of factory overhead applied on the basis of machine-hours, direct labor dollars, direct labor hours, or some similar basis, is used by many manufacturing companies. The predetermined overhead rate is usually revised periodically, but nevertheless leads each year to some underabsorbed or overabsorbed overhead. The auditor will ordinarily insist that any significant amount of overabsorbed overhead be applied to a proportionate reduction in inventory and cost of sales. Underabsorbed overhead should generally be written off as a cost of the period; if material, it should be separately disclosed in the income statement.

A distinction between factory overhead, on the one hand, and overhead costs pertaining to selling or general administration of the business, on the other, must be made under generally accepted accounting principles, since selling expenses and general administrative overhead are usually written off in the period incurred. The difference in the accounting treatment accorded to factory overhead and to "nonmanufacturing" overhead implies a fundamental difference between these two types of cost. Nevertheless, as a practical matter, it is often impossible to say with finality that a particular expenditure, such as the salary of a vice president in charge of production, should be classified as factory overhead, as general administrative expense, or perhaps divided between the two. Despite this difficulty, a vital procedure in the audit of cost of sales for a manufacturing concern is determining that factory overhead costs are reasonably allocated in the accounts. Failure to distribute factory costs to the correct accounts can cause significant distortions in the client's predetermined overhead rate and in over- or underapplied factory overhead. The auditor may find it necessary to obtain or prepare analyses of a number of the factory overhead subsidiary ledger accounts, and to verify the propriety of the charges thereto. Then, the auditor must determine the propriety of the total machine-hours, direct labor hours, or other aggregate allocation base used by the client to predetermine the factory overhead rate.

If standard costs are in use, it is desirable to compare standard costs with actual costs for representative items and to ascertain whether the standards reflect current materials and labor usage and unit costs. The composition of factory overhead, the basis for its distribution by department and product, and the effect of any change in basis during the year should be reviewed. The standard costs of selected products should be verified by testing computations, extensions, and footings and by tracing charges for labor, material, and overhead to original sources.

The auditor's study of a manufacturing company's cost accounting system should give special attention to any changes in cost methods made during the year and the effect of such changes on the cost of sales. Close attention should also be given to the methods of summarizing costs of completed products and to the procedures for recording the cost of partial shipments. (As pointed out in the spectacular Drayer-

Hanson case, lack of control over partial shipments may lead to gross misstatement of operating results.)

3. Evaluate internal controls for inventories and cost of sales.

The description and tests of the client's internal control for inventories and cost of sales provide the auditor with evidence as to weaknesses and strengths of the system. The auditor should appraise these weaknesses and strengths, and design the remainder of his audit program for inventories and cost of sales accordingly.

4. Participate in advance planning of physical inventory.

Efficient and economical inventory taking requires careful planning in advance. Cooperation between the auditor and client in formulating the procedures to be followed will prevent unnecessary confusion and will aid in securing a complete and well-controlled count. A first step in securing the desired elements of control and efficiency is the designation by the client of an individual employee, often a representative of the controller, to assume responsibility for the physical inventory. This responsibility will begin with the drafting of procedures and will carry through to the final determination of the dollar value of all inventories.

Advance planning will include:

a) Selection of the most advantageous date or dates for inventory taking.

b) Scheduling operations to minimize amount of work in process.

c) Determination of advisability of closing down entire plant or certain departments.

d) Segregation of obsolete and defective goods.

e) Designing of prenumbered inventory tags, summary sheets, and other necessary forms, preferably with copies for the use of the auditors.

f) Preparation of written instructions for all persons who are to participate in the physical inventory.

g) Arranging for control of goods received while inventory is being taken.

h) Arranging for services of engineers or other technicians needed to determine quantity or condition of certain goods or materials.

i) Planning control over all documents throughout the inventory taking, pricing, and summarizing.

Most important of all the preliminary work is that relating to the written procedures and instructions for the taking of the inventory. These instructions will normally be drafted by the client and reviewed by the auditor, who will judge their adequacy in the light of instructions used in previous years and the problems encountered in those years. If the instructions for taking inventory are adequate, then the auditor's responsibility during the count is largely a matter of seeing that the instructions are conscientiously followed.

Some companies prepare two sets of instructions for the physical inventory: one set for the supervisors who will direct the count and a second set for the employees who will perform the detailed work of counting and listing merchandise. A set of instructions prepared by the controller of a large clothing store for use by supervisors is illustrated in Figure 14–1.

In addition to a set of written instructions for supervisors, the clothing store previously mentioned also prepared a set of inventory instructions for the employees who were to participate in the count. These instructions were very specific and were thoroughly discussed with the employees prior to beginning the inventory. The inventory instructions prepared for employees are presented in Figure 14–2.

Advance planning by the auditor in charge is also necessary to assure efficient use of audit staff members during the inventory taking. The auditor in charge should determine the dates of the counts, number of auditors needed at each location, and the estimated time required. He should then assign auditors to specific locations and may in some cases provide them with a written statement of their duties. He may also wish to arrange for the cooperation of the client's internal auditing staff during the count, and possibly for the assistance of the company's engineers or other technicians.

When written instructions are prepared by the auditing firm for use of its staff in a particular engagement, these instructions are not made available to the client. Their purpose is to make sure that each auditor understands his assignment and can therefore work efficiently during the physical inventory. An example of inventory instructions prepared by a public accounting firm for the use of its own staff members is presented in Figure 14–3; these instructions relate to the same audit engagement described in the client's instructions to supervisors and employees illustrated in Figures 14–1 and 14–2. In every case, the audit staff members will have copies of the client's inventory instructions in their possession during the inventory observation.

5.   *Observe the taking of physical inventory.*

It is not the auditor's function to *take* the inventory or to control or supervise the taking; this is the responsibility of management. The auditor *observes* the inventory taking in order to satisfy himself that management is discharging its responsibility. In brief, observation of inventory taking gives the auditor a basis for an opinion as to the credibility of representations by management as to inventory quantities.

To observe the inventory taking, however, implies a much more active role than that of a mere spectator. Observation by the auditor also includes determining that all usable inventory owned by the client is

FIGURE 14–1

GLEN HAVEN DEPARTMENT STORES, INC.

Instructions for Physical Inventory,
August 4, 1974

TO ALL SUPERVISORS:

A complete physical inventory of all departments in each store will be taken Sunday, August 4, 1974, beginning at 8:30 a.m. and continuing until completed. Employees are to report at 8:15 a.m. to receive your final briefing on their instructions, which are appended hereto.

Each count team should be assigned and started by a supervisor, and should be periodically observed by that supervisor to assure that instructions are being complied with in the ·-counting and listing processes.

A block of sequential prenumbered inventory sheets will be issued to each supervisor at 8:00 a.m. August 4, for later issuance to count teams. Each supervisor is to account for all sheets--used, unused, or voided. In addition, each supervisor will be furnished at that time with a listing of count teams under his supervision.

When a count team reports completion of a department, that team's supervisor should accompany a representative of the independent auditors, McDonald & Company, in performing test counts. A space is provided on each inventory sheet for the supervisor's initials as reviewer. When the independent auditor has "cleared" a department, the supervisor responsible should take possession of the count sheets. All completed count sheets are to be placed in numerical sequence and turned over to me when the entire inventory has been completed.

Before supervisors and employees leave the stores Saturday evening, August 3, they are to make certain that "housekeeping" is in order in each department, and that all merchandise bears a price ticket.

If you have any questions about these instructions or any other aspect of the physical inventory, please see me.

J. R. Adams

J. R. Adams
Controller
July 24, 1974

FIGURE 14–2

GLEN HAVEN DEPARTMENT STORES, INC.

Instructions for Physical Inventory,
August 4, 1974

TO ALL EMPLOYEES:

A complete physical inventory of all departments in each store will be taken Sunday,
August 4, 1974, beginning at 8:30 a.m. and continuing until completed. You are to
report to your supervisor, R. W. Watson   , for assignment and final briefing at
8:15 a.m.

Inventory will be taken by two-member teams. One member will count and call
each stock item, the other will list each item on a prenumbered inventory sheet. All inventory sheets are to be returned to the supervisor from whom received, whether used,
unused, or voided. No voided or unused sheets should be destroyed.

Space is provided on the inventory sheets for listing department number, stock
number, description including season, quantity, market retail price, and initials of
counter and lister. No other markings or amounts should be listed on a sheet.

All boxed merchandise in a department is to be unpacked, counted by units, and
replaced in the box.

When counting for a department has been completed, the supervisor is to be
notified. He will review and test the counts together with a representative of the independent auditors, McDonald and Company. When test counts are completed and any
necessary corrections made, count teams will go to their next assignments.

Any questions concerning these instructions should be cleared with your supervisor
at the 8:15 a.m. briefing session.

J. R. Adams

J. R. Adams
Controller
July 24, 1974

FIGURE 14–3

CERTIFIED PUBLIC ACCOUNTANTS

Glen Haven Department Stores, Inc.
Inventory Observation—Instructions for Audit Staff
August 4, 1974

We will observe physical inventory taking at the following stores of Glen Haven Department Stores, Inc., on August 4, 1974:

Store	Store Manager	Our Staff
Wilshire	J. M. Baker	John Rogers, Fred Arnold
Crenshaw	Robert Bryan	Weldon Simpkins
Valley	Hugh Remington	Roger Dawson

Report to assigned stores promptly at 8:00 a.m. Attached are copies of the Company's detailed instructions to employees who are to take the physical inventories and to supervisors who are to be in charge. These instructions appear to be complete and adequate; we should satisfy ourselves by observation that the instructions are being followed.

All merchandise counted will be listed on prenumbered inventory sheets. We should make occasional test counts to ascertain the accuracy of the physical counts. Test counts are to be recorded in working papers, with the following information included:

    Department number
    Inventory sheet number
    Stock number
    Description of item, including season letter and year
    Quantity
    Selling price per price tag

We should ascertain that adequate control is maintained over the prenumbered inventory sheets issued. Also, we should prepare a listing of the last numbers used for transfers, markdowns, and markups in the various departments and stores. Inventory sheets are not to be removed from the departments until we have "cleared" them; we should not delay this operation.

Each staff member's working papers should include an opinion on the adequacy of the inventory taking. The papers should also include a summary of time incurred in the observation.

No cash or other cutoff procedures are to be performed as an adjunct to the inventory observation.

included in the count and that the client's employees comply with the written inventory instructions. As part of the process of observing the physical inventory, the experienced auditor will be alert to detect any obsolete or damaged merchandise included in inventory. Such merchandise should be segregated and written down to realizable value. In short, during the inventory observation the auditor is alert for, and follows up on, unusual problems either not anticipated in the client's written inventory instructions or improperly dealt with by the client's inventory teams.

The auditor will also make a record of the serial number of the final receiving and shipping documents issued before the taking of inventory so that the accuracy of the cutoff can be determined at a later date. Shipments or receipts of goods taking place during the counting process should be closely observed and any necessary reconciliations made. Observation of the physical inventory by the auditor also stresses close control over inventory tags or sheets. These should be prenumbered so that all tags can be accounted for.

Working papers will be prepared by each auditor participating in the observation of the inventory. These papers should indicate the extent of test counts, describe any deficiencies noted, and express an opinion as to whether the inventory appeared to have been properly taken in accordance with the client's instructions. The auditor in charge should prepare a concise summary memorandum indicating the overall extent of observation and the percentage of inventory value covered by quantity tests. The memorandum may also include comments on the consideration given to the factors of quality and condition of stock, the treatment of consigned goods on hand, and the control of shipments and receipts during the counting process. Figure 14–4 illustrates this type of memorandum.

Inventory verification when auditor is engaged after the end of the year. The auditor will, of course, not be able to observe a year-end physical inventory if his appointment as auditor is not made until after the end of the year.

A business desiring an independent audit should engage the auditor well before the end of the year, so that he can participate in advance planning of the physical inventory and be prepared to observe the actual counting process. Occasionally, however, an auditor is not engaged until after the end of the year and therefore finds it impossible to observe the taking of inventory at the close of the year. For example, the illness or death of a company's CPA near the year-end might lead to the engagement of new auditors shortly after the balance sheet date.

Under these circumstances, the auditor may conclude that sufficient evidence cannot be obtained concerning inventory to permit him to express an opinion on the overall fairness of the financial statements.

FIGURE 14–4

THE WILSHIRE CORPORATION
Comments on Observation of Physical Inventory   H-9

December 31, 1974

1. Advance Planning of Physical Inventory.

A physical inventory was taken by the client on December 31, 1974. Two weeks in advance of this date we reviewed the written inventory instructions prepared by Mr. L. D. Frome, Controller. These instructions appeared entirely adequate and reflected the experience gained during the counts of previous years. The plan called for a complete closing down of the factory on December 31, since the preceding year's count had been handicapped by movements of productive material during the counting process. Training meetings were conducted by Mr. Frome for all employees assigned to participate in the inventory; at these meetings the written instructions were explained and discussed.

2. Observation of Physical Inventory.

We were present throughout the taking of the physical inventory on December 31, 1974. Prior to the count, all materials had been neatly arranged, labeled, and separated by type. Two-man inventory teams were used: one man counting and calling quantities and descriptions; the other man filling in data on the serially numbered inventory tags. As the goods were counted, the counting team tore off the "first count" portion of the inventory tag. A second count was made later by another team working independently of the first; this second team recorded the quantity of its count on the "second count" portion of the tag.

We made test counts of the numerous items, covering approximately 30 percent of the total inventory value. These counts were recorded on our working papers and used as noted below. Our observation throughout the plant indicated that both the first and second counts required by the inventory instructions were being performed in a systematic and conscientious manner. The careful and alert attitude of employees indicated that the training meetings preceding the count had been quite effective in creating an understanding of the importance of an accurate count. Before the "second count" portions of the tags were removed, we visited all departments in company with Mr. Frome and satisfied ourselves that all goods had been tagged and counted.

No goods were shipped on December 31. We ascertained that receiving reports were prepared on all goods taken into the receiving department on this day. We recorded the serial numbers of the last receiving report and the last shipping advice for the year 1974. (See H-9-1.) We compared the quantities per the count with perpetual inventory records and found no significant discrepancies.

3. Quality and Condition of Materials.

Certain obsolete parts had been removed from stock prior to the count and reduced to a scrap carrying value. On the basis of our personal observation and questions addressed to supervisors, we have no reason to believe that any obsolete or defective materials remained in inventory. We tested the reasonableness of quantities of 10 items, representing 40 percent of the value of the inventory, by comparing the quantity on hand with the quantity used in recent months; in no case did we find that the quantity in inventory exceeded three months' normal usage.

V. M. H.
1/3/75

On the other hand, if circumstances are favorable, he may be able to satisfy himself concerning the inventory by alternative auditing procedures. These favorable circumstances might include the existence of strong internal control, perpetual inventory records, availability of working papers showing that the client had carried out a well-planned physical inventory at or near the year-end, and the making of test counts by the newly appointed auditor. If he is to express an unqualified opinion, his investigation of inventory must be thorough enough to compensate for the fact that he was not present when the inventory was taken. Whether such alternative auditing procedures will be feasible and will enable the auditor to satisfy himself depends upon the circumstances of the particular engagement.

5a. Make test counts and compare the counts with final summaries of inventories.

During his inventory observation, the auditor will make test counts of selected inventory items. The extent of the test counts will vary widely, dependent upon the circumstances of the individual case, but in general should cover a representative cross section of the stock on hand. All test counts should be recorded in the audit working papers for subsequent comparison with the completed inventory.

Serially numbered inventory count tags are usually attached to each lot of goods during the taking of a physical inventory. The design of the tag and the procedures for using it are intended to guard against two common pitfalls: (*a*) accidental omission of goods from the count, and (*b*) double counting of goods.

Many companies use two-man teams to count the inventories. Each team is charged with a sequence of the serially numbered tags and required to turn in any tags voided or not used.

The actual counting, the filling in of inventory tags, and the "pulling" of these tags are done by the client's employees. While the inventory tags are still attached to the goods, the auditor may make such test counts as he deems appropriate in the circumstances. He will list in his working papers the tag numbers for which test counts were made. The client will ordinarily not collect ("pull") the inventory tags until the auditor indicates that he is satisfied with the accuracy of the count.

In comparing his test counts to the inventory tags, the auditor is alert for errors not only in quantities but also in part numbers, descriptions, units of measure, and all other aspects of the inventory item. For test counts of work-in-process inventory, the auditor must ascertain that the percentage or stage of completion indicated on the inventory tag is appropriate.

If the test counts made by the auditor indicate discrepancies, the goods are recounted at once by the client's employees and the error corrected. If an excessive number of errors is found, the inventory for the entire department or even for the entire business should be recounted.

The information listed on the inventory tags is transferred by the client to serially numbered inventory sheets. These sheets are used in pricing the inventory and in summarizing the dollar amounts involved. After the inventory tags have been collected, the person supervising the inventory will ascertain that all tags are accounted for by serial number. The auditor should satisfy himself that numerical control is maintained over both inventory tags and inventory sheets.

The test counts and tag numbers listed by the auditor in his working papers will be traced to the client's inventory summary sheets. A discrepancy will be regarded not as an error in counting but as a mistake in copying data from the tags or as the result of a purposeful alteration of a tag.

The preceding discussion has assumed that inventory tags and summaries are prepared manually. Clients utilizing electronic data processing equipment may facilitate inventory counting and summarizing through the use of punched cards and "machine sensible" pencils. Tag numbers, part numbers, descriptions, and unit prices may be prepunched into cards utilized as inventory tags. Count teams then record counts with pencils that are computer sensible. The computer extends quantity times unit price for each punched card and prints out a complete inventory summary.

5b. Review the handling of goods held on consignment and determine that inventories do not include any items owned by others or properly chargeable to other asset accounts.

During the observation of physical inventories the auditor should make inquiries to ascertain whether any of the materials or goods on hand are the property of others, such as goods held on consignment or customer-owned materials sent in for machine work or other processing. Although such materials and merchandise are not to be included in inventory, their existence and quantity should nevertheless be verified. The auditor should also ascertain that no items properly chargeable to plant and equipment or other asset accounts have been included in inventory.

Audit procedures applicable to goods held by the client on consignment may include a comparison of the physical inventory with the records of consigned goods on hand, review of contracts and correspondence with consignors, and direct written communication with the consignor to confirm the quantity and value of goods held at the balance sheet date and to disclose any client liability for unremitted sales proceeds or from inability to collect consignment accounts receivable.

5c. *Verify existence of goods held by public warehouses and goods out on consignment.*

The examination of warehouse receipts is not a sufficient verification of goods stored in public warehouses. The AICPA has recommended direct confirmation in writing from outside custodians of inventories, and supplementary inquiries when the amounts involved represent a significant proportion of the current assets or of the total assets of a concern. These supplementary inquiries should, as a minimum, establish the existence, independence, and financial responsibility of warehouses, mills, or other concerns holding substantial quantities of goods belonging to the client. The auditor may refer to a business directory to verify the existence of a bonded public warehouse, or if the amounts are quite material, or any reason for doubt exists, he may decide to visit the warehouse, accompanied by a representative of the client, and to observe a physical inventory of the client's merchandise.

The verification of goods in the hands of consignees may conveniently be begun by obtaining from the client a list of all consignees and copies of the consignment contracts. Contract provisions concerning the payment of freight and other handling charges, the extension of credit, computation of commissions, and frequency of reports and remittances require close attention. After review of the contracts and the client's records of consignment shipments and collections, the auditor should communicate directly with the consignees and obtain full written information on inventory, receivables, unremitted proceeds, and accrued expenses and commissions as of the balance sheet date. Material quantities of goods in the hands of consignees at the close of the period may appear in the balance sheet as a separate classification of inventories.

Often, the client may own raw materials which are processed by a subcontractor before being used in the client's production process. The auditor should request the subcontractor to confirm quantities and descriptions of client-owned materials in his possession.

5d. *Review the cutoff of purchases and sales.*

An accurate cutoff of purchases is one of the most important factors in verifying the amount of the year-end inventory. Assume that a shipment of goods costing $10,000 is received from a supplier on December 31, but the purchase invoice does not arrive until January 2 and is entered as a January transaction. If the goods are included in the December 31st physical inventory but there is no December entry to record the purchase and the liability, the result will be to overstate both net income for the year and retained earnings, and to understate accounts payable, each error being in the full amount of $10,000 (ignoring taxes).

An opposite situation may arise if a purchase invoice is received and recorded on December 31, but the merchandise covered by the invoice is not received until several days later and is not included in the physical inventory taken at the year-end. The effect on the financial statements of recording a purchase without including the goods in the inventory will be to understate net income, retained earnings, and inventory.

These effects are the same regardless of whether the company uses the periodic inventory method or the perpetual inventory method. However, under the periodic inventory method, a cutoff error will also cause an error in the figure for cost of sales through use of an incorrect amount for purchases or ending inventory in computing the cost of sales. Under the perpetual inventory method, the cost of sales is not affected by an error in the cutoff of purchases; the cutoff error will, however, cause a discrepancy between the book figure for inventory and the physical count.

How can the auditor determine that the liabiity to suppliers has been recorded for all goods included in inventory? His approach is to examine on a test basis the purchase invoices and receiving reports for several days before and after the inventory date. Each purchase invoice in the files should have a receiving report attached; if an invoice recorded in late December is accompanied by a receiving report dated December 31 or earlier, the goods must have been on hand and included in the year-end physical inventory. However, if the receiving report carried a January date, the goods were not included in the physical count made on December 31.

A supplementary approach to the matching of purchase invoices and receiving reports is to examine the records of the receiving department. For each shipment received near the year-end, the auditor should determine that the related purchase invoice was recorded in the same period.

The effect on the financial statements of failing to include a year-end "in-transit purchase" as part of physical inventory is not a serious one, *provided* the related liability is not recorded until the following period. In other words, the primary point in effecting an accurate cutoff of purchases is that both sides of a purchase transaction must be reflected in the same accounting period. If a given shipment is included in the year-end inventory of the purchaser, the entry debiting Purchases and crediting Accounts Payable must be made. If the shipment is not included in the purchaser's year-end inventory, the purchase invoice must not be recorded until the following period.

Adjustments to achieve an accurate cutoff of purchases should of course be made by the client's staff; the function of the auditor should be to review the cutoff and satisfy himself the necessary adjustments have been properly made.

Chapter 13 included a detailed discussion of the audit procedures for determining the accuracy of the sales cutoff. The sales cutoff is mentioned again at this point to emphasize its importance in determining the fairness of the client's inventory as well as accounts receivable and sales.

5e. *Determine inventory quality and condition.*

The auditor's responsibility for determining quality or condition of inventories is less rigorous than his responsibility for determining existence and ownership of inventories, for he does not claim to be an expert in detecting deterioration or obsolescence of goods. However, an awareness of the problem and an alert attitude to recognize and act upon any evidence of unsatisfactory condition of goods is expected of the auditor.

To discharge his responsibility for inventory quality and condition, the auditor may have to rely upon the advice of an outside expert. For example, the auditor of a retail jeweler might request the client to hire an independent expert in jewelry to assist the auditor in identifying the precious stones and metals included in the client's inventory. Similarly, the auditor of a chemical producer might rely upon the expert opinion of an independent chemist as to the identity of components of the client's inventories.

The auditor should also be alert during the course of his inventory observation for any inventory of questionable quality or condition. Excessive dust or rust on raw materials inventory items may be indicative of obsolescence or infrequent use. Work-in-process inventories rejected by quality control inspectors are obviously of poor quality.

The auditor should also review perpetual inventory records for indications of slow-moving inventory items. Then, during the course of observing inventory taking, the auditor should examine these slow-moving items and determine that the client has identified the items as obsolete if appropriate.

6. *Review the bases and methods of inventory pricing.*

The auditor is responsible for determining that the bases and methods of pricing inventory are in accordance with generally accepted accounting principles. The auditor's investigation of inventory pricing will often emphasize the following three questions:

1. What method of pricing does the client use?
2. Is the method of pricing the same as that used in prior years?
3. Has the method officially selected by the client been applied consistently and accurately in practice?

For the first question—a method of pricing—a long list of alternatives is possible, including such methods as cost; cost or market, whichever is lower; the retail method; and quoted market price (as for metals and staple commodities traded on organized exchanges). The "cost" method of course includes many diverse systems, such as last-in, first-out; first-in, first-out; specific cost; average cost; and standard cost.

The second question raised in this section concerned a change in method of pricing inventory from one year to the next. For example, let us say that the client has changed from the first-in, first-out method to the last-in, first-out method. The cost of the ending inventory should be determined under both methods, if possible; the difference between the two amounts represents the dollar effect of the change in method upon the balance sheet and upon the year's earnings. This amount should be set forth in the income statement in accordance with the provisions of *APB Opinion No. 20*, "Accounting Changes." In addition, the nature and justification of the change in method of valuing inventory, and its effect on income, should be set forth in a note to the financial statements. Also, the auditor must insert a qualification in his report concerning the lack of consistency in the two years.

The third question posed dealt with consistent accurate application in practice of the method of valuation officially adopted by the client. To answer this question the auditor must test the pricing of a representative number of inventory items. The auditor's techniques for testing inventory pricing will be described in the three following procedures of this program.

In summary, it is important to emphasize that the auditor does not price the inventory. The client determines inventory prices; and he represents that a given method of pricing has been followed. The auditor's responsibility is to make sufficient tests to determine whether the client's representations are reasonably accurate.

7. Test pricing of raw materials or purchased merchandise.

The testing of prices applied to inventories of raw materials, purchased parts, and supplies by a manufacturing company is similar to the testing of cost prices of merchandise in a trading business. In both cases, cost of inventory items, whether last-in, first-out, first-in, first-out, average, or specific, is readily verified by reference to purchase invoices. In comparing inventory carrying values for raw materials or merchandise with prices shown on purchase invoices, the auditor should bear in mind that all trade discounts and rebates for quantity purchases should be deducted in the determination of costs, while cash discounts may or may not be deducted. The inventory prices may also properly include freight and insurance charges incurred in obtaining the goods.

An illustration of a working paper used by an auditor in making price tests of an inventory of raw materials and purchased parts is presented in Figure 14–5.

8. Determine reasonableness and accuracy of the pricing of finished goods and work in process.

Audit procedures for verification of the inventory values assigned to work in process and finished goods are not so simple and conclusive as in the case of raw materials or merchandise for which purchase in-

FIGURE 14–5

The Wilshire Corporation
Test of Pricing—Raw Materials and Purchased Parts (Fifo) H-5
December 31, 1974

Part No.	Description	Per Inventory Quantity Price	Per Vendor's Invoice Vendor	Date	No.	Quantity	Price
8Z 182	Aluminum 48x144x.025	910 sheets 10.10	Hardy & Co.	12/18/74	541E	1,000	10.10~
8Z 195	Aluminum 45x72x.032	804 sheets 9.01	Watson Mfg. Co.	11/29/74	2815	500	9.01~
				12/22/74	3207	500	9.01~
K1125	Stainless steel .025 x 23	80,625 lbs. .80	Ajax Steel Co.	12/3/74	K182	100,000	.80~
K1382	Stainless steel .031 x 17	65,212 lbs. .82	Ajax Steel Co.	12/3/74	K182	75,000	.82~
XL3925	10 H.P. Electronic motor	50 ea. 400.00	Cronyn Mfg. Co.	11/18/74	253	100	400.00~
XJ3821	¾ H.P. Electronic motor	645 ea. 30.50	Long & Co.	12/29/74	E3821	650	30.50~

Inventory value of raw materials and purchased parts selected
for price testing — $301,825.56

% of total raw materials and purchased parts selected for price
testing — $\frac{\$301,825.56}{\$503,615.10} = 60\%$

See audit program B-4 for method of selecting raw materials
and purchased parts for price testing.

~ - Inventory price appears reasonable.

V.M.H.
1/20/75

voices are readily available. To determine whether the inventory valuation method used by the client has been properly applied, the auditor must make tests of the pricing of selected items of finished goods and work in process. The items to be tested should be selected from the client's inventory summary sheets after the quantities established by the physical inventory have been priced and extended. Items of large total value may be selected for testing so that the tests will encompass a significant portion of the dollar amount of inventories. If statistical sampling is employed, the selection of items for testing will of course be on a random basis.

Let us assume that the client uses a job cost system and prices the inventory on a first-in, first-out basis. In this situation, the auditor may test the prices for finished goods by tracing the unit prices of selected products from the inventory sheets to the job cost cards. The auditor will already have determined during his study and evaluation of internal control the extent to which he may rely upon the client's job cost records. If the quantity of units on the most recently completed job covers most of the quantity in the year-end inventory, the cost per the job card should agree with the cost shown on the inventory sheet. If several completed jobs are included in the year-end inventory, it will be necessary to refer to additional job cost cards.

Next let us assume that the client's cost accounting system is known to have some weakness in internal control. In this case the auditor should examine the documents supporting cost accumulations on the job cards. For material cost, these documents will include material requisitions, perpetual inventory records for raw materials, and vendors' invoices. For the element of labor cost, the documents to be examined would include timecards showing hours worked on the job in question and pay rate authorizations from the personnel department for the workers involved.

Assuming that overhead has been allocated to the job cost card as a percentage of direct labor dollars, the auditor will compute the percentage relationship of overhead to labor cost on the job and compare this percentage with the overhead rate in use during the period. Of course, a predetermined overhead rate may vary significantly from the actual current level of overhead, and the auditor should verify the reasonableness of the overhead rate. The verification will consist of determining the total labor cost and total factory overhead for the current and preceding years. Attention should also be given to changes in the nature of items treated as overhead.

The auditor's approach to verifying items selected for testing from the work-in-process inventory follows a pattern similar to that described for finished goods. The total of the labor and overhead costs required to complete a job currently in process is of course not definitely determinable, but as a rule the overall reasonableness of the charges to date can be appraised by making comparisons with the costs of similar jobs completed in the recent past.

9. Apply "lower of cost or market" test to inventory prices.

Pricing the inventories at cost ordinarily leads to a satisfactory matching of costs and revenues. However, if evidence exists that the utility of goods when sold will be less than cost, the prospective loss should be recognized in the current period. There is no justification for carrying inventories at an amount in excess of net realizable value. The lower of cost or market rule is a common means of measuring any loss of utility in the inventories. Lower of cost or market valuation may be applied on an individual, group, or total inventory basis.

The AICPA, in discussing the lower of cost or market rule in *APB Accounting Principles,* issued the following warning:

In applying the rule, however, judgment must always be exercised and no loss should be recognized unless the evidence indicates clearly that a loss has been sustained. . . . Furthermore, where the evidence indicates that cost will be recovered with an approximately normal profit upon sale in the ordinary course of business, no loss should be recognized even though replacement or reproduction costs are lower.

For raw materials and purchased parts, the client will usually obtain replacement cost data from vendors' price sheets or direct quotations. Replacement cost for work in process and finished goods may be determined by reference to costs of products completed subsequent to the balance sheet date, or from cost estimates compiled by the client's personnel. If the inventory includes any discontinued lines, obsolete, or damaged goods, these items should be reduced to net realizable value, which is often scrap value.

ILLUSTRATIVE CASE. During the audit of an automobile agency, the auditor was observing the taking of the physical inventory of repair parts. He noticed a large number of new fenders of a design and shape not used on the current model cars. Closer inspection revealed that the fenders (with a total inventory valuation of several thousand dollars) were for a model of automobile made seven years ago. The records showed that only one of this type of fender had been sold during the past two years. The automobile dealer explained that these fenders had been included in the parts inventory when he purchased the agency two years ago, and that he had no idea as to why such a large stock had originally been acquired. He agreed that few, if any, of this model of fender would ever be sold. It had not occurred to him to write down the carrying value of these obsolete parts, but he readily agreed with the auditor's suggestion that the fenders, being virtually unsalable, should be reduced to scrap value.

10. *Obtain copy of the completed physical inventory and determine its clerical accuracy.*

The testing of inventory extensions and footings, though a fairly mechanical procedure, nevertheless often discloses substantial misstatements of physical inventories. The auditor may himself perform these tests; or he may request the client to obtain the services of a comptometer operator to perform the tests under the auditor's supervision.

Mere mechanical operation of an adding machine in a test of footings is often less effective than "sight-footing" to the nearest hundred dollars or thousand dollars. Any substantial footing error indicated by sight-footing may be verified by precise mechanical footing.

In testing extensions, the auditor should be alert for two sources of substantial errors—misplaced decimal points and incorrect extension of *count* units by *price* units. For example, an inventory listing that extends 1,000 units times $1.00C (per hundred) as $1,000 will be over-stated $990. An inventory extension of 1,000 sheets of steel times $1 per pound will be substantially understated if each sheet of steel weighs more than one pound.

11.   *Compare the completed physical inventory to perpetual inventory records.*

The auditor should compare the quantities and values of individual items per the physical inventory with the perpetual inventory records. The totals of various sections of inventory should also be compared with the corresponding control accounts. All substantial discrepancies should be fully investigated. The number, type, and cause of the discrepancies revealed by such comparisons are highly significant in appraising the adequacy of the system of internal control over inventories.

In the examination of concerns carrying on inventory counts continuously or at various times during the year, the auditor may gain considerable insight into the dependability of the records by a critical review of the adjustments arising from physical counts.

12.   *Test the reasonableness of inventories by comparison with prior years, by application of the gross profit percentage method, by computing the rate of turnover, and by reference to capacity of storage facilities.*

Gross errors in pricing, footings, and extensions of inventory, as well as the recording of fictitious transactions, may be disclosed by overall tests designed to establish the general reasonableness of the inventory figures.

A comparative summary of inventories classified by major types, such as raw materials, work in process, finished goods, and supplies, should be obtained or prepared. Explanations should be obtained for all major increases or decreases.

In certain lines of business, particularly retail and wholesale concerns, gross profit margins may be quite uniform from year to year. Any major difference between the ending inventory estimated by the gross profit percentage method and the count of inventory at year-end should be investigated fully. The discrepancy may reflect theft of merchandise, or unrecorded or fictitious purchases or sales. On the other hand, it may be the result of changes in the basis of inventory valuation or of sharp changes in sales prices.

Another useful test is the computation of rates of inventory turnover, based on the relationship between the cost of sales for the year and the average inventory as shown on the monthly financial statements. These turnover rates should be compared with the rates prevailing in prior years. A decreasing rate of turnover suggests the possibility of obsolescence or of unnecessarily large inventories. Deliberate stockpiling in anticipation of higher prices or shortages of certain strategic materials will of course be reflected by a declining inventory turnover rate. Rates of turnover are most significant when computed for individual products or by departments; if computed on a companywide basis, substantial declines in turnover in certain sections of the company's operations may be obscured by compensating increases in the turnover rates for other units of the organization.

13. *Determine whether any inventories have been pledged and review purchase and sales commitments.*

The verification of inventory includes a determination by the auditor as to whether any goods have been pledged or subjected to a lien of any kind. Pledging of inventories to secure bank loans should be brought to light when bank balances and indebtedness are confirmed. Examination of insurance policies may disclose a lien on inventory if endorsements making losses payable to a third party have been added to the policies. Replies to requests for confirmation of notes payable should be examined for evidence of liens, and a clear statement as to the existence of liens should be included in the inventory representations obtained from the client.

A record of outstanding purchase commitments is usually readily available, since this information is essential to management in maintaining day-to-day control of the company's inventory position and cash flow. The record of purchase commitments may be developed by the accounting department from copies of purchase orders. The total outstanding commitments will be reduced by every invoice received and processed.

In some lines of business it is customary to enter into firm contracts for the purchase of merchandise or materials well in advance of the scheduled delivery dates. Comparison by the auditor of the prices quoted in such commitments with the prices prevailing at the balance sheet date may indicate substantial losses if firm purchase commitments are not protected by firm sales contracts. Such losses should be reflected in the financial statements. A similar comparison of commitments and prevailing prices should be made near the end of the audit, since the relationship may have changed materially in the intervening period.

Purchase orders which may be canceled at the option of the buyer and orders which contain clauses providing for adjustment of prices to conform to changes in price indices or market quotations do not entail the possibility of loss inherent in fixed-price, noncancelable contracts and need not be disclosed in the financial statements in most cases.

The quantities of purchase commitments should be reviewed in the light of current and prospective demand, as indicated by past operations, the backlog of sales orders, and current conditions within the industry. If quantities on order appear excessive by these standards, the auditor should seek full information on this phase of operations. As a general rule, purchase commitments need not be mentioned in the financial statements unless significant losses are realized or the commitments are unusual in amount or nature. Nevertheless, purchase commitments should always be investigated by the auditor.

ILLUSTRATIVE CASE. A few years ago, the leading American manufacturers of aluminum anticipated that they would be unable to meet the rising demand for their product. Consequently, these companies entered into large, long-term contracts with the leading Canadian producer, calling for the purchase of many millions of dollars worth of aluminum annually for many years to come. Shortly afterwards the productive capacity of American aluminum fabricators increased to the point that it outstripped demand. The aluminum fabricators were then in a position for several years of being forced to purchase large quantities of aluminum from the Canadian producer at a time when they were closing down their own plants because of an inadequate demand for the product. The disclosure of purchase commitments in the financial statements, under these circumstances, is clearly essential if the reader is to obtain a satisfactory understanding of the business.

Sales commitments are indicated by the client's **backlog** of unfilled sales orders. Losses inherent in firm sales commitments are generally recognized in the lower of cost or market valuation of inventories, with "market" being defined as the net realizable value of the work-in-process or finished goods inventories applicable to the sales commitments. In addition, the backlog may include sales orders for which no production has been started as of the balance sheet date. The auditor must review the client's cost estimates for these sales orders. If estimated total costs to produce the goods ordered exceed fixed sales prices, the indicated loss and a related liability should be recorded in the client's financial statements for the current period.

In summary, the auditor must review the client's backlog to determine if there are any losses inherent therein. The auditor who does not study the backlog has not gathered sufficient competent evidence for inventories.

14. *Obtain and review an analysis of cost of sales.*

Much of the audit work necessary to verify cost of sales in a trading business has already been suggested in Chapter 13 dealing with the audit of sales and in the discussion of inventories in this chapter. Errors in cost of sales are usually caused by errors in beginning or ending inventories or from errors in accounting for purchases. The propriety of beginning and ending inventories is established in the verification of balance sheet items. The study and evaluation of internal controls for purchases were discussed earlier in this chapter.

It is axiomatic to the experienced auditor that nothing may be taken for granted in the process of verifying financial statements. As applied to the investigation of cost of sales, this means that in addition to the detailed testing of purchases and inventories, the auditor should review all general ledger accounts relating to cost of sales to make certain that they contain no apparent irregularities. Adjustments of substantial

FIGURE 14–6

The Constellation Company.
Acct. No. 501   Cost of Sales   R-1
Year Ended December 31, 1974

Month			Inventory Relief			Scrap Sales Proceeds	Under-(Over) absorbed Factory Overhead	Total
-------	--	--	Materials	Direct Labor	Factory Overhead			
Jan.			15 160 28	42 815 70 ×	64 223 55 ∧	(819 72)	1 214 68	122 594 49 ∧
Feb.			19 142 55 ×	47 922 18	71 883 27	(947 55) ⁿ	(881 19) ∧	136 119 31 ∧
Mar.			17 655 95	45 814 00	68 721 00 ∧	(742 88)	581 26	132 029 33 ∧
Apr.			20 944 16	50 222 16 ×	75 333 24	(1 482 67)	(987 44) ∧	144 029 45 ∧
May			19 446 82 ×	48 144 76 ×	72 217 14 ×	(1 289 77) ⁿ	(722 66)	137 957 29 ∧
June			22 814 70	52 581 22	78 871 83 ∧	(1 222 14)	381 14	153 426 75 ∧
July ①			21 214 14	51 582 16 ×	77 373 24 ×	(998 82)	(701 28)	148 469 44 ∧
Aug.			20 844 27 ×	51 018 00	76 527 00 ∧	(1 008 44) ⁿ	914 68 ∧	148 295 51 ∧
Sept.			19 842 10	49 827 14	74 740 71 ×	(882 92)	(481 16)	143 045 87 ∧
Oct.			22 822 90	53 018 10 ×	79 527 15 ∧	(1 871 28) ⁿ	714 28 ∧	154 211 15 ∧
Nov.			20 476 20 ×	48 218 70	72 328 05	(1 347 19)	(422 19)	139 253 57 ∧
Dec.			21 807 14	50 976 10 ×	76 464 15 ∧ ×	(1 548 02)	(781 10) ∧	146 918 21 ∧
			241 171 21 ∧	592 140 22 ∧	888 210 33 ∧	(14 000 40) ∧	(1 170 99) ∧	1 706 350 37 ∧

Dec. 31, 1974 Adjustment of perpetual inventory to physical inventory ③ { H-1   76 418 55
Write-off of loss on fixed price contract No. AF 219-716   H-4   22 841 16

                                                                              1 805 610 08
                                                                              C-2

Prepared by client

∧- Footed and cross-footed.
ⁿ- Computation tested – no exceptions.
×- Traced to relief of perpetual inventory accounts – no exceptions.
ʸ- Vouched proceeds to remittance advice from scrap dealer and to certified weight tickets – no exceptions.

① 150% of direct labor dollars. See R-1-1 for our satisfactory test of this predetermined rate.
② Net overabsorbed factory overhead is less than 1% of total factory overhead applied, hence immaterial.
③ See referenced working paper for satisfactory tests of these write-offs.
④ See H-3 for our satisfactory study of internal control for cost accounting system for year ended December 31, 1974.

                                                                              V. M. H.
                                                                              1/29/75
                                                                              14

amount should be investigated to the extent necessary to make their purpose clear to the auditor and to gain assurance that they do not represent manipulation designed to conceal irregularities. If this review of general ledger accounts were not made, the door would be left open for all types of gross errors to remain undetected—such obvious errors, for example, as closing miscellaneous revenue and expense into cost of sales.

In the audit of a manufacturing company the auditor must go beyond verification of the beginning and ending inventories of raw materials, work in process, and finished goods in order to establish the validity of the figures for cost of goods manufactured and sold during the period. Since the determination of cost of goods manufactured involves all the ramifications of (*a*) raw material purchases and issuances, (*b*) direct labor costs, and (*c*) distribution of overhead costs, the review of cost of sales of a manufacturing company is clearly a more complex task than for a retail store or a wholesale business.

The auditor of a manufacturer client should obtain from the client or prepare an analysis of cost of sales by month, broken down into raw materials, direct labor, and factory overhead elements. The analysis should also include a description of all unusual and nonrecurring charges or credits to cost of sales. Figure 14–6 illustrates an analysis of cost of sales for a manufacturing concern.

The extent of the auditor's verification of cost of sales for the year is largely dependent upon his evaluation of the client's cost accounting system. If the system is strong, the auditor may limit his tests to verifying that perpetual inventory records have been relieved for the cost of goods sold and that the predetermined factory overhead rate is reasonable. These tests are illustrated in Figure 14–6. A weak cost accounting system will necessitate extensive tests to determine that all goods sold are costed in reasonable amounts.

15. *Determine proper balance sheet presentation of inventories.*

One of the most important factors in proper presentation of inventories in the financial statements is disclosure of the inventory pricing method or methods in use. To say that inventories are stated at cost is not sufficient, because cost may be determined under several alternative assumptions, each of which leads to a substantially different valuation. *APB Accounting Principles* points out that:

It is important that the amounts at which current assets are stated be supplemented by information which reveals . . . for the various classifications of inventory items, the bases upon which their amounts are stated, and, where practicable, indication of the method of determining the cost—e.g., *average cost, first-in first-out, last-in first-out,* etc.

From the standpoint of analyzing the current earnings of the company, it is extremely important to know whether the reported profits have been inflated by price changes, as has often been the case under first-in, first-out, or that the effect of price rises has been largely excluded through the lifo method of valuation. The users of the financial statements also need to know whether the carrying value of inventory approximates current cost (as with first-in, first-out) or whether inventories are stated at cost of an earlier period (as with the Lifo method). If inventories are priced on the Lifo method, the disclosure of the current value of the inventory may facilitate analysis of the balance sheet by the banker, credit analyst, and others.

Other important points in presenting inventories in the financial statements include the following:

a)   Changes in methods of valuing inventory should be disclosed and the dollar effect and justification for the change reported, in accordance with *APB Opinion No. 20.* The auditor's report will contain a qualification in the opinion paragraph because of the lack of consistency between years.

b)   Separate listing is desirable for the various classifications of inventory, such as finished goods, work in process, and raw materials.

c)   If any portion of the inventory has been pledged to secure liabilities, full disclosure of the arrangement should be made.

d)   Purchase commitments need be disclosed only when extraordinary in nature or involving losses.

e)   Progress payments received on work in process under U.S. government contracts should be offset against work-in-process inventories in the balance sheet.

EXAMPLES OF DISCLOSURES OF INVENTORY PRICING METHODS. In many large companies the cost of certain portions of the inventory is determined on one basis and other portions of inventory on some other basis. Typical of the disclosure of inventory pricing methods are the following examples taken from published financial statements:

ALPHA PORTLAND CEMENT COMPANY

Inventories—at cost or market, whichever is lower:

Finished cement at cost under Lifo method......................	$ 2,547,980
Raw materials, in process, packages, and operating supplies principally at average cost..	1,907,376
Maintenance supplies and repair parts at or below cost..........	2,155,742

LEAR SIEGLER, INC.

Inventories—at the lower of cost (determined by the first-in, first-out method) or market:

Raw materials...	$16,969,758
Work in process.......................................	8,110,027
Finished goods.......................................	17,068,834
	$42,148,619

16. *In the first audit of a new client, investigate the beginning inventory.*

The need for the auditor to be present to observe the taking of the ending inventory has been strongly emphasized in auditing literature. However, the figure for beginning inventory is equally significant in determining the cost of sales and the net income for the year. In the initial examination of a new client, the auditor obviously will not have been present to observe the taking of inventory at the beginning of the year. What procedures can he follow to satisfy himself that the beginning inventory is fairly stated?

The first factor to consider is whether the new client was audited by another firm of independent public accountants for the preceding year. If a review of the predecessor firm's working papers indicates compliance with generally accepted auditing standards, the new auditors can accept the opening inventory with a minimum of investigation. That minimum might include the following steps: (*a*) study of the inventory valuation methods used; (*b*) review of the inventory records; (*c*) review of the inventory sheets used in taking the preceding year's inventory; and (*d*) comparison of the beginning and ending inventories, broken down by product classification.

If there had been no satisfactory audit for the preceding year, the investigation of the beginning inventory would include not only the procedures mentioned above but also the following steps: (*a*) discussion with the person in the client's organization who supervised the physical inventory at the preceding balance sheet date; (*b*) study of the written instructions used in planning the inventory; (*c*) tracing of numerous items from the inventory tags or count sheets to the final summary sheets; (*d*) tests of the perpetual inventory records for the preceding period by reference to supporting documents for receipts and withdrawals; and (*e*) tests of the overall reasonableness of the beginning inventory in relation to sales, gross profit, and rate of inventory turnover. An investigation along these lines will often give the auditor definite assurance that the beginning inventory was carefully compiled and reasonable in amount; in other cases these procedures may raise serious doubts as to the validity of the opening inventory figure. In these latter cases the auditor will not be able to issue an unqualified report as to the income statement. He may, however, be able to give unqualified approval to the balance sheet since this does not reflect the beginning inventory.

17. *Obtain from client a letter of representations on inventories.*

Public accounting firms generally obtain from clients a formal written statement concerning the overall accuracy of the inventories. The purpose of these representations is to emphasize to management that primary responsibility for the correctness of inventories and of the financial

FIGURE 14–7
Representations as to inventories

(Name of Accounting Firm)   Date _____
(Address)

Dear Sirs:

    In connection with your examination of the financial statements of the X Company, for the period ended December 31, 19‑‑, we make the following statements and representations concerning inventories:

    1. Inventories consisting of the following classifications:

Raw materials and purchased parts	$ XXXX
Work in process	$ XXXX
Finished goods	$ XXXX
Supplies	$ XXXX
Total	$ XXXX

were on hand December 31, 19‑‑, as determined by a physical inventory, taken under our supervision in accordance with written instructions.

    2. All quantities were determined by count, weight, or measurement.

    3. All inventories owned, and only inventories owned, are included in the above summary, and no inventories have been pledged or hypothecated.

    4. All liabilities for inventories have been recorded in the financial statements as of the above balance sheet date.

    5. All raw materials, purchased parts, and supplies are stated at the lower of cost or market, with cost determined by the first‑in, first‑out method after deduction of all trade discounts, consistent with the basis employed in the preceding period.

    6. Finished goods and work in process are stated at manufacturing cost, except for items having a lower net realizable value after proper allowance for completion and disposal costs, consistent with the basis employed in the preceding period.

    7. Proper provision has been made for obsolete, inactive, and damaged goods.

    8. There are no purchase commitments in excess of current market price as of the above balance sheet date.

    9. There are no sales commitments below inventory price and no purchase or sale commitments in excess of normal operations.

DATE _____   Signed _____
                                               Titles _____

statements as a whole rests with the client rather than with the auditor. Officers or other executives asked to sign such representations are prone to attach greater significance to the process of taking, pricing, and summarizing the inventory than they otherwise would. The obtaining of the inventory representations does not in any way reduce the scope of the examination to be made by the auditor; nor does it lessen his responsibility.

The points usually covered in the inventory representations include quantities, titles, prices, commitments, and condition. An example of a form of inventory representations in common use is shown in Figure 14–7.

GROUP I
REVIEW QUESTIONS

14–1.　Select the best answer for each of the following:

a)　A CPA's client maintains perpetual inventory records which he tests by physical count of items on a cycle basis during the year. Because of unique circumstances, the CPA does not participate in these physical inventory tests but satisfies himself as to the validity of the inventory records by other audit procedures. Inventories are a material factor in the determination of financial position and results of operation. The CPA's report should:

(1)　Be qualified as to scope only. *— if requested by client*

(2)　Contain a disclaimer of opinion.

(3)　Be qualified as to scope and opinion.

(4)　Be without qualification.

b)　For control purposes the quantities of materials ordered may be omitted from the copy of the purchase order which is—

(1)　Forwarded to the accounting department.

(2)　Retained in the purchasing department's files.

(3)　Returned to the requisitioner.

(4)　Forwarded to the receiving department.

c)　Marlin Company has an inventory of raw materials and parts consisting of thousands of different items which are of small value individually but significant in total. A fundamental control requirement of Marlin's inventory system is that—

(1)　Perpetual inventory records be maintained for all inventory items.

(2)　The taking of physical inventories be conducted on a cycle basis rather than at year-end.

(3)　The storekeeping function not be combined with the production and inventory record-keeping functions.

(4)　Materials requisitions be approved by an officer of the company. *Now flexible ... for 5¢ + 10¢ items*

d)　A CPA's client maintains perpetual inventory records. In the past all inventory items have been counted on a cycle basis at least once during the year and physical inventory differences have been minor. Now, the client wishes to minimize costs of conducting the physical inventory by changing to a sampling method in which many inventory items will not be counted during a given year. For purposes of expressing an opinion on his client's financial statements the CPA will accept the sampling method only if—

(1)   The sampling method has statistical validity.

(2)   A stratified sampling plan is used.

(3)   The client is willing to accept an opinion qualification in the auditor's report.

(4)   The client is willing to accept a scope qualification in the auditor's report. (AICPA, adapted)

14–2.   How does the independent auditor utilize the client's backlog of unfilled sales orders in the examination of inventories?

14–3.   What are cost accounting standards? *pricing mfg. products*

14–4.   What are general objectives or purposes of the CPA's observation of the taking of the physical inventory? (Do not discuss the procedures or techniques involved in making the observation.) (AICPA)

14–5.   For what purposes does the CPA make and record test counts of inventory quantities during his observation of the taking of the physical inventory? Discuss. (AICPA) *satisfy accuracy of counting provide evidence of extent of tests*

14–6.   What part, if any, does the independent auditor play in the planning for a client's physical inventory?

14–7.   For the past five years a CPA has audited the financial statements of a manufacturing company. During this period, the examination scope was limited by the client regarding the observation of the annual physical inventory. Since the CPA considered the inventories to be of material amount and he was not able to satisfy himself by other auditing procedures, he disclaimed an opinion on the financial statements in each of the five years.

The CPA was allowed to observe physical inventories for the current year ended December 31, 1974, because the client's banker would no longer accept the audit reports. In the interest of economy the client requested the CPA to not extend his audit procedures to the inventory as of January 1, 1974.

In his short-form report the CPA should mention his lack of observation of the January 1, 1974 inventory and his lack of application of other procedures to satisfy himself. He would then proceed as follows: (Select one of the following alternatives and justify your choice by a brief analysis of each alternative.)

a)   Issue an unqualified opinion only as to the balance sheet at December 31, 1974.

b)   Issue an unqualified opinion only as to the balance sheet at December 31, 1974 and disclaim an opinion on the results of operations and changes in financial position.

c)   Disclaim an opinion on the balance sheet at December 31, 1974 and the results of operations and changes in financial position for 1974, because of the significance of inventories in these financial statements.

d) Issue an unqualified opinion as to the balance sheet at December 31, 1974, and the results of operations for 1974, because his mention of the facts complies with the third standard of reporting that requires disclosure of the omission of any generally accepted auditing procedures. (AICPA, adapted)

14–8. Once the auditor has completed his test counts of the inventory, will he have any reason to make later reference to the inventory tags used by the client's employees in the counting process? Explain.

14–9. The client's cost system is often the focal point in the CPA's examination of the financial statements of a manufacturing company. For what purposes does the CPA review the cost system? (AICPA)

14–10. What charges and credits may be disclosed in the auditor's analysis of the Cost of Sales account of a manufacturing concern?

14–11. Explain the significance of the purchase order in attaining adequate internal control over purchase transactions.

14–12. What segregation of duties would you recommend to attain maximum internal control over purchasing activities in a manufacturing concern?

14–13. Do you believe that the normal review of purchase transactions by the auditor should include examination of receiving reports? Explain.

14–14. Many auditors feel that the substantiation of the figure for inventory is a more difficult and challenging task than the verification of most other items on the balance sheet. List several specific factors which support this view.

14–15. "A well-prepared balance sheet usually includes a statement that the inventories are valued at cost." Evaluate this quotation.

14–16. The Darnell Equipment Company uses the last-in, first-out method of valuation for part of its inventory and average cost for another portion. Would you be willing to issue an unqualified audit report under these circumstances? Explain.

14–17. "If the auditor can determine that all goods in inventory have been accurately counted and properly priced, he will have discharged fully his responsibility with respect to inventory." Evaluate this statement.

14–18. When perpetual inventory records are maintained, is it necessary for a physical inventory to be taken at the balance sheet date? Explain.

14–19. The controller of a new client informs you that most of the inventories are stored in bonded public warehouses. He presents warehouse receipts to account for the inventories. Will careful examination of these warehouse receipts constitute adequate verification of these inventories? Explain.

14–20. Assume that a manufacturing company which has been among your clients for many years changes its method of pricing inventories *must qualify (opinion) if valuation method of inventory pricing changed — inconsistency. requiring client footnote difference*

484 | Principles of auditing

during the current year. What effect, if any, will the change in pricing method have upon your audit procedures and audit report?

14–21. Hana Ranch Company, which has never been audited, is asked on October 1 by its bank to arrange for a year-end audit. The company retains you to make this audit and asks what measures, if any, it should take to ensure a satisfactory year-end physical inventory. Perpetual inventories are not maintained. How would you answer this inquiry?

14–22. Enumerate specific steps to be taken by an auditor to satisfy himself that a client's inventory has not been pledged or subjected to a lien of any kind. *1. confirmation with banks or loan co. 2. review insurance clause.*

GROUP II
QUESTIONS REQUIRING ANALYSIS

14–23. Select the best answer for the following and justify your choice by a brief analysis of each of the four alternatives.

Columbia Company stores a portion of its finished goods inventory in a reputable public warehouse. Certain customers have been authorized to make withdrawals at will from the public warehouse, which informs Columbia Company daily of the withdrawals and balances on hand. In connection with his examination of the financial statements of Columbia Company for the year ended February 28, 1974, the CPA generally will rely most upon his—

a) Examination of the report from the public warehouse for February 28, 1974.

b) Direct confirmation of the balances stored as of February 28, 1974. *(when internal control good)*

c) Observation of the physical inventory on February 28, 1974.

d) Observation of a daily physical inventory sometime during the year ended February 28, 1974. (AICPA, adapted)

14–24. You have been asked to examine the financial statements of Wilson Corporation, a roadbuilding contractor which has never before been audited by CPAs. During your interim work, you learn that Wilson excludes a significant inventory item from its annual balance sheet. This inventory item, which Wilson management claims is approximately the same amount each year, is gravel which has been processed for use in road building and is placed at different road construction sites wherever it might be used. The client states that any unused gravel at the completion of a construction contract is never moved to another job site; in fact, the gravel often disappears because of thefts during winter months when road construction is suspended.

Would you be willing to issue an unqualified audit report on the financial statements of Wilson Corporation? Explain.

14–25. You have been retained by a corporation engaged in the purchasing, raising, and selling of livestock to examine its financial statements for the year ended September 30, 1974. During your preliminary investigation, you learn that cattle inventory is a material asset in the balance sheet. The client's accounting records for cattle purchases, sales, and known death losses appear well maintained; however, reconciling the perpetual inventory of cattle with physical inventory appears to be less than satisfactory. Your test counts of cattle enclosed in selected fenced pastures indicate that only a few of the pasture counts agree with the perpetual inventory records. In most cases, discrepancies between actual counts and perpetual records occurred and ranged from small to quite substantial. From your inquiries of client personnel you learn that the cattle break pasture fences and mingle with the cattle in adjoining pastures or stray out on the nearby roads. Some pastures are unfenced because of rough terrain, and cattle roam into timbered or inaccessible areas where they cannot be counted.

What effect will these circumstances have upon your audit report opinion on the financial statements? Explain.

14–26. The Sherman Manufacturing Company employs standard costs in its cost accounting system. List the audit procedures that you would apply to satisfy yourself that Sherman's cost standards and related variance amounts are acceptable and have not distorted the financial statements. (Confine your audit procedures to those applicable to materials.) (AICPA, adapted)

14–27. At the beginning of your annual audit of The Seacrest Manufacturing Company's financial statements for the year ended December 31, 1974, the company president confides in you that an employee is living on a scale in excess of that which his salary would support.

The employee has been a buyer in the purchasing department for six years and has charge of purchasing all general materials and supplies. He is authorized to sign purchase orders for amounts up to $500. Purchase orders in excess of $500 require the countersignature of the general purchasing agent.

The president understands that the usual examination of financial statements is not designed, and cannot be relied upon, to disclose fraud or conflicts of interest, although their discovery may result. The president authorizes you, however, to expand your regular audit procedures and to apply additional audit procedures to determine whether there is any evidence that the buyer has been misappropriating company funds or has been engaged in activities that were a conflict of interests.

Required:

a)   List the audit procedures that you would apply to the company records and documents in an attempt to—

    (1)   Discover evidence within the purchasing department of defalcations being committed by the buyer. Give the purpose of each audit procedure.

(2)   Provide leads as to possible collusion between the buyer and suppliers. Give the purpose of each audit procedure.

b)   Assume that your investigation disclosed that some suppliers have been charging The Seacrest Manufacturing Company in excess of their usual prices and apparently have been making "kick-backs" to the buyer. The excess charges are material in amount.

What effect, if any, would the defalcation have upon (1) the financial statements that were prepared before the defalcation was uncovered and (2) your auditor's report? Discuss. (AICPA, adapted)

14–28.   A number of companies employ outside service companies which specialize in counting, pricing, extending and footing inventories. These service companies usually furnish a certificate attesting to the value of the inventory.

Assuming that the service company took the inventory on the balance sheet date:

a)   How much reliance, if any, can the CPA place on the inventory certificate of outside specialists? Discuss.

b)   What effect, if any, would the inventory certificate of outside specialists have upon the type of report the CPA would render? Discuss.

c)   What reference, if any, would the CPA make to the certificate of outside specialists in his short-form report? (AICPA)

14–29.   Santa Rosa Corporation is a furniture manufacturer employing approximately one thousand employees. On December 15, the corporation retained the firm of Warren and Wood, Certified Public Accountants, to perform a year-end audit. The president of the corporation explained that perpetual inventory records were maintained and that every attention was given to maintaining a strong system of internal control. A complete count of inventory had been made at November 30 by the company's own employees; in addition extensive test counts had been made in most departments at various intervals during the year. Although the company was not large, it employed an internal auditor and an assistant who had devoted their full time to analysis of internal control and appraisal of operations in the various organizational units of the company.

The certified public accountant who had audited the Santa Rosa Corporation for several years had died during the current year, and the company had decided to forego an annual audit. The physical inventory had therefore been taken at November 30 without being observed by an independent public accountant. Shortly thereafter, a major stockholder in the company had demanded that new auditors be retained. The president explained to Warren and Wood that the company was too far behind on its delivery schedules to take time out for another physical inventory but that all the papers used in the recent count were available for their review. The auditors reviewed these papers, made a thorough analysis of the internal controls over inventory, and made test counts at December 31 of large items representing 10 percent of the total value of inventory. The items tested were traced to the perpetual inventory records, and no significant discrepancies were found. Inventories at December 31 amounted to $4,000,000 out of total assets of $9,000,000.

Required:

Assume that the auditors find no shortcomings in any aspect of the examination apart from the area of inventories. You are to prepare:

a) An argument setting forth the factors that indicate the issuance of an unqualified audit report.

b) An opposing argument setting forth the factors that indicate the auditors should not issue an unqualified report.

14–30. One of the problems faced by the auditor in his verification of inventory is the possibility that slow-moving and obsolete items may be included in the stock of goods on hand at the balance sheet date. In the event that such items are identified in the inventory, their carrying value should be written down to an estimated scrap value or other recoverable amount.

Prepare a list of the auditing procedures that a CPA should employ to determine whether slow-moving or obsolete items are included in the inventory.

14–31. Assume that you are engaged in an audit of the financial statements of a manufacturing company and that you have asked the client to provide you with a letter of representations as to inventories.

Required:

a) Explain fully why it is desirable to obtain an inventory representations letter from the client.

b) Enumerate the specific statements or points of information that you would want the client to include in the representations letter.

c) Assume that the client refuses to sign an inventory representations letter. What effect would this have upon your audit and your report? Explain.

14–32. During your observation of the November 30, 1974 physical inventory of Jefferson, Inc., you note the following unusual items:

a) Electric motors in finished goods storeroom not tagged. Upon inquiry, you are informed that the motors are on consignment to Jefferson, Inc.

b) A cutting machine (one of Jefferson's principal products) in the receiving department, with a large "REWORK" tag attached.

c) A crated cutting machine in the shipping department, addressed to a nearby U.S. Naval Base, with a Department of Defense "Material Inspection and Receiving Report" attached, dated November 30, 1974 and signed by the Navy Source Inspector.

    d) A small, isolated storeroom with five types of dusty raw materials stored therein. Inventory tags are attached to all of the materials, and your test counts agree with the tags.

Required:

    What additional procedures, if any, would you carry out for each of the above? Explain.

14–33. Orlando Manufacturing Company retains you on April 1 to perform an audit for the fiscal year ending June 30. During the month of May you made extensive studies of the system of internal control over inventories.

    All goods purchased pass through a receiving department under the direction of the chief purchasing agent. The duties of the receiving department are to unpack, count, and inspect the goods. The quantity received is compared with the quantity shown on the receiving department's copy of the purchase order. If there is no discrepancy, the purchase order is stamped "O.K.—Receiving Dept." and forwarded to the accounts payable section of the accounting department. Any discrepancies in quantity or variations from specifications are called to the attention of the buyer by returning the purchase order to him with an explanation of the circumstances. No records are maintained in the receiving department, and no reports originate there.

    As soon as goods have been inspected and counted in the receiving department, they are sent to the factory production area and stored alongside the machines in which they are to be processed. Finished goods are moved from the assembly line to a storeroom in the custody of a stock clerk, who maintains a perpetual inventory record in terms of physical units but not in dollars.

    What weaknesses, if any, do you see in the internal control over inventories?

GROUP III
PROBLEMS

14–34. Western Meat Processing Company buys and processes livestock for sale to supermarkets. In connection with your examination of the company's financial statements, you have prepared the following notes based on your review of procedures:

    (1) Each livestock buyer submits a daily report of his purchases to the plant superintendent. This report shows the dates of purchase and expected delivery, the vendor and the number, weights and type of livestock purchased. As shipments are received, any available plant employee counts the number of each type received and places a check mark beside this quantity on the buyer's report. When all shipments listed on the report have been received, the report is returned to the buyer.

    (2) Vendors' invoices, after a clerical review, are sent to the buyer for

approval and returned to the accounting department. A disbursement voucher and a check for the approved amount are prepared in the accounting department. Checks are forwarded to the treasurer for his signature. The treasurer's office sends signed checks directly to the buyer for delivery to the vendor.

(3) Livestock carcasses are processed by lots. Each lot is assigned a number. At the end of each day a tally sheet reporting the lots processed, the number and type of animals in each lot, and the carcass weight is sent to the accounting department, where a perpetual inventory record of processed carcasses and their weights is maintained.

(4) Processed carcasses are stored in a refrigerated cooler located in a small building adjacent to the employee parking lot. The cooler is locked when the plant is not open, and a company guard is on duty when the employees report for work and leave at the end of their shifts. Supermarket truck drivers wishing to pick up their orders have been instructed to contact someone in the plant if no one is in the cooler.

(5) Substantial quantities of by-products are produced and stored, either in the cooler or elsewhere in the plant. By-products are initially accounted for as they are sold. At this time the sales manager prepares a two-part form: one copy serves as authorization to transfer the goods to the customer and the other becomes the basis for billing the customer.

Required:

For each of the numbered notes (1) to (5) above state:

a) What the specific internal control objective(s) should be at the stage of the operating cycle described by the note.

b) The control weaknesses in the present procedures, if any, and suggestions for improvement, if any. (AICPA)

14–35. On January 10, 1975 you were engaged to make an examination of the financial statements of Rath Motors Corporation for the year ended December 31, 1974. Rath has sold trucks and truck parts and accessories for many years but has never had an audit. Rath maintains good perpetual records for all inventories and takes a complete physical inventory each December 31. New trucks constitute the major portion of inventory.

The Parts Inventory account includes the $25,000 cost of obsolete parts. Rath's executives acknowledge these parts have been worthless for several years, but they have continued to carry the cost as an asset. The amount of $25,000 is material in relation to 1974 net income and year-end inventories but not material in relation to total assets or stockholders' equity at December 31, 1974.

Required:

a) List the procedures you would add to your inventory audit program for new trucks because you did not observe the physical inventory taken by the corporation as of December 31, 1974.

b) Should the $25,000 of obsolete parts be carried in inventory as an asset? Discuss.

c) Assume your alternative auditing procedures satisfy you as to the corporation's December 31, 1974 inventory but that you were unable to apply these alternative procedures to the December 31, 1973 inventory. Discuss (ignoring the obsolete parts) the effect this would have on your auditor's report in (1) the scope (or middle) paragraph and (2) the opinion paragraph. (AICPA, adapted)

14–36.   Your audit client, Household Appliances, Inc. operates a retail store in the center of town. Because of lack of storage space, Household keeps inventory that is not on display in a public warehouse outside of town. The warehouseman receives inventory from suppliers and on request from your client by a shipping advice or telephone call delivers merchandise to customers or to the retail outlet.

The accounts are maintained at the retail store by a bookkeeper. Each month the warehouseman sends to the bookkeeper a quantity report indicating opening balance, receipts, deliveries, and ending balance. The bookkeeper compares book quantities on hand at month-end with the warehouseman's report and adjusts his books to agree with the report. No physical counts of the merchandise at the warehouse were made by your client during the year.

You are now preparing for your examination of the current year's financial statements in this recurring engagement. Last year you rendered an unqualified opinion.

Required:

a) Prepare an audit program for the observation of the physical inventory of Household Appliances, Inc. (1) at the retail outlet and (2) at the warehouse.

b) As part of your examination would you verify inventory quantities at the warehouse by means of—
(1)   A warehouse confirmation? Why?
(2)   Test counts of inventory at the warehouse? Why?

c) Since the bookkeeper adjusts books to quantities shown on the warehouseman's report each month, what significance would you attach to the year-end adjustments if they were substantial? Discuss.

d) Assume you are unable to satisfy yourself as to the inventory at the audit date of Household Appliances, Inc. Could you render an unqualified opinion? Why? (AICPA, adapted)

14–37.   Barton Press Company is engaged in the manufacture of large-sized presses under specific contracts and in accordance with customers' specifications. Customers are required to advance 25 percent of the contract price. The company records sales on a shipment basis and accumulates costs by job orders. The normal profit margin over the past few years has been approximately 5 percent of sales, after providing for selling and administrative expenses of about 10 percent of sales. Inventory is valued at the lower of cost or market.

Among the jobs you are reviewing in the course of your annual examination of the company's December 31 financial statements is Job No. 2357, calling for delivery of a three-color press at a firm contract price of $50,000. Costs accumulated for the job at the year-end aggregated $30,250. The company's engineers estimated that the job was approximately 55 percent complete at December 31. Your audit procedures have been as follows:

(1) Examined all contracts, noting pertinent provisions.
(2) Observed physical inventory of jobs in process and reconciled details to job order accounts.
(3) Tested input of labor, material, and overhead charges into the various jobs to determine that such charges were authentic and had been posted correctly.
(4) Confirmed customers' advances at year-end.
(5) Reconciled work-in-process job ledger with control account.

Required:

With respect to Job No. 2357:

a) State what additional audit procedures, if any, you would follow and explain the purpose of the procedures.

b) Indicate the manner and the amount at which you would include Job No. 2357 in the balance sheet. (AICPA, adapted)

14–38. The internal control procedures relating to purchases of materials by the Scott Company, a medium-sized concern manufacturing special machinery to order, have been described by your staff assistant in the following terms:

"After approval by manufacturing department foremen, material purchase requisitions are forwarded to the purchasing department supervisor who distributes such requisitions to the several employees under his control. The latter employees prepare prenumbered purchase orders in triplicate, account for all numbers, and send the original purchase order to the vendor. One copy of the purchase order is sent to the receiving department where it is used as a receiving report. The other copy is filed in the purchasing department.

"When the materials are received, they are moved directly to the storeroom and issued to the foremen on informal requests. The receiving department sends a receiving report (with its copy of the purchase order attached) to the purchasing department and sends copies of the receiving report to the storeroom and to the accounting department.

"Vendors' invoices for material purchases, received in duplicate in the mailroom, are sent to the purchasing department and directed to the employee who placed the related order. The employee then compares the invoice with the copy of the purchase order on file in the purchasing department for price and terms and compares the invoice quantity with the quantity received as reported by the shipping and receiving department on its copy of the purchase order. The purchasing department employee also verifies discounts, footings, and extensions, and initials the invoice to indicate approval for payment. The invoice is then sent to the voucher section of the accounting department where it is coded for account distribution, assigned a voucher number, entered in the voucher register, and filed according to payment due date.

"On payment dates prenumbered checks are requisitioned by the voucher section from the cashier and prepared except for signature. After the checks are prepared they are returned to the cashier, who puts them through a check signing machine, accounts for the sequence of numbers, and passes them to the cash disbursements bookkeeper for entry in the cash disbursements book. The cash disbursements bookkeeper then returns the checks to the voucher section, which then notes payment dates in the voucher register, places the checks in envelopes, and sends them to the mailroom. The vouchers are then filed in numerical sequence. At the end of each month one of the voucher clerks prepares an adding machine tape of unpaid items in the voucher register and compares the total thereof with the general ledger balance and investigates any difference disclosed by such comparison."

Required:

Discuss the weaknesses, if any, in the internal control of Scott's purchasing and related procedures and suggest supplementary or revised procedures for remedying each weakness with regard to—

a) Requisition of materials.

b) Receipt and storage of materials.

c) Functions of the purchasing department.

d) Functions of the accounting department. (AICPA, adapted)

14–39. Virgil Company cans two food commodities which it stores at various warehouses. The company employs a perpetual inventory accounting system under which the finished goods inventory is charged with production and credited for sales at standard cost. The detail of the finished goods inventory is maintained on punched cards by the data processing department in units and dollars for the various warehouses.

Company procedures call for the accounting department to receive copies of daily production reports and sales invoices. Units are then extended at standard cost and a summary of the day's activity is posted to the Finished Goods Inventory general ledger control account. Next the sales invoices and production reports are sent to the data processing department. Every month the control account and detailed computer print-outs are reconciled and adjustments recorded. The last reconciliation and adjustments were made at November 30, 1974.

Your CPA firm observed the taking of the physical inventory at all locations on December 31, 1974. The inventory count began at 4 P.M. and was completed at 8 P.M. The company's figure for the physical inventory is $331,400. The general ledger control account balance at December 31 was $373,900, and the final computer run of the inventory punched cards showed a total of $392,300.

Unit cost data for the company's two products are as follows:

Product	Standard cost
A.............	$2.00
B.............	3.00

A review of December transactions disclosed the following:

(1) Sales invoice No. 1301, 12-2-74, was priced at standard cost for $11,700 but was listed on the accounting department's daily summary at $11,200.

(2) A production report for $23,000, 12-15-74, was processed twice in error by the data processing department.

(3) Sales invoice No. 1423, 12-9-74, for 1,200 units of product A, was priced at a standard cost of $1.50 per unit by the accounting department. The data processing department noticed and corrected the error but did not notify the accounting department of the error.

(4) A shipment of 3,400 units of product A was invoiced by the billing department as 3,000 units on sales invoice No. 1504, 12-27-74. The error was discovered by your review of transactions.

(5) On December 27 the Memphis warehouse notified the data processing department to remove 2,200 unsalable units of product A from the finished goods inventory, which it did without receiving a special invoice from the accounting department. The accounting department received a copy of the Memphis warehouse notification on December 29 and made up a special invoice which was processed in the normal manner. The units were not included in the physical inventory.

(6) A production report for the production on January 3 of 2,500 units of product B was processed for the Omaha plant as of December 31.

(7) A shipment of 300 units of product B was made from the Portland warehouse to Ken's Markets, Inc. at 8:30 P.M. on December 31 as an emergency service. The sales invoice was processed as of December 31. The client prefers to treat the transaction as a sale in 1974.

(8) The working papers of the auditor observing the physical count at the Chicago warehouse revealed that 700 units of product B were omitted from the client's physical count. The client concurred that units were omitted in error.

(9) A sales invoice for 600 units of product A shipped from the Newark warehouse was mislaid and was not processed until January 5. The units involved were shipped on December 30.

(10) The physical inventory of the St. Louis warehouse excluded 350 units of product A that were marked "reserved." Upon investigation it was ascertained that this merchandise was being stored as a convenience for Steve's Markets, Inc., a customer. This merchandise, which has not been recorded as a sale, is billed as it is shipped.

(11) A shipment of 10,000 units of product B was made on December 27 from the Newark warehouse to the Chicago warehouse. The shipment arrived on January 6 but had been excluded from the physical inventories.

Required:

Prepare a working paper to reconcile the balances for the physical inventory, Finished Goods Inventory general ledger control account, and the data processing department's detail print-out of finished goods inventory.

The following format is suggested for the working paper:

	Physical Inventory	General Ledger Control Account	Data Processing Department's Detail of Inventory
Balance per client.........	$331,400	$373,900	$392,300

(AICPA, adapted)

14–40. Webster Company, a processor of frozen foods, carries an inventory of finished products consisting of 50 different types of items valued at approximately $2 million. About $750,000 of this value represents stock produced by the company and billed to customers prior to the audit date. This stock is being held for the customers at a monthly rental charge until they request shipment and is not separated from the company's inventory.

The company maintains separate perpetual ledgers at the plant office for both stock owned and stock being held for customers. The cost department also maintains a perpetual record of stock owned. The perpetual records reflect quantities only.

The company does not take a complete physical inventory at any time during the year since the temperature in the cold-storage facilities is too low to allow one to spend more than 15 minutes inside at a time. It is not considered practical to move items outside or to de-freeze the cold-storage facilities for the purpose of taking a physical inventory. Due to these circumstances, it is impractical to test count quantities to the extent of completely verifying specific items. The company considers as its inventory valuation at year-end the aggregate of the quantities reflected by the perpetual record of stock owned, maintained at the plant office, priced at the lower of cost or market.

Required:

a) What are the two principal problems facing the auditor in the audit of the inventory? Discuss briefly.

b) Outline the audit steps that you would take to enable you to render an unqualified opinion with respect to the inventory. (You may omit consideration of a verification of unit prices and clerical accuracy.) (AICPA adapted)

14–41. Late in December, 1974 your CPA firm accepted an audit engagement at Local Jewelers, Inc., a corporation which deals largely in diamonds.

The corporation has retail jewelry stores in several Eastern cities and a diamond wholesale store in New York City. The wholesale store also sets the diamonds in rings and other quality jewelry.

The retail stores place orders for diamond jewelry with the wholesale store in New York City. A buyer employed by the wholesale store purchases diamonds in the New York diamond market, and the wholesale store then fills orders from the retail stores and from independent customers and maintains a substantial inventory of diamonds. The corporation values its inventory by the specific identification cost method.

Required:

Assume that at the inventory date you are satisfied that Local Jewelers, Inc. has no items left by customers for repair or sale on consignment and that no inventory owned by the corporation is in the possession of outsiders.

a) Discuss the problems the auditor should anticipate in planning for the observation of the physical inventory on this engagement because of the—

    (1) Different locations of the inventories.

    (2) Nature of the inventory.

b) (1) Explain how your audit program for this inventory would be different from that used for most other inventories.

    (2) Prepare an audit program for the verification of the corporation's diamond and diamond jewelry inventories, identifying any steps which you would apply only to the retail stores or to the wholesale store.

c) Assume that a shipment of diamond rings was in transit by corporation messenger from the wholesale store to a retail store on the inventory date. What additional audit steps would you take to satisfy yourself as to the gems which were in transit from the wholesale store on the inventory date? (AICPA)

GROUP IV
CASE STUDIES IN AUDITING

THE WESTERN TRADING COMPANY

14–42. The Western Trading Company is a sole proprietorship engaged in the grain brokerage business. At December 31, 1974 the entire grain inventory of the company was stored in outside bonded warehouses. The company's procedure of pricing inventories in these warehouses included comparing the actual cost of each commodity in inventory with the market price as reported for transactions on the commodity exchanges at December 31. A write-down was made on commodities in which cost was in excess of market. During the course of the examination the auditors verified the company's computations. In addition they compared the inventory prices with market prices at dates subsequent to the year-end. Before the end of the engagement the market declined sharply for one commodity until its market price was below the average inventory price. The auditors suggested that the inventory be written down to give effect to this decline in market price subsequent to December 31, 1974. The company agreed, and a write-down of $7,000 was made.

The auditors also examined the trading position of the company and found that there was a short position in grain trading; that is, the sales negotiated for future delivery exceeded the total of year-end inventory and purchase contracts. The indicated loss on these contracts was reflected in the financial statements. After the above adjustments, the final net income for the year amounted to $30,000.

At December 31, 1975, the auditors made a similar examination of the financial statements of The Western Trading Company. They found that the company had priced the inventory in the same manner as in 1974. The auditors followed procedures similar to those used in 1974, and at the end of their field work on February 2, 1976 noted that the inventories were priced at an amount that was not in excess of the market at that time. The trading position had been examined; the short position at the end of 1975 had an indicated gain of $4,000. No adjustment was proposed for this amount. Subsequent to the completion of the field work, but prior to the issuance of the audit report, there was a sharp decline in the market price of one commodity. The inventory was repriced by the auditors on the basis of the new market price, and the inventory value at December 31, 1975 was found to be in excess of market by approximately $21,000. The auditors proposed that the inventories be written down by $17,000 to this new market value, net of the gains on the subsequent sales. The management protested this suggestion, stating that in their opinion the market decline was only temporary and that prices would recover in the near future. They refused to allow the write-down to be made. Accordingly, the auditors took an exception in their audit report dated February 16, 1976, and the opinion paragraph of their report read as follows:

"Except for the effect of the failure to record the market decline in grain inventories discussed in Note 2 to the financial statements, in our opinion, the aforementioned financial statements present fairly the financial position of The Western Trading Company at December 31, 1975, and the results of its operations and the changes in its financial position for the year then ended, in conformity with generally accepted accounting principles. Except for the matter discussed in Note 2 to the financial statements, these accounting principles were applied on a basis consistent with that of the preceding year."

Note 2 stated:

"The company's grain inventories at December 31, 1974 were reduced by approximately $7,000 to reflect a decline in market value subsequent to that date. A similar market decline of approximately $21,000 subsequent to December 31, 1975 has not been recorded by the company. If this adjustment had been made as of December 31, 1975, the grain inventories shown on the accompanying balance sheet and the net income for the year would have been reduced by $21,000.

"At December 31, 1975, the net short market position of the company was 20,000 bushels of wheat; a gain of some $4,000 applicable thereto, based on the year-end market prices, had not been reflected in the accompanying financial statements."

Net income for the year 1975 amounted to $37,000 as shown by the company's income statement. Subsequent to the issuance of the auditor's report, the market reversed its downward trend and regained the level prevailing at February 2, 1976.

Required:

a) Does the "lower of cost or market" method include recognition of price declines subsequent to the balance sheet date? Explain.

b) To what extent should financial statements disclose by footnotes events subsequent to the balance sheet date?

c) If "adequate disclosure" of facts is achieved in the financial statements and accompanying notes, is the position taken by the auditors in their report thereby justified?

d) Were the auditors justified in issuing a qualified opinion in this case? Discuss fully, including alternative courses of action.

e) Would the entry proposed by the auditors have eliminated the necessity for a qualification if it had been made?

f) Was it necessary to comment on lack of consistency in valuation of inventories?

15

Property, plant, and equipment: Depreciation and depletion

THE TERM "property, plant, and equipment" includes all tangible assets with a service life of more than one year which are used in the operation of the business. Three major groups of such assets are generally recognized:

1. **Land.** Land used in the operation of the business has the significant characteristic of not being subject to depreciation.
2. **Buildings, machinery, equipment,** and **land improvements** such as fences and parking lots. Properties in this classification have limited lives and are subject to depreciation.
3. **Natural resources** (wasting assets) such as oil wells, coal mines, and tracts of timber. These assets are subject to depletion and should be present on the balance sheet as a separate subgroup.

Closely related to the property, plant, and equipment category are *intangible assets* such as patents, franchises, and leaseholds. However, intangible assets can more conveniently be considered along with deferred charges and prepaid expenses in Chapter 16.

The auditor's objectives in examination of property, plant, and equipment

In his examination of property, plant, and equipment, the auditor tries to determine: (*a*) the adequacy of internal control; (*b*) the existence and ownership of the plant assets; (*c*) the propriety of the valuation methods used; and (*d*) the reasonableness of the depreciation program.

Contrast with audit of current assets

In many companies the investment in plant and equipment amounts to 50 percent or more of the total assets. However, the audit work required to verify these properties is usually a much smaller proportion of the total audit time spent on the engagement. The verification of plant and equipment is facilitated by several factors not applicable to audit work on current assets.

Typically a unit of property or equipment has a high dollar value, and a relatively few transactions may lie behind a large balance sheet figure for plant and equipment. Secondly, there is usually little change in the property accounts from year to year. The Land account often remains unchanged for a long span of years. The durable nature of buildings and equipment also tends to hold accounting activity to a minimum for these accounts. By way of contrast, current assets such as accounts receivable and inventory may have a complete turnover several times a year.

In the discussion of inventories in Chapter 14, considerable attention was given to the problem of an accurate cutoff at the year-end. The auditor must make extensive tests to prove that the year-end cutoff of purchases and sales of merchandise is accurate, because an error in cutoff may cause an error of corresponding amount in the year's net income. Errors in making a cutoff of the year's transactions do not pose a comparable problem in the case of plant and equipment acquisitions; a cutoff error in recording the purchase or retirement of equipment will ordinarily not affect significantly the determination of net income for the year. Of course such errors could cause slight inaccuracies in depreciation, or in the timing of gains and losses on retirements.

Another important factor in explaining the relative speed and ease with which plant and equipment can be verified is that the auditor is not concerned with current realizable values. In the examination of current assets such as receivables, marketable securities, and inventories, one of the auditor's principal responsibilities is the determination of current realizable value. This objective is not carried over to the examination of plant and equipment, because these properties are not to be offered for sale. The auditor is not an appraiser of land values; he does not claim any skill in estimating the current market valuations of buildings or machinery. His opinion that a balance sheet is fairly stated is not intended as an assurance that the operating properties can be sold or replaced at the amounts listed.

The auditor's examination of property, plant, and equipment does not include a determination of the "adequacy" of insurance coverage for several reasons. The amount of insurance is logically related to current replacement value, and the auditor is not an appraiser of property values. Furthermore, the auditor's opinion on financial statements concerns the consistent application of generally accepted accounting principles rather than an evaluation of management's wisdom in deciding whether or not to carry insurance against some of the many risks inherent in property ownership.

Cost as the basis of valuation

Accounting authorities have long held that cost is the proper basis for valuing plant and equipment. The cost basis is a highly satisfactory one during periods of stable price levels, for it gives a degree of objectivity to the process of income measurement not otherwise obtainable. During periods of drastic price changes, however, the computation of depreciation expense in terms of the original cost of long-lived assets leads to the reporting of operating profits of questionable validity. The tremendous pressures generated by inflation and by mounting tax rates create a demand that some type of current value be substituted for historical cost figures. The base for depreciation provisions would then be more in keeping with current replacement costs. Recognition of the inadequacies of conventional methods of computing depreciation has increased in recent years as the underlying assumption of stable price levels has become more and more unrealistic.

Under present standards, however, cost is the only accepted basis for valuing plant and equipment. Financial statements which presented property, equipment, and related depreciation on a basis other than cost would not be in conformity with generally accepted accounting principles, and therefore could not receive unqualified approval from the auditor.

Use of a general price index to adjust depreciation

The AICPA has given extensive consideration to the feasibility of basing depreciation on replacement costs, in recognition of recent sharp increases in the prices of specific plant assets, but has so far concluded that to do so is neither practicable nor desirable.

The traditional objections to basing depreciation on replacement costs have stressed the difficulty of determining objective current value data for the variety of plant assets utilized by companies. The American Accounting Association took note of these objections in *A Statement of Basic Accounting Theory* issued in 1966, but nevertheless recommended presentation of "current costs" in columns parallel to the historical cost figures of conventional financial statements.

Recently, another approach has been suggested—the use of a general priced index to adjust depreciation. Depreciation would be converted from historical dollars to dollars of current general purchasing power by use of a price-level index such as the Gross National Product Implicit Price Deflator. This method would avoid the difficulty of determining valid replacement costs, yet achieve some meaningful matching of revenue and costs in terms of current dollars.

In *Financial Statements Restated for General Price-Level Changes* issued in 1969, the AICPA's Accounting Principles Board suggested the presentation of general price-level financial statements or data extracted therefrom as supplementary schedules, not in columns parallel to the historical-dollar data in financial statements. The board also advised that all general price-level information presented be based on **complete** general price-level calculations, not on partial computations such as depreciation.

In summary, although the Accounting Principles Board has sanctioned presentation of general price-level data as supplementary information, current practice calls for audited statements to present depreciation based on historical costs, regardless of certain recognized deficiencies in this approach.

Internal controls over plant and equipment

The principal purpose of internal controls relating to plant and equipment *is to obtain maximum efficiency from the dollars invested in plant assets.*

The amounts invested in plant and equipment represent a major portion of the total assets of many industrial concerns. The expenses of maintenance, rearrangement, and depreciation of these assets are a major factor in the income statement. The sheer size of the amounts involved makes carefully devised internal controls essential to the production of reliable financial statements. Errors in measurement of income will be material if assets are scrapped without their costs being removed from the accounts. The losses which inevitably arise from uncontrolled methods of acquiring, maintaining, and retiring plant and equipment are often greater than the risks of fraud in cash handling.

The plant and equipment budget

In large corporate enterprises the auditor may expect to find an annual plant budget used to forecast and control acquisitions and retirements of plant and equipment. Many small concerns also budget expenditures for plant assets. Successful utilization of a plant budget presupposes the existence of reliable and detailed accounting records for plant and equipment. A detailed knowledge of the kinds, quantities, and condition of existing equipment is an essential basis for intelligent forecasting of the need for replacements and additions to the plant.

Budgetary estimates of expenditures for plant and equipment will usually originate within the various operating divisions and will then be reviewed by the plant engineering department. The determination of costs may also require the cooperation of purchasing department personnel. Final approval of the budgetary estimates involves a critical review by the budget section of the accounting or finance division, emphasizing such considerations as attendant increases in property taxes, depreciation and insurance expense, the availability of funds, and the prospects for full utilization of the proposed addition throughout its useful life.

If the auditor is to perform the dual functions of verifying financial statements and rendering valuable services to management as analyst and consultant, his examination of plant and equipment may well include an appraisal of the methods of budget preparation and a review of the system of reporting variances between budgeted and actual expenditures for plant acquisitions. When the purpose of the audit is limited to the issuance of a short-form report, the time available will probably not permit a critical evaluation of the detailed steps in budget construction. The auditor may find, however, that this type of investigation has been performed by the internal auditing staff. Reference to the reports and working papers of the internal auditors is often a convenient method for the auditor to become familiar with the scope and dependability of the budgetary controls over plant and equipment.

If the auditor can satisfy himself that acquisitions of plant and equipment, whether by purchase or construction, are made in accordance with prior budgetary authorizations, and that any necessary expenditures not provided for in the budget are made only upon approval of a major executive, he will be able to minimize the routine testing of the year's acquisitions.

Other major control devices

Other important internal controls applicable to plant and equipment are as follows:

1. A subsidiary ledger consisting of a separate record for each unit of property. An adequate plant and equipment ledger, usually on magnetic tape or punched cards in large concerns, facilitates the auditor's work in analyzing additions and retirements, in verifying the depreciation provision and maintenance expenses, in comparing authorizations with actual expenditures, and in determining the extent of insurance coverage.

2. A system of authorizations requiring advance executive approval of all plant and equipment acquisitions, whether by purchase, lease, or construction. Serially numbered capital work orders are a convenient means of recording authorizations.
3. A reporting procedure assuring prompt disclosure and analysis of variances between authorized expenditures and actual costs.
4. An authoritative written statement of company policy distinguishing between capital and revenue expenditures. A dollar minimum will ordinarily be established for capitalization; any expenditures of lesser amount are automatically classified as charges against current revenue.
5. A policy requiring all purchases of plant and equipment to be handled through the purchasing department and subjected to standard routines for receiving, inspection, and payment.
6. Periodic physical inventories, designed to verify the existence, location, and condition of all property listed in the accounts and to disclose the existence of any unrecorded units.
7. A system of retirement procedures, including serially numbered retirement work orders, stating reasons for retirement and bearing appropriate approvals.

Audit working papers

Apart from a grouping sheet, the key working paper obtained or prepared by the auditor for property, plant, and equipment is a summary analysis such as that illustrated in Figure 15–1.

The significant point to note in this working paper (Figure 15–1) is the emphasis upon changes during the current period. The analysis serves as a basis for completion of comparable forms in the client's federal and state income tax returns and annual report to the SEC (if applicable); it also is often presented in a long-form audit report.

Among the other working papers commonly prepared in the audit of property, plant, and equipment are analyses of plant asset additions and retirements, analyses of repairs and maintenance expense accounts, and tests of depreciation provisions.

Initial audits and repeat engagements

The auditing procedures listed in subsequent pages are applicable to repeat engagements and therefore concern only transactions of the current year. In the auditor's first examination of a new client who has changed auditors, the beginning balances of plant and equipment may be substantiated by reference to the predecessor firm's working papers. If, in previous years, audits were made by other reputable firms of public accountants, it is not customary to go beyond a general review

FIGURE 15-1

The Manderville Corporation

Summary of Property, Plant and Equipment, and Accumulated Depreciation

December 31, 1974

K-1

Account No.	Description	Assets Balance 12/31/73	Additions	Retirements	Balance 12/31/74	Method	Rate	Accum. Depr. Balance 12/31/73	Provision	Retirements	Balance 12/31/74
151	Land	50,000.00	15,100.00		65,100.00						
152/3	Land Improvements	13,500.00	1,000.00		14,500.00 ✓	a.l.	5%	1,350.00	700.00		2,050.00 ✓
154/5	Buildings	450,000.00	49,500.00		499,500.00 ✓	a.l.	3%	29,202.00	14,242.00		43,452.00 ✓
156/7	Equipment	82,000.00	11,000.00	6,000.00	85,000.00 ✓	a.l.	10%	23,500.00	7,040.00	5,040.00	25,520.00 ✓
		593,500.00	76,600.00	6,000.00	664,100.00			54,052.00	22,002.00	5,040.00	71,022.00
			K-1-1		K				K-1-2	K-1-1	K

✓ — Footed plant and equipment subsidiary ledger
Cards. No exceptions.

V.M.H.
1/19/75

of the past history of the plant and equipment as recorded in the accounts.

In a first audit of a concern for which satisfactory audits by independent public accountants have not previously been made, the ideal approach is a complete historical analysis of the property accounts. By thorough review of all major charges and credits to the property accounts since their inception, the auditor can determine whether the company has consistently followed good accounting practices in recording capital additions and retirements. This review of the transactions of prior years should include verification of the cost of assets by examination of documentary evidence in much the same manner used in verifying changes of the current period.

If the client has been in business for a long period of years, the review of transactions in earlier years must necessarily be performed on a test basis in order to stay within reasonable time limits. However, the importance of an analysis of transactions of prior years deserves emphasis. Only by this approach can the auditor place himself in a sound position to express an opinion as to the propriety of the current period's depreciation. If repair and maintenance expenses have been capitalized, or asset additions have been recorded as operating expenses, or retirements of property have gone unrecorded, the entire depreciation program is invalidated regardless of the care taken in the selection of depreciation rates. The auditor should make clear to the client that the initial examination of plant and equipment requires procedures which need not be duplicated in subsequent engagements.

Audit program for property, plant, and equipment

The following procedures are typical of the work required in many engagements for the verification of property, plant, and equipment. The procedures for accumulated depreciation are covered in a separate program on pages 516–17.

1. Obtain a description of the internal control for property, plant, and equipment.
2. Test property, plant, and equipment transactions.
3. Evaluate internal control for property, plant, and equipment.
4. Determine that the plant and equipment ledger is in agreement with the control accounts.
5. Verify legal ownership of property, plant, and equipment.
6. Verify additions to property during the year.
7. Verify retirements of property during the year.
8. Make physical inspection of substantial additions and consider the need for a complete physical inventory of plant and equipment.

9. Obtain or prepare analyses of repair and maintenance expense accounts.
10. Review accounting policy for tools and patterns.
11. Investigate the status of property not in current use.
12. Obtain or prepare a summary analysis showing changes during the year in property owned.
13. Review rental revenue from land, buildings, and equipment.
14. Determine proper balance sheet presentation.

1. Obtain a description of the internal control for property, plant, and equipment.

In his study of internal control for plant and equipment, the auditor may utilize a written description, flowcharts, or an internal control questionnaire such as the following.

1. Are plant ledgers maintained?
2. Are plant ledgers regularly balanced with general ledger control accounts?
3. Do the plant ledgers include records of accumulated depreciation on individual units?
4. Are periodic physical inventories of plant and equipment taken and compared with the plant ledgers?
5. Do all units of equipment bear a metal tag with an identification number corresponding to the number on the detail plant records?
6. Are all plant assets recorded at cost?
7. Are periodic appraisals made for the purpose of establishing insurable values?
8. With respect to additions to plant and equipment:
    a) Are all additions controlled by a plant expenditure budget?
    b) Are variations between budget and actual cost of plant additions subject to review and approval of major executives?
    c) Are all purchases authorized in advance by appropriate officials?
    d) Are expenditures for construction or installation of plant and equipment by the company's own employees adequately controlled by means of construction work orders and detailed records of labor time and materials?
9. With respect to retirements of plant and equipment:
    a) Does the sale, transfer, or dismantling of equipment require written executive approval on specially designed, serially numbered forms?
    b) Does the accounting department receive a copy of each form used to authorize sale, transfer, or dismantling of equipment?
    c) Are the metal identification tags removed from equipment sold or scrapped, and forwarded to the accounting department?

d) Are the detail accounts for plant assets and related allowances for depreciation promptly adjusted when equipment is sold, dismantled, or transferred?

10. Are fully depreciated assets carried in the plant ledgers as long as these items remain in use?

11. Are small tools kept in designated locations under the custody of authorized employees?

12. Is there a written policy for the guidance of accounting personnel in distinguishing between capital expenditures and revenue expenditures?

13. Are detailed accounting records maintained showing the value and location of returnable containers?

2. Test property, plant, and equipment transactions.

Generally, the auditor need not design a special audit program for testing additions to and retirements of plant assets. The auditor's customary tests of purchases, accounts payable, and cash disbursements transactions will provide evidence as to the controls for additions to the property accounts; and the test of cash receipts will generally include the verification of sales of property and equipment.

3. Evaluate internal control for property, plant, and equipment.

The evaluation of internal control for plant assets includes an identification of weaknesses and unusual strengths in controls. The auditor then selects the audit procedures necessary to provide sufficient competent evidence as to existence, ownership, and valuation of the client's property, plant, and equipment, given the quality of the internal control for plant assets.

4. Determine that the plant and equipment ledger is in agreement with the control accounts.

Before a detailed analysis of changes in property accounts during the year is made, it is necessary to determine that the individual plant asset records in the subsidiary ledger agree in total with the balances in the general ledger control accounts. This is also a desirable prerequisite to any tests of the ledger by physical inspection of plant and equipment. Adding machine tapes prepared from the subsidiary property ledger should also be compared with the closing balances shown on the summary analysis obtained in procedure 12, below, and a notation of this comparison made on the analysis.

5. Verify legal ownership of property, plant, and equipment.

To determine that plant assets are the property of the client, the auditor looks for such evidence as a deed, title insurance policy, tax bills, receipts for payments to mortgagee, and fire insurance policies. In addition, the fact that rental payments are not being made is supporting evidence of ownership.

It is sometimes suggested that the auditor may verify ownership of real property and the absence of liens by examination of public records. This step is seldom taken, but a title search may in some circumstances be completed by a title insurance company for the auditor. Inspection of the documentary evidence listed above usually provides adequate proof of ownership. If some doubt exists as to whether the client has clear title to property, the auditor should obtain the opinion of the client's legal counsel.

In the first audit of a company, the auditor should obtain a copy of the deed for inclusion in the permanent file. The legal description in the deed should be compared with that in the title insurance policy or abstract of title. Possession of a deed is not proof of present owner-ship, because in the sale of real property a new deed is usually prepared and the seller may retain the old one. This is true of title insurance policies as well. Better evidence of continuing ownership is found in tax bills made out in the name of the client, and in fire insurance policies, rent payments from lessees, and regular interest payments to a mort-gagee or trustee.

The disclosure of liens on property will usually be made during the examination of liabilities, but in the audit work on plant and equipment the auditor should be alert for evidence indicating the existence of liens. Purchase contracts examined in verifying the cost of property may reveal unpaid balances and installment sales contracts. Insurance policies may contain "loss payable" endorsements in favor of a mortgagee or trustee.

The ownership of automobiles and trucks can readily be ascertained by the auditor by reference to certificates of title and registration documents. The ease of transfer of title to automotive equipment plus the fact that it is often used as collateral for loans makes it important that the auditor verify title to such property.

6. Verify additions to property during the year.

The vouching of additions to the property accounts during the period under audit is one of the most important steps in the verification of plant and equipment. The extent of the vouching is dependent upon the auditor's evaluation of internal control for plant and equipment ex-penditures. The vouching process utilizes a working paper analysis of the general ledger control accounts and will include the tracing of entries through the journals to the original documents, such as contracts, deeds, construction work orders, and authorization by directors.

The specific steps to be taken in investigating the year's property acquisitions will usually include the following:

a) Examine authorizations for all major acquisitions, including assets both purchased and constructed.

b) Review changes during the year in construction in progress and examine supporting work orders, both incomplete and closed.

c) Trace transfers from the Construction in Progress account to the property accounts, observing propriety of classification. Determine that all completed items have been transferred.

d) On a test basis, vouch purchases of plant and equipment assets to invoices, deeds, contracts, or other supporting documents. Test extensions, footings, and treatment of discounts.

e) Investigate all instances in which the actual cost of acquisitions substantially exceeded authorized amounts. Determine whether such excess expenditures were analyzed and approved by appropriate officials.

f) Investigate fully any debits to property accounts not arising from acquisition of physical assets.

g) Determine that the total contract price of any plant and equipment assets purchased on the installment plan is reflected in the asset accounts and that the unpaid installments are set up as liabilities. Ascertain that all plant and equipment "leases" that are in effect installment purchases are accounted for in a similar fashion. Interest charges should not be capitalized as a cost of the asset acquired.

h) Obtain for the working papers full information concerning any large uncompleted contracts for acquisitions of plant and equipment.

i) Discuss the year's additions with the architect, plant engineer, or building superintendent for the purpose of ascertaining generally that additions have not been charged to expense; that repairs, replacements, and renewals have not been improperly capitalized; and that units replaced, sold, or scrapped have been properly recorded.

Assets acquired in transactions involving trade-ins or exchanges should theoretically be valued at the total of the cash paid plus the cash value of the article traded in. This view represents a segregation of the transaction into its components—that is, a hypothetical sale of the asset disposed of and use of the sales proceeds along with other funds to buy new equipment. In practice the auditor usually finds trade-in transactions recorded in the manner required by income tax regulations. These regulations do not provide for recognition of gain or loss on such exchanges and specify a valuation for the new asset equal to the undepreciated cost of the trade-in plus any additional payments made or to be made. This procedure is acceptable because of its convenience and because the results do not differ appreciably from the theoretically desirable treatment.

Assets constructed by a company for its own use should be recorded at the cost of direct material, direct labor, and applicable overhead cost. However, auditors usually apply the additional test of comparing the total cost of self-constructed equipment with bids or estimated purchase prices for similar equipment from outside suppliers, and they take exception to the capitalization of costs substantially in excess of the amount for which the asset could have been purchased and installed.

Assets acquired from affiliated corporations, from promoters or stockholders, or by any other type of transaction not involving arm's length bargaining between buyer and seller, have often been recorded at inflated amounts. The auditor should inquire into the methods by which the sales price was determined, the cost of the property to the vendor, length of ownership by vendor, and any other available evidence which might indicate an arbitrarily determined valuation. When vendor and vendee are under common control, or for any reason arm's-length bargaining does not appear to have been present in the acquisition of plant and equipment, the balance sheet should contain full disclosure of the transaction, including cost to the vendor.

7.   *Verify retirements of property during the year.*

The principal purpose of this procedure is to determine whether any property has been replaced, sold, dismantled, or abandoned without having been properly accounted for in the records. Nearly every thorough physical inventory of plant and equipment reveals missing units of property: units disposed of without a corresponding reduction of the accounts.

It is not unusual for a factory supervisor to order that a machine be scrapped, without realizing that the accounting department has an interest in such action. How is the accounting department expected to know when a factory asset is retired? If a machine is sold for cash or traded in on a new machine, the transaction will presumably involve the use of documents, such as a cash receipts form or a purchase order; the processing of these documents may bring the retirement to the attention of alert accounting personnel. Not all employees are alert, however, and some are not sufficiently trained to recognize a clue to the retirement of a plant asset. Moreover, many plant assets are scrapped rather than being sold or traded in on new equipment; consequently, there may be no paper work to evidence the disappearance of the machine.

One method of guarding against unrecorded retirements is enforcement of a companywide policy that no plant asset shall be retired from use without prior approval on a special type of serially numbered work order. A copy of the retirement work order is routed to the accounting department. To supplement this policy, a physical inventory of plant and equipment should be taken at regular intervals, perhaps once a year. Together, these two measures provide reasonable assurance that retirements will be reflected in the accounting records.

What specific steps should the auditor take to discover any unrecorded retirements? The following measures are often effective:

a)　If major additions of plant and equipment have been made during the year, ascertain whether old equipment was traded in or superseded by the new units.

b)　Analyze the Miscellaneous Revenue account to locate any cash proceeds from sale of plant assets.

c)　If any of the company's products have been discontinued during the year, investigate the disposition of plant facilities formerly used in manufacturing such products.

d)　Inquire of executives and supervisors whether any plant assets have been retired during the year.

e)　Examine retirement work orders or other source documents for authorization by the appropriate official or committee.

f)　Investigate any reduction of insurance coverage to see whether this was caused by retirement of plant assets.

8.　*Make physical inspection of substantial additions and consider the need for a complete physical inventory of plant and equipment.*

It is customary for the auditor to make a physical inspection of any major items of plant and equipment acquired during the period under audit, but not to undertake a complete plant inspection. At first thought, it does not appear unreasonable that verification of the existence of plant and equipment listed in the statements and accounts could best be accomplished through physical inspection by the auditor. Auditing procedures with respect to inventory and other current assets call for physical inspection or confirmation; and the Securities and Exchange Commission has in *Accounting Series Release No. 19* expressed the opinion that audit procedures should include physical inspection of plant and equipment to supplement the examination of book entries. Current practice, however, does not include physical inspection as a standard procedure of verification, and casual inspection as part of a conducted plant tour can hardly be considered as verification. The omission of physical inspection from verification work in this area of the examination appears to be the result of several factors:

a)　The risk of loss from theft or disappearance is slight, as compared with cash or other current assets.

b)　Management has, in general, been reluctant to authorize frequent physical inventories of plant and equipment. This attitude is attributable to the cost and effort required for a physical inventory, and also may be based upon the outmolded notion that internal controls are applicable only to current assets.

c)　The variety, quantity, and location of plant and equipment in large enterprises make a physical inventory thereof difficult and time consuming. It can be more satisfactorily performed by the internal auditing staff than by outside auditors.

In certain lines of business—as, for example, construction work, where costly mobile equipment is often scrapped or sold upon authorization of a field supervisor—good audit practice would call for physical inspection as part of the verification procedures. In the audit of concerns owning substantial numbers of automobiles and trucks, physical inspection and verification of legal title are practicable and desirable measures. More extensive use of this approach to the verification of plant and equipment is to be recommended.

9.   Obtain or prepare analyses of repair and maintenance expense accounts.

The principal objective in analyzing repair and maintenance expense accounts is to discover items which should have been capitalized. Large concerns often have a written policy setting the minimum expenditure to be capitalized. For example, company policy may prescribe that no expenditure for less than $50 shall be capitalized regardless of the useful life of the item purchased. In such cases the auditor will analyze the repair and maintenance accounts with a view toward determining the consistency of application of this policy as well as compliance with generally accepted accounting principles. To determine that the accounts contain only bona fide repair and maintenance charges, the auditor will trace the larger expenditures to written authorizations for the transaction. Correctness of the amounts involved may be verified by reference to vendors' invoices, to material requisitions, and to labor timecards.

One particularly useful means of identifying capital expenditures buried in the repair, and maintenance accounts is to obtain or prepare an analysis of the monthly amounts of expense with corresponding amounts listed for the preceding year. Any significant variations from month to month or between corresponding months of the two years should be fully investigated. If maintenance expense is classified by the departments serviced, the variations are especially noticeable.

10.   Review accounting policy for tools and patterns.

The auditor should determine whether it is the client's policy to capitalize replacements of tools and patterns. Some concerns capitalize only the original stock and charge all replacements to expense; other concerns capitalize replacements and compute depreciation on them. During the course of his investigation of tools and patterns the auditor should determine that—

a)   The stated accounting policy is being consistently followed.
b)   The scrapping of tools and patterns is handled by acceptable accounting methods.

c) Tools and patterns applicable to obsolete or discontinued products are not being carried at amounts in excess of scrap value.

11. *Investigate the status of property not in current use.*

Land, buildings, and equipment not in current use should be thoroughly investigated to determine the prospects for their future use in operations. Plant assets which are temporarily idle need not be reclassified, and depreciation may be continued at normal rates. On the other hand, idle equipment which has been dismantled, or for any reason appears unsuitable for future operating use, should generally be written down to an estimated realizable value and excluded from the plant and equipment classification. In the case of standby equipment and other property not needed at present or prospective levels of operation, the auditor should consider whether the carrying value is proportionate to the prospect of future use.

12. *Obtain or prepare a summary analysis showing changes during the year in property owned.*

At this point in the audit, the auditor has verified the beginning balances of plant and equipment assets by reference to prior year's working papers or by carrying out procedures necessary in the audit of a new client. In addition, he has satisfied himself as to the additions and retirements of plant and equipment during the year. He may now obtain or prepare the summary analysis illustrated in Figure 15–1, and cross-index it to the analysis of additions and disposals.

13. *Review rental revenue from land, buildings, and equipment.*

Most manufacturing clients retain the usual risks and rewards of ownership in connection with their leasing activities, and thus qualify for the *operating method* of recording aggregate lease rentals over the lives of the leases, as described in *APB Opinion No. 7.*

In verifying rental revenue from land and buildings it is often desirable for the auditor to obtain or to sketch a map of the property and to make a physical inspection of each unit. This may disclose that premises reported as vacant are in fact occupied by lessees and producing revenue not reflected in the accounts. If the client's property includes an office or apartment building, the auditor should obtain a floor plan of the building as well as copies of all lease contracts. In this way he can account for all available rental space as revenue producing or vacant under terms of lease agreements and can verify reported vacancies by physical inspection at the balance sheet date. If interim audit work is being performed, vacancies should also be verified by inspection and discussion with management during each visit by the auditor during the year.

Examination of leases will indicate whether tenants are responsible for the cost of electricity, water, gas, and telephone service. These provisions should be reconciled with the handling of utility expense accounts. Rental revenue accounts should be analyzed in all cases, and the amounts compared with lease agreements and cash records.

14. Determine proper balance sheet presentation.

The AICPA *Accounting Principles Board Opinion No. 12* requires that the balance sheet, or notes thereto, disclose balances of major classes of depreciable assets. Accumulated depreciation may be shown by major class or in total, and the method or methods of computing depreciation should be disclosed.

In addition, adequate balance sheet presentation will ordinarily reflect the following principles:

a) Property, plant, and equipment can usually be summarized by the following major classes: Land and Land Improvements; Buildings and Leasehold Improvements; Machinery and Equipment; Furniture and Fixtures; and Construction in Progress.

b) Property not in current use should be segregated in the balance sheet.

c) Property pledged to secure loans should be clearly identified.

d) The basis of valuation should be explicitly stated. At present, cost is the generally accepted basis of valuation for plant and equipment; property not in use should be valued at estimated realizable value.

e) Material amounts of fully depreciated assets still in use should be disclosed in a note to financial statements.

f) Depreciation, amortization, and depletion allowances should be shown as deductions from the related asset accounts, not grouped with other "reserve" accounts.

Depreciation

The technical knowledge needed by the auditor includes a thorough understanding of the various alternative methods of computing depreciation. Only a brief general review of depreciation methods is appropriate, however, in an auditing text; the reader who desires comprehensive coverage should refer to textbooks in accounting theory.

The two general approaches to depreciation are known as the unit basis and the group (or composite) basis. These two approaches differ sharply in the procedure for handling retirements. Let us assume first that the unit approach is being used. When an asset is retired before the end of its estimated useful life, the depreciation actually taken is used in computing the gain or loss on the retirement. The group method, on the other hand, provides for assets to be classified in various functional groups with an estimated useful life for each group. It is recognized that some items in the group will have shorter lives than the average, and that other items will last longer than the estimated average for the group. When an item is retired, the cost is charged to the accumulated depreciation account and credited to the property account. No gain or loss is recognized because under this averaging method each unit retired is assumed to be fully depreciated. When the group approach is employed, depreciation charges are usually calculated on a straight-line basis. The unit approach is much more widely used than depreciation on a group basis, and this preference has been accentuated by the recent swing to declining-balance methods of depreciation which almost invariably are applied on a unit basis. In the remainder of this chapter, use of the unit approach is assumed; we are now ready to consider methods of computing depreciation charges.

Computation of depreciation charges.   Among the methods of computing depreciation charges most frequently encountered by the auditor are the straight-line method and declining-balance methods. Far less common, although quite acceptable, are methods based on units of output or hours of service. Since 1954 when the Internal Revenue Code gave approval to declining-balance methods of depreciation for the determination of taxable income, a great many concerns have adopted such methods, attracted by the immediate advantage of deferring tax payments and thereby conserving working capital. The most widely adopted types of declining-balance depreciation methods are (*a*) fixed-percentage-of-declining-balance, and (*b*) sum-of-the-years'-digits. The essential characteristic of these and other similar methods is that depreciation is greatest in the first year and becomes smaller in succeeding years.

The use of a declining-balance method for tax purposes does not necessarily mean that this method should also be used for general accounting purposes. Many accountants, however, believe that declining-balance methods constitute a logical and reasonable basis for allocating cost of property to operating periods, because, in general, plant assets render services of greater value in the earlier years of their useful lives. There is the additional argument that repairs and maintenance tend to be greater in later years, plus the factor of convenience in maintaining the records on the same basis used for tax purposes.

Review of depreciation rates.   In reviewing the client's depreciation rates, the auditor must satisfy himself that the estimates of useful lives are reasonable. Average useful lives for various types of assets are suggested in *Depreciation Guidelines and Rules,* issued by the Internal Revenue Service as Revenue Procedure 62–21, effective July 12, 1962, and in the U.S. Treasury Department publication *Asset Depreciation Range (ADR) System,* issued in July 1971.

The auditor's objectives in review of depreciation

The principal objectives of the auditor in reviewing depreciation methods and amounts are to determine (*a*) that the method in use is a reasonable one, (*b*) that it is being followed consistently, and (*c*) that the computations required by the chosen method are accurately made. A more detailed picture of the auditor's objectives is conveyed by the audit program in the following section. Methods of accounting for the Investment Credit are considered in Chapter 17, along with other income tax problems.

Audit program—depreciation and depreciation allowances

The following outline of procedures to be followed by the auditor in reviewing depreciation is stated in sufficient detail to be largely self-explanatory. Consequently, no point-by-point discussion will be presented. Techniques for testing the client's provision of depreciation for the year and for analyzing the accumulated depreciation accounts are, however, discussed immediately following the audit program.

1. Review the depreciation policies set forth in company manuals or other management directives. Determine whether the methods in use are carefully designed and intended to allocate costs of plant and equipment equitably over their useful lives. Consider the applicability of "Guideline Lives" promulgated by the Internal Revenue Service.

   a) Inquire whether any extra working shifts or other conditions of accelerated production are present which might warrant adjustment of normal depreciation rates.

   b) Discuss with executives the possible need for recognition of extraordinary obsolescence resulting from inventions, design changes, or economic developments.

2. Obtain or prepare a summary analysis (see Figure 15–1) of depreciation allowances for the major property classifications as shown by the general ledger control accounts, listing beginning balances, provisions for depreciation during the year, retirements, and ending balances.

   a) Compare beginning balances with the adjusted amounts in last year's working papers.

   b) Determine that the totals of accumulated depreciation recorded in the plant and equipment subsidiary records agree with the applicable general ledger control accounts.

3. Verify the provisions for depreciation.

   a) Compare rates used in current year with those employed in prior years and investigate any variances.

b) Review computations of depreciation provisions for a representative number of units and trace to individual records in property ledger. Be alert for excessive depreciation on fully depreciated assets.

c) Compare credits to accumulated depreciation accounts for year's depreciation provisions with debit entries in related depreciation expense accounts.

4. Verify deductions from accumulated depreciation for assets retired.

a) Trace deductions to the working paper analyzing retirements of assets during year.

b) Test accuracy of accumulated depreciation to date of retirement.

5. Review the most recent audit report on depreciation made by the auditors from the Internal Revenue Service. Determine whether provisions and rates have been adjusted, when necessary, to agree with the findings of the Internal Revenue Service.

6. Compare the percentage relationships between accumulated depreciation and related property accounts with that prevailing in prior years and discuss significant variations from the normal depreciation program with appropriate members of management.

Testing the client's provision for depreciation

An overall test of the annual provision for depreciation requires the auditor to perform the following steps:

a) List the balances in the various asset accounts at the beginning of the year.

b) Deduct any fully depreciated assets, since these items should no longer be subject to depreciation.

c) Add one half of the asset additions for the year.

d) Deduct one half of the asset retirements for the year (exclusive of any fully depreciated assets).

These four steps produce average amounts subject to depreciation at the regular rates in each of the major asset categories. By applying the appropriate rates to these amounts, the auditor determines on an overall average basis the amount of the provision for depreciation and compares his computation with the client's figures. Any significant discrepancy between the depreciation expense computed in this manner and the amounts set up by the client should be fully investigated.

Analysis of accumulated depreciation accounts

The summary analysis in Figure 15–1 included a listing of the accumulated depreciation corresponding to the major classifications of plant and equipment and showed for each valuation account the beginning balance, depreciation rate and amount provided during the year, total deductions of the period, and the ending balances. The purposes of the working papers prepared to support this summary analysis are: (1) to test the accuracy of the provision for depreciation, and (2) to classify and explain the deductions made from the accumulated depreciation accounts.

The testing of the current year's provision for depreciation has already been explained. We shall now consider the deductions made from the accumulated depreciation accounts during the year. Debit entries to accumulated depreciation accounts normally consist of charges for accumulated depreciation on units of property being retired, and occasionally of charges for extraordinary repairs believed to lengthen the useful life of an asset and thus "offset depreciation."

Ths propriety of the charges relating to the retirement of assets will have been verified in the analysis of the plant and equipment accounts. One of the tasks in that analysis was a study of assets retired, with emphasis being placed on the removal of original cost from the asset account and of accumulated depreciation from the valuation account. There is no reason to duplicate this verification in the analysis of accumulated depreciation accounts. On the summary analysis of accumulated depreciation in Figure 15–1, the deductions of accumulated depreciation for assets retired are cross-referenced to the working paper analysis of plant and equipment retirements.

If the examination of accumulated depreciation reveals charges for extraordinary repairs, the auditor should ascertain if these expenditures should properly have been recorded as repair expense or as additions to asset accounts. This investigation will include a review of documentary evidence such as repair work orders and vendors' invoices, and discussion with executives. After review of the available evidence, the auditor must decide whether the charges to the accumulated depreciation accounts were in accordance with accounting conventions for distinguishing between capital and revenue expenditures.

Audit procedures for depletion of natural resources

In the examination of companies operating properties subject to depletion (mines, oil and gas deposits, timberlands, and other natural resources), the auditor follows a pattern similar to that used in evaluating the provision for depreciation expense and accumulated depreciation. He seeks to determine whether depletion has been recorded consistently and in accordance with generally accepted accounting principles, and he tests the mathematical accuracy of the client's computations.

The depletion of timberlands is usually based on physical quantities established by cruising. The determination of physical quantities to use as a basis for depletion is more difficult in many mining ventures and for oil and gas deposits. The auditor often relies upon the opinions of mining engineers and geologists as to the reasonableness of the depletion rates being used for such resources.

If the number of tons of ore in a mining property could be accurately determined in advance, an exact depletion cost per ton could be computed by dividing the cost of the mine by the number of tons available for extraction. In reality the contents of the mine can only be estimated, and the estimates may require drastic revision as mining operations progress. Some companies, especially those engaged in the mining of nonferrous metals, make no provision for depletion and argue that reliable information simply is not available as to the future output of the mine. Accountants generally have insisted that provision for depletion is a necessary step in all extractive industries; admittedly the underlying estimates of physical quantity are subject to error, but income measurement reflecting the best available estimates of depletion will be more realistic and more useful than a determination of income without regard for depletion.

The auditor verifies the ownership and the cost of mining properties by examining deeds, leases, tax bills, vouchers, paid checks, and other records in the same manner that he verifies the plant and equipment of a manufacturing or trading concern. The costs of exploration and development work in a mine are customarily capitalized until such time as commercial production begins. After that date additional development work is generally treated as expense. The costs of drilling oil wells are usually capitalized. When an oil company leases land, it often makes an immediate payment followed by annual rental payments until production begins, after which time the landowner receives payment in the form of royalties. In the records of the oil company, the lease may be carried at the total of the payments made, including the cost of developmental work, with this total becoming the basis for depletion, or being written off if the property proves to be nonproductive. As an alternative some oil companies capitalize the bonus paid for a lease but treat rental payments as an immediate charge to expense.

For some extractive companies the cost of the mine or oil deposit is negligible and a "discovery" value or appraised value is substituted as the basis for computing depletion. The auditor's responsibility in this situation is the same as when he encounters appraised values on the books of a manufacturing or mercantile business; he must investigate the appraisal report, determine the basis of the appraisal values, trace the amounts from the report into the records, and insist upon appropriate disclosure in the financial statements.

The Internal Revenue Code permits depletion to be computed as a fixed percentage of the gross revenue from the property. The allowable rates of depletion at present range up to 22 percent of gross revenue for oil, gas, and certain other minerals. Although this approach to depletion is of great importance in the determination of taxable income, it is not acceptable for other purposes; cost is the usual basis for depletion for purposes other than taxation.

Examination of plant and equipment in advance of the balance sheet date

Most of the audit work on plant and equipment can conveniently be done in advance of the balance sheet date. For the initial audit of a new client, the time-consuming task of reviewing the records of prior years and establishing the beginning balances in the plant accounts for the current period should if possible be completed before the year-end.

In repeat engagements, as well as in first examinations, the study and evaluation of internal control can be carried out at any convenient time during the year. Many auditing firms lighten their year-end work loads by preliminary work during October and November, including the analysis of the plant and equipment ledger accounts for the first 9 or 10 months of the year. After the balance sheet date, the work necessary on property accounts is then limited to the final two or three months' transactions. One of the major problems in managing an accounting practice is arranging a uniform work load for the staff throughout the year. A step toward the solution of this problem lies in performing most of the work on plant and equipment in advance of the balance sheet date.

GROUP I
REVIEW QUESTIONS

15–1. Does the auditor question the useful lives adopted by the client for plant assets, or does he accept the useful lives without investigation? Explain.

15–2. Can the independent auditor make use of the "Guideline Lives" developed for depreciable assets by the Internal Revenue Service? Explain.

15–3. Should the independent auditor observe a physical inventory of property and equipment in every audit engagement? Discuss.

15–4. The Hamlin Metals Company has sales representatives covering several states and provides automobiles for all its salesmen and executives. Describe any special verification procedures you would consider appropriate for the company's fleet of over 100 automobiles, other than the verification procedures generally applicable to all property and equipment.

15–5. Explain the use of a "system of authorizations" for property and equipment acquisitions.

15-6. What types of expenditures may properly be charged against accumulated depreciation? *extraordinary repairs*

15-7. What is the principal objective of an auditor in analyzing a Maintenance and Repairs expense account? *follow generally accepted acct. periods; can it be capitalized.*

15-8. The Gibson Manufacturing Company acquired new factory machinery this year and ceased using the old machinery. The old equipment was retained, however, and is capable of being used if the demand for the company's products warrants additional production. How should the old machinery be handled in the accounts and on the financial statements?

15-9. What objections do businessmen have to the traditional practice of basing depreciation charges on original cost?

15-10. The Moultrie Company discovered recently that a number of its property and equipment assets had been retired from use several years ago without any entry being made. The company asks you to suggest procedures which will prevent unrecorded retirement of assets.

15-11. Does a failure to record the retirement of machinery affect net income? *yes,* Explain. *if fully depreciated, should still be shown in balance sheet.*

15-12. What documentary evidence is usually available to the auditor in the client's office to substantiate the ownership of property, plant, and equipment?

15-13. The auditor's verification of current assets such as cash, securities, and inventories emphasizes count, inspection, and confirmation to determine the physical existence of these assets. Should the auditor take a similar approach to establish the existence of the recorded plant assets? Explain fully.

15-14. The current assets of Miller Manufacturing, Inc. amount to $2,500,000, and are approximately equal in amount to the plant and equipment. You have audited the company for several years. Which group of assets should require more audit time? Give reasons.

15-15. You are making your first examination of the Clarke Manufacturing Company. Plant and equipment represent a very substantial portion of the total assets. What verification, if any, will you make of the balances of the ledger accounts for Plant and Equipment as of the beginning of the period under audit?

15-16. Should the auditor examine public records to determine the legal title of property apparently owned by the client? *don't rely on this*

GROUP II
QUESTIONS REQUIRING ANALYSIS

15-17. In connection with a recurring examination of the financial statements of the Louis Manufacturing Company for the year ended December 31, 1974, you have been assigned the audit of the Manufacturing Equipment, Manufacturing Equipment—Accumulated Depreciation, and Repairs to Manufacturing Equipment accounts. Your review of Louis' policies and procedures has disclosed the following pertinent information:

(1) The Manufacturing Equipment account includes the net invoice price plus related freight and installation costs for all of the equipment in Louis' manufacturing plant.

(2) The Manufacturing Equipment and Accumulated Depreciation accounts are supported by a subsidiary ledger which shows the cost and accumulated depreciation for each piece of equipment.

(3) An annual budget for capital expenditures of $1,000 or more is prepared by the budget committee and approved by the board of directors. Capital expenditures over $1,000 which are not included in this budget must be approved by the board of directors, and variations of 20 percent or more must be explained to the board. Approval by the supervisor of production is required for capital expenditures under $1,000.

(4) Company employees handle installation, removal, repair, and rebuilding of the machinery. Work orders are prepared for these activities and are subject to the same budgetary control as other expenditures. Work orders are not required for external expenditures.

Required:

a) Cite the major objectives of your audit of the Manufacturing Equipment, Manufacturing Equipment—Accumulated Depreciation, and Repairs to Manufacturing Equipment accounts. Do not include in this listing the auditing procedures designed to accomplish these objectives.

b) Prepare the portion of your audit program applicable to the review of 1974 additions to the Manufacturing Equipment account. (AICPA, adapted)

15–18. Your new client, Parsons Mfg. Co., Inc., completed its first fiscal year March 31, 1975. During the course of your examination you discover the following entry in the general journal, dated April 1, 1974:

Building............................	2,400,000	
Mortgage Payable..............		1,400,000
Common Stock................		1,000,000

To record (1) acquisition of building constructed by J. A. Parsons Construction Co. (a sole proprietorship); (2) assumption of Parson Construction Co. mortgage loan for construction of the building; and for (3) issuance of entire authorized capital stock (10,000 shares, $100 par value) to J. A. Parsons.

Required:

Explain how you would accomplish the following objective relating to audit of this client's plant and equipment: "Determine the propriety of the valuation methods used."

15–19. Hardware Manufacturing Company, a closely held corporation, has operated since 1965 but has not had its financial statements audited. The company now plans to issue additional capital stock expected to be sold to outsiders and wishes to engage you to examine its 1974 transactions and render an opinion on the financial statements for the year ended December 31, 1974.

The company has expanded from one plant to three plants and has frequently acquired, modified, and disposed of all types of equipment. Plant assets have a net depreciated value of 70 percent of total assets and consist of land and buildings, diversified machinery and equipment, and furniture and fixtures. Some property was acquired by donation from stockholders. Depreciation was recorded by several methods using various estimated lives.

Required:

a) May you confine your examination solely to 1974 transactions as requested by this prospective client whose financial statements have not previously been examined? Explain.

b) Prepare an audit program for the January 1, 1974 opening balances of the Land, Building, and Equipment and Accumulated Depreciation accounts of Hardware Manufacturing Company. You need not include tests of 1974 transactions in your program. (AICPA, adapted)

15–20. An executive of a manufacturing company informs you that no formal procedures have been followed to control the retirement of machinery and equipment. A physical inventory of plant assets has just been completed. It revealed that 25 percent of the assets carried in the ledger were not on hand and had presumably been scrapped. The books have been adjusted to agree with the physical inventory. You are asked to outline internal control practices to govern future retirements.

15–21. The balance sheet of a manufacturing company contained the following assets among others:

Petty cash............................... $ 500
Automobiles and trucks................... 42,000

The auditor counted the petty cash fund and found it to be intact. When he was ready to begin the verification of the Automobiles account, the client suggested that if counting the petty cash was the best way to verify it, a physical inspection of the automobiles might also be appropriate. The auditor agreed and made a careful inspection of the company's fleet of 15 new or near-new cars, all of which appeared to be in excellent condition and easily worth the amount shown on the books.

Did the physical inspection of the automobiles constitute as effective a verification as the count of petty cash? Explain.

15–22. List and give briefly the purpose of all audit procedures which might reasonably be applied by an auditor to determine that all property and equipment retirements have been recorded on the books. (AICPA)

15–23. Mr. Allen Fraser was president of three corporations: The Missouri Metals Corporation, The Kansas Metals Corporation, and The Iowa Metals Corporation. Each of the three corporations owned land and buildings acquired for approximately $20,000. An appraiser retained in 1974 estimated the value of the land and buildings in each corporation at approximately $200,000. The appraisals were recorded in the accounts. A new corporation, called The Midwest Corporation, was then formed, and Mr. Fraser became its president. The new corporation purchased the assets of the three predecessor corporations, making payment in capital stock. The balance sheet of The Midwest Corporation shows land and buildings "valued at cost" in the amount of $600,000, the book values to the vendor companies at the time of transfer to The Midwest Corporation. Do you consider this treatment acceptable? Explain.

GROUP III
PROBLEMS

15–24. The Equipment account in the general ledger of Caulfield Company, Inc. at March 31, 1975 appears as shown below. Caulfield maintains its accounts on a fiscal year ending March 31. The company uses straight-line depreciation, 10-year life, and 10 percent salvage value for all its equipment. The company takes a full-year's depreciation on all additions to equipment occurring during the fiscal year, and you may treat this policy as a satisfactory one for the purpose of this problem. The company has recorded depreciation for the fiscal year ended March 31, 1975.

Equipment

4-1-74 Bal. fund.	100,000
12-1-74	10,500
1-2-75	1,015
2-1-75	1,015
3-1-75	1,015

Upon further investigation, you find the following contract dated December 1, 1974 covering the acquisition of equipment:

List price	$30,000
5% sales tax	1,500
Total	$31,500
Down payment	10,500
Balance	$21,000
8% interest, 24 months	3,360
Contract amount	$24,360

Required:

Prepare in good form including full explanations the adjusting journal entry (entries) you would propose as auditor of the Caulfield Company, Inc. with respect to the equipment and related depreciation accounts at March 31, 1975.

15–25.   Terra Land Development Corporation is a closely held family corporation engaged in the business of purchasing large tracts of land, subdividing the tracts, and installing paved streets, and utilities. The corporation does not construct buildings for the buyers of the land and does not have any affiliated construction companies. Undeveloped land is usually leased for farming until the corporation is ready to begin developing it.

The corporation finances its land acquisitions by mortgages; the mortgagees require audited financial statements. This is your first audit of the company and you have now begun the examination of the financial statements for the year ended December 31, 1974.

Required:

The corporation has three tracts of land in various stages of development. List the audit procedures to be employed in the verification of the physical existence and title to the corporation's three landholdings. (AICPA, adapted)

15–26.   You are engaged in the examination of the financial statements of the Marshall Corporation for the year ended December 31, 1974. The accompanying analyses of the Property, Plant, and Equipment, and related Accumulated Depreciation accounts have been prepared by the client. You have traced the opening balances to your prior year's audit working papers.

MARSHALL CORPORATION
ANALYSIS OF PROPERTY, PLANT, AND EQUIPMENT, AND
RELATED ACCUMULATED DEPRECIATION ACCOUNTS
Year Ended December 31, 1974

ASSETS

Description	Final 12-31-73	Additions	Retirements	Per books 12-31-74
Land	$ 22,500	$ 5,000		$ 27,500
Buildings	120,000	17,500		137,500
Machinery and equipment	385,000	40,400	$26,000	399,400
	$527,500	$62,900	$26,000	$564,400

ACCUMULATED DEPRECIATION

Description	Final 12-31-73	Additions*	Retirements	Per books 12-31-74
Buildings	$ 60,000	$ 5,150		$ 65,150
Machinery and equipment	173,250	$39,220		212,470
	$233,250	$44,370		$277,620

* Depreciation expense for the year.

All equipment is depreciated on the straight-line basis (no salvage value taken into consideration) based on the following estimated lives: buildings, 25 years; all other items, 10 years. The company's policy is to take one half-year's depreciation on all asset acquisitions and disposals during the year.

Your examination reveals the following information:

(1) On April 1 the company entered into a 10-year lease contract for a die casting machine, with annual rentals of $5,000 payable in advance every April 1. The lease is cancelable by either party (60 days' written notice is required), and there is no option to renew the lease or buy the equipment at the end of the lease. The estimated useful life of the machine is 10 years with no salvage value. The company recorded the die casting machine in the Machinery and Equipment account at $40,400, the present discounted value at the date of the lease, and $2,020 applicable to the machine has been included in depreciation expense for the year.

(2) The company completed the construction of a wing on the plant building on June 30. The useful life of the building was not extended by this addition. The lowest construction bid received was $17,500, the amount recorded in the Buildings account. Company personnel were used to construct the addition at a cost of $16,000 (materials, $7,500; labor, $5,500; and overhead, $3,000).

(3) On August 18, $5,000 was paid for paving and fencing a portion of land owned by the company and used as a parking lot for employees. The expenditure was charged to the Land account.

(4) The amount shown in the machinery and equipment asset retirement column represents cash received on September 5 upon disposal of a machine purchased in July 1970 for $48,000. The bookkeeper recorded depreciation expense of $3,500 on this machine in 1974.

(5) Harbor City donated land and building appraised at $10,000 and $40,000, respectively, to Marshall Corporation for a plant. On September 1, the company began operating the plant. Since no costs were involved, the bookkeeper made no entry for the above transaction.

Required:

Prepare the formal adjusting journal entries that you would suggest at December 31, 1974 to adjust the accounts for the above transactions. Disregard income tax implications. The books have not been closed. Computations should be rounded-off to the nearest dollar. (AICPA, adapted)

15–27. You are the senior accountant in the audit of the Paulsen Grain Corporation, whose business primarily involves the purchase, storage, and sale of grain products. The corporation owns several elevators located along navigable water routes and transports its grain by barge and rail. Your assistant submitted the following analysis for your review:

PAULSEN GRAIN CORPORATION

ADVANCES PAID ON BARGES UNDER CONSTRUCTION—a/c 210
December 31, 1974

Advances made:

1-15-74—Ck. No. 3463—Jones Barge Construction Co.......	$100,000[1]
4-13-74—Ck. No. 4129—Jones Barge Construction Co.......	25,000[1]
6-19-74—Ck. No. 5396—Jones Barge Construction Co.......	63,000[1]
Total payments....................................	$188,000
Deduct cash received 9-1-74 from Eastern Life Insurance Co..	188,000[2]
Balance per general ledger—12-31-74.....................	–0–

[1] Examined approved check request and paid check and traced to cash disbursements record.

[2] Traced to cash receipts book and to duplicate deposit ticket.

Required:

a) In what respects is the analysis incomplete for audit purposes? (Do not include any discussion of specific auditing procedures.)

b) What two different types of contractual arrangements may be inferred from your assistant's analysis?

c) What additional auditing procedures would you suggest that your assistant perform before you accept the working paper as being complete? (AICPA)

16

Prepaid expenses, deferred
charges, and intangible assets

In terms of audit objectives and techniques, we can conveniently deal with prepaid expenses, deferred charges, and intangible assets in a single chapter. For all these groups we are interested in seeing that the amounts recorded as assets represent goods or services which will be useful in the production of revenue in one or more future periods. We must also stress the importance of a rational, systematic program for apportioning these assets to expense. With respect to balance sheet classification, prepaid expenses are included in the current asset section; however, deferred charges and intangible assets represent long-term prepayments which must be classified on the balance sheet as noncurrent assets.

PREPAID EXPENSES AND DEFERRED CHARGES

In the balance sheets of many companies the last item in the current asset section is "Prepaid expenses." A few companies prefer to use an alternative title such as "Short-term prepayments," or "Prepaid insurance, rents, etc." Typically the dollar amount of prepaid expenses represents only 1 or 2 percent of the total assets. The relatively small amounts involved explain why it is customary to combine the various types of prepaid expense, such as unexpired insurance, prepaid taxes, and prepaid rent, into a single figure for the balance sheet.

The auditor may occasionally encounter an account classification which includes under the heading of "Deferred Charges" many of the items described in this chapter as prepaid expenses or as intangible assets. The term "Deferred Charges" could be applied to the cost of any asset acquired for use in the operations of future periods, but the classification of "Intangible Assets" seems preferable for such costs as research and development, goodwill, organization costs, leaseholds, and patents.

Among the more important kinds of prepaid expenses encountered by the auditor are unexpired insurance, prepaid rent, prepaid taxes, prepaid interest, prepaid advertising, prepaid commissions to salesmen, advances to employees for traveling expenses, supplies, postage, and deposits. Included in the deferred charges category are long-term expense prepayments which do not qualify for inclusion in current assets because they produce benefits applicable to periods beyond the current operating cycle. Specific examples include the costs of employee training programs when new equipment is installed, costs of plant rearrangement, the costs of moving employees and equipment to new locations, and bond issue costs.

The comparatively small dollar amount of prepaid expenses and deferred charges suggests that the auditor should invest much less time in the verification of these asset groups than he does for such material assets as inventories, receivables, or plant and equipment. The amount of auditing work devoted to prepaid expenses and deferred charges should reflect the relative importance of these items to the financial statements as a whole.

Small items such as magazine subscriptions are generally treated as expense in the period paid. If this policy is followed consistently, there is no material distortion of operating results or financial position. Economy and simplicity of accounting routines are important factors in the formulation of accounting policies. If the auditor is to maintain the respect and confidence of business executives, he must avoid recommending costly adjustments of insignificant items which, from the standpoint of convenience and economy, are customarily charged to expense.

Internal control of prepaid expenses and deferred charges

Determination of the adequacy of internal controls over prepaid expenses and deferred charges is an essential step in the auditor's investigation of these items. In Chapter 5, internal control was stated to consist of all measures employed by a business for the purposes of (1) safeguarding assets, (2) promoting accuracy and reliability in accounting and operating data, and (3) encouraging and measuring compliance with company policy. When defined in this manner, the principles of internal control obviously apply to such items as prepaid expenses and deferred charges, as well as to cash receipts and disbursements.

Internal controls of particular significance in the area of prepaid expenses are (*a*) proper authorization of expenditures, and (*b*) maintenance of detailed accounting records showing the regular amortization or other disposition of the amounts recorded as prepayments. For example, good internal control practices for unexpired insurance include: (*a*) the placement of responsibility for adequate insurance coverage with an officer or major executive; (*b*) authorization of every expenditure for insurance by this executive based on a continuing review of adequacy of coverage; (*c*) the maintenance of an insurance register containing full information on all policies owned; (*d*) preservation and orderly filing of brokers' advices and other original documents authorizing and supporting insurance transactions; and (*e*) periodic investigation of insurance coverage, records, and related accounting procedures by the internal auditing staff.

The auditor's evaluation of the internal controls applicable to prepaid expenses and deferred charges will govern the scope and intensity of his audit of the year's transactions in exactly the same way as it guides and influences the extent of verification of other asset classifications.

The auditor's objectives in examination of prepaid expenses and deferred charges

In the examination of prepaid expenses and deferred charges the auditor's objectives are to determine (*a*) the adequacy of internal controls, (*b*) the validity of the expenditures originally charged to the asset accounts, (*c*) the propriety of carrying unexpired expenditures as assets, (*d*) the reasonableness of the amortization program, and (*e*) the proper recording of related liabilities. Accomplishment of these objectives requires a variety of audit procedures designed to fit the widely differing items included in the prepaid expense and deferred charge categories. Despite the dissimilarity of individual items, however, the following general techniques underlie most audit programs for prepaid expenses and deferred charges:

1. Look for weaknesses in the system of internal control over expenditures of these types and develop suggestions for their correction.
2. Obtain or prepare analyses of the accounts to determine their contents.
3. Examine supporting evidence, such as insurance policies, tax receipts, contracts, and invoices, to prove the correctness of costs charged to the asset accounts.
4. Review the client's procedures for allocation of expense to the periods benefited and determine the overall reasonableness and propriety of the amortization program.
5. Test the computation of the unamortized balances to be carried as assets and the expired amounts to be charged to expense accounts.

6. Examine the related liability accounts and ascertain that all liabilities are properly recorded.

The above brief, generalized program provides a base from which specific audit procedures and programs can be developed for each type of prepaid expense and deferred charge. A single comprehensive audit program for all prepaid expenses and deferred charges is not feasible because of the diverse nature of the costs involved and because of the variety of accounting policies currently applied to individual items in these categories.

Concurrent verification of related expense and liability accounts

Adequate verification of assets and liabilities often requires concurrent analysis of closely related revenue and expense accounts. The examination of buildings and machinery, for example, would be dangerously incomplete if analysis of the Repair Expense account were not included as part of the verification procedures, because expenditures properly chargeable to buildings and machinery occasionally are recorded as repair expense. Another obvious example is found in the balance sheet account Accumulated Depreciation, which could hardly be subjected to audit without concurrent examination of the Depreciation Expense account. This principle of concurrent investigation of closely related real and nominal accounts is equally applicable to the audit of prepaid expenses and deferred charges. The following schedule indicates various types of prepaid expenses and deferred charges, verification of which involves the concurrent analysis of related expense and liability accounts:

Asset account	*Related expense account*	*Related liability account*
1. Unexpired Insurance	1. Insurance Expense	1. Accrued Insurance Payable
2. Prepaid Taxes	2. Taxes Expense	2. Accrued Taxes Payable
3. Prepaid Rent	3. Rent Expense	3. Accrued Rent Payable
4. Prepaid Interest	4. Interest Expense	4. Accrued Interest Payable
5. Bond Issue Costs	5. Interest Expense	5. Bonds Payable

The verification of Prepaid Taxes, for example, requires reference to the same documents and other sources of evidence as does the verification of Taxes Expense and Accrued Taxes Payable. Thus, concurrent verification of related accounts avoids duplication of effort.

Audit working papers for prepaid expenses and deferred charges

Apart from required grouping sheets, the working papers for prepaid expenses and deferred charges are generally analyses of the accounts, showing details of beginning balances, charges, credits, and ending balances. Often, related expense and liability accounts are analyzed on the same working paper as the prepaid expense or deferred charge.

Unexpired insurance

One of the most common items of prepaid expense is unexpired insurance. The types of protection frequently encountered include fire, sprinkler leakage, theft, burglary, property damage and bodily injury, workmen's compensation, business interruption, and fidelity bonds.

Most clients have adequate internal control for unexpired insurance. The controller or other official periodically reviews adequacy of insurance coverage with the company's insurance broker, and comprehensive records such as an insurance register are maintained. In such cases, the auditor obtains a copy of the insurance register, or an analysis of the Unexpired Insurance ledger account, as a starting point.

The most efficient method of verifying unexpired insurance is by obtaining direct confirmation from the client's insurance broker. Brokers willingly provide the auditor with a listing of policy numbers, carriers, coverages, terms, premiums paid, and premiums billed but unpaid at the balance sheet date. In addition, if requested, the broker will indicate any "loss payable" clauses included in the policies.

After the auditor has compared the broker's listing with the analysis obtained from the client, he resolves any exceptions by examining the policies and, if necessary, communicating further with the broker. The auditor then completes his verification of unexpired insurance by comparing beginning balances to the previous year's working papers and by testing computations of insurance expense and ending unexpired and accrued insurance.

Accrued insurance premiums apply to the "reporting-type" policies. Coverages such as workmen's compensation, fire insurance on inventories, and product liability are based on insurable values which fluctuate during the year—payrolls, monthly inventory balances, and sales, respectively. Accordingly, *deposit* premiums are paid at the beginning of the policy year on these coverages, and *actual* premiums accrue monthly on values reported by the insured to the insurance carrier. Rates of accrual are set forth in the policy. Accrued premiums are often paid at the end of the policy year, with the deposit premium offset against the total accrued premiums.

The auditor should ascertain that deposit premiums are not being amortized and that actual premiums are being accrued in accordance with reported values and rates specified in the policies. Otherwise, insurance *expense* for the year may be substantially misstated.

In addition to accrued insurance, there may be liabilities for unpaid premium billings; as indicated above, the auditor may confirm these amounts with the insurance broker. In addition, "loss payable" clauses in fire insurance policies indicate a lien-holder's interest in the insured property; the auditor should determine that the related liability has been recorded.

If policies are carried with mutual insurance companies, there is the possibility that the insured may be called upon to pay an assessment if the insurance company sustains heavy losses; this contingency is so remote, however, that it is not customary to make any disclosure in the financial statements. Refunds or dividends from mutual companies are of more practical significance, and the auditor should make sure that any such items have been considered in the computation of prepaid insurance and insurance expense.

If internal control for unexpired insurance is weak, the auditor must perform a number of additional procedures. He will probably find it necessary to prepare a working paper analysis of unexpired insurance; in addition, he should obtain and examine all of the insurance policies. Missing insurance policies may be in the possession of creditors whose loans are secured by the insured assets. It may also be desirable to vouch all premiums and refunds for the period. Refunds may arise because of cancellation of policies or may represent "dividends" received from mutual insurance companies. In either case, verification is made by examination of credit memoranda from the insurance broker and by reference to the cash receipts journal. Particular attention is usually given to brokers' advices; these should be on hand even though the related insurance policies have been placed in the custody of secured creditors. Review of brokers' advices may consequently disclose the absence of insurance policies and the unrecorded pledging of assets.

Another important audit procedure when internal control for unexpired insurance appears weak is the review of reports submitted by the client under "reporting-type" policies. This procedure is necessary to ascertain that accrued premiums are properly computed and that the client is complying with the reporting requirements. Failure to comply may void the insurance coverage.

Taxes paid in advance

Prepaid taxes may include real and personal property taxes, license fees, and state franchise taxes. Consistency in the use of a given method of accounting for taxes is a consideration of prime importance; any one of several methods of assigning property taxes to specific periods is acceptable if consistently followed. In *APB Accounting Principles,* the AICPA expresses the opinion that—

Generally, the most acceptable basis of providing for property taxes is monthly accrual on the taxpayer's books during the fiscal period of the taxing authority for which the taxes are levied. The books will then show, at any closing date, the appropriate accrual or prepayment.

Variations in state and local laws are largely responsible for the great variety of methods of accounting for taxes; familiarity with the tax statutes is, therefore, a prerequisite to evaluation by the auditor of the accounting procedures employed.

In the verification of prepaid taxes the following audit procedures are suggested:

1. Obtain an analysis of prepaid taxes, taxes expense, and accrued taxes.
2. Vouch tax payments to supporting paid checks and tax bills.
3. Test computations of tax prepayments, accruals, and expense.

The analysis of tax accounts should show: (*a*) the type of tax, (*b*) the period covered, (*c*) the amounts of tax, (*d*) the basis of the levy, (*e*) the amount prepaid or accured, and (*f*) the current expense.

Tax payments are vouched to the tax bills and cash records. A careful review of the paid tax bills will provide much of the information needed in the working papers. Normally, the taxes paid are prorated on a straight-line basis over the periods assumed to be benefited.

The analysis of tax accounts may include various items for which accruals, rather than prepayments, exist. In such cases, accrued taxes should not be netted against prepaid taxes. Proper handling requires that the accruals be adequately cross-referenced to the auditor's working papers for liabilities and shown on the balance sheet as current liabilities.

Rent paid in advance

Prepaid rent includes only the prepayment of amounts applicable to the ensuing operating cycle. For example, a 10-year lease may require that rent for the 10th or final year under the lease be paid in advance at the time of signing the contract. Such an advance payment does not qualify as part of current prepaid expenses; it should be classified as a deferred charge and placed among "Other assets" on the balance sheet. Prepayments for a period longer than one month should be recognized as assets and included in prepaid expenses to the extent that the prepayment falls within the next operating cycle.

The following procedures are suggested as being generally applicable to the audit of prepaid rent and rent expense:

1. Obtain copies of all leases for the permanent file and review all provisions affecting the financial statements.
2. Obtain analyses of Prepaid Rent and Rent Expense and test computations thereof by reference to the lease copies.

3. Vouch rent payments to paid checks and other supporting documents.
4. Consider whether any leases should be accounted for as installment purchases.

In many lease contracts the periodic rental is not a fixed amount but a percentage of the volume of sales or other base. Verification of rent payments and expense under such conditions will obviously require careful study of the lease agreement. In addition, the lessee is sometimes required to pay the taxes on the leased property, and in such cases may choose to classify the payments as rent rather than as taxes. Rented property may be subleased in part to other concerns, and the revenue realized credited to rent expense. Rental revenue collected in advance from subleases may have been recorded as an offset against prepaid rent. All such payments and collections should be verified by the auditor and reconciled with the terms of lease contracts. The offsetting of rental revenue and expense is not desirable from the standpoint of statement presentation if the amounts are significant.

The problem of leases which are in effect installment purchases will be discussed in this chapter under "Leases and leasehold improvements."

Other prepaid expenses

There are a number of miscellaneous items which may be included as prepaid expense in addition to the major groups described in preceding sections of this chapter. Examples are postage on hand and advertising paid in advance. Others, such as prepaid interest, prepaid royalties, and prepaid commissions, are appropriately audited in conjunction with the verification of the related liability accounts. Advances to employees for travel expenses, though theoretically prepaid expenses, are usually controlled and classified as accounts receivable, as discussed in Chapter 13. Similarly, factory and office supplies inventories are a form of prepaid expense but are better controlled and accounted for as inventories.

Although expenditures for advertising and promotional activities often yield some benefits in the following accounting period, conservative accounting practice calls for an immediate charge to expense for most such outlays. The auditor should satisfy himself that any advertising or other selling expenses deferred to future periods will produce definite benefits in those periods. Advertising of an institutional nature is regarded as expense of the period in which the advertising appears in publications or on radio or television.

Advertising paid in advance may include: (1) the unexpired cost of contracts with advertising agencies, newspapers, periodicals, etc.; and (2) the cost of advertising supplies on hand. The total cost of advertising contracts may be prorated to the periods benefited by any reasonable method.

Concerns having substantial mailing costs, such as mail-order houses and stockbrokers, may defer postage on hand as a prepaid expense. In the audit of businesses which incur large amounts of postage expense, the auditor may wish to verify entries in the Prepaid Postage and Postage Expense accounts. The adequacy of the system of internal control, as well as the materiality of the amounts involved, must be considered in determining whether such verification is appropriate. Purchases of stamps and metered postage may be traced to the cash disbursements records and to post office receipts. The total purchases adjusted by the beginning and ending postage inventories indicate postage expense for the period and may be traced to the ledger accounts for postage expense. The system of departmental distribution of postage expense should be reviewed and comparisons made with departmental expense totals for prior years.

If other expenditures are to be deferred as prepaid expenses, the decision to do so and the computations underlying the division of the outlay between current expense and prepaid expense will generally be made by the client's staff, not by the auditor. In such cases it is the responsibility of the auditor to determine the propriety of the amount charged to current expense and of the amount carried forward as applicable to operations of future periods. The audit function consists of reviewing and testing the decisions and supporting computations made by the client and of determining whether the decisions reached year by year constitute in their entirety a consistent and logical accounting policy.

Deferred charges

Some deferred charges do not present any special auditing problems because their periods of benefit to the client are easily determinable. For example, the prepayment of the 10th-year rent for a 10-year lease (discussed under "Rent paid in advance" in this chapter) can be verified by confirmation with the lessor and by reference to terms of the lease. Material prepaid insurance premiums for periods longer than one year (or one operating cycle) may be verified in the same manner as short-term unexpired insurance. Bond issue costs (discussed in Chapter 18) benefit the client over the life of the bond issue.

On the other hand, deferred charges for costs of employee training programs, costs of plant rearrangement, and costs of relocating employees and equipment present auditing problems because the periods benefited by the expenditures are not readily determinable. A specific example may serve to illustrate the problem more forcibly. A merchandising corporation doing a worldwide business moved its home office from New York to California in the belief that certain administrative and operating economies would result from the new location. The corporation paid the moving expenses of its entire home-office staff, in addition to the costs of transporting records and equipment. The total cost of the move was in excess of one million dollars, and if treated as an expense of the current period would have caused the year's net income to drop substantially below the earnings of previous years. Assuming that the company's expectation of operating economies as a result of the move was well founded, the most appropriate classification of the costs of moving is that of a deferred charge to expense. The determination of the write-off period is necessarily an arbitrary one. Most auditors would probably urge that the costs be written off over a period of not more than five years.

Preoperating costs. Preoperating costs, or start-up costs, are a unique type of deferred charge incurred only at the start-up of a business enterprise or a new division or product line. Preoperating costs are not to be confused with organization costs (discussed in a later section of this chapter) because organization costs are incurred only in the formation of the corporate legal entity and not in the beginning of the business operations.

Preoperating costs include expenditures for services prior to beginning operations, such as rent, salaries and wages, utilities, and janitorial services. Charging these expenditures to accounting periods prior to the beginning of operations would result in operating statements showing no revenue, numerous expenses, and net losses. On the other hand, to defer these costs for amortization after operations begin necessitates estimating periods to be benefited by the preoperating costs—a problem which has no easy solution. Most auditors would probably favor the client's write-off of preoperating costs during the first fiscal year of operations.

Suspense accounts. A suspense account is a temporary resting place for charges which cannot be properly classified on the basis of information presently available. The costs of preliminary surveys and investigations for construction projects not yet formally approved are often charged to a suspense account pending the issuance of a capital work order. If the project is not authorized, the accumulated charges will be written off to expense; if the project is approved, these expenditures will be reclassified as construction in progress.

Use of suspense accounts should be held to a minimum, for their very nature makes them susceptible to abuse. Unless the account is frequently reviewed by someone in authority, expenditures once charged to Suspense are apt to remain there long after the reason for such classification has ceased to exist. Losses should be recognized as such and not concealed by classification as suspense charges. Thorough analysis of suspense accounts is, therefore, an essential part of the audit. As a result of this analysis, reclassification of the charges to specific asset or expense accounts should be made wherever possible.

INTANGIBLE ASSETS

Among the more prominent examples of intangible assets are goodwill, organization costs, research and development costs, patents, copyrights, trademarks, trade names, franchises, distributorships, leaseholds, and leasehold improvements. Characteristically, these assets are long-lived, at least to the extent of not qualifying as current assets. Since they are lacking in physical substance, their value lies in the rights or economic advantages afforded by their ownership. Also because of the lack of physical substance, intangible assets may be more difficult to identify than units of plant and equipment. When a client treats an expenditure as creating an intangible asset, the auditor must look for objective evidence that a genuine asset has come into being.

Generally accepted accounting principles for intangible assets

Accounting Principles Board Opinion No. 17 established the current accepted accounting standards for intangible assets. Major provisions are summarized in the following paragraph of the *Opinion:*

> The Board concludes that a company should record as assets the costs of intangible assets acquired from others, including goodwill acquired in a business combination. A company should record as expenses the costs to develop intangible assets which are not specifically identifiable. The Board also concludes that the cost of each type of intangible asset should be amortized by systematic charges to income over the period estimated to be benefited. The period of amortization should not, however, exceed forty years.

The board also concluded that the straight-line method of amortization should be applied to intangible assets unless a company can demonstrate that another systematic method is more appropriate. With respect to the difficult issue of determining periods for amortization of intangible assets, the board suggested considering the following factors:

a) Legal, regulatory, or contractual provisions may limit the maximum useful life.

b) Provisions for renewal or extension may alter a specified limit on useful life.

c) Effects of obsolescence, demand, competition, and other economic factors may reduce a useful life.

d) A useful life may parallel the service life expectancies of individuals or groups of employees.

e) Expected actions of competitors and others may restrict present competitive advantages.

f) An apparently unlimited useful life may in fact be indefinite and benefits cannot be reasonably projected.

g) An intangible asset may be a composite of many individual factors with varying effective lives.

The auditor's objectives in examination of intangible assets

The auditor's objectives in the examination of intangible assets are to determine (*a*) the adequacy of internal controls; (*b*) the authorization for acquisition, sale, licensing, or write-off; (*c*) the basis of valuation; (*d*) the reasonableness of amortization; (*e*) the appropriate balance sheet presentation; and (*f*) the propriety of accounting for revenue earned on intangibles.

The varying character of items included in the classification of intangible assets prevents the development of a single audit program for this group. In lieu thereof, the appropriate steps to be taken by the auditor will be presented as each major type of intangible asset is discussed in the following pages.

Internal control

The significance of internal control varies greatly from one type of intangible asset to the next. In the auditor's verification of goodwill, for example, the question of internal control may be limited to determining that charges to the account and amortization entries were authorized by directors or appropriate executives. In the verification of patents and related licensing agreements, on the other hand, the auditor may attach great importance to the effectiveness of the internal control procedures for allocation of development costs and collection of royalty revenue arising from licensing agreements.

Since internal control may represent a significant factor in the audit of certain intangible assets but may be a minor consideration in the examination of others, no general discussion of internal control will be presented in this chapter. In outlining the audit work required for certain intangible assets, however, significant applications of internal control will be described.

Acquisition of intangibles from insiders

In his investigation of the valuation of intangible assets, the auditor should give particular attention to transactions not characterized by arm's-length bargaining. The acquisition of intangible assets from directors, stockholders, promoters, or affiliated or predecessor enterprises—particularly if payment is made by other means than cash—inevitably raises the question of overvaluation of assets. One of the traditional abuses of corporate authority has been the issuance of a corporation's own stock to insiders in exchange for intangible assets of dubious value. The auditor should ascertain, if possible, the cost of such intangibles to the sellers and should determine whether the services of qualified independent appraisers were employed in fixing the cost of the corporation. The relationship between the parties to such transactions should be fully disclosed in the financial statements.

ILLUSTRATIVE CASE. The audited balance sheet of Thomascolor, Incorporated, included in a registration statement filed with the SEC, showed total assets of approximately $2,552,000. Included in the balance sheet was following item:

Patents and patent applications (representing the amounts of such
assets as carried on the books of predecessor interests plus the
excess of the stated value of common stock issued therefor over the
net assets acquired as shown by the books of such predecessor interests) —(Note 2)... $2,014,941.03
    Note 2 read in part as follows:

The amount of $2,014,941.03 at which the item "Patents and Patent Applications" is carried in the above balance sheet represents the valuation of such patents and patent applications by the Directors and is based upon the par value of the 579,800 shares of class A Stock of $5 par value less 81,377 $27/49$ shares returned to treasury and on 10 cents per share for the 100,000 shares class B issued therefor with adjustments for other assets acquired and liabilities assumed.

Said valuation does not purport to be the cost to the original owners.

In an investigation of Thomascolor, Incorporated reported in *Accounting Series Release No. 73*, the SEC found that the valuation of patents and patent applications was merely a balancing figure. The valuation was substantially in excess of the aggregate amounts in the books of related predecessor companies from which the patents were acquired, and had no relation to actual values. The CPA firm which expressed an unqualified opinion on Thomascolor's financial statements was suspended from appearing or practicing before the SEC for a 10-day period.

Audit working papers for intangible assets

The examination of intangible assets does not pose any unusual problems in the preparation of audit working papers. Intangible assets are not generally combined for balance sheet presentation; hence a grouping sheet for "Other Assets" is unnecessary. For most of the intangibles, such as goodwill, organization costs, patents, and franchises, the principal working paper is an analysis of one or more ledger accounts. This form of analytical working paper for organization costs is illustrated in Figure 16–1.

FIGURE 16–1

The Gibraltar Company
Acct. No. 168   Organization Costs   U-18
June 30, 1972 and Succeeding Years

Date	Refer-ence	Payee	Description	Amount
3/1/72	CD-1	Thomas & Jones	Legal fees re incorporation	2 000 00 ✓
4/15/72	CD-1	Martin & Loren, CPAs	Accounting fees re incorporation	1 100 00 ✓
5/1/72	CD-1	R. W. Blackstone	Promotional services as incorporator	7 600 00 ✓
6/10/72	CD-2	Secretary of State	Incorporation fees	400 00 ✓
6/15/72	CD-2	R. W. Blackstone	Travel costs re incorporation	800 00 ✓
6/25/72	CD-2	Public Secretaries, Inc.	Secretarial services re incorporation	800 00 ✓
6/30/72			Balance, 6/30/72 ⓞ C-1	12 700 00
6/30/73	J 73-119		Amortization, 2½%-Y/e 6/30/73	(317 50)
6/30/73			Balance, 6/30/73 C-1	12 382 50
6/30/74	J 74-125		Amortization, 2½%-Y/e 6/30/74	(317 50)
6/30/74			Balance, 6/30/74 C-1	12 065 00

✓ – Examined paid check and supporting statement
    or check request.

ⓞ – Date The Gibraltar Company began business.

V. M. H.
7/15/72
7/6/73
7/2/74

Goodwill

Goodwill arises most frequently in a business combination—the bringing together of a corporation and one or more incorporated or unincorporated businesses into one accounting entity. *Accounting Principles Board Opinion No. 16* provides that when a business combination is accounted for as a *purchase,* the acquiring company must allocate the cost of an acquired business to the assets acquired and liabilities assumed. First, a portion of the cost must be allocated to all identifiable tangible and intangible assets acquired and liabilities assumed—usually in amounts equal to their respective fair values at date of acquisition. Then, the excess, if any, of the cost of the acquired company over the sum of the amounts assigned to identifiable assets less liabilities assumed is recorded as goodwill. Thus, goodwill is valued on a residual basis in a business combination.

Audit program for goodwill. The auditing work to be performed in the verification of goodwill can be summarized in the following specific steps:

1. Obtain or prepare an analysis of the Goodwill account for the entire period from its inception to the date of audit. For repeat engagements, the analysis will, of course, be limited to the current period.
2. Determine that all charges to the account were properly authorized by the board of directors.
3. Examine the original documents and authorizations supporting the allocation of a lump-sum purchase price among identifiable tangible and intangible assets and liabilities, and goodwill. Consider the reasonableness of the allocation.
4. Review the program of amortization or arbitrary write-off to determine authorization, reasonableness, and consistency of application.

In the initial audit of a client, the Goodwill account should be analyzed for the entire period from its inception up to the date of audit. The information derived from this analysis should be recorded in the permanent file so that the audit work in subsequent engagements can be limited to transactions of the year under audit. Full information should be obtained concerning the purchase transaction leading to the recognition of goodwill in the accounts.

The auditor should be alert to detect any unsual charges to the Goodwill account representing deviations from the cost principle. Examples of such charges include the capitalization of promotional expenses, research and development expenditures, and extraordinary advertising outlays. Since charges to the Goodwill account are infrequent and associated with highly significant events in the life of the enterprise, the auditor should expect to find all charges to the account supported by formal action of the board of directors.

In the examination of contracts involving the lump-sum purchase of a business, the auditor should investigate the basis employed for allocation of the total cost between identifiable tangible and intangible assets and liabilities, and goodwill. The reports of qualified independent appraisers should be reviewed by the auditor as an aid to judging the objectivity and general reasonableness of such allocations. Increasing recognition of the need for adequate informative disclosure in corporate financial statements demands that the auditing profession go beyond a mere comparison of ledger balances and directors' resolutions in verifying the valuations placed on intangible assets. The auditor's responsibility to investors who act in reliance upon his professional skill and integrity requires that he evaluate the reasonableness of costs allocated to intangible assets.

In reviewing the program of goodwill amortization the auditor should stress the need for consistency; the amortization of goodwill should not be used as a device for equalizing the profits of successive years by varying the amount of amortization expense to be recognized. The auditor should also consider the propriety of the amortization period selected for goodwill by the client.

Organization costs

The process of forming a corporation or reorganizing an existing corporate entity may entail substantial expenditures. Typical of the costs of organizing a corporation are legal and accounting fees, payments to promoters, state incorporation fees, traveling expenditures, and fees of incorporators during the organizational period. Miscellaneous other expenditures made prior to the formation of the corporation may be clearly associated with the creation of the corporate organization rather than with production of revenue. Costs incurred in the issuance of capital stock are not organization costs, but offsets against the proceeds received for the stock. Preoperating costs are not organization costs.

It is sometimes suggested that organization costs be treated as expense at the time incurred; such treatment is undesirable, however, because the financial statements would indicate a dissipation of invested capital. Charging organization costs to expense would place an unwarranted burden on the operations of the first period, for the benefits derived from these expenditures are no more applicable to the first year of corporate existence than to any succeeding year. Capitalization of organization costs is, therefore, warranted from the viewpoint of accounting theory.

When payment for organization costs is made by issuance of the corporation's own securities, the amount to be recorded may be based on (a) the fair value of the services received, or (b) the current market value of the securities. The par value or other face value of the securities issued in payment for organizational services is not a satisfactory indicator of the dollar amount involved. Adequate informative disclosure is particularly important for transactions of this nature; the valuation basis used in determining the amount of organization costs arising from noncash transactions should be disclosed in the financial statements.

Audit program for organization costs.   Verification of organization costs during the first audit of a client's records will include an analysis of the ledger account. All items of significant amount should be vouched to original documents and authorizations by stockholders and directors. Particular attention should be given to any charges to the account resulting from noncash transactions. Charges representing payments to directors, officers, or stockholders should also be explored fully. An appropriate form of working paper for analysis of the Organization Costs account is illustrated in Figure 16–1. (See p. 541.)

At the conclusion of his investigation the auditor should have satisfied himself as to the content of the Organization Costs account, the valuation basis employed for noncash expenditures, the sufficiency of authorizations and the propriety of the amortization policy. Write-offs are often credited directly to intangible asset accounts, but the use of valuation accounts is also acceptable. Under no circumstances should the auditor condone irregular amortization of organization costs which distorts periodic net income and conceals significant variations in earnings.

If the working papers summarizing the investigation of organization costs made during the initial examination are preserved in the permanent file and made available during subsequent engagements, very little additional work will be required. The account is normally inactive after the first year or two of the corporation's existence; and once the auditor has satisfied himself as to its contents, the only work required in succeeding audits is the review of amortization entries. Reorganization of a corporation warrants the capitalization of legal and accounting fees and other costs similar to those chargeable to organization costs when the corporation was first established. Any unamortized costs of the original organization, however, should be written off at the time of reorganization.

Patents

A patent is a document issued by the federal government granting an exclusive right for the manufacture, use, or sale of a machine, design, or process for a period of 17 years. If the original device or process is modified in some manner, the patent may be renewed for a second term of 17 years. Patents may be sold or assigned. In contrast with such intangibles as goodwill and organization costs, patents are assets which may be sold separately from the business and which may have a realizable value even though the business is terminated.

Valuation of patents. The proper valuation basis for recording patents in the accounts is cost. If a patent is purchased, its cost consists of the purchase price plus any incidental charges such as commissions, legal and filing fees, or other expenditures necessary to establish and defend title to the patent.

When patents are purchased for cash in an arm's-length transaction with outsiders, valuation at acquisition cost is a simple and definite process. If patents are acquired from promoters, directors, major stockholders, or affiliated corporations, however, the objective nature of the cost determination is lost, particularly if payment is made in shares of stock rather than in cash. If directors are cast in the roles of both buyers and sellers in a transaction involving the acquisition of patents or other intangibles, those circumstances should be disclosed in notes to the financial statements.

When patents are developed by engineers or other employees of the client, accounting theory favors the capitalization of all applicable research and development costs, including material, labor, and overhead. Legal fees, filing costs, and any expenditures incurred in establishing title to the patent should be charged to the Patents account. Costs incurred but not recovered in successful litigation involving the validity of patents should logically be added to the cost of the patent. Any damages recovered over and above costs incurred constitute an extraordinary gain. An unsuccessful lawsuit which has the result of invalidating the patent leaves no alternative but to write off as a loss the unamortized cost of the patent along with any expenditures incurred in the course of the litigation.

Amortization of patents. The useful life of a patent may be considerably shorter than its legal life. The amortization program should be based on the estimated useful life of the asset, but under no circumstances should be extended beyond the legal life. If the patent loses its productive value earlier than anticipated, the unamortized cost should immediately be written off.

Licensing agreements and royalty revenue. A licensing agreement is a contract in which the owner of a patent, or "licensor," authorizes another party, called the "licensee," to make use of the patented device or process. The consideration for such use is often a fixed sum for each unit of product manufactured or sold with the aid of the patented item. A minimum annual royalty is also provided in most licensing agreements. These contracts often contain clauses permitting the licensor to examine the accounting and production records of the licensee for the purpose of verifying the amount of royalties accrued. The auditor may often find it desirable to analyze the Royalty Revenue account concurrently with his verification of patents.

Audit program for patents.   The Patents account is often a control account summarizing the unamortized cost of a number of patents acquired at different dates and under varying circumstances. The audit of this account, therefore, often requires the preparation of a separate working paper for each patent, containing evidence of the following investigative steps performed by the auditor:

1. Review of authorizations by directors for the purchase, development, valuation, licensing, and sale of patents.
2. Verification of the costs incurred through purchase or development of the patent, and of any costs relating to the defense of title.
3. Verification of legal ownership of the patent.
4. Review of the amortization policy, noting authorization by directors, consistency of application, and conformance with generally accepted accounting principles for recording cost expiration.
5. Investigation of the present use of patents, with consideration being given to the advisability of writing off any costs represented by patents not currently productive.
6. Examination of licensing agreements and resulting revenue, including analysis of the revenue accounts and review of reports from licensees.
7. Consultation with officers and with the client's legal counsel to determine the significance of any current or contemplated patent litigation.

As in the case of other long-lived assets, the investigative work required in the initial audit engagement will normally be much more extensive than is required in subsequent examinations. By reference to the permanent file, the auditor can, during repeat engagements, limit his work to the analysis of the current year's changes. This must be accompanied, however, by determination of the present use being made of the patents, the need for change in the amortization program in the light of current developments, and the current status of patent litigation.

Research and development costs

A determination of the development costs which should be capitalized is not a simple matter in large corporations maintaining research and experimental departments on a permanent basis. A large part, if not all, of the expenditures of a research department may be necessary if the enterprise is to maintain its competitive position in the industry.

From such substantial and continuous research programs, patents of substantial value will occasionally be developed. In theory, the expenditures relating to each research project should be segregated and capitalized in those instances in which valuable patents result. From the standpoint of accounting theory, expenditures made in development of patents should be capitalized. But in view of the practical difficulties of distinguishing the particular research projects which will ultimately lead to valuable patent rights, the auditor may expect to find the bulk of research and development expenditures treated as expense in the period incurred.

Although research and development costs are generally charged to expense in the year incurred, the deferral and amortization of these costs constitute acceptable practice if adequate evidence exists that the costs will be recovered through future sales of the new products under development. The examination of costs in the area of research and development will stress budgetary control, prior authorization of expenditures, authorization of deferrals, and a logical plan for amortization for any amounts carried forward to subsequent years. Under no circumstances should the auditor give approval to the deferral of research costs applicable to projects which have been terminated or which for other reasons appear unrelated to future revenue.

Leases and leasehold improvements

A lease is a contract providing for the rental of real or personal property, usually for a period of years. A leasehold is defined as the right to the use of property held under a lease. The owner of the property is called the "lessor," and the tenant is described as the "lessee." In recent years the leasing of all types of business property has become very common. Not only land and buildings, but automobiles, machinery, office equipment, and many other kinds of assets are acquired by lease rather than by purchase in an increasing number of companies. The question posed by this new trend of business practice is the extent to which leased properties should be shown as assets in the balance sheet. In considering what constitutes proper presentation of leases in financial statements, the auditor is guided in large part by the accounting principle of adequate informative disclosure.

Disclosure of leases in financial statements. Guidelines for reporting leases in the financial statements of lessees are presented in *Opinion No. 5* of the AICPA's Accounting Principles Board. The board concluded that leases which are in substance *purchases* of property should be recorded as such. In contrast, leases which merely convey the right to *use* property, without an equity in the property accruing to the lessee, should be disclosed in notes to the financial statements.

The board furnished two principal and four corollary criteria for determining whether a lease is in substance a purchase. The board also held that leases between related parties should often be treated as purchases, even though the criteria for a purchase are not met.

If a lease is deemed to be a purchase, the property and the related obligation should be presented in the balance sheet as a plant asset and a liability, respectively, at the discounted amount of all future lease rental payments. "Future lease rental payments" are defined to exclude taxes and operating expenses. The asset should be depreciated over its estimated useful life, rather than over the initial period of the lease. On the other hand, bona fide leases are disclosed in a note to the financial statements. The note should include minimum annual rentals, periods covered by the leases, current-year rentals if significantly different from minimum rentals, types of property leased, obligations assumed or guarantees made under the leases, and any restrictions imposed by the leases.

Sale and leaseback transactions.   In recent years, many large organizations have sold their buildings and equipment to investors who simultaneously lease the property back to the seller. The objective of the seller is to free invested capital for operating activities rather than having large sums invested in plant and equipment. *Opinion No. 5* considers sale and leaseback transactions to be generally interdependent. Accordingly, material gains or losses resulting from sales and leasebacks of property should be amortized, net of income tax effect, over the life of the lease, as an adjustment to rent expense for a bona fide lease or to depreciation for a "purchase" lease.

Audit program—leases and leasehold improvements.   In the audit of a business making extensive use of leased property, the auditor's primary concern is to determine that lease transactions are subject to adequate internal control and that the accounting records reflecting these transactions are accurate and complete. The following specific audit procedures are designed to accomplish these objectives:

1. Review the internal control procedures governing the formation or purchase of lease contracts and the making of subleases.
2. Obtain copies of all leases for the permanent file and review for significant clauses such as the following:
    a)   Description of the leased property.
    b)   Names and titles of the parties signing the lease.
    c)   Duration of the lease and date signed.
    d)   Amount of rent or method of computation of rent when based on sales or profits.
    e)   Rental payment dates and periods covered.
    f)   Amount of deposit, if any, and interest thereon.
    g)   Amount of bonus, if any, paid to secure lease.

h) Provision for alteration of leased property and condition of property when returned to owner.

i) Responsibility for payment of costs of maintenance, repairs, insurance, and taxes.

j) Option to purchase property and to apply rental payments against purchase price.

3. Consider whether any of the leases are in substance purchases, necessitating the recognition of assets and liabilities in the client's balance sheet.

4. Analyze ledger accounts for leaseholds and leasehold improvements and determine propriety of charges thereto.

5. Review the program for amortization of leaseholds and leasehold improvements.

6. Review estimates of costs of restoring property to required condition at end of lease and determine that these estimates are properly reflected in the accounts.

7. Determine that client is performing all duties required under the lease contract with respect to insurance, repairs, and taxes.

8. Determine what information will constitute adequate informative disclosure of leases in the financial statements and most appropriate method of presentation.

Other intangible assets

Other intangible assets sometimes encountered by the auditor include copyrights, trademarks and trade names, franchises, and distributorships (or commercial franchises). A copyright is an exclusive legal right to reproduce, publish, and sell a literary, musical, or artistic work for a maximum period of 56 years. A trademark, label, or trade name may be registered with the federal government as a means of establishing its legal ownership. Registration is for a period of 30 years but is renewable. A franchise granted by a governmental unit to a private corporation consists of the privilege of using public property in providing such essential services as transportation, communications, and the transmission of gas and electricity.

Distributorships (or commercial franchises) consist of an exclusive right to market the products or services of a well-known company in a given area. Such a franchise may be a most significant factor in successful merchandising for such fields as automobiles, motels, restaurants, and many other goods and services. The contract creating a commercial franchise may be terminable at the option of either part or may extend over a specified time period. The appropriate valuation basis is cost whether the franchise was acquired directly from the issuing company or was purchased from another franchisee. Amortization of a franchise should extend over the indicated period of useful existence.

Audit procedures for copyrights, trademarks, franchises, and distributorships are similar to those for other intangible assets. The auditor prepares or obtains analyses of the ledger accounts, determines the propriety and authorization of charges to the accounts, and considers the reasonableness of the amortization programs.

Time of examination

Many of the auditing procedures described in this chapter can be performed in advance of the balance sheet date. The opportunities for lightening the year-end work load by doing preliminary work on deferred charges and intangible assets are comparable to those described in Chapter 15 for plant and equipment. Turnover is not rapid in these asset categories, and the amounts verified in October or November are often little changed by the end of December. Consequently, the time required at the year-end to complete the working papers developed during the interim audit work is usually not extensive.

Deferred charges and intangible assets acquired during the year must be verified as to cost and proper authorization for the transaction. All such acquisitions (and sales as well) may be verified during the year; transactions during the last few months will then be the only matters requiring review at the end of the period. The minutes of directors' meetings may also be examined on an interim basis to establish the authorization for purchases, sales, and amortization programs for intangibles. A final review of minutes must of course be made after the close of the year to complete this audit procedure.

GROUP I
REVIEW QUESTIONS

16–1. What similarities are there in the auditor's objectives in the examination of (*a*) property, plant, and equipment; (*b*) prepaid expenses and deferred charges; and (*c*) intangible assets?

16–2. What are preoperating costs?

16–3. How is a valuation for goodwill determined in a business combination accounted for as a purchase?

16–4. In your first examination of the financial statements of Hancock Mfg. Co., a company never previously audited, you find among the company's total assets of $1 million an intangible asset entitled "Deferred Research and Development Costs" in the amount of $200,000. What evidence would you require to support the treatment of these costs as intangible assets?

16–5. What factors determine the amortization policy for intangible assets?

16–6. State two important aspects of internal control over all types of prepaid expenses and deferred charges.

16–7. During your audit of Simpson Corporation you find that the company has a number of insurance policies and maintains an insurance register. You obtain the policies from the treasurer in connection with your review of unexpired insurance. What specific points should be observed in inspecting these policies?

16–8. In your first examination of Rochester Company you are impressed by the superior earnings of the company, which appear to be caused by such factors as excellent management and strategic location. During the year under audit goodwill in the amount of $40,000 was placed on the books by authority of a resolution of the board of directors. The president explains that this action was taken because this amount of goodwill had been written off as an extraordinary item several years previously when the company was operating at a loss. The goodwill had originally been recorded at cost as part of the purchase of a going business. The president believes that the present earnings show that the previous write-off of goodwill was unwarranted. What position would you take?

16–9. Enumerate the various kinds of expenditures properly included in organization costs.

16–10. In discussing the verification of prepaid expenses by an auditor, a student of auditing made the following statement: "If the auditor finds that the expenditures originally charged to the prepaid expense accounts were valid and properly recorded, and he finds that these amounts have been amortized systematically, he can give full approval to inclusion of these assets in the balance sheet." Do you agree? Explain.

16–11. Should the verification of prepaid taxes be combined with the examination of taxes expense and accrued taxes? Explain.

16–12. May any charges properly be made to organization costs after operations have begun? Explain.

16–13. The Atlantic Manufacturing Company leased a tract of land and storage building for a period of 10 years at an annual rental of $6,000. Terms of the lease required immediate payment of the first and last years' rent. How should this prepayment be disclosed in the financial statements?

16–14. What documents would ordinarily be examined by the auditor in his verification of (a) prepaid rent and (b) prepaid insurance?

16–15. Reynolds Television Company has been carrying on a very costly advertising campaign for the past three months. The expense of this campaign is far in excess of the company's normal advertising expenditures and is regarded by management as a radical step designed to place the company in a strategic position in the community. Management proposes to charge the costs of the campaign to the Goodwill account. Would you approve? Explain.

16–16. What points deserve attention by the auditor in the verification of organization costs?

16–17. May the cost of patents developed within a company be capitalized and amortized on the same basis as patents purchased from outsiders?

16–18. The time required for verification of various asset groups such as cash and inventories will vary from one audit to another, but certain tendencies as to relative time requirements are usually apparent. You are to rate the following asset groups first on the basis of the relative amount of audit time usually required and secondly on the basis of the relative amount of difficulty likely to be encountered by the auditor. Prepare two separate lists: one in order of time requirements; and the other in order of relative difficulty.

a)   Cash.
b)   Investments in securities.
c)   Accounts receivable.
d)   Notes receivable.
e)   Inventories.
f)   Prepaid expenses.
g)   Deferred charges.

GROUP II
QUESTIONS REQUIRING ANALYSIS

16–19. You are engaged in the first audit of Martin Corporation, for the year ended August 31, 1974. In your review of the client's general ledger, you discover an account entitled "Suspense," with a balance of $250,000. Your investigation discloses that the $250,000 represents part of the purchase price of all of the assets of a sole proprietorship, Lewis Company. The purchase agreement, dated February 28, 1974, provides for a total purchase price of $1,000,000. According to the minutes, Martin's directors assigned $750,000 of the purchase price to the tangible assets and identifiable intangible assets of Lewis Company based on their fair values at February 28, 1974. The controller of Martin Corporation informs you that neither he nor the directors could decide how to account for the remaining $250,000 of the purchase price.

Required:

Assuming you are satisfied with the allocation of the $750,000, how would you advise the Martin controller to account for the $250,000 balance of the suspense account? Explain.

16–20. A client engaged in the operation of intercontinental airline routes has made large expenditures in the current year to acquire new large aircraft and has also expended large amounts for training programs to prepare flight crews and ground personnel to operate and maintain the new models of aircraft. The client is currently considering whether to treat the expenditures for training programs as expenses of the current year or as capital expenditures to be amortized over the next several years. He inquires whether you favor one or the other of these approaches and whether you would be willing to give an unqualified audit report regardless of which method is selected.

16–21. During the course of your annual audit of a manufacturing company, one of your assistants, who has been engaged in the verification of prepaid expenses, reports that he has discovered that a significant portion of the company's inventory has been pledged as collateral for a loan. Explain how audit work relating to prepaid expenses would have led to discovery of the pledge of inventory as collateral.

16–22. The Vinton Corporation occupies four similar buildings, three of which are owned and the other rented. You are making your first audit of Vinton Corporation, which maintains its records on a calendar year basis. In studying the lease contract of the nonowned building you find that the rent is $600 a month payable in advance on the 10th of each month. The records show that payment covering the period from December 10 to January 10 was made on January 9 and was charged to expense at that time. The controller of Vinton Corporation informs you that it has been the company's practice for many years to charge each rental payment to expense when paid and not to make any year-end adjustment of rental expense. Under these circumstances would you propose an adjustment entry to defer that portion of the rent applicable to the succeeding year?

16–23. A new client, Dalton Engineering Company, is primarily known for its development of new products. The company carries on continuous and extensive research designed to produce new products of commercial value, and it consistently charges the cost of research to current operations. You discover that in January 1970 a large-scale research project called "Project Pace" was begun with the objective of developing an important new machine. Work continued on this project until January 1974, at which time the patent was applied for on the machine and the project was closed. Because the company had a precisely designed objective for this project and was highly confident that the research would result in the obtaining of a patent, the research costs of "Project Pace" were accumulated in an asset account. The accumulated balance in this account was transferred to the Patents account at June 30, 1974, when a patent was granted.

You are to design an audit program for the patent acquired as the result of "Project Pace," assuming that you are auditing Dalton Engineering Company for the first time at December 31, 1974. (AICPA, adapted)

16–24. Shortly after you were retained to examine the financial statements of Case Corporation, you learned from a preliminary discussion with management that the corporation had recently acquired a competing business, the Mall Company. In your study of the terms of the acquisition, you find that the total purchase price was paid in cash and that the transaction was authorized by the board of directors and fully described in the minutes of the directors' meetings. The only aspect of the acquisition of the Mall Company which raises any doubts in your mind is the allocation of the total purchase price among the several kinds of assets acquired. This allocation, which had been specifically approved by the board of directors of Case Corporation, placed very high values on the tangible assets acquired and allowed nothing for goodwill.

You are inclined to believe that the allocation of the lump-sum price to the several types of assets was somewhat unreasonable, because the total price for the business was as much or more than the current replacement cost of the tangible assets acquired. However, as an auditor, you do not claim to be an expert in property values. Would you question the propriety of the directors' allocation of the lump-sum purchase price? Explain fully.

GROUP III
PROBLEMS

16–25.   You are examining the financial statements of Aby Company, a retail enterprise, for the year ended December 31, 1974. The client's accounting department presented you with an analysis of the Prepaid Expenses account balance of $31,400 at December 31, 1974 as shown below:

ABY COMPANY
ANALYSIS OF PREPAID EXPENSES ACCOUNT
December 31, 1974

Description	*Balance December 31, 1974*
Unexpired insurance:	
Fire	$ 750
Liability	4,900
Utility deposits	2,000
Loan to officer	500
Purchase of postage meter machine, one half of invoice price	400
Bond discount	3,000
Advertising of store opening	9,600
Amount due for overpayment on purchase of furniture and fixtures	675
Unsaleable inventory—entered June 30, 1974	8,300
Contributions from employees to employee welfare fund	(275)
Book value of obsolete machinery held for resale	550
Funds delivered to Skyhigh Stores with purchase offer	1,000
Total	$31,400

Additional information includes the following:

(1)   Insurance policy data:

Type	*Period covered*	*Premium*
Fire	12-31-73 to 12-31-75	$1,000
Liability	6-30-74 to 6-30-75	9,500

(2) The postage meter machine was delivered in November and the balance due was paid in January. Unused postage of $700 in the machine at December 31, 1974 was recorded as expense at time of purchase.

(3) Bond discount represents the unamortized portion applicable to bonds maturing in 1975.

(4) The $9,600 paid and recorded for advertising was for the cost of an advertisement to be run in a monthly magazine for six months, beginning in December 1974. You examined an invoice received from the advertising agency and extracted the following description:

Advertising services rendered for store opened in
November 1974.......................... $6,900

(5) Aby has contracted to purchase Skyhigh Stores and has been re-required to accompany its offer with a check for $1,000 to be held in escrow as an indication of good faith. An examination of paid checks revealed the check had not been returned from the bank through January 1975.

Required:

Assuming that you have examined acceptable underlying audit evidence, prepare a working paper to show the necessary adjustments, corrections, and reclassifications of the items in the Prepaid Expenses account. In addition to the information shown in the above analysis, the following column headings are suggested for your working paper:

Adjustments and Reclassifications		Prepaid Expenses Adjusted Balance December 31, 1974	Disposition of Adjustments and Reclassifications				
			Expense Debit (Credit)	Accts. Rec.— Other	General		
Debit	Credit				Account	Debit	Credit

(AICPA, adapted)

16–26. During your first audit of the financial statements of Forrest Corporation, you observe that the balance sheet at December 31, 1974 includes the item, Patents, at cost, $56,340. Through inspection of ledger accounts, you find the following information applicable to one patent acquired in 1960:

1970	Legal costs incurred in defending the validity of the patent..	$4,500
1972	Legal costs in prosecuting an infringement suit............	3,300
1972	Legal costs (additional) in the infringement suit...........	1,020
1972	Cost of improvements (unpatented) on the patented device...	2,700

There are no credits in the account and no allowance for amortization has been set up on the books for any of the patents. There are three other patents issued in 1968, 1970 and 1971; all were developed by the staff of the client. The patented articles are presently very marketable, but are estimated to be in demand only for the next few years.

Required:

a) What auditing procedures for all the patents should be included in your audit program and what details of patented articles should appear in the permanent file?

b) Discuss the items included in the patent account from an accounting standpoint. (AICPA, adapted)

16–27. Meadowbrook Corporation, a newly organized company engaged in the retailing of men's clothing, has retained you to audit its financial statements at December 31, of the first year of operation. The president of the corporation informs you that certain stockholders have voiced opposition to some of the operating policies of the new enterprise, and he is therefore very anxious that the financial statements for this first year show an impressive profit. He therefore suggests that the following items, which were originally entered in operating expense accounts, be transferred to an asset classification such as prepaid expenses, deferred charges, or intangible assets, thus reducing the amount of expenses allocated to the first year of operations. The company's accounts are maintained on a calendar year basis, but the president emphasizes that in his judgment the benefits derived from many of the expenditures during this first year will extend beyond the December 31 cutoff.

(1) Rent of store for months of February and March. The store was leased on February 1, but two months were spent in equipping the store and it was not opened for business until April 1. Monthly rental is $700.

(2) Fees paid to a firm of certified public accountants who designed the accounting system and various forms and reports presently in use— $800.

(3) Costs incurred in October after six months of operation for the purpose of rearranging store layout—$900.

(4) Salaries of officers and wages of clerks applicable to period prior to opening for business on April 1—$3,000.

(5) Charges for paving parking lot and landscaping land in front of store. This work was approximately 90 percent complete as of December 31, and an invoice had been received from the contractor for work performed to December 31 in the amount of $6,500. Of this total, $5,200 was applicable to the parking lot and $1,300 was incurred for landscaping. The president explained that he had requested the bill be sent before the close of the year so that he could take advantage of this expenditure for income tax purposes, but that he was now more interested in showing an impressive profit for the first year of operations than he was in minimizing the current year's tax bill. He added that the work would not be completed until sometime in January and would normally not have been billed until that time.

(6) Payment to Flood-Lite, Incorporated, a service organization, for a year's contract calling for the maintenance of the various lighting fixtures used in the parking lot and to illuminate outdoor advertising displays. The contract was signed on August 15 and provided for all necessary maintenance work for 12 months from that date. By paying in advance, the company secured the contract for $600. If paid

on a monthly basis, the cost of each month's service would have been $55.

(7) Purchase of a television set to be given away to a customer in a drawing to be held on January 15. The television set had been purchased and placed on display in the store on December 1, with a sign indicating it to be the first prize in the drawing to be held six weeks later. The president explained that although the set had been charged to Advertising Expense when purchased, he believed it would be better accounting practice to treat it as advertising expense of the period in which it was actually given away. Cost of the set and other related prizes was $900.

Required:

State your opinion concerning the proper accounting treatment of each of the above listed items. In drafting your answer, use a separate paragraph for each item and label it with an identifying number, as above. State fully the reasoning underlying your decision in each case. Also state any assumptions which you consider necessary to a conclusive answer, and indicate any alternative decisions which you would consider acceptable.

16–28. You have assigned your assistant to the examination of the Victor Sales Company's fire insurance policies. All audit procedures with regard to the fire insurance register have been completed (i.e., vouching, footing, examination of paid checks, testing computations of insurance expense and prepayments, tracing of expense charges to appropriate expense accounts, etc.). Your assistant has never examined fire insurance policies and asks for detailed instructions.

Required:

a) In addition to examining the policies for the amounts of insurance and premiums and for effective and expiration dates, to what other details should your assistant give particular attention as he examines the policies? Give the reasons for examining each detail. (Confine your comments to fire insurance policies covering buildings, their contents, and inventories.)

b) After reviewing your assistant's working papers, you concur in his conclusion that the insurance coverage against loss by fire is inadequate and that if loss occurs the company may have insufficient assets to liquidate its debts. After a discussion with you, management refuses to increase the amount of insurance coverage.

    (1) What mention will you make of this condition and contingency in your short-form report? Why?

    (2) What effect will this condition and contingency have upon your opinion? Give the reasons for your position. (AICPA, adapted)

16–29. During your first examination of Bolt Co., a newly organized corporation, you find a ledger account entitled "Organization, Promotion, and Development Costs" in which the following entries were made during the first year of operation:

Date		Explanation	Debit	Credit
January	6	Legal fees—incorporation..............	20,000	
		Fees and taxes—charter..............	1,200	
February	1	Stock certificates....................	1,000	
March	1	Leasehold...........................	32,500	
March	20	Travel re location of branch...........	2,800	
April	1	Advertising.........................	25,000	
April	1	Bond discount.......................	30,000	
May	1	Advertising.........................	20,000	
May	30	Engineering research.................	8,000	
July	30	Engineering research.................	10,500	
September	1	Advertising.........................	18,000	
September	10	Entertainment—opening of branch.....	3,500	
November	15	Installation—cost system.............	2,800	
December	31	Engineering research.................	18,100	
December	31	Damage suit........................	5,000	
December	31	Amortization........................		19,840

Investigation of the supporting evidence for these transactions disclosed the following information:

(1) A corporate charter providing for perpetual existence was obtained on January 6. The legal fees were incurred exclusively for the purpose of incorporation.

(2) The leasehold was obtained March 1 and runs for a period of 20 years. In addition to the cash payment made on this date to secure the lease, the company agreed to an annual cash rental of $3,600. The leased premises included an old frame apartment building estimated to be worth $6,000. This building was moved to another location to make way for construction of a new business building suitable for the company's operations. The old building was sold for $5,000, but moving costs of $3,200 were incurred. The net proceeds were credited to Miscellaneous Revenue.

(3) Travel expenditures amounting to $2,800 were reimbursed to the treasurer of the company, who had investigated several possible sites for a branch to be established by the company.

(4) Advertising expenditures were stated by the president to represent an initial campaign designed to make the community familiar with the name and products of the new company. He stated further that this campaign had been completed as of December 31, and that further advertising would involve only moderate charges which would be treated as operating expense.

(5) Engineering research represented the costs of perfecting several electrical devices which the company planned to place in production in the near future.

(6) The bond discount represented the excess of the face value of an issue of $1,000,000 of first-mortgage, 5 percent, 20-year bonds over the net proceeds. The bonds were sold through an underwriter on April 1; the semiannual interest payment dates are April 1 and October 1.

(7) Elaborate opening ceremonies with an orchestra, refreshments, and numerous prizes were conducted on September 10 to acquaint the public with the sales branch opened by the company on that date.

(8) The company engaged a firm of certified public accountants to design and install a cost accounting system for the manufacturing operations.

(9) The settlement of the damage suit by a cash payment of $5,000 resulted from smoke damage to adjoining property caused by the company's operations. This situation is not likely to recur in view of a change in the operating procedures.

(10) The amortization of this account at December 31 was made in accordance with a resolution of the board of directors. You determine that the amount of amortization provided is reasonable for the research and development costs.

A profit of $247,600 was realized during the first year according to the company's books.

You are to prepare appropriate audit working papers showing your analysis of this account and also to draft any necessary adjusting journal entries, except for income taxes.

GROUP IV
CASE STUDIES IN AUDITING

SOUTHERN TELEVISION, INC.

16–30. You have been engaged by Mr. J. K. Shell, a practicing attorney, to audit the financial statements of Southern Television, Inc., for the year ended December 31, 1974. Mr. Shell is secretary of the corporation and is also a major stockholder. The company is in the second year of its existence but has not previously been audited by independent certified public accountants. The only activities during the first year of the corporate existence consisted of organization, construction of plant, and other preliminary work.

The corporation's accountant presents to you the following balance sheet which he had prepared from the books as of December 31, 1974.

ASSETS

Accounts receivable—stockholders	$ 50,000	
Other current assets (net)	30,000	
Total Current Assets		$ 80,000
Transmitter and equipment (net)	$250,000	
Other property and equipment (net)	50,000	
Total Property and Equipment		300,000
Organization costs		20,000
Goodwill		35,000
Deferred interest		15,000
Total Assets		$450,000

LIABILITIES AND STOCKHOLDERS' EQUITY

Current liabilities			$ 75,000
Long-term liabilities (secured)			240,000
Total Liabilities			$315,000
Common stock issued		$150,000	
Deficit, January 1, 1974	$ 5,000		
Operating loss for 1974	10,000	15,000	135,000
Total Liabilities and Stockholders' Equity			$450,000

Your examination reveals that the accounts receivable from stockholders represent funds borrowed by the corporation on its property and equipment and advanced to Mr. Shell, who used the money to pay the indebtedness he had incurred to buy stock in the corporation. The item of organization costs includes $1,000 attributable to formation of the corporation and $19,000 representing fees of attorneys and engineers who represented the corporation in obtaining its franchise from the Federal Communications Commission. Goodwill represents the par value of stock issued to executives of the company in exchange for services (including the securing of certain preliminary approvals from the FCC) rendered during the period before the corporations received its charter. Deferred interest, which appears on the balance sheet at $15,000, represents finance charges for the purchase of equipment.

The permit for the issuance of stock obtained from the Corporation Commissioner of the state requires the corporation to receive full value for the par value of the shares issued.

Required:

a) What course would you pursue in each of the following situations? It is known that an adverse opinion in your report would seriously curtail the corporation's line of credit.

   (1) You have proposed to reverse the entry of goodwill, debiting the amount instead to Discount on Common Stock. Mr. Shell has objected to your proposal. He states that the board of directors has fixed the value of the promotional services rendered at $35,000, and that the board's finding is prima facie evidence of the value.

   (2) The corporation's chief engineer, who is also vice president, has urged that $15,000 of the $19,000 cost of appearances before the FCC be charged to the cost of Transmitter and Equipment rather than to Organization Costs where it now appears. The amounts involved were expended for such projects as maps of the proposed broadcast pattern, securing FCC approval on the design of the station, and acceptance of the completed installation.

   (3) In discussions of the $50,000 debt owed by Mr. Shell to the corporation, he stated that he considered the corporation had repaid him the money which he had put into it, that he still owned all his stock in the corporation, but that he had orally agreed not to withdraw any dividends from the company until the other stockholders had received dividends equaling their original investment.

   As you talk to Mr. Shell, who in his capacity as an attorney handled the incorporation of the company, you have considerable doubt as to the legality of some of the corporate transactions. However, you realize that Mr. Shell is also quite sensitive on the subject of unauthorized practice of law.

b) In addition to discussing the problems of accounting, balance sheet presentation, and report writing involved here, give your suggestions as to how negotiations with Mr. Shell should be conducted.

17

Accounts payable and other liabilities

Now THAT the several chapters dealing with the verification of assets have been completed and we are ready to consider the examination of liability accounts, it is appropriate to compare and contrast the auditor's work on assets with the work to be done on liabilities. In the verification of every asset the auditor is constantly on guard against *overstated* asset values. Accounting records which overstate the amount of cash on hand or on deposit are usually suggestive of fraud, and the auditor's approach to this danger is a careful count of cash on hand and confirmation of amounts shown as on deposit with banks. Similarly, the threat of an overstated or fictitious account receivable necessitates direct communication with customers. The possibility of an overstated inventory requires that the auditor observe the physical count of goods. In carrying out these audit procedures the auditor is, of course, on the alert for all types of errors, but he is particularly aware of the dangers of overstatement of asset accounts.

The auditor's concern with possible overstatement of asset values arises from the fact that creditors and investors may sustain serious losses if they extend credit in reliance upon financial statements with inflated asset valuations. Secondly, any theft from the company by dishonest employees usually involves the abstraction of cash and improper entries in the accounts to conceal the theft. The question of legal liability on the part of certified public accountants is usually illustrated by cases in which auditors failed to detect material overstatement of assets.

In the study of audit work on liabilities, the point to be emphasized

561

is this: An *understatement of liabilities* will exaggerate financial strength of a company and conceal fraud just as effectively as *overstatement of assets.* Furthermore, the understatement of liabilities is usually accompanied by understatement of expenses and overstatement of net income. Audit procedures for liabilities should be designed to detect understatement, just as audit procedures for assets are designed to detect overstatement.

To overstate an asset account usually requires an improper entry in the accounting records, as by the recording of a fictitious transaction. Such improper entries can be detected by the auditor through verification of the individual items making up the balance of an asset account. Once a fictitious entry is detected, the individual responsible for the fraud has little alternative but to admit his acts. By way of contrast, it is possible to understate a liability account merely by failing to make an entry for a transaction creating a liability. The omission of an entry is less susceptible of detection than is a fictitious entry. If the omission is detected, there is at least a possibility of passing it off as an accidental error. Auditors have long recognized that the most difficult type of fraud to detect is fraud based on the nonrecording of transactions. Once transactions are entered in the records, there are many verification techniques available.

Another point of difference between the auditor's work on assets and liabilities is that liabilities generally do not present a problem of valuation. The amount of a liability is usually a matter of fact, whereas the proper valuation of an asset is a matter of opinion. (Income taxes payable represent a prominent exception to this generalization.) Much of the audit time devoted to assets is concerned with the propriety of the valuation methods used by the client. Consequently, the audit time required for verification of liability accounts may be considerably shorter than for verification of corresponding dollar amounts in asset accounts. Contingent liabilities, of course, do raise the question of valuation.

Meaning of accounts payable

In a broad sense, accounts payable include not only amounts owing for merchandise and materials but all obligations of a business except those evidenced by bonds and notes. Apart from the purchase of materials and merchandise, other transactions giving rise to accounts payable include the acquisition of plant and equipment and the incurring of various types of production costs, as well as selling and administrative expenses. Taxes, wages, salaries, light, power, rent, and a host of other items all result in liabilities which must be verified, classified, recorded, and paid by the client. The auditor's verification of these liabilities will ordinarily be broken down into separate phases corresponding to balance sheet captions, such as "Accounts payable—trade," "Accounts payable—officers and employees," and "Accrued liabilities."

Trade accounts payable are those current liabilities arising from the purchase of goods and services from trade creditors and are generally evidenced by invoices or statements received from the creditors. Other types of accounts payable are those current liabilities for which the company acts as fiduciary, such as taxes withheld from employees' salaries, unclaimed wages, and customers' deposits. *Accrued liabilities* generally accumulate as a result of the company's contractual or legal obligation to pay salaries, pensions, interest, rent, taxes chargeable to expense, and obligations under product warranties. The company seldom receives invoices or statements for accrued liabilities.

In terms of auditing procedures, liabilities arising from transactions with outside suppliers differ significantly from payroll and other obligations originating within the company. Moreover, purchases of merchandise and materials make up the major portion of accounts payable transactions and require a corresponding amount of auditing activity. For these reasons. it is convenient to center the discussion at present on trade accounts payable and to deal separately with other current liabilities such as accrued expenses, taxes, and deferred credits to revenue.

The auditor's objectives in examination of accounts payable

The principal objectives of the auditor in his examination of accounts payable are to: (*a*) determine the adequacy of internal controls for the processing and payment of vendors' invoices; (*b*) prove that the amount shown on the balance sheet is in agreement with the supporting accounting records, and (*c*) determine that all liabilities existing at the balance sheet date have been recorded.

Internal control

In thinking about internal control for accounts payable, it is important to recognize that the accounts payable of one company are the accounts receivable of other companies. It follows that there is little danger of permanently overlooking or misplacing a liability because creditors will naturally maintain complete records of their receivables and will speak up if payment is not received. A company may, therefore, choose to minimize its record keeping of liabilities and to rely on creditors to call attention to any delay in making payment. This viewpoint is not an endorsement of inaccurate or incomplete records of accounts payable but merely a recognition that the self-interest of creditors constitutes a protective feature of accounting for payables which is not present in the case of accounts receivable.

Discussions of internal control applicable to accounts payable are often extended to cover the functions of purchasing and receiving, as well as the activities of the accounts payable department. This is not surprising, for the end objective of controls in this area of operations is to provide assurance that the company receives value for all payments made; and this, in turn, requires proof that goods have been received in proper quantity and condition before invoices are approved. A first essential of adequate control is the segregation of duties so that a cash disbursement to a creditor will be made only upon approval of the purchasing, receiving, accounting, and finance departments. All purchase transactions should be evidenced by serially numbered purchase orders, copies of which are sent to the accounts payable department for comparison with vendors' invoices and receiving reports.

The receiving department should be independent of the purchasing department. Receiving reports should be prepared for all goods received. These documents should be serially numbered and prepared in a sufficient number of copies to permit prompt notification of receipts to the accounts payable department, purchasing department, and stores department. In smaller companies, vendors' packing slips are often utilized as receiving reports.

Within the accounts payable department, all forms should be stamped with the date and hour received. Vouchers and other documents originating within the department can be controlled through the use of serial numbers. Each step in the verification of an invoice should be evidenced by the entering of a date and signature on the voucher. The most effective means of assuring that routine procedures, such as the proof of extensions and footings and the review of the propriety of discounts taken, are consistently carried out is the requirement that a designated employee sign the voucher as each step in verification is completed. Comparison of the quantities listed on the invoice with those shown on the receiving report and purchase order, if carefully made, will prevent the payment of charges for goods in excess of those ordered and received. Comparison of the prices, discounts, and terms of shipment as shown on the purchase order and on the vendor's invoice provides a safeguard against the payment of excessive prices.

Separation of the function of invoice verification and approval from that of cash disbursement is another step which tends to prevent error or fraud. Before invoices are approved for payment, written evidence must be presented to show that all aspects of the transaction have been verified.

Another control procedure which the auditor may expect to find in a well-managed accounts payable department is regular monthly balancing of the detailed records of accounts payable to the general ledger control. These trial balances should be preserved as evidence of the performance of this procedure and as an aid in localizing any subsequent errors.

Monthly statements from vendors should be reconciled with the accounts payable ledger or list of open vouchers, and any discrepancies fully investigated. In some industries it is common practice to make advances to vendors which are recovered by making percentage deductions from invoices. When such advances are in use, the auditor should ascertain what procedures are followed to assure that deductions from the invoices are made in accordance with the agreement.

Internal control and the computer

The substantial volume of accounts payable transactions of a company makes processing of payables an effective application of a computer. The traditional accounts payable subsidiary ledger is seldom found in a computerized payables system; instead, invoices are processed by a voucher system for payment within the discount or credit period. Periodically, a computer print-out of purchasing volume from each vendor is provided for use by the purchasing department. In addition, the computer may be programmed to print out unpaid accounts payable vouchers for each vendor, for use by internal auditors or independent auditors.

With the increased utilization of electronic computers, some changes in the traditional procedures for accounts payable have become desirable. One large company, for example, has overcome the difficulties of converting the variety of invoices and statements received from vendors to computer input form by dispensing with these documents entirely. Instead, the uniform company purchase orders, supported by comparable receiving reports, serve as the source data for credits to accounts payable.

Another accounts payable shortcut method is the "purchase order draft" system. In this, a company remits to its vendor a purchase order form with an attached draft executed in blank to the vendor. Upon shipment of the order, the vendor completes the draft for the purchase price net of any cash discount and deposits the draft in his bank. The purchaser's bank notifies him that the draft has cleared, and upon verification of the order the draft is paid for by the purchaser's check and is processed by the computer.

It is evident that the system described above, which short-cuts or eliminates a number of the traditional controls associated with the accounts payable function, must be adequately safeguarded to prevent substantial losses. The participating vendors should be carefully screened, partial shipments should not be accepted, and purchase prices should be agreed upon in advance. In addition, the draft form should have imprinted on its face a dollar limitation, and the clearing bank should be furnished a list of participating vendors and authorized draft signers. Receiving and inspection functions should be thoroughly carried out.

Audit working papers for accounts payable

In addition to the grouping sheet for accounts payable, the principal working papers are schedules or trial balances of the various types of accounts payable at the balance sheet date. In addition, the auditor usually prepares a listing of unrecorded accounts payable discovered during the course of the audit, as illustrated in Figure 17–2.

Audit program

The examination of trade accounts payable usually requires audit work along the following lines. The first three procedures are performed as a part of the study and evaluation of internal control for accounts payable. The remainder of the audit program is performed on or subsequent to the balance sheet date.

Study and evaluation of internal control for accounts payable:

1. Obtain a description of internal control for accounts payable.
2. Test accounts payable transactions:
   a) Verify postings to Accounts Payable control account for a test period.
   b) Vouch to supporting documents all postings in selected accounts of the accounts payable subsidiary ledger.
   c) Review the handling of cash discounts.
3. Evaluate internal control for accounts payable.

Procedures for accounts payable at balance sheet date:

4. Obtain or prepare a trial balance of accounts payable as of the balance sheet date.
5. Reconcile the trial balance total to the general ledger control account.
6. Vouch balances payable to selected creditors to supporting documents.
7. Reconcile liabilities with monthly statements from creditors.
8. Consider confirming accounts by direct correspondence if statements from creditors are not available.
9. Compare cash disbursements subsequent to the balance sheet date with the accounts payable trial balance.
10. Trace balances owing to affiliated companies to books of respective companies, or confirm by correspondence if books are not available.

11. Investigate debit balances for collectibility and reclassify if substantial in amount.
12. Ascertain that liability to consignors for merchandise sold has been recorded.
13. Search for unrecorded accounts payable.
14. Obtain a letter of representations from client regarding the inclusion of all liabilities.
15. Determine proper balance sheet presentation of accounts payable.

1. *Obtain a description of internal control for accounts payable.*

The following questionnaire enumerates many of the matters to be investigated by the auditor in making a study of the internal control for accounts payable:

1. Is the accounts payable department clearly designated as the group responsible for verification and approval of invoices for payment?
2. Is the accounts payable department independent of—
   a) The purchasing department?
   b) Other persons requesting specific expenditures?
   c) Cashier or persons signing checks?
   d) The receiving department?
3. Do the procedures for verification of invoices in the accounts payable department require a signature on every voucher to show that the following steps have been taken:
   a) Comparison of quantities billed on the invoice with quantities called for on the purchase order and shown as received by the receiving report?
   b) Comparison of the prices, discounts, credit period, and terms of shipment per the invoice with those specified on the purchase order?
   c) Proof of the clerical accuracy of the invoice with respect to extensions, footings, and deduction of discounts?
4. Is an accounts payable trial balance prepared monthly and balanced to the general ledger control account?
5. Are monthly statements from vendors regularly reconciled with accounts payable ledgers or open vouchers?
6. Are returned purchases controlled in a manner which assures that the vendor will be charged therefor?
7. Are advance payments to vendors recorded as receivables and controlled in a manner which assures that they will be recovered by offset against vendors' invoices?
8. If payments are made to vendors for shipments direct to customers, are the procedures in use adequate to assure that the sales are billed to customers?
9. Is there an adequate record of open purchase orders and commitments?
10. Are debit memos issued to vendors for discrepancies in invoice prices, quantities, or computations? Are these memos approved by an executive outside the accounts payable department?

11. Are debit balances in vendors' accounts brought to the attention of the credit and purchasing departments?

12. Are there established procedures to call attention to invoices not paid within the discount period?

2a. Verify postings to Accounts Payable control account for a test period.

A procedure necessary to establish the validity of the balance shown by the general ledger control account for accounts payable consists of tracing postings for one or more months to the voucher register and cash disbursements journal. Any postings to the control account from the general journal during this test period should also be traced. This work is performed prior to the audit date as part of a general test of postings to all records. At the same time, the auditor should scrutinize all entries to the control account for the entire period under audit and should investigate any unusual entries.

2b. Vouch to supporting documents all postings in selected accounts of the accounts payable subsidiary ledger.

Testing the accuracy of the voucher register or the accounts payable ledgers by tracing specific items back through the cashbook, purchases journal, and other journals to original documents, such as purchase orders, receiving reports, invoices, and paid checks, is necessary to determine the adequacy of the system of internal control. If the functions of purchasing, receiving, invoice verification, and cash disbursement are delegated to separate departments and internal controls appear adequate, the tracing of individual items from the ledgers to the original records may be undertaken only to the extent necessary to determine that the system is operating properly.

2c. Review the handling of cash discounts.

Some concerns record purchase invoices in the voucher register at the net amount after deduction of any available cash discounts. This method is desirable for companies which regularly take all discounts offered, since it minimizes bookkeeping effort and states liabilities at the amounts required for their payment. No purchase discount column will appear in the voucher register when this method is used. Occasionally, some delay in the processing of an invoice will prevent payment being made within the discount period. In such cases the amount of the check will exceed the recorded liability, and the excess will be offset in the cash disbursements journal by a debit entry in a column headed "Discounts Lost."

It is also acceptable practice to record invoices at the gross amount before deduction of cash discounts. Under this procedure the cash disbursements journal usually contains a credit column for "Cash Discount on Purchases." An alternative procedure is to use a discount column in the voucher register, with the liability recorded at the net amount and the Purchases account debited for the gross amount.

The auditor's concern with purchase discounts is based on the possibility of fraudulent manipulation by employees and also on the possibility of accidental loss through failure to take discounts. Numerous case histories of fraud relating to cash disbursements have involved the drawing of checks for the gross amount of an invoice paid within the discount period. The dishonest employee was then in a position to request a refund from the creditor, to substitute the refund check for currency, and to abstract cash in this amount without any further manipulation of the records.

The most convenient test of discounts when these are recorded separately is to compute the ratio of cash discounts earned to total purchases during the period and to compare this ratio from period to period. Any significant decrease in the ratio indicates a change in terms of purchases, failure to take discounts, or fraudulent manipulation.

3.   *Evaluate internal control for accounts payable.*

Completion of the preceding audit procedures enables the auditor to evaluate internal control for accounts payable. The internal control evaluation provides the basis for selecting the necessary audit procedures for verification of accounts payable at the balance sheet date.

4.   *Obtain or prepare a trial balance of accounts payable as of the balance sheet date.*

The purpose of this procedure is to prove that the liability figure appearing in the balance sheet is in agreement with the individual items comprising the detail records. A second purpose is to provide a starting point for the auditor's testing procedures: from the list of vouchers or accounts payable he will select a representative group of items for careful examination.

Large companies with numerous accounts payable usually furnish the auditor with a computer-prepared trial balance. For a lesser volume of accounts, a manually completed listing may be used. In either case, the auditor should verify the footing and the accuracy of individual amounts of the trial balance.

5.   *Reconcile the trial balance total to the general ledger control account.*

As stated in the preceding section, the obtaining or preparation of a trial balance of individual vouchers payable or accounts payable is a first step toward proving the validity of the amount to be presented as accounts payable in the balance sheet. If the schedule of individual items does not agree in total with the control account, the cause of the discrepancy must be investigated. In most situations the auditor will arrange for the client's staff to locate such errors and make the necessary adjustments. Agreement of the control account and the list of individual account balances is not absolute proof of the total indebtedness; invoices received near the close of the period may not be reflected in either the control account or the subsidiary records, and other similar errors may exist without causing the accounts to be out of balance.

6. Vouch balances payable to selected creditors to supporting documents.

Another procedure for establishing the validity of the client-prepared trial balance of accounts payable is the vouching of selected creditors' balances to supporting vouchers, invoices, purchase orders, and receiving documents. This work, generally performed on a test basis, also establishes additional evidence as to the status of internal control for accounts payable.

Many companies use a voucher system; and in this case, the verification of the individual vouchers is most conveniently made at the balance sheet date, when they will all be together in the unpaid voucher file. The content of the unpaid voucher file changes daily; as vouchers are paid, they are removed from the file and filed alphabetically by vendor. Consequently, it is very difficult to determine at a later date what vouchers were outstanding at the year-end.

If the auditor cannot be present at the balance sheet date, he should ask the client to prepare a list of vouchers at that date with sufficient identifying data for each voucher to permit its being located some weeks later. This listing of vouchers payable at the end of the year should show the names of vendors, voucher numbers, dates, and amounts.

7. Reconcile liabilities with monthly statements from creditors.

In some companies it is a regular practice each month to reconcile vendors' statements with the detailed records of payables. If the auditor finds that this reconciliation is regularly performed by the client's staff, he may limit his own review of vendors' statements to establishing that the reconciliation work has been satisfactory.

If the client's staff has not reconciled vendors' statements and accounts payable, the auditor will generally do so. If internal control for accounts payable is weak, the auditor may control incoming mail to assure that all vendors' statements received by the client are made available to the auditor. Among the discrepancies often revealed by reconciliation of vendors' statements are charges by the vendor for shipments not yet received or recorded by the client. Normal accounting procedures do not provide for recording invoices as liabilities until the merchandise has been received. These in-transit shipments should be listed and a decision reached as to whether they are sufficiently material to warrant being recorded. A strictly theoretical approach would often call for an adjusting entry to include year-end shipments in the inventory as "Merchandise in Transit." In practice, however, the auditor often concludes that such an adjustment would not cause a sufficient change in the financial statements to be worth suggesting.

In judging the materiality of unrecorded liabilities, consideration should be given to the related unrecorded debits. If recording the transaction would mean adding an asset as well as a liability, the effect on the financial statements would be less significant than recording an invoice of like amount for which the debit belonged in an expense account. The auditor must be sure, however, that invoices have been recorded as liabilities for all goods received and included in the year-end inventory.

Other discrepancies revealed by the reconciliation of clients' accounts payable with vendors' statements include discounts taken but disallowed, returned purchases for which credit has not been given, disputes over defective merchandise, and cash payments in transit at the balance sheet date from the client to vendors. These payments should appear as outstanding checks in the bank reconciliation for the balance sheet date.

8. *Consider confirming accounts by direct correspondence if statements from creditors are not available.*

Confirmation of accounts payable by direct correspondence with creditors is not a universal or mandatory procedure, as is the confirmation of accounts receivable. However, in many engagements the confirmation of at least a few accounts with creditors is advisable.

If confirmation of accounts payable is undertaken, confirmation requests should be mailed to suppliers from whom substantial purchases have been made during the year, regardless of the balances of their accounts at the balance sheet date. These suppliers can be identified by reference to the accounts payable subsidiary ledger, or by inquiry of purchasing department personnel. Other accounts warranting circularization by the auditor include those for which monthly statements are not available, accounts reflecting unusual transactions, accounts with parent or subsidiary corporations, and accounts secured by pledged assets.

The confirmation letter affords an opportunity to inquire into purchase commitments as well as to establish the facts concerning completed transactions. The letter shown in Figure 17–1 illustrates the points generally covered.

Why is confirmation of accounts payable not a mandatory procedure as is the confirmation of receivables? One reason is that the greatest hazard in the verification of liabilities is the existence of unrecorded liabilities. To confirm the *recorded accounts payable* contributes little or nothing to determining whether any *unrecorded accounts payable* exist. Secondly, the auditor will find in the client's possession externally created evidence such as vendors' invoices and statements which substantiate the

FIGURE 17–1

The Palermo Co.

1435 EAST FIFTH STREET, LOS ANGELES, CALIFORNIA 90024

December 31, 1974

The Creditor Corporation
1822 Skyline Drive
Chicago, Illinois 60606

Dear Sirs:

Will you please send directly to our auditors, Adams and Barnes, Certified Public Accountants, an itemized statement of the amount owed to you by us at the close of business December 31, 1974. Will you also please supply the following information:

Amount not yet due $_____

Amount past due $_____

Amount of purchase commitments $_____

Description of any collateral held _____

_____

A business reply envelope addressed to our auditors is enclosed. A prompt reply will be very much appreciated.

Very truly yours,

J. A. McBride

The Palermo Company
J. A. McBride
Controller

accounts payable. No such external evidence is on hand to support accounts receivable. Finally, many of the recorded liabilities as of the balance sheet date will be paid before the auditor completes his examination. The act of payment serves further to substantiate the authenticity of recorded liabilities. Of course some accounts receivable are also collected during the course of an audit, but often the receivables of greatest significance to the auditor will not be promptly collected, and confirmation is the only external evidence of their validity. For all these reasons, the audit procedure of confirmation is of less importance for accounts payable than for accounts receivable.

9. **Compare cash disbursements subsequent to the balance sheet date with the accounts payable trial balance.**

The comparison of cash disbursements occurring after the balance sheet date with the accounts payable trial balance is an excellent means of disclosing any unrecorded accounts payable. All liabilities must eventually be paid, and will, therefore, be reflected in the accounts when paid if not when incurred. By close study of payments made subsequent to the balance sheet date, the auditor may find some items that should have appeared as liabilities on the balance sheet. Regular monthly expenses, such as rent and utilities, are often posted to the ledger accounts directly from the cash disbursements journal without any account payable or other liability having been set up. Of course after having located such items the auditor may decide against proposing any adjusting entry, but it is still essential that he have all the facts about omitted liabilities before he reaches a decision as to the materiality of these items.

The auditor's comparison of cash disbursements occurring after the balance sheet date with the accounts payable trial balance also furnishes evidence of the validity of the recorded payables.

Payments subsequent to the balance sheet date should be scrutinized for the entire period of audit field work. Some clients retain copies of all checks issued; other clients maintain a cash disbursements journal only. In either case, the auditor should account for the numerical sequence of all checks issued subsequent to the balance sheet date, through the date of completion of field work.

10. **Trace balances owing to affiliated companies to books of respective companies, or confirm by correspondence if books are not available.**

Transactions with parent or subsidiary corporations are often not conducted on the same basis as transactions with outsiders, and they deserve special attention from the auditor. Unusual items, such as charges for machinery and equipment borrowed from an affiliated company, may be intermingled with outright purchase transactions. One ledger account is often used to record all transactions between two related concerns.

Such an account obviously may have either a debit or credit balance and must be analyzed to determine the proper presentation in the balance sheet. Whenever feasible, reconciliation of the account by reference to both sets of books is desirable. If this cannot be done, confirmation of the balance is essential. If another staff member or office of the auditor's firm is examining the financial statements of the affiliate, that staff member or office should be requested to process the confirmation.

11.   *Investigate debit balances for collectibility and reclassify if substantial in amount.*

Debit balances in accounts payable arise from a variety of sources, including the return of merchandise after payment has been made, duplicate payments, payment of excessive amounts, advances to suppliers, outright loans, and incorrect postings. Old debit balances may reflect disputed items for which collection is doubtful. The auditor should make sufficient investigation to satisfy himself as to the nature and collectibility of any substantial amounts. If collectible, these should be reclassified as assets for statement purposes rather than offset against accounts with credit balances.

If a vendor company is also a customer, a single ledger account is sometimes used to record both purchase and sales transactions. This is particularly likely to occur in the case of affiliated companies. Unless the right of offset exists by law or by agreement, such an account should, of course, be divided into the receivable and payable elements for balance sheet presentation.

12.   *Ascertain that liability to consignors for merchandise sold has been recorded.*

A review of the agreements with consignors is, of course, a prerequisite to the analysis of consignment transactions. The terms of these contracts often call for the rendering of "account sales" and the remittance of sales proceeds on a weekly or monthly basis. Sales of consigned goods shortly before the close of the period may not have been set up as a liability to the consignor; this is the central point of the auditor's inquiry. To determine that the liability to the consignor is correctly stated as of the balance sheet date will usually require these steps: tracing sales invoices to the liability account, a review of the computation of commissions, and determining the disposition of freight and handling charges applicable to the consigned goods.

13.   *Search for unrecorded accounts payable.*

Throughout his examination of accounts payable, the auditor is alert for any indication that liabilities may have been omitted from the records. The six preceding audit procedures are directly or indirectly concerned with bringing unrecorded accounts payable to light. In addition, there are several other sources of potential unrecorded accounts payable:

a) Unmatched invoices and unbilled receivers. These documents are "work in process" in a voucher system. The auditor should review such unprocessed documents at the balance sheet date to ascertain that the client has recorded an account payable where appropriate.

b) Unpaid vouchers entered in the voucher register subsequent to the balance sheet date. The auditor's scrutiny of these records may uncover an item which should have been booked as of the balance sheet date.

c) Invoices received by the client after the balance sheet date. Not all vendors bill promptly when goods are shipped or services are rendered. Accordingly, the auditor's review of invoices received by the client in the post-balance sheet period may disclose unrecorded accounts payable as of the balance sheet date.

d) Other audit areas. A variety of unrecorded accounts payable may be discovered during the course of the entire audit. Examples are customers' deposits recorded as credits to accounts receivable; obligations for securities purchased but not "settled" at the balance sheet date; unbilled contractor or architect fees for a building under construction at the audit date; and unpaid attorney or insurance broker fees. In all areas of the audit, the auditor should be alert for unrecorded payables.

A form of audit working paper used to summarize unrecorded accounts payable discovered by the auditor is illustrated in Figure 17–2.

When unrecorded liabilities are discovered by the auditor, the next question is whether the omissions are sufficiently material to warrant proposing an adjusting entry. Will the adjustment cause a sufficient change in the financial statements to give a different impression of the company's current position or of its earning power? As previously indicated in the discussion of the reconciliation of vendors' statements with accounts payable, auditors seldom propose adjustments for the purpose of adding shipments in transit to the year-end inventory unless the shipments are unusually large.

As a further illustration of the factors to be considered in deciding upon the materiality of an unrecorded transaction, let us use as an example the December 31, 1974 annual audit of a small manufacturing company in good financial condition with total assets of $1 million and preadjustment net income of $50,000. The auditor's procedures bring to light the following unrecorded liabilities:

a) An invoice for $700, dated December 30, 1974, and bearing terms of f.o.b. shipping point. The goods were shipped on December 30 but were not received until January 4. The invoice was also received and recorded on January 4.

FIGURE 17–2

The Palermo Company
Unrecorded Accounts Payable   M-1-1
December 31, 1974

Invoice Date	No.	Vendor and Description	Account charged	Amount
12/31/74	285	Hages Mfg. Co.- invoice & shipment in transit	Inventory	10 650 00
—	—	Fox & Williams-unpaid legal fees- see M-4	Legal Expense	1 000 00
12/28/74	428	Hart & Co.- machinery repairs (paid 1/18/75)	Repairs Exp.	12 600 00
12/31/74	—	Allen Enterprises-Dec., 1974 account sales for consigned goods	Sales	25 680 00
—	—	Grant Co.-shipment received 12/31/74 per receiver no. 2907; invoice not yet received	Inventory	15 820 00
—	—	Arthur & Baker-earned but unpaid architects' fee for building under construction-see K-5	Construction in Progress	23 370 00
				89 120 00
				M-1

A.J.E. 8	131	Inventory	26 470 00	
	156	Construction in Progress	23 370 00	
	401	Sales	25 680 00	
	518	Legal Expense	1 000 00	
	527	Repairs Expense	12 600 00	
	203	Accounts Payable - Trade		89 120 00
		To record unrecorded accounts payable at 12/31/74		

Above payables were developed principally in the audit of accounts payable. See audit program B-4 for procedures employed.

V.M.H.
1/28/75

In considering the materiality of this omission, the first point is that net income is not affected. The adjusting entry, if made, would add equal amounts to current assets (inventory) and to current liabilities, hence would not change the amount of working capital. The omission does affect the current ratio very slightly. The auditor would probably consider this transaction as not sufficiently material to warrant adjustment.

b) Another invoice for $2,000 dated December 30, 1974 and bearing terms of f.o.b. shipping point. The goods arrived on December 31 and were included in the physical inventory taken that day. The invoice was not received until January 8 and was entered as a January transaction.

This error should be corrected because the inclusion of the goods in inventory without recognition of the liability has caused an error of $2,000 in net income (before income taxes) for the year 1974. Since the current liabilities are understated, both the amount of working capital and the current ratio are exaggerated. The owners' equity is also overstated. These facts point to the materiality of the omission and constitute strong arguments for an adjusting entry.

c) An invoice for $700 dated December 31 for a new office safe. The safe was installed on December 31, but the invoice was not recorded until paid on January 15. Since the transaction involved only asset and liability accounts, the omission of an entry did not affect net income. However, working capital and the current ratio are affected by the error since the debit affects a noncurrent asset and the credit affects a current liability. Most auditors would probably not propose an adjusting entry for this item.

d) An invoice for $1,500 dated December 31, 1974 for advertising services rendered during October, November, and December. The invoice was not recorded until paid on January 15.

The argument for treating this item as sufficiently material to warrant adjustment is based on the fact that net income is affected, as well as the amount of working capital and the current ratio. The adjusting entry should probably be recommended in these circumstances.

The preceding examples suggest that a decision as to the materiality of an unrecorded transaction hinges to an important extent on whether the transaction affects net income. Assuming that an omitted transaction does affect net income and there is doubt as to whether the dollar amount is large enough to warrant adjustment, the auditor should bear in mind that approximately half of the effect of the error on net income is eliminated by the present high level of corporate income taxes. In other words, an adjusting entry to bring on the books an omitted expense item of $500 will reduce net income after federal income taxes by only about $250. If the adjusting entry is not made, the only ultimate effect is a shift of $250 between the net income of two successive years. As a general rule, the auditor should avoid proposing adjusting entries for errors in the year-end cutoff of transactions unless the effect on the statements is clearly significant. However, it should be borne in mind that a number of insignificant individual errors may be material in their cumulative effect on the financial statements.

14.   Obtain a letter of representations from client regarding the inclusion of all liabilities.

Most public accounting firms obtain written representations from clients concerning nearly all financial statement items. Although some accountants do not utilize representations by clients to this extent, it is standard practice to obtain a statement signed by an officer that all known liabilities are reflected in the financial statements. Such a representation does not reduce the auditor's responsibility but it often serves as an effective reminder to executives that management is primarily responsible for the fairness of financial statements.

The liability representations should be on the client's own letterhead and should show the titles of the offices signing the statement. A representation concerning contingent liabilities is illustrated in Chapter 18; the liability representation in Figure 17–3 is designed to cover direct liabilities.

FIGURE 17–3

The Palermo Co.

1435 EAST FIFTH STREET, LOS ANGELES, CALIFORNIA 90024

January 20, 1975

Adams and Barnes
Certified Public Accountants
8261 Washington Drive
Los Angeles, California 90018

    In connection with your examination of our financial statements for the year ended December 31, 1974, we represent that to the best of our knowledge and belief all liabilities of the corporation at December 31, 1974, have been recorded in the accounts as of that date, with the exception of small recurring expense items which are treated as expense when paid each month. No assets of the company have been pledged.

_____
(President)

_____
(Controller)

15. *Determine proper balance sheet presentation of accounts payable.*

Proper balance sheet presentation of accounts payable requires segregation of the following groups, if material:

a) Accounts payable to trade creditors.
b) Accounts payable to affiliates.
c) Accounts payable to directors, principal stockholders, officers, and employees.

Accounts payable secured by pledged assets should be disclosed in the balance sheet or a note thereto, and cross-referenced to the pledged assets.

Accounts payable should always be stated net of trade discounts. Cash discounts may or may not be deducted, depending upon the established procedures of the company in recording invoices.

OTHER LIABILITIES

Notes payable are discussed in the next chapter. In addition to the accounts payable previously considered, other important items included in the current liability section of the balance sheet are:

a) Amounts withheld from employees' pay.
b) Sales taxes payable.
c) Unclaimed wages.
d) Customers' deposits.
e) Liabilities for fines or other penalties.
f) Accrued liabilities.
g) Deferred credits to revenue.

Auditing procedures applicable to these various types of liabilities vary sufficiently to warrant separate consideration of each. Space limitations do not permit as full a discussion as was accorded accounts payable, but the major auditing problems and procedures will be briefly presented.

Amounts withheld from employees' pay

Payroll deductions are notoriously numerous; among the more important are social security taxes and individual income taxes. Although the federal and state governments do not specify the exact form of records to be maintained, they do require that records of amounts earned and withheld be adequate to permit a determination of compliance with tax laws.

Income taxes withheld from employees' pay and not remitted as of the balance sheet date constitute a liability to be verified by the auditor.

Accrued employer payroll taxes may be audited at the same time. This verification usually consists of tracing the amounts withheld to the payroll summary sheets, testing computations of taxes withheld and accrued, determining that taxes have been deposited or paid in accordance with the federal and state laws and regulations, and reviewing quarterly tax returns.

Payroll deductions are also often made for union dues, charitable contributions, retirement plans, insurance, savings bonds, and other purposes. In addition to verifying the liability for any such amounts withheld from employees and not remitted as of the balance sheet date, the auditor should review the adequacy of the withhholding procedures and determine that payroll deductions have been properly authorized and accurately computed.

Sales taxes payable

In many sections of the country, business concerns are required to collect sales taxes imposed by state and local governments on retail sales. These taxes do not represent an expense to the business; the retailer merely acts as a collecting agent. Until the amounts collected from customers are remitted to the taxing authority, they constitute current liabilities of the business. The auditor's verification of this liability includes a review of the client's periodic tax returns. The reasonableness of the liability is also tested by a computation applying the tax rate to total taxable sales. In addition, the auditor should examine a number of sales invoices to ascertain that customers are being charged the correct amount of tax. Debits to the liability account for remittances to the taxing authority should be traced to copies of the tax returns and should be vouched to the paid checks.

Unclaimed wages

Unclaimed wages are, by their very nature, subject to misappropriation. The auditor is, therefore, particularly concerned with the adequacy of internal control over this item. A list of unpaid wages should be prepared after each payroll distribution and recorded in the accounts. The payroll checks should not be left for more than a few days in the payroll department. Prompt deposit in a special bank account provides much improved control. The auditor will analyze the Unclaimed Wages account for the purpose of determining that (1) the credits represent all unclaimed wages after each payroll distribution, and (2) the debits represent only authorized payments to employees, remittances to the state under unclaimed property laws, or transfers back to general funds through approved procedures.

Customers' deposits

Many business concerns require that customers make deposits on returnable containers, and public utilities and common carriers may require deposits to guarantee payment of bills or to cover equipment on loan to the customer. A review of the procedures followed in accepting and returning deposits should be made by the auditor with a view to disclosing any shortcomings in internal control. There have been many instances in which deposits shown by the records as refunded to customers were in fact abstracted by employees.

The verification, in addition to a review of procedures, should include the listing of the individual deposit cards and a comparison of the total with the general ledger control account. If deposits are interest-bearing, the amount of accrued interest should also be verified. As a general rule, the auditor does not attempt to confirm deposits by direct communication with customers; but this procedure is desirable if the amounts involved are substantial or the internal control procedures are considered to be deficient.

Liabilities for fines or other penalties

In Chapter 10 the point was made that the auditor must be familiar with federal and state laws and regulations that affect his client's financial statements. If the auditor discovers that the client has apparently violated a law or regulation, he should discuss the matter with management and legal counsel of the client company and consider the possibility of a liability for a fine or penalty.

Penalties known as *liquidated damages* are often specified in a production contract in the event that scheduled delivery dates or performance specifications are not met for the product. The auditor should determine if the client is, or obviously will be, in violation of such contractual provisions; if so, the client should record a liability for the liquidated damages.

Accrued liabilities

Most accrued liabilities represent obligations payable sometime during the succeeding period for services or privileges received prior to the balance sheet date. Examples include interest payable, accrued property taxes, accrued payrolls and payroll taxes, income taxes payable, and amounts accrued under service guarantees.

Unlike accounts payable, which result from executed contracts, accrued liabilities pertain to services of a continuing nature, with the related expense often measured on a time basis. The basic auditing steps for accrued liabilities are:

1. Examine any contracts or other documents on hand which provide the basis for the accrual.
2. Appraise the accuracy of the detailed accounting records maintained for this category of liability.
3. Test the computations made by the client in setting up the accrual.
4. Determine that accrued liabilities have been treated consistently at the beginning and end of the period.

The computation of the amount of an accrued liability is a routine accounting function which should be performed by the client's staff before the auditor begins his verification. If this work has not been performed prior to the auditor's arrival, he should request that it be done as quickly as possible. If a shortage of competent personnel in the client's employ makes it necessary that the auditor assume the responsibility for computation of accruals, it should be recognized that he is going beyond normal auditing functions. This is a situation commonly encountered, however, in the examination of small concerns.

If the accounting records are well maintained and internal control is reasonably satisfactory, there is no need for the auditor to make an independent computation of accrued liabilities. He should merely review the methods employed in setting up the accruals and test the arithmetical accuracy of the computations made by the employees of the company.

Accrued property taxes.   In Chapter 16 it was pointed out that accrued property taxes may appropriately be verified in conjunction with the audit of prepaid property taxes. In any event, property tax payments are usually few in number and substantial in amount. It is, therefore, feasible for the audit working papers to include an analysis showing all of the year's transactions. Tax payments should be verified by inspection of the tax bills issued by governmental units and by reference to the related paid checks. If the tax accruals at the balance sheet date differ significantly from those of prior years, an explanation of the variation should be obtained. It is of utmost importance that the auditor verify that tax bills have been received on all taxable property, or that an estimated tax has been accrued.

Accrued payrolls.   The examination of payrolls from the standpoint of appraising the adequacy of internal controls and substantiating the expenditures for the period under audit is considered in Chapter 20. The present consideration of payrolls is limited to the procedures required for the verification of accrued payrolls at the balance sheet date.

Accrued gross salaries and wages appear on the balance sheets of virtually all concerns. The correctness of the amount accrued is significant in the determination of total liabilities and also in the proper matching of costs and revenue. The dates of payment usually differ for company officers, office employees, and factory employees; and the liability for each class of payroll is separately determined. The verification procedure consists principally of comparing the amounts accrued to the actual payroll of the subsequent period and reviewing the method of allocation at the cutoff date. Payments made at the first payroll dates of the subsequent period are reviewed to determine that no unrecorded payroll liability existed as of the balance sheet date.

A more exact determination of the accrued payroll at the year-end is made by some companies which compute the precise earnings of each employee for the fractional period. This method has the advantage of reflecting the overtime pay applicable to the days in question. When the allocation method previously described is in use, any significant variations in overtime from one period to the next may cause a degree of error. When overtime pay is a significant element, the auditor may compare the total payrolls of several periods to make sure that an allocation based on the period following the year-end produces a representative amount.

Pension plan accruals. In recent years formal contracts for pension plans have become standard practice. Along with the increase in number of pension plans has come a tendency toward larger payments and broader coverage. The employer is usually obligated to make regular payments into a pension fund administered by a trustee. This change in the character of pension programs has raised accounting questions as to the best method of allocating pension costs and recognizing pension plan liabilities. Informal, noncontractual arrangements of pensions determined on a case-by-case basis by an employer do not create the same issues and are not included as pension plans within the meaning of this discussion.

With the present-day pattern of employer-employee relationships, we may reasonably assume that a formal pension plan once adopted will continue indefinitely. This assumption of permanence is realistic, even though the wording of the plan calls for periodic review and permits discontinuance after a specified period. The total cost of a pension plan cannot be exactly computed in advance because of the number of variable factors, such as employee turnover, length of life of covered employees, and decisions by employees as to the exact time of retirement within the authorized period. Reasonably accurate estimates can however be computed by actuarial methods, thus permitting pension costs to be accounted for on an accrual basis.

When a pension plan is first adopted, some employees will already be approaching retirement age after long service with the company. The pension plan will usually recognize and give credit for past services as a qualifying factor. Pension costs may therefore conveniently be viewed as falling into two major categories: (*a*) costs based on past services rendered prior to the adoption or amendment of the pension plan, and (*b*) costs attributable to present and future services of employees. The purpose of a company in adopting a pension plan is to obtain *future* benefits from improved employee relations and a more competitive position in the labor market; consequently, all costs including past service costs should be treated as operating expenses of the present and future periods. Past service costs should not be charged to Retained Earnings, as some companies have been inclined to do.

Accounting for the cost of pension plans is highly complex. The auditor reviewing a client's pension costs and accruals should be familiar with the definitive pronouncement on the subject, the AICPA's *Accounting Principles Board Opinion No. 8*, "Accounting for the Cost of Pension Plans."

Auditing procedures for the accrued liability for pension costs include a review of the pension plan copy in the permanent file, confirmation of the client's pension cost for the period by direct correspondence with the client's actuary, and analysis of the related liability account, including confirmation of payments to the trustee, if appropriate.

Accrued vacation pay. Closely related to accrued salaries and wages is the liability which may exist for accrued vacation pay. This type of liability arises from two situations: (1) an employee entitled by contract to a vacation during the past year may have been prevented from taking it by an emergency work schedule, and (2) an employee may be entitled to a future vacation of which part of the cost must be accrued to achieve a proper matching of costs and revenue.

The auditor's verification of accrued vacation pay may begin with a review of the permanent file copy of the employment contract or agreement stipulating vacation terms. The computation of the accrual should then be verified both as to arithmetical accuracy and for agreement with the terms of the company's vacation policy. The auditor should also ascertain whether the expense provision offsetting the vacation accrual qualifies as a federal income tax deduction. If not, income tax allocation will be required.

Service guarantees. The products of many companies are sold with a guarantee of free service or replacement during a rather extended warranty period. The costs of rendering such services should preferably be recognized as expense in the year the product is sold rather than in a later year in which the replacement is made or repair service performed. If this policy is followed, the company will make an annual charge to expense and credit to a liability account based on the amount of the year's sales and the estimated future service or replacement. As repairs and replacements take place the costs will be charged to the liability account.

The auditor should review the client's annual provision for estimated future expenditures and compute the percentage relationship between the amount in the liability account and the amount of the year's sales. If this relationship varies sharply from year to year, the client should be asked for an explanation. The auditor should also review the charges month by month to the liability account and be alert for the "burial" of other expenses in this account. Sudden variations in the monthly charges to the liability account require investigation. In general, the auditor should satisfy himself that the balance in the liability account for service guarantees moves in reasonable relationship with the trend of sales and is properly segregated into current and long-term portions in the balance sheet.

Current income tax laws prohibit the deduction of provisions for service guarantees; deductions are permitted only when actual expenditures are incurred. Accordingly, the auditor should ascertain that the client is properly accounting for income taxes allocable to the nondeductible provisions.

Accrued commissions and bonuses. Accrued commissions to salesmen and bonuses payable to managerial personnel also require verification. The essential step in this case is reference to the authority for the commission or bonus. The basic contracts should be examined and traced to minutes of directors' meetings. If the bonus or commission is based on the total volume of sales or some other objective measure, the auditor should verify the computation of the accrual by applying the prescribed rate to the amount used as a base.

The appearance of prepaid commissions in the records indicates that salesmen are permitted to draw funds in anticipation of future earnings from commissions. A drawing account is maintained for each salesman, and this account is charged with payments to the salesman and credited with his commission earnings. A debit balance in the account represents the excess of drawings over earnings to date and is classified as a prepaid expense, on the assumption that it will be absorbed against future commissions. In his examination of prepaid commissions to salesmen the auditor attempts to determine whether such prepayments are accurately stated, have been properly authorized, and can reasonably be recovered through normal operations.

Income taxes payable. Federal, state, and foreign income taxes on corporations represent a material factor in determining both net income and financial position. The auditor cannot express an opinion on either the balance sheet or income statement of a corporation without first satisfying himself that the provision for income taxes has been properly computed. In the audit of small and medium-sized companies it is customary for the audit engagement to include the preparation of the client's tax returns. If the income tax returns have been prepared by the client's staff or other persons, the auditor must nevertheless verify the reasonableness of the tax liability if he is to express an opinion on the fairness of the financial statements. In preforming such a review of a tax return prepared by the client's staff or by others, the auditor may sometimes discover an opportunity for a tax saving which has been overlooked; obviously such a discovery tends to enhance the client's appreciation of the services rendered by the auditor.

For business organized as single proprietorships or partnerships, no provision for income taxes appears on the income statement because taxes on the profits of these enterprises are payable by the individual owner or owners.

Taxable income often differs from income as determined in the accounts and presented in the financial statements. If the difference between income as determined for tax purposes and income as determined by applying generally accepted accounting principles is substantial, allocation of income taxes is necessary to avoid a distortion of net income. Assume, for example, that a corporation adopts the sum-of-the-years'-digits or double-declining-balance method of computing depreciation for tax purposes but continues to use straight-line depreciation in its financial statements and accounting records. In the first years after adoption of the "rapid write-off" method of depreciation, the depreciation expense deduction on the tax return will be larger than the straight-line depreciation expense shown on the income statement.

In this situation if the income statement shows as income tax expense the amount of taxes actually payable for the year, the after-tax net income will be increased because of the reduction in the current year's taxes. However, this apparent rise in net income may be misleading because within a few years the depreciation available for tax purposes will have dropped below that being shown on the books under the straight-line method and the taxes payable in these later years will be larger than normal for the income being reported on the income statement. To avoid this artificial shifting of income, the AICPA, in *Accounting Principles Board Opinion No. 11*, has urged that income taxes be allocated between periods as are other expenses. This allocation may be made by recognizing as tax expense in the early years the additional taxes which will be payable in subsequent years when depreciation for tax purposes has fallen below depreciation per the books. Since the debit to income tax expense in the early years will be larger than the tax liability of those years, the excess credit is made to a Deferred Income Taxes account. In later years when the increased taxes are payable, the debit entry will be to the deferred credit account for Deferred Income Taxes. The effect of this allocation of income taxes is to cause the income tax expense of each year's income statement to bear the normal relationship to the reported income before taxes.

Other examples of the need for allocation of income taxes include provision for unrealized losses or expenses which relate to current operations but cannot be deducted for tax purposes until a later period, and extraordinary gains or losses which are reported separately from the results of ordinary operations in the income statement and included in the determination of taxable income as well. The income taxes applicable to extraordinary items should be applied to reduce the gains or losses, so that these items are presented in the income statement net of their tax effects.

The Revenue Act of 1962 provided an incentive to businessmen to modernize plant and equipment through the use of an Investment Credit. Since 1962 the Investment Credit has been successively suspended or repealed, then reinstated. It appears that the Investment Credit may be an element of federal fiscal policy for some years to come. The Investment Credit is a percentage (usually 7 percent) of the cost of certain depreciable assets. The amount of the credit available in any one year is deducted from the income tax payable for that year.

At present, two methods of accounting for the Investment Credit are in use. One, favored by the AICPA's Accounting Principles Board, allocates the credit ratably over the productive life of the acquired property in the computation of net income. The alternative "flow-through" method applies the credit as a reduction of federal income taxes in the year in which the credit arises. In either method, full disclosure of the method followed and amounts involved, if material, is necessary.

The Income Taxes Payable account should be analyzed and all amounts vouched to paid checks, income tax returns, or other supporting documents. The final balance in the Income Taxes Payable account will ordinarily equal the computed federal, state, and foreign taxes on the current year's operations less any payments thereon. The account may also contain unpaid taxes of prior years or items in dispute.

In addition to reviewing the computation of the income tax liability for the current year, the auditor should determine the date to which returns for prior years have been examined by the Treasury Department, or applicable state or foreign taxing authorities, and the particulars of any disputes or additional assessments. Review of the reports of revenue agents is also an essential step. In a first engagement the auditor should review all prior years' tax returns, especially those not yet examined by revenue agents, to make sure that there has been no substantial underpayment of taxes which would warrant presentation as a liability.

Accrued professional fees. Fees of professional firms include charges for the services of attorneys, public accountants, consulting engineers, and other specialists, who often render services of a continuing nature but present bills only at infrequent intervals. By inquiry of officers and review of corporate minutes, the auditor may learn of professional services received for which no liability has yet been reflected in the accounts. Review of the expense account for legal fees is always mandatory because it may reveal damage suits, tax disputes, or other litigation warranting disclosure in the financial statements. Fees of public accountants for periodic audits are properly reflected in the accounts of the year subsequent to the period under audit. Accruals are desirable, however, for any other accounting services completed but unbilled as of the balance sheet date.

Deferred credits to revenue

Deferred credits to revenue represent collections in advance for services to be rendered subsequent to the balance sheet date. Items for which payment in advance is commonly required include rentals, interest, subscriptions, tuition, insurance premiums, and outstanding tickets and coupons redeemable in merchandise or services.

Some deferred credits will have been verified during the examination of related asset and revenue accounts. The amount of interest to be deferred, for example, will be verified as part of the examination of notes receivable and interest earned. Similarly, the amount of rent to be deferred may have been verified during the review of the rental revenue account. Working papers prepared during the investigation of deferred credits should in all instances be cross-referenced to the analyses of related asset and revenue accounts so that duplication of investigative work may be avoided.

The principal objectives of the auditor's work on deferred credits are to determine (1) that revenue is reflected in the period in which it is earned, and (2) that no obligation for the rendering of future services is omitted from the balance sheet.

The computations necessary in determining the amount of rent or other type of revenue to be deferred should be made by the client's accounting staff, not by the auditor. The audit function is merely to review the computations for clerical accuracy and to determine the propriety of the allocation between periods. In the audit of some small concerns operating without competent accounting personnel, it may be necessary for the auditor to make independent computations of revenue to be deferred; but this is not a normal auditing procedure.

Deferred gross profit on installment sales. For concerns selling merchandise under long-term installment contracts, the auditor should first review the accounting method used in measuring gross profit earned on these sales and the consistency of its use from year to year. If the special installment method, which recognizes gross profit on the basis of collections rather than at the time of sale, is in use, the auditor should verify the computations underlying the gross profit percentage figure. This percentage, when applied to contracts outstanding, produces the portion of gross profit unearned as of the balance sheet date. Departmental gross profit rates may be used to reflect more accurately the profit margins on various types of merchandise. If the number of installment notes on hand is few but the amounts are large, the auditor may find it advantageous to maintain a continuing analysis summarizing the transactions and profit recognized for each period. The limited acceptability of the special installment method is discussed in Chapter 13.

Balance sheet presentation

Accrued expenses—interest, taxes, rent, and wages—are included in the current liability section of the balance sheet. These items are generally combined into one figure. However, any liability of material amount should be separately listed.

Federal, state, and foreign income taxes payable are usually material in amount and should be listed as a separate item. Although the tax liability is usually an estimated amount rather than a final determination, there is little justification for including the word "reserve" in the title of the income tax liability, or in any other liability of estimated amount. Neither is there any justification for placing so-called "liability reserves" midway between the liability and owners' equity sections, as has been done in some published financial statements. In short, liabilities should be clearly identified as such, regardless of whether the amount is precisely determined or merely estimated.

Deferred federal income taxes resulting from tax allocations should be classified as current liabilities if they relate to current assets. Otherwise, deferred federal income taxes are classified as long-term. Deferred Investment Credits may be included in the long-term liability section of the balance sheet. Unused income tax loss or Investment Credit carryforwards are disclosed in notes to the financial statements as contingent assets, unless sufficient evidence is available to record them as real assets.

Deferred credits to revenue for such items as rent or interest collected in advance which will be taken into earnings in the succeeding period are customarily included in current liabilities. Deposits on contracts and similar advances from customers are also accorded the status of current liabilities because the receipt of an advance increases the current asset total and because the goods to be used in liquidating the advance are generally included in current assets.

Time of examination

The nature and amount of trade accounts payable may change greatly within a few weeks' time; consequently, the auditor's verification of these rapidly changing liabilities is most effective when performed immediately after the balance sheet date. As stressed at the beginning of this chapter, failure to record a liability will cause an exaggeration of financial position; if audit work on accounts payable is performed prior to the balance sheet date, the possibility exists that the client may fail to record important liabilities coming into existence during the remaining weeks of the year under audit. For this reason many auditors believe that most of the audit work on accounts payable should be performed after the balance sheet date. Certainly, the auditor's search for unrecorded liabilities must be made after the balance sheet date, because this search is concentrated on the transactions occurring during the first few weeks of the new year.

Some current liability accounts other than accounts payable are more suitable for preliminary audit work. The documents relating to accrued property taxes, for example, may be available in advance of the balance sheet date. Amounts withheld from employees' pay can conveniently be examined before the end of the year. The propriety of amounts withheld and of amounts remitted to the tax authorities during the year can advantageously be verified before the pressure of year-end work begins. The working papers relating to such liability accounts may then be completed very quickly after the books have been closed.

GROUP I
REVIEW QUESTIONS

17–1. A CPA examines all unrecorded invoices on hand as of February 28, 1975, the last day of field work. Which of the errors listed below has the best chance of being detected by this auditing procedure?
   a)   Accounts payable are overstated at December 31, 1974.
   b)   Accounts payable are understated at December 31, 1974.
   c)   Operating expenses are overstated for the 12 months ended December 31, 1974.
   d)   Operating expenses are overstated for the two months ended February 28, 1975. (AICPA, adapted)

17–2. Compare the auditor's approach to the verification of liabilities with his approach to the verification of assets.

17–3. What are "liquidated damages"?

17–4. Describe two changes in the traditional processing procedures for accounts payable which have been brought about by the increased utilization of electronic computers.

17–5. What disclosure is customarily made in a corporate balance sheet concerning income tax liabilities?

17–6. Most auditors are interested in performing as many phases of an examination as possible in advance of the balance sheet date. The verification of accounts payable, however, is generally regarded as something to be done after the balance sheet date. What specific factors can you suggest that make the verification of accounts payable less suitable than many other accounts for interim work? *searching for unrecorded liabilities -*

17-7.   In achieving adequate internal control over operations of the accounts payable department, a company should establish procedures that will insure that extensions and footings are proved on all invoices and that the propriety of prices is reviewed. What is the most effective means of assuring consistent performance of these duties? *2 duties*

17-8.   Which do you consider the more significant step in establishing strong internal control over accounts payable transactions: the approval of an invoice for payment, or the issuance of a check in payment of an invoice?

17-9.   What use should be made of monthly statements for vendors by operating personnel in the accounts payable department? *reconcile*

17-10. Is the confirmation of accounts payable by direct communication with vendors as useful and important an audit procedure as is the confirmation of accounts receivable? Explain fully. (AICPA) *no; monthly stmt from outside*

17-11. During the verification of the individual invoices comprising the total of accounts payable at the balance sheet date, the auditor discovered some receiving reports indicating that the merchandise covered by several of these invoices was not received until after the balance sheet date. What action should the auditor take?

17-12. What do you consider to be the most important single procedure in the auditor's search for unrecorded accounts payable? Explain. *review cash disbursements, transactions for 2 or 3 wks after balance sheet date*

17-13. The Vernon Corporation records its liabilities in accounts payable subsidiary ledgers. The auditor decided to select some of the accounts for confirmation by direct communication with vendors. The largest volume of purchases during the year had been made from Downey Supply Company, but at the balance sheet date this account had a zero balance. Under these circumstances should the auditor send a confirmation request to Downey Supply Company or would he accomplish more by limiting his confirmation program to accounts with large year-end balances?

17-14. What audit procedure would you recommend for the verification of balances owed to affiliated companies?

17-15. Outline a method by which the auditor may test the propriety of cash discounts taken on accounts payable. *ratios*

17-16. For what documents relating to the accounts payable operation would you recommend the use of serial numbers as an internal control procedure? *every document use! ① purchase orders ② closing inventories ③ receiving reports ④ vouchers ⑤ remittance advices*

17-17. What internal control procedure would you recommend to call attention to failure to pay invoices within the discount period? *voucher register*

17-18. As part of the investigation of accounts payable, auditors sometimes vouch entries in selected creditors' accounts back through the journals to original documents such as purchase orders, receiving reports, invoices, and paid checks. What is the principal purpose of this procedure? *test internal control check accuracy of recording.*

17–19. If accounts with a few creditors represent the major portion of the total outstanding accounts payable, what special verification would you suggest for these accounts?

17–20. List three different transactions which may lead to debit balances in accounts payable. Assuming that the debit balances are large enough to justify reclassification, indicate the most appropriate asset account title to be used.

17–21. The operating procedures of a well-managed accounts payable department will provide for the verification of several specific points before a vendor's invoice is recorded as an approved liability. What are the points requiring verification?

17–22. List the major responsibilities of an accounts payable department.

17–23. Would you, as an auditor, take exception to the practice followed by some small businesses of not recording invoices until the time of payment?

17–24. Is the auditor concerned with invoices and debit memoranda recorded during his examination but subsequent to the balance sheet date? Explain.

17–25. Outline a procedure by which the auditor may determine the accuracy of any amounts owed to consignors.

17–26. Outline the procedure you would follow in verifying accrued tax liabilities relating to payrolls.

17–27. "Deferred credits to revenue are often verified during the examination of related asset and revenue accounts." Explain and illustrate this quotation by use of specific examples.

17–28. What are the principal objectives of the auditor with respect to the examination of deferred credits to revenue?

GROUP II
QUESTIONS REQUIRING ANALYSIS

17–29. In connection with his examination of the financial statements of the Thames Corporation, a CPA is reviewing the Federal Income Taxes Payable account.

Required:

a) Discuss reasons why the CPA should review federal income tax returns for prior years and the reports of internal revenue agents.

b) What information will these reviews provide? (Do not discuss specific tax return items.) (AICPA, adapted)

17–30. You were in the final stages of your examination of the financial statements of Cameron Corporation for the year ended December 31, 1974 when you were consulted by the corporation's president who believes there is no point to your examining the 1975 voucher register and testing data in support of 1975 entries. He stated that (*a*) bills pertaining to 1974 which were received too late to be included in the December voucher register were recorded as of the year-end by the corporation by journal entry, (*b*) the internal auditor made tests after the year-end, and (*c*) he would furnish you with a letter representing that there were no unrecorded liabilities.

Required:

a) Should a CPA's test for unrecorded liabilities be affected by the fact that the client made a journal entry to record 1974 bills which were received late? Explain.

b) Should a CPA's test for unrecorded liabilities be affected by the fact that a letter is obtained in which a responsible management official represents that to the best of his knowledge all liabilities have been recorded? Explain.

c) Should a CPA's test for unrecorded liablities be eliminated or reduced because of the internal audit tests? Explain.

d) Assume that the corporation, which handled some government contracts, had no internal auditor but that an auditor for a federal agency spent three weeks auditing the records and was just completing his work at this time. How would the CPA's unrecorded liability test be affected by the work of the auditor for a federal agency?

e) What sources in addition to the 1975 voucher register should the CPA consider to locate possible unrecorded liabilities? (AICPA, adapted)

17–31. The partnership of Fenton and Wagner has followed the policy of paying pensions to selected employees who retire after long service with the company. The amount of the pension has in most cases been approximately half the salary rate of the employee at the date of his retirement, but the partners have varied this method of computation in accordance with the personal circumstances of the retiring employee and the overall value of his services to the company. At present there are 35 employees who have been with the company for more than 15 years and who will presumably continue until they reach retirement age. One of the partners asks you whether the balance sheet of the company should include a long-term liability for the estimated amount to be paid to these employees as pensions.

17–32. The Emmett Company engages your services to perform a year-end audit for the year 1974. The income for the year was approximately $800,000 before taxes, and retained earnings on December 31, 1974 amounted to $610,000. The company has filed a federal income tax return for 1974 indicating a total tax of $400,000. In addition, you find that the Internal Revenue Service has disallowed part of the depreciation deductions claimed in 1971 and 1972 on certain equipment. The additional income tax liability resulting from the disallowances in 1971 and 1972 amounts to $50,000. The depreciation claimed in returns filed for 1971 through 1974 was on a consistent basis. Upon examination by the IRS of the years 1973 and 1974, the anticipated disallowances will result in a further additional income tax liability for each year of $20,000. Your examination disclosed no questionable items other than depreciation deductions.

Required:

Give the balance sheet presentation of the federal income taxes payable in the following situations:

a) The company has agreed to the disallowances and has accepted but not paid the Internal Revenue Service's assessment of $50,000.

b) The company has been advised by its counsel that the disallowances are improper and has notified the Internal Revenue Service that the disallowances will be contested. (AICPA, adapted)

17–33. Compare the confirmation of accounts receivable with the confirmation of accounts payable under the following headings:

a) Generally accepted auditing procedures. (Justify the differences revealed by your comparison.)

b) Form of confirmation requests. (You need not supply examples.)

c) Selection of accounts to be confirmed. (AICPA)

17–34. During the course of any audit, the CPA is always alert for unrecorded accounts payable or other unrecorded liabilities.

Required:

For each of the following audit areas, (1) describe an unrecorded liability which might be discovered, and (2) state what auditing procedure(s) might bring it to light.

a) Construction in progress (property, plant, and equipment).

b) Prepaid insurance.

c) License authorizing the client to produce a product patented by another company.

d) Minutes of directors' meetings.

17–35. Describe the audit steps that would generally be followed in establishing the propriety of the recorded liability for federal income taxes of an established corporation which you are auditing for the first time. Consideration should be given the status of (a) the liability for prior years, and (b) the liability arising from the current year's income. (AICPA)

17–36. In the course of your initial examination of the financial statements of the Modern Stores Company, you ascertain that of the substantial amount of accounts payable outstanding at the close of the period, approximately 75 percent is owing to six creditors. You have requested that you be permitted to confirm the balances owing to these six creditors by communicating with the creditors, but the president of the company is disinclined to approve your request on the grounds that correspondence in regard to the balances—all of which contain some overdue items—might give rise to demands on the part of the creditors for immediate payment of the overdue items and thereby embarrass the Modern Stores Company.

In the circumstances, what alternative procedure would you adopt in an effort to satisfy yourself that the books show the correct amounts payable to these creditors? (AICPA, adapted)

17–37. You are engaged in auditing the financial statements of Ward Company, a large independent contractor. All employees are paid in cash because Ward's controller believes this arrangement reduces clerical expenses and is preferred by the employees.

During the audit you find in the petty cash fund approximately $200 of which $185 is stated to be unclaimed wages. Further investigation reveals that the controller has installed the procedure of putting any unclaimed wages in the petty cash fund so that the cash can be used for disbursements. When the claimant to the wages appears, he is paid from the petty cash fund. The controller contends that this procedure reduces the number of checks drawn to replenish the petty cash fund and centers the responsibility for all cash on hand in one person inasmuch as the petty cash custodian distributes the pay envelopes.

Required:

a) Does Ward Company's system provide proper internal control of unclaimed wages? Explain fully.

b) Because Ward's controller insists on paying salaries in cash, what procedures would you recommend to provide better internal control over unclaimed wages? (AICPA, adapted)

17–38. A manufacturing company has elected to treat the Investment Credit arising from the purchase of assets which qualify for this credit under the terms of the Internal Revenue Code, as a reduction in taxes otherwise applicable to the year in which the credit arises, instead of reflecting the credit in net income over the life of the assets. The method has been adequately disclosed in footnotes to financial statements. In order to conform with the standards of reporting regarding the use of generally accepted principles of accounting, a CPA preparing a short-form report under the above circumstances should proceed as follows: (Select one alternative and defend your selection.)

a) He should include a middle paragraph describing the procedure followed by the company and disclaim an opinion on the fairness of presentation of the financial statements as a whole due to this deviation from generally accepted principles of accounting.

b) He should indicate this deviation from generally accepted principles of accounting, and, depending upon the materiality of the amount involved, issue a qualified opinion or an adverse opinion.

c) Even though this method is acceptable and may be used in accordance with generally accepted principles of accounting, the CPA should disclose in the middle paragraph of his report the effect of the method elected and compare it to the effect of an alternative method. An unqualified opinion may be rendered by the CPA.

(d) While the method of reporting the investment credit in net income over the life of acquired assets is considered to be preferable, the alternative method of treating the credit as a reduction of taxes of the year in which the credit arises is also acceptable, and an unqualified opinion may be rendered by the CPA. (AICPA, adapted)

GROUP III
PROBLEMS

17–39. During your audit of the Border Corporation for 1974 you find that the corporation plans to install the following purchase order draft system for paying vendors:

(1) The corporation will issue a draft in the form of a blank draft attached to the purchase order for purchases. The purchase order draft (POD) form will combine a purchase order (upper half of form) with a blank draft (lower half of form), and the two documents will be prenumbered with the same number and perforated so that the draft can be easily detached.

(2) The purchasing department will be responsible for this issuance and the PODs will be valid for a period of 90 days from the date of issuance. Each of eight buyers will maintain a supply of PODs. The supply will be replenished as needed.

(3) The cashier's department will maintain a log of the numbers of the PODs given to each buyer. Unissued PODs will be kept in a safe in the cashier's office. The POD form will consist of five parts, which will be distributed as follows:

(a) Copy No. 1 will be the purchase order and will be mailed to the vendor.

(b) Copy No 2 will be sent to the receiving department.

(c) Copy No. 3 will be sent to the accounting department.

(d) Copy No. 4 will be filed numerically in the purchasing department.

(e) Copy No. 5 will be kept by the buyer for follow-up purposes.

(4) When the purchase order is issued, the buyer will enter the quantity, unit price, extended amount, and the total estimated amount of the order on the upper half of the POD form. The draft will be made out in the vendor's name, dated and signed by the buyer. The original of the five-part form will then be mailed to the vendor.

(5) The vendor will enter his invoice number, quantity, unit price, and total amount of goods to be shipped in the space provided on the draft. When the goods are shipped the vendor will enter the total amount of the shipment on the face of the draft and present the completed draft to the bank for payment. No partially filled orders will be accepted. Vendors who deliver a quantity less than that ordered must receive a new purchase order for additional quantities to be delivered.

(6) The bank will honor the draft if it has not matured, stamp it "Paid," and charge the amount to the corporation's general cash account. The bank will send the paid draft to the cashier's department daily.

After reviewing the paid drafts the cashier's department will prepare an adding machine tape of the amounts and enter the total each day in the cash disbursements journal, debiting Accounts Payable. The paid drafts will then be sent to the purchasing department.

(7) When the goods are received, the receiving department will compare the quantity of items received to copy No. 2 of the POD, indicate the date the goods are received, initial copy No. 2 and route it to the purchasing department. The purchasing department will match the receiving department's copy No. 2 with the paid POD received from the cashier's department and enter the account distribution on the description section of the draft. The extensions of unit prices multiplied by quantities entered by the vendor will be verified and the receiving department's copy No. 2 attached to the paid draft and the documents sent to the accounting department.

(8) The accounting department will charge the appropriate asset or expense accounts at the time the paid drafts are recorded in the accounts payable register. The drafts, together with the related receiving reports, will then be filed by vendor.

Required:

a) The controller of the corporation requests your aid in preparing a memorandum informing the bank of the new "POD" procedures. List the instructions that you would recommend be given to the bank regarding the POD bank account and the payment of POD drafts.

b) The internal control procedures within the corporation with regard to purchases in general are excellent. Suggest additional internal control measures needed for the use of purchase order drafts and verification of paid and unpaid PODs. (AICPA, adapted)

17–40. In the discussions with officers of the Morris Company prior to the beginning of your 1974 annual examination of the financial statements, you learn that on October 31, 1974 the company entered into an agreement with the union representing its employees that included a plan for employee pensions. The effective date of the contract and its pension provisions was January 1, 1975, provided, however, that the pension provisions would be effective only if ratified by the stockholders prior to March 31, 1975. Ratification took place on January 6, 1975. The contract, including the pension provisions, was for a two-year term expiring December 31, 1976.

The pension provisions read that an employee of the Morris Company is to receive a pension for life if he (a) shall reach the age of 65, (b) shall have been employed by the company at least 10 years at the date of his retirement, and (c) shall actually retire during the effective period of the contract.

The monthly amount of the pension shall be $40 for each year of service with the company, less any old-age benefits to which the employee is entitled under the federal social security program.

The company shall pay into a trust fund in five annual installments, the first in 1975, a sufficient amount to provide for the pensions of those who retire within the contract period.

In the course of your discussions with officers of the Morris Company concerning the pension agreement, the controller pointed out that the amount of the pension benefits depends on past services and suggested that the cost of benefits for services rendered prior to January 1, 1975, by those employees who are expected to be eligible to retire in 1975 and 1976, should be charged to retained earnings in full in 1975. The treasurer of the company expressed the opinion that the charge to retained earnings should be made in 1974, the year in which the contract was signed. The president suggested that the cost of benefits for services rendered prior to January 1, 1975 be charged to expense in the year the employee retired. Another executive urged that these costs be charged to expense as the pensions are funded.

Required:

a) State which of the above suggestions you would favor and give reasons underlying your choice. If none of the proposed plans meets with your approval, indicate what course of action you would recommend.

b) State how the pension agreement should be disclosed in the financial statements for the years ended December 31, 1975 and December 31, 1976. (State specifically whether the trust fund should appear among the company's assets, and give reasons for your decision.) (AICPA, adapted)

17-41. In 1974 your client, Video Corporation, was licensed to manufacture a patented type of television tube. The licensing agreement called for royalty payments of 10 cents for each tube manufactured. What procedures would you follow in connection with your regular annual audit as of December 31, 1974 to satisfy yourself that the liability for royalties is correctly stated? (AICPA, adapted)

17-42. Ventura Grain and Milling Company decided to stimulate the sale of its flour by including a coupon, redeemable for 50 cents, in every 25- and 50-pound sack of flour produced subsequent to October 1, 1974. The company estimates that 150,000 coupons will be in the hands of customers before completion of the promotional campaign on March 31, 1975.

Upon commencing your year-end work on January 10, 1975 for the calendar year ended December 31, 1974, you are requested by the controller of Ventura Grain and Milling Company to review the accounting records and the internal controls applicable to the flour coupons.

In your review of the accounting records and the system of internal control, you learned the following:

(1) A perpetual record of coupons received, damaged, and used is kept by the production superintendent. Coupons received from the printer are entered from a copy of the receiving ticket, damaged coupons are reported orally by a line foreman, and coupons used are entered from a copy of the production report of sacks of flour packed. A

summary of the perpetual record as of December 31, 1974 is as follows:

Coupons received to date........................	150,000
Coupons damaged and destroyed.................	(2,000)
Coupons included in 25-pound sacks of flour.......	(50,000)
Coupons included in 50-pound sacks of flour.......	(25,000)
On hand per record............................	73,000

(2) Unused coupons are kept in a storeroom with stationery and supplies and are readily accessible. No count of coupons within a package is made as they are received from the printers; however, the number of packages times the indicated amount in each package is recorded on a receiving ticket which is later agreed, in the office, with a copy of the vendor's invoice.

(3) Coupons are sometimes damaged by the machinery which mechanically inserts them in the sacks. The production superintendent said that he thought that the line foreman destroyed these coupons. As previously mentioned, the number of damaged coupons is reported to the production superintendent orally each day by the line foreman.

(4) The line foreman takes a quantity of unused coupons from the storeroom each day, based upon scheduled production for that day.

(5) Correspondence containing coupons mailed to the company for redemption is first opened in the mail department. The coupons are then sent to the cashier department, where they are redeemed in cash out of a fund especially set up for that purpose. The cashier places a 50-cent piece in a self-addressed envelope, seals the envelope, and returns it to the mail department for ultimate disposition. The cashier stamps the coupon paid with the date of payment.

(6) Once each week the cashier's coupon fund is reimbursed in the same manner as any other imprest fund.

(7) Complaints from customers not receiving their 50-cent pieces are sent to the cashier for disposition.

You also learned that a physical inventory of unused coupons was taken on December 31, 1974. It was found that 71,250 coupons were on hand. As of December 31, 1974 flour containing 50,000 coupons had been sold to the company's retail outlets. In addition, by December 31, 1974, 37,500 coupons had been redeemed and paid; and it was estimated that only 50 percent of the remaining coupons outstanding at that time would be redeemed.

Required:

a) Prepare a report to the controller as to weaknesses in the present control procedures in regard to handling redeemable coupons and your recommendations for improvement.

b) Prepare an adjusting journal entry setting up the company's liability for unredeemed coupons as of December 31, 1974. Show your method of computing the liability. (AICPA, adapted)

17–43. Dowling Company manufactures household appliances that are sold through independent franchised retail dealers. The electric motors in the appliances are guaranteed for five years from the date of sale of the appliances to the consumer. Under the guaranty defective motors are replaced by the dealers without charge.

Inventories of replacement motors are kept in the dealers' stores and are carried at cost in Dowling Company's records. When the dealer replaces a defective motor, he notifies the factory and returns the defective motor to the factory for reconditioning. After the defective motor is received by the factory, the dealer's account is credited with an agreed fee for the replacement service.

When the appliance is brought to the dealer after the guaranty period has elapsed, the dealer charges the owner for installing the new motor. The dealer notifies the factory of the installation and returns the replaced motor for reconditioning. The motor installed is then charged to the dealer's account at a price in excess of its inventory value. In this instance, to encourage the return of replaced motors, the dealer's account is credited with a nominal value for the returned motor.

Dealers submit quarterly inventory reports of the motors on hand. The reports are later verified by factory salesmen. Dealers are billed for inventory shortages determined by comparison of the dealers' inventory reports and the factory's perpetual records of the dealers' inventories. The dealers order additional motors as they need them. One motor is used for all appliances in a given year, but the motors are changed in basic design each model year.

Dowling Company has established an account, Estimated Liability for Product Guaranties, in connection with the guaranties. An amount representing the estimated guaranty cost prorated per sales unit is credited to the Estimated Liability account for each appliance sold and the debit is charged to a Provision account. The Estimated Liability account is debited for the service fees credited to the dealers' accounts and for the inventory cost of the motors installed under the guaranties.

The engineering department keeps statistical records of the number of units of each model sold in each year and the replacements that were made. The effect of improvements in design and construction is under continuous study by the engineering department, and the estimated guaranty cost per unit is adjusted annually on the basis of experience and improvements in design. Experience shows that for a given motor model, the number of guaranties made good varies widely from year to year during the guaranty period, but the total number of guaranties to be made good can be reliably predicted.

Required:

a) Prepare an audit program to satisfy yourself as to the propriety of the transactions recorded in the Estimated Liability for Product Guaranties account for the year ended December 31, 1974.

b) Prepare the working paper format that would be used to test the adequacy of the balance in the Estimated Liability for Product Guaranties account. The working paper column headings should describe clearly the data to be inserted in the columns. (AICPA, adapted)

GROUP IV
CASE STUDIES IN AUDITING

Charles Company

17–44. Able and Baker, Certified Public Accountants, had audited the financial statements of the Charles Company for several years. The client was a construction company having total assets of $2.5 million and stockholders' equity of $1 million.

   During the fiscal year ended February 28, 1974, the client had entered in its records a judgment payable for $35,000. The judgment was based on a suit against the Charles Company involving nonperformance under the terms of a contract. The suit was originally decided in favor of the Charles Company in a circuit court case. In April, 1974 the state supreme court reversed the earlier decision and remanded the case to the circuit court. In view of the reversal by the supreme court, the Charles Company concluded that the $35,000 judgment would have to be paid and entered the amount as an extraordinary loss in its records for the fiscal year ended February 28, 1974.

   Immediately after the case was remanded to the circuit court, the Charles Company instituted an appeal in the district court. This was done against the advice of counsel. The client insisted on this course because it felt that additional favorable evidence had been uncovered.

   During the audit of the client's financial statements for the year ended February 28, 1975 it became obvious to the auditors that Mr. Charles, president of the Charles Company, was unhappy about the results of operations for that year. His own tentative estimate of pretax income was $33,000. While he was concerned with the fact that this amount would not have a favorable effect on the company's creditors, he appeared to be primarily concerned with the company's tax picture for that year. From a tax viewpoint, the $33,000 amount included capital gains of $65,000 and an ordinary loss of $32,000. He pointed out that unless the ordinary earnings exceeded the capital gains, the company would lose part or all of the beneficial treatment usually derived from capital gains. The president's attitude became even more apparent when upon a review of the auditors' proposed adjustments, he objected strenuously to any adjustments which would reduce earnings even further. The net result of all the adjustments was minor. The auditors' working papers showed essentially the same figures as those listed above after all the adjustments were made.

   At the conclusion of the engagement Mr. Charles was asked to sign a liability representation. The partner in charge of the engagement specifically pointed out, among other things, the usual comment pertaining to the existence on any contingent liabilities. At this point Mr. Charles, recognizing the possibility of increasing pretax income through this means, decided that the judgment payable which had been entered in the previous year now should be considered as a contingent liability. The result would be an increase of Charles Company's pretax income from $33,000 to $68,000. In the company's income tax return, the $68,000 would be broken down as ordinary earnings—$3,000, and capital gains—$65,000.

Mr. Charles said that his treatment was justified by the fact that the appeal to the district court was still pending and that its final result could not be predicted. He felt that a credit to current year's income was justified by the fact that the new evidence was discovered during the current year.

Able and Baker questioned this treatment. They doubted that the new evidence could even be introduced at the appeal stage. They contended that unless they had assurance that the new evidence which the president referred to could be introduced and that it was so conclusive as to refute completely the basis for the earlier ruling, they had no basis for sanctioning the reversal of the previous year's entry, particularly when the effect was to double the current year's pretax income. However, having high regard for the company's legal counsel, they said that they would not protest the entry reversing the previous year's entry and treating the judgment as a contingent liability if the company's attorney indicated in writing that this treatment was proper. It was further agreed that the $35,000 should be taken into current year's income if the attorney would indicate that the liability had changed from a real liability to a contingent liability because of specific happenings during the year under review. The company's attorney stated the following facts: The newly discovered evidence indicated to him that a fraud had been perpetrated against the Charles Company. He stated that if the true facts could be presented to the court, the judgment should be reversed. He also stated that a previous move to introduce these facts was defeated and that a previous move for a new trial was also defeated. The attorney stated "the main difficulty was a technical one of getting the courts to review the matter."

After considerable discussion, the attorney's final conclusion was as follows: "While we had expressed some doubts as to the successful outcome of the appeal, there is unquestionable merit, equitably as well as legally, in the appellant's position, and it may prevail."

Able and Baker felt that the attorney's opinion did not justify the reversal of the recorded liability. Mr. Charles continued to express confidence in the outcome of the legal proceedings and insisted that the liability be removed from his balance sheet and that the $35,000 be included in income. Mr. Charles was adamant in his position and reminded Able and Baker that the financial statements were those of the client.

The lower portion of the statement of income and retained earnings, which follows, shows how the item was taken into income:

Loss before income tax credits..............................		$ (32,000)
Federal and state income tax credits.......................		(16,000)
Loss before extraordinary items...........................		$ (16,000)
Extraordinary items:		
Gain on sale of marketable securities, net of applicable income taxes of $16,250............	$48,750	
Reversal of previously recorded liability, less applicable income taxes of $17,500............	17,500	66,250
Net income...		$ 50,250
Retained earnings at beginning of year.....................		340,000
Retained earnings at end of year...........................		$390,250

NOTE: Federal and state income tax rates assumed to be an aggregate of 50 percent on ordinary earnings and 25 percent on capital gains.

In addition to a standard scope paragraph, the following middle paragraph appeared in the auditors' report:

During the year ended February 28, 1975, the company reversed a previously recorded liability for $35,000 and credited income for that amount. The $35,000, which had originally been recorded as a liability during the preceding fiscal year, is the amount of a judgment which a supplier obtained against the company. The company contends that the judgment was obtained by fraudulent representations, but has been unsuccessful to date in obtaining a reversal of the judgment. We believe that there was insufficient support for reversing the entry made in the preceding year and that the inclusion of $35,000 in income is not in accordance with generally accepted accounting principles.

The opinion paragraph contrained an adverse opinion on the statement of income and retained earnings and a qualified opinion on the balance sheet and the statement of changes in financial position.

Able and Baker believed so strongly that the client's position was erroneous that they felt that they could not prepare the federal and state income tax returns on that basis. Accordingly they prepared and submitted to the client tax returns which showed the $35,000 extraordinary item as an adjustment to the retained earnings balance at March 1, 1974 rather than as taxable income. The company then prepared its own returns, including the item as income and deleting all references to Able and Baker's having prepared the returns.

Required:

a) Do you think that sufficient grounds existed for reversing the previously recorded liability?

b) If the reversal mentioned above is in order, would you approve a credit to current year's income in the amount of $35,000?

c) What would you have said in the audit report if you had been in Able and Baker's place?

d) Would you have prepared the tax returns as Able and Baker did had you been in their place?

18

Interest-bearing debt and interest expense: Contingent liabilities and commitments

BUSINESS enterprises obtain substantial amounts of their financial resources by borrowing. Short-term bank loans, evidenced by notes payable, are commonly used to finance inventories and other short-term working capital requirements; commercial paper may also be used for this purpose. Closely held companies may also borrow on a short-term basis from stockholders, directors, or officers. Purchases of small components of plant assets may be financed on an installment credit basis, including a lease which is in substance an installment purchase. Long-term debt, issued either to the public or to an institutional investor in a "private placement," is often incurred to finance the purchase of another company or of substantial amounts of plant and equipment. The judicious use of debt financing in conjunction with equity financing and resources provided by profitable operations enables a business to maximize the return on its assets.

A business with an excellent credit reputation may find it possible to borrow from a bank on a simple unsecured note. A business of lesser financial standing may find that the obtaining of bank credit requires the pledging of specific assets as collateral; or that it must agree to certain restrictive covenants, such as the suspension of dividends and other protective provisions during the term of the loan; or that a loan is obtainable only if the signature of a cosigner of greater financial strength can be obtained on the note. The issuance of notes payable in the settlement of past-due accounts payable is obviously an indication of serious financial weakness.

Long-term debt is usually substantial in amount and often extends for periods of 30 years or more. Debentures, secured bonds, and notes payable (sometimes secured by mortgages or trust deeds) are the principal types of long-term debt. Debentures are backed only by the general credit of the issuing corporation and not by liens on specific assets. Since in most respects debentures have the characteristics of other corporate bonds, we shall use the term *bonds* to include both debentures and secured bonds payable.

The formal document creating bonded indebtedness is called the *indenture or trust indenture.* When creditors supply capital on a long-term basis, they often insist upon placing certain restrictions on the company. For example, the indenture often provides that a company may not declare dividends unless the amount of working capital is maintained above a specified amount. The acquisition of plant and equipment, or the increasing of managerial salaries, may be permitted only if the current ratio is maintained at a specified level and if net income reaches a designated amount. Another device for protecting the long-term creditor is the requirement of a sinking fund or redemption fund to be held by a trustee. If these restrictions are violated, the indenture may provide that the entire debt is due on demand.

Fashions change in securities as for merchandise and services. In recent years convertible subordinated debentures have become very popular. These securities are subordinate to other types of creditors' claims and may be converted into common stock in a specified ratio at the option of the holder. A full description of these special features, such as the conversion privilege, should be presented in the notes accompanying the financial statements.

The auditor's objectives in examination of interest-bearing debt

The objectives of the auditor in his examination of interest-bearing debt are to determine that (a) internal controls are adequate; (b) all interest-bearing debt of the client has been recorded and represents bona fide obligations issued in accordance with federal and state laws; (c) interest payable and interest expense have been accurately computed, including the amortization of bond discount or premium; (d) the client company has met all requirements and restrictions imposed upon it by debt contracts; and (e) the interest-bearing debt and related expenses are properly presented in the financial statements and adequate informative disclosure is achieved.

Internal control over interest-bearing debt

Effective internal control over interest-bearing debt begins with the authorization to incur the debt. The bylaws of a corporation usually require that borrowing be approved by the board of directors. The treasurer of the corporation will prepare a report on any proposed financing, explaining the need for funds, the estimated effect of borrowing upon future earnings, the estimated financial position of the company in comparison with others in the industry both before and after the borrowing, and alternative methods of raising the amount desired. Authorization by the board of directors will include review and approval of such matters as the choice of a bank, the type of security, the choice of a trustee, registration with the SEC, agreements with investment bankers, compliance with requirements of the state of incorporation, and listing of bonds on a securities exchange. Bonds should be serially numbered by the printer and kept in the custody of an officer of the corporation. The signing and countersigning of bond certificates, notes, and mortgage or trust deed documents should not take place until the time for issuance. The board of directors should receive a report stating the net amount received and its disposition, as for acquisition of plant assets, addition to working capital, or other purposes.

When an independent trustee for long-term debt is not employed, an officer of the corporation should be given direct responsibility for maintenance of the required records. Even though the services of an independent trustee are employed, the issuing company will usually maintain a bond or note register to show the amount of the indebtedness issued, canceled, and currently outstanding. If the loan is obtained directly from a bank, insurance company, or other single creditor, there is, of course, no need for such subsidiary records; the original amount of the loan and any subsequent reductions can be recorded in a general ledger account.

Proper authorization procedures are important for the redemption or cancellation of bonds, as well as for the original issuance of the securities. If the company employs a trustee, the reacquired certificates may be destroyed by the trustee and a cremation certificate issued to the company. If bonds are reacquired directly by the issuing company, they should be canceled and attached to the stubs in the certificate book. All certificate numbers should be accounted for periodically and at the final redemption of the issue. The authorization procedures should also provide for bonds reacquired for a sinking fund. These are customarily turned over to the trustee, but in any event the acquisition should be reflected in the accounts of the issuing company.

The most effective internal control is obtained when the indenture lodges the responsibility for the sinking fund, as well as the functions of issuance and cancellation, with a trustee. The trustee is charged with the protection of creditors' interests and must continuously review the company's compliance with the provisions of the indenture.

Interest payments on bonds, notes, and mortgages or trust deeds. The auditor's appraisal of internal controls relating to bonds, notes, and mortgages or trust deeds must also extend to the handling of interest payments. In the case of a note, mortgage, or trust deed, there may be only one recipient of interest, and the disbursement may be controlled in the same manner as other cash payments. For large, widely distributed bond issues, interest coupons attached to the bonds provide an effective means of control. As the coupons are presented for payment, they are canceled and preserved in a specially designed book. The total cash disbursements for interest may then be reconciled to the number of coupons collected. This approach should be supplemented by the maintenance of standard controls over the signing and issuance of interest checks. When the bonds are registered and the corporation knows the names of the holders, it is sometimes desirable to install a system whereby checks are addressed and written by a computer master tape or addressograph plates, which may be reused many times. These tapes or plates must be kept in safe custody and released only for authorized use.

Many corporations assign the entire problem of paying interest to the trustee. Highly effective control is then achieved, since the company will issue a single check for the full amount of the periodic interest payment. Upon receipt of this check the trustee will make payment for coupons presented, cancel the coupons, and file them numerically. A second count of the coupons is made at a later date; the coupons are then destroyed and a cremation certificate delivered to the issuing company. The trustee does not attempt to maintain a list of the holders of coupon bonds, since these securities are transferable by the mere act of delivery. If certain coupons are not presented for payment, the trustee will hold the funds corresponding to such coupons for the length of time prescribed by statute. In the case of registered bonds, the trustee will maintain a current list of holders and will remit interest checks to them in the same manner as dividend checks are distributed to stockholders.

Audit working papers

A copy of the indenture relating to a bond issued should be placed in the permanent file. Analyses of ledger accounts for notes and bonds payable and the related accounts for interest and discount or premium should be obtained for the current working papers file. A grouping sheet is seldom required for short-term notes payable or for long-term debt.

Internal control questionnaire

The auditor's appraisal of the internal control procedures affecting interest-paying debt may be facilitated by investigation of the factors listed in the following questionnaire.

1. Are interest-bearing liabilities incurred only under authorization of the board of directors?
2. Has the board of directors specified banks from which loans may be obtained?
3. Is the renewal of notes payable subject to the same controls as original issuance?
4. Is an independent trustee employed to account for all bond issuances, cancellations, and interest payments?
5. If the company does not employ an independent trustee—
    a) Are unsigned bonds and notes in the custody of an officer?
    b) Are bond and note certificates prenumbered by the printer?
    c) Are certificates unsigned until the time they are issued?
    d) Are surrendered certificates and interest coupons properly canceled and preserved?
    e) Are interest checks under proper control?
    f) Are unclaimed interest checks properly accounted for and kept in safe custody?
6. Are records of interest-bearing debt under the control of a responsible official and inaccessible to other employees?
7. Are detail records of interest-bearing debt reconciled to periodic statements of trustees and to the general ledger by an employee not responsible for maintaining the detail records?
8. Are adequate records maintained for collateral pledged as security for interest-bearing debt?
9. Are paid notes canceled and retained?
10. Are treasury bonds kept in adequate safekeeping?

Audit program for interest-bearing debt

Audit procedures appropriate for the verification of interest-bearing debt include the following:

1. Obtain or prepare analyses of interest-bearing debt accounts and related interest, premium, and discount accounts.
2. Examine copies of notes and mortgages or trust deeds payable.
3. Obtain copy of indenture for bonds payable and review its important provisions.
4. Trace authority for issuance of interest-bearing debt to the corporate minutes.
5. Determine that debt issuance is in accordance with applicable state and federal securities laws.
6. Vouch interest-bearing debt transactions for the year to supporting documents.
7. Confirm interest-bearing debt with appropriate third parties.
8. Examine treasury bonds and reconcile to the general ledger.

9. Verify computation of interest expense, interest payable, and amortization of discount or premium.
10. Determine that all provisions of the indenture have been met.
11. Review notes paid or renewed since the balance sheet date.
12. Determine proper balance sheet presentation of interest-bearing debt, interest payable, and premium or discount.

1. *Obtain or prepare analyses of interest-bearing debt accounts and related interest, premium, and discount accounts.*

A working paper analysis for notes payable is very similar to the analysis of notes receivable illustrated in Chapter 13 (Figure 13–2). A notes payable analysis shows the beginning balance, if any, of each individual note; additional notes issued and payments on notes during the year; and the ending balance of each note. In addition, the beginning balances of interest payable or prepaid interest, interest expense, interest paid, and ending balances of interest payable or prepaid interest, are presented in the analysis working paper.

An analysis of the Notes Payable account will serve a number of purposes: (*a*) the payment or other dispostion of notes listed as outstanding in the previous year's audit can be verified; (*b*) the propriety of individual debits and credits can be established; and (*c*) the validity of the year-end balance of the account is proved through the step-by-step verification of all changes in the account during the year. Such a detailed analysis of notes payable is feasible and justified because there are normally not very many transactions and the dollar amounts are relatively large. Analysis of the Notes Payable account will also give the auditor an understanding of the purposes for which the company utilizes notes payable and will enable him to form an opinion as to the quality of the accounting routines followed.

In the first audit of a client, the auditor will analyze the ledger accounts for Bonds Payable, Bond Issue Costs, and Bond Discount (or Bond Premium) for the entire period since the bonds were issued. A working paper used in analyzing the Bonds Payable, Bond Issue Costs, and Bond Discount accounts is illustrated in Figure 18–1. This working paper is placed in the auditor's permanent file; in subsequent examinations any further entries in the accounts may be added to the analysis. In this way the preparation of detailed analyses of these accounts during each repeat engagement is avoided. This practice is appropriate because these accounts usually change very little over a period of years. On the other hand, Interest Expense and Interest Payable are more active accounts which should, therefore, be analyzed separately during each engagement.

An analysis of the Mortgages Payable account should also be designed in a form permitting the addition of information in subsequent years

FIGURE 18–1

The Torino Corporation   Permanent File

Bonds Payable, Bond Issue Costs, and Bond Discount   U–6

6%, 20-year Debenture due 7-1-93   December 31, 1973

Date			Bonds Payable Acct. No. 220	Bond Issue Costs Acct. No. 185	Bond Discount Acct. No. 221
7-1-73	Issue at 98 to underwriting syndicate x		10 000 000 –n		200 000 –n
7-2-73	Bond issue costs paid:				
	Printing charges			3 500 –y	
	Legal fees			5 000 –y	
	Audit fees			5 500 –y	
	SEC registration fee			2 000 –y	
			10 000 000 –	16 000 –	200 000 –
7/1-12/31/73	"Interest method" amortization of discount - at 3.088% semiannual rate				(2 624 –) y
	straight-line amortization of issue costs			(400 –) y	
	Balances 12-31-73	C-1	10 000 000 –c	15 600 –	197 376 –
1/1-12/31/74	Amortization as above			(800 –) y	(5 494 –) y
	Balances 12-31-74	C-1	10 000 000 –c	14 800 –	191 882 –

n – Traced net proceeds to cash receipts records.
x – Traced authorization to minutes of 5-22-73 directors' meeting (U-3); see U-6-1 for copy of Prospectus filed with SEC.
y – Vouched to paid check and invoice or statement
y – Computation verified (amortization methods are in accordance with directors' resolution of 7-22-73)
c – Confirmed

V.M.A.
1-5-74
1-3-75

and should be made part of the permanent audit file. The analysis should include a detailed description of the mortgage or trust deed, the total initial amount, installment payments, and the balance outstanding.

If the analysis of interest-bearing debt is prepared by the client's employees, the auditor should compare the individual items listed with entries in the detailed records. The footings of the analyses should be proved and compared with the balances of the control accounts in the general ledger. In addition, the footings of the control accounts should be tested. Any discrepancy between the auditor's analyses and the balances of the control accounts must, of course, be investigated. Common causes of such discrepancies include failure to enter installment payments in the detailed records and making credit entries to the control account for the net proceeds, rather than for the face amount, when notes are issued with interest included in the face amount.

2. *Examine copies of notes and mortgages or trust deeds payable.*

The auditor should examine the client's copies of notes payable and mortgages and trust deeds payable as of the balance sheet date. The original documents will of course be in the possession of the respective payees; but the auditor should make certain that the client has retained copies of the debt instruments and that their details correspond to the analyses obtained in the first procedure of this audit program.

3. *Obtain copy of indenture for bonds payable and review its important provisions.*

In the first audit of a client or upon the issuance of a new bond issue, the auditor will obtain a copy of the bond indenture for the permanent file. The indenture should be carefully studied, with particular attention to the following points:

a) Amount of bonds authorized for issuance.

b) The principal amount of each bond.

c) The interest rates and dates of payment and the method of payment.

d) The maturity date of the issue, or, if serial bonds are issued, the periodic installment dates.

e) A description of the pledged property.

f) The provision for retirement or conversion, including computation of the conversion price.

g) Any sinking fund provisions.

h) The various restrictions on working capital, maintenance of the property, insurance of pledged assets, etc., that may be required.

i) Provisions concerning the disposition of funds provided by the issue.

j) Name and address of trustee.

k) The trustee's duties and responsibilities.

l) The basis of any additional bond issues.

4. Trace authority for issuance of interest-bearing debt to the corporate minutes.

The authority to issue interest-bearing debt generally lies in the board of directors. To determine that the bonds outstanding were properly authorized, the auditor should, therefore, read the passages in the minutes of directors' (and stockholders') meetings concerning the issuance of debt. The minutes will usually cite the applicable sections of the corporate bylaws permitting the issuance of debt instruments and may also contain reference to the opinion of the company's counsel concerning the legality of the issue. Such information should then be traced by the auditor to the original sources. Adequate notes should be prepared for the audit working papers showing the extent of the auditor's investigation of authorization for the debt issue.

The purpose and authorization of a mortgage or trust deed payable deserve consideration because in some instances partnership agreements and articles of incorporation may forbid the incurring of a mortgage or trust deed lien. This information is also necessary for the auditor to determine that the funds arising from the loan have been expended in the manner intended by the partners, owners, or directors. Unauthorized mortgages or inconsistencies in the use of the borrowed funds should be mentioned in the auditor's working papers.

5. Determine that debt issuance is in accordance with applicable state and federal securities laws.

The auditor is not qualified to pass on the legality of a bond issue; this is a problem for the company's attorneys. The auditor should be familiar, however, with the principal provisions of the federal Securities Act of 1933 and of the corporate "blue sky" laws of the client's state of incorporation. He should ascertain that the client has obtained an attorney's opinion on the legality of the bond issuance, including the indenture's compliance with the provisions of the federal Trust Indenture Act of 1939. In doubtful cases he should consult the client's legal counsel.

The auditor must also ascertain that a mortgage is recorded in order to gain assurance of the validity of a mortgage bond or note issue. If he does not inspect public records, an alternative procedure consists of obtaining a statement from the client's attorney to the effect that the mortgage has been recorded. This may be supplemented by an inspection of the receipt from the county clerk for the recording fee. Again it should be noted that this is a procedure which will be undertaken only during a first audit or after a new bond or mortgage note issue.

6. Vouch interest-bearing debt transactions for the year to supporting documents.

The auditor must satisfy himself that transactions in interest-bearing debt accounts were valid. To accomplish this objective, the auditor traces the cash received from the issuance of notes, bonds, or mortgages to the validated copy of the bank deposit slip and to the bank statement. Any remittance advices supporting these cash receipts are also examined.

The auditor finds further support for the net proceeds of a bond issue by reference to the underwriting agreement and to the Prospectus filed with the SEC. In a private placement of a debt issue, the principal supporting document is usually a contract between the issuer and the institutional investor. In either a public or private offering of debt, the difference between the net proceeds and the face amount of the debt represents the discount or premium on the debt. The auditor vouches bond issue costs to supporting paid checks and to invoices or statements from attorneys, CPAs, printers, and the SEC.

In addition to verifying the proceeds of a debt issue, the auditor must ascertain that the funds were expended for the purposes intended by the client. The directors' minutes, indenture, and Prospectus should contain clear statements as to projected uses of funds obtained from interest-bearing debt.

Debits to a Notes Payable or a Mortgages Payable account generally represent payments in full or in installments. The auditor should examine paid checks for these payments; in so doing, he will also account for payments of accrued interest. The propriety of installment payments should be verified by reference to the repayment schedule set forth in the note or mortgage copy in the client's possession.

A comparison of canceled notes payable with the debit entries in the Notes Payable account provides further assurance that notes indicated as paid during the year have, in fact, been retired. The auditor's inspection of these notes should include a comparison of the maturity date of the note with the date of cash disbursement. Failure to pay notes promptly at maturity is suggestive of serious financial weakness. Payment prior to maturity, on the other hand, may be accompanied by a reduction in the amount of the liability on noninterest-bearing notes. The auditor should ascertain whether any such saving of interest by early payment has been properly recorded. Other points to be verified include the authenticity of the signatures and the unmistakable evidence of cancellation.

There is seldom any justification for a paid note to be missing from the files; a receipt for payment from the payee of the note is not a satisfactory substitute. If, for any reason, a paid note is not available for inspection, the auditor should review the request for a check or other vouchers supporting the disbursement and should discuss the transaction with an appropriate official.

In examining the canceled notes the auditor should also trace the disposition of any collateral used to secure these notes. A convenient opportunity for diversion of pledged securities or other assets to an unauthorized use may be created at the time these assets are regained from a secured creditor.

Debit entries in a Bonds Payable account are best verified by direct communication with the trustee, as described in the next portion of this audit program.

7.   *Confirm interest-bearing debt with appropriate third parties.*

Notes payable to banks are confirmed as part of the confirmation of bank balances. The standard bank confirmation form illustrated in the chapter on cash (Figure 11–2, p. 348) includes a request that the bank prepare a list of all borrowings by the depositor. The primary objective of this inquiry is to bring to light any unrecorded notes. As mentioned previously in the discussion of bank accounts, confirmation requests should be sent to all banks with which the client has done business during the year, since a note payable to a bank may be outstanding long after a deposit account has been closed.

Confirmation requests for notes payable to payees other than banks should be drafted on the client's letterhead stationery, signed by the controller or other appropriate executive, and mailed by the auditor. Payees should be requested to confirm dates of origin, due dates, unpaid balances of notes, interest rates and dates to which paid, and collateral for the notes. If any notes payable have been subordinated—that is, made subject to prior settlement of some other obligation—the holders of the notes should be requested to acknowledge such agreement.

The auditor may also substantiate the existence and amount of a mortgage or trust deed liability outstanding by direct confirmation with the mortgagee or trustee. The information received should be compared with the client's records and the audit working papers. When no change in the liability account has occurred in the period under audit, the only major procedure necessary will be this confirmation with the creditor. At the same time that the mortgagee or trustee is asked to confirm the debt, he may be requested for an opinion as to the company's compliance with the mortgage or trust deed agreement.

Figure 18–2 illustrates a form which enables the CPA to verify interest-bearing debt arising from secured transactions in which the client is the debtor. This form is mailed by the auditor to the filing officer of the appropriate public office to obtain information regarding financing statements required to be filed for secured transactions under the Uniform Commercial Code.

Bond transactions can usually be confirmed directly with the trustee. The information to be included in the trustee's statement of the year's transactions may be as follows:

a)   Exact description of the issue, maturity dates, and interest rates.

b)   Bonds redeemed or purchased for the treasury during the year.

c) Bonds converted to stock during the year.

d) Sinking fund transactions during the year.

e) Bonds outstanding at balance sheet date.

f) Securities and cash in the sinking fund.

g) Total trustee fees billed for the year and amount unpaid at the end of the year.

An example of a confirmation statement obtained from the trustee of a bond issue is presented in Figure 18–3. The information obtained is used to verify the data shown in the account analysis of bonds payable, bond issue costs, and unamortized discount illustrated in Figure 18–1. The total amount outstanding on the balance sheet date should of course agree with the company's books. If a difference exists, it may have been caused by the clients' failure to record a transaction reported by the trustee. An adjustment of the unamortized premium or discount and bond issue costs is required each time a company reacquires its own bonds through purchase or conversion to stock. Occasionally auditors find that the acquisition of bonds has been recorded but that no entry has been made to reduce proportionately the total issue costs, premium, or discount applicable to the issue.

When the trustee reports any conversions, cancellations or redemptions during the period under audit, the auditor will inspect the canceled certificates or the trustee's cremation certificate to determine that proper evidence exists for the reduction in bonds outstanding. This objective may also require tracing the reported cash outlays to the cash records. When bonds are canceled, it is important to note that any coupons which had not been redeemed are canceled or cremated. On the other hand, if the trustee reports additional issuances of bonds during the period, the CPA will trace the proceeds to the cash records to ascertain that the issuing corporation has received proper payment for these additional sales. In this case the auditor should determine that any coupons for interest prior to the date the bonds were sold have been retained by the issuing corporation and mutilated to prevent their being redeemed.

ALTERNATIVE PROCEDURES IN ABSENCE OF A TRUSTEE. When an indenture does not provide for the services of a trustee, the auditor may direct his verification along the following lines:

a) Inspect unissued bonds on hand to determine that all numbers are accounted for.

b) Verify all sales and purchases to cashbooks, bank statements, and vouchers.

c) Reconcile subsidiary records for bonds payable with the general ledger control account.

d) Confirm registered bonds with the holders.

FIGURE 18–2

REQUEST FOR INFORMATION OR COPIES. Present in Duplicate to Filing Officer

1. INFORMATION REQUEST. Filing officer please furnish certificate showing whether there is on file any presently effective financing statement naming the Debtor listed below and any statement of assignment thereof, and if there is, giving the date and hour of filing of each such statement and the names and addresses of each secured party named therein.

1A. DEBTOR (LAST NAME FIRST)		1B. SOC. SEC. OR FED. TAX NO.
1C. MAILING ADDRESS	1D. CITY, STATE	1E. ZIP CODE

1F.

Date_____19_____   Signature of Requesting Party_____

2. CERTIFICATE:

FILE NUMBER	DATE AND HOUR OF FILING	NAME(S) AND ADDRESS(ES) OF SECURED PARTY(IES) AND ASSIGNEE(S), IF ANY

The undersigned filing officer hereby certifies that the above listing is a record of all presently effective financing statements and statements of assignment which name the above debtor and which are on file in my office as of_____19____at_____ ___M.

_____19_____
(DATE)

_____
(FILING OFFICER)

By:_____

3. COPY REQUEST. Filing officer please furnish_____copy(ies) of each page of the following statements concerning the debtors listed below ☐ Financing Statement ☐ Amendments ☐ Statements of Assignment ☐ Continuation Statements ☐ Statement of Release ☐ Termination Statement ☐ All Statements on file.

FILE NUMBER	DATE OF FILING	NAME(S) AND MAILING ADDRESS(ES) OF DEBTOR(S)	DEBTORS SOC. SEC. OR FED. TAX NO.

Date_____19_____   Signature of Requesting Party_____

4. CERTIFICATE

The undersigned filing officer hereby certifies that the attached copies are true and exact copies of all statements requested above.

_____19_____
(DATE)

_____
(FILING OFFICER)

By:_____

5.   **Mail Information or Copies to**

NAME
MAILING
ADDRESS
CITY AND
STATE

FIGURE 18–3
Trustee's reply to confirmation request

THE LAKESIDE TRUST COMPANY

P.O. BOX 1357 E,   CHICAGO, ILLINOIS 60601

January 12, 1975

McArthur and Company
Certified Public Accountants
97 Green Street
Chicago, Illinois 60610

Dear Sirs:

In reply to the request of The Torino Corporation, concerning their 6 percent, 20-year, Debenture Bonds, we are pleased to provide the following information based on our records as of December 31, 1974:

Issued and outstanding at December 31, 1974 . . . . $10,000,000

There were no acquisitions or issuances of bonds of this issue during the year ended December 31, 1974. The bonds are not convertible, and no sinking fund is required under the indenture. Our fees billed during the year ended December 31, 1974 totaled $6,240, none of which remained unpaid at December 31, 1974.

Very truly yours,
The Lakeside Trust Company

Vice President

These procedures are intended to provide the same assurances as the steps previously described for companies utilizing the services of an independent trustee.

8.   Examine treasury bonds and reconcile to the general ledger.

Some companies reacquire their own bonds in the open market or directly from bondholders for the purpose of reissuing them at a later date. These bonds are usually carried in a Treasury Bonds account. To verify this item, the auditor will trace all debits for treasury bonds reacquired (and all credits for reissuances) directly to the minutes authorizing these transaction and to the cash records. He will inspect and count the bonds in the treasury and reconcile the total amount to the general ledger account. At the same time the auditor can conveniently review any gains or losses from dealings in treasury bonds, and the effect of these transactions on unamortized issue costs, discount or premium.

Occasionally a corporation may elect to deliver treasury bonds or unissued bonds to creditors as security for other loans. One supplementary objective of the inspection of treasury bonds and unissued bonds is to disclose the existence of any such loans which the client might have obtained but failed to record. The auditor may also make direct inquiries as to whether treasury bonds have been used as collateral, and whether at the balance sheet date there were any loans so secured.

9.   Verify computation of interest expense, interest payable, and amortization of discount or premium.

Interest expense is of special significance to an auditor because it indicates the amount of outstanding liabilities. In other words, close study of interest payments is a means of bringing to light any unrecorded interest-bearing liabilities.

Verification of interest expense and interest payable for notes, mortgages, or trust deeds payable is usually a simple matter. The auditor tests the propriety of the client's interest expense and payable computations, which are set forth in the working paper analyses of the related notes or mortgages obtained in the first procedure of this audit program. In addition, the auditor should examine paid checks supporting interest payments and review confirmations received from note payees or mortgagees to verify the dates to which interest on each note or mortgage has been paid.

In his review of vouchers payable and cash records for the period between the balance sheet date and the completion of the audit field work, the auditor should also be alert for any interest payments which do not correspond to notes shown as outstanding at the balance sheet date. This is one more step in the auditor's search for unrecorded liabilities.

If bonds were issued at par and the interest payment dates coincided with the company's fiscal year, the proof of bond interest expense would be simple indeed. The auditor would need only to multiply the stated interest rate times the face value of bonds outstanding. Such a simplified situation is of course seldom found in practice. The total bond interest expense for the period usually reflects not only the interest actually paid and accured but also amortization of bond premium or discount and costs of issuance. Current fees of the trustee may also be included.

The nominal interest on the bonds should be verified by computation (interest rate times face value). Checks drawn in payment of interest are traced to the cash records. Any balance of interest expense which remains unpaid at the balance sheet date is traced to an accrued liability account. Canceled coupons (or the trustee's cremation certificate covering such coupons) are examined and reconciled with the cash interest payments. If the payment of interest to bondholders is handled through the independent trustee, a direct confirmation of the trustee's transactions for the period under review should be obtained. All cash transactions will be vouched to the underlying documents showing authority for interest payments.

The amortization of bond issue costs and premium or discount is verified by computation. In making these computations the auditor should give attention to any charges arising because of refunding or the acquisition by the company of its own bonds. If the current fees of the trustee are charged to the Interest Expense account, these expenses should be traced to the trustee's statements and to the confirmation letter.

10. *Determine that all provisions of the indenture have been met.*

Bond issues generally impose upon the borrowing company a number of restrictions and prohibitions—all designed to protect the interests of the bondholders. The following points are typical of these requirements:

a) The maintenance of specified ratios, especially for working capital.
b) The restriction of dividends to a specified proportion of earnings.
c) The maintenance of sinking funds.
d) The repair, maintenance, and insurance of pledged property.
e) The prohibition of further long-term borrowing, except under stipulated conditions.

The auditor will already have accumulated information bearing on many of these points. Adequate comments should be included in the audit working papers as to the company's compliance with the provisions of the indenture. If the company has not complied fully with the requirements, the auditor should inform both the client and the client's counsel of the violation; explanation of the extent of noncompliance should also be included in the client's financial statements and possibly in the audit report. In some cases of violation the entire bond issue may be due and payable on demand, and hence a current liability.

11.   *Review notes paid or renewed since the balance sheet date.*

If any of the notes payable outstanding at the balance sheet date are paid before completion of the audit engagement, the auditor is provided with an opportunity for verification of these items. Renewal of notes maturing shortly after the balance sheet date may alter the auditor's thinking as to the proper classification of these liabilities.

In Chapter 13, dealing with notes receivable, emphasis was placed on the necessity of close scrutiny of loans to officers, directors, and affiliates because of the absence of arm's-length bargaining in these transactions. Similar emphasis should be placed on the examination of notes payable to insiders or affiliates, although the opportunities for self-dealing are more limited than with receivables. The auditor should scan the notes payable records for the period between the balance sheet date and the completion of his examination so that he may be aware of any unusual transactions, such as the reestablishment of an "insider" note which had been paid just prior to the balance sheet date.

12.   *Determine proper balance sheet presentation of interest-bearing debt, interest payable, and premium or discount.*

Bankers and other prospective creditors study the current liability section of a balance sheet very closely for clues to a company's credit status. The presence of unsecured bank loans indicates financial strength and good credit standing. In the evaluation of secured bank loans, the nature of the assets pledged is of great significance. The pledging of government bonds, for example, indicates a strong financial position coupled with a policy decision to retain the bonds and borrow money rather than to sell the bonds. The pledging of inventory or of accounts receivable as security for loans is quite another matter and suggests a hardpressed financial situation.

Because of the interest of creditors in the current liability section of the balance sheet and the inferences which may be drawn from various uses of notes payable, adequate informative disclosure is extremely important. Classification of notes by types of payees, as well as by current or long-term maturity, is desirable. Separate listing is needed for notes payable to banks, notes payable to trade creditors, and notes payable to officers, directors, stockholders, and affiliates. The pledging of assets to secure notes should be disclosed, preferably in a note to the balance sheet. In the event of financial difficulties and dissolution, creditors expect to share in the assets in proportion to their respective claims; and if choice assets, such as current receivables, have been pledged to one creditor, the risk to unsecured creditors is increased. Current liabilities should include not only those notes maturing within a period of 12 months (or a longer operating cycle) but also any installments currently payable on long-term obligations such as mortgages. If notes bear the personal endorsement or guarantee of officers or directors, this fact should also be disclosed as a significant element in the appraisal of financial position.

The essential point in balance sheet presentation of long-term liabilities is that they be adequately and fully described. Each category of long-term debt should be stated under a separate title, which includes:

1. The precise name of the debt.
2. The total amount authorized and issued.
3. The interest rate and the maturity dates.
4. A cross-reference to any assets pledged as security for the liability.
5. Any conversion rights.
6. Any subordination of long-term debt to other liabilities.

LONG-TERM DEBT PAYABLE IN CURRENT PERIOD. It is general practice to include under long-term liabilities all debts which will not mature within the ensuing operating cycle and any debt which will mature but which will not be liquidated from current assets. In other words, any bonds or notes falling due in the coming operating cycle which are to be refunded or paid from special funds will be classed as long-term obligations regardless of maturity date. Conversely, any debt maturing currently and payable from current assets will be a current liability. This distinction is necessary to present a picture of the working capital showing clearly the amount of current funds and the liabilities payable therefrom.

RESTRICTIONS IMPOSED BY LONG-TERM DEBT AGREEMENTS. Most long-term debt agreements contain clauses limiting the borrowing company's right to pay dividends. Such a restriction is vitally significant to investors in common stocks. Consequently, the nature of the restriction should be clearly set forth by a footnote to the balance sheet. An example adapted from a published financial statement follows:

The long-term notes payable contain restrictions on the payment of common stock dividends. The notes provide that the Company may not pay dividends (except in common stock of the Company) if, since July 31, 1970, the aggregate thereof, plus dividends paid on preferred stock and net expenditures for the reacquisition of common stock, will exceed consolidated net income (as defined) since that date plus $5,000,000. Approximately $12,000,000 of consolidated earnings retained in the business at July 31, 1974 is free of this restriction.

UNAMORTIZED BOND ISSUE COSTS AND PREMIUM OR DISCOUNT. Unamortized bond issue costs are a deferred charge and should be included in the Other Assets section of the balance sheet. Unamortized premium should be added to the face amount of the bonds or debentures in the liability section of the balance sheet. Similarly, unamortized discount should be deducted from the face amount of the debt. These methods of presentation are sanctioned by *APB Opinion No. 21*, "Interest on Receivables and Payables."

APB Opinion No. 21 also requires the imputation of an appropriate interest rate to a long-term liability which is either noninterest bearing on its face or which has an interest rate clearly out of line with prevailing rates for comparable debt instruments. Such an interest imputation results in unamortized premium or discount.

Treasury Bonds. Some accountants have argued that treasury bonds being held for reissuance constitute a valid asset. In theory, however, a bond payable reacquired by the issuing company in advance of the maturity date is little different from a promissory note paid prior to maturity. Both constitute evidence that former indebtedness has been liquidated; neither represents anything of value owned. Treasury bonds need not be distinguished from unissued bonds in the balance sheet and are properly shown as a deduction from the amount of bonds authorized in arriving at the amount outstanding.

Time of examination

The review of internal control over interest-bearing debt may be carried out in advance of the balance sheet date. Analysis of the ledger accounts for interest-bearing debt and interest expense takes very little time in most audits because of the small number of entries. Consequently, most auditors prefer to wait until the end of the year before analyzing these accounts.

Throughout this chapter emphasis has been placed on the auditor's concern over a possible understatement of liabilities; audit procedures intended to bring to light any unrecorded liabilities cannot very well be performed in advance of the balance sheet date. Such steps as the confirmation of outstanding interest-bearing debt, the verification of accrued interest, and the investigation of notes paid or renewed shortly after the balance sheet date must necessarily await the close of the period being audited. We must conclude therefore that the opportunities for performing audit work in advance of the balance sheet date are much more limited in the case of interest-bearing debt than for most of the asset groups previously discussed.

CONTINGENT LIABILITIES

Contingent liabilities may be defined as potential obligations which may in the future develop into actual liabilities or may dissolve without necessitating any outlay. The crucial characteristic of contingent liabilities is *uncertainty;* whether they will or will not develop into real liabilities cannot be determined as of the date of the balance sheet.

Among the more important types of contingent liabilities are the following:

1. Notes receivable discounted.
2. Accommodation endorsements and other guarantees of indebtedness.
3. Accounts receivable sold or assigned with recourse.
4. Renegotiation of U.S. government contracts.
5. Pending litigation.
6. Income tax disputes.

The principal auditing problem involved is that of ascertaining the existence of contingent liabilities. Because of the uncertainty factor, most of the items listed will not appear in the accounts, and a systematic search is required if the auditor is to have reasonable assurance that no important contingent liability has been overlooked. The procedures to be undertaken by the auditor vary with the nature of the contingent item, and hence a discussion of procedures to be followed is most conveniently presented by considering briefly each of the principal sources of contingent liabilities.

1. *Notes receivable discounted.*

The determination of the contingent liability for notes receivable discounted is one of the essential steps in the verification of notes receivable and was discussed in Chapter 13.

The auditor's determination of the contingent liability existing at the balance sheet date may be begun by obtaining or preparing a schedule of notes receivable discounted. These should be verified by confirmation from the bank or other holders. The usual form of confirmation request used in verifying bank balances contains a section for the listing of contingent liabilities.

In addition to inquiring from banks as to the existence of contingent liabilities, the auditor should review the credits to the Notes Receivable account to see whether any of these entries represent discounting transactions rather than collections of maturing notes. Other desirable procedures include making inquiry of officers and reviewing the minutes of directors' meetings for resolutions authorizing the discounting of receivables.

2. *Accommodation endorsements and other guarantees of indebtedness.*

The endorsement of notes of other concerns or individuals is very seldom recorded in the accounts but may be reflected in the minutes of directors' meetings. The practice is more common among small concerns—particularly when one person has a proprietary interest in several companies. Officers, partners, and sole proprietors of small organizations should be questioned as to the existence of any contingent liability from this source. Inquiry should also be made as to whether any collateral has been received to protect the company. The auditor may suggest the desirability of maintaining a record of any accommodation endorsements by inclusion of a pair of memorandum accounts in the general ledger.

A corporation sometimes guarantees the payment of principal and/or interest on bonds or notes issued by affiliated companies. Information concerning such guarantees is usually presented in detail in the minutes of directors' meetings. A company cannot guarantee its own obligations, for it is already fully committed to pay its debts. The following note illustrates the disclosure of a contingent liability arising from guaranteeing securities of affiliates:

> The Company has guaranteed payment of liabilities of affiliates in the amount of $2,500,000. Additional loans by insurance companies to affiliates in the amount of $2,000,000 are to be guaranteed by the Company under an existing agreement.

3. *Accounts receivable sold or assigned with recourse.*

When accounts receivable are sold or assigned *with recourse,* a guarantee of collectibility is given. Authorization of such a transaction should be revealed during the auditor's reading of the minutes, and a clue may also be found during the examination of transactions and correspondence with financial institutions. Confirmation by direct communication with the purchaser or assignee is necessary for any receivables sold or assigned.

4. *Renegotiation of U.S. government contracts.*

Companies engaged in production under U.S. government contracts may be required to refund excessive profits realized on such work. Contractors must submit to the Renegotiation Board an annual report summarizing the contractor's operations and profits and setting forth any special factors peculiar to the company's financing, organization, and operation which may have a bearing on the determination of "reasonable profits." All reports are examined by the board. Those showing renegotiable profits which are obviously not excessive are disposed of by a clearance, and the contractor is so notified. Reports indicating possible excessive profits are reviewed based on the following statutory factors:

a) Efficiency of the contractor.
b) Reasonableness of costs and profits.
c) Stockholders' equity of the contractor.
d) Extent of risk assumed by the contractor.

e) Nature and extent of the contractor's contribution to the defense effort.

f) Character of contractor's business.

If the board makes a determination of excessive profits, the contractor, if aggrieved, may petition the Tax Court of the United States for a redetermination. Any amounts refundable by the contractor are generally net of any federal income taxes which have been paid or assessed thereon.

The renegotiation settlement applicable to sales of a given year will not be completed until some time subsequent to the balance sheet date; hence it is customary for the client to disclose in the financial statements whether a refund may be required and to indicate the terms of the most recent renegotiation settlement. The following note is typical:

Approximately $85,000,000 of the Company's sales during 1974 are subject to the profit limitations of the Renegotiation Act. However, it is not expected that any substantial refund will be required, and no provision therefore has been made in the accounts. Review by the Government of the operations for all years through 1973 has resulted in a determination that no refunds were required.

5. *Pending litigation.*

The likelihood of an adverse decision in any lawsuit or claims pending against the company can best be appraised by the client's legal counsel, and it is standard procedure for the auditor to request the client's attorneys to express an opinion as to the probable outcome of any pending litigation. Many attorneys, however, are reluctant to take a definite position on such cases, and the auditor may find it necessary to accept financial statement disclosure limited to a description of the suit and a resumé of its present status. Protection against possible losses from claims filed against the company is sometimes afforded by insurance. The following footnote to the financial statement of an aircraft manufacturer illustrates the method of disclosing this type of contingent liability:

A number of suits are pending against the Company as the result of accidents in prior years involving airplanes manufactured by the Company. It is believed that insurance carried by the Company is sufficient to protect it against loss by reason of suits involving the lives of passengers and damage to aircraft. Other litigation pending against the Company involves no substantial amount or is covered by insurance.

The balance sheet of another large corporation contained the following note concerning contingent liabilities:

The Company has suits pending against it, some of which are for large amounts. The Company is advised by counsel that, while it is impossible to ascertain the ultimate legal and financial responsibility in respect to such litigation as of December 31, 1974, it is his opinion that the ultimate liability will not be materially important in relation to the total assets of the Company.

6. Income tax disputes.

The necessity of estimating the income tax liability applicable to the year under audit was discussed in Chapter 17. In addition to the taxes relating to the current year's income, uncertainty often exists concerning the amount ultimately payable for prior years. A lag of two or three years often exists between the filing of income tax returns and the final settlement after review by the Internal Revenue Service. Disputes between the taxpayer and the IRS may create contingent liabilities not settled for several more years. The auditor should determine whether internal revenue agents have examined any returns of the client since the preceding audit, and if so, whether any additional taxes have been assessed.

General audit procedures

Although audit procedures vary with the individual type of contingent liability, the following steps are taken in most audits as a means of discovering these potential obligations:

1. Review the minutes of directors' meetings to the date of completion of field work. Important contracts, lawsuits, and dealings with subsidiaries are typical of matters discussed in board meetings which may involve contingent liabilities.
2. Request client's attorneys to advise the auditor directly of—
    a)   All claims and lawsuits threatening or pending.
    b)   Tax assessments proposed or made.
    c)   Any other contingent liabilities of which the attorneys have knowledge.
    d)   Unbilled legal fees, if any.
3. Send standard bank confirmation request to all banks with which the client has done business during the year. This standard form includes a request for information on any indirect or contingent liabilities of the client.
4. Review correspondence with financial institutions for evidence of accommodation endorsements, guarantees of indebtedness, or sales or assignments of account receivable.

Liability representations

Since contingent liabilities are often not entered in the accounting records, the officers of the company may be the only persons aware of the contingencies. It is therefore important that the auditor should ask the officers to disclose all contingent liabilities of which they have knowledge. To emphasize the importance of the request and to guard against any possible misunderstanding, the officers should be asked to sign a written statement such as the one illustrated in Figure 18–4, as of a date near the end of the field work.

Balance sheet presentation

Although textbooks in accounting theory discuss methods of presenting contingent liabilities within the body of the balance sheet, current practice almost universally relies upon supporting footnotes as a means of disclosure. This permits presentation of the pertinent facts in some detail. It is customary to include in the balance sheet proper a reference to the footnote so that all readers will be made aware of the existence of the contingent liabilities.

Some concerns have listed so-called "reserves for contingencies" on the balance sheet midway between the liability and stockholders' equity sections. This practice creates confusion as to whether the reserve was created by a charge against revenue or by appropriation of retained earnings. It also leaves room for doubt as to what amount is intended to represent the total stockholders' equity of the company. In some cases it appears that management has created reserves for the purpose of arbitrarily shifting income from one period to another. Such practices do untold harm by destroying public confidence in financial statements and in the integrity of the accounting profession. It is doubtful whether such reserves serve any constructive purpose; if used at all, they should be included in the stockholders' equity section and clearly labeled as part of retained earnings. Presentation of information concerning contingent liabilities should be limited to specific factual situations, such as accommodation endorsements, guarantees and pending lawsuits. To fill the financial statements with vague generalities about the uncertainties of the future is more akin to fortune telling than financial reporting.

COMMITMENTS

Closely related to contingent liabilities are obligations termed *commitments.* The auditor may discover during his examination many of the following commitments: inventory purchase commitments, contracts for the construction of plant and equipment, pension or profit-sharing plans, long-term leases of plant and equipment, employee stock option plans, and employment contracts with key officers. A common characteristic of these commitments is the contractual obligation to issue stock or assets *in the future* for goods or services to be received *in the future*.

FIGURE 18–4

Georgetown Enterprises Inc.

1451 WATERSHED AVENUE, ALBANY, NEW YORK 12221

January 28, 1975

Rogers and Heart, CPAs
4243 Exeter Street
Albany, New York 12244

Dear Sirs:

To the best of our knowledge and belief, the Company had no contingent liabilities at December 31, 1974, except as shown below:

Contingent Liability for:	Estimated Amount
Notes receivable discounted . . . .$	None
Accommodation endorsements and other guarantees of indebtedness . .	None
Accounts receivable sold or assigned with recourse	None
Renegotiation of U.S. government contracts	None
Pending litigation.	None
Income tax disputes	None
Other	None

A. G. Robertson
President

R. W. Watson
Controller

All classes of material commitments may be described in a single note to financial statements; or they may be included in a "Commitments and Contingent Liabilities" note.

GROUP I
REVIEW QUESTIONS

18–1. How are contingent liabilities presented in financial statements?

18–2. If the federal income tax returns for prior years have not as yet been reviewed by federal tax authorities, would you consider it necessary to disclose this situation in the financial statements? Explain.

18–3. Explain the meaning of the term "liability representation."

18–4. The Palmer Company has issued a number of notes payable during the year, and several of these notes are outstanding at the balance sheet date. What source of information should the auditor use in preparing a working paper analysis of the notes payable?

18–5. What is the principal reason for verifying the Interest Expense account in conjunction with the verification of notes payable?

18–6. Are contingent liabilities ordinarily recorded in the accounts? Explain.

18–7. Suggest two important audit procedures commonly used to verify the contingent liability from discounting of notes receivable.

18–8. The Logan Company, which is in a strong financial position, has on several occasions agreed to assist some of its customers by placing accommodation endorsements on their promissory notes to banks. What method would you suggest to the client to insure that contingent liability from such actions is not overlooked at the time of preparing financial statements?

18–9. Audit programs for verification of accounts receivable and notes receivable often include investigation of selected transactions occurring after the balance sheet date as well as transactions during the year under audit. Is the auditor concerned with note payable transactions subsequent to the balance sheet date? Explain.

18–10. Is the confirmation of notes payable usually correlated with any other specific phase of the audit? Explain.

18–11. What is the meaning of the term "commitment" as used in accounting?

18–12. What constitutes adequate informative disclosure for long-term liabilities in the balance sheet?

18–13. Long-term creditors often insist upon placing certain restrictions upon the borrowing company for the term of the loan. Give three examples of such restrictions and indicate how each restriction protects the long-term creditor.

18–14. Most corporations with bonds payable outstanding utilize the services of a trustee. What relation, if any, does this practice have to the maintenance of adequate internal control?

18–15. In addition to verifying the recorded liabilities of a company, the auditor must also give consideration to the possibility that other unrecorded liabilities exist. What specific steps may be taken by the auditor to determine that all of his client's interest-bearing liabilities are recorded?

18–16. During your first audit of the Giles Corporation for the year ended December 31, 1974, you are informed by the president that the corporation has been unable to make a $100,000 sinking fund contribution required as of December 15, 1974, under the terms of a bond indenture. The president asks you whether this amount should appear as a current liability or a long-term liability, and whether, if properly disclosed in the financial statements, it must be mentioned in your audit report.

18–17. An assistant auditor was assigned by the auditor in charge to the verification of long-term liabilities. Some time later he reported to the auditor in charge that he had determined that all long-term liabilities were properly recorded and that all recorded long-term liabilities were genuine obligations. Does this determination constitute a sufficient examination of long-term liabilities? Explain.

18–18. "An auditor is not qualified to pass on the legality of a bond issue; this is a problem for the company's attorneys. It is therefore unnecessary for the auditor to inspect the bond indenture." Criticize this quotation.

18–19. Should the audit working papers for debentures payable be placed in the permanent file or in the file of working papers for the current audit? Why?

18–20. The Schofield Corporation has recently issued a large amount of bonds payable and is required to make semiannual contributions to a sinking fund under the control of an independent trustee. What audit procedures are appropriate in connection with the sinking fund?

18–21. What information should be requested by the auditor from the trustee responsible for an issue of debentures payable?

GROUP II
QUESTIONS REQUIRING ANALYSIS

18–22. Select the best answer choice for each of the following and justify your selection in a brief statement.

  a) A covenant in Milton Company's indenture for an outstanding 1965 issue of mortgage bonds requires the maintenance at all times of a current ratio in excess of 2 to 1. The indenture also provides that should any covenant be violated, the bond trustee has the option of requiring immediate payment of the principal due.

    A CPA is engaged in the initial examination of the financial statements of Milton Company for the year ended December 31,

1974. He notes that the current ratio has not met indenture requirements since 1969 and is 1.7 to 1 at December 31, 1974. The bond trustee has been furnished financial statements yearly and has not questioned the failure to comply with the covenant; in response to a standard confirmation letter the trustee indicated that to the best of his knowledge there had been no covenant violations to December 31, 1974. Under the circumstances the CPA should—

(1)   Rely upon the bond trustee's confirmation and require no reclassification or further inquiry.

(2)   Require reclassification of the bonds payable as a current liability.

(3)   Request that the management letter of representations explicitly refer to the noncompliance with the covenant and management's expectation that the trustee will take no action.

(4)   Request that Milton Company obtain a waiver of the requirement from the bond trustee.

b)   A CPA analyzes the accrued interest payable account for the year, recomputes the amounts of payments and beginning and ending balances, and reconciles to the interest expense account. Which of the following errors or questionable practices has the best chance of being detected by the CPA's audit procedures?

(1)   Interest revenue of $52 on a note receivable was credited against miscellaneous expense.

(2)   A provision of the company's loan agreement was violated. Common dividends are prohibited if income available for interest and dividends is not three times interest requirements.

(3)   Interest paid on an account payable was charged to the raw material purchases account.

(4)   A note payable had not been recorded. Interest of $150 on the note was properly paid and was charged to the interest expense account. (AICPA, adapted)

18–23.   You are the audit manager for the April 30, 1974 examination of the financial statements of Midwest Grain Storage, Inc., a new client. The company's records show that as of April 30, 1974 approximately 15 million bushels of various grains are in storage for the Commodity Credit Corporation, an agency of the U.S. government.

In your review of the audit senior's working papers, you ascertain the following facts:

(1)   All grain is stored under a Uniform Grain Storage Agreement, which holds Midwest responsible for the quantity and quality of the grain.

(2)   Losses due to shrinkage, spoilage, and so forth are inherent in the storage of grain. Midwest's losses, however, have been negligible due to the excellence of its storage facilities.

(3)   Midwest's insurance covers the grain fully for such risks as fire, flood, vandalism, etc.

(4) Midwest carries a warehouseman's bond covering approximately 20 percent of the value of the stored grain.

In the "contingent liabilities" section of the working papers, the senior has made the following notation: "I propose recommending to Midwest's controller that the contingent liability for grain spoilage and shrinkage be disclosed in a note to the financial statements."

Required:

Do you concur with the senior's proposal? Explain.

18–24. You are engaged in the examination of the financial statements of Marshall, Inc., a publicly owned company, for the year ended August 31, 1974. Marshall's August 31, 1974 balance sheet, reflecting all of your audit adjustments accepted by the client to date, shows total current assets, $5,000,000; total current liabilities, $2,000,000; and stockholders' equity, $3,500,000. Included in current liabilities are two unsecured, 6 percent notes payable—one payable to United National Bank in the amount of $400,000 due October 31, 1974, the other payable to First State Bank in the amount of $300,000 due September 30, 1974. On September 30, the last scheduled date for your audit field work, you learn that Marshall, Inc. is unable to pay the $309,000 maturity value of the First State Bank note; that Marshall executives are negotiating with First State Bank for an extension of the due date of the note; and that nothing definite has been decided as to the extension.

Required:

Should this situation be described in notes to Marshall, Inc.'s August 31, 1974 financial statements? Explain.

18–25. Linda Reeves, CPA, receives a telephone call from her client, Maximus Company. The company's controller states that the board of directors of Maximus has entered into two contractual arrangements with the company's former president, who has recently retired. Under one agreement, Maximus Company will pay the ex-president $900 per month for five years if he does not compete with the company during that time in a rival business. Under the other agreement, the company will pay the ex-president $600 per month for five years for such advisory services as the company may request from the ex-president.

Maximus's controller asks Miss Reeves whether the balance sheet as of the date the two agreements were signed should show $18,000 in current liabilities and $72,000 in long-term liabilities, or whether the two agreements should be disclosed in a contingent liabilities note to the financial statements.

Required:

How should Linda Reeves reply to the Maximus controller's questions? Explain.

18–26. Wilson Hall, CPA, is engaged in the examination of Garrett Company's financial statements for the year ended December 31, 1974. During the course of his field work, Mr. Hall accumulates the following audit evidence for a $100,000 note receivable from Memphis Mfg. Co., Inc., a customer of Garrett Company:

> Date of note: November 1, 1974
> Due date: May 1, 1975
> Interest: 6 percent payable in full at maturity of note
> Discounting: December 1, 1974 with First Northern Bank, discount rate 8 percent

A Dun & Bradstreet, Inc. credit report in Mr. Hall's working papers, dated January 22, 1975, reports that Memphis Mfg. Co., Inc. is in the process of liquidation and that Memphis's management estimates that creditors will receive 25 cents on the dollar.

How should Mr. Hall advise Garrett Company to present the note receivable from Memphis Mfg. Co., Inc. in the balance sheet for December 31, 1974? Explain.

18–27. The only long-term liability owed by Rogers Corporation is a note payable for $100,000 secured by a mortgage on the company's plant and equipment. You have audited the company annually for the last three years, during which time there has been no change in the principal amount of the note. The maturity date is 10 years from the current balance sheet date. All interest payments have been made promptly in accordance with the terms of the note. Under these circumstances, what audit work, if any, is necessary with respect to this long-term liability during your present year-end audit?

18–28. During your annual audit of the Cook Manufacturing Company, your assistant reports to you that although a number of entries were made during the year in the general ledger account, Notes Payable to Officers, he decided that it was not necessary to audit the account because it had a zero balance at year-end.

Required:

Do you agree with your assistant's decision? Discuss. (AICPA)

18–29. In an audit of a corporation that has a bond issue outstanding, the trust indenture is reviewed and confirmation as to the issue is obtained from the trustee. List eight matters of importance to the auditor that might be found either in the indenture or in the confirmation obtained from the trustee. Explain briefly the reason for the auditor's interest in each of the items. (AICPA)

18–30. You are retained by the Columbia Corporation to make an examination of its financial statements for the fiscal year ended June 30, 1974, and you begin work on July 15. Your survey of internal control indicates a fairly satisfactory condition, although there are not enough employees to permit extensive subdivision of duties. The company is one of the smaller units in the industry but has realized net income of about $70,000 in each of the last three years.

Near the end of your field work you overhear a telephone call received by the president of the company while you are discussing the audit with him. The telephone conversation indicates that on May 15, 1974 the Columbia Corporation made an accommodation endorsement of a 60-day, $30,000 note issued by a major customer, Brill Corporation, to its bank. The purpose of the telephone call from Brill was to inform your client that the note had been paid at the maturity date. You had not been aware of the existence of the note prior to overhearing the telephone call.

Required:

a)   Do you think the auditor would be justified from an ethical standpoint in acting on information acquired in this manner?

b)   Should the balance sheet as of June 30 disclose the contingent liability? Give reasons for your answer.

c)   Prepare a list of auditing procedures which might have brought the contingency to light. Explain fully the likelihood of detection of the accommodation endorsement by each procedure listed.

GROUP III
PROBLEMS

18–31.   You were engaged to examine the financial statements of Ronlyn Corporation for the year ended June 30, 1974.

On May 1, 1974 the corporation borrowed $500,000 from Second National Bank to finance plant expansion. The long-term note agreement provided for the annual payment of principal and interest over five years. The existing plant was pledged as security for the loan.

Required:

a)   What are the audit objectives in the examination of long-term debt?

b)   Prepare an audit program for the examination of the long-term note agreement between Ronlyn and Second National Bank. (AICPA, adapted)

18–32.   In your first audit of Hydrafoil Company, a manufacturer of specially designed boats capable of transporting passengers over water at very high speeds, you find that sales are made to commercial transportation companies. The sales price per unit is $200,000, and with each unit sold, the client gives the purchasing company a certificate reading as follows:

Hydrafoil Company promises to pay to _____ the sum of $12,000 when the boat designated as Serial No. _____ is permanently retired from service and evidence of such retirement is submitted.

The president of Hydrafoil Company explains to you that the purpose of issuing the certificate is to insure contact with the customer when he is in the market for new equipment. You also learn that the company makes no journal entry to record a certificate when it is issued. Instead, the company charges an expense account and credits a liability account $100 per month for each outstanding certificate, based on the company's experience that its hydrafoil boats will be rendered obsolete by new more efficient models in approximately 10 years from the date of sale.

Required:

Do you concur with Hydrafoil Company's accounting for the certificates? You may assume that the 10-year life of the product (and therefore of the certificates) is an accurate determination. Explain your position clearly.

18–33. Prepare an audit program which would bring to light various types of contingent liabilities and commitments. (The program should be in **general terms** for **each** area covered and should **describe** briefly the **type** of contingent item which might be found under each step. Ignore the fact that several of the steps in the program might normally be included in programs for other parts of your examination.) (AICPA)

18–34. The following covenants are extracted from the indenture of a bond issue of Thorne Company. The indenture provides that failure to comply with its terms in any respect automatically advances the due date of the loan to the date of noncompliance (the regular due date is 20 years hence). Give any audit procedures or reporting requirements you feel should be taken or recognized in connection with each one of the following:

(1) "The debtor company shall endeavor to maintain a working capital ratio of 2 to 1 at all times; and in any fiscal year following a failure to maintain said ratio, the company shall restrict compensation of officers to a total of $100,000. Officers for this purpose shall include chairman of the board of directors, president, all vice presidents, secretary, controller, and treasurer."

(2) "The debtor company shall keep all property which is security for this debt insured against loss by fire to the extent of 100 percent of its actual value. Policies of insurance comprising this protection shall be filed with the trustee."

(3) "The debtor company shall pay all taxes legally assessed against property which is security for this debt within the time provided by law for payment without penalty, and shall deposit receipted tax bills or equally acceptable evidence of payment of same with the trustee."

(4) "A sinking fund shall be deposited with the trustee by semiannual payments of $300,000, from which the trustee shall, in his discretion, purchase bonds of this issue." (AICPA, adapted)

18–35. In an examination of the Ludlow Corporation at December 31, 1974 you have learned that the following situations exist. No entries in respect thereto have been made in the accounting records. What **entries** would you recommend and what **disclosures,** if any, would you suggest for these situations in the financial statements for December 31, 1974?

(1) The Ludlow Corporation has guaranteed the payment of interest on the 10-year, first-mortgage bonds of the Kipling Company, an affiliate. Outstanding bonds of the Kipling Company amount to $150,000 with interest payable at 5 percent per annum, due June 1 and December 1 of each year. The bonds were issued by the Kipling Company on December 1, 1972, and all interest payments have been met by that company with the exception of the payment due December 1, 1974. The Ludlow Corporation states that it will pay the defaulted interest to the bondholders on January 15, 1975.

(2) During the year 1974, the Ludlow Corporation was named as defendant in a suit for damages by the Dalton Company for breach of contract. An adverse decision to the Ludlow Corporation was rendered, and the Dalton Company was awarded $40,000 damages. At the time of the audit, the case was under appeal to a higher court.

(3) On December 23, 1974, the Ludlow Corporation declared a common stock dividend of 1,000 shares, par $100,000, of its common stock, payable February 2, 1975, to the common stockholders of record December 30, 1974. (AICPA, adapted)

18–36. Palmdale Company sold bonds of the par value of $1,000,000 on January 1, 1974. The bonds were due serially $100,000 on December 31, 1974 and annually thereafter. Interest at the rate of 5 percent is payable semiannually on June 30 and December 31 of each year. The bonds refer to a trust indenture naming the Lancaster Trust Company as trustee. All principal and interest payments to the bondholders are specified to be made by the trust company, and the indenture also states that Palmdale Company shall pay all maturing principal and interest amounts to the trustee on the due dates.

On June 30, 1974 the company paid $25,000 to the trustee and charged this amount to interest. On December 31, 1974 the company paid $125,000 to the trustee and charged $100,000 to the Bond account and $25,000 to Interest.

You are the auditor of Palmdale Company and have received confirmation from the trustee as of December 31, 1974, stating that interest coupons maturing June 30, 1974 have been paid in the amount of $23,900 and interest coupons maturing December 31, 1974 have been paid in the amount of $800; also that bonds maturing December 31 have been paid in the amount of $13,000. The trustee also reports that he has on hand a cash balance of $112,300 in favor of Palmdale Company. The paid bonds and coupons referred to by the trustee had been returned to the company and were inspected by you.

How should Palmdale Company treat the outstanding bonds, interest coupons, and cash balance in the hands of the trustee in the company's balance sheet of December 31, 1974? (AICPA, adapted)

18–37. Mr. Robert Hopkins was the senior office employee in the Griffin Equipment Company and enjoyed the complete confidence of the owner, William Barton, who devoted most of his attention to sales, engineering, and production problems. All financial and accounting matters were entrusted to Mr. Hopkins, whose title was office manager. Mr. Hopkins had two assistants, but their only experience in accounting and financial work had been gained under Hopkins' supervision. Mr. Barton had informed Hopkins that it was his responsibility to keep him (Barton) informed on financial position and operating results of the company but not to bother him with details.

The company was short of working capital and would occasionally issue notes payable in settlement of past-due open accounts to suppliers. The situations warranting issuance of notes were decided upon by Mr. Hopkins, and the notes were drawn by him for signature by Mr. Barton. Mr. Hopkins was aware of the weakness in internal control and finally devised a scheme for defrauding the company through understating the amount of notes payable outstanding. He prepared a note in the amount of $24,000 payable to a supplier to whom several invoices were past due. After securing Mr. Barton's signature on the note and mailing it to the creditor, Mr. Hopkins entered the note in the Notes Payable account of the general ledger as $4,000, with an offsetting debit of $4,000 to the creditor's account.

Several months later when the note matured, a check for $24,000 plus interest was issued and properly recorded, including a debit of $24,000 to the Notes Payable account. Mr. Hopkins then altered the original credit in the account by changing the figure from $4,000 to $24,000. He also changed the original debit to Accounts Payable from $4,000 to $24,000. This alteration caused the Notes Payable account to have a balance in agreement with the total of other notes outstanding. To complete the fraud, Mr. Hopkins called the supplier to whom the check had been sent and explained that the check should have been for only $4,000 plus interest.

Mr. Hopkins explained to the supplier that the note for $24,000 had originally been issued in settlement of a number of past-due invoices but that while the note was outstanding, checks had been sent in payment of all the invoices. "In other words," said Mr. Hopkins over the telephone, "we made the mistake of giving you a note for those invoices and then going ahead and sending you checks for them as soon as our cash position had improved. Then we paid the note at maturity. So please excuse our mistakes and return the overpayment." After reviewing the record of invoices and checks received, the supplier agreed he had been overpaid by $20,000 plus interest and promptly sent a refund which Mr. Hopkins abstracted without making any entry in the accounts.

Required:

a) Assuming that an audit by an independent CPA was made while the note was outstanding, do you think that the $20,000 understatement of the Notes Payable account would have been detected? Explain fully the reasoning underlying your answer.

b) If the irregularity was not discovered while the note was outstanding, do you think that an audit subsequent to the payment of the note would have disclosed the fraud? Explain.

c) What internal control procedures would you recommend for the Griffin Equipment Company to avoid fraud of this type?

GROUP IV
CASE STUDIES IN AUDITING

Brown Construction Corporation

18–38. Jones and Miller, CPAs, have been assisting the Brown Construction
Corporation, contractors, in their accounting problems. In the summer
of 1974, Mr. Brown called Mr. Jones and told him that he would
like to have a complete audit of the company's financial statements
for the year ended June 30, 1974, since the bank and also the Department of Public Works, State of California, had requested audited
statements.

Mr. Jones discussed the outlines of an audit plan with Mr. Black,
the senior accountant familiar with the corporation's affairs, and sent
him out to start the audit.

As part of the examination, Mr. Black reviewed all expense accounts for items which should possibly have been capitalized. One
recurring charge of $5,140, appearing in the May and June entries
in the Equipment Rental account, attracted Mr. Black's attention.
The invoices supporting the charges bore the name of a local firm
of construction equipment dealers. The body of the invoices read,
"For equipment leased to you per our agreement, $5,140."

Mr. Black asked to see the agreement and any other correspondence related to the transaction. The agreement was in the form
of a lease, stating that the dealers had leased to Brown Construction
Corporation six pieces of equipment for a period of 10 months,
at a monthly rental of $5,140. The lease specified that the lessors
retained all property rights, title, etc., to the equipment and that
the Brown Construction Corporation was to return the equipment
at the end of the 10 months. It also required the corporation to
pay all expenses of maintenance and licenses, if any, and to insure
the equipment against loss in the amount of $53,000, in favor of
the lessors.

The correspondence covering this transaction included several
printed prospectuses of the equipment covered by the lease agreement, pencil notes, and a typed letter from the lessor, listing the
equipment and its sales price, a financing charge, and sales tax in
the total amount of $53,600. There was also a notation on the margin
of the letter, showing the total of $53,600, deducting 10 payments
of $5,140 each, and a remainder of $2,200.

Mr. Black made careful and extensive working paper notes on
his findings and discussed them with Mr. Jones. They both felt that
the transaction was more in the nature of a purchase than a lease,
especially in a view of the size of the monthly "rental" in relation
to the value of the equipment rented. Mr. Jones called the president
of the Brown Construction Corporation, who told him that Brown
was renting the equipment but that there was a verbal understanding
that the corporation could buy the equipment at the end of the

10 months' lease by paying $2,200. The president insisted, however, that he did not believe the corporation would buy the equipment, although to date, rental payments aggregating $20,560 had been made.

Mr. Black drafted a proposed adjusting entry to reflect a purchase of equipment of $53,000, a current liability of $42,720, and depreciation for two months. When Mr. Black submitted the proposed adjusting entry to the president of the Brown Construction Corporation for his approval, Mr. Brown protested strongly against the conversion, as he called it, of a simple equipment lease into a purchase arrangement.

Required:

a) Was Mr. Jones justified in considering the transaction to be a purchase? Explain.
b) Could the auditors express an unqualified opinion if Mr. Brown refused to record Mr. Black's proposed adjustment?
c) Assume that the Brown Construction Corporation had current assets of $100,000 and a current ratio of 2 to 1 before the audit adjustment on the equipment. Would the treatment of the transaction have a material effect on the financial picture of the corporation?
d) What effect, if any, will a decision either way have on the current and future income statements?
e) If you had to argue either side, what additional steps would you take to support your reasoning?
    (1) As the corporation's president.
    (2) As Mr. Jones, CPA.

19

Owners' equity

MOST OF THIS chapter is concerned with the audit of the stockholders' equity accounts of corporate clients; the audit of owners' equity in partnerships and sole proprietorships is discussed briefly near the end of the chapter.

The examination of owners' equity differs from the audit of assets and liabilities in that transactions are generally few in number but material in amount. Consequently, each transaction requires careful attention. In many audit engagements, however, the auditor will find that no change has occurred during the current year in the Capital Stock account and perhaps only one or two entries have been made in the Retained Earnings account. Under these circumstances the audit time required will be very small in relation to the dollar amounts in these accounts. The Capital Stock account often has a larger balance than the Cash account, but the audit work required for capital stock is usually far less.

The auditor's objectives in examination of owners' equity

The auditor's principal objectives in his examination of owners' equity are: (a) to evaluate the internal control over stock certificates, stock transactions, and dividend payments; (b) to determine that all transactions during the year affecting owners' equity accounts were properly authorized and recorded; (c) to determine that legal requirements relating to corporate capital have been met; and (d) to determine that owners' equity is properly presented in the balance sheet.

To accomplish these objectives, the auditor will need some familiarity with federal and state laws concerning securities and also with the rules and regulations of the Securities and Exchange Commission.

Internal control for owners' equity

There are three principal elements of strong internal control over capital stock and dividends. These three elements are (1) the proper authorization of transactions by the board of directors and corporate officers; (2) the segregation of duties in handling these transactions (especially the use of independent agents for stock registration and transfer and dividend payments); and (3) the maintenance of adequate records.

Control of capital stock transactions by board of directors

All capital stock transactions should receive formal advance approval by the board of directors. The audit procedures for verifying an entry in a Capital Stock account should therefore include tracing the entry to an authorization in the minutes of directors' meetings.

Let us consider for a moment some of the specific steps relating to capital stock transactions which require authorization by directors. The board of directors must determine the number of shares to be issued and the price per share; if an installment plan of payment is to be used, the terms must be prescribed by the board. If plant and equipment, services, or any considerations other than cash are to be accepted in payment for shares, the board of directors must set the valuation on the noncash assets received. In recent years many "growth companies" have made acquisitions of other companies by issuance of convertible preferred shares and other securities in exchange for the outstanding stock of the companies being acquired. The terms of such corporate acquisitions naturally require approval of the board of directors prior to the making of the acquisition offer. Transfers from retained earnings to the Capital Stock and Paid-In Capital accounts, as in the case of stock dividends, are initiated by action of the board. Stock splits and changes in par or stated value of shares also require formal authorization by the board.

Authority for all dividend actions rests with the directors. The declaration of a dividend must specify not only the amount per share but also the date of record and the date of payment.

If a corporation handles its own capital stock transactions rather than utilizing the services of an independent registrar and stock transfer agent, the board of directors should pass a resolution designating those officers who are authorized to (*a*) sign stock certificates, (*b*) maintain records of stockholders, (*c*) have custody of unissued certificates, and (*d*) sign dividend checks. The signatures of two officers are generally required on stock certificates.

Independent registrar and stock transfer agent

In appraising the adequacy of internal controls over capital stock the first question that the auditor considers is whether the corporation employs the services of an independent stock registrar and a stock transfer agent or handles its own capital stock transactions. Internal control is far stronger when the services of an independent stock registrar and a stock transfer agent are utilized, because the banks or trust companies acting in these capacities will have the necessary experience, the specialized facilities, and the trained personnel to perform the work in an expert manner. Moreover, by placing the responsibility for handling capital stock certificates in separate and independent organizations, the corporation achieves to the fullest extent the internal control concept of separation of duties. The New York Stock Exchange and most other exchanges require that listed corporations utilize the services of an independent registrar. Corporations with more than one issue of capital stock usually retain a different financial institution to act as registrar for each issue.

The primary responsibility of the stock registrar is to avoid any overissuance of stock. The danger of overissuance is illustrated by the old story of a promoter who sold a 25 percent interest in a new corporation to each of 10 investors. To prevent such irregularities, the registrar must verify that stock certificates are issued in accordance with the articles of incorporation and formal authorizations by the board of directors. The registrar obtains copies of the documents authorizing the total shares to be issued and maintains detailed records of total shares issued and canceled. Each new certificate must be presented to the registrar for examination and registration before it is issued to a stockholder. The dangers of fraud and accidental error relating to improper issuance of stock certificates are obviously greatly reduced when an independent registrar is employed.

Large corporations and medium-sized ones with actively traded securities employ independent stock transfer agents. Although the stock transfer agent maintains a record of the total shares outstanding, his primary responsibility is the task of maintaining detail stockholder records and carrying out transfers of stock ownership. The appointment of an independent transfer agent requires a formal resolution by the board of directors.

The procedures for transfer of stock are governed by provisions of the Uniform Commercial Code, in effect in most states, and also by the regulations of the stock exchanges. The objectives of these procedures are to insure that forged or altered certificates are not negotiated, that "stop orders" are placed in effect for lost certificates, that laws levying taxes on the transfer of securities are complied with, and that up-to-date records are maintained showing the name and address of each stockholder and the number of shares owned. The rights of a stockholder—to receive dividends when declared, to vote, to subscribe to new issues in proportion to present holdings, and to share in the proceeds of dissolution—obviously cannot be observed if the records of stockholders are inaccurate or incomplete. Moreover, the courts have placed the responsibility for propriety of stock transfers upon the officers of the corporation.

Recently, the New York Stock Exchange modified its requirement that the independent registrar and stock transfer agent be separate entities. Now, a bank which meets specified requirements for net assets, insurance, and internal accounting controls may serve as both registrar and transfer agent for a single corporation.

The stock certificate book

If the corporation does not utilize the services of an independent registrar and stock transfer agent, these functions are usually assigned by the board of directors to the secretary of the company. The stock certificates should be serially numbered by the printer; and from the time of delivery to the company until issuance, they should be in the exclusive custody of the designated officer. The internal auditing staff of the corporation may periodically examine the unissued stock certificates and review the procedures being followed to determine their effectiveness and the extent of compliance with established policies.

The certificates are often prepared in bound books, with attached stubs similar to those in a checkbook. Each stub shows the certificate number and contains blank spaces for entering the number of shares represented by the certificate, the name of the stockholder, and the serial number of any previously issued certificate surrendered in exchange for the new one. Certificates should be issued in numerical sequence and not signed or countersigned until the time of issuance. When outstanding shares are transferred from one holder to another, the old certificate is surrendered to the company. After careful inspection of the signature of the transferor and other details, the designated officer cancels the old certificate by perforation and attaches it to the corresponding stub in the certificate book.

The stockholders' ledger

The stock certificate book is not in itself an adequate record of the capital stock outstanding. The certificates appear in the book in serial number order, and a single stockholder may own several certificates listed at various places in the certificate book.

A stockholders' ledger provides a separate record for each stockholder, thus making it possible to determine at a glance the total number of shares owned by any one person. This record may be used in compiling the list of dividend checks or for any other communication with shareholders. The stockholders' ledger may be maintained by the secretary of the corporation, by a stock transfer department, or in the accounting department.

Other records significant in the maintenance of adequate internal control for capital stock include stock transfer journals, files of receipts for certificates delivered, and records of the signatures of shareholders. These records should be under the control of an officer of the corporation and not accessible to employees.

The acquisition of treasury stock by a corporation requires authorization by the board of directors. If reacquired shares are to be held for possible reissuance, they should be registered in the name of the corporation and kept under the same type of control applicable to investments in securities of other companies. Reissuance of treasury shares also requires authorization by the board of directors.

Internal control over other paid-in capital and retained earnings

The major consideration in the internal control over paid-in capital items and retained earnings is that all entries be made only after proper approval of an executive officer. In many cases the board of directors will provide the authorization for entries in these accounts. As an additional control, periodically, the controller should review all entries to retained earnings and other capital accounts to determine their propriety.

Internal control over dividends

The nature of internal control over the payment of dividends, as in the case of stock issuance, depends primarily upon whether the company performs the function of dividend payment itself or utilizes the services of an independent dividend-paying agent. If an independent dividend-disbursing agent is used, the corporation will provide the agent with a certified copy of the dividend declaration and with a check for the full amount of the dividend. The bank or trust company serving as stock transfer agent is usually appointed to distribute the dividend, since it maintains the detail records of stockholders. The agent issues dividend checks to the individual stockholders and sends the corporation a detailed list of the payments made. The use of an independent fiscal agent is to be recommended from the standpoint of internal control, for it materially reduces the possibility of fraud or error arising in connection with the distribution of dividends.

In a small corporation not utilizing the services of a dividend-paying agent, the responsibility for payment of dividends is usually lodged with the treasurer or secretary. After declaration of a dividend by the board of directors, the secretary prepares a list of stockholders as of the date of record, the number of shares held by each, and the amount of the dividend each is to receive. The total of these individual amounts is proved by multiplying the dividend per share by the total number of outstanding shares.

A separate dividend bank account is then opened by the deposit of a check drawn for the total amount of the dividend. Dividend checks of a distinctive color and controlled by serial numbers are drawn payable to individual stockholders in the amounts shown on the list described above. The secretary submits the stockholder list and the dividend checks to the treasurer for approval and signature. The checks should be reconciled by the treasurer with the total of shares outstanding and mailed without again coming under control of the officer who prepared them.

As the dividend checks are paid and returned by the bank, they should be matched with the check stubs or marked paid in the dividend check register. A list of outstanding checks should be prepared monthly from the open stubs or open items in the check register. This list should agree in total with the balance remaining in the dividend bank account. It is to be expected that some dividend checks will be long outstanding. Eventually, unclaimed dividends may be returned to retained earnings if this is permitted by state corporation laws. In states having unclaimed property laws, unclaimed dividends revert to the state at the end of a statutory period.

Audit working papers for owners' equity

In addition to the grouping sheet for owners' equity accounts, an analysis of each equity account is prepared by the auditor for the permanent file. A detailed analysis is essential for all aspects of a stock option plan: options authorized, issued, and outstanding. For a closely held corporation not served by a transfer agent, the auditor will often prepare for the permanent file a list of shareholders and the number of shares owned by each.

Internal control questionnaire

A typical internal control questionnaire for owners' equity follows:

CAPITAL STOCK:

1. Does the company utilize the services of an independent registrar and stock transfer agent?
2. If not—
   a) Are unissued certificates under numerical control?
   b) Are canceled certificates mutilated to prevent further use?
   c) Are unissued certificates in the custody of an officer?
   d) Is there definite prohibition against signing certificates in blank?
3. Are state tax stamps attached to the stubs?
4. Are issues and retirements made only on proper authority?
5. Is treasury stock in the company's name rather than in the name of the treasurer or other officer?
6. Are stockholder ledgers and transfer journals maintained?
7. Are subsidiary records and the stubs of the stock certificate book frequently balanced to the control account?

DIVIDENDS:

1. Is an independent disbursing agent employed?
2. Is a separate dividend bank account maintained?
3. Are dividend checks reconciled to stockholder records before mailing?
4. Are undelivered checks immediately redeposited in a separate account?

MISCELLANEOUS:

1. Are journal vouchers used for all entries to paid-in capital, retained earnings, or other capital accounts?
2. Are entries in owners' equity accounts reviewed periodically by the controller?

Audit program—capital stock

The following procedures are typical of the work required in many engagements for the verification of capital stock:

1. Review articles of incorporation, bylaws, and minutes for provisions relating to capital stock.
2. Obtain or prepare an analysis of the Capital Stock account.
3. Confirm shares outstanding with the independent registrar and stock transfer agent.
4. Account for all proceeds from stock issues.
5. Examine all canceled certificates.
6. Account for all certificate numbers.
7. Reconcile stockholder records and stock certificate book with general ledger control account.

8. Review for proper use of stock transfer tax stamps.
9. Inspect treasury shares on hand and reconcile.
10. Determine compliance with stock option plans and with other restrictions and preferences pertaining to capital stock.
11. Obtain for income tax returns the total number of shares owned by officers.

1. *Review articles of incorporation, bylaws, and minutes for provisions relating to capital stock.*

In a first audit, copies of the articles of incorporation, bylaws, and minutes of the meetings of directors and stockholders obtained for the permanent file should be carefully read. All provisions of significance from an accounting standpoint should be underscored or otherwise highlighted for followup during the audit.

The time devoted to reading the minutes of directors' and stockholders' meetings of earlier years will depend upon all the circumstances of the engagement. If the corporation has been audited previously by other certified public accountants, less emphasis is placed on reading the minutes of prior years. An extensive discussion of the auditor's review of corporate minutes has already been presented in Chapter 10.

The information required by the auditor for each issue of capital stock includes the number of shares authorized and issued, par or stated value if any, dividend rates, call and conversion provisions, stock splits, and stock options. By gathering evidence on these points, the auditor will have some assurance that capital stock transactions and dividend payments have been in accordance with legal requirements and specific authorizations by stockholders and directors. Also, he will be able to judge whether the balance sheet contains all necessary information to describe adequately the various stock issues and other elements of corporate capital.

2. *Obtain or prepare an analysis of the Capital Stock account.*

In an initial audit engagement, Capital Stock accounts should be analyzed from the beginning of the corporation to provide the auditor with a complete historical picture of corporate capital. This approach is comparable to that employed for plant and equipment; in both cases the auditor requires assurance as to the propriety of the balances at the beginning of the period under audit. Analysis of capital stock includes an appraisal of the nature of all changes and the vouching of these changes to the supporting documents and records. All journal entries should be inspected to determine that they represent bona fide charges or credits to the accounts and that they were properly authorized. Special attention should be given to the recording of original and subsequent issues, the capitalization of retained earnings when stock dividends are issued, and the reduction of stated or par values in quasi reorganizations. These transactions are vouched by tracing them to the original documents, the most important of which is the minutes book. All capital stock transactions should bear the authority of the board; therefore, every entry in the accounts should have some reference in the minutes. In addition, the auditor may obtain from the client's legal counsel an opinion as to the legality of all prior stock issuances.

The analysis of Capital Stock accounts may be prepared in such a manner as to permit additions during subsequent audit engagements. After the initial audit, if the analysis is kept in a permanent file, all that will be necessary is to record the current period's increases and decreases and to vouch these transactions. The auditor will then have a working paper showing all changes in capital stock from the inception of the corporation.

3. *Confirm shares outstanding with the independent registrar and stock transfer agent.*

The number of shares issued and outstanding on the balance sheet date may be confirmed by direct communication with the independent

FIGURE 19–1
Confirmation request sent to independent registrar

The Fairway Corporation

SAN FRANCISCO, CALIFORNIA 94108

December 31, 1974

The Manhattan Trust Company
New York, N.Y. 10014

Dear Sirs:

To facilitate our annual audit now being conducted by Douglas, Dumfries and Company, will you please confirm directly to them the following information concerning our capital stock issues:

a) The number of shares of our 6 percent cumulative $100 par value preferred stock issued as of December 31, 1974.
b) The number of shares of our no-par value common stock issued as of December 31, 1974.

An envelope addressed to our auditors is enclosed for your reply.

Very truly yours,
The Fairway Corporation

J. B. Phillips

Controller

FIGURE 19–1 (continued)
Reply by independent registrar to confirmation request

 The Manhattan Trust Co.

New York, N.Y. 10014

January 5, 1975

Douglas, Dumfries, and Company
Certified Public Accountants
National Petroleum Building
San Francisco, California 94108

Dear Sirs:

As independent registrar for the Fairway Corporation, we wish to report the
following facts as shown by our records as of December 31, 1974 with respect to
the Corporation's capital stock.

	Shares Issued
Preferred stock, 6 percent cumulative, $100 par value	None
Common stock, no-par value	56,000

Very truly yours,
The Manhattan Trust Company

Wayne Burgin
Wayne Burgin
Vice President

registrar and the stock transfer agent. An illustration of a confirmation
request and the reply received from the independent registrar is presented in Figure 19–1. Confirmation replies should be sent directly to
the auditor, not to the client. All information contained in these replies
should be traced to the corporate records and a reconciliation made
between the records and confirmations, if necessary. It is essential that
the general ledger control accounts agree with the amount of stock
issued as reported by the independent registrar and stock transfer
agent. Because of the strong internal controls usually maintained over
stock certificates, it is not customary to communicate with individual
stockholders in establishing the number of shares outstanding.

When a corporation acts as its own transfer agent and registrar, the auditor must adopt alternative procedures as nearly as possible equivalent to direct confirmation with outside parties. These procedures are described in subsequent steps in this audit program.

4.   *Account for all proceeds from stock issues.*

Closely related to the analysis of Capital Stock accounts is the audit procedure of accounting for the receipt and proper disposition of all funds derived from the issuance of capital stock. The proceeds should be traced to the cash records and bank statements. In this connection, it is essential that the auditor be familiar with any underwriting contracts, SEC registration statements, or state stock issuance permits, so that he can determine the propriety of amounts reported as receipts from stock issues. These documents provide necessary information as to issuance prices, the net cash consideration to be received by the corporation, and the use of the proceeds.

When assets other than cash are received as consideration for the issuance of capital stock, the entire transaction requires the most careful study. Generally the value of plant assets, patents, services, etc., received in exchange for capital shares depends upon the decision of the board of directors. State laws frequently provide that in the absence of fraud this valuation must be accepted as valid. However, the auditor should bear in mind during his study of such transactions that the SEC has on numerous occasions held that the valuation placed on property acquired from promoters in exchange for capital stock was excessive and that, in fact, the shares were issued at a discount equal to the excess of the recorded value over the fair value of the property.

While tracing the proceeds of capital stock issues, the auditor will determine the propriety of all allocations between amounts credited to Capital Stock accounts and amounts applicable to other Paid-In Capital accounts. In many states the issuance of stock at a discount is permitted only under certain conditions. Although the auditor cannot pass on the legality of any such issue, he should, when the circumstances warrant, obtain the opinion of legal counsel on a stock issue. If the stock carries no par value, the amount to be credited to the capital stock account depends upon state laws. The amount of the credit may be (1) the total consideration received, (2) the declared or stated value, or (3) a prescribed minimum amount. The auditor should be familiar with the legal requirements and should determine that they have been observed in the particular case. In all examinations, he is interested in determining that the capital stock is fairly stated in accordance with accepted legal and accounting requirements.

5.   *Examine all canceled certificates.*

An adequate system of internal control for corporations not utilizing the services of an independent registrar and stock transfer agent requires that all canceled stock certificates be perforated or marked in a manner precluding the possibility of further use. Canceled certificates should be attached to the corresponding stubs in the stock certificate book and permanently preserved. If reacquired certificates are not properly canceled, the danger exists that they may be fraudulently reissued by officers or employees. Such unauthorized reissuance would create an excess of capital stock outstanding over the amount properly issued and reflected in the accounts. Auditors will, therefore, examine all canceled stock certificates on hand, noting in particular that they have been effectively voided.

6. *Account for all certificate numbers.*

The audit working papers should include a record of the last certificate number issued during the year. Reference to the working papers for the preceding audit, combined with the verification of certificate numbers issued during the current period, will enable the auditor to account for all certificates by serial number.

A working paper prepared during the auditor's examination of the stock certificate book of a small closely held corporation is designed to be utilized during several audits; it may be retained in the permanent file or forwarded to successive current files. In addition it is desirable for the auditor to inspect the unissued certificates to determine that all certificates purported to be unissued are actually on hand and blank. In this connection it is sometimes advocated that the auditor confirm directly with the printer the number of certificates printed and delivered, and the serial numbers used.

7. *Reconcile stockholder records and stock certificate book with general ledger control account.*

The general ledger account for capital stock shows the total par value or stated value of all shares outstanding, plus any treasury shares. The subsidiary records for capital stock contains an account for each stockholder. The stock certificate book contains all canceled certificates and also open stubs for outstanding certificates. These three records must be reconciled by the auditor to establish the amount of oustanding stock, and to rule out the possibility of an overissuance of shares. If this verification were not made, it would be possible for a dishonest official to issue unlimited amounts of stock and to withhold the proceeds from such sales.

A trial balance of the subsidiary stockholder records may be obtained from the client or prepared by the auditor, and compared with the general ledger control account. Any discrepancies should be resolved. In conjunction with this procedure, the total shares outstanding, as shown by the stock certificate book stubs, should also be reconciled with the control account and with the subsidiary trial balance. These procedures assure the auditor of the accuracy of the ledger account balances for capital stock.

8.   *Review for proper use of stock transfer tax stamps.*

Some state governments impose taxes on the original issue and subsequent transfers of capital stock. These taxes are collected through the sale of tax stamps to the issuing corporation, with the provision that the stamps be affixed to the certificate stubs upon issuance or transfer of shares. Since the statutes provide penalties for failure to use these stamps, auditors should scrutinize the certificate books to determine that the proper amount of stamps has been affixed to the stubs.

9.   *Inspect treasury shares on hand and reconcile.*

Treasury stock is capital stock originally issued as fully paid and subsequently reacquired, but not retired, by the issuing corporation. These shares may be acquired by donation from shareholders, by purchase on the open market, by acceptance for the cancellation of a debt, or in exchange for assets. Corporations often purchase their own shares in order to make required distributions of shares under employee stock purchase plans or executive stock option plans. Various state laws have specific regulations regarding the acquisition of treasury stock, and the auditor should be familiar with these laws. Perhaps the most common regulation is that an amount of retained earnings equivalent to the cost of the treasury shares be restricted.

The restriction of retained earnings is intended for the protection of creditors. When a corporation reacquires shares of its own stock by purchase, it is handing out cash to stockholders, just as when a cash dividend is paid. The cash payment for purchase of shares may go to only a few of the stockholders, but the drain on the company's assets is just as real as if the payment had been divided proportionately among all stockholders as in the case of a dividend.

ILLUSTRATIVE CASE.   To emphasize the essential similarity between the purchase of treasury stock and the payment of cash dividends, let us consider the case of Century Corporation, which has 100 stockholders, each of whom owns 10 shares of stock. Century Corporation decides to reacquire 100 shares of its stock and does so by purchasing one share from each of the 100 stockholders. Cash flows from the corporation to the stockholders, and after the transaction, each stockholder owns the same percent (1 percent) of the outstanding stock as before. Obviously such a purchase of stock has much the same effect from the viewpoint of creditors of the corporation as if a cash dividend had been paid.

Total cash payments to stockholders should not exceed total earnings or an impairment of the original contributed capital will result. This original contributed capital is intended to stand as a permanent buffer between corporate creditors and any operating losses which the company may incur. Consequently, in most states, a corporation is not permitted to impair its permanent contributed capital by handing out cash to its shareholders in excess of earnings, regardless of whether these cash payouts are in the form of dividends or in payments for reacquired shares. In all but a few states, payments for treasury shares are charged to the Treasury Stock account and therefore do not reduce the Retained Earnings account. Unless the Retained Earnings account is restricted by the cost of treasury shares purchased, a corporation conceivably might impair its permanent capital by paying cash dividends in the full amount of the Retained Earnings account. Of course most corporations do not consider paying dividends to the full amount of earnings.

The Treasury Stock account should be analyzed and a list showing the number of shares of treasury stock on hand compiled from the analysis. All certificates on hand may then be inspected. The individual certificates are compared to the list to determine the accuracy of the Treasury Stock account. Each certificate should be examined to ascertain that it is in the name of the corporation or that it has been properly endorsed with a power of attorney. If the certificates are not on hand, they should be confirmed directly with the holders.

In his review of treasury stock transactions, the auditor should refer to permanent file copies of the minutes of directors' meetings to determine that (*a*) the acquisition or reissuance of treasury stock was authorized by directors, and (*b*) the price paid or received was in accordance with prices specified by the board.

In verifying the cost of treasury stock acquired, the auditor will also examine the paid checks. If the purchase was made through a stock broker, the broker's advice of purchase should also be examined. Reissuances of treasury stock should be verified in a parallel manner, including the tracing of the proceeds of reissuance into the bank account.

Gains on reissuance of treasury stock represent an increase in contributed capital and should be credited to a Paid-In Capital account, not to Retained Earnings or to current income. Losses on sales of treasury stock should be charged against Paid-In Capital to the extent of any previous gains from treasury stock transactions. Any further losses on treasury stock may be charged against Retained Earnings.

In summary, the auditor's review of treasury stock transactions will make clear whether these transactions were properly authorized by the board of directors and will also determine that the recording methods used were in conformity with generally accepted accounting principles and with state statutes.

10. *Determine compliance with stock option plans and with other restrictions and preferences pertaining to capital stock.*

Many corporations grant stock options to officers and key employees as an incentive-type compensation plan. For example, a corporation with stock selling in the open market for $30 a share on December 31, 1974 might agree to sell 50,000 additional shares to its management group at a price of $30 at any time during the next five years. Any rise in the market price of the stock will obviously benefit the holders of stock options. When stock options are granted, a portion of the authorized but unissued stock must be held in reserve by the corporation so that it will be in a position to fulfill the option agreements. Similarly, corporations with convertible debentures or convertible preferred stocks outstanding must hold in reserve a sufficient number of common shares to meet the demands of preferred stockholders and debenture holders who may elect to convert their securities into common stock.

The auditor must become thoroughly familiar with the terms of any stock options and with the conversion features in debenture bonds and preferred stock, so that he can determine whether the financial statements make adequate disclosure of these agreements. He must also verify the shares issued during the year through conversion or exercise of stock options and must ascertain that the number of shares held in reserve at the balance sheet date does not exceed the corporation's authorized but unissued stock. The following footnote to a corporate balance sheet is suggestive of the work done by the auditor along these lines:

At December 31, 1974, 2,033,982 shares of Common Stock were reserved for the following purposes: (*a*) 228,079 shares for conversion of 4 percent Convertible Subordinated Debentures; (*b*) 1,293,103 shares for conversion of 5 percent Convertible Subordinated Debentures; (*c*) 512,800 shares for Qualified Stock Option Plans.

Of the 512,800 shares reserved for Qualified Stock Option Plans, options for 71,763 shares, including options presently exercisable for 9,943 shares, are outstanding at prices ranging from $12 to $16.51 a share under two 1969 Plans, and options for 391,013 shares are outstanding at prices ranging from $19.02 to $26.72 a share under the 1973 Plan. These prices are 100 percent of the market prices on the dates the options were granted or accepted, adjusted to give effect to stock dividends paid subsequent to those dates.

Other restrictions and preferences pertaining to capital stock include the callable and cumulative provisions frequently attached to preferred stock. Most preferred stocks are callable at specified prices slightly above par; and the auditor must ascertain that any program of reacquiring shares accurately carries out the call provisions of the issue. The cumulative provision found in many preferred stocks must be considered by the auditor in reviewing the propriety of dividend payments and in determining the disclosure to be made of any arrearage of preferred dividends. If redemption funds are required by the terms of preferred stock issues, the auditor should ascertain that the funds are being accumulated as scheduled.

11.   Obtain for income tax returns the total number of shares owned by officers.

Federal income tax returns for corporations, as well as some state returns, require the percentages of corporate stock owned by each officer. The auditor should obtain this information from the client, the independent stock transfer agent, or from his stock certificate working paper. In this way, the later preparation of income tax returns will be facilitated.

Additional paid-in capital

"Additional paid-in capital" and similar expressions are terms used to describe capital contributed by stockholders in excess of the par or stated value of the shares. The verification of additional paid-in capital requires reference to transactions in capital stock; consequently, the audit work on additional paid-in capital is usually performed concurrently with the examination of capital stock.

Paid-in capital often arises from transactions such as the following:

1. Par value stock is issued at a price in excess of par; par value is often as low as $10, $5, or even $1 per share. The excess of the issuance price over par is often very substantial and is credited to an account entitled Premium on Capital Stock, or Paid-In Capital in Excess of Par Value.
2. No-par-value stock is issued. A portion of the proceeds is designated by the board of directors as capital stock and the remainder as additional paid-in capital.
3. Stock dividends are declared. When the market value of the outstanding stock is higher than the par value, it is accepted accounting practice to debit Retained Earnings for an amount equal to the market value of the dividend shares. The offsetting credits are to the Capital Stock account for the par value of the dividend shares and to Paid-In Capital in Excess of Par Value for the remainder of the amount of retained earnings being capitalized.
4. Convertible preferred stock (often with a par value of $100 per share) is converted by the holders into common stock with much smaller par value or perhaps into common stock of the no-par variety. The excess of the par value of the shares converted over the par or stated value of the common shares issued in exchange is credited to an Additional Paid-In Capital account. Similar accounting treatment applies to conversions of convertible bonds or debentures.
5. Additional paid-in capital of a subsidiary acquired in a pooling of interests is credited to Additional Paid-In Capital on the parent's books.

Paid-in capital arising from transactions in preferred stock should be recorded in a separate account from capital contributed by common stockholders. If the preferred stock issue is eliminated through conversion or redemption, however, any remaining paid-in capital becomes part of the common stock equity and may be combined with paid-in capital from common stock transactions.

Audit procedures—additional paid-in capital

The objective of the auditor is to determine that all entries in the Additional Paid-In Capital accounts represent properly authorized transactions, recorded in accordance with generally accepted accounting principles. To achieve this objective the auditor obtains or prepares an analysis of the Additional Paid-In Capital accounts. In the initial audit of a client, this analysis must begin with the very first entries in these accounts—which often means the date of organization of the corporation. Since this analysis consists mainly of identifying credit entries arising from capital stock transactions, the work is most conveniently done as part of the examination of capital stock. The auditor must satisfy himself that stockholder contributions have been properly divided between Capital Stock and Additional Paid-In Capital.

Credits from other sources, such as the declaration of stock dividends and from treasury stock transactions, should be verified by reference to the original documents and authorizations. Debit entries to Additional Paid-In Capital accounts are not frequent in most companies; one basis for debit entries is the redemption of preferred stock at a price in excess of par value. Costs associated with the issuance of capital stock, except for costs incurred in a business combination accounted for as a pooling of interests, are properly chargeable to Additional Paid-In Capital. The auditor should be alert for any unjustified debit entries in the Additional Paid-In Capital accounts; some companies have sought to dispose of extraordinary losses by charging Additional Paid-In Capital, and others have attempted to write off discount on capital stock in this manner.

The work required in an initial examination with respect to analysis of Additional Paid-In Capital accounts for prior years may be considerably reduced if audits have been made in the past by other firms of certified public accountants. However, there is seldom enough activity in accounts of this type to make the analysis a difficult task.

The process of analyzing the Additional Paid-In Capital accounts will usually lead the auditor to authorizations in the minutes of directors and stockholders. Conversely, a reading of the minutes may bring to light the authorization of other transactions which should have resulted in entries in the Additional Paid-In Capital accounts, but which were improperly placed in other accounts.

Audit program—retained earnings and dividends

A suggested audit program for retained earnings and dividends includes the following steps:

1. Analyze retained earnings and appropriations of retained earnings.
2. Investigate any prior period adjustments to retained earnings.
3. Review dividend procedures for both cash and stock dividends.

1. Analyze retained earnings and appropriations of retained earnings.

The analysis of retained earnings and any appropriations of retained earnings should cover the entire history of these accounts. Such an analysis is prepared for the permanent file and added to each year.

Credits to the Retained Earnings account ordinarily represent amounts of net income transferred from the Income Summary account. In addition the account may contain credits derived from reserves which have been discontinued and restored to retained earnings. The auditor's verification of these entries will include reference to the action of the board of directors in discontinuing reserves and tracing the contra entries for the year's net income. The Retained Earnings account may also be credited in a business combination accounted for as a pooling of interests.

Debits to the Retained Earnings account may include entries for net losses, cash and stock dividends, and for the creation or enlargement of appropriated reserves. The auditor's verification of dividends will be discussed in the third step of this audit program. Debit entries to the Retained Earnings account for the purpose of creating reserves for contingencies or other appropriations of retained earnings require specific authorization by the board of directors. The only verification necessary for these entries is to ascertain that the dates and amounts correspond to the actions of the board.

Appropriations of retained earnings appear to be made less commonly now than they were a few years ago. The decline in use of these reserves created from retained earnings may reflect a growing awareness that such segregations of retained earnings seldom serve any constructive purpose and are sure to create confusion and misunderstanding on the part of some readers of the financial statements.

Under no circumstances should operating expenses or losses be absorbed against reserves created from retained earnings. Such misuse of reserves would cause operating expenses to be entirely omitted from the determination of net income and consequently would cause an overstatement of that highly significant figure.

2. Investigate any prior period adjustments to retained earnings.

Accounting Principles Board Opinion No. 9, "Reporting the Results of Operations," established the concept of *prior period adjustments,* which in single-year financial statements are treated as restatements of the beginning retained earnings balance, net of applicable income taxes. Prior period adjustments were defined as material adjustments having the following characteristics:

1. Specifically identifiable with and directly related to the business activities of prior periods.
2. Not attributable to economic events occurring subsequent to the date of the prior periods' financial statements.

3. Primarily dependent upon determinations by persons other than management and not reasonably susceptible to estimation prior to such determination.

The board concluded that prior period adjustments as thus defined are extremely rare, citing as examples material, nonrecurring settlements of income taxes or renegotiation proceedings, as well as some settlements resulting from litigation. Normal, recurring corrections and adjustments resulting from the use of estimates inherent in the accounting process, such as revisions of estimated lives of depreciable assets and relatively immaterial adjustements of liabilities provided in prior periods, are specifically excluded from the prior period adjustments classification.

Accounting Principles Board Opinion No. 20, "Accounting Changes," extended prior period adjustment accounting to the following:

1. Correction of an error in financial statements of a prior period discovered subsequent to issuance of the statements.
2. Three changes in accounting principle: A change from the Lifo method of inventory pricing to another method; a change in the method of accounting for long-term construction contracts; and a change to or from the "full cost" method of accounting used in the extractive industries.

In view of the preceding discussion, the auditor should investigate any charges or credits to retained earnings which the client has labeled as prior period adjustments, to determine that the criteria of *APB Opinion No. 9* or *APB Opinion No. 20* have been met. The auditor should insist that any extraordinary gains or losses which the client has allocated to retained earnings be removed and presented separately in the income statement, net of applicable income tax effects.

3.   *Review dividend procedures for both cash and stock dividends.*

In the verification of cash dividends the auditor will usually perform the following steps:

a)   Determine the dates and amounts of dividends authorized.
b)   Verify the amounts paid.
c)   Determine the amount of any preferred dividends in arrears.
d)   Review the treatment of unclaimed dividend checks.

In the verification of stock dividends there is the additional problem of determining that the proper amount has been transferred from the Retained Earnings account to the Capital Stock and Additional Paid-In Capital accounts. In recent years the payment of frequent small stock dividends has been increasingly popular. A stock dividend amounting to 4 or 5 percent of the outstanding stock often has had no apparent effect on the market price per share of the stock, particularly when the shares carried a reputation for regular cash dividends of stable amount. Many companies became impressed with the apparent fact that small stock dividends cost the company nothing and would be welcome to shareholders *if there were no proportionate decline in the market price per share of stock.* Such an increase in the number of outstanding shares would, of course, indicate a greater amount of cash dividends in the future if the established cash dividend per share were maintained. Some companies, however, apparently seeking to take advantage of the trend toward greater use of stock dividends, have distributed small stock dividends and concurrently reduced or eliminated cash dividends. It is difficult to see that such action confers any benefit on shareholders.

ILLUSTRATIVE CASE. Martin Corporation, a large manufacturing enterprise with capital stock listed on the New York Stock Exchange, had been paying a quarterly cash dividend of 25 cents per share for several years. When the company's earnings fell during a period of keen competition in the industry, all cash dividends were suspended and the company announced that for the foreseeable future it intended to pay no cash dividends but to distribute a 4 percent stock dividend each year. A spokesman for the company made clear that no plans had been made for the resumption of cash dividends nor was there any present idea of what the cash dividend rate might be when and if cash dividends were resumed. Under the circumstances the issuance of an annual stock dividend would appear to serve no purpose other than to placate those uninformed stockholders who did not understand the basic distinction between cash dividends and stock dividends.

Regardless of the logic underlying the decision to issue small stock dividends, it is the responsibility of the auditor to see that the amount transferred from Retained Earnings to Capital Stock and Additional Paid-In Capital corresponds to the *fair market value* of the shares at the date of the dividend declaration. The use of fair market value as a measure of the amount of retained earnings to be capitalized for each dividend share has been consistently supported by the Securities and Exchange Commission, and has also received the recommendation of the AICPA. Par or stated value per share is not an acceptable alternative, since this amount is often far different from fair market value. The transfer from retained earnings to permanent capital accounts of an amount equal to the fair market value of the dividend shares eliminates the possibility that earnings which the shareholder assumes were distributed by means of the stock dividend can later be distributed through another dividend action.

The above line of reasoning is not applicable to large stock dividends, since these are essentially similar to stock splits undertaken for the purpose of reducing the market price per share to a more convenient level and thus encouraging wider distribution of the company's stock. For large stock dividends (perhaps above 20 percent) there is no reason to capitalize a greater amount of retained earnings than the par or stated value of the dividend shares. Most common stocks issued in recent years carry low par amounts. It is common to encounter stocks with par value of $1 or $5 selling for prices of $50 to $100. In these circumstances there is obviously a great difference between the use of par value and fair market value in determining the amount of retained earnings to be capitalized when a stock dividend is declared.

When reviewing his copy of the directors' meetings minutes, one of the items the auditor should note is the date and amount of each dividend declaration. This serves to establish the authority for dividend disbursements. The dividend payments may then be verified by obtaining the list of shareholders as of the dividend date and multiplying the total number of shares by the dividend rate per share set forth in the minutes. The accuracy of these dividend lists may be verified by tracing them to the subsidiary stockholders ledger on a test basis. The total dividend payment may also be verified by multiplying the number of shares in the general ledger control account by the amount per share. Although the auditor is not expected to pass on the legality of dividends, he may satisfy himself that dividends paid are in general correct. In special situations the auditor may request the client's legal counsel for an opinion as to the legality of dividends declared.

The auditor's review of dividend declarations may reveal the existence of cash dividends declared but not paid. These declared but unpaid dividends must be shown as liabilities in the balance sheet. The auditor may also review the procedures for handling unclaimed dividends and may ascertain that these items are recognized as liabilities. The amount of any accumulated dividends in arrears on preferred stock should be computed. If a closely held company has irregular dividend declarations or none at all, the auditor should consider whether the federal penalty surtax or unreasonably accumulated earnings might be assessed.

Donated capital

Donated capital represents the fair value of any assets contributed to a corporation by persons or organizations other than shareholders. For example, a city may donate a building site to a manufacturing concern as a means of attracting new enterprises to the community.

In the audit of the Donated Capital account, the objectives of the auditor are: (*a*) to establish the propriety of the amounts originally entered in the account; (*b*) to determine the nature of any changes which have been recorded; and (*c*) to determine that any restrictions imposed by the donor are being observed. The logical starting point is to analyze the account. Credit entries should be vouched to the gift contract or agreement or to the appraiser's report. This will serve to establish the opening balances and any additions. Any debits to the account should be carefully investigated. Perhaps the only charges properly made against donated capital are for the costs of acquiring the gift; these costs may be vouched to the cash records.

Time of examination

The ledger accounts for capital stock, additional paid-in capital, and retained earnings ordinarily receive very few entries during the year. Consequently, most auditors feel that nothing can be gained by making a preliminary analysis of these accounts for a fraction of the year. It is usually more efficient to make the analysis in one step after the close of the period. Other audit procedures, such as the examination of the stock certificate book or the confirmation of outstanding shares with the independent registrar and stock transfer agent, are also performed at the year-end. In the first audit of a new client, some preliminary work can advantageously be done in obtaining and reviewing copies of the articles of incorporation and bylaws, and in analyzing the capital accounts. For repeat engagements, however, there is usually little opportunity to perform audit work on owners' equity accounts before the end of the period.

FINANCIAL STATEMENT PRESENTATION

Adequate informative disclosure is a critical requirement for stockholders' equity. All changes during the year in each of the equity accounts must be disclosed. If many transactions have affected these accounts, a statement of stockholders' equity is appropriate. Otherwise, a statement of retained earnings, together with footnote disclosure of any changes in contributed capital, may be presented.

Capital stock

The presentation of capital stock on the balance sheet should include a complete descriptions of each issue. To enable the investor or financial analyst to make a close appraisal of a stock issue, the following data should be provided in the owners' equity section, or in notes thereto:

1. Exact title of the issue; par or stated value; dividend rate, if any.
2. For preferred stock, the extent of dividend preference, call provisions, conversion privileges, and aggregate liquidation rights.
3. Number of shares authorized, issued, in treasury, and outstanding.
4. Per share and aggregate amounts of cumulative preferred dividends in arrears.

5. Information as to shares reserved for stock option plans and for conversion of bonds or preferred stock. The number of shares reserved for outstanding stock warrants, subscribed but unissued stock, stock dividends declared but undistributed, and stock to be issued in completion of a business combination, should also be disclosed.

Treasury stock is preferably shown in the owners' equity section, at cost, as a deduction from the combined total of contributed capital and retained earnings. The laws of some states require a different accounting treatment for treasury stock. The balance sheet should disclose retained earnings restricted under state law because of treasury stock acquisitions. The presentation of treasury stock as an asset is still encountered on a few published financial statements. Such treatment is to be discouraged; if the auditor accepts such classification, he should at least insist upon clear-cut identification of the "asset" as the company's own shares. Dividends are not to be paid on treasury shares; to do so would lead to an overstatement of the company's revenue.

Other paid-in capital

Since low-par stock and no-par stock have largely superseded the $100 par value share for common stock, a major portion of the capital contributed by stockholders does not appear in the Capital Stock account but under a title such as "Additional Paid-In Capital" or "Paid-In Capital in Excess of Par Value." A subtotal combining capital stock and paid-in capital is desirable. This presentation will emphasize that from an economic standpoint, all contributed capital is normally to be maintained permanently for the protection of creditors and to assure the continued existence of the corporation.

Retained earnings

The term "Retained Earnings" has generally displaced "Earned Surplus" in published financial statements. Other terms enjoying a significant degree of use include "Retained Income," "Earnings Retained for Use in the Business," and "Earnings Reinvested in the Business."

Changes in retained earnings during the year may be shown in a separate statement or combined with the income statement. The combined statement of income and retained earnings appears to be continuing in popularity. In this form of presentation the amount of retained earnings at the beginning of the year is added to the net income figure, dividends paid are subtracted from the subtotal, and the final figure represents the new balance of retained earnings.

Amounts placed in reserve accounts by appropriation of retained earnings are still part of total retained earnings. They should be presented as separate items, but in a position where they may be added to the portion of retained earnings presently available for dividends. The term "reserve" should not be used in any sense other than for appropriations of retained earnings. This usage has been recommended by the AICPA; if it is observed, the term "reserve" will appear only in the owners' equity section of the balance sheet.

One of the most significant points to consider in determining the presentation of retained earnings in the balance sheet is the existence of any restriction on the use of this retained income. Agreements with banks, bondholders, and other creditors very commonly impose limitations on the payment of dividends. These restrictions must be fully disclosed in the notes to financial statements.

AUDIT OF SOLE PROPRIETORSHIPS AND PARTNERSHIPS

In general the same principles described for the audit of corporate capital are applicable to the examination of the capital accounts and drawing accounts of a sole proprietorship or partnership. Analyses are made of all proprietorship accounts from the beginning of the business; the initial capital investment and any additions are traced to the cash and asset records; and the net income or loss for the period and any withdrawals are verified. In the case of a sole proprietorship, a common source of difficulty is the practice of intermingling business and personal transactions, making it necessary for the auditor to segregate personal net worth from business capital. Otherwise, the procedures of analyzing capital and drawings and the vouching of all entries apply.

Intermingling of business and personal transactions. In the audit of a sole proprietorship the auditor often finds that many personal expenses of the owner have been paid with business funds and charged as business expenses. It is extremely difficult to segregate many types of expenditures as between business and personal, because the business and social activities of the proprietor of a small business are likely to be very closely interwoven. Moreover, a tendency exists to classify borderline or doubtful items as business expense, since this classification makes them deductible in the determination of taxable income. On the other hand, the auditor may occasionally find that expenses of the business have been paid from the proprietor's personal funds without any reflection in the accounts. In some cases, business and personal funds and transactions may be continually intermingled without any effort to make a distinction.

A theoretical answer to this problem would, of course, require that the auditor insist that all personal expenditures be excluded from the proprietorship accounts. Any such expenditures paid with company funds should, by means of adjusting entries, be transferred from expense accounts to the owner's drawing account. Through discussions with the client and a report on internal control the auditor may point out the desirability of a careful distinction between business and personal funds.

As a practical matter, however, it may as well be recognized that the auditor's work in this area is necessarily quite limited. In many sole proprietorships there is little internal control, and consequent limited assurance of the dependability of the accounting records. The auditor can, and should, question any substantial expenditures which do not appear to be of a business nature; but unless the facts are quite apparent, he is seldom in a position to challenge any explanation offered by the proprietor. Moreover, it would not serve the primary purposes of the audit to expend a large amount of time in seeking to make precise distinctions between business and nonbusiness expenditures when the amounts involved are comparatively small.

Procedures for audit of partners' accounts. A most significant document underlying the partnership form of organization is the articles of copartnership. The auditor is particularly interested in determining that the distribution of net income has been carried out in accordance with the profit-sharing provisions of the partnership agreement. Maintenance of partner's capital accounts at prescribed levels and restriction of drawings by partners to specified amounts are other points often covered in the agreement; compliance with these clauses should be verified by the auditor in determining the propriety of the year's entries in the capital accounts. Partners' loan accounts also require reference to the partnership contract to determine the treatment intended by the partners.

Occasionally an auditor may find that a partnership is operating without any written agreement of partnership. This situation raises a question of whether profits have been divided in accordance with the understanding existing between the partners. The auditor may appropriately suggest that the firm develop a written partnership contract; for his own protection the auditor may wish to obtain from each partner a written statement confirming the balance in his capital account and his approval of the method used in dividing the year's earnings.

GROUP I
REVIEW QUESTIONS

19-1.   The CPA's examination normally would not include (select one):
   a)   Determining that dividend declarations have been in compliance with debt agreements.

b)   Tracing the authorization of the dividend from the directors' minutes.

c)   Detail tracing from the dividend payment list to the capital stock records.

d)   Reviewing the bank reconciliation for the imprest dividend account. (AICPA, adapted)

19–2.   How can the independent auditor determine the propriety of charges or credits to retained earnings which the client has identified as prior period adjustments?

19–3.   Contrast the auditor's responsibility in the examination of the capital and drawing accounts of a partnership with his responsibility relating to the stockholders' equity accounts of a corporation.

19–4.   Corporations sometimes issue their own capital stock in exchange for services and various assets other than cash. As an auditor, what evidence would you look for to determine the propriety of the values used in recording such transactions?

19–5.   In your second annual examination of a corporate client you find a new account in the general ledger, "Treasury Stock," with a balance of $10,500. Describe the procedures you would follow to verify this item.

19–6.   In examining the financial statements of Foster Company, you observe a debit entry for $20,000 labeled as "Dividends" in the Retained Earnings account. Explain in detail how you would verify this entry.

19–7.   A staff assistant reported to the auditor in charge that the Retained Earnings account of the Olympic Corporation contained a debit entry on December 15 for $100,000, which he had been informed represented a dividend. In his review of cash disbursements, however, he had found the total of dividend checks issued to be less than half this amount. What is the most probable explanation of this situation?

19–8.   Compare the auditor's examination of owners' equity with his work on assets and liabilities. Among other factors to be considered are the relative amounts of time involved and the character of the transactions to be reviewed.

19–9.   What do you consider to be the most important internal control device which a corporation can adopt with respect to capital stock transactions?

19–10.   What working papers, if any, should be prepared for the auditor's permanent file in connection with the examination of Capital Stock accounts or Partners' Capital accounts?

19–11.   With respect to the examination of the Capital Stock account, how does the work in an initial audit differ from that required in a repeat engagement?

19–12.   During your first audit of Garvey Manufacturing Company, you find that extraordinary losses caused by a three-month strike had amounted to $210,000. At the beginning of the year the retained earnings amounted to $150,000 and paid-in capital in excess of par value totaled $400,000. Earnings for the year were reported by the company as $80,000, but the strike loss of $210,000 had been charged directly to the paid-in capital in accordance with a resolution by the board of directors. Would you take exception to this treatment? Explain.

19–13.   Comment on the desirability of audit work on the owners' equity accounts prior to the balance sheet date.

19–14.   Name three situations which might place a restriction on retained earnings limiting or preventing dividend payments. Explain how an auditor might become aware of each such restricting factor.

19–15.   The Delta Company has issued stock options to four of its officers permitting them to purchase 5,000 shares each of common stock at a price of $25 per share at any time during the next five years. The president asks you what effect, if any, the granting of the options will have upon the balance sheet presentation of the owners' equity accounts.

19–16.   Describe the significant features of a stock certificate book, its purpose, and the method of using it.

19–17.   What use is made of the stock certificate book by the auditor?

19–18.   Are the procedures for transfer of capital stock prescribed by statute or devised by the issuing corporation? Explain.

19–19.   What is the primary responsibility of an independent registrar?

19–20.   Some corporations use a separate bank account for the payment of dividends. What advantages are gained by this practice?

19–21.   "If an independent dividend-paying agent is employed by a corporation, the directors are relieved of the task of determining when dividends may properly be paid." Do you agree? Explain.

19–22.   The Powell Corporation was organized in 1950 and has grown slowly but steadily since that time. You are retained to make an examination for the first time in 1974. With respect to the Capital Stock account, how far back should your analysis extend?

19–23.   In his first examination of the Wright Corporation, an auditor verified all items on the balance sheet other than retained earnings; he also noted that the figure for retained earnings was the proper amount to put the statement in balance. Is any additional verification of the retained earnings figure necessary? Explain.

19–24.   What errors are commonly encountered by the auditor in his examination of the capital and drawing accounts of a sole proprietorship?

19–25.   In your examination of Kelley Corporation you find that two 10 percent stock dividends were distributed during the year. On what basis would you expect the charges to Retained Earnings to be computed?

19–26.   How are changes in contributed capital during a period disclosed in the financial statements?

GROUP II
QUESTIONS REQUIRING ANALYSIS

19–27. John Selby, CPA, is near completion of the field work in the examination of Emerson Company's financial statements. The financial statements which Mr. Selby is examining were drafted by Emerson Company's controller; and the balance sheet does not present the number of shares of authorized capital stock. In Mr. Selby's opinion, all other financial statement disclosures are adequate. In response to Mr. Selby's inquiry, the controller states that he believes authorized capital stock is irrelevant data and that he prefers to have the balance sheet as free from "clutter" as possible.

Required:

Can John Selby express an unqualified opinion on the financial statements of Emerson Company drafted by the controller? Discuss.

19–28. Dumont Company was incorporated July 10, 1974 with an authorized capital as follows:

Common stock, Class A, 20,000 shares, par value $25 per share
Common stock, Class B, 100,000 shares, par value $5 per share

The Capital Stock account in the general ledger is credited with only one item in the year, 1974, representing capital stock sold for cash, at par, as follows:

Class A, 12,000 shares
Class B, 60,000 shares

The sum of open certificate stubs in the stock certificate books at December 31, 1974 indicates that 82,000 shares of stock were outstanding.

Required:

a) State possible explanations for this apparent discrepancy.
b) State the steps you would take to determine the cause of the discrepancy. (AICPA, adapted)

19–29. Gibson Corporation has outstanding one issue of 5 percent cumulative, convertible $100 par preferred stock, as well as an issue of no-par common stock. Dividends have been paid regularly on both stocks until the present year, when the company showed a substantial loss because of a strike which shut down all operations for several months.

At the directors' annual "dividend meeting" on December 1, a decision was reached to pay no more dividends until the company's plants had been modernized and the cash position improved. The

Retained Earnings account was several times as large as a normal year's dividend payments but cash was critically low.

With regard to the failure to pay dividends on the preferred stock, the following alternative suggestions were made by various directors:

a)   Charge Retained Earnings for the amount of the regular dividend on the preferred and show the dividend payable as a current liability.

b)   Same as (a), but classify the dividend payable as a noncurrent liability.

c)   Make no mention of the omitted dividends in the balance sheet.

d)   Attach a footnote to the balance sheet stating the per share and aggregate amount of dividends in arrears on the preferred stock.

e)   Create a reserve for dividends in arrears out of retained earnings and list this account in the owners' equity section of the balance sheet.

Evaluate each of these suggestions.

19–30.   What would be your procedure in an audit of a partnership if your examination disclosed that—

a)   The division of profits and the capital contributed by each partner does not agree with the partnership agreement?

b)   A partner had died in the year under examination but no recognition of this fact was shown on the books?

c)   A partner had sold his share during the year to one of his co-partners, but this sale was not reflected in the accounts?

d)   A new partner was admitted during the year? (AICPA)

19–31.   Several years ago the board of directors of EDP Corporation authorized the creation of a Reserve for Development of Electronic Computers by a charge to the Retained Earnings account. Until the present year expenditures for research and development had been fairly consistent at about 5 percent of sales and had been treated as operating expense. In the present year, however, the corporation increased its research and development program substantially, and it is estimated that expenditures for the program will approximate 12 percent of the current year's sales. The directors propose to charge the portion in excess of 5 percent of sales to the Reserve for Development of Electronic Computers. Would you as an auditor take exception to the action proposed by the board of directors?

19–32.   Raymond Company found itself short of cash in 1974 and decided to forego cash dividends in favor of a 4 percent stock dividend. The dividend was declared on April 30, at which time the company's stock was selling at $25 a share. The date of record was May 15, and the date of distribution June 10. The outstanding shares prior to the dividend numbered 800,000 with a par value of $10 each; the original issuance price of these shares had been $15. In your first examination of the company at December 31, 1974, you observed that the only effects of the stock dividend had been a transfer of $320,000 from the Retained Earnings account to the Capital Stock account and an increase in the number of outstanding shares to 832,000. Was the stock dividend properly recorded? Explain fully.

GROUP III
PROBLEMS

19–33. You were engaged on May 1, 1975 by a committee of stockholders to perform a special audit as of December 31, 1974 of the stockholders' equity of Hamilton Corporation. The stock is actively traded on a stock exchange. The group of stockholders who engaged you believe that the information contained in the stockholders' equity section of the published annual report for the year ended December 31, 1974 is not correct. If your examination confirms their suspicions, they intend to use your report in a proxy fight to gain control of Hamilton Corporation.

Management agrees to permit your audit but refuses to permit any direct confirmation with stockholders. To secure management's cooperation in the audit, the committee of stockholders has agreed to this limitation and you have been instructed by the committee to limit your audit procedures in this respect. You have also been instructed to exclude the audit of revenue and expense accounts for 1974.

Required:

a) Prepare a general audit program for the usual examination of the stockholders' equity section of a corporation's balance sheet, assuming no limitation upon the scope of your examination. Exclude the audit of revenue and expense accounts.

b) Describe any special auditing procedures you would undertake in view of the limitations and other special circumstances of your examination of Hamilton Corporation's stockholders' equity accounts. (AICPA, adapted)

19–34. You are engaged in the audit of a corporation whose financial statements have not previously been audited by you. The corporation has both a stock transfer agent and an independent registrar for its capital stock. The transfer agent maintains the record of stockholders, and the registrar determines that there is no overissue of stock. Signatures of both are required to validate stock certificates.

It has been proposed that confirmations be obtained from both the transfer agent and the registrar as to the stock outstanding at balance sheet date. If such confirmations agree with the books, no additional work is to be performed as to capital stock.

If you agree that obtaining the confirmations as suggested would be sufficient in this case, give the justification for your position. If you do not agree, state specifically all additional steps you would take and explain your reasons for taking them. (AICPA, adapted)

19–35.   You are engaged in the audit of Jensen Corporation, a new client, at the close of its first fiscal year, April 30, 1974. The books had been closed prior to the time you began your year-end field work.

You review the following stockholders' equity accounts in the general ledger:

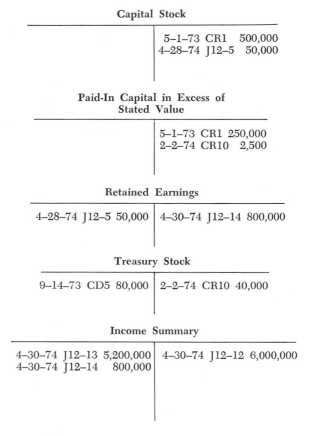

Capital Stock

	5–1–73 CR1 500,000
	4–28–74 J12–5 50,000

Paid-In Capital in Excess of Stated Value

	5–1–73 CR1 250,000
	2–2–74 CR10 2,500

Retained Earnings

4–28–74 J12–5 50,000	4–30–74 J12–14 800,000

Treasury Stock

9–14–73 CD5 80,000	2–2–74 CR10 40,000

Income Summary

4–30–74 J12–13 5,200,000	4–30–74 J12–12 6,000,000
4–30–74 J12–14 800,000	

Other information in your working papers includes the following:

(1)   Jensen's articles of incorporation filed April 17, 1973, authorize 100,000 shares of no-par-value capital stock.
(2)   Directors' minutes include the following resolutions:
    4–18–73.   Established $50 per share stated value for capital stock.
    4–30–73.   Authorized issue of 10,000 shares to an underwriting syndicate for $75 per share.
    9–13–73.   Authorized acquisition of 1,000 shares from a dissident holder at $80 per share.
    2–1–74.   Authorized reissue of 500 treasury shares at $85 per share.
    4–28–74.   Declared 10 percent stock dividend, payable May 18, 1974 to stockholders of record May 4, 1974.

(3) The following costs of the May 1, 1973 and February 2, 1974 stock issuances were charged to the named expense accounts: Printing Expense, $2,500; Legal Fees, $12,000; Accounting Fees, $10,000; SEC Fees, $7,500.

(4) Market values for Jensen Corporation capital stock on various dates were:

9–13–73	$78.50
9–14–73	79.00
2–2–74	85.00
4–28–74	90.00

(5) Jensen Corporation's combined federal and state income tax rates total 55 percent.

Required:

a) Adjusting journal entries at April 30, 1974.

b) Stockholders' equity section of Jensen Corporation's April 30, 1974 balance sheet.

19–36. You are a CPA engaged in an examination of the financial statements of Young Corporation for the year ended December 31, 1974. The financial statements of Young Corporation have not been audited by a CPA in prior years.

The stockholders' equity section of Young Corporation's balance sheet at December 31, 1974 follows:

STOCKHOLDERS' EQUITY

Capital stock—10,000 shares of $10 par value authorized; 5,000 shares issued and outstanding	$ 50,000
Capital contributed in excess of par value of capital stock	32,580
Retained earnings	47,320
Total Stockholders' Equity	$129,900

Young Corporation was founded in 1968. The corporation has 10 stockholders and serves as its own registrar and transfer agent. There are no capital stock subscription contracts in effect.

Required:

Prepare the detailed audit program for the examination of the three accounts comprising the stockholders' equity section of Young Corporation's balance sheet. (Do not include in the audit program the verification of the results of the current year's operations.) (AICPA, adapted)

19–37. You are engaged in the audit of the financial statements of Armstrong Mfg. Co., Inc. for its second year of operations. Financial statements for the preceding year, which included net income of $22,500, were not examined by independent CPAs. Your engagement includes preparation of the company's federal and state income tax returns for the year under audit.

The company's statement of income, prepared by the controller, is as follows:

ARMSTRONG MFG. CO., INC.

SATEMENT OF INCOME

Year Ended September 30, 1974

Net sales....................................	$2,000,000
Costs and expenses:	
Cost of sales...............................	1,400,000
Selling, general and administrative..........	500,000
Interest..................................	30,000
Federal and state income taxes..............	38,500
	$1,968,500
Net Income...............................	$ 31,500

During the course of your examination you learn that manufacturing overhead had been excluded from the valuation of Armstrong's inventories at first-in, first-out cost. Overhead thus excluded amounted to $100,000 at September 30, 1973 and $160,000 at September 30, 1974. Armstrong's federal and state income tax returns for the year ended September 30, 1973 were prepared by Armstrong's controller on the same basis as the financial statements for that year. The company's combined federal and state income tax rates total 55 percent. Any deficiency in income taxes paid for the fiscal year ended September 30, 1973 would be subject to an annual interest rate of 6 percent, computed from the due date (December 15, 1973) to September 30, 1974.

Required:

a)   Draft a proposed adjusting journal entry to correct the exclusion of manufacturing overhead from inventories.

b)   How should you advise Armstrong Mfg. Co., Inc., regarding the income tax returns for the year ended September 30, 1973.

GROUP IV
CASE STUDIES IN AUDITING

CONTRACTOR'S INSPECTION & DISBURSEMENT SERVICE, INC.

19–38.   Contractor's Inspection & Disbursement Service, Inc., furnishes a control service for building contractors. Contractors of limited financial standing are required by certain lending institutions to engage such a service to make regular progress inspections of their projects and to control the disbursement of funds advanced to the contractor by the lenders. The funds are advanced by the bank and deposited in a separate bank account for each contractor; the service controls these accounts. Disbursements are made on the basis of approved invoices supported by release and lien waivers where necessary.

One of the larger financial institutions has become apprehensive over the financial condition of Contractor's Inspection & Disbursement Service, Inc., and has threatened to discontinue referrals of its borrowers to this service unless the stockholders' equity of the corporation can be increased to at least $150,000. The financial position of the service at present is as follows:

ASSETS

Cash............................	$ 25,000
Accounts receivable...............	200,000
Other assets......................	25,000
Total........................	$250,000

LIABILITIES AND STOCKHOLDERS' EQUITY

Accounts payable..................	$ 50,000
Deferred revenue..................	125,000
Stockholders' equity...............	75,000
Total........................	$250,000

NOTE: This statement does not include any funds held for account of contractors.

The present billing procedure of the service is to bill the contractor as soon as construction begins and the first funds are received from the bank. In most cases the fee is payable out of the first advance from the bank, so that accounts receivable are generally collected promptly; in some agreements the fee is not payable until the construction is completed. At the time the fee is billed, deferred revenue is credited, and this deferred revenue is subsequently taken into income pro rata over the period of construction. Therefore, there is always a substantial balance of deferred revenue representing the advance charges for control services that have not been rendered.

The stockholders of the company either do not have the necessary additional capital required by the lending institution or they are reluctant to transfer such capital from other investments. Therefore, the controller has proposed the following:

A new corporation, called "Contractor's Inspection & Disbursement Company," will be formed. To it will be transferred all collectible accounts receivable, as well as cash and other assets, and all liabilities except the deferred revenue. After this transfer the balance sheet of the new company will appear as follows:

ASSETS

Cash............................	$ 25,000
Accounts receivable..............	150,000
Other assets.....................	25,000
Total.......................	$200,000

LIABILITIES AND STOCKHOLDERS' EQUITY

Accounts payable.................	$ 50,000
Capital stock....................	150,000
Total.......................	$200,000

The balance sheet of Contractor's Inspection & Disbursement Service, Inc. (the old company), will appear as follows:

ASSETS

Cash...............................	–0–
Accounts receivable..................	$ 50,000
Other assets........................	–0–
Investment in Contractor's Inspection & Disbursement Company..............	150,000
Total...........................	$200,000

LIABILITIES AND STOCKHOLDERS' EQUITY

Deferred revenue.....................	$125,000
Stockholders' equity..................	75,000
Total...........................	$200,000

To compensate for the failure to transfer the deferred revenue to the new company, the old company will sign an agreement guaranteeing to complete any control contracts which the new company may be financially unable to carry out, and to take over certain problem jobs when they arise. (In the past the old company has frequently had to take over a contractor's work and finish up the job when the contractor got hopelessly delinquent.) Through this agreement the old company intends to indemnify the new company for any such occurrences. The old company will adjust the balance of deferred revenue on its books at the end of each year to show the correct amount of deferred revenue.

In establishing accounting policies for the new company, the controller proposes to take all fees into income as they are billed, without any deferral. He says he is justified in doing this because many companies operate on a cash basis and he feels such a procedure is in order if it helps accomplish the objective of increasing the stockholders' equity of the organization to the level of $150,000 as required by the bank. He also points out that income tax regulations require the inclusion of deferred revenue in taxable income when it is received. Thus the method of accounting adopted for the new company would be in accordance with income tax reporting requirements.

The controller has outlined this procedure to the bank official handling the case, and this official has agreed that the proposed reorganization will be satisfactory to the bank. However, you were not present during the conference, and there is nothing in writing to assure you that the bank official fully understood just what was being done. It is understood that the bank will be given financial statements of only the new company and that they no longer will be interested in the old company.

You were asked to perform an examination and submit an opinion as to the opening balance sheet of the new company in a report to the bank. Your engagement also comtemplates making annual audits of the new company.

Required:

a) What kind of an opinion would you give on the opening balance sheet?

b) In your report at the end of the first year can you give an opinion that the income statement presents fairly the results of operations for the year? Explain fully.

20

Further verification of revenue and expenses

ONE OF the most significant changes in accounting practice in recent years has been the increased importance placed upon the income statement. A generation ago the balance sheet was regarded as the all-important end product of the accounting process; but today, with greater and greater emphasis being placed upon corporate earnings as an indicator of the health and well-being of our industrialized economy, the income statement has come to be of fundamental importance to management, stockholders, employees, and government. The relative level of corporate earnings is now a key factor in the determination of such issues as wage negotiations, income tax rates, price controls, subsidies, and government fiscal policy. It must be remembered that the function of the independent public accountant is to give integrity to financial statements—to give assurance to all who use these statements, including management, employees, investors, and government, that the net earnings reported each year have been determined in accordance with generally accepted accounting principles, in an unbiased manner, and on a basis consistent with that of the preceding year. Acceptance of this responsibility is the best evidence that public accounting has reached the status of a profession. The development of the profession during the past few decades is most apparent when we recall that a generation ago auditors were largely concerned with protecting creditors against overstatement of asset values.

676

The auditor's approach to verification of income

Accountants generally agree that the measurement of income is the most important single function of accounting. A fair and informative income statement is then surely as important as, if not more important than, the balance sheet. Nevertheless, audits continue to be organized in terms of balance sheet topics. The verification of revenue and expense accounts represents a much smaller segment of an audit than does the examination of assets, liabilities, and owners' equity. The allocation of space in auditing textbooks follows a similar pattern.

Why should audits be organized in terms of verifying balance sheet items? Would it be equally efficient to begin an examination with the verification of revenue and expenses, and to treat the investigation of assets and liabilities as a secondary matter? There are a number of reasons why auditors prefer to follow a balance sheet approach in planning an audit. Not the least of these reasons is the factor of custom and tradition. Audits by independent public accountants had their beginnings in serving the needs of bankers and merchandise creditors who required trustworthy balance sheets as a basis for the extension of short-term credit. The need for audited financial statements for credit purposes is probably still the greatest motivating factor leading to independent audits of small business concerns. The work patterns of auditors were well established long before businessmen became accustomed to public release of information about operating results.

As the significance of the income statement increased, auditors began to verify income statement accounts concurrently with related balance sheet accounts. Depreciation expense, for example, is most conveniently verified along with the plant and equipment accounts; once the cost and existence of depreciable assets is established, the verification of depreciation expense is merely an additional step. On the other hand, to verify depreciation expense without first establishing the nature and amount of assets owned and subject to depreciation would obviously be a cart-before-the-horse approach. The same line of reasoning tells us that the auditor's work on inventories, especially determining that inventory transactions were accurately cut off at the end of the period, is a major step toward the verification of the income statement figures for sales and cost of sales.

In other words, much of the audit work associated with balance sheet topics such as plant and equipment, or notes payable, consists of verification of related revenue and expenses. In the same way much of the material in the preceding 9 chapters of this book has related to income statement accounts, although the sequence of topics has followed a balance sheet arrangement.

The greater amount of emphasis placed on balance sheet topics in auditing textbooks is also explained by the importance of the problem of asset valuation. Valuation principles differ for the various asset groups, and audit objectives and procedures differ accordingly for these groups. Such disparity is not found in the verification of most revenue and expense accounts. The most difficult issues to be faced by the auditor in verifying revenue and expenses are valuation problems, and these problems have been considered in the preceding chapters dealing primarily with balance sheet accounts.

When the balance sheets at the beginning and end of an accounting period have been fully verified, the net income for the year is fairly well established, although considerable additional work remains to be done before the auditor can express his professional opinion that the income statement "presents fairly" the results of operations.

Now that we have considered at length the reasons for the organization of an audit (and an auditing textbook) in terms of balance sheet topics, let us emphasize the fact that the auditor's review of revenue and expense transactions should be much more than an incidental by-product of his examination of assets and liabilities.

Critical examination of revenue and expense accounts may bring to light errors, omissions, and inconsistencies not disclosed in the examination of balance sheet accounts. Examples of such deficiencies in accounting for revenue and expense transactions include: failure to distinguish properly between capital and revenue expenditures; failure to prepare invoices for certain shipments; errors in the pricing, extension, and footings of sales invoices; and issuance of credit memoranda granting credit to customers for sales returns when, in fact, the merchandise in question has not been returned.

Audit by comparison

The monthly totals of individual revenue and expense accounts should be compared with the corresponding monthly figures of the preceding year. This comparison may disclose variations caused by unusual items which warrant investigation. Comparison of budgeted amounts with actual revenue and expenses may also draw the auditor's attention to areas requiring detailed analysis. Significant variations should be fully explored with a view toward the development of suggestions to management of means of reducing expenses and expanding revenue. The relative profitability or unprofitability of particular products or territories, as well as the development of significant trends in certain types of revenue and expense, may be disclosed by this process of "auditing by comparison." The value of auditing services is certain to be increased in the eyes of management if the auditor will expand this approach to include a thorough appraisal of the methods of controlling both revenue and expenses.

Conservatism in the measurement of income

Conservatism in the valuation of assets means that when two (or more) reasonable alternative values are indicated, the accountant will choose the lower of the two. Of course the principles used in valuing assets such as inventory and accounts receivable also have an effect upon the measurement of income. The traditional policy of choosing the lower of two possible valuations for an asset has the supplementary effects of minimizing net income for the current period and also of minimizing owners' equity. The doctrine of conservatism is a powerful force influencing distinctions between capital and revenue expenditures; this force is always exerted in favor of treating borderline cases as expenses of the period.

Another aspect of conservatism in the measurement of income is the policy of not recording revenue until the point of delivery of goods or services; at this point the revenue is realized through the receipt of cash or the acquisition of a receivable or the equivalent. The other side of income measurement is the recognition of expenses; in this area conservatism requires that all expenses associated with the revenue of the period be recognized, even though some of these expenses (as for pension plans or for the warranty of products sold) are not subject to precise measurement until a later date.

Most auditors have a considerable respect for the doctrine of conservatism. In part this attitude springs from the concept of legal liability to third parties. Bankers, creditors, and investors who have sustained losses as a result of the failure of auditors to detect overstated assets and exaggerated earnings have time and again collected heavy damages from public accounting firms and have ruined many a professional reputation. Financial statements which **understate** financial position and operating results almost never lead to legal action against the auditors who approve these statements. Nevertheless leaders of the public accounting profession must recognize that overemphasis on conservatism in financial reporting is a narrow and shortsighted approach to meeting the needs of the business community. To be of greatest value, financial statements should present fairly rather than understate financial position and operating results.

Time of examination

The audit of revenue and expense accounts stresses the review of internal control and the testing of transactions, rather than the observation inspection, and confirmation of year-end balances as in the case of balance sheet accounts. Consequently, most of the audit work can advantageously be performed before the end of the year.

REVENUE

Audit objectives

In the examination of revenue, the principal objectives of the auditor are (a) to study and evaluate internal control, with particular emphasis upon the use of accrual accounting to record revenue; (b) to verify that all earned revenue has been recorded and all recorded revenue has been earned; and (c) to identify and interpret significant trends and variations in the dollar amounts of various categories of revenue.

Relationship of revenue to balance sheet accounts

The auditor's review of sales activities was considered in connection with accounts receivable in Chapter 13. As pointed out previously, most revenue accounts are verified by the auditor in conjunction with the audit of a related asset or liability. The following list summarizes the revenue verified in this manner:

Balance sheet item	*Revenue*
Accounts receivable	Sales
Notes receivable	Interest earned
Securities and other investments	Interest, dividends, gains on sales
Property, plant, and equipment	Rent, gains on sale
Intangible assets	Royalties earned
Deferred revenue	Related revenue earned such as subscription revenue and tuition revenue

A common characteristic of the revenue items listed above is that most, if not all, are accounted for on the accrual basis. Accrual basis accounting for revenue results in strengthening internal control, because it requires the recording of a receivable when the revenue is earned. Once the receivable is recorded, some follow-up is inevitable. Additional assurance is provided that attention will be drawn to any delay in the receipt of cash or any failure to record a cash receipt. For example, if dividends earned are recorded as receivables by an accrual entry at the date of record, any failure to receive or to record dividend checks will be readily apparent.

Miscellaneous revenue

One category of revenue not included in the above listing but of interest to the auditor is miscellaneous revenue. Miscellaneous revenue, by its very nature, is a mixture of minor items, some nonrecurring and others likely to be received at irregular intervals. Consequently, many companies do not accrue such revenue but merely debit Cash and credit Miscellaneous Revenue when cash is received. The weakness inherent in this procedure is not of particular significance if the amounts involved are minor and infrequent. However, the weakness can become serious if revenue of substantial amount is misclassified as Miscellaneous Revenue, a practice sometimes followed because of its convenience.

ILLUSTRATIVE CASE. An old story in public accounting circles concerns the auditor who inquired of a new client how extensive was the classification by the company of revenue and expenses. "Just two of each," was the reply, "general and miscellaneous."

For the reasons indicated above, the auditor should obtain an analysis of the Miscellaneous Revenue account. Among the items the auditor might find improperly included as miscellaneous revenue are the following:

a) Collections on previously written-off accounts or notes receivable. These collections should be credited to the allowance for uncollectible accounts and notes.

b) Write-offs of old outstanding checks or unclaimed wages. In many states unclaimed properties revert to the state after statutory periods; in such circumstances these write-offs should be credited to a liability account rather than to miscellaneoues revenue.

c) Proceeds from sales of scrap. Scrap sales proceeds should generally be applied to reduce cost of sales, under by-product cost accounting principles.

d) Rebates or refunds of insurance premiums. These refunds should be offset against the related expense or unexpired insurance.

e) Proceeds from sales of plant assets. These proceeds should be accounted for in the determination of the gain or loss on the assets sold.

The auditor should propose adjusting journal entries to classify correctly any material items of the types described above which have been included in miscellaneous revenue by the client. Before concluding the work on revenue, the auditor should perform the "audit by comparison" techniques described earlier in this chapter and investigate unusual fluctuations. Material amounts of unrecorded revenue may be discovered by this procedure, as well as significant misclassifications affecting revenue accounts.

EXPENSES

The auditor's work relating to purchases and cost of sales was covered along with inventories in Chapter 14. We are now concerned with audit objectives and procedures for other types of expenses.

Audit objectives

In his examination of payrolls, selling expenses, and general and administrative expenses, the auditor studies and evaluates the internal controls in force and tries to determine whether expenses have been recognized in the proper accounting period. In other words, he wants evidence that expenses have been properly matched with revenue. He also considers whether expenses have been properly classified and are reasonable in amount as compared with budget estimates, with expenses of prior years, and the sales of the current year.

The work required to attain these objectives has in large part already been performed in connection with the verification of balance sheet accounts. Let us consider for a moment the number of expense accounts for which we have already outlined verification procedures in the chapters dealing with balance sheet topics:

Relationship of expenses to balance sheet accounts

Balance sheet item	*Expenses (and costs)*
Accounts and notes receivable	Uncollectible accounts and notes expense
Inventories	Purchases and cost of sales
Property, plant, and equipment	Depreciation, repairs and maintenance, and depletion expense
Prepaid expenses and deferred charges	Various related expenses such as rent, property taxes, advertising, postage, and others
Intangible assets	Amortization expense
Accrued liabilities	Commissions, fees, bonuses, product warranty expenses, and others
Interest-bearing debt	Interest expense

In the following sections we shall complete our review of expenses by considering additional audit objectives and procedures for payrolls, and for selling and general administrative expenses, other than those listed above. The audit of payroll is presented as a unit without regard to the division of salaries and wages between manufacturing operations and other operations. Manufacturing salaries and wages are of course charged to inventories, either directly or by means of the allocation of factory overhead.

The budget—a vital element in controlling costs and expenses

In approaching the examination of costs and expenses, perhaps the most important single question to raise is the following: "Does the client have a good budgeting program?" The existence of a good budgeting program means that department heads, foremen, and other supervisors who authorize expenditures have prepared a year in advance a statement of the expenses which must be incurred for a given volume of operations. These estimates of expenses to be incurred have been assembled and summarized by the accounting department, and reviewed and approved by top management. A definite plan of operations exists; standards of performance have been set; and month by month the costs and expenses actually incurred are carefully compared with the amounts shown by the budget. Any significant discrepancy between estimated expenses and actual expenses immediately receives the attention of management, and the supervisor responsible for the expenses in question is called upon for an explanation. When a budgeting program of this type is in operation, the integrity of the accounts is greatly increased: the opportunities for misclassification of expenses, for omission of transactions, and for fraud are reduced to a minimum.

Much of the audit work on costs and expenses may therefore be devoted to a study of the client's budget program. If the auditor finds that the client does not prepare a budget, or merely makes a pretense of using budgetary techniques, the conduct of the audit must be modified accordingly. One of the most effective substitutes for comparison of actual expenses with budgeted expenses is to compare the expenses of each month with the expenses of the corresponding month for the preceding year. Other procedures to be stressed in the absence of budgetary controls include close review of variations in gross profit margins and extensive analysis of ledger accounts for expenses.

Payrolls

The payroll in many companies is by far the largest operating cost, and therefore deserves the close attention of the auditor. In the past, payroll frauds were common and often substantial. Today, however, payroll frauds are more difficult to conceal for several reasons: (*a*) extensive subdivision of duties relating to payroll, (*b*) use of computers for preparation of payrolls, and (*c*) necessity of frequent reports to government, listing employees' earnings and tax withholdings.

The principal objectives of the auditor in the examination of payrolls are:

1. To determine that the authorized records and procedures are so designed and operated as to provide adequate internal control.
2. To determine that the client has complied with government regulations concerning social security taxes, unemployment insurance, workmen's compensation insurance, wages and hours, income tax withholding, and other federal, state, and local requirements concerning employment.

3. To determine that the company is complying with terms of union agreements as to wage rates, vacation pay, and similar items.
4. To suggest methods of simplifying and improving payroll procedures.

Internal control

The establishment of strong internal control over payrolls is particularly important for several reasons. The possibility of large-scale fraud is greater in the handling of payroll than for most phases of operations. Payroll frauds have often involved listing fictitious persons on the payroll, overpaying employees, and continuing employees on the payroll after their separation from the company. A second reason for emphasizing internal control over payrolls is that a great mass of detailed information concerning hours worked and rates of pay must be processed quickly and accurately if workers are to be paid promptly and without error. Good employee relations demand that paychecks be ready on time and be free from error. As pointed out in previous chapters, internal control is a means of securing accuracy and dependability in accounting data as well as a means of preventing fraud.

Still another reason for emphasizing the importance of internal control over payrolls is the existence of various payroll tax laws and income tax laws which require that certain payroll records be maintained, and that payroll data be reported to the employee and to governmental agencies. Complete and accurate records of time worked are also necessary if a company is to protect itself against lawsuits under the Wages and Hours law.

Methods of achieving internal control

Budgetary control of labor costs. To control payroll costs means to avoid waste and to obtain the maximum production from the dollars expended for services of employees. As a means of establishing control over payroll costs, many companies delegate to department heads and other supervisors responsibility for the control of costs in their respective units of the business. The supervisor may be requested at the beginning of each year to submit for the budget an estimate of his labor costs for the coming period. As the year progresses and actual labor costs are compiled, the controller submits monthly reports to top management comparing the budgeted labor costs and the actual labor costs for each department. The effectiveness of this control device will depend largely upon the extent to which top management utilizes these reports and takes action upon variances from the budget.

Reports to governmental agencies. Another important internal control over payroll lies in the necessity of preparing reports to government agencies showing the earnings and tax deductions for all employees. This type of control is not concerned with holding labor costs to a minimum but is an effective means of preventing and detecting payroll fraud. Now that every employee must have a social security number and the employer must report earnings and deductions for each employee, the opportunities for payroll fraud are greatly reduced. In a few cases, falsified reports to government agencies have been prepared as part of a payroll fraud, but this involves such extensive scheming and falsification of records as to make fraud of this type rather unlikely.

Subdivision of duties. Most important of all internal controls over payroll is the division of payroll work among several departments of the company. Payroll activities include the functions of employment, timekeeping, payroll preparation and record keeping, and the distribution of pay to employees. For strong internal control, each of these functions should be handled by a separate department of the company. Combination of these functions in a single department or under the authority of one person opens the door to payroll fraud. These several phases of payroll activities will now be considered individually.

The employment function

The first significant step in building a strong system of internal control over payrolls is taken by the personnel department when a new employee is hired. At this point, the authorized rate of pay should be entered on a pay rate card. The employee should also sign a payroll deduction card, specifying any amounts to be withheld, and a withholding tax exemption certificate. These records should be kept in the personnel department, but a notice of the hiring of the new employee, the rate of pay, and the payroll deductions should be sent to the payroll department. Notice of employment and of the authorized pay rate is also sent to the head of the department in which the employee is to work.

Under no circumstances is the payroll department justified in adding a name to the payroll without having received the formal authorization notice from the personnel department. When an employee's rate of pay is changed, the new rate will be entered on the pay rate card maintained in the personnel department. An authorization for the new rate must be sent to the payroll department before the change can be made effective on the payroll. Upon the termination of an employee, notice of termination is sent from the personnel department to the payroll department. The work of the payroll department and the propriety of names and pay rates used in preparing the payroll, therefore, rest upon formal documents originating outside the payroll department.

An adequate system of internal control demands that the addition and removal of names from the company payroll, as well as rate changes and reclassification of employees, be evidenced by written approval of an executive in the personnel department and by the head of the operating department concerned. To permit the payroll department to initiate changes in pay rates or to add names to the payroll without formal authorization from the personnel department is to invite payroll fraud.

Timekeeping

The function of timekeeping consists of determining the number of hours (or units of production) for which each employee is to be paid. The use of automatic time-recording equipment is of considerable aid in establishing adequate internal control over the timekeeping function. Reports prepared by timekeepers who travel through the plant and contact an employee only once or twice during the day may be less dependable than time reports prepared by foremen whose supervisory duties keep them in continuous contact with a small group of employees.

Internal control can be improved by the practice of regular comparison of the time reports prepared by timekeepers or foremen with time clock records showing arrival and departure times of employees. If pay is based on piecework, a comparison may be made between the reports of units produced and the quantities which are added to the perpetual inventory records.

Salaried employees receiving a fixed monthly or weekly salary may not be required to use time clocks. Some companies require salaried employees to fill out a weekly or semimonthly report indicating the time devoted to various activities. If a salaried employee is absent, the department head usually has authority to decide whether a pay reduction should be made.

Undesirable practices related to the timekeeping function include permitting employees to maintain their own records of time worked or units completed and basing payment on these records without any independent verification. Combination of the timekeeping function with that of payroll preparation is also extremely dangerous from an internal control standpoint. If time clock records are to contribute significantly to internal control, it is imperative that each employee punch his own timecard and no other. Any overtime worked by employees paid on an hourly basis should be approved in writing by the appropriate supervisor.

Payroll records and payroll preparation

The payroll department has the responsibility of computing the amounts to be paid to employees, and of preparing all payroll records.

It is imperative that the payroll department should *not* perform the related functions of timekeeping, employment, or distribution of pay to employees. The output of the payroll department may be thought of as (1) the payroll checks (or pay envelopes if wages are paid in cash); (2) individual employee statements of earnings and deductions; (3) a payroll journal, (4) an employees' ledger, summarizing for each employee his earnings and deductions; (5) a payroll distribution schedule, showing the allocation of payroll costs to direct labor, overhead, and various departmental expense accounts; and (6) quarterly and annual reports to the government showing employees' earnings and taxes withheld. If the client utilizes an electronic data processing installation, many of these functions may be delegated to the data processing department.

The computation of the payroll is made from the work hours reported by the timekeeping department and from authorized pay rates and payroll deductions. These source documents have already been mentioned in discussing the work of related departments.

The auditor may find payroll records and procedures varying in complexity from a manual "write it once" system to the most sophisticated computerized techniques. However, he should expect the client's system to include such basic records as timecards, payroll journals, labor distributions, and employee earnings records.

Distributing paychecks or cash to employees

The distribution of paychecks or pay envelopes to employees is the task of the paymaster. If employees are paid in cash, a copy of the payroll register is forwarded from the payroll department and the paymaster uses this record as a guide to filling the payroll envelopes. These envelopes should preferably be prepared by the payroll department. If employees are paid by check, the checks may be made ready for signature in the payroll department and forwarded to the paymaster for signature.

The paymaster handles large amounts of checks and cash; consequently, his work usually comes under the treasurer's department. Under no circumstances should the signed payroll checks or pay envelopes containing cash be returned to the payroll department. Neither is it acceptable to turn paychecks or pay envelopes over to supervisors in the operating departments for distribution to employees. The function of distribution of paychecks should be lodged exclusively with a paymaster, and he should perform no payroll activity other than distribution of checks or cash. When the paymaster delivers a check to an employee, he will require proof of identity by presentation of a badge or signing of a receipt. A check or pay envelope for an absent employee should be retained and never turned over to a fellow employee for delivery. When the absentee later picks up his pay, he should be required to sign a receipt for it.

Most companies which pay employees by check use a special payroll bank account. A voucher for the entire amount of the weekly payroll may be prepared in the general accounting department based on the payroll summary prepared in the payroll department. This voucher is sent to the treasurer, who issues a check on the general bank account for the amount of the payroll. The check is deposited in the special payroll bank account, and checks to individual employees are drawn on this bank account. It is also the practice of some companies to have printed on the check a statement that this type of check is not valid if issued for an amount in excess of a specified dollar amount, such as $500 or $1,000.

The payment of employees in cash is undesirable from the standpoint of internal control but is a practice still followed by a significant number of companies. Reasons advanced to justify meeting a payroll in cash include inadequate banking facilities in the area, employee attitudes, and a desire on the part of management to eliminate the need for check signing and bank reconciliations. When employees are paid in cash, one check is written and cashed for the entire amount of the payroll. The paymaster fills the envelopes with cash and inserts a form listing the gross earnings, deductions, and net pay.

In small concerns it is not uncommon to find that the person compiling the payroll also fills the pay envelopes and distributes them to employees. This combination of duties affords no protection against payroll fraud. The functions of timekeeping, payroll preparation, and distribution of pay envelopes must be segregated if satisfactory control is to be exercised over wages paid in cash.

Another desirable control device is to obtain a receipt from each employee showing the pay period, gross earnings, deductions, cash payment, and signature of employee. To obtain an adequate receipt, some concerns prepare regular paychecks but pay employees in cash upon endorsement of the paycheck by the employee. The paychecks are then deposited by the company and serve as detailed support for the cash distributed.

If wages are paid in cash, any unclaimed wages should be deposited in the bank and credited to a special liability account. Subsequent disbursement of these funds to employees will then be controlled by the necessity of drawing a check and preparing supporting documents. The auditor should investigate thoroughly all debits to the Unclaimed Wages account. The dangers inherent in permitting unclaimed pay envelopes to be retained by the paymaster, returned to the payroll clerk, or intermingled with petty cash should be obvious.

Internal control questionnaire for payroll

The following list of questions indicates numerous points to be investigated by the auditor in obtaining a description of internal control over payroll activities:

1. Are employees paid by check?
2. Are payroll checks prenumbered?
3. Is a payroll bank account operated on an imprest basis used for all payroll purposes?
4. Are spoiled payroll checks voided in a manner which prevents reuse and filed in numerical sequence with paid checks?
5. Is a check protector in use?
6. Are the various phases of payroll work—such as timekeeping, compilation of payroll, writing of paychecks or filling of pay envelopes, and distribution of payments to employees—assigned to independent departments or divided among a sufficient number of persons?
7. Is there reasonable rotation of duties among timekeepers, paymasters, and employees preparing payrolls?
8. Are all clerical operations involved in preparation of the payroll subjected to independent proof and verification before distribution of the payroll?
9. Are undelivered payroll checks forwarded by the paymaster to an appropriate official for deposit after a specified period of time?
10. Are time reports signed by foremen?
11. Are additions to and separations from the payroll and changes in rates made effective through formal authorization by an appropriate executive?
12. Does the internal auditing department observe the distribution of payroll checks at unannounced intervals?
13. Is the payroll bank account reconciled monthly by employees having no other connection with payroll work?
14. Does the reconciliation of the payroll bank account include examination of endorsements on paid checks, accounting for the numerical sequence of checks, and comparison of checks with the payroll records?
15. If payrolls are distributed in cash, are appropriate safeguards, such as the following, in use:
    a) Armored-car service?
    b) Paymasters rotated frequently?
    c) Receipts obtained from employees?
    d) Receipts compared with payroll by employee having no other connection with payroll activities?

Audit program for payrolls

The following audit procedures are representative of the work generally needed to establish the propriety of payments for salaries, wages, bonuses, and commissions:

1. Obtain a description of the internal control for payrolls.

2. Make a detailed test of payroll transactions for one or more pay periods, including the following specific procedures:
   a) Trace names and wage or salary rates to records maintained by personnel department.
   b) Trace time shown on payroll to timecards and time reports signed by foremen.
   c) If payroll is based on piecework rates rather than hourly rates, reconcile earnings with production records.
   d) Determine basis of deductions from payroll and compare with records of deductions authorized by employees.
   e) Test extensions and footings of payroll.
   f) Compare totals of payroll with totals of payroll checks issued.
   g) Compare total of payroll with total of labor cost summary prepared by cost accounting department.
   h) If wages are paid in cash, compare receipts obtained from employees with payroll.
   i) If wages are paid by check, compare paid checks with payroll and compare endorsements to signatures on withholding tax exemption certificates.
   j) Review subsequent payment of unclaimed wages, comparing receipts with payroll records, wage rates, and time reports.
3. Determine that payrolls for the year do not exceed the number of weekly or monthly pay periods and that all payrolls have been properly approved.
4. If wages are paid in cash, appraise the control procedures applicable to the filling and distribution of pay envelopes.
5. Plan a surprise observation of one of the regular payoffs, including control of payroll records and an accounting for all employees listed.
6. Observe the use of time clocks by employees checking in, and investigate timecards not used.
7. Obtain or prepare a summary of compensation of officers for the year and trace to contracts, minutes of directors' meetings, or other authorization.
8. Investigate any extraordinary fluctuations in salaries, wages, and commissions.
9. Compute compensation earned under profit-sharing plans.
10. Test commission earnings by examination of contracts and detailed supporting records.
11. Test pension payments by reference to authorized pension plans and to supporting records.

The fifth procedure in the above list calling for the auditor to plan a surprise observation of a regular distribution of paychecks to employees deserves special consideration. The auditor's objective in observing firsthand the distribution of checks or cash to employees on a regular payday is to satisfy himself that every name on the company payroll is that of a bona fide employee presently on the job. This audit procedure is particularly desirable if the various phases of payroll work are not sufficiently segregated by departments to afford good internal control. The history of payroll frauds shows that permitting one person to have custody of employment records, timecards, paychecks, and employees' earnings records has often led to the entering of fictitious names on the payroll, and to other irregularities such as use of excessive pay rates and continuance of pay after the termination of an employee.

The auditor's observation of a payoff should be on a surprise basis and may conveniently be done at some time other than the peak of the audit work season. Efficient planning of the payoff distribution requires that the auditor know in advance the general procedure and timing of payroll preparation and distribution. Without any prior announcement the auditor should appear on a regular payday and take control of the paychecks or pay envelopes. Before the distribution to employees is begun, the auditor will compare the name and amount on each check or envelope with the corresponding entry in the payroll register. He must make sure that he has a check or envelope for every item on the payroll register. The footings of the payroll register should also be verified so that there is no doubt that the auditor is accounting for the distribution of every dollar of the payroll. In a business so large that the auditor cannot conveniently observe the distribution of the entire payroll, the test may be limited to one or more selected departments.

After satisfying himself that he has in his possession all checks or envelopes comprising the payroll, the auditor will accompany the paymaster on his round of the plant. The whole procedure will be meaningless unless the auditor establishes definitely the identity of each employee receiving payment.

Audit program for selling, general, and administrative expenses

For other expenses not verified in the audit of balance sheet accounts, the following audit procedures are appropriate. The extent to which the first four procedures are applied is dependent upon the auditor's evaluation of internal control for expenses.

1. Compare actual expenses and budgeted expenses.
2. Compare monthly operating expenses with those of the prior year, both in dollar amounts and expressed as a percentage of net sales.
3. Investigate all significant variations disclosed by comparison of expenses with the budget and with figures of prior years.

4. Obtain or prepare analyses of expense accounts selected as a result of the above three procedures.
5. Obtain or prepare an analysis of professional fees expense.
6. Obtain or prepare analyses of critical expenses in income tax returns.

1. Compare actual expenses and budgeted expenses.

The effectiveness of a good budget program in controlling expenses was discussed earlier in this chapter. In the examination of companies which prepare budgets, the auditor should compare actual and budgeted expenses, and analyze variances from budgets. Often management will have investigated thoroughly the variances from the budget and will be able to provide logical explanations. The existence of a good budget program may reduce considerably the audit time which otherwise would be devoted to analysis of expense accounts.

2. Compare monthly operating expenses with those of the prior year, both in dollar amounts and expressed as a percentage of net sales.

Even though a budget is not in use by the client, the auditor may still apply the principle of "audit by comparison" by obtaining or preparing analyses which compare the various operating expenses month by month with the figures for corresponding months of the preceding year. One of the audit objectives for expenses previously mentioned was determining whether expenses had been correctly classified. The issue of classification is most important as between factory overhead costs, on the one hand, and selling and general administrative expenses, on the other. Factory overhead costs may properly be carried forward as part of inventory cost, whereas the expenses of selling and general and administrative functions are generally deducted from revenue in the period incurred. Consequently, an error in classification may cause an error in the net income of the period. The auditor's review of the propriety of classification of expenses can conveniently be linked with the comparison of monthly amounts of the various expenses. Comparison of yearly totals is accomplished by inclusion of figures for the preceding year on the auditor's grouping sheets or working trial balance, but this step should be supplemented by comparison of expenses on a month-by-month basis.

3. Investigate all significant variations disclosed by comparison of expenses with the budget and with figures of prior years.

The principal method of investigating significant variations in expenses is analysis of ledger accounts. Entries in the expense accounts are traced back to the voucher register, or to the cash disbursements journal if the company records expenses only at time of making payment. From these books of original entry, reference may be made to invoices, receiving reports, purchase orders, or other supporting evidence.

4. Obtain or prepare analyses of expense accounts selected as a result of the above three procedures.

As a result of the above three procedures, the auditor will have chosen certain expense accounts for further verification. The client should be requested to furnish analyses of the accounts selected, together with related vouchers and other supporting documents, for the auditor's review. An illustration of an expense account analysis is presented in Figure 20–1.

Which expense accounts are most likely to contain errors and are most important for the auditor to analyze? Generally auditors have found that the accounts for traveling expense, entertainment, contributions.

FIGURE 20–1

Cheviot Corporation
Acct. no. 547 — Professional Fees — R-3-7
Year Ended December 31, 1974

Date	Reference	Payee	Description	Amount
Various	Various	Hempstead & Hempstead	Monthly legal services retainer – 12 x #500 n	6 000 –
3/5/74	CD411	James & Williams, CPAs	Fee for 1973 audit	4 500 – n
5/2/74	CD602	Hempstead & Hempstead	Fee for legal services relating to acquisition of real estate adjoining San Diego plant	1 000 – n
9/18/74	CD1018	Hempstead & Hempstead	Legal fees for review and modification of installment sales contract forms	400 – n
12/31/74			Balance per ledger	11 900 –

A.J.E. 41 To capitalize 5/2/74 disbursement as part of cost of land K-1 — (1 000 –)

10 900 –
R-3

Prepared by client

n – Examined statement and duplicate check in payment thereof.

V.M.H.
1/12/75

professional fees, officers' compensation, repairs and maintenance, and miscellaneous expense should be analyzed.

5. Obtain or prepare an analysis of professional fees expense.

As indicated in the preceding paragraph, the auditor should analyze professional fees expense. This analysis will often disclose legal and audit fees properly chargeable to costs of issuing stock or debt instruments, or to costs of acquiring subsidiaries. A study of professional fees expense for a new client will inform the auditor of fees charged by the predecessor CPA. Also, the analysis of professional fees expense furnishes the names of attorneys to whom letters should be sent requesting information as to litigation, contingent liabilities, etc. Figure 20–1 illustrates an analysis of professional fees expense.

6. Obtain or prepare analyses of critical expenses in income tax returns.

Income tax returns in use at present generally require "schedules" for officers' salaries, taxes, contributions, and casualty losses. In addition, officers' expense account allowances are presented in the analysis of officers' salaries. Accordingly, the auditor should obtain or prepare analyses of any of these expenses which were not analyzed in connection with the audit of payrolls or the fourth procedure of this audit program. The auditor should bear in mind that details of these expenses will probably be closely scrutinized when the state or federal revenue service representatives examine the client's tax returns.

INCOME STATEMENT PRESENTATION

Extraordinary gains and losses

In 1966 the Accounting Principles Board, in *Opinion No. 9,* "Reporting the Results of Operations," settled the long-standing dispute over financial statement presentation of extraordinary gains and losses. In sanctioning the "all-inclusive" income statement, the board concluded that net income should reflect all items of profit and loss recognized during the period except prior period adjustments, and that extraordinary items should be shown separately as an element of net income. The board identified extraordinary items as infrequent events and transactions of material effect which are not considered to be recurring factors in the ordinary operations of the business. Examples cited were the following:

1. Sale or abandonment of a plant or a significant segment of the business.
2. Sale of an investment not acquired for resale.
3. Write-off of goodwill due to unusual events or developments during the period.

4. Condemnation or expropriation of properties.
5. Major devaluation of a foreign currency.

The board also specified that certain gains or losses, regardless of amount, are not extraordinary items and should be included in the determination of income before extraordinary items. Examples furnished were write-downs of receivables, inventories, or research and development costs; adjustments of accrued contract prices; and gains or losses from fluctuations of foreign exchange.

ILLUSTRATIVE CASE. In 1973 the Rapallo Company sold the oldest of its three plants, which had been idle much of the time in recent years. This old plant was fully depreciated on the company's books, and the sale resulted in a nonrecurring profit of over $3 million. In the succeeding year operating earnings improved greatly. The comparative income statement for the two years combined with a statement of retained earnings included the following:

	Year ended December 31,	
	1974	1973
Income before extraordinary item....................	$18,721,450	$16,067,600
Gain on sale of plant, net of applicable income taxes of $900,000...	....	2,700,000
Net income..	$18,721,450	$18,767,600
Retained earnings at beginning of year..............	46,974,600	34,207,000
Total...	$65,696,050	$52,974,600
Cash dividends—$1 per share.......................	6,000,000	6,000,000
Retained earnings at end of year....................	$59,696,050	$46,974,600

The most significant point revealed in this comparative income statement is that the Rapallo Company's earnings from regular operations rose by nearly $3 million in 1974, an increase of over 16 percent. Stockholders, bankers, and other outsiders interested in the progress of the company will make important decisions on the strength of this sharp upward movement of earnings. However, the total net earnings reported for 1973 and 1974 are about the same because the net income of the earlier year was inflated by a large nonrecurring profit from the sale of plant and equipment. If this extraordinary gain were not clearly shown as a separate item, the readers of the comparative income statement might miss the key point that operating results improved sharply from 1973 to 1974.

Accounting Principles Board Opinion No. 20, "Accounting Changes," requires income statement presentation similar to extraordinary items for all except three types of changes in accounting principle. Emphasizing that these cumulative effects are *not* extraordinary items, the *Opinion* requires the presentation of the cumulative effects in the income statement between the captions *extraordinary items* and *net income.* (Chapter 19 described the three changes of accounting principle which are accorded treatment similar to *prior period adjustments.*)

The independent auditor should study the items presented in the client's income statement as extraordinary items or cumulative effects of changes in accounting principle, and determine whether the criteria of the relevant Accounting Principles Board *Opinions* have been met.

How much detail in the income statement?

One of the more interesting problems of statement presentation of revenue and expenses is the question of how much detailed operating information may be disclosed without aiding competitors or otherwise harming the interests of the client. As a minimum, the income statement should show the net sales revenue, cost of sales, selling expenses, general and administrative expenses, income taxes, income before extraordinary items, extraordinary items, cumulative effects of changes in accounting principle, and net income.

Reporting earnings per share

After the net income figure, per share figures should be reported for income before extraordinary items, cumulative effects of accounting changes, and net income. The computations should be based upon the weighted average number of actual and "equivalent" common shares outstanding during the year. In addition to these "primary" earnings per share figures, pro forma "fully diluted" earnings per share figures should generally be reported, under the assumption of full conversion of all outstanding convertible debentures and comparable securities which are not "common stock equivalents." These disclosures are required by *Accounting Principles Board Opinion No. 15,* "Earnings per Share."

Reporting by conglomerates and other diversified companies

The corporate merger movement in recent years has created many large "conglomerate" corporations by bringing together companies in quite unrelated industries. Although the word *conglomerate* is usually applied to a business combination created by mergers, other companies have achieved the same degree of diversification among unrelated industries through internal development and expansion. The term *diversified company* is therefore more appropriate for our use in considering the special financial reporting problems created by the emergence of this new type of business entity.

For the diversified company carrying on operations in several unrelated industries, we may well question whether the traditional form of income statement constitutes a fair presentation. Would the income statement be more useful to financial analysts and others if it showed separately the revenue and operating results of the various industry segments comprising the diversified company? In the past an investor or financial analyst could easily associate a given corporation with a specific industry. Since this is hardly possible for many of the new large diversified companies, a worthwhile analysis of the income statement may require disclosure of profitability of the several industry segments.

In *Statement No. 2,* "Disclosure of Supplemental Financial Information by Diversified Companies," the Accounting Principles Board of the AICPA took notice of this issue, suggesting that diversified companies consider voluntary disclosure of supplemental financial information as to the various industry segments of their business. The board offered no specific guidelines, pending a study and the issuance of a formal *Opinion* on the matter.

A study group of the Financial Executives Institute recommended that diversified companies report sales or other gross revenue and the relative percentage contribution to net income of any separate industry segment producing 15 percent or more of the company's gross revenue. The SEC accepted this proposal for companies with total sales and revenue of $50 million or less; for larger companies the SEC enacted a more stringent rule which requires them to report net sales and the contribution to net income of each product line contributing 10 percent or more to total net sales or net earnings.

GROUP I
REVIEW QUESTIONS

20–1. Select the best answer choice for each of the following:

  a) A CPA compares the client's 1974 revenue and expenses with those of the prior year and investigates all changes exceeding 10 percent. Which error or questionable practice has the best chance of being detected by the CPA's procedures?

  (1) The cashier began lapping accounts receivable in 1974.
  (2) Because of worsening economic conditions, the 1974 provision for uncollectible accounts was inadequate.
  (3) The client changed its capitalization policy for small tools in 1974.
  (4) An increase in property tax rates has not been recognized in the client's 1974 accrual.

  b) An example of an internal control weakness for payroll is to assign to a department supervisor the responsibility for:

  (1) Distributing payroll checks to subordinate employees.
  (2) Reviewing and approving time reports for subordinates.
  (3) Interviewing applicants for subordinate positions prior to hiring by the personnel department.
  (4) Initiating request for salary adjustments for subordinate employees.

  c) From the standpoint of good internal control, distribution of payroll checks to employees is best handled by the

    (1) Treasurer's department.

    (2) Personnel department.

    (3) Payroll accounting section.

    (4) Departmental supervisors. (AICPA, adapted)

20–2. Identify three revenue accounts which are verified during the audit of balance sheet accounts; also identify the related balance sheet accounts.

20–3. Identify three items which are often misclassified as miscellaneous revenue and state how the misclassified items should be accounted for.

20–4. How is the "audit by comparison" technique applied in the verification of revenue?

20–5. Both management and auditors attach greater importance to the income statement today than they did in the past. What explains this change in viewpoint?

20–6. Despite the increased importance accorded to the income statement in recent years, audits by independent public accountants continue to be organized in terms of balance sheet topics. Why?

20–7. Identify three expense accounts which are verified during the audit of balance sheet accounts; also identify the related balance sheet accounts.

20–8. For what expense accounts should the auditor obtain or prepare analyses to be used in preparation of the client's income tax returns?

20-9. When you are first retained to examine the financial statements of the Welch Equipment Company you inquire whether a budget is used to control costs and expenses. The controller replies that he personally prepares such a budget each year, but that he regards it as a highly confidential document. He states that you may refer to it if necessary, but he wants you to make sure that no employee of the firm sees any of the budget data. Comment on this use of a budget.

20–10. What influence does the existence of a good budgeting program in the client's business have on the conduct of an audit?

20–11. During an initial audit, you observe that the client is not complying with federal regulations concerning wages and hours. Would you (*a*) report the violation to regulatory authorities, (*b*) discuss the matter with the client, (*c*) ignore the matter completely, (*d*) withdraw from the engagement, or (*e*) follow some other course of action? Explain.

20–12. What division of duties among independent departments is desirable to achieve maximum internal control over payrolls?

20–13. What specific steps are suggested by the phrase "detailed test of payroll transactions"?

20–14. What safeguards should be employed when the inaccessibility of banking facilities makes it desirable to pay employees in cash?

20–15. You are asked by a client to outline the procedures you would recommend for disposing of unclaimed wages.

20–16. What auditing procedure can you suggest for determining the reasonableness of selling, general, and administrative expenses?

20–17. What are *extraordinary items?*

20–18. How does the independent auditor determine the propriety of extraordinary items in the client's income statement?

20–19. What rule did the SEC enact for disclosures of operating details on the income statements of diversified companies?

GROUP II
QUESTIONS REQUIRING ANALYSIS

20–20. The Lambert Company owed real estate taxes of $1,972. Through error Morton Bryant, who served the company as office manager, cashier, and bookkeeper, paid the tax bill twice. Realizing his error after having mailed the second check, he wrote to the city officials requesting a refund.

When the refund was received some weeks later, Mr. Bryant substituted the check from the city for cash receipts and abstracted $1,972 in currency.

Would this error and theft probably be discovered in an audit by independent public accountants? Indicate what auditing procedure, if any, would disclose the facts.

20–21. Farlow Corporation, a client, calls you on September 25 for advice on financial statement presentation of a gain on the sale of a 5 percent investment in stock of a principal supplier. The stock was acquired March 18, 1972 for $100,000 to strengthen relations with the supplier and was sold September 24, 1974 for $150,000. No dividends were received by Farlow on the investment. Exclusive of the gain on the stock, Farlow estimates pretax income of $100,000 for the year ending December 31, 1974. Assume combined federal and state income tax rates of 55 percent on ordinary income and 35 percent on capital gains.

Required:

How would you advise Farlow Corporation to present the gain in financial statements? Explain.

20–22. State what documents or evidence the auditor would examine in the verification of each of the following:

    a) Advertising expense, where advertising is placed through an agency.

    b) Advertising expense, where advertising is placed directly in newspapers by the client.

   c)   Royalty expense.
   d)   Repair expense. (AICPA)
20–23.   Stevens Corporation is highly diversified, with divisions which manu-
         facture and sell antibiotics, dairy products, hospital supplies, toiletries,
         and chemicals. In what form should the income statement of Stevens
         Corporation be prepared?
20–24.   The general ledger of the Linfield Manufacturing Company contains
         a Payroll Clearing account. Debits to the account originate in the
         payroll section of the factory accounting office. Credits to the account
         originate in the cost distribution section. The company does not
         use standard or estimated costs. On the assumption that there is
         effective internal control over payrolls you are to—
   a)   State the information needed by the payroll section and indicate
         the source of this information.
   b)   State the information needed by the cost distribution section
         and the source of the information.
   c)   State the principal controls over the payroll in the system as you
         have described it. (AICPA)

GROUP III
PROBLEMS

20–25.   Howell Manufacturing Company employs about 50 production work-
         ers and has the following payroll procedures.
            The factory foreman interviews applicants and on the basis of
         the interview either hires or rejects the applicants. When the appli-
         cant is hired he prepares a W–4 form (Employee's Withholding
         Exemption Certificate) and gives it to the foreman. The foreman
         writes the hourly rate of pay for the new employee in the corner
         of the W–4 form and then gives the form to a payroll clerk as
         notice that the worker has been employed. The foreman verbally
         advises the payroll department of rate adjustments.
            A supply of blank timecards is kept in a box near the entrance
         to the factory. Each worker takes a timecard on Monday morning,
         fills in his name, and notes in pencil on the timecard his daily arrival
         and departure times. At the end of the week the workers drop the
         timecards in a box near the door to the factory.
            The completed timecards are taken from the box on Monday
         morning by a payroll clerk. Two payroll clerks divide the cards
         alphabetically between them, one taking the A to L section of the
         payroll and the other taking the M to Z section. Each clerk is fully
         responsible for her section of the payroll. She computes the gross
         pay, deductions and net pay, posts the details to the employees'
         earnings records, and prepares and numbers the payroll checks. Em-
         ployees are automatically removed from the payroll when they fail
         to turn in a timecard.
            The payroll checks are manually signed by the chief accountant
         and given to the foreman. The foreman distributes the checks to

the workers in the factory and arranges for the delivery of the checks to the workers who are absent. The payroll bank account is reconciled by the chief accountant, who also prepares the various quarterly and annual payroll tax reports.

Required:

List your suggestions for improving Howell Manufacturing Company's system of internal control for factory hiring practices *and* payroll procedures. (AICPA, adapted)

20–26. Your client is a shopping center with 30 store tenants. All leases with the store tenants provide for a fixed rent plus a percentage of sales, net of sales taxes, in excess of a fixed dollar amount computed on an annual basis. Each lease also provides that the landlord may engage a CPA to audit all records of the tenant for assurance that sales are being properly reported to the landlord.

You have been requested by your client to audit the records of Traders Restaurant to determine that the sales totaling $390,000 for the year ended December 31, 1974, have been properly reported to the landlord. The restaurant and the shopping center entered into a five-year lease on January 1, 1974. Traders Restaurant offers only table service. No liquor is served. During meal times there are four or five waitresses in attendance who prepare handwritten prenumbered restaurant checks for the customers. Payment is made at a cash register, manned by the proprietor, as the customer leaves. All sales are for cash. The proprietor also is the bookkeeper. Complete files are kept of restaurant checks and cash register tapes. A daily sales book and general ledger are also maintained.

Required:

List the auditing procedures that you would employ to verify the total annual sales of Traders Restaurant. (Disregard vending machine sales and counter sales of chewing gum, candy, etc.) (AICPA)

20–27. You are examining the financial statements of a moderate-sized manufacturing corporation, with the objective of issuing an unqualified opinion. There is some internal control, but the office and bookkeeping staff comprises only three persons. You decide to test two months' transactions in detail. The sales are $1 million per year.

Submit a detailed, explicit audit program setting forth the steps you believe are necessary in connection with the following expense accounts. (The total of one year's charges in each account is set forth opposite each caption):

Advertising	$60,000
Rent	8,000
Salesmen's Commissions	39,000
Insurance	4,000

(AICPA, adapted)

20–28.   The Professional Women's Association of Lexington is made up of
women in the various professions, including CPAs. From the start
it has been exempt from federal and state income taxes, other than
payroll.

The dues for members are $40 a year, after an initiation fee
of $100. The association has had a consistent policy of operating
on a cash basis. It does not deposit initiation fees received with
applications and does not consider them as revenue until the membership committee has acted thereon. Then the successful applicants'
fees are deposited and the unsuccessful applicants' checks are returned to them.

The fiscal year ends August 31. Each year the directors choose
a CPA to make a thorough audit; and no one is allowed to audit
two consecutive years. For the year ended August 31, 1974 you
have been selected for the first time, but you are solemnly warned
that the directors will not tolerate any suggestion of putting the
accounts on an accrual basis. You accept. An adequate fee is provided.

The secretary furnishes you with the following information:

Membership at September 1, 1973..........		2,980
Elected during year......................	123	
Dropped for nonpayment of dues...........	15	
Died....................................	37	
Expelled................................	1	53
Net gain................................		70

Your examination of records shows the following:

Notices that "dues are due" are sent out in August. Dues for
a full year, not to be prorated, must be paid when elected to membership. Prior to the end of the preceding fiscal year 410 members
had paid their dues and in the current fiscal year 457 members
had paid their dues for the year beginning September 1, 1974. One
of these who had died very suddenly on August 30, 1974 is included
in the 37 above. No refunds are made for deaths taking place after
the fiscal year begins; however, refunds of one half of the dues are
made to expelled members. There were 36 applications pending
at August 31, 1974. During the course of your audit, the committee
met and approved 34. You further find that at the **beginning** of
the year there were 47 such applications and that 45 had been
acted upon favorably and are included in the 123 above.

The directors are interested in learning if there is a substantial
difference between the revenue from dues on a cash basis as compared to the accrual basis.

Required:

a)   Prepare an analysis of revenue from membership showing:

(1)   Changes in members.

(2)   Revenue from initiation fees.

(3)   Revenue from dues for the year, accrual basis.

(4) Revenue from dues for the year, cash basis.

(5) Total revenue from membership, cash basis.

(6) Reconciliation of the cash basis revenue from dues to the accrual basis.

b) What other audit procedures would you use to verify the revenue from membership? Give reasons. (AICPA, adapted)

20–29. Bay State Loan Company has 100 branch loan offices. Each office has a manager and four or five subordinates who are employed by the manager. Branch managers prepare the weekly payroll, including their own salaries, and pay employees from cash on hand. The employee signs the payroll sheet signifying receipt of his salary. Hours worked by hourly personnel are inserted in the payroll sheet from timecards prepared by the employees and approved by the manager.

The weekly payroll sheets are sent to the home office along with other accounting statements and reports. The home office compiles employee earnings records and prepares all federal and state payroll tax returns from the weekly payroll sheets.

Salaries are established by home office job-evaluation schedules. Salary adjustments, promotions, and transfers of full-time employees are approved by a home office salary committee based upon the recommendations of branch managers and area supervisors. Branch managers advise the salary committee of new full-time employees and terminations. Part-time and temporary employees are hired without referral to the salary committee.

Required:

a) How might funds for payroll be diverted in the above system?

b) Prepare a payroll audit program to be used in the home office to audit the branch office payrolls of Bay State Loan Company. (AICPA, adapted)

20–30. The review of the system of internal control by an independent CPA is fundamental in every examination of financial statements upon which he must express an opinion.

You have been engaged to examine the financial statements of a manufacturing company which pays all payrolls in currency.

Required:

a) State what questions you would ask in your review of the system of internal control and procedures relative to payrolls. (The answer may be in the form of an appropriate questionnaire.)

b) Give your reasons for asking the above questions, including an explanation of how you would use the questions in deciding on the effectiveness of the control over payrolls. (AICPA, adapted)

20–31. You are engaged in your first audit of Sloane Pest Control Company for the year ended December 31, 1974. The company began doing business in January 1974, and provides pest control services for industrial enterprises.

Additional information:

(1) The office staff consists of a bookkeeper, a typist, and the president, Richard Sloane. In addition, the company employs 20 servicemen on an hourly basis, who are assigned to individual territories to make both monthly and emergency visits to customers' premises. The servicemen submit weekly time reports which include the customer's name and the time devoted to each customer. Time charges for emergency visits are shown separateiy from regular monthly visits on the report.

(2) Customers are required to sign annual contracts which are pre-numbered and prepared in duplicate. The original is filed in numeri-cal order by contract anniversary date, and the copy is given to the customer. The contract entitles the customer to pest control services once each month. Emergency visits are billed separately.

(3) Fees for monthly services are payable in advance—quarterly, semi-annually or annually—and are recorded on the books as "revenue from services" when the cash is received. All payments are by checks received by mail.

(4) Prenumbered invoices for contract renewals are prepared in tripli-cate from information in the contract file. The original invoice is sent to the customer 20 days prior to the due date of payment, the duplicate copy is filed chronologically by due date, and the triplicate copy is filed alphabetically by customer. If payment is not received by 15 days after the due date, a cancellation notice is sent to the customer and a copy of the notice is attached to the customer's con-tract. The bookkeeper notifies the servicemen of all contract cancella-tions and requires written acknowledgement of receipt of such notices. Mr. Sloane approves all cancellations and reinstatements of contracts.

(5) Prenumbered invoices for emergency services are prepared weekly from information shown on servicemen's time reports. The custo-mer is billed at 200 percent of the serviceman's hourly rate. These invoices, prepared in triplicate and distributed as shown above, are recorded on the books as "revenue from services" at the billing date. Payment is due 30 days after the invoice date.

(6) All remittances are received by the typist, who prepares a daily list of collections and stamps a restrictive endorsement on the checks. A copy of the list is forwarded with the checks to the bookkeeper, who posts the date and amount received on the copies of the invoice in both the alphabetical and chronological files. After posting, the copy of the invoice is transferred from the chronological file to the daily cash receipts binder, which serves as a subsidiary record for the cash receipts book. The bookkeeper totals the amounts of all remittances received, posts this total to the cash receipts book and attaches the daily remittance tapes to the paid invoices in the daily cash receipts binder.

(7) The bookkeeper prepares a daily bank deposit slip and compares the total with the total amount shown on the daily remittance tapes. All remittances are deposited in the bank the day they are received. (Cash receipts from sources other than services need not be considered.)

(8) Financial statements are prepared on the accrual basis.

Required:

List the audit procedures you would employ in the examination of the Revenue from Services account for 1974. (AICPA, adapted)

GROUP IV
CASE STUDIES IN AUDITING

PHOENIX PIPELINE COMPANY

20-32. The Phoenix Pipeline Company was organized a year ago to construct a pipeline across several states from certain oil fields to the industrial and residential consumers of utilities in several large cities. The pipeline is still being constructed, and it is not expected to be completed for about six months. You were asked to give an unqualified opinion to the following statements:

BALANCE SHEET

ASSETS

Current Assets:	
Cash...	$14,000,000
Land purchased for resale........................	800,000
Total Current Assets...........................	$14,800,000
Construction in progress...........................	23,600,000
Unamortized debt issue costs......................	500,000
Total Assets.................................	$38,900,000

LIABILITIES AND STOCKHOLDERS' EQUITY

Current liabilities................................	$ 2,000,000
Long-term debt....................................	18,400,000
Common stock.....................................	18,000,000
Retained earnings.................................	500,000
Total Liabilities and Stockholders' Equity.......	$38,900,000

INCOME STATEMENT

Revenue:	
Interest charged to outsiders......................	$ 80,000
Interest charged to construction...................	1,975,000
Total Revenue...............................	$ 2,055,000
Expenses:	
Interest on long-term debt........................	$ 1,100,000
Amortization of debt issue costs..................	51,000
Other expenses...................................	400,000
Federal and state income taxes....................	252,000
Total Expenses..............................	$ 1,803,000
Net Income......................................	$ 252,000

The interest charged to construction is based on the funds invested in the construction of the pipeline at the maximum rate allowed by government regulatory agencies involved. The pipeline company will be under supervision of these agencies and will only be allowed gas transmission rates high enough to yield the legal rate of return on the amount invested in the facilities. Charging interest as a cost of construction, a practice permitted by the regulatory agencies, therefore increases the rate base.

Land purchased for resale is shown as a current asset because the company acquired this land for the construction of its office building and has a commitment from a large insurance company to purchase this land and the building as soon as it is completed. The land and building will then be leased back to the Phoenix Pipeline Company by the insurance company.

Required:

a) Would you as independent auditor regard the capitalization of interest during construction as acceptable practice by a regulated utility company? By an unregulated industrial company? Explain fully.

b) Assuming a "normal" interest rate of 6 percent, how was the $1,975,000 of interest charged to construction probably computed?

c) What position would you as a CPA take if accounting practices required by a public utility regulatory commission differed from generally accepted accounting principles?

d) Can you express an unqualified opinion on the statements as presented?

e) Can an unqualified opinion be given if additional information and explanations are included in footnotes to the statements?

20–33.   Timber Products Corporation

During the first audit of the Timber Products Corporation, the auditor found the payroll activities to be concentrated in the hands of an experienced and trusted employee, Richard Cardiff. Mr. Cardiff prepares a payroll register from timecards. The register is presented for approval of the treasurer, who then issues a check for the total amount of the payroll. Mr. Cardiff cashes this check, fills pay envelopes for all of the company's 400 hourly employees, and distributes the pay envelopes to the employees.

In verifying the hourly payroll, the auditor selected two test periods, the first week in July and the second week in December. For these test periods, he proved the accuracy of the footings and the extensions on the payroll register. The totals shown by the payroll register corresponded with the checks issued for the total payrolls. Employee names and rates of pay were traced to a file of employment cards, maintained by Mr. Cardiff. These cards indicated the date of employment, the job classification, and the hourly rate of pay. When an employee was reclassified to a higher pay classification, the date and nature of the reclassification were noted on these cards. When an employee terminated, his card was transferred to another file.

In support of the hours worked during the test period, the auditor found timecards on file for all employees, showing time of arrival and departure each day. Mr. Cardiff stated that he personally observed the punching in and out of employees and had custody of the timecards.

Mr. Cardiff produced for inspection by the auditor an envelope containing $27 in cash, which he stated to be the pay due a former employee who had left in the middle of November without claiming the fraction of a week's pay due him.

The auditor's examination of the payroll register, employment rate cards, and checks for the total payroll during the two periods selected for testing revealed no discrepancies. A comparison of the payroll during the year under audit with the payroll for the two preceding years on a month-to-month basis indicated no significant variation. The auditor also compared the number of employees in each job classification with the number employed in such jobs in the two preceding years and compared the rates of pay for various jobs during the three-year period. He noted that the output of the company during these three years had been fairly stable. Inquiries made of officers substantiated this lack of trend and evoked the observation that profits were down slightly.

Officers and supervisory employees of the company were paid by check on a monthly basis. The auditor traced these payments to salary authorizations in the minutes of directors' meetings and found no exceptions. Although his tests had served to substantiate the accuracy of the payroll records, the auditor felt somewhat concerned over the lack of internal control caused by the delegation of so much responsibility to Mr. Cardiff. Consequently, the auditor decided to extend his work by being present to observe employees punching in and out of the plant on the time clock, and by observing (on a surprise basis) the distribution of pay envelopes by Mr. Cardiff to the employees.

The auditor's observation of employees arriving at and leaving the plant disclosed no improper use of timecards. When the auditor appeared without warning on payday and informed Mr. Cardiff that he wished to observe the distribution of pay envelopes, Mr. Cardiff expressed some impatience with this step. Mr. Cardiff explained that he had a very busy day in prospect and proposed to distribute pay envelopes at intervals during the day as his other duties took him to various parts of the plant. The auditor insisted on carrying out this observation of the payoff and accompanied Mr. Cardiff until the last pay envelope had been delivered, although this process was interrupted a good many times while Mr. Cardiff attended to other matters. Mr. Cardiff knew all of the 400 employees personally and did not require any identification from them. The auditor inquired if the employees were required to carry identification badges, but was informed that this practice had been abandoned because the plant was small enough that Mr. Cardiff knew each employee. Furthermore, when badges had been required in prior years, employees frequently came to work without them. When an employee reported for work without a badge, he was refused admission to the plant, but this practice led to so much lost time and employee resentment that the company had discontinued the use of badges. Mr. Cardiff added that since the use of badges had been discontinued, each employee was required to sign a receipt for his pay.

Since his surprise observation of the payoff and his other verification procedures had revealed no irregularities, the auditor concluded that the payroll records were dependable, despite the concentration of duties in the hands of Mr. Cardiff. Other phases of the audit were completed satisfactorily, and an unqualified audit report was issued by the auditor.

Several months later, sudden illness of Richard Cardiff caused an officer of the company to take over the payroll work temporarily. The officer discovered that 10 fictitious names were on the payroll and had been on the payroll continuously for three years, with a consequent loss to the company of approximately $150,000. The company sought to recover a part of its losses from the auditor on the grounds that he must have been guilty of gross negligence not to have discovered that approximately 2½ percent of the payroll was entirely fictitious. The auditor attempted to defend himself against the charges by emphasizing his surprise observation of the payoff, which he stated was evidence of his having gone beyond normal auditing procedures in recognition of the weakness in internal control. The auditor contended that a "padded payroll" could not have avoided detection by this test, but Mr. Cardiff explained that during the payday in question, when accompanied by the auditor, he had delivered five extra pay envelopes to one employee and five more to another, both employees being good friends of his and willing to "help him out of a tight spot."

The pay envelopes delivered to these employees had been presented to them at various hours during the day at various locations in the plant, and the auditor had apparently not remembered having seen the employees previously.

Required:

a) Did the examination conform to generally accepted auditing standards? Explain.

b) Discuss the purpose and effectiveness of the auditor's observation of the distribution of pay to employees.

c) Do you believe the Timber Products Corporation had a valid claim against the auditor? Explain.

d) Would this payroll fraud have been prevented if the company had paid its employees by check rather than in cash? Explain.

21

Financial statements and
audit reports

THE REPORTING phase of an auditing engagement begins when the independent auditor has completed his field work and his proposed adjustments have been accepted and recorded by the client. Before writing his report, the auditor must review the client-prepared financial statements for form and content, or draft the statements himself on behalf of the client.

FINANCIAL STATEMENTS

The financial statements on which the independent auditor customarily reports are the balance sheet, the income statement, the statement of retained earnings, and the statement of changes in financial position. Often, the statement of retained earnings is combined with the income statement. In some cases the retained earnings statement may be expanded to a statement of stockholders' equity. Financial statements are generally presented in comparative form for the current year and the preceding year, and are accompanied by explanatory footnotes. The financial statements for a parent corporation are usually consolidated with those of the subsidiaries.

Preceding chapters have commented in detail on the financial statement presentation of specific items. Accordingly, the discussion of financial statements in this chapter will be confined to the more general aspects.

709

Working papers supporting financial statements

Working balance sheet and working income statement. The auditor who utilizes grouping sheets instead of a working trial balance will include in his working papers a working balance sheet and working income statement. These two working papers summarize the various grouping sheets, and also include those individual ledger accounts which are presented as separate captions in the financial statements. The dollar amounts in a working balance sheet and working income statement

FIGURE 21–1

Proctis Company, Inc.
Working Balance Sheet   C-1
December 31, 1974

Working Paper Refer.	Acct No.	Caption	Final 12/31/73	Per Books 12/31/74	Adjustments Dr.(Cr.)	Adjusted 12/31/74	Reclassification Dr.(Cr.)	Final 12/31/74
		Assets						
		Current Assets						
E		Cash	481 413	742 186		742 186		742 186
F-1	111	Marketable Securities	—	149 413		149 413		149 413
G		Accounts Rec.–Net	2 298 722	2 053 918	(91 096)	1 962 822		1 962 822
H		Inventories	2 701 814	2 942 117	(129 799)	2 812 318		2 812 318
J-2		Prepaid Expenses	118 322	125 829		125 829		125 829
		Total	5 600 271	6 013 463		5 792 568		5 792 568
K		Property & Equip.–Net	2 982 431	2 997 433	32 766	3 030 199		3 030 199
			8 582 702	9 010 896	(188 129)	8 822 767		8 822 767
		Liabilities & Equity						
		Current Liabilities:						
M-4	201	Notes Payable	500 000	450 000		450 000		450 000
M-1		Accounts Payable	1 651 126	1 585 839	(76 585)	1 662 424		1 662 424
M-2	221	Income Taxes Payable	127 000	323 000	⑤ 132 000	191 000		191 000
M-3		Other Accrued Liab.	321 418	385 014		385 014		385 014
		Total	2 599 544	2 743 853		2 688 438		2 688 438
N		Long-Term Liabilities	2 000 000	1 960 000		1 960 000		1 960 000
P		Stockholders' Equity	3 983 158	4 307 043	132 714	4 174 329		4 174 329
			8 582 702	9 010 896	188 129	8 822 767		8 822 767

V.M.H.
2/24/75

should agree with the client-prepared financial statements, or with the statements drafted by the auditor on the client's behalf.

A working balance sheet and working income statement for Process Company, Inc. are illustrated in Figures 21–1 and 21–2. Notice particularly the following features of these illustrations:

1. Account numbers are included for individual general ledger accounts presented as separate financial statement captions (Notes Payable, for example, is Account 201).

FIGURE 21–2

Process Company, Inc.
Working Income Statement   C-2
Year Ended December 31, 1974

Working Paper Acct. Refs.	No.	Caption	Final 12/31/73	Per Books 12/31/74	Adjustments Dr. (Cr.)	Adjusted 12/31/74	Reclassifications Dr. (Cr.)	Final 12/31/74
Q	700	Net Sales	21 422 719	23 814 882		23 814 882		23 814 882
		Costs and Expenses:						
R-1		Cost of Sales	19 344 703	20 941 887	232 296	21 174 183		21 174 183
R-2		Selling, General and Administrative Exp.	1 713 878	2 124 810	32 418	2 157 228		2 157 228
R-4	582	Interest	110 200	101 300		101 300		101 300
M-2	601	Income Taxes	127 000	323 000	⑤(132 000)	191 000		191 000
			21 295 801	23 490 997	132 714	23 623 711		23 623 711
P		Net Income	126 918	323 885	132 714	191 171		191 171

V.M.H.
2/24/75

2. All captions are cross-referenced to supporting grouping sheets, schedules, or analyses.
3. The only individual adjusting journal entry posted to the working statements is number 8, which affects individual accounts listed in the working statements. Totals of all other adjustments are carried forward from the applicable grouping sheets.

Consolidating working papers.   The audit working papers for a client which issues consolidated financial statements should include a consolidating balance sheet and consolidating statement of income and retained earnings, as well as a summary of consolidating adjustments and eliminations. These working papers may be prepared by the client or by the auditor. If prepared by the client, the working papers must of course be thoroughly verified.

A textbook devoted to the principles of auditing cannot explore the many complex problems associated with consolidations. However, the auditor must be familiar with the proper handling of these problems in order to judge the propriety of the client's consolidation techniques, or to complete the consolidation himself. An important aspect of consolidating working papers is that separate *financial statements* are combined, rather than *trial balances* as often illustrated in advanced accounting textbooks.

Balance sheet

The comparative balance sheets presented in most audit reports are in *account* form, with assets on the left and liabilities and stockholders' equity on the right. Assets and liabilities are classified into current and noncurrent categories. Occasionally, the *financial position* form of balance sheet is used. This form shows current assets minus current liabilities, plus other assets, minus other liabilities, and thereby reaches a residual amount equal to stockholders' equity.

A minimum of detail is included in most audit report balance sheets. Footnotes are utilized to achieve adequate informative disclosure when more detail is required.

Income statement

The income statement, like the balance sheet, is preferably prepared in comparative form to show changes from the preceding year. Both the single-step form of statement and the multiple-step statement are widely used, although the latter has been declining in popularity. The single-step statement in which all costs and expenses are totaled and subtracted from the total of all revenue affords a concise and understandable picture to the general public. For the professional analyst the multiple-step statement with expenses separated by major functions of the business may be preferable. In both forms of statements it is imperative that any extraordinary gains or losses of material amount be shown separately, so that the reader can observe the year-to-year trend of income from operations. In addition, earnings per share should be presented in the income statement.

Statement of retained earnings

The statement of retained earnings is frequently combined with the statement of income. In the absence of prior period adjustments and creation or elimination of reserves, a comparative statement of retained earnings should include only beginning balances, net income or loss for the periods, dividends declared, and ending balances.

If substantial changes in contributed capital have occurred during a given year, the statement of retained earnings may be expanded to a statement of stockholders' equity. This statement, usually presented for the current year only, shows beginning balances, additions, deductions, and ending balances for capital stock and all other components of the stockholders' equity.

Statement of changes in financial position

A statement of changes in financial position is a basic financial statement, along with the balance sheet and statement of income and retained earnings. The statement should disclose all important aspects of the reporting company's financing and investing activities, regardless of whether cash or other working capital components are affected.

Notes to financial statements

As indicated previously, notes to financial statements are utilized to achieve adequate disclosure when information in the financial statements is insufficient to attain this objective. Although the notes, like the financial statements themselves, are representations of the client, the auditor generally assists in drafting the notes. The writing of notes to financial statements is a challenging task because complex issues must be summarized in a clear and concise manner.

Among the many items requiring footnote disclosure are the following:

1. Significant accounting policies.
2. Business combinations consummated during the period.
3. Pledged assets and related liabilities.

4. Investments in common stock (other than marketable securities).
5. Long-term liabilities, including imputed interest, if any.
6. Contingent assets and liabilities.
7. Commitments.
8. Restrictions on retained earnings.
9. Changes in contributed capital (if not presented in a separate statement of changes in stockholders' equity).
10. Liquidation value of preferred stock.
11. Cumulative preferred dividends in arrears.
12. Substantial differences between book and taxable income.
13. Basis for computing earnings per share.
14. Subsequent events.

The first footnote listed above was recommended by the Accounting Principles Board in *Opinion No. 22,* "Disclosure of Accounting Policies." A "Summary of Significant Accounting Policies" note should now include information on accounting principles and their application which in the past was customarily scattered throughout a number of footnotes. Among the accounting policies which may be included in the first footnote (or separately, preceding notes to the financial statements) are the following:

1. Nature of, justification for, and effect of a change in accounting principle.
2. Effect of change in accounting estimate.
3. Nature of, reasons for, and effect of change in reporting entity.
4. Principles of consolidation.
5. Basis of valuation and amortization of assets.
6. Translation of foreign currencies.
7. Recognition of revenue from leasing and franchising operations.
8. Recognition of profit on long-term construction-type contracts.

In drafting or revising proposed notes to financial statements, the auditor should consider two important guidelines. First, notes should not be utilized to *correct* improper financial statement presentations. Second, notes should be worded to *inform,* not *confuse,* the reader of the financial statements. A great deal of rewriting, editing, and polishing is required to finalize notes which are in accord with these guidelines.

AUDIT REPORTS

The expressing of an independent and expert opinion on the fairness of financial statements is the most important and valuable service rendered by the public accounting profession. This independent opinion may be expressed through either a short-form or long-form report, or both types of reports may be issued for a single audit engagement. The short-form report, consisting of a concise description of the scope of the examination and a statement of the auditor's opinion on the financial statements, was illustrated and discussed in Chapter 1. The long-form report, although popular for many years, is seldom issued today. Long-form reports, with their extensive supplementary details, are very expensive to draft and process. In addition, the supplementary details are available in the client's internal records; therefore, the long-form report, unless required by a bank or other outsider, is often considered nonessential and not the most efficient utilization of the auditor's time.

In this chapter we shall first restate and develop further some of the most important ideas concerning the short-form report, and then turn our attention briefly to long-form audit reports and reports to the SEC. In addition to audit reports on financial statements, we shall consider the use of special reports to clients, in which the customary wording of the standard short-form report does not apply.

The standard short-form audit report

For convenient reference the standard short-form of audit report which was introduced and discussed in Chapter 1 is presented again:

We have examined the balance sheet of XYZ Company as of December 31, 19__ and the related statements of income and retained earnings and changes in financial position for the year then ended. Our examination was made in accordance with generally accepted auditing standards, and accordingly included such tests of the accounting records and such other auditing procedures as we considered necessary in the circumstances.

In our opinion, the aforementioned financial statements present fairly the financial position of XYZ Company at December 31, 19__, and the results of its operations and the changes in its financial position for the year then ended, in conformity with generally accepted accounting principles applied on a basis consistent with that of the preceding year.

Discontinuance of the term "audit certificate"

In the early days of public accounting, the auditor's report was called a certificate. The choice of this term was unfortunate to some extent, because to many people the word "certificate" conveyed the idea that the auditor was issuing a guarantee of absolute correctness of the financial statements. The auditor is in no position to guarantee the "correctness" of financial statements for several reasons. In the first place, his audit does not include a detailed verification of all transactions or even an inspection of all assets owned. The auditor reaches his conclusion about financial statements through evaluation of the system of internal control and the making of a limited number of tests of the accounts.

Secondly, there are so many alternative accounting methods (as in the valuation of inventory) falling within the concept of "generally accepted accounting principles" that no one set of statement data may be considered as the only "correct" presentation. Finally, financial statements always contain many estimates or approximations (as for depreciation rates and for the collectibility of receivables) which are incompatible with the idea of absolute precision and truth in reporting on financial position and operating results.

The nature of the accounting process and of auditing standards are such that the auditor may reasonably express an opinion as to the overall fairness of the financial statements, but he cannot issue a "certificate" or "guarantee" of correctness. The term "certificate" has therefore been largely replaced by such terms as auditor's report, auditor's opinion, accountant's report, report of independent public accountants and short-form report. Once a technical term has gained widespread use, however, it is not easily eradicated, and one still finds the term "certificate" used to a considerable extent both in auditing literature and discussions with clients.

Some attorneys prefer that the audit report be entitled a "certificate" because the Securities Act of 1933 and some SEC regulations refer to the "certificate" of the independent public accountant. However, in practice, the SEC accepts audit reports with titles of "opinion" and "report" as well as that of "certificate." In fact, the SEC's recent amendments of *Regulation S—X*, issued in 1972, omit any reference to "audit certificate."

Restatement of basic points concerning the short-form report

Among the major points made in Chapter 1 concerning the standard short-form report were the following:

1. The financial statements (including notes thereto) are the statements of the client, not of the auditor. The auditor's product is his report, in which he expresses his opinion about the client's financial statements.
2. The statement in the audit report that an examination has been made in accordance with "generally accepted auditing standards" refers to an official statement of standards adopted by the membership of the American Institute of Certified Public Accountants. This official set of standards includes general standards (such as independence), standards of field work (such as the gathering of sufficient evidence), and standards of reporting. In this chapter we are particularly concerned with standards of reporting. Four standards of reporting have been enunciated by the AICPA and deserve careful attention. These four standards require:

a) A clear statement as to whether the financial statements are prepared in accordance with generally accepted principles of accounting.

b) A statement as to the consistency with which accounting principles have been applied in the current and preceding periods.

c) Adequate disclosure in the financial statements (or notes thereto).

d) Clear indication of the character of the examination and the degree of responsibility assumed by the auditor. This fourth standard of reporting has not always been easy to enforce; it will be discussed at more length later in this chapter.

3. The auditor's opinion indicates whether the financial statements "present fairly. . . ." The quality of "fairness" in financial statements means freedom from bias and adequate informative disclosure of material facts.

4. The auditor's opinion that the financial statements were prepared in conformity with "generally accepted accounting principles applied on a basis consistent with that of the preceding year" gives assurance to bankers, stockholders, and other interested persons that these statements may reasonably be compared with the company's statements in prior years, and with statements of other companies in the industry. The banker or stockholder is thereby enabled to weigh the merits of one company against another.

No official list of "generally accepted accounting principles" exists, but as pointed out in Chapter 1, the Accounting Principles Board's *Basic Concepts and Accounting Principles Underlying Financial Statements of Business Enterprises* has contributed a great deal to the understanding of the composition of accounting principles. The Financial Accounting Standards Board, as successor to the Accounting Principles Board, may be expected to continue the development of uniform standards and practices on major accounting questions.

Reporting on audits of sole proprietorships

One of the AICPA standards of reporting states that "informative disclosures in the financial statements are to be regarded as reasonably adequate unless otherwise stated in the report." Let us apply this standard to the problem of income taxes payable by the owners of unincorporated businesses. Income taxes on the profits of sole proprietorships and partnerships are payable by the owners as individuals, and are usually not shown in the financial statements of the business. In many cases, however, the proprietor or partner will withdraw cash from the business when the time arrives to pay the tax liability.

To insure that the reader of an audit report on a sole proprietorship or partnership does not overlook the probability that business funds will be withdrawn to make payment of the owner's income taxes, the notes to financial statements or the audit report may appropriately include a comment that the financial statements do not reflect any provision for income taxes, but that the income is taxable to the proprietors.

Another problem peculiar to reporting on a sole proprietorship arises when the owner has other business interests in addition to the concern being audited. To meet standards of adequate disclosure the auditor should clearly identify the business entity on which he is reporting and point out that the financial statements pertain to that entity alone, and do not portray other resources or liabilities of the proprietor.

The scope paragraph of the standard short-form audit report might be modified as follows to fit the needs of a sole proprietorship:

We have examined the balance sheet of William Kerr & Company (a sole proprietorship) as of December 31, 19___ and the related statements of income and proprietor's capital and changes in financial position for the year then ended. The financial statements are for the business entity known as William Kerr & Company and reflect the assets, liabilities, proprietor's capital, revenue and expenses recorded in the books of account maintained at 2311 West Third Avenue, Long Beach, California. Our examination was made in accordance with generally accepted auditing standards, and accordingly included such tests of the accounting records and such other auditing procedures as we considered necessary in the circumstances.

Reporting on audits of personal financial statements

Financial statements for individuals have been audited and made public by a number of political candidates in recent years. Personal financial statements are also often required for credit applications and for income tax and estate tax planning. To provide guidelines for such statements, the AICPA has issued an Industry Audit Guide entitled *Audits of Personal Financial Statements.* The Guide states that the basic financial statements for individuals or families—the statement of assets and liabilities and the statement of changes in net assets—should utilize dual money columns, one for *cost* and the other for *estimated value.* The statements should reflect the accrual basis of accounting, including income tax allocation for differences between cost and tax bases, and provision in the "estimated value" column for accrued income taxes on unrealized appreciation of assets.

An unqualified audit report for personal financial statements includes the two paragraphs of the standard short-form report, expressing an opinion only on the *cost* column amounts in the financial statements. In a third paragraph, the auditor asserts that he has determined that the *estimated value* column amounts are presented on the bases described in the statements or footnotes. He does not express an opinion on the amounts shown as estimated values.

Expression of an opinion by the CPA

The principal alternatives in reporting may be summed up as follows:

1. An unqualified opinion.
2. A qualified opinion.
3. An adverse opinion.
4. A disclaimer of opinion.

These alternatives are based on the fourth standard of reporting adopted by the membership of the AICPA, which reads as follows:

The report shall either contain an expression of opinion regarding the financial statements, taken as a whole, or an assertion to the effect that an opinion cannot be expressed. When an over-all opinion cannot be expressed, the reasons therefore should be stated. In all cases where an auditor's name is associated with financial statements the report should contain a clear-cut indication of the character of the auditor's examination, if any, and the degree of responsibility he is taking.

This standard does not prevent the CPA from expressing separate opinions on the balance sheet and the income statement. For example, he may express an unqualified opinion on the balance sheet and disclaim an opinion or express a qualified or adverse opinion on the income statement.

Unqualified opinion

The unqualified opinion (illustrated on page 715) is, of course, the most desirable opinion from the client's point of view. The auditor expresses an unqualified opinion on the client's financial statements when there has been no unresolvable restriction on the scope of his examination and he has no significant exceptions as to the accounting principles reflected in the financial statements, the consistency of their application, and the adequacy of informative disclosures in the financial statements.

A modification of the conventional unqualified opinion is sometimes appropriate when the principal auditor shares responsibility for an engagement with another CPA firm. The two courses of action open to the principal auditor in this situation are described as follows in *Statement on Auditing Procedure No. 45*, "Using the Work and Reports of Other Auditors":

If the principal auditor decides to assume responsibility for the work of the other auditor insofar as that work relates to the principal auditor's expression of an opinion on the financial statements taken as a whole, no reference should be made to the other auditor's examination. On the other hand, if the principal auditor decides not to assume that responsibility, his report should make reference to the examination of the other auditor and should indicate clearly the division of responsibility between himself and the other auditor in expressing his opinion on the financial statements.

For example, if the principal auditor engages the services of another CPA whose professional reputation and independence are satisfactory, the principal auditor usually pays the fee of the second auditor and assumes full responsibility for the work done. It is unnecessary for the principal auditor to mention in the audit report that he utilized the services of an agent. In some cases, however, the client may act directly to retain a second reputable firm of auditors to examine the records of a distant branch; in these circumstances the auditors examining the home office might not accept responsibility for the work of the other auditors and may consequently disclose in the scope paragraph the use of other public accountants for the examination of the branch. An unqualified opinion may be issued if neither auditor had any significant exceptions; however, the report should be worded to show the joint responsibility for the opinion, as in the following illustration:

We have examined the consolidated balance sheet of XYZ Company and subsidiaries as of December 31, 19___ and the related consolidated statements of income and retained earnings and changes in financial position for the year then ended. Our examination was made in accordance with generally accepted auditing standards, and accordingly included such tests of the accounting records and such other auditing procedures as we considered necessary in the circumstances. We did not examine the financial statements of ABC Company, a consolidated subsidiary, which statements reflect total assets and revenue constituting 20 percent and 22 percent, respectively, of the related consolidated totals. These statements were examined by other auditors whose report thereon has been furnished to us and our opinion expressed herein, insofar as it relates to the amounts included for ABC Company, is based solely upon the report of the other auditors.

In our opinion, based on our examination and the report of other auditors, the aforementioned consolidated financial statements present fairly the financial position of XYZ Company and subsidiaries at December 31, 19___, and the results of their operations and the changes in their financial position for the year then ended, in conformity with generally accepted accounting principles applied on a basis consistent with that of the preceding year.

Conditions preventing issuance of an unqualified opinion

The auditor is not always able to give the "clean bill of health" indicated by the model report on page 715. Among the reasons which may prevent the issuance of an unqualified opinion are the following:

1. The examination may not have been made in accordance with generally accepted auditing standards.

   a) The CPA may not be independent with respect to a company for which he has prepared unaudited financial statements. For example, a company's controller, although perhaps a licensed CPA, is not independent with respect to that company.

   b) Internal control may be so seriously inadequate that a satisfactory examination cannot be performed within reasonable time limits.

   c) The financial statements may have been prepared from the books without audit. The independent public accountant is sometimes requested to prepare financial statements for internal use or for presentation to a bank without making any effort at verification. A slight variation is found when the auditor is authorized to make only a limited examination of specified accounts such as cash.

   d) The client may place restrictions on the scope of the auditor's examination, as for example, not permitting the confirmation of accounts receivable, not taking a physical inventory, which the auditor must observe, or not permitting the auditor to visit a distant branch location where an important portion of the company's assets are located.

   e) For reasons beyond the control of the client or the auditor, it may not have been possible to perform certain necessary auditing procedures. In a first audit if inventory records and internal controls are very poor, there may be no way to verify the beginning inventory; consequently, the cost of sales and net income for the year cannot be satisfactorily verified. Another example is that of the company whose records have been partially destroyed by fire or flood. Substantial uncertainty with respect to the outcome of a pending lawsuit may prevent the auditor from obtaining satisfactory evidence as to the contingent liability status of the lawsuit.

2. The financial statements may not have been prepared in accordance with generally accepted accounting principles. When the auditor finds that assets have been improperly valued, that liabilities have been omitted, or that other violations of generally accepted accounting principles exist, his first reaction will be to attempt to persuade management to revise the statements. In most cases management will agree, and the deficiencies will be remedied; occasionally, however, management will not agree to the changes considered necessary by the auditor, and consequently an unqualified opinion cannot be issued.

3. Accounting principles may not have been applied consistently as

compared with the preceding year. An unqualified audit report cannot be issued if the company has changed its method of inventory valuation, if it has adopted a new method of computing depreciation, or has made other material changes in accounting principle as compared with the preceding year.

4. The financial statements may not present fairly the client's financial position and operating results. Fairness in financial statements often hinges on the issue of what constitutes adequate informative disclosure. Assume, for example, that pending legislation indicated that a certain type of business, such as the operation of a race track, may soon be outlawed. Disclosure of this threat to continued existence of the business is essential to a fair presentation. A similar contingency requiring disclosure is the existence of claims in the process of litigation.

Qualified opinion

A qualified opinion is a modification of the unqualified opinion stating that *"except for"* the effects of some limitation on the scope of the examination or some unsatisfactory financial statement presentation, the financial statements are fairly presented. If a scope limitation resulted from the inability of the auditor to resolve some uncertainty, the words *"subject to"* are included in the opinion paragraph.

The materiality of the exception governs the use of the qualified opinion. The exception must be sufficiently significant to warrant mentioning in the auditor's report, but it must not be so significant as to necessitate a disclaimer of opinion or an adverse opinion. In consequence, the propriety of a qualified opinion in the event of a significant exception is a matter for careful professional judgment by the auditor.

For example, if the company being audited is contesting deficiencies in income taxes proposed by the Internal Revenue Service for prior years, it may be impossible for the auditor to determine the extent of the company's liability, if any. The following report illustrating this situation clearly indicates the nature of the qualification!

We have examined the balance sheet of XYZ Company as of June 30, 19__ and the related statements of income and retained earnings and changes in financial position for the year then ended. Our examination was made in accordance with generally accepted auditing standards, and accordingly included such tests of the accounting records and such other auditing procedures as we considered necessary in the circumstances. We could not satisfy ourselves as to the amount, if any, of the Company's income tax liability for prior years, described in Note 6 to the financial statements.

In our opinion, subject to any adjustments which may result from the final determination of the Company's income tax liability for prior years as indicated in Note 6 to the financial statements, the aforementioned financial statements present fairly the financial position of XYZ Company at June 30, 19___, and the results of its operations and the changes in its financial position for the year then ended, in conformity with generally accepted accounting principles applied on a basis consistent with that of the preceding year.

Even though the scope of the examination has not been limited by the client, the auditor sometimes must qualify his opinion because he does not agree with the accounting principles used in preparing the statements. In most cases when the auditor's objections are carefully explained, the client will agree to change the statements in an acceptable manner. If the client does not agree to make the suggested changes, the auditor will be forced to qualify his opinion, or if the exception is sufficiently material, to issue an adverse opinion. As an example of a qualified opinion, the following paragraphs might be inserted following the usual scope paragraph:

In view of the age of certain large accounts receivable, it is our opinion that the allowance for uncollectible accounts should be substantially larger than has been provided by management.

In our opinion, except for the valuation of accounts receivable and the related effect upon net income, the aforementioned financial statements present fairly the financial position of XYZ Company at December 31, 19___, and the results of its operations and the changes in its financial position for the year then ended, in conformity with generally accepted accounting principles applied on a basis consistent with that of the preceding year.

A qualified opinion must also be issued by the auditor if the client fails to provide a statement of changes in financial position to accompany a balance sheet and statement of income and retained earnings. In this case, the qualification is necessitated by inadequate disclosure.

Consistency qualifications. If a company makes a change in accounting principle (including a change in the reporting entity), the nature of, justification for, and effect of the change is reported in a note to the financial statements for the period in which the change was made. Any such change having a material effect upon the financial statements will also require qualification of the auditor's opinion even though he is in full agreement with the change. An example follows:

In our opinion, the aforementioned financial statements present fairly the financial position of XYZ Company at December 31, 19___, and the results of its operations and the changes in its financial position for the year then ended, in conformity with generally accepted accounting principles which, except for the change (with which we concur) in the method of valuing raw materials described in Note 1, to the financial statements, have been applied on a basis consistent with that of the preceding year.

In the preceding example, Note 1 would describe fully the nature of and justification for the change in method of valuation of raw materials, and the related effect upon net income. If the auditor did not concur with any aspects of the change or its disclosure, he would qualify his opinion or issue an adverse opinion, as appropriate.

A change in accounting estimate, such as the estimated useful life of a patent, and a changed condition unrelated to accounting, such as the sale of a plant, do not require a consistency qualification by the auditor if they are properly disclosed in notes to the financial statements. However, if financial statements of the prior year are not restated to reflect a pooling of interests effected during the current year, and the prior year statements are presented for comparative purposes, the auditor must take exception to the inconsistency of the comparative statements.

If the auditor is reporting on the financial statements for the first accounting period of a newly organized company, no previous accounting period exists. Accordingly, the auditor should not refer to consistency, unless there had been a change in accounting principle during the first accounting period which had not been retroactively applied for the entire period.

"Explained opinions."   Some audit reports have been issued containing a qualification worded in such a cautious manner that it could be interpreted as no qualification at all. Typically the opinion paragraph following an ambiguous qualification might contain the expression "with the foregoing explanation as to inventories, the accompanying financial statements present fairly. . . ." Such indecisive or contradictory audit reports are not satisfactory. The acceptable alternatives in such cases are to issue an unqualified opinion, or a qualified opinion which incorporates the words *"except for"* or *"subject to."*

Adverse opinion

An adverse opinion is the opposite of an unqualified opinion; it is an opinion that the financial statements *do not* present fairly the financial position, results of operations, and changes in financial position of the client, in conformity with generally accepted accounting principles. When the CPA expresses an adverse opinion, he must have no unresolved scope qualifications; he must have accumulated sufficient evidence to support his unfavorable opinion.

The CPA should express an adverse opinion if the statements are so lacking in fairness that a qualified opinion would not be warning enough. If the CPA knows the statements to be an unfair presentation, he cannot properly disclaim an opinion. Whenever he issues an adverse opinion (probably a rare occurrence), he should disclose his reasons in a middle paragraph of the audit report.

Adverse opinions are rare, because most clients follow the recommendations of the independent auditor with respect to fair presentation in financial statements. An important source of adverse opinions is the actions of regulatory agencies which prescribe practices not in accordance with generally accepted accounting principles. Consider, for example, a savings and loan association which is prohibited by state law from accruing earned but uncollected loan interest in its balance sheet and statement of income. In view of the materiality of accrued interest, the audit report would probably contain the following paragraphs in addition to the standard scope paragraph:

In accordance with regulations of the state savings and loan commission, the financial statements do not include accrued interest on loans approximating $450,000 at December 31, 19___. The effect of this omission, which in our opinion is not in accordance with generally accepted accounting principles, is to understate total assets at December 31, 19___ by approximately $450,000 and to understate net income for the year then ended by approximately $200,000.

In view of the materiality of the amounts described in the preceding paragraph, in our opinion the aforementioned financial statements do not present fairly the financial position of XYZ Savings and Loan Association at December 31, 19___, and the results of its operations and the changes in its financial position for the year then ended, in conformity with generally accepted accounting principles.

Disclaimer of opinion

A disclaimer of opinion is no opinion. A disclaimer is required when substantial restrictions upon the scope of the auditor's examination or other conditions preclude his compliance with generally accepted auditing standards. Examples of such restrictions or conditions follow.

Auditor not independent. A CPA who is not independent in fact or in appearance with respect to a company cannot comply with the generally accepted auditing standard requiring an independence in mental attitude in all matters relating to the assignment. In such circumstances, the CPA must disclaim an opinion. The AICPA's Committee on Auditing Procedure has suggested the following language for the independence disclaimer:

We are not independent with respect to XYZ Company, and the accompanying balance sheet as of December 31, 19___ and the related statements of income and retained earnings and changes in financial position for the year then ended were not audited by us; accordingly, we do not express an opinion on them.

Unaudited financial statements. Certified public accountants often draft financial statements for clients without performing an examination of the statements in accordance with generally accepted auditing standards. Two common examples are financial statements prepared as an adjunct to "write-up" work for small clients and interim financial statements drafted for fiscal-year audit clients.

The AICPA's Committee on Auditing Procedure, in *Statement on Auditing Procedure No. 38*, considered the problem of unaudited financial statements prepared by a CPA. The Committee's conclusions included the following:

1. The CPA has no responsibility to apply any auditing procedures to unaudited financial statements.
2. A disclaimer of opinion should accompany unaudited financial statements prepared by a CPA, and each page of the financial statements should be clearly marked as *"unaudited."* Suggested wording for the disclaimer is as follows:

    The accompanying balance sheet of XYZ Company as of December 31, 19__ and the related statements of income and retained earnings and changes in financial position for the year then ended were not audited by us and accordingly we do not express an opinion on them.

3. Financial statements drafted for a client's internal use may not include all notes or other disclosures necessary for adequate informative disclosure. In such cases, the CPA's disclaimer should include this fact.
4. If a CPA knows that unaudited financial statements intended to be distributed to external users are not in accordance with generally accepted accounting principles or do not contain adequate informative disclosures, he should insist upon appropriate revision or should state his reservations in his disclaimer of opinion. If necessary, he should withdraw from the engagement.

Restrictions imposed by client. In many engagements, the client will impose restrictions limiting the auditor's compliance with generally accepted auditing standards. A common example is the prohibition of inventory observation. Since inventories are usually an important factor in determining both financial position and operating results, the auditor (if prohibited by the client from observing the physical inventory) must qualify the scope paragraph of his report. Generally failure to observe the physical inventory will represent such a material shortcoming in the scope of the examination that the auditor will not be able to express an opinion on the fairness of the statements taken as a whole. The audit report under these circumstances should include a disclaimer of opinion along the following lines:

We have examined the balance sheet of XYZ Company as of December 31, 19___ and the related statements of income and retained earnings and changes in financial position for the year then ended. Our examination was made in accordance with generally accepted auditing standards, and accordingly included such tests of the accounting records and such other auditing procedures as we considered necessary in the circumstances, except as noted in the following paragraph.

In accordance with your instructions we did not observe the taking of the physical inventory at December 31, 19___. Accordingly, we do not express any opinion concerning the inventory stated at $23,418,221 in the accompanying balance sheet.

Because the inventory at December 31, 19___ enters materially into the determination of financial position and results of operations, we do not express an opinion on the aforementioned financial statements taken as a whole.

Failure to visit branches. Many companies maintain sales offices or other types of branches or divisions in locations far removed from the home office. The question then arises as to whether an examination "in accordance with generally accepted auditing standards" will require that the auditor visit the branch office. In other words, must the auditor qualify his report if the client is not willing to bear the expense necessary for the auditor to visit a distant branch office?

An answer to this question hinges on the relative importance of the operations carried on at the branch and the proportion of the company's assets which are located at the branch. Assume, for example, that a Chicago company maintains a Denver sales office. All of the accounting records are kept at the home office in Chicago. Sales orders obtained by employees in Denver are sent to Chicago; the merchandise is shipped to the customer from the Chicago plant; the billing is prepared at the Chicago office; and the account receivable record is maintained there. The only assets located in the Denver office are some office equipment and a petty cash fund. Under these circumstances there is no reason for the auditor to visit the Denver sales office. After completing an examination at the home office in Chicago he may issue an unqualified report.

To illustrate a different situation, let us assume that a Los Angeles company maintains a branch in Dallas. Approximately one quarter of the company's inventories are located in Dallas, and the Dallas office also bills its customers directly, maintains records of accounts receivable, and collects the receivables. Even though three quarters of the company's operations and resources are located in Los Angeles, it would be impossible for the auditor to make a satisfactory examination or to issue an unqualified report without visiting the Dallas branch to verify the inventories and receivables and otherwise review the internal control and records of that office. Examination of the records in Dallas by the company's internal auditing staff would not be an acceptable substitute for a visit by the independent CPA. However, it would be possible to retain the services of a Dallas firm of CPAs to do the necessary work at the branch and thereby conform with generally accepted auditing standards, as discussed on page 720.

In between the two examples cited, some difficult borderline cases could be encountered. No fixed percentages or other arbitrary rules can be used to determine how important a branch operation must be in order to require a visit by the auditor. In these situations as in other phases of an audit, the professional judgment of the CPA must be employed to reach a decision based on study of all the relevant circumstances. When the auditor is not authorized to visit a branch, the result may be a disclaimer of an opinion on the financial statements; in other cases, however, as previously illustrated, there may be no significant consequences and an unqualified report may be issued.

Major uncertainty affecting a client's business. If substantial uncertainty exists as to the outcome of an important matter affecting the client's financial statements, the auditor may not be able to accumulate sufficient competent evidential matter and hence must disclaim an opinion. For example, consider a business which is unable to meet all liabilities that are due. It is questionable whether such a client should be considered a going concern; the auditor may be forced to disclaim an opinion under these circumstances.

A report in which the auditor disclaims an opinion on the fairness of the financial statements is not likely to be of much use to the client. Consequently, the auditor should consider at the beginning of the engagement what obstacles may exist to his expression of an opinion and should reach an understanding with the client as to any special problem that may prevent the endorsement of the statements.

Piecemeal opinions

When the auditor finds himself forced to disclaim an opinion for reasons other than client-imposed restrictions, or to express an adverse opinion on the overall fairness of the financial statements, he may nevertheless be able to express a piecemeal opinion indicating the fairness of certain items in the statements. For example, let us assume that the auditor has completed an examination unlimited in scope and has found all accounts satisfactory except those relating to inventory, which is not properly valued. Because inventory is quite material and affects the income statement, balance sheet, and statement of changes in financial position, the auditor must express an adverse opinion on the statements as a whole. He can, however, also express a piecemeal opinion naming other accounts such as Cash, Accounts Receivable, and Plant an̲d̲ ̲E̲q̲u̲i̲p̲m̲e̲n̲t̲ ̲w̲h̲i̲c̲h̲ ̲a̲r̲e̲ ̲f̲a̲i̲r̲l̲y̲ ̲s̲t̲a̲t̲e̲d̲. Naming the accounts is preferable to such expressions as "all other accounts" because retained earnings, taxes payable, cost of sales, and other items may be unfairly stated because of their relationship to inventories. The piecemeal opinion should be carefully worded so that it clearly does not contradict or outweigh the adverse opinion or disclaimer of opinion on the fairness of the statements as a whole. In addition, the auditor must have accumulated sufficient competent evidence on the financial statement components covered by the piecemeal opinion to assure himself that they are fairly stated on an individual basis.

"Comfort" clause in audit report

"Comfort" clauses or statements of "negative assurance" have sometimes been included in audit reports to comfort or reassure a client when the auditor cannot express an unqualified opinion. For example:

Our examination did not include confirmation of accounts receivable or observation of physical inventory. Consequently, we do not express an opinion on the fairness of the financial statements as a whole. However, nothing came to our attention which would lead us to question the fairness of the amounts shown for receivables and inventories.

The purpose of such a statement is to soften the disclaimer of opinion and to avoid giving the impression of a blunt denial of responsibility by the auditor. Such statements are likely to be misleading; they encourage the reader to believe that the amounts shown for receivables and inventory are dependable. Furthermore, they are a violation of the AICPA reporting standards which include a requirement that "in all cases where the auditor's name is associated with financial statements the report should contain a clear-cut indication of the character of the auditor's examination, if any, and the degree of responsibility he is taking."

For the auditor to report that "nothing came to his attention" which would cause him to doubt the amounts shown for receivables or inventory creates confusion as to what responsibility, if any, the auditor is assuming. If he made no investigation of these items, then there was little opportunity for anything unfavorable to come to his attention. If he did perform audit work on these items, the procedures followed were inadequate to give him a basis for an opinion. The less work an auditor performs on an engagement, the more readily he might resort to a comfort statement. From any standpoint a comfort clause in an audit report appears to be contradictory to straightforward candid reporting. The use of a comfort clause in letters for underwriters is a separate issue considered later in this chapter.

Miscellaneous aspects of the short-form report

The short-form audit report is generally addressed to the board of directors of the client. If stockholders concur in the directors' appointment of the auditors, the report may be addressed jointly to directors and stockholders. The report is usually dated as of the day the audit field work was completed, regardless of the date the report is actually issued. The completion of audit field work in most cases also signifies the completion of all important audit procedures. However, if an event subsequent to the date of field work completion, but prior to issuance of the audit report, requires disclosure in a note to the audited financial statements, the auditor has two options for dating his report. He may use "dual dating" such as "Feburary 10, 19—, except for Note 7 as to which the date is February 22, 19—"; or he may date his report as of the later date. If the auditor chooses the second option, he should return to the client's premises and apply additional auditing procedures described in Chapter 7 up to the later date.

Comparative financial statements. If the short-form report applies to comparative financial statements for the current year and the prior year, the auditor should comment upon the prior year's statements in his report. If the statements of the prior year were unaudited, they should clearly and conspicuously be marked unaudited, and the auditor should insert in the scope paragraph of the report a disclaimer similar to the following:

We did not examine the financial statements for the prior year and accordingly do not express an opinion on them.

More frequently, the auditor has also examined and reported upon the prior year's statements. In this event, the scope paragraph should have the following added sentence:

We have previously made a similar examination of the financial statements for the prior year.

Any significant exceptions to the prior year's statements should be disclosed by the auditor in his current report.

Long-form reports

Long-form audit reports contain information to supplement and analyze the basic financial statements. Reporting standards require that the auditor indicated the responsibility he assumes with respect to the supplementary information. If the auditor has examined the information, he should express an opinion on its fairness; otherwise, he must disclaim an opinion.

An unqualified opinion on supplementary information is customarily expressed in a third paragraph following the two standard short-form report paragraphs, as follows:

The accompanying supplementary information has been subjected to the tests and other auditing procedures applied in the examination of the financial statements mentioned above and, in our opinion, is fairly stated in all respects material in relation to the financial statements taken as a whole.

Content of supplementary information. Supplementary information presented in a long-form report customarily includes many of the following:

1. Comparative summary of operations, stressing changes in dollar amounts and in percentage relationships.
2. Operating ratios.
3. Comparative summary of financial position and measurement of changes.
4. Details of selected balance sheet items such as receivables and inventories.
5. Supporting analyses of selling and administrative expenses and property and related depreciation accounts.

In addition, general price-level financial information may be included with supplementary information.

The inclusion of supplementary information in the long-form report should not be regarded as a satisfactory substitute for adequate informative disclosure in the basic financial statements. Furthermore, nothing in the supplementary information should contradict data in the financial statements or in the auditor's opinion.

Reports to the SEC

Many audit clients are subject to the financial reporting requirements of the federal laws administered by the SEC. Two principal laws, the Securities Act of 1933 and the Securities Exchange Act of 1934, provide for a multitude of reports requiring audited financial statements. The most important of these reports, or *forms,* are the following:

1. Forms S–1, S–7, or S–16. These forms are the "registration statements" for clients planning to issue securities to the public.
2. Form 10. This is the principal device for registering securities for trading on a national securities exchange.
3. Form 10–K. This report is filed annually with the SEC by companies subject to the periodic reporting provisions of the Securities Acts.

4. Proxy Statement. Companies planning to solicit proxies for the election of directors at shareholders' meetings are often required to submit audited financial statements in the proxy statements mailed to shareholders.
5. Form 8–K. This is a "current report" filed for any month in which significant events occur for a company subject to the Securities Acts. If the significant event is the acquisition of another business, audited financial statements of the acquired business are often required in the current report.

The preceding points represent only a brief summary of the complex reporting requirements of the SEC. The auditor dealing with these reports should be well versed in the requirements of each form, as well as in the provisions of the SEC's *Regulation S–X*, which governs the form and content of financial statements and supporting schedules required to be filed with the various forms.

Special reports

The standard short-form audit report which we have considered in some detail is appropriate when the auditor makes an examination of basic financial statements for a business concern operated for profit. These basic financial statements are designed to show financial position, results of operations, and changes in financial position. However, the independent CPA may also be retained to report on many other types of financial data. He may be engaged to verify the calculation of an insurance claim, a profit-sharing bonus, or the amount to be paid under an agreement for the purchase of a business. A borrowing agreement with banks or other creditors may require approval by an independent accountant of statements as to compliance with terms of the contract.

The special reports used by the CPA for engagements of these types do not require him to express an opinion as to whether the data under examination are in conformity with generally accepted accounting principles. He should indicate, however, whether the data present fairly what they purport to show.

To define a *special report* is difficult because of the variety of the situations and purposes served by such reports. One common characteristic of special reports is that the standard wording of the short-form report is not applicable. It is not applicable for several reasons: the absence of intent to present financial position and changes therein or operating results; the fact that some of the standards of reporting may not fit the engagement; and in some cases the fact that the fundamental purpose of the report may be to convey recommendations for managerial action. To make clear the role of special reports in public accounting, we shall now review some of the more important types of special reports.

Letters for underwriters. Investment banking firms which underwrite a securities issue often request the independent auditor who examined the financial statements and schedules included in the registration statement to issue a letter for the underwriters. This letter, commonly called a "comfort letter," usually covers the following:

1. A statement as to the auditor's independence.
2. An opinion as to whether the audited financial statements and schedules included in the registration statement comply in all material respects with the applicable requirements of the Securities Act of 1933 and related rules and regulations of the SEC.
3. "Negative assurances" as to whether any unaudited financial statements and schedules included in the registration statement comply with the 1933 Act and SEC pronouncements, and are fairly presented on a basis consistent with the audited financial statements and schedules included in the registration statement.
4. "Negative assurances" as to whether during a specified period following the date of the latest financial statements in the registration statement there had been any change in long-term debt or capital stock, or any decrease in other specified financial statement items.

Letters for underwriters are highly specialized and require a great deal of skill and care in their writing. The independent auditor engaged in writing a letter for underwriters should consult *Statement on Auditing Procedure No. 48,* "Letters for Underwriters," which contains detailed instructions for and illustrations of typical letters.

Reports on acquisition investigations. Corporations which stress growth through the acquisition of other companies may use their internal audit staffs to conduct investigations of companies considered as merger prospects. As an alternative, the acquisition-minded corporation may request its CPA firm to perform such investigations.

The scope of an acquisition investigation may vary from a comprehensive "opinion audit" to a brief visit limited to inspection of facilities and records and interviews with key personnel.

A tentative acquisition proposal usually contains a number of representations by the company seeking to be acquired, on such matters as the condition and salability of inventories and the collectibility of receivables. Often a CPA firm is retained by the prospective purchaser to perform an investigation of sufficient scope to verify these representations.

An illustration of a CPA's report on a brief investigation of a prospective acquisition is presented in Figure 21–3. In this illustration, we are

FIGURE 21-3

CERTIFIED PUBLIC ACCOUNTANTS

CHICAGO, ILLINOIS

The Board of Directors
Venus Industries, Inc.

At your request, we completed on May 21, 1974 a limited investigation of
Andrews Mfg. Co., Inc., which you are considering for acquisition. Our investigation did not constitute an examination of financial statements in accordance with
generally accepted auditing standards, and accordingly we do not express an independent auditor's opinion on the data presented below, or upon the unaudited balance
sheet of Andrews Mfg. Co., Inc. at April 30, 1974.

Comments on the scope of our investigation and our findings follow.

Plant and equipment

Andrews Mfg. Co., Inc. occupies a 10,000 square feet building located in the
Highland Park section of Los Angeles at 418 West Avenue 48. We were informed that
the building is leased for $700 per month under a lease expiring in 1976.

Approximately two thirds of the building is occupied by the manufacturing facilities; the remainder consists of general and sales offices. Both the machinery and the
office equipment appear to be old but well maintained. The April 30, 1974 unaudited
balance sheet of Andrews reflects machinery and equipment at cost less accumulated
depreciation, in the net amount of $282,000. Double-declining-balance depreciation
methods have been used for all types of depreciable assets.

Key personnel

We were introduced to the following offices and employees:

> Joseph B. Andrews, President
> J. C. Wharton, Vice President — Sales
> Alvis J. Terry, Vice President — Manufacturing
> Elaine L. (Mrs. Joseph B.) Andrews, Secretary
> R. W. Spencer, Treasurer - Controller
> Ronald Jamison, General Manager

All of these individuals cooperated fully in our investigation. In general, their
answers to our questions and the information which they volunteered indicated a strong

FIGURE 21–3 (continued)

ROBERTS & CO.   2

interest in the company and enthusiasm for its product.

Books and records

   Andrews maintains a minutes book, stockholder records, general journal, general ledger, sales journal, voucher register, job cost ledger, plant ledger, cash receipts journal, and check register. All records are handwritten. The records were posted through April 30, 1974, the date of the most recent financial statements (see statements appended hereto). The volume of recorded transactions in April, 1974 was as follows: general journal entries— 13; sales invoices — 148; credit memos — 3; vouchers —57; cash receipts — 121; checks written — 88.

   Joseph Andrews informed us that the financial statements of Andrews Mfg. Co., Inc. have never been audited.

Capital structure

   The articles of incorporation, filed with the California Secretary of State October 18, 1952, authorize 10,000 shares of no-par capital stock. A California Corporation Commission permit dated October 29, 1951 approves the issuance of 5,000 shares to Joseph B. Andrews for $10,000 cash.

Income taxes

   Federal income tax returns and California franchise tax returns for Andrews are on file from October 31, 1952, the company's first fiscal year, through October 31, 1973. None of the returns showed evidence of having been prepared by an outsider. No returns report a net operating loss. The most recent federal income tax return examined by the Internal Revenue Service is 1971. We were informed by Mr. Spencer that no deficiency assessments remain unpaid.

Inventories

   Andrews Mfg. Co., Inc. produces three styles of binoculars. The company accounts for inventory by the periodic method; hence no general ledger cost valuation of inventory was available at May 21, 1974. Mr. Terry estimated the inventory cost to be $115,000. (At October 31, 1973, the inventory reported in the tax returns was $89,000. The inventory in the attached unaudited financial statements for April 30, 1974 — $112,000 —was estimated by the gross profit method, according to Mr. Spencer.)

   Inventory storage and safeguards appeared adequate. The production process seemed to be efficient and expeditious. We were informed, by Messrs. Terry and Spencer, that binoculars are typically produced in lots of 25, with costs accounted for under a job order system utilizing a periodic inventory.

FIGURE 21–3 (concluded)

ROBERTS & CO.   3

The Andrews Company has used the Lifo method of inventory valuation for the last 10 years.

Receivables

No notes receivable are reflected in the general ledger at April 30, 1974. Accounts receivable reported in the unaudited balance sheet at that date aggregated $74,000, net of a $5,000 allowance for losses. Mr. Spencer considers the allowance to be adequate, despite the existence of $15,000 accounts receivables more than 90 days past due.

Payables

Accounts payable and accrued liabilities in the April 30, 1974 unaudited balance sheet totaled $85,000. There are no recorded notes payable, and the federal payroll and income taxes and California franchise and payroll taxes are paid to date, according to Mr. Spencer. Mr. Spencer furnished us with an aged trial balance of trade accounts payable as of May 20, 1974; it showed $35,000 payables past due and $53,000 current. Mr. Andrews informed us that the shortage of working capital in the face of increasing sales volume prompted his interest in the possibility of acquisition by Venus Industries, Inc.

Sales and gross profit trends

Net sales reported in the recent federal income tax returns are as follows: 1973 — $1,815,000; 1972 — $1,592,000; 1971 — $1,218,000; 1970 — $948,000; 1969 — $860,000. The unaudited income statement for the six months ended April 30, 1974 reflects net sales of $965,000. Computed gross profit percentages ranged from a low of 38 percent (1971) to a high of 42 percent (six months ended April 30, 1974).

The use by Andrews of double-declining-balance depreciation and the Lifo method of inventory have caused net income and balance sheet amounts to be substantially lower than would have been produced through use of other acceptable alternative accounting methods.

Our findings were developed during a one-day visit to Andrews Mfg. Co., Inc. If you would like further information, please call on us.

Roberts & Co. CPA.s

assuming that the company under investigation took the initiative in suggesting acquisition. The CPA's client is sufficiently interested to make a very limited investigation which will be followed by more intensive studies if the preliminary report indicates a promising situation. Because this investigation was limited and preliminary, it required only one day's field work by the CPA.

Reports on cash basis statements.   Is an independent public accountant justified in issuing the standard short-form report for a small business or nonprofit organization which uses the cash basis of accounting? This question is a practical one, for many such organizations do retain CPAs and request that all work necessary be done to permit issuance of an unqualified audit report.

It is sometimes argued that if an organization does not have significant amounts of inventory, plant and equipment, or accrued revenue and expenses, financial statements prepared on the basis of cash receipts and disbursements will be approximately the same as if prepared on the accrual basis. Even if we grant that cash basis statements for *some* organizations in *some* years will not differ significantly from statements based on the accrual basis, this line of argument still appears to ignore the real issue. That issue may be stated as follows: Are cash basis statements prepared in accordance with "generally accepted accounting principles" as that phrase is used in the standard audit report? The answer is *no*. However, this fact does not condemn the cash basis of accounting nor prevent the auditor from expressing an opinion on cash basis statements. It is important that cash basis financial statements disclose that the reporting is being done on the cash basis. A footnote may be used to call attention to the omission of any material items which would have been included if the statements had been prepared on the accrual basis.

Financial statements prepared on the cash basis of accounting do not present fairly either financial position or changes therein or operating results for the period; such statements merely summarize the cash transactions for the period. The auditor's opinion attached to cash basis statements may serve a very useful purpose, but the opinion should omit any reference to generally accepted accounting principles and should recognize the statements for what they are.

The following wording is suggested:

We have examined the statement of assets, liabilities, and capital (prepared on a cash basis) of XYZ Company as of December 31, 19___, and the related statement of cash receipts and disbursements for the year then ended. Our examination was made in accordance with generally accepted auditing standards and accordingly included such tests of the accounting records and such other auditing procedures as we considered necessary in the circumstances.

The statements have been prepared on the cash basis of accounting and therefore do not purport to show financial position, changes in financial position or operating results as do statements prepared on the accrual basis in accordance with generally accepted accounting principles.

In our opinion, the aforementioned financial statements summarize fairly the cash position at December 31, 19___, and the cash transactions for the year then ended.

The essence of the audit report is the expression of an opinion as to whether the statements fairly present what they purport to present. The wording of the report will vary from case to case in order to give an accurate indication of the content of the statements, for the cash basis or modified cash basis sometimes includes accounting records of various assets other than cash.

Reports on internal control.   Reports on internal control were discussed and illustrated in Chapter 5, "Internal Control." The desirability of standardized language for these reports is worth reemphasizing at this time.

Reports on statements of nonprofit organizations.   Some of the accounting practices long established and widely used by nonprofit organizations such as hospitals and universities are not in accord with generally accepted accounting principles. The independent auditor preferably should report on the conformity of the organization's financial statements with generally accepted accounting principles, although some CPA firms continue to issue reports indicating whether their clients' financial statements are in accord with established accounting practices for nonprofit organizations in the particular field.

Cash forecasts.   CPAs often assist their clients in the preparation of cash forecasts and other budgetary or pro forma projections. Rule 204 of the AICPA's *Rules of Conduct* prohibits expressing an opinion on or otherwise vouching for the achievability of the forecast. Accordingly, a report accompanying a cash forecast should define the scope of the work, identify the underlying assumptions supporting the forecast, and disclaim any opinion as to the forecast's achievability.

Reports on incomplete financial presentations.   The CPA is sometimes requested to examine the computation of costs under a fixed-price government contract, or perhaps to study the probable impact of future conversion of convertible debentures or preferred stock. In reporting on such examinations, the CPA should state what information is covered by his report, the basis on which the information was prepared, and whether in his opinion the information is presented fairly on the stated basis.

Financial statements and audit reports for "conglomerate" enterprises

The rapid growth of large, highly diversified "conglomerate" organizations in recent years has triggered criticisms of the traditional consolidated financial statements issued by such enterprises. Financial analysts and other interested parties have complained of the lack of comparability of one conglomerate's financial statements with those of another conglomerate, and with statements for companies in the same industries as segments of the conglomerates. As a result of this criticism, many diversified enterprises have been presenting supplementary financial information in their published reports, such as revenue and profits by industry segment.

The AICPA's Accounting Principles Board encouraged such voluntary disclosures. Meanwhile, pending a release by the Financial Accounting Standards Board on the propriety and acceptability of such supplementary data in terms of generally accepted accounting principles, the independent auditor may be reluctant to express an opinion on the supplementary data. If the information appears in the general section of an annual report to shareholders, separate from the basic financial statements, the independent auditor has not in the past assumed responsibility for these data. Recent court decisions, however, suggest an expansion of the CPA's legal responsibility for the validity of supplementary information in various parts of published annual reports.

Audit reports—a look to the future

The CPA sometimes encounters clients who will not authorize a complete or standard examination. For example, some clients may restrict the scope of the audit by declining to conduct a physical inventory, or by refusing to permit the CPA to confirm accounts receivable. Unless the auditor can compensate for such omissions by alternative auditing procedures (and usually this is not possible), he must usually disclaim an opinion on the financial statements as a whole. However, when the CPA issues a report after conducting a limited and incomplete audit, his name becomes associated with the financial statements and lends authority to them. Bankers, investors, creditors, and other nonaccountants are likely to hold the CPA responsible for any errors or deficiencies in the financial statements, regardless of the precise wording of his report.

Of course the CPA may be able to avoid legal liability by pointing to the carefully worded qualifications in his report, but this will not soften the anger of persons who have sustained losses by relying upon financial statements with which the CPA was associated.

Audit reports are sometimes criticized as skillfully drawn defensive devices to protect the auditor. If the auditor cannot persuade the client to authorize a standard examination, he is in a sense forced to protect himself against possible lawsuits by carefully wording his report to limit the responsibility he accepts. The report which is carefully worded to protect the auditor who has made only a partial examination is probably not of much practical value to users of financial statements, and it is very likely to be misinterpreted. The nonaccountant reader is usually not able to assess the meaning of technical phrases by which the auditor limits his responsibility. In other words, the users of audit reports quite naturally expect that an audit by a CPA will be an adequate one, and the financial statements to which a CPA lends his name will be fair and dependable.

Earlier in this chapter it was stated that CPAs often assist their regular fiscal year audit clients in the preparation of unaudited quarterly financial statements. These statements serve as the basis for quarterly unaudited earnings reports required by the SEC and by stock exchanges. In some cases, rosy performances portrayed by three quarters' unaudited earnings reports have disappeared in the audited income statement for the complete fiscal year. Financial analysts have been urging that CPAs perform audits of quarterly earnings reports; this recommendation should not be taken lightly by professional accountants and their clients. Recent pronouncements by the SEC indicate that the Commission will soon require that independent CPAs review quarterly reports to be filed with the Commission.

If the CPA is to live up to the image he has created in the public mind, he should refuse to permit his name to be associated with financial statements unless he is permitted to make a standard examination. Further, he should refuse to issue any report unless he can endorse the statements without qualification. Such a policy is far removed from current practice but appears to be a worthwhile goal for the public accounting profession. Of course clients will, in the future as at present, sometimes need partial examinations and special investigations. Accounting firms can properly provide investigative and analytical services without issuing any kind of an opinion on the client's financial statements or otherwise associating themselves as CPAs with such statements.

Example of short-form report

An actual example of a well-prepared audit report and the related financial statements offers the best means of illustrating the concepts presented in this chapter. A short-form report prepared by a national firm of certified public accountants is presented in the following pages. The report concerns Kaufman and Broad, Inc., a company listed on the New York Stock Exchange.

△ Kaufman and Broad, Inc.
and Consolidated Subsidiaries

Consolidated Balance Sheet
Assets

	November 30 1971	November 30 1970
Current Assets:		
Cash	$ 8,718,000	$ 6,296,000
Short-term investments	9,795,000	5,115,000
Receivables:		
Closing proceeds due from mortgage companies	3,436,000	2,267,000
Trade	10,125,000	6,773,000
Mortgages	7,887,000	4,569,000
Other	7,555,000	4,795,000
Inventories:		
Homes, lots and improvements in production	87,208,000	77,530,000
Land under development and land purchase options	23,750,000	20,035,000
Prepaid expenses	1,204,000	861,000
Total current assets	159,678,000	128,241,000
Investments and Advances:		
Sun Life Insurance Company of America—at cost	52,100,000	
Other unconsolidated subsidiaries—at equity	10,944,000	10,425,000
Joint ventures and partnerships—at equity	2,129,000	2,101,000
Total investments and advances	65,173,000	12,526,000
Other Assets:		
Manufacturing equipment, model home furnishings, etc.—at cost less accumulated depreciation and amortization: 1971—$2,338,000; 1970—$1,790,000	6,260,000	3,361,000
Deferred financing expense—net of amortization	943,000	959,000
Trademarks and brand names	4,253,000	4,253,000
Dealer distribution systems	2,557,000	2,557,000
Goodwill—net of amortization	4,989,000	5,119,000
Total other assets	19,002,000	16,249,000
Total	$243,853,000	$157,016,000

See accompanying notes.

Liabilities and Shareholders' Equity

	November 30 1971	November 30 1970
Current Liabilities:		
Unsecured notes payable	$ 8,278,000	$ 5,187,000
Accounts payable and other liabilities	31,536,000	22,061,000
Mortgages and land contracts payable	31,378,000	29,066,000
Income taxes payable	17,112,000	9,428,000
Total current liabilities	88,304,000	65,742,000
5% subordinated notes due April 1, 1994— partially convertible	11,200,000	15,000,000
6% subordinated convertible debentures due December 1, 1995	24,950,000	25,000,000
6¾% capital notes due August 10, 1977	3,072,000	3,072,000
8% sinking fund debentures due February 1, 1979	4,300,000	4,656,000
Shareholders' Equity:		
Capital stock:		
Preferred stock—Series A, $1.50 cumulative convertible, without par value; outstanding: 450,912 shares	13,527,000	
Common stock—par value $1.00; outstanding: 1971—14,196,041 shares; 1970—5,966,439 shares	14,196,000	5,966,000
Capital surplus	59,434,000	21,419,000
Retained earnings	24,870,000	16,161,000
Total	$243,853,000	$157,016,000

△Kaufman and Broad, Inc.
and Consolidated Subsidiaries

Statement of Changes in Consolidated Financial Position

	November 30 1971	1970
Source of Working Capital:		
Income before equity in earnings of unconsolidated subsidiaries ($210,000 in 1971 and $113,000 in 1970)	$ 9,728,000	$ 6,467,000
Depreciation and amortization (straight-line method)	1,149,000	777,000
Total from operations	10,877,000	7,244,000
Net proceeds received from sale or conversion of:		
Subordinated indebtedness	3,811,000	32,001,000
Stock options and warrants	5,246,000	890,000
Capital stock issued re Sun Life	50,715,000	
Total	70,649,000	40,135,000
Application of Working Capital:		
Cash dividends	1,229,000	1,128,000
Decrease in long-term indebtedness	4,206,000	6,700,000
Investment in Sun Life	52,100,000	
Other investments and advances	337,000	6,522,000
Increase in other assets — net	3,902,000	9,388,000
Total	61,774,000	23,738,000
Increase in Working Capital	$ 8,875,000	$16,397,000
Working Capital Changes:		
Cash and short-term investments	$ 7,102,000	$(4,219,000)
Receivables and prepaid expenses	10,942,000	6,131,000
Inventories	13,393,000	36,825,000
Unsecured notes, mortgages and land contracts payable	(5,403,000)	(11,040,000)
Accounts payable	(9,475,000)	(6,033,000)
Income taxes	(7,684,000)	(5,267,000)
Increase in Working Capital	$ 8,875,000	$16,397,000

Statement of Consolidated Shareholders' Equity

	Capital Stock	Capital Surplus	Retained Earnings
Balance at November 30, 1969	$ 5,870,000	$20,625,000	$10,709,000
Net income			6,580,000
Cash dividends ($.10 per share)			(1,128,000)
Exercise of common stock options	96,000	794,000	
Balance at November 30, 1970	5,966,000	21,419,000	16,161,000
Net income			9,938,000
Cash dividends ($.10 per share)			(1,229,000)
Transfer to common stock of amount equal to par value of stock issued as a result of two-for-one stock split	6,266,000	(6,266,000)	
Exercise of common stock options and common stock purchase warrants	355,000	4,891,000	
Conversion of subordinated indebtedness	144,000	3,667,000	
Acquisition of Sun Life (Preferred stock, $13,527,000; Common stock, $1,465,000)	14,992,000	35,723,000	
Balance at November 30, 1971	$27,723,000	$59,434,000	$24,870,000

⚌ Kaufman and Broad, Inc.
and Consolidated Subsidiaries

Statement of Consolidated Income

	November 30	
	1971	1970
Sales	$227,434,000	$152,347,000
Cost of Sales	183,644,000	119,962,000
Gross Profit	43,790,000	32,385,000
Expenses:		
Marketing	9,502,000	7,045,000
Customer financing	4,153,000	4,300,000
General and administrative	8,844,000	6,836,000
Interest—net	2,315,000	1,872,000
Other—net	297,000	(99,000)
Total expenses	25,111,000	19,954,000
Income Before Income Taxes	18,679,000	12,431,000
Income Taxes	8,741,000	5,851,000
Net Income	$ 9,938,000	$ 6,580,000
Per Common Share — assuming no dilution	$ .82	$ .56
Per Common Share — assuming full dilution	$ .74	$ .51

Opinion of Independent
Certified Public Accountants

HASKINS & SELLS   One Wilshire Building

Certified Public Accountants   Los Angeles 90017

To the Shareholders and Directors of Kaufman and Broad, Inc.:

We have examined the consolidated balance sheet of Kaufman and Broad, Inc. and consolidated subsidiaries as of November 30, 1971 and 1970 and the related statements of consolidated income, shareholders' equity, and changes in financial position for the years then ended. Our examination was made in accordance with generally accepted auditing standards, and accordingly included such tests of the accounting records and such other auditing procedures as we considered necessary in the circumstances.

In our opinion, the above-mentioned financial statements present fairly the financial position of Kaufman and Broad, Inc. and consolidated subsidiaries at November 30, 1971 and 1970 and the results of their operations and the changes in their financial position for the years then ended, in conformity with generally accepted accounting principles consistently applied.

January 31, 1972   *Haskins & Sells*

△ Kaufman and Broad, Inc. and Consolidated Subsidiaries

Notes to Consolidated Financial Statements

1. *General*

The accompanying consolidated financial statements include all subsidiaries of the Company except Nation Wide Cablevision, Inc., Sun Life Insurance Company of America, International Mortgage Company and First Northern Company. Such subsidiaries have been excluded from consolidation because of the lack of similarity of their activities to those of the Company. The Company's equity in net income of unconsolidated subsidiaries, approximately $210,000 in 1971 and $113,000 in 1970, and the minority interest in the net income of majority-owned subsidiaries (which is not significant) are included in other expenses.

The combined condensed balance sheet of the unconsolidated mortgage companies as of November 30, 1971 and 1970, was as follows:

	1971	1970
Assets:		
Cash	$ 337,000	$ 288,000
Mortgages receivable held for sale (collateralized to notes payable)	37,664,000	17,688,000
Other assets	1,677,000	1,120,000
Total	$39,678,000	$19,096,000
Liabilities:		
Notes payable to banks	$37,323,000	$16,259,000
Intercompany payables	1,256,000	2,003,000
Other liabilities	397,000	272,000
Shareholder's equity	702,000	562,000
Total	$39,678,000	$19,096,000

The accounts of foreign subsidiaries have been translated into United States dollars at appropriate rates of exchange; unrealized foreign exchange profits have not been included in income. The consolidated financial statements include the following amounts related to French and Canadian operations: total assets and total liabilities of $55,085,000 and $29,324,000, respectively, at November 30, 1971, and $47,902,000 and $33,498,000, respectively, at November 30, 1970; and net income of $2,819,000 and $1,361,000, respectively, for the years ended November 30, 1971 and 1970.

Goodwill is being amortized over 40 years.

2. *Other Receivables:*

Other receivables consist principally of progress billings on uncompleted contracts, escrow deposits and amounts due from municipalities and utilities.

3. *Inventories:*

Inventories are stated at the lower of accumulated actual cost or market. Substantial portions of the inventories are subject to mortgages and land contracts payable. Interest and property taxes are capitalized on land until the time of the first home delivery and thereafter are expensed.

4. *Income Taxes:*

Income tax expense includes deferred taxes of approximately $4,609,000 and $3,617,000 for the years 1971 and 1970 respectively. Deferred taxes payable amounted to approximately $11,620,000 and $7,011,000 at November 30, 1971 and 1970, respectively. Deferred taxes result principally from accelerated charge-off of interest, property taxes, marketing expenses and start-up costs of new divisions associated with on-site housing and factory housing operations, installment sales of vacation housing sites, accelerated depreciation of cable television assets and taxes payable only upon repatriation of foreign earnings.

5. *Subordinated Indebtedness:*

The 5% subordinated notes are payable in annual installments of $750,000 from 1984 through 1988, and $1,500,000 from 1989 through 1993, with final maturity in 1994. Prior to March 31, 1976, a maximum of $5,200,000 of the principal amount of the notes may be converted into common stock of the Company at $13.33 a share.

Sinking fund requirements of $1,250,000 a year for the 6% subordinated convertible debentures commence in 1981. The debentures are convertible into common stock of the Company at $26.75 a share.

In December, 1971, the Company purchased substantially all of the 8% sinking fund debentures which were scheduled for maturity in installments through February, 1979.

6. *Capital Stock and Capital Surplus:*

The Board of Directors of the Company declared a two-for-one stock split on July 8, 1971 (effected in the form of a stock dividend on the outstanding common stock of the Company).

On April 15, 1971, the shareholders approved an increase in authorized common stock from 15,000,000 to 25,000,000 shares. There are also 2,000,000 shares of preferred stock authorized, of which 450,912 shares have been designated as $1.50 Cumulative Convertible Series A Preferred Stock, all of which were issued in connection with the Sun Life acquisition. The Series A shares are convertible into 315,638 shares of common stock and have a liquidation preference of $13,527,000.

As of November 30, 1971, the Company has reserved 1,099,882 shares of its common stock for possible issuance under outstanding common stock purchase warrants. The warrants are exercisable prior to March, 1974 at $10.84 a share. The Company has also reserved 1,638,438 common shares for possible issuance upon conversion of the 5% subordinated notes, the 6% subordinated convertible debentures and the Series A Preferred Stock and 607,408 common shares for issuance under stock option plans.

Common shares issued upon exercise of stock options during 1971 and 1970 amounted to 109,846 and 192,010, respectively. There were options outstanding at November 30, 1971 and 1970 for 383,-053 and 423,644 common shares, respectively, and the aggregate purchase price of all outstanding stock options was $6,067,000 and $4,916,000, respectively. Options were exercisable at November 30, 1971 for 80,580 shares of common stock. At November 30, 1971 options for 224,355 shares of common stock were available for grant to officers and other key employees.

7. *Commitments and Contingent Liabilities:*

Commitments and contingent liabilities include the usual obligations of on-site and factory housing producers for the completion of contracts and those incurred in the ordinary course of its business. The Company has land options and option type agreements covering land, if purchased, of $39,608,000 and $48,589,000 at November 30, 1971 and 1970, respectively. The Company is also contingently liable as guarantor of certain obligations of its unconsolidated subsidiaries aggregating approximately $16,500,000 at November 30, 1971.

The Company is committed under lease agreements, relating principally to office and factory housing facilities, to make annual lease payments ranging from approximately $900,000 in 1972 to approximately $600,000 in 1976, with a total commitment during such period of approximately $3,800,000.

8. *Per Share Computations:*

Earnings per common share—assuming no dilution has been based on the weighted average number of shares of common stock outstanding during each year. Earnings per common share — assuming full dilution has been based on the assumptions that all outstanding stock options and stock purchase warrants were exercised as of the later of the beginning of the respective years or on the dates issued and proceeds therefrom used to retire common stock and that the outstanding 5% subordinated notes were converted on date of issuance.

9. *Sun Life Insurance Company of America:*

On November 19, 1971, the Company purchased all of the outstanding stock of Sun Life Insurance Company of America in exchange for 1,465,464 shares of common stock and 450,912 shares of Series A Convertible Preferred Stock. The cost of the investment in Sun Life is stated at the fair value of the shares of stock issued plus related acquisition costs. The excess of the $52,100,000 cost of the investment in Sun Life over the $50,500,000 fair value of Sun Life's net assets at date of acquisition, $1,600,000, will be amortized ratably over forty years commencing in 1972. The Company has not included any income from Sun Life in the accompanying financial statements. Net income of Sun Life in accordance with generally accepted accounting principles has not been determined for 1971 because recent events have delayed the promulgation of accounting principles for life insurance companies. Therefore, pro forma earnings for 1971 and 1970 giving effect to the Sun Life acquisition are not presented.

The condensed statutory balance sheet of Sun Life as of December 31, 1971, based upon financial statements reported upon by independent auditors other than Haskins & Sells, was as follows:

Assets:

Bonds and stocks	$107,454,000
Mortgage and policy loans	94,100,000
Real estate	8,825,000
Other	16,676,000
Total	$227,055,000

Liabilities:

Policy and claim reserves	$182,972,000
Other liabilities	13,261,000
Stockholder's equity	30,822,000
Total	$227,055,000

Assets and liabilities are stated at values based on accounting practices prescribed or permitted by the Insurance Department of the State of Maryland. These practices differ in certain respects from generally accepted accounting principles commonly applied by other enterprises.

GROUP I
REVIEW QUESTIONS

21–1.   Select the best answer choice for each of the following:
  a)   An auditor's opinion exception arising from a limitation on the scope of his examination should be explained in—
    (1) A footnote to the financial statements.
    (2) The auditor's report.
    (3) Both a footnote to the financial statements and the auditor's report.
    (4) Both the financial statements (immediately after the caption of the item or items which could not be verified) and the report.
  b)   Footnotes to financial statements should not be used to—
    (1) Describe the nature and effect of a change in accounting principle.
    (2) Identify substantial differences between book and taxable income.
    (3) Correct an improper financial statement presentation.
    (4) Indicate bases for valuing assets.
  c)   Assuming that none of the following have been disclosed in the financial statements, the most appropriate item for footnote disclosure is the—
    (1) Collection of all receivables subsequent to year-end.
    (2) Revision of employees' pension plan.
    (3) Retirement of president of company and election of new president.
    (4) Material decrease in the advertising budget for the coming year and its anticipated effect upon income.
  d)   While assisting Phoenix Company in the preparation of un-audited financial statements, James Jackson, CPA, noted the Phoenix had increased property, plant, and equipment to reflect a recent property appraisal. In this circumstance Mr. Jackson's reporting responsibility is met by—
    (1) Issuing the statements on plain paper without reference to the CPA.
    (2) Advising Phoenix's management of the deviation from generally accepted accounting principles.
    (3) Describing the deviation from generally accepted accounting principles in his disclaimer of opinion.
    (4) Stating in his disclaimer of opinion that Phoenix's financial statements are unaudited.
  e)   The primary responsibility for the adequacy of disclosure in the financial statements and footnotes rests with the—
    (1) Partner assigned to the engagement.
    (2) Auditor in charge of field work.
    (3) Staff assistant who drafts the statements and footnotes.
    (4) Client.

f) The use of an adverse opinion generally indicates—

(1) Uncertainty with respect to an item that is so material that the auditor cannot form an opinion on the fairness of presentation of the financial statements as a whole.

(2) Uncertainty with respect to an item that is material but not so material that the auditor cannot form an opinion on the fairness of the financial statements as a whole.

(3) A violation of generally accepted accounting principles that has a material effect upon the fairness of presentation of the financial statements but is not so material that a qualified opinion is unjustified.

(4) A violation of generally accepted accounting principles that is so material that a qualified opinion is not justified.

g) The use of a disclaimer of opinion might indicate that the auditor—

(1) Is so uncertain with respect to an item that he cannot form an opinion on the fairness of presentation of the financial statements as a whole.

(2) Is uncertain with respect to an item that is material but not so material that he cannot form an opinion on the fairness of presentation of the financial statements as a whole.

(3) Has observed a violation of generally accepted accounting principles that has a material effect upon the fairness of presentation of financial statements but is not so material that a qualified report is unjustified.

(4) Has observed a violation of generally accepted accounting principles that is so material that a qualified opinion is not justified.

h) An auditor's "subject to" report is a type of—

(1) Disclaimer of opinion.

(2) Qualified opinion.

(3) Adverse opinion.

(4) Standard opinion.

i) Generally the auditor's opinion on financial statements should be dated to coincide with the—

(1) Balance sheet date.

(2) Completion of all important audit procedures.

(3) Closing of the client's books.

(4) Transmittal of the report to the client.

j) Gregory George, a candidate for the state legislature, is preparing personal financial statements for submission to the electorate. Mr. George's statement of assets and liabilities should be prepared on the—

(1) Cost basis.

(2) Basis of cost adjusted for general price-level changes.

(3) Lower of cost or estimated value basis.

(4) Bases of both cost and estimated value.

(AICPA, adapted)

21–2. Write a disclaimer of opinion which should accompany financial statements examined by a CPA who owns a material direct financial interest in his audit client. (AICPA)

21–3. How does a piecemeal opinion differ from a qualified opinion?

21–4. Why does the expression of a piecemeal opinion with respect to specific items require a more extensive examination of such items than would ordinarily be required if the auditor were expressing an opinion on the financial statements taken as a whole? (AICPA)

21–5. Why is it important that a piecemeal opinion be carefully worded? (AICPA)

21–6. What is the function of notes to financial statements?

21–7. List five items generally covered in notes to financial statements.

21–8. Your client refuses to include a statement of changes in financial position in his financial statements for the current year. Would this prevent you from issuing an unqualified audit report?

21–9. Describe the reports customarily filed by a company subject to the reporting requirements of the SEC.

21–10. How do special reports differ from the standard short-form audit report?

21–11. Your client wishes you to issue an unqualified audit report to accompany a cash forecast supporting the client's application for a bank loan. Can you comply with the client's request? Explain.

21–12. How does the auditor utilize a working balance sheet and working income statement included with his working papers?

21–13. Carroll Electronics Corporation has been a client of yours for the last several years. At the beginning of 1974 the company changed its method of inventory valuation from average cost to Lifo. The change, which had been under consideration for some time, was in your opinion a logical and proper step for the company to take. What effect, if any, would this change have upon your short-form audit report for the year ended December 31, 1974?

21–14. List several factors which would prevent the issuance of an unqualified audit report.

21–15. In the annual examination of the Rogers Company the auditors did not confirm accounts receivable from customers, at the client's request. During the course of the examination, virtually all of the accounts receivable outstanding at the balance sheet date were collected and the auditors examined the checks and remittance advices received from customers. Under these circumstances, can the auditors issue an unqualified report? Explain.

21–16. Describe the kinds of information generally included in long-form audit reports.

GROUP II
QUESTIONS REQUIRING ANALYSIS

21–17. Select the best answer choice for each of the following and justify your selection with a brief sentence:

a) An exception in the auditor's report because of the lack of consistent application of generally accepted principles most likely would be required in the event of—

(1) A change in the rate of provision for uncollectible accounts based upon collection experience.

(2) The original adoption of a pension plan for employees.

(3) Inclusion of a previously unconsolidated subsidiary in consolidated financial statements.

(4) The revision of pension plan actuarial assumptions based upon experience.

b) A CPA is completing his examination of the financial statements of Juneau Service Company for the year ended April 30, 1974. During the year Juneau's employees were granted an additional week's vacation, and this had a material effect upon vacation pay expense for the year and accrued liability for vacation pay at April 30, 1974. In the opinion of the CPA, this occurrence and its effects have been adequately disclosed in a footnote to the financial statements. In his auditor's report, the CPA normally will—

(1) Omit any mention of this occurrence and its effects.

(2) Refer to the footnote in his opinion paragraph but express an unqualified opinion.

(3) Refer to the footnote and express an opinion that is qualified as to consistency.

(4) Insist that comparative income statements for prior years be restated or express an opinion that is qualified as to consistency.

c) A CPA is completing an examination of the financial statements of Proshek Trucking Company. The company had been depreciating its trucks over an eight-year period but determined that a more realistic life is 10 years and based this year's depreciation provision upon that life. The change and the effects of the change have been adequately disclosed in a note to the financial statements. If the CPA agrees that the change in estimated life was properly made, he should—

(1) Omit mention of the change in his report because it results from changed conditions, is not a change in accounting principle and has been properly disclosed.

(2) Recognize this change as one that involves a choice be-

tween two generally accepted principles of accounting and qualify his report as to consistency.

(3) Render an unqualified opinion provided that comparative income statements for prior years are restated based upon the 10-year life.

(4) Insist that comparative income statements for prior years be restated and render an opinion qualified as to consistency.

d) A CPA was engaged to examine the consolidated financial statements of Kauffman Tool Company and its Canadian subsidiary. He arranged for a reputable firm of Canadian chartered accountants to conduct the examination of the Canadian subsidiary's financial statements. The CPA reviewed both the audit program and the working papers prepared by the Canadian firm and is willing to accept full responsibility for the performance of the examination of the subsidiary's financial statements. The Canadian chartered accountants expressed an unqualified opinion on the subsidiary's financial statements, and the CPA has no exceptions on the parent's statements or the procedures used to prepare the consolidated statements. Under these circumstances, the CPA's report on the consolidated statements—

(1) Should include a piecemeal opinion covering the parent's statements and a qualified opinion as to the Canadian subsidiary.

(2) Need make no reference to the chartered accountant's examination.

(3) Must include a reference to the chartered accountant's examination in the scope paragraph or a middle paragraph together with an unqualified opinion paragraph.

(4) Must include a qualification of the opinion paragraph stating that the CPA's unqualified opinion is based in part upon the chartered accountant's examination. (AICPA, adapted)

21–18. Dale Goodman, CPA, is examining the financial statements of Madison Company for the year ended March 31, 1974. At Madison's request, the confirmation of accounts receivable and observation of the physical inventory are omitted from this examination. Since he cannot express any opinion as to receivables and inventory, Mr. Goodman omits all normal auditing procedures related to those accounts. Receivables and inventory account for 60 percent of the total assets.

Mr. Goodman decides to express a piecemeal opinion and proposes the following report:

To: The Board of Directors
Madison Company

We have examined the balance sheet of Madison Company as of March 31, 1974 and the related statements of income and retained earnings and changes in financial position for the year then ended. Our examination was made in accordance with generally accepted auditing standards, and accordingly included such tests of the accounting records and such other procedures as we considered necessary in the circumstances, except that we did not communicate with debtors to confirm accounts receivable balances or observe and test the methods used in the determination of inventory quantities.

With the exception of accounts receivable and inventories, our examination indicated that all other accounts were maintained, and the aforementioned financial statements were prepared, in accordance with generally accepted accounting principles applied on a basis consistent with that of the preceding year. However, because of the materiality of accounts receivable and inventories, we are unable to express an independent accountant's opinion as to the fairness of presentation of the accompanying financial statements taken as a whole.

Dale Goodman, CPA

April 26, 1974

Required:

a)   Discuss whether Mr. Goodman is justified in expressing a piecemeal opinion in the specific situation where Madison Company has limited the scope of his examination.

b)   Without prejudice to your answer for part (a), assume that a piecemeal opinion is justified. List deficiencies in the form and content of Mr. Goodman's proposed report. (AICPA, adapted)

21–19.   You are engaged in the examination of the financial statements of Rapid, Inc. and its recently acquired subsidiary, Slow Corporation. In acquiring Slow Corporation during 1974, Rapid, Inc. exchanged a large number of its shares of common stock for 90 percent of the outstanding common stock of Slow Corporation in a transaction that was accounted for as a pooling of interests. Rapid, Inc. is now preparing the annual report to shareholders and proposes to include in the report combined financial statements for the year ended December 31, 1974 with a footnote describing its exchange of stock for that of Slow Corporation. Rapid, Inc. also proposes to include in its report the financial statements of the previous year as they appeared in Rapid, Inc.'s 1973 annual report along with a five-year financial summary from Rapid's prior annual reports, all of which had been accompanied by your unqualified auditor's opinion.

Required:

a)   Discuss the objectives or purposes of the standard of reporting which requires the auditor's report to state whether generally accepted accounting principles have been consistently observed over the past two periods.

b)   Describe the treatment in the auditor's report of interperiod changes having a material effect on the financial statements arising from—

(1)   A change in accounting principle.

(2)   Changed conditions which necessitate accounting estimate changes but which do not involve changes in accounting principle.

(3)   Changed conditions unrelated to accounting.

c) (1) Would the financial reporting treatment proposed by Rapid, Inc. for the 1974 annual report be on a consistent basis? Discuss.

(2) Describe the auditor's report which should accompany the financial statements as proposed by Rapid, Inc. for inclusion in the annual report. (AICPA, adapted)

21-20. *Comment upon the following:* "The standard short-form (audit) report . . . was adopted in substantially its present form nearly 40 years ago. Considerable accounting literature has been devoted to the wording used in it, and its intended meaning is fairly well understood by the accounting profession and by the more sophisticated users of auditor's reports. However, despite continuous efforts on the part of the profession to educate the vast mass of less sophisticated users—those who consciously, but somewhat innocently, rely on the reports—the auditor's role still seems to be mostly misunderstood. Most users think of the financial statements themselves, and probably even more so the notes, as comprising part of the auditor's report rather than being the representations of management. The report itself does little to dispel this notion or to make clear that the auditor is only expressing his opinion on management's report."

21-21. Criticize the following audit report.

June 2, 1974

Mr. Richard Thomas
Thomas Enterprises

We have examined the accounts and records of Thomas Enterprises (a sole proprietorship) as at April 30, 1974 and present herewith a statement of financial position as at April 30, 1974 and the related statement of income for the year then ended.

Our examination included such tests as we considered necessary to generally satisfy ourselves as to the reasonableness of the aforementioned statements. However, we did not perform all tests required by statute so that we might issue an independent accountant's opinion.

Farley, Jackson & Co., CPAs

21-22. At the beginning of your examination of the financial statements of Western Insurance Company, the president of the company requested that in the interest of efficiency, you coordinate your audit procedures with the audit being conducted by the state insurance examiners for the same fiscal year. The state examiners audited the asset accounts of the company while you audited the accounts for liabilities, stockholders' equity, revenue, and expenses. In addition you obtained confirmations of the accounts receivable and were satisfied with the results of your audit tests. Although you had no supervisory control over the state examiners, they allowed you to review and prepare extracts from their working papers and report. After reviewing the state examiners' working papers and report to your complete satisfaction, you are now preparing your short-form report.

Required:

What effect, if any, would the above circumstances have on your short-form audit report? Discuss. (AICPA, adapted)

21–23. Nugent Company was seeking a substantial bank loan for a period of six months and was asked by the bank to support its application with a complete report including forecasts of expected cash receipts and disbursements, and expected sales and earnings for the coming year. The bank made clear that it wished to know exactly how the company planned to obtain the funds to repay the loan.

The controller of Nugent Company compiled a detailed forecast for the coming year and requested the public accounting firm which was just completing the annual audit to attach a brief statement to the forecast indicating that the estimates were reasonable in relation to operations of prior years and were based upon information drawn from the accounting records.

What action do you think the public accounting firm should take?

21–24. What type of audit report would be issued in each of the following cases? Justify your choice.

a) Balsam Corporation is engaged in a hazardous trade and cannot obtain insurance coverage from any source. A material portion of the corporation's assets could be destroyed by a serious accident. The corporation has an excellent safety record and has never suffered a catastrophe. *Unqualified – No footnote Required*

b) Dogwood Corporation owns properties which have substantially appreciated in value since the date of purchase. The properties were appraised and are reported in the balance sheet at the appraised values with full disclosure. The CPA believes that the values reported in the balance sheet are reasonable. *Adverse*

c) The CPA is examining the financial statements which are to be included in the annual report to the stockholders of Elm Corporation, a regulated company. Elm Corporation's financial statements are prepared as prescribed by a regulatory agency of the U.S. government, and some items are not presented in accordance with generally accepted accounting principles. The amounts involved are material and are adequately disclosed in footnotes to the financial statements.

d) Linden Corporation has material investments in stocks of subsidiary companies. Stocks of the subsidiary companies are not actively traded in the market, and the CPA's engagement does not extend to any subsidiary company. The CPA is able to satisfy himself that all investments are carried at original cost, and he has no reason to suspect that the amounts are not stated fairly.

e) Quassia Corporation has material investments in stocks of subsidiary companies. Stocks of the subsidiary companies are actively traded in the market, but the CPA's engagement does not extend to any subsidiary company. Management insists that all investments shall be carried at original costs, and the CPA is satisfied that the original costs are fairly stated. The CPA believes that the client will never ultimately realize a substantial portion of the investments, and the client has fully disclosed the facts in footnotes to the financial statements. (AICPA, adapted)

21-25. Upon completion of the examination of his client's financial statements the CPA, in his report, must either express an opinion or disclaim an opinion on the statements taken as a whole. His opinion may be unqualified, qualified, or adverse. Under certain circumstances he may issue a piecemeal opinion.

Required:

a) Under what general conditions may a CPA express an unqualified opinion on his client's financial statements?

b) Define and distinguish among (1) a qualified opinion, (2) an adverse opinion, and (3) a disclaimer of opinion on the statements taken as a whole.

c) Discuss the circumstances under which a CPA may issue a piecemeal opinion, including the relationship, if any, of a piecemeal opinion to (1) a qualified opinion, (2) an adverse opinion, (3) a disclaimer of opinion on the statements taken as a whole, and (4) an unqualified opinion. (AICPA)

21-26. A CPA was engaged by Lane Nursing Home to prepare, on the CPA's stationery and without audit, financial statements for 1974 and its 1974 income tax returns. From the accounting and other records the CPA learned the following information about the Nursing Home:

(1) Lane Nursing Home is a partnership that was formed early in 1974. The nursing home occupies a large old mansion that stands on a sizable piece of land beside a busy highway. The property was purchased by the partnership from an estate that out-of-state heirs wanted to settle. The heirs were unfamiliar with the local real estate market and sold the property at the bargain price of $10,000 for the house and $5,000 for the land.

(2) A few weeks after the purchase the partnership employed a competent independent appraisal firm that appraised the house at $100,000 and the land at $50,000.

(3) The property was then written up on the partnership books to its appraisal value, and the partners' capital accounts were credited with the amount of the write-up.

(4) Additional funds were invested to convert the mansion into a nursing home, to purchase the necessary equipment and supplies, and to provide working capital.

Required:

a) Assume that the CPA prepared the financial statements of the Lane Nursing Home from the accounting records, placed them on his stationery, and labeled each page "Prepared Without Audit." In accordance with the client's preference, the assets were reported only at appraisal values. Under the circumstances presented, what is the CPA's responsibility, if any, to disclose the method of valuation of the assets? Discuss.

b) In this situation, how does the CPA's responsibility for disclosure of the valuation basis of the assets differ, if at all, from the responsibility he would have had if he had made a typical examination of the financial statements?

c) In this situation, would it be proper for the CPA to prepare, and sign as preparer, the 1974 federal and state income tax returns of the partnership if the mansion is shown on the income tax return at its appraisal value? Discuss. (AICPA, adapted) **No**

21–27. Marlene Rogers, after several years' experience on the audit staff of a national firm of certified public accountants, opened her own public accounting office in partnership with another young accountant. In a discussion with one of the clients of the new firm, Miss Rogers placed great emphasis upon the importance of a well-designed system of internal control. She pointed out the usefulness of internal control to management and also the importance of a careful evaluation of internal control by an auditor as a basis for determining the extent and nature of tests to be made.

The client appeared to be quite favorably impressed with Miss Rogers' emphasis upon internal control and explained that for years he had encouraged the development of strong internal controls in his company. On the following day, the client requested that the short-form report to be issued upon completion of the examination include a statement that the auditors had made a thorough review of the system of internal control. He also requested that the report contain a formal expression of opinion by the auditors as to the adequacy of the system of internal control.

What answer do you believe Miss Rogers should make to the client, and what special statement, if any, should be included in the wording of the audit report?

21–28. Douglas McGraw, senior partner in a small public accounting firm, received a telephone call at 11 o'clock one morning from R. J. Dunn, owner of the Dunn Manufacturing Corporation. Mr. Dunn stated that he needed a balance sheet of his business by 2 o'clock that afternoon to use in a meeting with a banker. He urged that Mr. McGraw come over at once and prepare the statement from the books. Mr. McGraw had rendered a variety of accounting services for the Dunn Manufacturing Corporation over a period of 20 years. These services had included audits, preparation of tax returns, the design of accounting systems, and other management advisory services. An audit had not been performed for several years. R. J. Dunn was a widely known figure in the community and had recommended Mr. McGraw to other businessmen on several occasions.

What response do you think Mr. McGraw should have made to the request from R. J. Dunn?

GROUP III
PROBLEMS

21–29. Webster Corporation, an audit client of yours, is a manufacturer of consumer products and has several wholly owned subsidiaries in foreign countries which are audited by other independent auditors in those countries. The financial statements of all subsidiaries were properly consolidated in the financial statements of the parent company and the foreign auditors' reports were furnished to your CPA firm.

   You are now preparing your auditor's opinion on the consolidated balance sheet and statements of income and retained earnings and changes in financial position for the year ended June 30, 1974. These statements were prepared on a comparative basis with those of last year.

   Required:

   a) How would you evaluate and accept the independence and professional reputations of the foreign auditors?

   b) Under what circumstances may a principal auditor assume responsibility for the work of another auditor to the same extent as if he had performed the work himself?

   c) Assume that both last year and this year you were willing to utilize the reports of the other independent auditors in expressing your opinion on the consolidated financial statements but were unwilling to take full responsibility for performance of the work underlying their opinions. Assuming your examination of the parent company's financial statements would allow you to render an unqualified opinion, prepare (1) the necessary disclosure to be contained in the scope paragraph and (2) the complete opinion paragraph of your auditor's report.

   d) What modification(s), if any, would be necessary in your auditor's opinion if the financial statements for the prior year were unaudited? (AICPA, adapted)

21–30. The following draft of an audit's report has been submitted to you for review:

   To: Eric Jones, Chief Accountant
         Sunshine Manufacturing Co.

   We have examined the balance sheet of Sunshine Manufacturing Company for the year ended August 31, 1974 and the related statements of income and retained earnings and changes in financial position. Our examination included such tests of the accounting records and such other auditing procedures as we considered necessary in the circumstances, except that, in accordance with your instructions, we did not count the buyers' cash working fund.

   In our opinion, subject to the limitation on our examination discussed above, the accompanying balance sheet and statements of income and earned surplus and changes in financial position present fairly the financial position of the Sunshine Manufacturing Company at August 31, 1974, and the results of its operations and the changes in its financial position for the year then ended.

Frank George & Co.

August 31, 1974

It has been determined that:

(1) Except for the omission of the count of the buyers' cash working fund, there were no scope restrictions placed on the auditor's examination.

(2) Sunshine Manufacturing Company has been in continuous operation since 1946, but its financial statements have not previously been audited.

Required:

a) Assuming that Frank George & Co. was able to perform alternative auditing procedures to satisfactorily substantiate the buyers' cash working fund and purchases through the fund, identify and discuss the deficiencies in the auditor's report.

b) Assuming that Frank George & Co. was unable to satisfactorily substantiate the buyers' cash working fund and purchases through the fund by alternative auditing procedures, discuss the appropriateness of the opinion qualification proposed in Frank George & Co.'s report.

c) Discuss the potential consequences to the CPA of issuing a substandard report or failing to adhere in his examination to generally accepted auditing standards. (AICPA, adapted)

21–31. In prior years your client, Preston, Inc., a manufacturing company, has used an accelerated depreciation method for its depreciable assets for both federal and state income taxes and financial reporting. At the beginning of 1974 the corporation changed to the straight-line method for financial reporting. As a result, depreciation expense for the year was $200,000 less for financial reporting than for income tax reporting, an amount which you consider to be material. The corporation did not use interperiod income tax allocation in 1974. Taxable income for 1974 was $600,000. Assume that the federal income tax rate was 48 percent and ignore state and local income taxes.

Required:

a) Financial statement presentation:
   (1) Describe the effects of the accounting change on Preston's 1974 balance sheet, income statement and statement of changes in financial position. Cite specific amounts in your answer.
   (2) Explain what disclosure of the accounting change should be made in Preston's 1974 financial statements.

b) Auditor's report:
   (1) Assuming that the financial statement disclosure is con-

sidered to be adequately informative, discuss the effects that the change in depreciation methods should have on auditor's report.

(2) Assuming that the financial statement disclosure of the change in depreciation methods is not considered to be adequately informative, discuss the effects on the auditor's report.

(3) Discuss whether the auditor's report should indicate approval of the change in depreciation methods.

(4) Discuss the effects on the auditor's report of the failure to use interperiod income tax allocation. (AICPA, adapted)

21–32. You are completing an examination of the financial statements of Sherman Manufacturing Corporation for the year ended February 28, 1974. Sherman's financial statements have not been examined previously. The controller of Sherman has given you the following draft of proposed footnotes to the financial statements:

SHERMAN MANUFACTURING CORPORATION

NOTES TO FINANCIAL STATEMENTS
Year Ended February 28, 1974

Note 1. Because we were not engaged as auditors until after February 28, 1973, we were unable to observe the taking of the beginning physical inventory. We satisfied ourselves as to the balance of physical inventory at February 28, 1973 by alternative procedures.

Note 2. With the approval of the Commissioner of Internal Revenue, the company changed its method of accounting for inventories from the first-in, first-out method to the last-in, first-out method on March 1, 1973. In the opinion of the company the effects of this change on the pricing of inventories and cost of goods manufactured were not material in the current year but are expected to be material in future years.

Note 3. The investment property was recorded at cost until December 1973 when it was written up to its appraisal value. The company plans to sell the property in 1974, and an independent real estate agent in the area has indicated that the appraisal price can be realized. Pending completion of the sale the amount of the expected gain on the sale has been recorded in a deferred credit account.

Note 4. The stock dividend described in our May 24, 1974 letter to stockholders has been recorded as a 105 for 100 stock split-up. Accordingly, there were no changes in the stockholders' equity account balances from this transaction.

Note 5. For many years the company has maintained a pension plan for certain of its employees. Prior to the current year pension expense was recognized as payments were made to retired employees. There was no change in the plan in the current year, but upon the recommendation of its auditor, the company provided $64,000, based upon an actuarial estimate, for pensions to be paid in the future to current employees.

Required:

For each Note 1 to 5 discuss:

a) The note's adequacy and needed revisions, if any, of the financial statements or the note.

b)   The necessary disclosure in or opinion modification of the
auditor's report. (For this requirement assume the revisions suggested in part (a), if any, have been made.)

Complete your discussion of each note (both parts [*a*] and [*b*])
before beginning discussion of the next one. (AICPA, adapted)

21–33.   Colton Electronics produces electronic components for sale to manufacturers of radios, television sets, and phonographic systems. In
connection with her examination of Colton's financial statements
for the year ended December 31, 1974 Donna Olds, CPA, completed
field work two weeks ago. Mrs. Olds now is evaluating the significance
of the following items prior to preparing her auditor's report. Except
as noted none of these items have been disclosed in the financial
statements or footnotes.

Item 1.   Recently Colton interrupted its policy of paying cash dividends quarterly to its stockholders. Dividends were paid regularly through
1973, discontinued for all of 1974 in order to finance equipment for the
company's new plant and resumed in the first quarter of 1975. In the
annual report dividend policy is to be discussed in the president's letter
to stockholders.

Item 2.   A 10-year loan agreement, which the company entered into
three years ago, provides that dividend payments may not exceed net income earned subsequent to the date of the agreement. The balance of
retained earnings at the date of the loan agreement was $298,000. From
that date through December 31, 1974 net income has totaled $360,000
and cash dividends have totaled $130,000. Based upon these data the
staff auditor assigned to this review concluded that there was no retained
earnings restriction at December 31, 1974.

Item 3.   The company's new manufacturing plant building, which cost
$600,000 and has an estimated life of 25 years, is leased from the Sixth
National Bank at an annual rental of $100,000. The company is obligated
to pay property taxes, insurance, and maintenance. At the conclusion of
its 10-year noncancelable lease, the company has the option of purchasing
the property for $1. In Colton's income statement the rental payment is
reported on a separate line.

Required:

For each item 1 to 3 discuss:

a)   Any additional disclosure in the financial statements and footnotes that the CPA should recommend to her client.

b)   The effect of this situation on the CPA's report upon Colton's
financial statements. For this requirement assume that the client
did not make the additional disclosure recommended in part (*a*).

Complete your discussion of each item (both parts [*a*] and [*b*])
before beginning discussion of the next item. The effects of each
item on the financial statements and the CPA's report should be
evaluated independently of the other items. The cumulative effects
of the three items should not be considered. (AICPA, adapted)

21–34.   The following audit report was rendered by independent public accountants at the conclusion of their first examination of Wilton Company:

To: The Board of Directors
      Wilton Company

We have examined the balance sheet of Wilton Company as of December 31, 1974, and the related statements of income and retained earnings and changes in financial position for the year then ended. Our examination was made in accordance with generally accepted auditing standards, and accordingly included such tests of the accounting records and such other auditing procedures as we considered necessary in the circumstances. We did not visit the company's Atlanta, Georgia branch, but we were able to satisfy ourselves by other means concerning the properties and operations of the branch.

In our opinion, the aforementioned financial statements present fairly the financial position of Wilton Company at December 31, 1974, and the results of its operations and the changes in its financial position for the year then ended, in conformity with generally accepted accounting principles applied on a basis consistent with that of the preceding year.

February 20, 1975

Warren, Knowles and Company
Certified Public Accountants

The Atlanta, Georgia branch of the company mentioned in the scope section of the audit report carries on sales and warehousing functions. Approximately 30 percent of the total inventories at December 31 were held at the Atlanta branch. The branch obtains all of its merchandise from the home office of the company; shipments to the branch are reflected in perpetual inventory records maintained at the home office. The branch carries on its own billing and collection activities and maintains accounts receivable records. The physical inventory taken on December 31 at the branch was observed by the company's internal auditor, who during the year also made a number of studies of internal control over billing and collection activities at the branch.

Although the independent auditors did not visit the branch, they verified the branch bank accounts by direct confirmation with the bank and by preparing bank reconciliations from bank statements obtained directly from the bank. A trial balance of accounts receivable at the branch was obtained by the independent auditors, and confirmation procedures were satisfactorily completed. The auditors also determined that the shipments of merchandise to the branch during the year were in line with the sales reported by the branch and with its reported inventories at the end of the year. They obtained the duplicate copies of the serially numbered sales invoices used by the branch and balanced these documents against monthly sales for three months of the year. The auditors' verification of the inventories located at the home office included all customary procedures and disclosed no significant discrepancies. In general, the auditors were favorably impressed with the quality of the accounting records and with the internal control in force.

In view of the fact that the auditors did not visit the branch, do you consider that they were justified in issuing the audit report set forth above? Explain fully.

21–35. Your client, Morton Company, requests your assistance in rewriting the footnote presented below, to make it clearer and more concise.

> *Note 6.* The indenture relating to the long-term debt contains certain provisions regarding the maintenance of working capital, the payment of dividends, and the purchase of the company's capital stock. The most restrictive of these provisions requires that: (*a*) working capital will be maintained at not less than $4,500,000; (*b*) the company cannot pay cash dividends or purchase its capital stock, if after it has done so, working capital is less than $5,000,000; and (*c*) cash dividends paid since January 1, 1970, plus the excess of capital stock purchased over the proceeds of stock sold during the same period, cannot exceed 70 percent of net earnings (since January 1, 1970) plus $250,000. At December 31, 1974, $2,441,291 of retained earnings was available for the payment of dividends under this last provision, as follows:

Net earnings since January 1, 1970	$5,478,127
70% of above	$3,834,688
Additional amount available under indenture	250,000
	$4,084,688
Cash dividends paid since January 1, 1970	1,643,397
Retained earnings available	$2,441,291

Required:

Rewrite the footnote in accordance with your client's instructions.

21–36. Jiffy Clerical Services is a corporation which furnishes temporary office help to its customers. Billings are rendered monthly based on predetermined hourly rates. You have examined the company's financial statements for several years. Following is an abbreviated statement of assets and liabilities on the modified cash basis as of December 31, 1974:

Assets:	
Cash	$20,000
Advances to employees	1,000
Equipment and autos, less accumulated depreciation	25,000
Total Assets	$46,000
Liabilities:	
Employees' payroll taxes withheld	$ 8,000
Bank loan payable	10,000
Estimated income taxes on cash basis profits	10,000
Total Liabilities	$28,000
Net Assets	$18,000
Represented by:	
Common stock	$ 3,000
Cash profits retained in the business	15,000
	$18,000

Unrecorded receivables were $55,000 and payables were $30,000.

Required:

a) Prepare the report you would issue covering the statement of assets and liabilities as of December 31, 1974, as summarized above, and the related statement of cash revenue and expenses for the year ended that date.

b) Briefly discuss and justify your modifications of the conventional report on accrual basis statements.

21–37. Following are the financial statements of Page Manufacturing Corporation and the auditor's report of examination for the year ended January 31, 1974. The examination was conducted by John Smith, an individual practitioner, who has examined the corporation's financial statements and reported on them for many years.

March 31, 1974

To: Mr. Paul Page, President
      Page Manufacturing Corporation

I have examined the Balance Sheet of the Page Manufacturing Corporation and the related statement of income and retained earnings.

These statements present fairly the financial position and results of operations in conformity with consistent generally accepted principles of accounting. My examination was made in accordance with generally accepted auditing standards, and accordingly included such tests of the accounting records an such other auditing procedures as I considered necessary in the circumstances.

(Signed)   *John Smith*

PAGE MANUFACTURING CORPORATION
STATEMENTS OF CONDITION
January 31, 1974 and 1973

ASSETS

	1974	1973
Current Assets:		
Cash	$ 43,822	$ 51,862
Accounts receivable—pledged—less allowances for doubtful accounts of $3,800 in 1974 and $3,000 in 1973 (see note)	65,298	46,922
Inventories, pledged—at average cost, not in excess of replacement cost	148,910	118,264
Other current assets	6,280	5,192
Total Current Assets	$264,310	$222,240
Fixed Assets:		
Land—at cost	$ 38,900	$ 62,300
Buildings—at cost, less accumulated depreciation of $50,800 in 1974 and $53,400 in 1973	174,400	150,200
Machinery and equipment—at cost, less accumulated depreciation of $30,500 in 1974 and $25,640 in 1973	98,540	78,560
Total Fixed Assets	$311,840	$291,060
Total Assets	$576,150	$513,300

LIABILITIES AND STOCKHOLDERS' EQUITY

Current Liabilities:

Accounts payable...........................	$ 27,926	$ 48,161
Other liabilities.............................	68,743	64,513
Current portion of long-term mortgage payable.....................................	3,600	3,600
Income taxes payable........................	46,840	30,866
Total Current Liabilities....................	$147,109	$147,140

Long-Term Liabilities:

Mortgage payable...........................	90,400	94,000
Total Liabilities...........................	$237,509	$241,140

Stockholders' Equity:

Capital stock, par value $100, 1,000 shares authorized, issued and outstanding.................	$100,000	$100,000
Retained earnings...........................	238,641	172,160
Total Stockholders' Equity..................	$338,641	$272,160
Total Liabilities and Stockholders' Equity.....	$576,150	$513,300

NOTE: I did not confirm the balances of the accounts receivable but satisfied myself by other auditing procedures that the balances were correct.

PAGE MANUFACTURING CORPORATION

INCOME STATEMENTS

For the Years Ended January 31, 1974 and 1973

	1974	*1973*
Income:		
Net sales..........................	$884,932	$682,131
Other income......................	3,872	2,851
Total..........................	$888,804	$684,982
Costs and expenses:		
Cost of goods sold..................	$463,570	$353,842
Selling expenses....................	241,698	201,986
Administrative expenses.............	72,154	66,582
Provision for income taxes...........	45,876	19,940
Other expenses.....................	12,582	13,649
Total..........................	$835,880	$655,999
Net Income........................	$ 52,924	$ 28,983

Required:

List and discuss the deficiencies of the Page Manufacturing Corporation financial statements and the auditor's report prepared by John Smith. Your discussion should include justifications that the matters you cited are deficiencies. (Do not verify the addition of the statements. Assume that the addition is correct.) (AICPA, adapted)

GROUP IV
CASE STUDIES IN AUDITING

PUSHBUTTON MACHINERY COMPANY

21–38. Pushbutton Machinery Company, manufacturers of machine tools, expanded rapidly for some years to supply the increased needs of industry. One of the last phases of this expansion program was the construction of a large plant in one of the major cities of the Pacific Coast. This plant was begun in 1970 but was not completed and ready for operation until 1973. By that time the company's operations had decreased so that the additional capacity provided by the West Coast plant was no longer needed. The plant was operated for a year, but in the spring of 1974, the board of directors of Pushbutton Machinery Company decided to put the plant up for sale. Production was stopped on April 30, 1974, and the plant was used only for storage pending a sale at a satisfactory price.

The condensed balance sheet of the company at December 31, 1974 was as follows:

ASSETS

Current assets............................		$ 5,000,000
Plant and equipment......................	$20,000,000	
Less: Accumulated depreciation...........	10,000,000	10,000,000
Other assets..............................		1,000,000
Total Assets.......................		$16,000,000

LIABILITIES AND STOCKHOLDERS' EQUITY

Current liabilities........................		$ 3,000,000
Long-term liabilities......................		4,000,000
Stockholders' equity:		
Capital stock..........................	$ 6,000,000	
Retained earnings......................	3,000,000	9,000,000
Total Liabilities and Stockholders' Equity...........................		$16,000,000

The cost of the West Coast plant was $4,000,000, and the accumulated depreciation to April 30, 1974, was $100,000. Earnings for the calendar year 1974 were $300,000 after taxes, including $150,000 of expenses applicable to the West Coast plant since its shutdown.

When the auditors began their examination of the company's financial statements for the year ended December 31, 1974, they asked about the status of the West Coast plant. They were informed that several inquiries had been received from prospective purchasers but no definite offers had been made. The auditors then asked what the company expected to receive from the sale of the plant. The management stated that the company would probably incur a loss on the sale but would not estimate what the loss might be. However, the senior on the engagement learned from the company's controller that the loss might range between $1,000,000 and $2,000,000, based on discussions with realtors and others.

After a thorough review of this matter, the auditors met with the audit committee of the board of directors and recommended the following presentation for the financial statements:

(1)   Segregate the West Coast plant from the plant and equipment section of the balance sheet and show it as a separate item captioned "Plant and equipment held for sale, at cost less accumulated depreciation."
(2)   Set out the expenses of $150,000 since the shutdown date as a separate item on the income statement.
(3)   Provide a reserve from retained earnings for the estimated loss to be incurred on the sale of the plant, assuming that this loss would be material.

The committee agreed with the first two suggestions but refused to set up a reserve for the potential loss. They admitted that a loss would probably be incurred on the sale of the plant and affirmed that the amount could be as much as $2,000,000, but they believed that the establishment of the reserve would be detrimental to negotiations with any prospective purchasers. The auditors then stated that they would have to qualify their opinion if no reserve was provided.

Accordingly, the audit report contained this paragraph after the standard introductory paragraph:

"The Company's West Coast plant, carried at $3,900,000, has not been used for production since April 1974, and is currently being offered for sale. The amount that may be realized from the disposition of this property is not now determinable but may be less than the carrying value shown in the accompanying balance sheet."

The auditor's opinion then said "Except for any adjustment which may be required to reflect a possible loss on the disposition of the West Coast plant, in our opinion, the aforementioned financial statements present fairly, etc."

Required:

a)   If a CPA gives unqualified approval to financial statements containing provision for a possible large loss on sale of plant and equipment, is he responsible for the accuracy of the estimate of loss? Is this different from forecasting future earnings?
b)   Should the independent auditors be influenced by the fact that disclosure of the estimated amount of a possible future loss on sale of a closed plant might be detrimental to the client in negotiating a sale of the closed plant? Explain.
c)   Do you believe that the auditors should have qualified their opinion or disclaimed an opinion under the circumstances given above? Why?
d)   What evidence should be contained in the audit working papers to support the auditors' decision to qualify the opinion or to disclaim an opinion?
e)   Do you agree with the presentation of this matter in the financial statements as recommended by the auditors? What other methods of presentation might be acceptable?

Index